REA's Test Prep Books Are The Best!
(a sample of the hundreds of letters REA receives each year)

" REA's *SAT Subject Test: Math Level 2* test prep definitely
helped boost my score.... "
Student, Portland, OR

" My students report your chapters of review as the most valuable single
resource they used for review and preparation. "
Teacher, American Fork, UT

" Your book was such a better value and was so much more complete than
anything your competition has produced — and I have them all! "
Teacher, Virginia Beach, VA

" Compared to the other books that my fellow students had, your book was
the most useful in helping me get a great score. "
Student, North Hollywood, CA

" Your book was responsible for my success on the exam, which helped me get
into the college of my choice... I will look for REA the next time I need help. "
Student, Chesterfield, MO

" Just a short note to say thanks for the great support your book gave me in
helping me pass the test... I'm on my way to a B.S. degree because of you! "
Student, Orlando, FL

(more on next page)

(continued from front page)

" I am writing to congratulate you on preparing an exceptional study guide. In five years of teaching this course, I have never encountered a more thorough, comprehensive, concise and realistic preparation for this examination. "
Teacher, Davie, FL

" I have found your publications, *The Best Test Preparation...*, to be exactly that. "
Teacher, Aptos, CA

" I used your book to prepare for the test and found that the advice and the sample tests were highly relevant... Without using any other material, I earned very high scores and will be going to the graduate school of my choice. "
Student, New Orleans, LA

" I used your *CLEP Introductory Sociology* book and rank it 99% — thank you! "
Student, Jerusalem, Israel

" Your *GMAT* book greatly helped me on the test. Thank you. "
Student, Oxford, OH

" I recently got the *French SAT II* Exam book from REA. I congratulate you on first-rate French practice tests."
Instructor, Los Angeles, CA

" Your *AP English Literature and Composition* book is most impressive."
Student, Montgomery, AL

" The REA *LSAT* Test Preparation guide is a winner! "
Instructor, Spartanburg, SC

The Best Test Preparation for the

SAT Subject Test
World History

With REA's TEST*ware*® on CD-ROM

Deborah Vess, Ph.D.
Professor of History and Interdisciplinary Studies
Department of History, Geography, and Philosophy
Georgia College and State University

Additional Practice Test by
Lynn Elizabeth Marlowe, M.A.

Research & Education Association
Visit our website at
www.rea.com

Research & Education Association
61 Ethel Road West
Piscataway, New Jersey 08854
E-mail: info@rea.com

The Best Test Preparation for the
SAT SUBJECT TEST IN WORLD HISTORY
With TEST*ware*® on CD-ROM

Printed in the United States of America

Library of Congress Control Number 2006927475

International Standard Book Number 0-7386-0251-5

CONTENTS

ABOUT OUR AUTHORS

Deborah Vess, Ph.D., is Professor of History and Interdisciplinary Studies at Georgia College & State University in Milledgeville, Georgia. She holds a Ph.D. in history from the University of North Texas, with areas of expertise in integrative studies, Church history, medieval monasticism, and gender issues. She co-founded and edited *Magistra: a Journal of Women's Spirituality*, served as Joint Editor for *Vox benedictina: A journal of women's and monastic studies*, and as Internet Review Editor for *The History Computer Review*. Dr. Vess has been active in promoting the use of technology in education, and has received an international exemplary course award from WEBCT for an online U.S. history core course now used in the University System of Georgia.

In 1996, the University System of Georgia Board of Regents named Dr. Vess a Distinguished Professor of Teaching and Learning. In 2001, she received the University System's Board of Regents Research in Undergraduate Education Award. In addition to numerous local awards, she has twice received an Excellence in Teaching Award from the National Institute of Staff and Organizational Development. In 1999, she was named a Carnegie Scholar with the Carnegie Foundation for the Advancement of Teaching. She has published articles in *Inventio, The History Teacher, Teaching History, The American Benedictine Review, Proteus, Mystics Quarterly, Word and Spirit,* and other publications.

Lynn Elizabeth Marlowe, M.A., received her M.A. degree from New York University and has taught at several colleges including Los Angeles City College, Chaffey College, and Pasadena City College.

AUTHOR ACKNOWLEDGMENT

Dr. Vess wishes to extend special thanks to Cathy Locks, Instructional Support Specialist in the Office of Electronic Instructional Services, Georgia College and State University, for her help developing the course review material devoted to the Revolutions of 1848, World War I and II, the Unification of Italy and Germany, and the Cold War.

ABOUT RESEARCH & EDUCATION ASSOCIATION

Founded in 1959, Research & Education Association (REA) is dedicated to publishing the finest and most effective educational materials—including software, study guides, and test preps—for students in middle school, high school, college, graduate school, and beyond.

REA's Test Preparation series includes books and software for all academic levels in almost all disciplines. REA publishes test preps for students who have not yet entered high school, as well as high school students preparing to enter college. Students from countries around the world seeking to attend college in the United States will find the assistance they need in REA's publications. For college students seeking advanced degrees, REA publishes test preps for many major graduate school admission examinations in a wide variety of disciplines, including engineering, law, and medicine. Students at every level, in every field, with every ambition can find what they are looking for among REA's publications.

REA's series presents tests that accurately depict the official exams in both degree of difficulty and types of questions. REA's practice tests are always based upon the most recently administered exams, and include every type of question that can be expected on the actual exams.

REA's publications and educational materials are highly regarded and continually receive an unprecedented amount of praise from professionals, instructors, librarians, parents, and students. Our authors are as diverse as the subject matter represented in the books we publish. They are well known in their respective disciplines and serve on the faculties of prestigious colleges and universities throughout the United States and Canada.

We invite you to visit us at *www.rea.com* to find out how "REA is making the world smarter."

STAFF ACKNOWLEDGMENTS

In addition to our author, we would like to thank Larry B. Kling, Vice President, Editorial, for supervising development; John Cording, Vice President, Technology, for coordinating the design and development of REA's TEST*ware*® software; Pam Weston, Vice President, Publishing, for setting the quality standards for production integrity and managing the publication to completion; Diane Goldschmidt, Associate Editor, for project management and post-production quality assurance; Christine Reilley and Anne Winthrop Esposito, Senior Editors, for their editorial contributions; Heena Patel and Michelle Boykins, Technology Project Managers, for their design contributions and software testing efforts; Jeff LoBalbo, Senior Graphic Artist, for his graphic arts contributions and post-production file mapping; and Christine Saul, Senior Graphic Artist, for designing our cover.

We also gratefully acknowledge Niles Holt for his technical review; Sally Wood for copyediting, and the team at Aquent Publishing Services for typesetting this edition.

SAT Subject Test World History

Excelling on the SAT World History Subject Test

INTRODUCTION

EXCELLING ON THE SAT WORLD HISTORY SUBJECT TEST

ABOUT THIS BOOK AND TEST*ware*®

This book provides you with an accurate and complete representation of the SAT World History Subject Test. Inside you will find a complete course review designed to provide you with the information and strategies needed to do well on the exam, as well as two practice tests based on the actual exam. The practice tests contain every type of question that you can expect to appear on the SAT World History Subject Test. Following each test you will find an answer key with detailed explanations designed to help you master the test material.

Practice Tests 1 and 2 are also included on the enclosed TEST*ware*® CD. The software provides the benefits of instantaneous, accurate scoring and enforced time conditions.

ABOUT THE TEST

Who Takes the Test and What Is It Used for?

Students planning to attend college take the SAT World History Subject Test for one of two reasons:

    (1) Because it's an admission requirement of the college or university to which they are applying,

    or

(2)   To demonstrate proficiency in world history.

Many colleges use the SAT Subject Tests for admission or for course placement. Used in combination with other background information (your high school record, scores from other tests, teacher recommendations, etc.), these tests provide a dependable measure of academic achievement and help predict future performance.

Who Administers the Test?

The SAT World History Subject Test is developed by the College Board and administered by Educational Testing Service (ETS). The test development process involves the assistance of educators throughout the country, and is designed and implemented to ensure that the content and difficulty level of the test are appropriate.

When Should the SAT World History be Taken?

If you are applying to a college that requires Subject Test scores as part of the admissions process, you should take the SAT World History Subject Test toward the end of your junior year or at the beginning of your senior year. If your scores are being used only for placement purposes, you may be able to take the test later in your senior year. Make sure to contact the colleges to which you are applying for more specific information.

If possible take the SAT World History test soon after completing your course of study in the subject, while the material is still fresh in your mind.

When and Where is the Test Given?

The SAT World History Subject Test is administered six times a year at many locations throughout the country, mostly high schools. The test is given in October, November, December, January, May, and June.

To receive information on upcoming administrations of the exam, consult the publication *Taking the SAT Subject Tests,* which may be obtained from your guidance counselor or by contacting:

College Board SAT Program
P.O. Box 6200
Princeton, NJ 08541–6200
Phone: (609) 771-7600
Website: *www.collegeboard.com*

Is there a Registration Fee?

You must pay a registration fee to take the SAT World History test. Consult the publication *Taking the SAT Subject Tests* for information on the fee structure. Financial assistance may be granted in certain situations. To find out if you qualify and to register for assistance, contact your academic advisor.

HOW TO USE THIS BOOK AND TEST*ware*®

What Do I Study First?

Remember that the SAT World History Subject Test is designed to test knowledge that has been acquired throughout your education. Therefore, the best way to prepare for the exam is to refresh yourself by thoroughly studying our review material and taking the sample tests provided in this book. They will familiarize you with the types of questions, directions, and format of the SAT World History Subject Test.

To begin your studies, read over the reviews and the suggestions for test-taking, take Practice Test 1 on CD-ROM to determine your area(s) of weakness, and then restudy the review material, focusing on your specific problem areas. The course review includes the information you need to know when taking the exam. Make sure to follow up your diagnostic work by taking Practice Test 2 on CD-ROM to become familiar with the format of the SAT World History Subject Test.

When Should I Start Studying?

It is never too early to start studying for the SAT World History test. The earlier you begin, the more time you will have to sharpen your skills. Do not procrastinate! Cramming is *not* an effective way to study, since it does not allow you the time needed to learn the test material. The sooner you learn the format of the exam, the more comfortable you will be when you take it.

CONTENT AND FORMAT OF THE SAT WORLD HISTORY TEST

The World History is a one-hour exam consisting of 95 multiple-choice questions. Each question has five possible answer choices, lettered (A) through (E). Topics cover the entire history of the world, from ancient times to the present, including all inhabitable continents.

The following tables summarize the distribution of topics covered on the SAT World History exam:

Chronological Material Covered	Approx. Percentage of Questions on the test
Pre-History and Civilizations to 500 C.E.	25
500 to 1500 C.E.	20
1500 - 1900 C.E.	25
Post - 1900 C.E.	20
Cross-chronological	10

Geographical Material Covered	Approx. Percentage of Questions on the test
Europe	25
Africa	10
Southwest Asia	10
South and Southeast Asia	10
East Asia	10
The Americas (excluding the U.S.)	10
Global or Comparative	25

Scoring the SAT World History

The SAT World History Test, like all other Subject Tests, is scored on a 200-800 scale.

How Do I Score My Practice Test?

Your exam is scored by crediting one point for each correct answer and deducting one-fourth of a point for each incorrect answer. There is no deduction for answers that are omitted. Use the worksheet below to calculate your raw score and to record your scores for the two practice tests in this book.

Scoring Worksheet

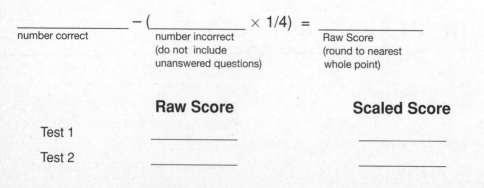

_____ − (_____ × 1/4) = _____

number correct   number incorrect   Raw Score
                        (do not include   (round to nearest
                        unanswered questions)   whole point)

	Raw Score	**Scaled Score**
Test 1	_____	_____
Test 2	_____	_____

Calculating Your Scaled Score

Scores on the SAT World History Subject Test range from 200 to 800. This table shows you how to convert your raw score to a scaled score.*

SAT WORLD HISTORY
PRACTICE-TEST SCALED SCORE CONVERSION TABLE

Raw Score	Scaled Score	Raw Score	Scaled Score	Raw Score	Scaled Score
95	800	55	630	15	430
94	800	54	630	14	430
93	800	53	620	13	420
92	800	52	610	12	420
91	800	51	610	11	410
90	800	50	600	10	410
89	800	49	600	9	400
88	800	48	590	8	390
87	800	47	590	7	380
86	800	46	580	6	380
85	800	45	570	5	370
84	790	44	570	4	360
83	790	43	560	3	360
82	790	42	560	2	350
81	780	41	550	1	350
80	770	40	550	0	340
79	770	39	540	-1	330
78	760	38	540	-2	320
77	750	37	530	-3	310
76	740	36	530	-4	310
75	740	35	520	-5	300
74	730	34	510	-6	290
73	720	33	510	-7	280
72	720	32	510	-8	270
71	710	31	500	-9	260
70	710	30	500	-10	250
69	700	29	490	-11	250
68	700	28	490	-12	240
67	690	27	490	-13	230
66	690	26	480	-14	220
65	680	25	480	-15	210
64	680	24	470	-16	200
63	670	23	470	-17	200
62	670	22	460	-18	200
61	660	21	460	-19	200
60	660	20	450	-20	200
59	650	19	450	-21	200
58	650	18	450	-22	200
57	640	17	440	-23	200
56	640	16	440	-24	200

* **The scores you achieve on our practice tests will strongly approximate your performance on the SAT World History. Strict correlations cannot be assumed.**

STUDYING FOR THE TEST

It is very important to choose the time and place for studying that works best for you. Some students may set aside a certain number of hours every morning to study, while others may choose to study at night before going to sleep. Other students may study during the day, while waiting on a line, or even while eating lunch. Only you can determine when and where your study time will be most effective. Be consistent and use your time wisely. Work out a study routine and stick to it!

When you take the practice tests, try to make your testing conditions as much like the actual test as possible. Turn your television and radio off, and sit down at a quiet table free from distraction. Make sure to time yourself with a timer.

As you complete each practice test, score your test and thoroughly review the explanations to the questions you answered incorrectly; however, do not review too much at any one time. Concentrate on one problem area at a time by reviewing the questions and explanations, and by studying our review until you are confident you completely understand the material.

Keep track of your scores. By doing so, you will be able to gauge your progress and discover general weaknesses in particular sections. You should carefully study the reviews that cover your areas of difficulty, as this will build your skills in those areas.

TEST-TAKING TIPS

Although you may be unfamiliar with standardized tests such as the SAT World History Subject Test, there are many ways to acquaint yourself with this type of examination and help alleviate your test-taking anxieties. Listed below are ways to help you become accustomed to the SAT World History test, some of which may apply to other standardized tests as well.

Become comfortable with the format of the exam. When you are practicing to take the SAT World History Subject Test, simulate the conditions under which you will be taking the actual test. Stay calm and pace yourself. After simulating the test only a couple of times, you will boost your chances of doing well, and you will be able to sit down for the actual exam with much more confidence.

Know the directions for the test. Familiarizing yourself with the directions and format of the exam will not only save you time, but will also ensure that you are familiar enough with the test to avoid nervousness (and the mistakes caused by being nervous).

Do your scratchwork in the margins of the test booklet. You will not be given scrap paper during the exam, and you may not perform scratchwork on your answer sheet. Space is provided in your test booklet to do any necessary work or draw diagrams.

If you are unsure of an answer, guess. However, if you do guess, guess wisely. Use the process of elimination by going through each answer to a question and ruling out as many of the answer choices as possible. By eliminating three answer choices, you give yourself a fifty-fifty chance of answering correctly since there will only be two choices left from which to make your guess.

Mark your answers in the appropriate spaces on the answer sheet. Each numbered row will contain five ovals corresponding to each answer choice for that question. Fill in the circle that corresponds to your answer darkly, completely, and neatly. You can change your answer, but remember to completely erase your old answer. Any stray lines or unnecessary marks may cause the machine to score your answer incorrectly. When you have finished working on a section, you may want to go back and check to make sure your answers correspond to the correct questions. Marking one answer in the wrong space will throw off the rest of your test, whether it is graded by machine or by hand.

You don't have to answer every question. You are not penalized if you do not answer every question. The only penalty you receive is if you answer a question incorrectly. Try to use the guessing strategy, but if you are truly stumped by a question, you do not have to answer it.

Work quickly and steadily. You have a limited amount of time to work on each section, so you need to work quickly and steadily. Avoid focusing on one problem for too long. Taking the practice tests in this book will help you to learn how to budget your time.

Before the Test

Make sure you know where your test center is well in advance of your test day so you do not get lost on the day of the test. On the night before the test, gather together the materials you will need the next day:

- Your admission ticket
- Two forms of identification (e.g., driver's license, student identification card, or current alien registration card)
- Two No. 2 pencils with erasers

- Directions to the test center

- A watch (if you wish) but not one that makes noise, as it may disturb other test-takers

On the day of the test, you should wake up early (it is hoped after a decent night's rest) and have a good breakfast. Dress comfortably, so that you are not distracted by being too hot or too cold while taking the test. Also, plan to arrive at the test center early. This will allow you to collect your thoughts and relax before the test, and will also spare you the stress of being late. If you arrive after the test begins, you will not be admitted and you will not receive a refund.

During the Test

When you arrive at the test center, try to find a seat where you feel you will be comfortable. Follow all the rules and instructions given by the test supervisor. If you do not, you risk being dismissed from the test and having your scores canceled.

Once all the test materials are passed out, the test instructor will give you directions for filling out your answer sheet. Fill this sheet out carefully since this information will appear on your score report.

After the Test

When you have completed the SAT World History Subject Test, you may hand in your test materials and leave. Then, go home and relax!

When Will I Receive My Score Report and What Will It Look Like?

You should receive your score report about five weeks after you take the test. This report will include your scores, percentile ranks, and interpretive information.

SAT Subject Test World History

Course Review

CHAPTER 1

THE PREHISTORIC ERA

Scientists currently estimate the age of the universe to be roughly 13.6 billion years old. The term "**prehistoric**" refers to the period before approximately 3000 B.C.E., when written records first appeared in Mesopotamia. The historic era represents a small fraction of the human past, from about 3000 B.C.E. to the present time. The terms "prehistoric" and "historic" do not so much describe the type of cultures that existed as they describe the ways that modern historians study them. The historical method emphasizes the use of written primary sources or firsthand accounts of the past. Traditionally, the written record has been considered the most important kind of primary source, whereas in the prehistoric periods, scholars must rely on fossil evidence and artifacts, or objects actually made by human hands. The term "prehistoric," then, simply refers to the vast period before there were written records. The time line on the following page reviews the major outlines of the prehistoric era that are important for understanding the human past.

THE PALEOLITHIC ERA

Human cultures first appeared in the **Paleolithic** era, which means "Old Stone Age." Scholars often characterize the early periods of the human past by the materials used, and stone was the primary medium of toolmaking in the Paleolithic era. There were a variety of hominids that lived during this vast period of time. Contrary to popular belief, hominids or early humans did not live at the same time as dinosaurs, which had become extinct long before the evolution of hominids began. Hominids are a subclass of the primate order, and are characterized by flattened nails and stereoscopic vision. Due to the increased development of their eyes, hominids had smaller noses and a diminished sense of smell as compared to other primates and, consequently, developed a longer, flatter face. Modern humans are classified as hominids of the primate order, and the hominid cultures of the prehistoric era were the predecessors of modern human cultures.

◀——— TIMELINE CHRONOLOGY ———▶

2,500,000 B.P. (The abbreviation means "before the present.")	The Paleolithic Era or Old Stone Age The rise of the hominids occurs during this period, including *australopithecene*, *Homo habilis*, and *Homo erectus*. Stone is the primary medium out of which hominids from *Homo habilis* onward make tools.
100,000 B.P.	*Homo erectus* migrates from Africa to the Middle East. *Homo erectus* has the capacity to make and control fire, which many believe enabled them to leave Africa. By 25,000 years ago, humans had reached the east from Africa.
85,000 B.P.	Neanderthal (*Homo sapiens*) flourishes.
35,000 B.P.	Cro-Magnon (*Homo sapiens sapiens*) first appears in Europe.
10,000 B.C.E. (The abbreviation means "before the common era.")	The beginning of the Neolithic Era, or New Stone Age During the Neolithic era, urban centers develop, such as Jericho and Catul Huyuk. Stone is still the primary medium for making tools and building, but tool-making is more sophisticated.
8000 B.C.E.	Agriculture first appears in the Middle East in Jericho and gradually spreads throughout the world, reaching the Americas last.
3000 B.C.E.	Writing first appears; the beginning of the historic era. The earliest writing, cuneiform, appears in Mesopotamia.

Lucy and Australopithecene

Anthropologists tell us that the single most important event in human history occurred during the prehistoric era, when hominids first learned to walk upright rather than on all fours. The anthropologist Donald Johansson believes that the first hominid to walk upright was the famous Lucy, a diminutive *australopithecene* female about four-and-one-half feet tall. *Australopithecenes* had pelvises adapted to upright walking at least part of the time. Lucy is also famous because she is the only hominid whose remains have been found in such a state of completion. By contrast, the first example discovered of an *australopithicene* was the Taung baby, whose skull only was found in South Africa in 1924. Darwin's *Origin of the Species,* written in the nineteenth century, argued that all life evolved through the process of natural selection, in which only the most fit survived. Darwin also wrote that humans and apes evolved from a common ancestor, and Johansson believes that *australopithecene* is the "missing link" between humans and the great apes. For Johansson, Lucy is the point at which these two lines diverged, her line leading to modern humans, the other to the modern great apes. There have been a number of famous forgeries claiming to be the missing link, such as the Piltdown man, and these have since been discredited.

Other Hominids

The oldest hominids are found in Africa in the Olduvai Gorge, located on the east coast of Africa in modern Tanzania. *Homo habilis*, or "human with ability," left the most primitive tools on the lowest level of the Gorge. Their crude hand tools, primarily made by chipping flakes off the side of stones, are known as the Olduwan Industry. *Homo erectus,* or "upright human," was first discovered in Trinil, Java, in 1891. Another famous discovery was the Peking man, which was a fragment of a *Homo erectus* cranium found in China in 1929. Based on the charred remains of wood and other materials found at campsites, scientists know that *erectus* had the ability to control fire. Many anthropologists speculate that this capacity was what allowed *erectus* to leave the continent of Africa and migrate to other parts of the world. The fact that the oldest hominids are found in Africa, and that there is the most genetic diversity among modern Africans, leads scholars to believe that human life originated in Africa and then gradually spread elsewhere. This argument is called the "out of Africa" thesis. Recent finds in other parts of the world, such as China, Australia, and Germany, however, are raising questions about the "out of Africa" thesis, as some of these hominids appear to be as old as those found in Africa.

The tools of *erectu*s are called the Acheulian industry, and they have been found in close proximity to the charred remains of *Homo habilis* campsites, suggesting that these two hominids may have lived side-by-side.

Neanderthal

Homo sapiens, or "knowing human," was another step along the evolutionary path for early humans. Remains of a *Homo sapiens* creature known as Neanderthal were first uncovered in 1856 in the Neander Valley, Dusseldorf, Germany. The word "Neanderthal" comes from the Neander Valley; the suffix "-thal" means valley. Remains of Neanderthal have also been found in France, Italy, Belgium, Greece, the Czech Republic, Slovakia, North Africa, and the Middle East.

Neanderthal lived in glacial periods 85,000 to 35,000 years ago and was adapted to cold weather by its short, stout, muscular body and large nose. The old view of Neanderthal as incompletely erect and walking with bent knees was based on a misconception. The original find was of an arthritic individual who would have indeed walked more like an ape than like a modern human. Neanderthal had a much larger brain than modern humans and its stout bones were adapted for heavy lifting. Neanderthal was a cave dweller who lived in a hunting and gathering culture in small bands of ten to fifteen people. He used tools for hunting.

The Shanidar cave in the Zagros Mountains of modern Iraq is the site of the most famous Neanderthal find. The site is 60,000 years old and contains a gravesite of an individual in a fetal position. Pollen grains, some of which are still used in herbal medicine today, were scattered around the grave in an orderly pattern, suggesting a burial rite and possible belief in an afterlife. The grave was in the cave, where the band lived, suggesting that they wanted to keep the dead with them and had concern for them. The individual was seriously injured and his injuries had occurred at least twenty years before his death; he was missing part of his arm and half of his face was smashed. Such an individual would have been incapable of surviving on his own, suggesting communal concern for his welfare. Neanderthal is the first evidence of a cohesive, caring human community.

Neanderthal, or *Homo sapiens*, became extinct around 35,000 years B.C.E. Scholars speculate that disease or lack of adaptation to warmer climates might account for the extinction, which occurred roughly at the end of the last great ice age when the glaciers were starting to retreat. Another theory is that Neanderthal was annihilated by a newer and more superior species, Cro-Magnon (*Homo sapiens sapiens*), that was beginning to flourish in Europe about this time. Some anthropologists speculate that Neanderthal is not really extinct, as it might have been genetically absorbed into the new group. Some suggest northern European stock is the product of such intermingling, but others argue that Neanderthal represents a separate hominid line from that of modern humans and that it was too different from Cro-Magnon to have genetically intermingled.

Cro-Magnon

Cro-Magnons were highly skilled at hunting, and there are many sites where thousands of animal carcasses have been discovered. In Torralba, Spain, Cro-Magnon herded animals together, chased them off cliffs, and harvested their flesh. Cro-Magnon humans *(Homo sapiens sapiens)* were first discovered in Europe in 1868 in the Cro-Magnon cave; their remains have also been uncovered in Italy and Great Britain. Remains have been found dating from 35,000 to 10,000 years ago. Cro-Magnon had a smaller brain than Neanderthal, but a more modern appearance. Cro-Magnon was an expert at making tools and also was the first artist in human history, embellishing tools and the walls of caves with beautiful art. Cro-Magnon tools are known as Aurignacian tools and include such beautiful and functional items as the laurel leaf flint knife.

Paleolithic Cave Art

Cro-Magnon art reflects the emphasis of early humans on the hunt. One of the most famous examples is the cave of Lascaux in France, accidentally discovered by four boys in 1940 when their dog fell into a hole in the ground. The Cro-Magnon artists of Lascaux painted mainly large animals, such as reindeer and bison. Early humans derived their daily sustenance from the hunt, and there are many aspects of the cave art that suggest it had a magical, ritualistic function. The location of the art, for example, is puzzling. The cave of Lascaux is very long, deep, and narrow, and much of the art is painted in very hard to reach places. There are often several layers of paintings, one on top of another. This suggests the actual location of the cave was sacred, as artists tended to return there repeatedly. There are also nick marks on the walls, suggesting that early humans reenacted the hunt there. There are very few images of humans in these caves, and those that exist seem to have animal characteristics as well. The sorcerer in the Tres Freres cave in France and the human-like image in the Well Shaft at Lascaux seem to be images of shamans. In modern hunting and gathering cultures, the shaman is often an important figure. He intercedes with the spiritual world, and often wears a mask made to resemble an animal or pieces of clothing made from animal skins. Since Cro-Magnon believed that the images in these caves were magical, the presence of a shaman would help to ward off evil. These images indicate the close relationship between early humans and nature, upon which they depended for their daily survival.

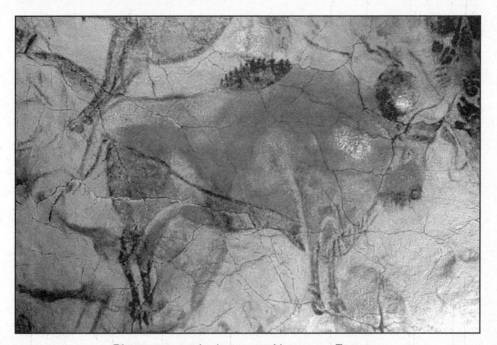

Bison cave art in the cave of Lascaux, France.

Paleolithic Venus Figurines

Other commonly found objects in Paleolithic caves are Venus figures, such as the Laussel Venus and the Venus of Willendorf. These figurines are feminine and have enlarged body parts associated with fertility. There are no identifiable features on their faces, making them more general symbols of fertility rather than images of individual women. The Laussel Venus symbolizes the unity of the human world and the natural world. She holds what appears at first glance to be a horn. Animals with horns regenerate them periodically, so the horn is a symbol of rebirth or renewal. If so, the horn and her prominent childbearing features suggest fertility. Alternatively, it has been suggested that this object represents the moon; there are markings on it that represent the number of days in the cycles of the moon. The Venus simultaneously holds her stomach, suggesting that the cycles of human life are in harmony with those of the natural universal order. These mother earth goddesses represent the dependence of early humans on their mother earth from day to day. Female fertility goddesses were very common in the ancient world, and scholars speculate that the earliest human cultures were female-centered and, since almost all ancient cultures had important fertility goddesses, some have suggested there was a universal cult of the mother earth.

Modern Hunters and Gatherers

There continue to be hunting and gathering cultures in the modern world that are similar to that of Cro-Magnon Paleolithic culture. These include the Guanches from the Canary Islands, the Australian Aborigines, and the !Kung in Africa. The human race first evolved from hunting and gathering cultures, and many modern humans continue to live that way today.

Just as there were a variety of hominids in the prehistoric era, humans continue to be varied today, from the African Negroids to the Asian Mongoloids to the Australoids to the American Indians to the peoples of the Pacific Islands to the Caucasians. Most sociologists argue that race is not an objective construct, but rather a social one. Nevertheless, the ways we differentiate people today may help us relate to the diverse world of prehistoric humans, where many different hominids existed side-by-side along with their different toolmaking cultures.

Human Migration

A major theme of world history is **migration**. Humans migrated from Africa to the Middle East by 100,000 years ago, to Australia by 50,000 years ago, and to the east by 25,000 years ago. They migrated 15,000 years ago to North America across the Bering Strait, a strip of land no longer in existence that connected Siberia with the Americas. Humans reached South America by 10,000 B.C.E.

THE NEOLITHIC ERA AND THE DEVELOPMENT OF AGRICULTURE

The **Neolithic Revolution**, or New Stone Age, occurred somewhere around 10,000 B.C.E. and continued to 3000 B.C.E. During the New Stone Age, humans developed more refined tools, but more importantly, they developed the beginnings of agriculture and urban centers. Organized cultivation of crops may have arisen by mistake when early humans noticed that dropped seeds resulted in plants. It is also likely that hunters and gatherers sometimes cultivated crops to a certain extent.

New Urban Centers

The development of organized agriculture along with the domestication of animals led to the development of urban centers; as some scholars have remarked, "without agriculture there is no culture." The development of agriculture created a stable supply of food, and therefore more leisure time to produce art and other cultural items; the new food supply created a new use for containers, such as pottery, to cook, preserve, and transport the food. Many beautiful examples of Neolithic art are found on pottery. There were no permanent dwellings in Paleolithic hunting and gathering times, as hunters and gatherers of necessity were constantly on the move. Agriculture enabled humans to stay in one place, giving rise to civilization. The word "civilization" derives from the Latin word "civilis" meaning "political or civic." Two of the most important Neolithic cities were **Jericho** in the Middle East, which earliest remains date to 8000 B.C.E., and **Catul Hayuk**, located in modern Turkey. Agriculture first evolved in the Middle East and then spread to other parts of the world. Twelve crops were cultivated here, including nuts, fruits, and three kinds of wheat. Agriculture later arose in the Balkans in 6500 B.C.E. In southeastern Asia, rice was cultivated by 5000 B.C.E.; around the Yellow and Wei Rivers, the centers of early Chinese civilizations, rice was first cultivated around 6000 B.C.E.; and along the Indus River Valley in India, wheat and barley were cultivated around 6000 B.C.E. In Mesoamerica, Native Americans developed agriculture between 7000 and 5000 B.C.E. Their primary crops were maize (a very hardy form of corn), beans, and squash. Along with agriculture came the domestication of animals, such as dogs.

In the new urban centers, a division of labor arose; some inhabitants performed cooking chores, others were farmers, others hunters, and so on. There was also an economic organization, which grew out of the need to conduct trade. The complexity of trade once agriculture developed probably prompted the need for written records. Civilization created the need for more complex governments and written laws. Civilization prompted the development of morality, as family and marriage laws are often related to property concerns.

CHAPTER 2

THE FIRST CIVILIZATION: MESOPOTAMIA

GEOGRAPHY OF ANCIENT MESOPOTAMIA AND CULTURAL PESSIMISM

Mesopotamia is known as "the cradle of world civilization." It is the earliest known civilization, and Mesopotamians produced the earliest written records, including the first unified code of law. Mesopotamians also invented the wheel, the calendar, and the clock. Mesopotamian writing is called **cuneiform**, a word that means "wedge-shaped" writing. They wrote on clay tablets with wedge-shaped instruments called styluses. Henry Creswick Rawlinson deciphered cuneiform in the nineteenth century C.E. by comparing cuneiform text on the Rock of Behistun about the ancient Persian ruler Darius to the same text in Old Persian, which scholars knew how to read.

Ancient Mesopotamia was located between the Tigris and the Euphrates rivers; in fact, the word "Mesopotamia" means "the land between two rivers." The rivers provided an abundant source of water and very fertile plains, ideal conditions for agriculture. The first settlements in Mesopotamia date back to 4000 B.C.E. Geography played an important role in the creation of the Mesopotamian worldview. The flooding of the Tigris and Euphrates rivers was unpredictable and disastrous; flooding often destroyed city-states in an instant. Many creation stories from the region, such as the *Epic of Gilgamesh*, describe a disastrous flood that wiped out the earth; these stories were likely based on actual events. The constant and unpredictable flooding partially accounts for the very grim view of life evident in the *Epic of Gilgamesh*. In the epic, the first immortal man, Utnapishtim, tells the hero Gilgamesh that the god Enlil sent the flood because humans were too noisy and irritated the gods. When Utnapishtim survives, Enlil is enraged and "rewards" him with immortality, a gift Utnapishtim assures Gilgamesh is no favor. Every day, he says, is like every other day, the days continuing on in dreary bleakness without end.

Another contributing factor to the overall pessimism of Mesopotamian culture was the competition for land and water resources. Due to the need for large amounts of land, there was fairly wide separation between settlements. Several independent city-states arose in southern Mesopotamia, such as Uruk, where the Sumerian king list records the beginning of the reign of Gilgamesh in 2700 B.C.E., and Ur, the original home of **Abraham**, patriarch of the Hebrews and Arabs. Southern Mesopotamia is known as Sumer, and each of these city-states had its own government, customs, and deities. Their common customs and culture are referred to as "Sumerian." Empires did not arise in Mesopotamia until Sargon the Great unified the region in the twenty-fourth century B.C.E. In any case, both the Sumerian city-states and the later Mesopotamian empires proved notoriously unstable. The competition for land and water rights led to almost continuous conflict between city-states. In fact, the earliest recorded treaty in world history resolved a conflict over irrigation rights between the Sumerian city-state of Lagash and its neighbors.

The geographical features of Mesopotamia also contributed to the lack of stability, as there were no natural barriers to protect the city-states from outside invaders. Throughout Mesopotamian history, there was a constant stream of conquering peoples such as the Assyrians and Amorites. Combined with the continuous conflict between city-states, Mesopotamians never developed a continuous and long-lived empire, as did Egypt. Rather, Mesopotamian history is one of constant invasion and conquest and is the story of successive cultures that borrowed from each other. The omnipresence of war is evident on the Standard of Ur, a music box used as an object of leisure but decorated with scenes of war. In the opening lines of the *Epic of Gilgamesh*, one of the chief sins of Gilgamesh was to have let the walls of his city-state crumble, again reflecting the omnipresent threat of invasion. The political turmoil that characterized ancient Mesopotamia is still a feature of this region today, which is currently known as Iraq.

The importance of the rivers as well as the ideology of warfare can be seen in Mesopotamian mythology. According to the creation myth of the Mesopotamians, in the beginning Ocean and Chaos began to merge, but Chaos tried to make herself supreme. Marduk, the creator god, killed Chaos by splitting her in half, from which came the heavens and the earth. The tears that flowed down her face from the pain became the Tigris and the Euphrates rivers. Marduk then kneaded the wet earth and created humans. As we have seen, according to the *Epic of Gilgamesh*, eventually the gods grew weary of the noise made by the troublesome humans and sent a flood to destroy them. The gods sent a heavenly bull to inflict revenge on Gilgamesh, but instead it killed his friend Enkidu. On his deathbed, Enkidu had a vision of the underworld, and told Gilgamesh that there the kings were now servants of the gods, and all one could find there was dust and darkness. Enkidu told Gilgamesh that the gods play with humans like puppets on strings, having a contest to see what misery they can inflict. From the creation myths to the collapse of the Assyrian empire in 612 B.C.E., the devastating flooding of the rivers and the bleak nature of brutal warfare colored Mesopotamian culture. Mesopotamians were not sure they could even turn to the gods for compassion; they were simply at the mercy of a brutal environment whose purpose and plan they did not know. Nevertheless, the hero Gilgamesh tested the limits of human achievement by searching for immortality and, although he did not succeed, the gods granted him a certain kind of immortality through his everlasting fame.

Although the Mesopotamians were rather pessimistic about the benevolence of the gods, they continued to worship them devoutly and perform sacrifices to them. In the *Epic of Gilgamesh,* the goddess Siduri told Gilgamesh to "live for the moment" and to learn to enjoy every minute of life. The Mesopotamians were never sure of what the future held, but they tried to find happiness in the moment and protection by offering whatever sacrifices they could to the gods. Every city-state had at its center and at its highest point a step-like structure called a ziggurat, or temple. Religious ceremonies were performed here, but scribes also learned to read and write here in the eddubas or "tablet houses," so-called because Sumerians wrote on clay tablets. At the foot of the ziggurat, there was a marketplace. The king, who was also chief priest, controlled this important religious and social center. Gilgamesh was said to be two-thirds god and one-third man, so Mesopotamian society was a theocracy, a system of government in which religion and politics were not separate. In Mesopotamia, the chief priest/king was considered to be semi-divine. The fact that the ziggurat was the center of education, religion, government, and trade illustrates an important feature of the ancient world. The ancient world did not distinguish between history, mythology, religion, or other areas as separate endeavors or areas of knowledge.

THE RISE OF EMPIRES IN MESOPOTAMIA

Several different peoples conquered Mesopotamia and established empires there. The following time line summarizes the main empires of ancient Mesopotamia.

◄──────────── **TIMELINE CHRONOLOGY** ──────────►

2340 B.C.E.	Sargon the Great establishes the Akkadian Empire.
2113 B.C.E.	Sargon's empire begins to collapse. Ur-Nammu restores it for a brief period.
1800 B.C.E.	The Amorites conquer Mesopotamia and establish their capital at Babylon. During this period, Hammurabi compiles the first unified code of law, the Code of Hammurabi.
1000 B.C.E.	The Assyrians conquer the Babylonians and establish their capital at Nineveh, where the tablets recording the *Epic of Gilgamesh* are later found.
612 B.C.E.	The Chaldeans conquer the Assyrian capital of Nineveh and establish an empire known as the Neo-Babylonian empire. Its most famous ruler is Nebuchadnezzar.
539 B.C.E.	The Persians, under Cyrus the Great, conquer the Chaldeans or Neo-Babylonians. The Persians would rule until the expansion of Islam engulfed the region in the seventh century C.E.

The Akkadians

Sargon I (the Great) created the first true empire in Mesopotamia with his capital at Akkad. His empire is known as the Akkadian Empire. Sargon lived sometime around 2340 B.C.E., and some aspects of his legend are reminiscent of the story of Moses contained in the Hebrew scriptures. According to legend, his mother launched him on the Euphrates in a reed basket. A farmer found him and raised him. He displayed prodigious abilities and became the cupbearer to the King of Kish. The cupbearer was the king's most trusted servant; he tasted his food and drink to make sure it was not poisoned before the king ate it. Sargon, however, overthrew the king. He then proceeded to conquer important Sumerian city-states, such as Uruk, Ur, Lagash, and also Elam. One of the texts on the Rock of Behistun was written in the Akkadian style of cuneiform. His grandson Naram-Sin, about whom we know very little, continued Sargon's empire. Although Sargon created an empire that lasted for 200 years, his empire collapsed in 2100 B.C.E.

The Babylonians or Amorites

In 1800 B.C.E., the Amorites conquered much of Mesopotamia and destroyed whatever of Sargon's empire the dynasty of Ur-Nammu had managed to preserve. At that time, the extent of Mesopotamian power increased from an area less than fifty miles in radius to one that extended from the Persian Gulf to beyond Turkey. The Amorite capital was **Babylon**, and the Amorites themselves are better known as Babylonians. Babylon was an economic and cultural crossroads of the ancient world. The Babylonians were most notable for creating two of the seven wonders of the ancient world: the hanging gardens of Babylon (created during the Neo-Babylonian era) and the beautiful blue-tiled gate of Ishtar that guarded the entrance to the city. The Babylonians were pioneers in mathematics and created a base 60 number system, which still influences the world today from the division of the hour into minutes and the minute into seconds to the 360-degree circle. The Babylonians were also leaders in astronomy, and observed and recorded eclipses. They charted the movements of the planets, discovered satellites around Saturn, distinguished stars from planets, and knew that the true length of the solar year was 365 and 1/4 days. Their interest in astronomy was due to their belief that planets had souls and were animate, and that their movements represented the will of the gods and foreshadowed events on earth. They built incredible architectural works, such as their famous ziggurat dedicated to the god Marduk. The ziggurat in Babylon was built in seven layers representing the planets, all colored differently. The ziggurat served as an observatory as well as a religious temple. The height of the great ziggurat of Babylon may have been the basis for the biblical story of the tower of Babel, according to which humans were punished for their attempt to reach the heavens by being unable to understand their many languages. In Babylon, literally, the ziggurat reached the heavens and here there were many languages spoken. The Babylonians also created the Code of Hammurabi and first wrote down the collection of stories known as the *Epic of Gilgamesh.*

The **Code of Hammurabi**, compiled in 1750 B.C.E., was not the world's first law code, but rather the first unified code of law. Hammurabi borrowed the best laws from various Mesopotamian city-states and compiled them into one code of law for the entire land. In the preface to the code, Hammurabi states that it was a gift of the god Marduk. The fact that the code was said to derive from the gods gave it a special authority, and Hammurabi tells us in the epilogue to the code that it should, consequently, last for all eternity and never be modified. In the preface to the code, Hammurabi states that its purpose was to preserve right and justice in the land. The code was a civil code of law, which means it provided for punishments for particular crimes. It contained no broad principles that could be applied to other cases not mentioned, such as the United States Constitution; rather, it was a collection of test cases with punishments to correspond. The main legal principle of the code was "an eye for an eye, a tooth for a tooth"; in other words, punishments were meted out according to the crime committed. For example, if a surgeon performed an operation and the patient died, the surgeon might lose his hand; if an architect designed a defective building that collapsed and killed the owner's son, his son would also be killed. Punishments, however, varied according to class. The principle "an eye for an eye" was applied only when the two parties were of the same class, as for example, if a freeman (the Mesopotamian word for noble) injured another freeman. There were three classes in Mesopotamia: the upper class made up of government officials, soldiers, and priests; the middle class of artisans; and the lower class of peasants and slaves. If someone from the class of freeman injured a slave, punishment would not be meted out according to the principle "an eye for an eye; a tooth for a tooth"; rather, punishment would be reduced to a mere fine. Slaves were treated as property in ancient Mesopotamia. As city-states rose and fell and empires came and went, captured citizens often were enslaved. Mesopotamians could also sell themselves or their wives and children into slavery for limited periods.

Code of Hammurabi, c. 1760 B.C.E.

Despite the harsh treatment of slaves in the code, Mesopotamian laws were rather liberal for their time for slaves. Slaves did have the right to intermarry with the free classes and their children would be free. Slaves could also give testimony in court and earn their freedom. There was more mobility of social class in ancient Mesopotamia than in other ancient empires, again perhaps due to the uncertainties of war. Further, those who were freeborn might be punished by slavery; for example, the punishment for a woman who committed adultery and whose husband chose to spare her was to become a slave in his household. Alternatively, those who were freeborn might sell themselves into slavery to pay their debts.

The distinctions in the code between classes must be understood in the context of the times. The upper class was the backbone of the state in a war-like culture; they were indispensable for defense. Slaves, on the other hand, were commodities of war.

The code also preserved certain rights for women and children. The dowry, usually an amount of money or other property brought into the marriage by the bride and her family, belonged to the woman, and if she was divorced without reason, it remained in her possession. Although a husband might take another wife without proving his first wife incompetent or that she had committed some wrong, he had to continue to care for his present one in the manner to which she was accustomed. If a man's wife became sick, he had to continue to care for her until she died, but he was often allowed to take another wife. If a husband did not return from war, the code gave the woman the right to remarry to ensure her well-being. If he later returned and had not been guilty of desertion, his wife had to return to him, even if she had remarried. In this case, if she had born her new husband children, the children stayed with their father. These laws gave women considerable protection. On the other hand, adultery was punished by death unless the husband chose to spare his wife, in which case she and her lover became his slaves. Children also had rights; a father could not disinherit his son on the first attempt. He had to prove continuous wrongdoing through a second trial. On the other hand, a child who struck his father would have his hands cut off.

There were also laws governing the conduct of trials. Judges who made mistakes where the evidence was clearly present were run out of the city-state. Further, consumers were protected from medical malpractice and also from a number of other business situations. The Code of Hammurabi was one of the most influential law codes in history, and it would later influence the laws of social justice found in Hebrew society and recorded in the Torah, as well as Islamic law.

The Assyrians

Despite their cultural achievements and legacy of law, Babylon fell to the **Assyrians** in 1000 B.C.E. The Assyrians were a military society whose most important god was Ashur, the god of war. The Assyrians used cruel and repressive tactics even at home; they fueled their military machine through encouraging a high birthrate and made abortion punishable by death. The Assyrian Empire created one of the first organized and well-trained armies; they were the first truly militaristic society in world history. One reason for their success was the iron weapons they used. Soldiers were rewarded for every severed head they brought back. They were ordered to take no hostages, and often beat in the heads of those they captured, cut off extremities of nobles and those in power, roasted people over slow fire, and deported entire populations to diffuse cultures. One famous relief shows an Assyrian soldier gouging out the eyes of a victim while the head was held in place with a string through the lips. Ashurbanipal was the most famous and brutal of Assyrian kings (d. 626 B.C.E.). He was also noteworthy for devotion to learning and created a library of 30,000 volumes. The capital of the Assyrian Empire was Nineveh, and several tablets with portions of the *Epic of Gilgamesh* were found here dating to the ninth century B.C.E. The *Epic of Gilgamesh*, like almost every ancient text, was told orally for hundreds of years before it was first written down by the Babylonians. The tablets found in Nineveh contain several versions of some of the tales in the epic, and it is unclear how they all fit together. Nineveh is also famous for its biblical connections. According to the Hebrew scriptures, God ordered the prophet Jonah to preach to the inhabitants of Nineveh; when he refused, a whale swallowed him. In the eighth century B.C.E., the Assyrians destroyed the northern kingdom of the Hebrews, Israel. The Assyrian Empire collapsed in 612 B.C.E. when the Chaldeans captured their capital city of Nineveh.

The Chaldeans or Neo-Babylonians

The **Chaldeans** restored much of the grandeur of the Babylonian Empire and, for that reason, the Chaldean Empire is also known as the Neo-Babylonian Empire. The Hanging Gardens of Babylon, built on top of the king's palace by **Nebuchadnezzar II**, were known as one of the seven wonders of the ancient world. Nebuchadnezzar built the gardens for his wife, who was a Mede (the predecessors of the Persians). Her homeland was a very lush and beautiful region with lots of vegetation and Nebuchadnezzar intended to replicate. Hydraulic pumps concealed in columns of the palace carried water to the trees on the top. The vegetation was reportedly so lush that the women of the royal harem could walk about unveiled, unseen by the citizens below. Although some scholars now doubt that the gardens were actually located in Babylon as some famous ancient travelers fail to mention them, they remain one of the most important wonders of the ancient world.

Nebuchadnezzar and the Hebrew Rebels

Nebuchadnezzar created an enormous empire by ruthlessly subjugating neighboring peoples, including those of Judea. His subjugation of the Hebrews is documented in the Hebrew book of Daniel. The Hebrew prophet Daniel describes Nebuchadnezzar's court as magnificent and enormously wealthy, attended by astronomers and governmental officials who were all carefully educated. Nebuchadnezzar was an absolute monarch, who could make or break a career with a word. He was given to sharp swings of mood and had a fierce temper. When threatened by rebellion, he committed atrocious acts. Nebuchadnezzar murdered the Hebrew rebel Zedekiah's sons before his very eyes and then put out his eyes. According to Daniel, Nebuchadnezzar had a strange dream and sought advice from Daniel, who told him that he would be removed from office for seven years as a result of an odd and strange disease. Within a year, Nebuchadnezzar did become ill with what scientists now think was lycanthropy. Lycanthropy results in loss of erect posture, rejection of all human food, and preference for walking on all fours. The king became a maniac. He lived in the open twenty-four hours a day, fed on herbs, rejected clothing, and became covered with a dense coat of hair. Daniel had prophesied that the illness would not be permanent, and after seven years Nebuchadnezzar was miraculously cured. He ruled until his death in 562 B.C.E., at about the age of 80.

The Persians

The Neo-Babylonian Empire fell to the **Persians** in 539 B.C.E. The Persians were Indo-Europeans who established a vast, tolerant, and ecumenical empire in the sixth century B.C.E. Persia was known as Elam during Sumerian and Babylonian times; today it is known as Iran. Ancient Persia was bounded by the Indus Valley, the Tigris and Euphrates rivers, and the Caucasus mountains. The empire had a high plateau in its center; in the center of the plateau were two large deserts. The Medes, who united earlier than the Persians, originally ruled Persia. In 550 B.C.E., Cyrus, chief of the Persian tribes, defeated the Medes. In 546 B.C.E., Cyrus went on to conquer Anatolia on the coast of Asia Minor. Anatolia gave the Persians access to seaports and thus to trade. Eventually, access to the sea would bring the Persians into conflict with the Greek colonies and the Greeks on the mainland. This series of conflicts is known as the Persian wars. The Persians then turned to Babylon and captured it in 539 B.C.E. These conquests were the beginning of the Achaemenid Empire, and Cyrus also ended the exile of the Jews in Babylon. Under **Darius I** (522–486 B.C.E.), the Persians achieved peace and prosperity. The stability, peace, and cosmopolitan nature of the government created an era known as the *Pax Archaemenica*.

Darius instituted a uniform system of coinage, standard weights and measures, a postal service, a calendar from Egypt, and a law code. He led expeditions into Eastern Europe all the way to the Danube and also into India, where he established the Hindush satrap. He led expeditions from the Indus River to the Red Sea. At one point, Darius even thought of building a canal from the Nile to the Red Sea, which might have made the fifteenth-century C.E. expeditions of Portugal around the coast of Africa unnecessary.

The Organization of the Persian Empire

The Persian Empire was organized into provinces or satrapies. The land of Medes was the first province, and at the height of Persian power there were some twenty such satrapies, each ruled by a provincial governor. Governors could not become too powerful, as in each province there was a military official. The king received tribute from the satraps, as well as recruits for the army. The Persian army was very well trained and at its heart was an elite core of 10,000 soldiers known as the Immortals, so-called because no matter how many died on the battlefield, the next day there were still 10,000 Immortals. The Immortals figured prominently in the Persian wars with the Greeks.

Kings ruled by "election of the gods" and were just and tolerant of all religions. The Persians were a very eclectic, tolerant, and prosperous culture, who traded with most of western Asia along the Royal Road. The Royal Road was a 1,600-mile-long stretch of road, the equivalent of a modern-day journey from New York to Dallas, Texas, and connected the capital of Susa to Sardis, a Greek port. In antiquity, this road took the ordinary person three months to traverse. There were 111 stations along the way, and royal couriers using horses could cross it in a week. The Royal Road helped fuse the kingdom together, as did the imposition of an official language, Aramaic, the same language spoken by the historic Christ.

Susa and Persepolis

There were two capitals of the Persian Empire, **Susa** and **Persepolis**. Susa was the setting of the biblical book of Esther, and a citadel that was reached by a stairway topped Persepolis. It contained monumental buildings and a huge royal audience hall. Architects and stonemasons from throughout the empire including Greece, Egypt and other regions, could be found working in the capitals.

Zoroastrianism

The Persians also contributed a religion known as **Zoroastrianism**. The prophet **Zoroaster** (or Zarathustra) (628–551 B.C.E.) founded Zoroastrianism. The main text we have for this tradition dates from the third century C.E. and is known as the *Zend Avesta*. According to this much later text, in his youth, Zoroaster had visions and conversations with divine beings. He became a wandering preacher who urged the Persians to abandon sacrifice to all minor deities, and to be more humane towards animals in sacrifice. He taught a dualist religion in which good battled evil. Good was symbolized by light while evil was symbolized by darkness. Fire was thought of as divine since it was a form of light. The god of good was Ahura Mazda, and immortal holy ones or forces of good, such as obedience, truth, law, and immortality, assisted him. His twin, Ahriman, was banished from heaven to hell, where he reigned as the embodiment of evil. Zoroaster urged the Persians to "turn from the lie (druj) to the truth (asha)."

Zoroaster taught that people are creations of the good god and have the free will to turn either towards good or evil. In the end, humans will be judged according to the Book of Life, in which all deeds are recorded. Zoroastrians did not burn or bury the dead as they considered soil and fire to be sacred. There was a priesthood known as the Magi, who absolved sins and meted out atonement and repentance. Some historians argue that the Zoroastrian concept of good vs. evil influenced Christianity, as did its concept of life after death, the importance of good works, and its cult of Magi, who are mentioned in the Christian gospels as among the first visitors to the infant Jesus.

An important tradition within Zoroastrianism was the cult of Mithraism. According to legend, Mithras was born on December 25, the date of the winter solstice when the sun returns from south of the equator and is reborn. Mithras was sent by Ahura Mazda to redeem the earth. After the first century of the common era, Mithraism was a widespread cult in ancient Rome, and in later Roman versions of this myth Mithras slaughtered a holy bull while on earth. Initiates bathed in the blood of the bull and also ate a sacred meal from its shoulder. The similarity of Christianity to Mithraism was one of the reasons Christianity spread rather slowly through the Roman Empire.

Zoroastrianism became the state religion of the Persian Empire following the conversion of the Persian kings. Darius, for example, was a convert to Zoroastrianism. The Persian Empire collapsed after Muslim invasions in the seventh century C.E.

CHAPTER 3

THE HITTITES

The **Hittites** were one of the most important empires of antiquity to rule Mesopotamia. They were Indo-Europeans who invaded and conquered the Old Babylonian empire in Mesopotamia (1900–1600 B.C.E.). The homeland of the Hittites was known as *Hatti* and was in Central Anatolia. Archaeologists discovered a huge cache of 10,000 Hittite tablets in 1906 in the Hittite capital Hattusas, located near the modern Turkish town of Boghazkoy about 210 kilometers east of Ankara. The Hittites adopted many Mesopotamian customs and also spread Mesopotamian culture in the near east. Whereas the Code of Hammurabi and later Assyrian codes mandated "an eye for an eye" policy and often the death penalty, Hittite laws were more merciful. The Hittites flourished from 1600 to 1200 B.C.E., and developed the use of iron. Their iron tools enabled them to become serious threats on the battlefield, and Egypt fought wars with them from 1300 to 1200 B.C.E. Ramses II in Egypt, for example, fought vigorously against the Hittites. After the Battle of Kadesh, Ramses negotiated a treaty with the Hittites and then married a Hittite princess. The Hittites, like many other cultures, collapsed in the set of disasters that occurred at the end of the second millennium B.C.E. Around the thirteenth century B.C.E., a wave of famines and other natural disasters brought about the collapse of the Hittites, as well as the Mycenaeans. Even Egypt had problems from the migrations of the Peoples of the Sea.

CHAPTER 4

EGYPT: THE GIFT OF THE NILE

GEOGRAPHY OF ANCIENT EGYPT

When the Greek historian Herodotus visited Egypt in the sixth century B.C.E., he called it "the Gift of the Nile." Like Mesopotamia, Egypt was dependent on a river and the fertile soil it deposited for the rise of its civilization. Ancient Egyptian culture was centered on a very small but fertile strip of land only ten to twenty miles wide.

The geography of the Nile River Valley created a stable and isolated region in which Egyptian culture could flourish uninterrupted by outside invaders. Consequently, the Egyptians developed a very positive view of life and the afterlife. The Nile River is the longest river in the world, and its annual period of inundation was regular and predictable. The flood waters deposited very fertile soil and agriculture flourished. The Nile was difficult to navigate due to several cataracts, areas where several small tributaries intersect to create white-water rapids. In fact, it was not until the twentieth century that explorers traced the Nile back to its source, Lake Victoria. To the west of the Nile was the world's largest desert, the Sahara, which takes its name from the Arabic word for "tan," the color of the sand. North Africa was not very populous in antiquity and presented no threat of invasion, and high cliffs protected the eastern side of the Nile. These natural barriers kept invaders out of the Nile River Valley.

These features of the Nile allowed the native culture to flourish without interference. Herodotus, who lived in the Golden Age of ancient Greece, was so impressed by the monumental ruins of Egypt that he called it "a land and works beyond expression great." Nevertheless, scholars have argued that Egyptian culture was rather stagnant during the Old Kingdom. During the

Old Kingdom, bureaucracy remained unchanged for centuries and so did the basic way of life; in fact, if one travels up and down the Nile River today, one can still see modern Egyptians using ancient tools, such as the shadoff, which is used to pull water from the river. Although the Egyptians had a more positive view of life and the afterlife than did the Mesopotamians, they also had a much more rigid social structure in which there was little mobility.

Scholars have more information about ancient Egypt than about ancient Mesopotamia. The hot, dry climate contributed to the preservation of documents written on papyrus, whereas the clay tablets of Mesopotamia dissolved in the flooding of the Tigris and Euphrates. The hot, dry weather also produced the first mummies through a natural process of dehydration in the desert sand. Egyptology first emerged as an area of interest following the late eighteenth-century expedition of Napoleon to Africa. He and his men uncovered many artifacts, including the Rosetta Stone, which recorded a decree in honor of the pharaoh Ptolemy V in Greek, Egyptian hieroglyphics (the language used for official and religious documents), and Demotic (the everyday script of Egypt). Since Greek was a well-known language, the nineteenth-century French scholar Jean Francois Champollion deciphered hieroglyphics by comparing the Egyptian texts to the Greek text. Unfortunately, according to legend, Napoleon's men destroyed many other artifacts, such as the Sphinx, whose nose they are said to have knocked off. Very likely this is untrue, but it has remained a legend for centuries.

Manetho, a third-century B.C.E. Egyptian priest, first divided Egyptian history into thirty-one dynastic periods. Modern scholars divide Egyptian history into three main periods based on the stability of the government, with two additional periods before and after. The three main periods of Egyptian history are the **Old Kingdom**, the **Middle Kingdom**, and the **New Kingdom**. The period before the Old Kingdom is the Archaic era, and the period after the New Kingdom is the late period.

The Archaic Era

The **Archaic Era** began in 3100 and lasted until 2700 B.C.E. Greek writers claimed that Menes founded the first dynasty in 3000 B.C.E. and first united Upper and Lower Egypt. The Narmer palette credits Narmer with these deeds, and scholars continue to debate whether these two figures are the same person. Scholars had also debated whether Menes was a mythological figure, but if he is the same person as Narmer, the Narmer palette confirmed his historic existence. Narmer (Menes) was also the first to wear the double crown of Egypt. The double crown is a combination of the symbols of Upper and Lower Egypt, the papyrus and lotus plants. The palette shows Narmer vanquishing his enemies; the two lions with their necks and heads intertwined symbolize the unity of Upper and Lower Egypt. Upper Egypt was the southernmost area along the Nile Valley, while Lower Egypt was the region nearest the Nile River Valley Delta. The Nile flows from south to north, which accounts for Lower Egypt being to the north of Upper Egypt. Egypt was the most stable when Upper and Lower Egypt were unified, and unification of these two regions helps to determine the dividing points between the various eras of Egyptian history.

The Old Kingdom

The **Old Kingdom** lasted from 2700 to 2200 B.C.E. and represents the third through the sixth dynasties. During this period, Egypt was isolated and uninfluenced by outside cultures. The geography of the region created a very stable environment. During the Old Kingdom the cult of the pharaoh was created, the bureaucracy of Egypt was established, and monumental constructions such as the pyramids were built. Egyptians considered their pharaoh to be fully divine, and he was known as the living Horus and the Osiris of the Underworld. The myth of Osiris created the cult of the pharaoh. Scholars do not know whether Osiris was an actual historic ruler, but the ancient Egyptians believed that he was. According to legend, Osiris was a ruler who was very much loved by his people. His brother Seth was very jealous of him, and one day while Osiris was walking along the Nile he snuck up from behind and slaughtered Osiris. He cut him into little pieces and threw them into the Nile River. Osiris's wife, Isis, and the falcon-headed god Horus collected the pieces and put him together. Horus later defeated Seth. Osiris had conquered death, and thus every pharaoh was revered as the lord of the underworld and as the living Horus on earth. When Egyptians passed into the underworld, they believed that Osiris himself would judge their deeds. The pharaoh was the center of Egyptian civilization. Scholars have often said that in Egypt there were only two classes of people: the pharaoh and everyone else. In fact, one can symbolize Egyptian social structure as a pyramid with the pharaoh on top and the rest of the Egyptian population on various levels beneath.

As a tribute to the immense power of the pharaoh, the Egyptians built enormous pyramids to ensure the passage of the pharaoh's *ka* to the underworld. The first pyramid builder was Sneferu who experienced several failures, such as the Bent Pyramid, but who nonetheless developed the techniques well enough for his children and grandchildren, Cheops, Khefren, and Mycerinus, to build the Great Pyramids of Giza. The famous sphinx is connected to the second pyramid at Giza for Khefren, but recent controversial geological studies have suggested it may be much older than the pyramids.

It took a vast bureaucracy to manage the enormous task and cost of constructing the pyramids. The Vizier, who ran daily affairs in Egypt, was the most important official. Priests also had a great deal of power due to the extensive focus of the Egyptians on afterlife. The Egyptians had a very positive view of afterlife, as reflected by the collection of poems known as *The Book of Dead*. According to "The Negative Confession," one of the texts from this collection, the Egyptians valued many of the same virtues as do many modern societies. The Egyptians considered beating one's family or slaves, stealing, and damming up the Nile so as to withhold life-giving water to be evil. The text also made clear that one should not trespass one's boundaries with the gods. The Egyptians believed that Osiris would reward good deeds with an afterlife that in many ways would be like life itself. Perhaps the form of the Negative Confessions influenced the Hebrew Ten Commandments, seven of which are in negative form.

By the fifth dynasty, the priests had become extremely powerful. The last pharaoh of the Old Kingdom, Pepi II of the sixth dynasty, ruled for some ninety years. To balance the rising power of the priesthood with his own power, he gave away pharaonic power and decentralized the government. Although Pepi reigned for almost a century in this precarious state, his successors were unable to hold power. The decline in the pharaoh's power can be seen in the title he took as "Son of Re" as opposed to Re himself.

The First Intermediate Period

The **First Intermediate period** lasted from 220 to 2050 B.C.E. During this period, there was political chaos as four dynasties competed for power. There were two dynasties at Memphis and two more at Herakleopolis, comprising the seventh, eighth, ninth, and tenth dynasties.

The Middle Kingdom

The **Middle Kingdom** lasted from 2050 to 1652 B.C.E. and represented restoration of unity and stability after the collapse of the Old Kingdom. The eleventh dynasty at Thebes reestablished control in 2000 B.C.E. The twelfth dynasty, also located in Thebes, reunited Upper and Lower Egypt. The main god of Thebes was Amon, and during this period the Thebans fused their mythology of Amon with that of the earlier god, Re. Amon-Re would be one of the most important deities worshipped throughout the remainder of Egyptian history.

The Second Intermediate Period

The **Second Intermediate** period lasted from 1567 to 1085 B.C.E. It began during the thirteenth dynasty, with a series of ineffective rulers. For most of this period Upper and Lower Egypt were not united, and there was civil warfare. The Hyksos, a group of people who came from Palestine, established a rival dynasty during this period. This was the first time Egypt had to deal with foreign influence.

The New Kingdom

The **New Kingdom** prospered from 1567 and lasted until 1085 B.C.E. It began when the eighteenth-dynasty pharaoh Ahmose I defeated the foreign Hyksos and reunited Upper and Lower Egypt. Thebes was once again the capital of Egypt. The New Kingdom was a very prosperous period marked by a new kind of pharaoh who excelled on the battlefield. Thutmose I, for example, expanded Egypt to the fourth cataract to the south and to Palestine and Syria in the east. His daughter, Hatshepsut, became the most important of six women in Egyptian history to wield power as regent or even, as in her case, as pharaoh. Hatshepsut ruled as regent for her stepson Thutmosis III, and then declared herself pharaoh shortly after she took power. While other New Kingdom pharaohs concentrated on conquest, Hatshepsut sent an expedition to Punt in Africa and engaged in trade. Thutmosis III defaced her monuments after he took power and became one of the greatest warriors of the New Kingdom. He led seventeen successful campaigns that led to 100 years of prosperity.

One of the more interesting pharaohs of the New Kingdom was Amen-hotep IV, who changed his name to Akhenaton in honor of the god he served, Aton. Akhenaton, or "he who is beneficial to Aton," reformed Egyptian religion with his wife Nefertiti and created a new style of realistic art at his new capital of Akhetaton, now Tel el-Amarna. His religious revolution marked the first expression of monotheism in the world but his son, Tutankamun, who died while still a young man of nineteen years, quickly overturned it. Tutankamun's tomb in the Valley of the Kings, excavated by Howard Carter, is one of the richest archaeological finds in Egyptian history.

Ramses II (the Great) was another important pharaoh of the New Kingdom. He defeated the Hittites at the famous battle of Kadesh. Although he failed to conquer them completely as a result of the battle, he negotiated an important treaty with them and sealed the alliance by his marriage to a Hittite princess. Ramses II remains larger than life in the many monumental structures built to honor him, such as the temple of Abu Simbel and the Ramesseum. Ramses may have been the pharaoh of the exodus, though many scholars put forward several other possibilities.

In 1200 B.C.E. a new group of people of diverse ethnicity, known as the Peoples of the Sea, began to enter Egypt. Their arrival began the decline of Egypt's traditional power structure that led to the late period.

The Late Period

Following the New Kingdom pharaohs, Egypt entered a long period of decline in which it would become part of several other empires. In the seventh century B.C.E. the Assyrians conquered Egypt. In 525 B.C.E. the

Persians conquered Egypt. In the fourth century B.C.E. Alexander the Great would proclaim himself the "son of Re" and bring Egypt into the Hellenistic world. One can still see the Greek influence on Egyptian architecture from the conquests of Alexander. Under the Ptolomies, the last pharaohs, Egypt became part of the Roman Empire.

CHAPTER 5

THE HEBREWS

The Torah refers to the **Hebrews** as the "fewest of all people." Politically, the Hebrew kingdoms flourished only during the forty-year reign of Solomon in the tenth century B.C.E. Nevertheless, the "fewest of all people" have had an immeasurable impact on the development of the world, as their ancient customs gave rise to three of the world's major religions, including Judaism and its offspring, Christianity, and Islam. It is important to remember that the early Christians were all Jews, including the historic Jesus; Ishmael, father of the Arab nations, was the firstborn son of Abraham, patriarch of the Hebrews, through his concubine Hagar, making the Jews and Arabs ancient cousins. The Qur'an contains a history of the Hebrew prophets and Abraham and Ishmael, as well as stories of Jesus.

Although the Hebrew scriptures were never meant to be histories in the modern sense of the word, these texts do contain references that are historically useful. For example, genealogies and references to ancient peoples and kingdoms can be compared to other sources. The Hebrew scriptures were, however, composed in the same way as many other texts in the ancient period. The life of Abraham, patriarch of the Hebrews, dates to 1800 B.C.E., yet the oldest texts we have of the Hebrew scriptures date to the ninth century B.C.E. This is approximately the same era in which the Greek epics the *Iliad* and *Odyssey* and the *Epic of Gilgamesh* were first recorded in written form. The present form of the biblical texts is not found in written form until the second century C.E.

The Torah, or Pentateuch, is the foundation of Judaism. The word "Pentateuch" comes from the root "pent," meaning five. The Torah includes the books of Genesis, Exodus, Leviticus, Deuteronomy, and Numbers. These books are traditionally credited to Moses. There is no mention of Moses as author of the Torah in the Torah itself, but the book of Nehemiah, which chronicles the return of the Hebrews from Babylon, tells us that Ezra in the fifth century B.C.E. brought out the "book of the law of Moses" (Nehemiah 8:1). Most scholars, however, believe that there were several authors involved in the creation of these texts.

Another issue of great importance is how one defines the group of people referred to as Hebrews. Today, the descendants of the ancient Hebrews are mainly known as "Jews," as they are the survivors of the Hebrew kingdom of Judah. It is unclear whether the Hebrews were of a homogenous ethnicity; clearly, they spoke a Semitic language. However, their scriptures seem to define them by a set of practices contained in the Torah. Chief among these practices was the *bris*, or circumcision of male infants at eight days of age. Modern Jews are also very difficult to categorize; Jews can be found all over the world, and today are not a single ethnicity but a very diverse collection of peoples. Further, many people identify themselves as Jews who do not practice Judaism.

HEBREW ORIGINS

Hebrew history begins with the life of Abraham, who lived in Ur in Mesopotamia around 1850 B.C.E. The era from 1850 to 1250 B.C.E. in Hebrew history is known as the time of the patriarchs and is recounted in the book of Genesis. Abraham was originally called Abram, and he rejected worship of the traditional deities of Mesopotamia. Abram left Ur, crossed into what is modern-day Israel, and eventually migrated to the Nile delta. The origins of the word "Hebrew" are difficult to trace. After Abraham left Ur, the Hebrews became a nomadic people; the word "abiru," meaning "dusty ones," may be the root of the modern word. Alternatively, Abram crossed the Euphrates, and the word "ibri" in Hebrew means "from the other side."

In Egypt, the Lord made one of several covenants with Abram promising to reward him with numerous descendants. Abram's name became Abraham, which means "father of a host of nations," and he later had two sons. His first son, Ishmael, was born of his concubine Hagar. His wife Sara had been barren, but in their later years Sara conceived and gave birth to Isaac. According to Genesis, Sara was concerned for Isaac's inheritance and status, and had Abraham expel Hagar and Ishmael. This expulsion is an important story in the Qur'an and the religion of Islam, as it was Ishmael who is credited with being the father of the Arab nations. Isaac, on the other hand, is the beginning of the Hebrew line. The twelve tribes of Israel descended through Isaac's son Jacob, renamed "Israel" or "the soldier of God." The covenant also promised that Abraham and his descendants would receive the land of Canaan. The symbol of the covenant was the *bris*, or circumcision, which physically distinguished the Hebrews from other peoples.

The Exodus

In the thirteenth century B.C.E., the books of Exodus, Deuteronomy, Numbers, and Joshua relate the exodus from Egypt under the leadership of **Moses** and the eventual settlement of the Hebrews in "the promised land." The story of Moses, whom his mother placed in a reed basket and set afloat on the Nile, is very similar to that of Sargon the Great, who founded the Akkadian Empire. Moses was discovered by an Egyptian princess and raised as a prince, and later discovered his heritage. Moses became the first prophet in Hebrew history. During the wandering in the desert, Moses went up to Mt. Sinai and brought back the ten words, or ten commandments, to the Hebrews. Moses received a new covenant and ordered the construction of the ark of the covenant to house the tablets he had brought down from Sinai. The ark was the physical dwelling place of a transcendental God. The Hebrews believed the presence of God to be so powerful that only the holiest priest could see the ark; all others would die immediately.

The covenant between the Hebrew God and Moses found in the book of Exodus is very similar to ancient treaties known as vassal treaties made in the Middle East between a powerful lord and a vassal who does not have the same status. The Mosaic covenant in Exodus follows this form with one exception, it contains no list of gods to witness the treaty. Later prophets, such as Jeremiah, reworded the covenant to emphasize that the Hebrews were to be the chosen people of their God.

The Ten Commandments

The covenant is what bound the ancient Hebrews together. The Torah contains over 770 commandments, but the most well-known of those may be the so-called **Ten Commandments**, which are often regarded as a summary of the covenant. Seven of these commandments begin with "Thou shalt not," or what we earlier referred to as negative theology. The Egyptian Book of the Dead may have influenced their form of expression. The Ten Commandments were remarkable in that they applied equally to all members of society; unlike the Code of Hammurabi, they do not apply differently to different classes.

The Kabbalah

Moses brought the Ten Commandments down from Sinai, but there is also a belief that he received a great deal of revelation that was never written down. This belief in an oral tradition ultimately grew into **Kabbalah**, or mystical Judaism. Kabbalists interpret the Torah in part through an oral tradition that they believe began with Moses. Kabbalists argue that the Torah tells one how, whereas Kabbalah tells one why. The main text of the Kabbalah tradition is the Zohar, which dates from the Roman period.

The Wandering in the Desert

According to the Hebrew Scriptures, the Hebrews continued to wander in the desert for forty years. Many modern archaeologists have tried to find evidence of the wanderings of thousands of people, but to date none has been found. This is one of the puzzling aspects of the Hebrew Scriptures. The Scriptures do not give exact enough references for us to know the path traveled in those years; in fact, there is great debate about exactly where Mt. Sinai is located. The monastery of St. Catherine, on the Sinai peninsula, has long maintained that it is located where the burning bush was located; however, other scholars suggest that Mt. Sinai is located elsewhere on the peninsula.

The Promised Land

The Hebrew texts chronicle the eventual arrival of the Hebrews in "the promised land" or the region known as Palestine in Roman times. The word "Palestine" comes from the Roman word to describe the Philistines. Under the leadership of Joshua, the Scriptures relate a victory over the Canaanites and the settlement of the Hebrews in the region of modern Israel. There is little archaeological evidence to support this account of a military conquest of the Holy Land. The Scriptures interpret what skirmishes did occur as an act in which their God delivered them from bondage and enabled them to found the kingdom of Israel.

The Judges and the Formation of the Hebrew Monarchy

The twelve tribes of Israel were ruled by judges from 1130 to 1020 B.C.E. The various decisions of the judges and the history of the Hebrews are chronicled in the book of Judges. The judges resisted the idea of a centralized government, as they believed only their god should be regarded as king.

Saul, The First King

The first Hebrew king to unite the twelve tribes was **Saul**, who reigned from 1020 to 1000 B.C.E.

David and the Foundation of Jerusalem

Saul's son-in-law **David** reunited the twelve tribes after his father-in-law's death. As a young shepherd boy, we first hear of David in connection with the Philistines; according to the Scriptures, he killed Goliath with his slingshot. David reigned from 1000 to 970 B.C.E., made Jerusalem his capital, and built the city to house the ark of the covenant. **Jerusalem** is the holiest city in the world for Jews and also for Christians. It is also considered holy for Muslims as it marks the site of Muhammad's Night Journey and

Ascension into Heaven. The presence of the ark there made Jerusalem the center of the Hebrew religion as well as its political center.

The Prosperity Under Solomon

David's son **Solomon** reigned from 970 to 930 B.C.E. This brief period was the most prosperous period in Hebrew history. Solomon built a magnificent temple for the ark in Jerusalem.

Meggido

The magnificence of Solomon's reign is seen in such ruins as **Meggido**, where there was a stable large enough for 500 horses. Meggido was located on an important trade route linking Egypt with the Near East. Moreover, Egypt had been the dominant power in the Middle East for over 2,000 years before Abraham. The Persian, Assyrian, and Babylonian empires balanced the power of Egypt to the east of Israel. The Hebrew kingdoms became the crossroads where these powers often struggled for supremacy, and Meggido overlooked the site of important battles. The name "meggido" derives from the word *Harmageddon*; Meggido was so well-known in the ancient world as the center of conflict in the Middle East that the author of the Book of Revelation, a Christian text, places the final conflict between good and evil at Armageddon or Meggido. Thutmosis III fought many battles for control of Meggido.

The Queen of Sheba

Solomon's wisdom and wealth also attracted people from many neighboring kingdoms, including the **Queen of Sheba**. Some scholars suggest she was from Ethiopia, while most scholars today argue that she was from the Saudi Arabian peninsula.

Despite the prosperity of Israel under Solomon, the foundations for the destruction of unity were already laid. Solomon heavily taxed the tribes to centralize the government, ignoring tribal loyalties and other issues. His successor, his son Rehoboam, had even less understanding of old tribal issues.

Disintegration of the Hebrew Kingdom of Solomon

After the death of Solomon, the unity of the twelve tribes disintegrated. Solomon's kingdom was split in half, Israel in the north and Judah in the south. Considerable tension erupted between the tribes during this period, and the Hebrew scriptures are very critical of Rehoboam and other rulers of the northern kingdom as well as the rulers of Judah.

The Northern Kingdom of Israel

The word "Israelite" refers to the inhabitants of the kingdom of Israel, named for Isaac's son Jacob, who was given the name "Israel" or "soldier of

God." The capital of the northern kingdom was Samaria. The Scriptures are very critical of the northern rulers, and in the period following the collapse of Solomon's empire, many prophets arose, including Elijah, Elisha, Amos, and Hosea. The prophets argued that the kings of the north had abandoned the covenant, and they urged reform of the state and religion in order to avoid destruction.

The Ten Lost Tribes of Israel

The Assyrians conquered Israel in 722 B.C.E. The Hebrew tribes dispersed, giving rise to the search for the "ten lost tribes" of Israel. There are various hypotheses about what happened to these ten tribes. One scholar has suggested that the tribes eventually migrated to the Americas, and, although most scholars do not accept this hypothesis, the Church of Jesus Christ of Latter-day Saints, or the Mormons, is based on this idea. Mormons also believe that Christ made an appearance in the Americas after his resurrection to descendants of the ten lost tribes.

Another thesis maintains that many of the ten tribes migrated to Europe, where they helped to lay the foundation for later European culture. The most credible of all these hypotheses is that the ten lost tribes fled to Judah, whose population doubled shortly after the conquest of Israel by the Assyrians.

The Southern Kingdom of Judah

Judah was the southern kingdom of the Hebrews. The word "Jew" refers to the inhabitants of Judah. In the period following the collapse of Solomon's empire, prophets arose in both the northern and southern kingdoms. Isaiah was one of the most important prophets, and he served the kings of Judah. In Christian times, Isaiah's words would be interpreted as prophesying the coming of Christ.

The Babylonian Captivity

The population of Judah doubled after the conquest of Israel, and it may be that Jews, or descendants of the tribe of Judah, include descendants of many of the so-called "ten lost tribes of Israel." The Babylonians conquered Judah in 586 B.C.E. and brought many inhabitants to Babylon. This period is known as the Babylonian Captivity and is chronicled in the second book of Kings, chapters 24–25, and in the books of Ezra and Nehemiah, which deal mainly with the later return of the Jews. During this fifty-year period, Jews attempted to preserve their identity. Rabbis, or teachers, taught Hebrew history and religion in the synagogues. This period is also the likely date for the beginnings of the Talmud, or rabbinical commentary on the Torah. The Talmud contains explications of such customs as the *bar mitzvah*, wedding rituals, and Kosher laws for the preparation of food.

The Persians liberated the Jews when they conquered Babylon and allowed them to return to Jerusalem. There was a great deal of resentment towards those who had remained in Judah; when the Jews returned after the Babylonian captivity, they refused to allow those who had remained to help rebuild the kingdom. The tension between these two factions is evident in the Christian Scriptures in the references to the Jews and Samaritans. Jerusalem was located in Judah.

The Second Temple

When the Persians conquered Babylon, Cyrus the Great allowed the Jews to return to the Holy Land. They built a second temple under the leadership of Ezra and Nehemiah. Herod the Great, a Roman ruler, greatly expanded the temple. The Romans razed the temple in 70 C.E. and again in 132 C.E.

The Wailing or Western Wall

The only remaining wall of the second temple is the western wall or "**wailing wall**." This is the holiest site in the Jewish world today. Jews go there to pray for the return of their temple and to lament its destruction. The sound that is often heard during these prayers is similar to wailing; hence, the origin of the name "wailing wall." Orthodox Jews separate the men from the women; the men's section is to the left, while the women's section on the wall is to the right.

Muslim Structures

Today, the **Dome of the Rock** shrine and the **al-Aqsa mosque** are located on the temple mount. Orthodox Jews believe that this sacred ground has been profaned by the presence of these Muslim structures. Jews believe the temple mount is holy; since no one knows the exact location of the ark in the Holy of Holies in the ancient temple, Orthodox Jews will not set foot anywhere on the mount.

Mysteries of the Bible

We know more about the ark of the covenant than perhaps any other artifact in history; the Hebrew Scriptures are very detailed about its appearance, construction, and even the material out of which it was made. One of the greatest mysteries in biblical scholarship, however, is the fate of the ark of the covenant. Roman reliefs show an object being carried off that might have been the ark. Some scholars suggest that the ark made its way to Ethiopia after the temple was destroyed the second time, where inhabitants still believe it is kept. Others suggest it may have been buried under Jerusalem, but the modern government of Israel refuses to give permission for the extensive excavations needed. Still others believe that the ark is located near Qum'ran by the Dead Sea, where the Dead Sea Scrolls were discovered.

The Diaspora

The destruction of the temple in Jerusalem also led to a widespread diaspora of the Jewish people. Jews live in every nation of the world today and have suffered many waves of persecution. In the 1890s, Theodor Herzl founded the movement known as Zionism, which sought to create a homeland for Jews. Although Zionists did not originally insist that a Jewish state be recreated in the same location as the historic Hebrew kingdoms, following World War II Jews began to return in great numbers to their ancient homeland, culminating in the controversial creation of the state of Israel in 1949.

The Cultural Contributions of the Hebrews: Judaism

The chief tenet of Judaism is a monotheistic belief in one god. The development of monotheism was a long process, but itculminated in the development of a very abstract concept of God. The Hebrew texts forbade the making of images, a prohibition that also appears in the Qur'an, the main text of Islam. The Hebrew God is limitless and cannot be limited by either images or concrete names. At the burning bush, the deity tells Moses that his "name" is Yahweh. In Hebrew, which has no vowels, the "name" is YHWH, the root word for "existence." Therefore, what the deity tells Moses is that it and only it exists. This four-letter word is called the Tetragrammaton, and it refers to the unnameable being worshiped by the Hebrews.

We interpolate the vowels in YHWH to get the word "Yahweh"; the word is considered so sacred it cannot be uttered. Later, Latin writers transliterated the word from YHWH to JHVH, or Jehovah.

This very abstract concept of God differs greatly from the anthropomorphic concepts of God seen in Egypt and Mesopotamia, where the gods were often represented as half human and half animal. The Hebrew God was also depicted as loving and compassionate towards its creations, unlike the gods of the *Epic of Gilgamesh*. The Hebrew God is also predictable and offers a rational covenant to his people, promising them prosperity in return for obedience.

The Hebrew story of creation in Genesis captures the rational nature of this deity. Creation occurs over the course of six days, and on the seventh, God rests. The texts tell us that God looked back on what He had done and said, "behold it is good." This vision of life is in stark contrast to the pessimism of Mesopotamia; for the Hebrews, God created humans in the image of God and were not subject to nature, but given power over it.

The Hebrew Scriptures also contain a flood epic that is similar in some ways to that of Gilgamesh but very dissimilar in others. While the flood epic in Gilgamesh is pessimistic in tone, that of the Hebrews is optimistic. After the flood, the rainbow appears as a promise that there will be no further destruction.

CHAPTER 6

INDIAN CIVILIZATION THROUGH THE MAURYAN EMPIRE

OVERVIEW

The earliest culture on the subcontinent of India was located in the Indus River Valley and is the third ancient river valley civilization. Later Indian cultures were centered on the **Ganges River**, which many Hindus regard as a deity. While the ancient inhabitants of India did not necessarily develop powerful, enduring physical empires, they developed an empire of the spirit that has lasted longer than that of any other religious tradition. The Hindu texts are the world's oldest religious texts in continuous use, and the values expressed in these texts, such as *ahimsa* or nonviolence, have influenced great world leaders from Mohandas Gandhi to Martin Luther King, Jr. One-seventh of the world's population today is Hindu.

The Indian origin of many important contributions has sometimes been forgotten, as they have often been attributed to other civilizations. For example, the numbers Western cultures use today are called Arabic numerals, but they were actually invented in India. The Arabs transmitted Indian mathematics to the European world after the Islamic conquest of India. Ancient Indian scholars developed the ideas of infinity, the cube root, and algebra. They also had a notion of a unified world order, *rta,* without which modern science would be impossible.

Ancient Indians were also pioneers in the use of iron steel. They were the earliest to weave cotton into cloth. The design of their looms later spread to

Europe, where their method of programming the design of the cloth inspired the invention of the punch cards used by the first computers to read data!

The Indus River Valley Civilization: The Twin Capitals of Harappa and Mohenjo-Daro

The Indus River is located in the northernmost reaches of the Indian subcontinent. There were two important centers of civilization here, the twin capitals of Harappa and Mohenjo-Daro, nearly identical cities located 400 miles apart from one another. The culture here is commonly called the Harappan culture, as most of the important discoveries came from the city of Harappa. Harappa was first excavated in the 1850s while the British were building a railroad across India; a worker found a small clay brick with an inscription. Scholars still have not deciphered the language of Harappa; this language was not related to Sumerian cuneiform, and many believe it was from the Dravidian family of languages. The Harappans recorded texts on tiny clay seals with images of animals. Some of these images are very similar to the Brahman bull that is venerated in India today. The Brahman bull is considered sacred by Hindus, and they believe it cannot be killed even for food, although thousands of modern Indians live in poverty. Hindus believe that the Brahman bull was the mount of one of their most important deities, Shiva, and also that the bull was one of the incarnations of Brahma, another important deity.

Unfortunately, when the inscriptions were found in the nineteenth century, the British were in the midst of an Imperialist expansion in India and were not interested in uncovering ancient Indian cultures. Rudyard Kipling, a British poet, wrote of the "White Man's Burden," indicating the European belief in the superiority of their culture over that of the Third World. Much of the brick from Harappa was used as ballast for the British railroads. It was not until the early twentieth century that scholars returned to Harappa. A close study of geographic and other references in the **Rig Veda**, the earliest Vedic text, led to the rediscovery of the ancient Indus River Valley culture.

Artifacts from Harappa date back to 2500 B.C.E., and there are many other aspects of Harappan culture that resemble practices of modern Hinduism. Both Harappa and Mohenjo-Daro were very well-planned cities laid out on a grid as most modern cities with streets intersecting each other at right angles. City blocks and buildings were uniform in structure between Harappa and Mohenjo-Daro, suggesting a centralized government. Although this hypothesis has recently been called into question, the similarity of the structures within each city and between the cities also resembles the modern Hindu belief in the unity of all life. The homes of the upper classes, however, are clearly distinguishable from those of the workers; similarly, later Hinduism would distinguish between the Brahmin, or priest caste, and the Sudra, or lowest caste of workers. The cities were also noteworthy for their system of running water and sewers.

Each city had a citadel surrounded by a wall, suggesting that the citadel was a sacred place worthy of special protection. In Mohenjo-Daro, there was a large basin known as the Great Bath, as it was lined with tar, making it watertight and suitable for bathing. It was also large enough to accommodate fifteen people, perhaps the number of priests they had.

The Harappan emphasis on cleanliness evident in their focus on a supply of running water was unique in the ancient world. Only the Hebrews and Romans could equal it, and these were both later cultures. Their attention to cleanliness also reminds one of the modern Hindu water rituals of purification, such as bathing in the Ganges.

In Harappa, there were very few weapons found but quite a number of toys, suggesting that the culture had plenty of leisure time and, therefore, few enemies to worry about. Harappa was likely a peaceful society. These aspects of the two cities also resemble many modern Hindu practices and beliefs, as modern Hindus have reverence for all life forms and practice nonviolence.

The earliest Hindu texts date from the later Aryan period, but given the similarity of Harappan practices to those of later Hinduism, scholars speculate on whether the culture who wrote the Hindu texts, the Aryans, borrowed many beliefs and practices from the Indus River Valley culture.

The Decline of the Harappan Civilization

The Harappan civilization began to decline around 1900 B.C.E., when its ports were suddenly abandoned for unknown reasons. Simultaneously, the construction of the homes and buildings was less proficient, and the pottery declined in quality. Scholars offer many possible explanations for the collapse of Harappa, including evidence that natural resources declined. There is evidence that excessive irrigation of the land led to the buildup of salts and alkalines. Second, the two cities may have declined due to flooding. Archaeological evidence shows that parts of Mohenjo-Daro had to be rebuilt several times after floods destroyed them. Finally, there is some evidence of a violent invasion, as there was a cache of unburied skeletons in Mohenjo-Daro with severe injuries including dismemberment. In fact, we know that by 1800 B.C.E. a new group of Indo-European people had migrated to India, the Aryans. They came from Asia and eventually conquered north India. The most likely explanation for the demise of the Harappan culture is a combination of all three possibilities.

The Vedic Period

The Aryans were part of an extremely widespread and important series of migrations. The Indo-European peoples spread to many parts of the world, including Greece, Iran (a word derived from the Sanskrit word "Arya," for noble), Italy, and numerous other locations.

In India, they created the set of traditions known as **Hinduism**. The period from 1700 to 500 B.C.E. is known as the Vedic period. The word "Veda" means "knowledge." The Aryans wrote the Vedas in Sanskrit, and the earliest of the Vedic texts, the *Rig Veda*, reveals much about their warlike culture, as their chief deity, Indra, was a god of war. The *Rig Veda* is a collection of 1,028 hymns.

Early Hinduism was very polytheistic in nature; Hindus worshiped Indra as well as numerous other deities. In fact, it has been said that there are 330 million gods in Hinduism, though, of course, such a large number is meant to convey the fact that Hinduism has a very large pantheon of deities that cannot in the end be counted. Hindu temples are very elaborate structures with literally thousands of carvings of gods and goddesses. Among the deities worshiped are Shiva the destroyer god, Ganesha the elephant god, Krishna, and many others. The *Rig Veda* also records the formation of the **castes** from the self-sacrifice of the deity Purusha. The caste system did not exist in India before the arrival of the Aryans, who were in the minority of the population. The caste system evolved in order to subjugate the native population of India. The Aryans were lighter skinned than were the native Indians; therefore, the caste system separated the natives or Dasa from their new masters. The highest caste was the Brahmin, or priests; then the Kshatriya, or warrior caste; then the Vaisya, or the herders, farmers, traders, and merchants; and then Sudra, or the slave and servant class. The class below the Sudra were the pariahs, or untouchables, those considered to be outside Indian society.

Since the twentieth century, the caste system has no longer been legally sanctioned in India, yet it is still practiced socially. Similarly, though it is no longer legal to discriminate against people on the basis of race in the United States, many members of minority groups continue to experience unequal treatment.

The Late Vedic or Brahamanic Age

As Hinduism evolved, however, many texts reflected a growing awareness of the unity of all reality. The Hindu concept of *Brahman*, or the total of all reality, is radically different from the Hebrew concept of God. The Hebrew deity is something apart from its creations; it is transcendent. The Hindu concept of *Brahman*, however, is of an imminent divine reality, present in the world and actually one with it.

The period from 1000 to 500 B.C.E. is called the late Vedic or Brahamanic Age. During this period, several classics of Indian literature were produced, including the *Mahabharata*, the world's longest poem about the power struggle of two clans. A subsection of the *Mahabharata* is the *Bhaga-*

vad Gita, a discussion between the warrior Arjuna and the god Krishna. In response to Arjuna's concerns about the possibility of killing members of his own clan, Krishna develops the idea of the *atman*, or the eternal self, which has always existed and will always exist; it cannot be destroyed. According to the Hindu concept of *samsara* or reincarnation, the *atman* lives eternally in innumerable bodies or life forms.

While in any incarnation, the *atman* has a **dharma**, or duty that it must fulfill. Krishna tells Arjuna, the warrior, that his duty is to fight the righteous battle of good against evil, which is more important than one person's particular family ties or interests. For the Hindu, each caste has its own dharma, and one's duty in life is to fulfill one's dharma to the best of one's ability. In perfectly fulfilling one's dharma, Hinduism teaches that one is freed from all karma, or the effects of action. Krishna tells Arjuna in the *Gita* that freedom from action is obtained through the path of renunciation. Once one is freed of action or karma, the Hindu attains unity with *Brahman,* called *moksha.*

The most abstract account of the unity of all reality is found in the *Upanishads,* the last of the Vedic texts to be written. The *Upanishads* were written in the eighth century B.C.E. The *Upanishads* record the dialogue between a master and his student; the word "Upanishads" means "teachings received at the foot of the master." The *atman,* said to be the only truly real aspect of life in the *Gita*, is now said to be one with the essence of all reality, *Brahman*. The Hindu *Brahman* is not physical, and it cannot be perceived, seen, or heard through the five senses.

According to Hinduism, then, life is really about growing in self-knowledge. The more one truly understands reality the more one knows the true self, the *atman*, and the more one knows that the *atman* and the *Brahman* are one. Once one attains such knowledge there is no longer a self at all, as the self becomes one with all reality. The ultimate goal of the Hindu is to understand the illusory quality of any particular life and any notion of the self as distinguished from all others. The self, the *Upanishads* tell us, is the *atman-Brahman*, the unity in *moksha* with all of reality. It is ironic that for the Hindu coming to know the self means losing the self.

Hinduism has no founder and no body of canonical texts that every Hindu must practice. The concept of *Brahman* as the totality of reality allows Hindus to accept any tradition as a path to *moksha*. Hindus believe all are Hindus, that all are on separate paths that will eventually meet in the same place, that reality in which all are one, *Brahman*. Hindus continue to worship many deities as they believe *Brahman* to be limitless, while the human mind in any one lifetime is finite. The 330 million deities are all aspects of that single reality, *Brahman,* presented to one in a way the human mind can grasp.

Three of these deities tend to be most predominant: Brahma, the creator god; Vishnu, the preserver; and Shiva, the destroyer. These three deities represent the cyclic nature of all reality, as from creation comes preservation, yet ultimately created things are destroyed. From the remnants of destruction new life often comes, as when the charred remains of a forest fertilize the ground for new growth. A phallus often symbolizes the god Shiva, for his legends are associated with acts of rape. While rape is a destructive force, it also can bring new life. The Hindu trinity of Brahma, Vishnu, and Shiva symbolizes the continuing cycle of reality of which we are all a part. No one of these deities are separate from the whole, rather they are aspects of it that can be conveniently discussed.

Hinduism is practiced today in many parts of the world, but most predominantly in India and Southeast Asia. Among the many famous Hindu sites is the massive complex at Angkor Wat in Cambodia, the center of the powerful Khmer kingdom abandoned in 1432 C.E.

Buddhism

Buddhism is another important world tradition to have emerged in the axis age. Prince **Siddhartha Gautama** was born into the warrior caste in 563 B.C.E. He died in 485 B.C.E., having become "awake." The number of legends that surround the life of the Buddha would rival the size of the Himalayas if stacked one atop the other. For many centuries, scholars were uncertain whether there ever was a historic Buddha or whether he was a legendary figure who exemplified the teachings of Buddhism. In the nineteenth century C.E., however, an inscription was discovered on a stone that decisively proved the historic existence of the Buddha.

According to legend, Queen Maya had a painless birth and the trees bent down to help her deliver her son. He was called "Siddhartha," or "he whose purpose is fulfilled." Immediately after birth, Siddhartha stood up and walked, leaving lotus plants in his footsteps. The lotus plant is a very beautiful plant that quickly withers, symbolizing the Buddhist belief in the transience of life.

Shortly after the birth, Queen Maya died, another symbol of the passing of one life form into another. Before the birth, Hindu ascetics had prophesied that Queen Maya's son would either be a prince like his father or a Buddha. His father chose for him the former life, and for twenty-nine years he kept his son enclosed within the palace walls. He was given every luxury imaginable, and married a beautiful young woman who bore him a son, Rahula. According to legend, he knew nothing of pain or suffering during those years.

Suddenly, at the age of twenty-nine, Siddhartha began to notice the noise which came from outside the palace walls. He became curious about the world outside, and told his father that he intended to journey outside the palace to discover the world. His father was concerned that he would encounter the nature of the world, its pain, suffering, disease, and misery. To counter that possibility he sent along a companion who was to keep Siddhartha from seeing such painful sights.

Life is often unpredictable, and as Siddhartha and the companion journeyed outside the palace they encountered the **four great sights**. The first great sight was of old people, withered with arthritis and other signs of age. Siddhartha had never known anything like this; he had known only beauty and happiness. He turned to his companion and asked for an explanation. In reply, his companion told him, "That is old age." Siddhartha was puzzled, and as they continued their journey they came across the second great sight: they saw a sick person writhing on the ground in pain. Again, Siddhartha asked for an explanation. In reply, his companion told him, "That is illness." Even more puzzled, Siddhartha continued his journey. He and his companion came upon the third great sight, the funeral procession of a man followed by his weeping daughter and widow. Siddhartha again turned to his companion and asked for an explanation. His companion replied, "That is death." At this point, having seen old age, illness, and death for the first time, Siddhartha was completely puzzled by these mysteries of life. He started to return to the palace, and just as he was almost there he saw the fourth great sight: an ascetic holding his one possession, the empty bowl which he used to beg for food. The ascetic, however, had a serene smile. Now, completely mystified, Siddhartha knew his companion could offer no explanations. His previous explanations had explained nothing. At this point, Siddhartha experienced that deep psychological pain that comes from not knowing the meaning of life or death, of pain or happiness.

When Siddhartha returned to the palace, he vowed to leave again and not return until he had understood those four great sights. On the night of the great renunciation, Siddhartha told his father, wife, and child good-bye, and journeyed with his companion to some forests where Hindu ascetics lived and meditated. At this point, he told his companion good-bye, for he knew that no one else could answer his questions. The answers had to come from within.

Siddhartha spent several years in the forest with the ascetics, and eventually they looked to him as a master. He endured tremendous deprivation, fasting on a grain of rice and a small drink of muddy water every day. He became emaciated. Although Siddhartha attained the Hindu ideal of renunciation, he had not yet attained understanding of the four great sights. He vowed to sit under a Bodhi or Bo tree until enlightenment came, and in a flash of insight he suddenly understood the Four Noble Truths that became the basis for all of his teachings.

The Four Noble Truths and the Middle Path

According to the **Four Noble Truths**, understanding begins when one accepts that life is full of suffering. Just as Siddhartha had seen suffering in three of the four great sights, all people, no matter where or when they live, endure suffering. Suffering permeates life, as illustrated by the Buddha's encounter with an old woman who wanted to resurrect her son who had recently died. The Buddha told the old woman to go and find a mustard seed from a house where no one had died. The woman searched for months and returned empty-handed, telling the Buddha that "the people tell me the living are few but the dead are many." The Buddha then explained the truth about suffering to her.

Had Buddha stopped here, his teachings would have been very pessimistic, yet the second noble truth tells us that suffering comes from desire, or attachment to things that are not permanent. The Buddhist teaches that everything is transient. We live; we die. Plants flourish and wither; nothing remains forever. Under the Bodhi tree, the Buddha realized that even the *atman*, or the self, was an illusion. The Hindu demon Mara tempted him with women and other luxuries. When Buddha understood the self as illusory, all temptation vanished, and he placed his hand to the ground calling the earth as his witness. The idea of the self as distinct leads to more and more desire; the self wants to keep not only the self but all things it desires with it. Nothing, however, lasts, and once one realizes this truth one is able to detach oneself from transient things.

The third noble truth teaches that detachment leads to **Nirvana**. Just as the Hindu taught that the cycle of samsara, or reincarnation, ended with *mokshe*, so, too, the Buddha taught that the cycle of life ends with Nirvana. Nirvana, however, is a difficult concept to grasp, as it represents more of a psychological state than the Hindu concept of *mokshe*. Anyone, at any time, can attain Nirvana through understanding the Four Noble Truths and practicing the middle path. Nirvana is a psychological acceptance of the world as transient and of the unreality of the self. When a disciple asked the Buddha to explain Nirvana, he asked him,

"Is there such a thing as the wind?"

The disciple replied, "Of course there is."

Buddha then asked, "What is its color, shape, thickness?"

The disciple replied, "It has no color, shape, or thickness."

Buddha asked, "Can one touch it and can it be shown?"

The disciple replied, "No, it cannot be touched and it cannot be shown."

Buddha then asked, "If it cannot be shown, how do you know it exists?"

The disciple replied, "I am positive it exists, even if it cannot be seen."

The disciple then concluded, "Nirvana is like that. It cannot be touched or seen, but we are positive it exists."

The fourth noble truth teaches one how to attain Nirvana. As he meditated with the ascetics, the Buddha came to realize that the severe path of

Statue of Bhudda

Hindu asceticism and renunciation did not bring one to enlightenment; neither had the other extreme, his life of luxury and complete contentment. The Buddha taught the Middle Path, a path of moderation and balance accessible to all.

The Eightfold Path of Right Conduct

The Buddha also taught the eightfold path of right conduct, which included:

Right Understanding

Right Belief

Right Speech (never to lie or slander anyone)

Right Behavior (never to steal or kill, and never to do anything one might later regret)

Right Occupation (never to choose an occupation that one might consider bad)

Right Effort (always to avoid evil and strive for good)

Right Contemplation (of the Four Noble Truths with calmness and detachment)

Right Concentration (the path to peace)

Differences between Hinduism and Buddhism

The Buddha denied the existence of the *atman*. He believed that people were not born into castes, but only born with the propensity to do good or evil. He also taught that sacrifice to deities was worthless. When asked by followers whether he was a god, he replied, "I am awake." Buddha forbade his followers from worshiping him as a god. Life in the sixth century B.C.E. in India was very difficult, and the Buddha's doctrine of Nirvana appealed to many for whom the thought of endless *samsara* and infinite numbers of painful lives was hard to bear. Nevertheless, Buddhism spread slowly at first in India; the Buddha's rejection of the caste system conflicted with the main stream of belief. Further, the Hindu concept of *Brahman* was able to absorb almost any tradition, and many aspects of Buddhism were reabsorbed into Hinduism. Hindus explain the Buddha as an incarnation of Krishna, just as they explain the historic Jesus and Muhammad as incarnations of Krishna.

Women and Buddhism

The Buddha preached his first sermon at the Deer Park in Benares to the five ascetics of the forest. Although the Buddha had women followers, in its early days the order of Buddhist monks, the *Sangha*, was made up of only men. Hindus taught that one must be a man before one can achieve *mokshe*, and the prohibition of women in the early Sangha was consonant with this tradition. According to legend, the Buddha's aunt, Queen Maha-Prajapati, had to fight for admission to the Sangha and was eventually admitted. Today, Buddhist nuns continue the tradition that started with Queen Maha-Prajapati.

The Mauryan Empire

Chandragupta Maurya founded the Mauryan Empire in the wake of the conquests of Alexander the Great. Following a bloody battle at Kalinga, Chandragupta's grandson **Ashoka** converted to Buddhism and became the first Buddhist ruler of India. Ashoka issued his edicts on many Rock Pillars throughout India, many marking the path to holy sites associated with the Buddha or celebrating events of his life. He also erected many stupa designed to house relics of the Buddha. The round shape of the stupa symbolizes the cosmic consciousness of the Buddha, as do the round protrusions on many statues of the Buddha. During Ashoka's reign, he emphasized the traditional

Buddhist ideal of taking "refuge in the *dharma*, the *Sangha,* and the Buddha," symbolized by three lions that often adorned the tops of the Rock Pillars. Ashoka attempted to spread Buddhism through the conquest of righteousness, without force and with tolerance for diversity. Although there is some suspicion that he used Buddhism in his early days to further his political ends, Ashoka was the greatest ruler in Indian history, and one of the most humane and benevolent monarchs in all of world civilization.

The Spread of Buddhism

Buddhist temples are found throughout the world, but the greatest concentration of Buddhists is in Southeast Asia, Laos, Thailand, Tibet, China, and Japan. Buddhism spread to China in the first or second century C.E., where the Chinese initially rejected the wandering monks who had left behind their families and shaved their heads. The Chinese were also puzzled by the notion of reincarnation, but despite the fact that Buddhist teaching conflicted with Chinese values, Buddhism eventually took root. The Chinese translated the Buddhist sutras, and in so doing, fused many of the Buddha's teachings with those of Confucius and other important Chinese thinkers. Chinese Buddhists, however, created some of the world's greatest Buddhist art, as seen especially in the caves of Magao along the frontiers of China. Here, thousands of caves are adorned with paintings and enormous statues of the Buddha. In the fourth century C.E., Chinese Buddhist monks began to make pilgrimages to India. The most famous Chinese pilgrim was Xuan Zang, who made a sixteen-year-long pilgrimage to India in the seventh century C.E. in search of Buddhist sutras. These Chinese pilgrim monks largely traveled across the legendary Silk Road.

Buddhism also spread to Japan, where the Japanese created a unique version of Buddha's teachings, Zen Buddhism. Zen Buddhists are known for the use of rock gardens to meditate. The rocks are often arranged in groups of three to symbolize heaven, earth, and humanity. The formations are also asymmetrical, to symbolize the uneven and imperfect nature of life.

Mahayana and Therevada Buddhism

Over the centuries, Buddhism evolved into two main traditions: Mahayana Buddhism and Therevada Buddhism. These two traditions differ on the issue of how to interpret the Buddha's teachings as reflected in the Tripitaka, or Three Baskets of Wisdom. Mahayana Buddhism is known as the greater vehicle and treats the Buddha as a deity. Mahayana Buddhists practice many rituals and emphasize the Buddha's value of compassion. Mahayana Buddhists also believe that salvation is achieved with others, and they venerate saints known as Bodhisattvas, those who have achieved Nirvana but remain behind to teach.

Therevada Buddhism, by contrast, is known as the lesser vehicle and also as Hinnayana Buddhism. Therevada Buddhists believe that Buddhism is for monks and regard the Buddha as a teacher. They avoid rituals and believe salvation is the concern of the individual. Therevada Buddhism is primarily practiced in Southeast Asia (Vietnam and Laos).

Tibetan Buddhists

Ironically, the arrival of Islam virtually extinguished Buddhism in the land of its birth. Buddhism took root, though, in Tibet in the fourth century B.C.E. Monasteries, such as Drepung Loseling, often had as many as 15,000 Buddhist monks, and the **Dalai Lama**'s residence, Poltala palace, was also the center of Tibetan government. In fact, it was considered a family's sacred duty to give a child to the monastery to be trained. Today, however, the Chinese conquest of Tibet is forcing many Buddhist monks and nuns to make the arduous trek over the Himalayas from Tibet to return to the land of the Buddha's birth. The leader of the modern Tibetan Buddhists is his holiness the fourteenth Dalai Lama, who has returned to India to live in the shadow of the Himalayas, where the Buddha was born. Tibetan Buddhists are a strong force for world peace. Their famous sand mandalas are meant to summon forth the spirits of the deities and to help bring about world peace; yet in typical Buddhist fashion, after days and days of arduous work, the mandalas are scooped into a bag and deposited in a river. This act emphasizes the transience of all life, yet water from the rivers travels to the world's oceans, where it evaporates and eventually returns to the earth as rain. In this way, Tibetan Buddhists hope to spread their prayers for world peace throughout the world, bringing to life the teachings of the ancient "awakened one."

CHAPTER 7

CHINA THROUGH
THE HAN

The Chinese are a people devoted to the ancient past. **Confucius**, the great axis-age philosopher, based his entire system of thought on the ancient models of the Zhou Dynasty. Confucius argued that to be a transmitter of past wisdom and morality was superior to being an innovator, and that the best models of society and virtue were to be found in the past. For followers of Confucius in China, "progress" is made not by going forward and getting away from the past, but by returning as closely as possible to its ideals.

Confucianism is an ancient school of thought based on more ancient ideals of the Zhou; even those ideals were based on a remote era when the Heavenly Emperors ruled, an era more mythological than historical. The completeness of the past dominates life for the Chinese. All those who have gone before lead those who live in the present, and the worship of ancestors ties each Chinese to their mythical past and to each other. Confucius articulated the role of the emperor as father to an extended family composed of all Chinese. The Chinese family is the basis of "religion" in China, and China's most noteworthy minds, including Confucius, based their notion of virtue on reverence for the family and respect for authority. Chinese society is a corporate society that downplays the individual in favor of the common good.

GEOGRAPHY, AGRICULTURE, THE FAMILY, AND THE PEASANT IN ANCIENT CHINA

Agriculture evolved as early as 8000 B.C.E. in northern China around fertile river valleys. The Yellow River was one of the most important of these river systems. This river is often called "China's Sorrow," as throughout history there have been many devastating floods that have killed thousands. The

Yellow River is a very turbulent river, which the Chinese crossed by inflating goat skins and creating rafts from them. Chinese culture arose on the small plots in valleys around the Yellow River. The family unit cultivated these plots. The influence of early Chinese agriculture around the Yellow River is still felt in the importance of the family unit in Chinese society. The oldest male was the head of the Chinese family; next in order of importance were the sons, from oldest to youngest; last in importance were the women of the family, from the oldest, the mother, to the youngest daughter.

The chief crop cultivated in ancient and modern China was rice or millet. Rice is a very efficient source of nutrition, but it must be cultivated primarily by hand. Rice sprouts are allowed to grow into shoots and then transplanted by hand into paddies, where they are later harvested by hand. Throughout Chinese history, the special care demanded by the rice plant meant that the vast majority of Chinese lived in the countryside and worked at manual labor. Women played an important role in the fields, and for centuries have been the most significant group of laborers in China. Just as historical records of the lives of women are scant, so, too, are records of the lives of the majority of the world's population, the peasants and laborers. Today, as in antiquity, the vast majority of Chinese live in the countryside in impoverished villages. Chinese peasants still live primarily within the family unit in these villages.

THE PREHISTORIC ERA

The **Prehistoric era** in Chinese history is the era before the Hsia Dynasty and is primarily dominated by the mythological stories of the **Heavenly Emperors**. Scholars have never been able to authenticate these stories, but for quite some time they also thought that the Shang and Hsia dynasties were mythological in nature.

Whether the stories of the Heavenly Emperors are mythological or not, they represent many elements of traditional Chinese beliefs and practices and also define the ideal emperor and state. The myths of five of these emperors give us the greatest insight into the evolution of Chinese culture. The emperor Fu Hsi created the *I Ching,* a text that is made up of long and short lines representing the balance between yin and yang. The Chinese believe that the combination of lines allows one to foretell the future. The emperor Shan Nung gave the Chinese the plow and the marketplace, two quintessential elements of an agricultural community. The emperor Huang Ti developed fire. If we look at what these three emperors gave the Chinese and compare these ideas to those of other cultures, we notice that most other cultures credit such developments to the gods, whereas the Chinese credit them to the emperors. The Chinese did not worship deities in the same way as the Mesopotamians, Egyptians, and Hebrews; rather, they worshiped their ancestors and also the emperor. Huang Ti also had twenty-five sons, from whom the feudal families of the Zhou era traced their heritage. The story of Huang Ti and his twenty-five sons illustrates the idea of China as an extended family. The sixth-century B.C.E. sage Confucius based his entire system of virtue on the family unit.

The emperor Ti Yao illustrates the concept of virtue determining the emperor, which was later articulated by Confucius. Ti Yao grew old and needed a successor, but distrusted his own son. He thought his son was immoral and shiftless, and so he went in search of a worthy successor. He found such a young man, one who was moral, hard working, and learned. However, he did not know his own family origins, as his mother was a prostitute. Nevertheless, Ti Yao ceded the throne to this young man, as his ability and inner virtue made him more fit for the throne than those whose genealogy made them candidates for it.

The Chinese creation myth also illustrates some very important Chinese concepts. According to Chinese belief, the universe was created from a giant egg, from which emerged the first cosmic man, Pan Ku. Pan Ku labored to construct the universe we know, and as he worked, his breath became the wind, his sweat the rivers, his hair the grass, and the tiny bugs on his body—lice—became humans. For the Chinese, one's identity comes from one's place in the family unit and larger social organizations. The Chinese ideal of humanity is a communal one, where individualism is de-emphasized in favor of the community. In our discussion of the Hsia (Xia) Dynasty, we shall see that the ideal emperor is one who sacrifices his own interests for those of the community. So, too, the ideal citizen serves others before himself. In the **Taoist** tradition, which began in the sixth century B.C.E., humans are a part of the Tao, which is a cosmic force that determines life. In Taoist art, humans are often seen as tiny specks within vast landscapes, reflecting the same viewpoint of the creation myth as to the place of humans within the grand scheme of things. In many ways, the Chinese have never moved away from the Prehistoric era in terms of the traditional values reflected in these stories.

The Hsia (Xia) Dynasty

For many years, scholars thought the **Hsia (Xia) Dynasty** (before 2000 B.C.E. to 1570 B.C.E.) was a mythological dynasty. Its founder was a Heavenly Emperor, Yu, who taught the Chinese how to manage the flooding of the Yellow River. Yu left his family behind and walked through China for ten years in order to help his people. At the end of the ten years, he returned a cripple. The emperor Yu illustrates the Confucian notion of the self-sacrificing and virtuous emperor who rules for the good of society. Scholars have recently unearthed artifacts that suggest that the Hsia Dynasty was actually an historic dynasty.

The Shang Dynasty

The first solidly authenticated dynasty in Chinese history is the **Shang Dynasty** (1570–1045 B.C.E.). It was thought that the Shang were another mythological dynasty until the twentieth century. The Shang used tortoise shells for divination and in their cult of ancestor worship. The chief priest was the oldest male in each family, and he would burn the shells and interpret the answers to the questions written on them depending on where the shell cracked. The use of tortoise shells in ancestor worship made literacy a necessity, and the Chinese were the most literate culture in the world for centuries.

The Shang were a warrior people, who moved their capital several times. The walls of the city of Ao, their sixth capital, aptly show their warrior culture, as they were thirty feet thick in places. The Shang buried their warriors with jade, as they believed it had magical properties. Jade is not indigenous to the area dominated by the Shang so we know they had established trading networks outside their dominions. The Shang also placed ritual vessels in the tombs, and Chinese skill in bronze casting was unequalled for centuries. The Shang also buried their warriors with live servants, in much the same way as the inhabitants of ancient Ur in Mesopotamia buried their royalty.

The Shang Dynasty was centered around the Yellow River. A slave revolt in the eleventh century B.C.E. overthrew the dynasty.

The Zhou Dynasty

The **Zhou Dynasty** (1045–403 B.C.E.) was centered around the Wei River Valley, and the sixth-century B.C.E. sage Confucius based his moral and ethical system on the Zhou rulers. For Confucius, the best models of virtue were in the distant Chinese past. The Zhou had overthrown the Shang during a massive slave revolt, and so had to establish their legitimacy. They argued that the last of the Shang rulers was immoral and that the "mandate of heaven" was withdrawn from him and his dynasty and given to the Zhou, who were moral. The Zhou modeled their idea of the state and the emperor on the heavens, specifically after the polestar, or the north star, a fixed point in the northern sky around which other stars revolve. For the Zhou, the emperor was the polestar, the center of Chinese society. The *Classic of History* or *Shu Jing* is a very important collection of documents from seventeen hundred years of Chinese civilization. Although many of these texts were reconstructed during the Han Dynasty, they give us much insight into the Zhou system of government and moral value that became the basis for Confucianism in the axis age.

Under the Zhou, China was a feudal society in which great and powerful nobles lived on fortified estates and lands and governed their own states. The law of primogeniture was important in this system, as all the possessions of the father passed to his eldest son, thereby preserving the family wealth and power. The legacy of the Zhou feudal structure is still seen in China today, where there are only approximately 400 family names despite the ethnic diversity of China. The emperor Shi Huang Ti would later unify China, thus limiting the number of family names in the country.

The capital of the Zhou Dynasty was Xian, which was also the beginning of the famous Silk Road. Xian was an important center for centuries, and was also the location near which the tomb of the first emperor of China, Shi Huang Ti, was constructed.

The Western Zhou

The western Zhou collapsed in 771 B.C.E. According to legend, the emperor had a concubine who was quite fond of watching the army assembled with all of its beautifully colored armor and banners. The emperor had routinely summoned them to please her on the pretext that invaders were coming. In 771 B.C.E., there really was a crisis, but when the emperor summoned the troops, no one came!

The Eastern Zhou

The Zhou also had an eastern capital, Loyang, where they maintained power from 722 to 481 B.C.E. Unlike many cities that were administrative centers of government, Loyang was a center for religious rites, which betrayed the weakness of the eastern Zhou. In 403 B.C.E., the eastern Zhou collapsed, followed by the period of warring states.

The Warring States Period

In the period following the collapse of the eastern Zhou from 403 to 221 B.C.E., the feudal lords of China vied for power, and the states of China were not united. The chaos of the Warring States Period created a desire for order, and the great Chinese schools of the axis age, such as Confucianism and Daoism, arose in response to the political and social chaos of the Warring States Period. It was during this time that the Confucian emphasis on learning led to the rise of the *shih* scholars. The *shih* scholars dominated the administrative apparatus of China for centuries, as these offices were determined by the Confucian idea of merit.

THE HUNDRED SCHOOLS OF CHINESE PHILOSOPHY

During the axis age in the sixth century B.C.E., the sages Confucius and Lao Tzu responded to the chaos surrounding the decline and collapse of the Zhou Dynasty by developing philosophies designed to promote order.

Confucius

Kong Fuzi was born in 551 B.C.E. and was a member of the minor noble family Kong. His name means "master Kong" in Chinese and has been anglicized as "**Confucius**." Although Confucius rose to a prominent position in the government of his native province Lu, political intrigue forced him from the government and he became a wandering teacher. He wrote no texts himself, but his followers collected his sayings and organized them. The most famous collection of Confucian teachings is the *Analects*. Confucius taught through parables and short aphorisms, which illustrate concepts rather than attempt to prove them. His teachings form the basis of Chinese culture and were themselves based on earlier traditions going back to the Zhou and the Chinese mythology surrounding the Heavenly Emperors. Confucius was not an innovator, but was a respecter of ancient traditions and customs. For Confucius, the most excellent models of virtue were to be found in the past, particularly in the Zhou Dynasty. Confucius did not consider himself to be a "sage," or extremely wise man; he simply saw himself as one who respected tradition and upheld the ways of the past. Respect for the past would restore balance, harmony, and order to society and to an individual's own life. Confucianism eventually formed the basis for Chinese culture and profoundly influenced Japanese and Korean culture.

The Nature of Confucianism

Although Confucianism is often practiced religiously, it is not a religion. In the *Analects,* Confucius refused to address questions about the afterlife or the spirit world, as he believed he had no knowledge of such things. Confucianism is not a lofty system of thought on transcendent deities and the afterlife; rather it is a practical system of ethics designed to produce a well-ordered person and state.

The Virtuous Man

Confucius was concerned above all else with virtue and with the virtuous individual. He did not regard himself as an especially brilliant thinker or sage. This is an important point, as Confucius insisted that the virtuous life is open to all and can be followed by any ordinary person. For Confucius, filial piety, or the respect of children for their elders, particularly their male elders, was the basis of all morality. In other words, family relationships formed the basis for a strong society.

The Rule of Propriety and the Way or Dao

The **Rules of Propriety** governed Chinese behavior and helped to develop virtuous behavior. One learned to follow these rules and to become virtuous through training. Virtue was not inborn for Confucius, but rather was a learned behavior. Through watching and imitating the virtuous behavior of one's parents and others in society, particularly the emperor, one learns to be virtuous. After years of performing virtuous actions, one becomes virtuous and can always be relied upon in any situation to be virtuous. For the truly virtuous person, rules and their enforcement are no longer necessary. Virtue becomes the essence of that person's character and will always dictate correct action, no matter the circumstances. Outer behavior is not to be identified with virtue. Behavior can help one learn and develop virtue, but inner virtue is something apart from mere actions. When there are no external factors that compel obedience, the truly virtuous person can be trusted to act properly as a result of his own inner being. So important was inner virtue that Confucius taught one to follow the Way or Dao simply for the sake of the Way rather than for the sake of reward or punishment.

These teachings helped to develop a meritocracy in China, or the idea that government should be conducted by those whose virtue and learning merited their positions of authority and respect. In other words, heredity was meaningless; only ability and inner virtue determined one's advancement.

It was particularly important for government officials to be virtuous. Confucius argued that if one governed people well for several decades or centuries, there would no longer be a need for the death penalty or other harsh punishments. People would submit to virtuous rulers, whereas they would revolt from dishonest ones. Confucianism was a practical form of action accessible to all that sought to create a virtuous society governed by virtuous rulers, a society in which one knew his place and kept it, in which one had respect for those above him and treated those beneath him with benevolence.

Lao Tzu and Daoism

Lao Tzu's historic existence, unlike that of Confucius, cannot be decisively verified or rejected. The great Han historian Ssu ma Ch'ien wrote the first biography of Lao Tzu in the second to the first century B.C.E. According to legend, Lao Tzu, known as the wise old dragon, was born in 604 B.C.E. and lived until 517 B.C.E. He was conceived by a shooting star and was carried in his mother's womb for sixty-two years. When he was born, he had a long mane of white hair. This is an interesting legend, as the dragon is the symbol of the heavens and imperial power, while the Chinese calendar is a sixty-two-year calendar. In other words, Lao Tzu's wisdom was identified with the wisdom of the heavens themselves. Lao Tzu became a *shih* scholar during the last years of the Zhou Dynasty, and, like Confucius, became very disenchanted with the collapse of order. According to legends, as Lao Tzu was attempting to leave China, he was detained at the last pass across the frontiers. A guard forced him to record the fruits of his wisdom before being allowed to exit. The result became known as the *Dao de Jing*, or *The Classic of the Way and of Virtue.*

The language of the *Dao de Jing*, however, is clearly from the Han era; we cannot know how much of this text actually represents the teachings of Lao Tzu, much less can we know whether Lao Tzu ever actually existed.

According to legend, Confucius once met the "old dragon" Lao Tzu, who was the older scholar. Lao Tzu was unimpressed with Confucius, and believed him vain and arrogant for attempting to define the Dao through his "Rules of Propriety." Lao Tzu rejected the Confucian notion that the Rules of Propriety might capture the path to virtue. This was due to his belief that the Dao was not to be equated with filial piety or with any other system of morality or learning, as the Dao itself was limitless and inexpressible. It could not be named or otherwise described, as any attempt to do so would necessarily limit the Dao. The Dao encompassed everything.

Therefore, the Daoist ideal of the sage was quite different from that of Confucius, who advocated learning and study in order to cultivate virtue. Lao Tzu argued that, "when we renounce learning we have no troubles. If we could renounce our sageness and discard our wisdom, it would be better for the people a hundredfold. If we could renounce our benevolence and discard our righteousness, the people would again become filial and kindly. If we could renounce our artful contrivances and discard our scheming for gain, there would be no thieves and robbers."

Daoist Nonaction or *Wu Wei*

This passage is a direct attack on the Confucian ideal of wisdom and benevolence. Lao Tzu argues that any system of rules or laws captures only a part of the Dao and therefore necessarily limits a person's innate response. Any system of laws creates disorder, since laws define crimes and criminals. Without laws, there are no crimes nor can there be criminals. Therefore, the Daoist sage and the Daoist emperor best manage affairs through the philosophy of nonaction or *wu wei,* which means noninterference with the natural path of things.

The Daoist confidence in human nature is boundless; unlike Confucius, who believed virtue must be learned, Lao Tzu believed following the Way would occur naturally if people were left without interference. Lao Tzu rejected the idea of meritocracy and instead sought a state where the true sage could become like an uncarved block of marble. Just as a sculptor can take the block and create any form with it, so, too, the Daoist sage could be able to adapt to any circumstances, as he held to no rigid school of thought nor any preconceived path of action.

A common misinterpretation of Daoism is to assume that Daoists advocate no action at all; however, the philosophy of nonaction simply means acting in accordance with the Dao and not interfering with the natural path of things. For the Daoist, not interfering with the natural path of humans through artificial laws that can only capture part of the Dao will lead to a harmonious society.

Historically, it has often been said that the Chinese are Confucians in their daily life and Daoists in their private life. Confucianism helped the Chinese in their daily affairs, while Daoism spoke to their more esoteric and private spiritual desires.

The Ch'in Empire

Shi Huang Ti was the first emperor in Chinese history. He was born in the third century B.C.E. and was the illegitimate son of an official in the provinces of Ch'in. The name Shi Huang has special meaning. The word "Shi" means "first" and the words "Huang Ti" refer to one of the Heavenly Emperors of Chinese mythology, whose contribution to Chinese culture was the gift of fire and whose twenty-five sons became the basis of the feudal families of the Zhou Dynasty. Shi Huang Ti was the first to unite the warring provinces of China.

The Great Wall of China

When Shi Huang Ti united the warring provinces, he tore down the internal walls that divided them and erected one wall around his new China. This wall is now known as the **Great Wall of China**. The Wall is the only structure visible with the naked human eye from the surface of the moon, and it is about thirty-five feet high and wide enough for two or three chariots to ride side by side. The Great Wall is not a single wall but rather a series of walls constructed over several centuries of China's history. Most of what can be seen of the Great Wall today was built during the Ming Dynasty, which came to power in the fourteenth century C.E. Most of the wall was constructed primarily through the rammed earth technique, where two walls are filled with earth. Some of the older sections of the wall are only earth, which is still packed so tightly that one can barely chisel it out. The Wall was built on very mountainous terrain and it extends for about 1,500 *li* (approximately 4,500 miles) along the northern borders of China.

It is still difficult to imagine how the workers were able to achieve such an enormous engineering feat, and the Chinese have many legends about its construction. According to legend, Shi Huang Ti had a magic bludgeon that was able to knock down entire mountains with a single blow. He also had a magic stallion who reared up and pawed the earth at strategic points. Here, the Chinese built watchtowers, where thousands of soldiers once stood guard on the frontiers of China. The towers were built only as far away from one another as a smoke signal could travel. There are also many legends about why the Wall was built. Some say that the Chinese believed that evil spirits could only travel in a straight line, and so the Wall was built to keep out the spirits. Others believe the Wall was constructed to keep out the Hsiun Nu (often identified with the Huns), who terrorized the Chinese frontiers during this period. If that is why the Wall was built, it is one of the most unsuccessful structures in history, as it never succeeded at keeping out invaders. China is the only culture that has attempted to literally wall itself in, and the Wall is more of a symbol that divided China from the rest of the world than an effective barrier.

One other hypothesis has been given for the construction of the Wall. It is argued that once Shi Huang Ti had won his victory over the other Chinese provinces, there was nothing to keep his army busy, so they were put to work on the Wall. Whatever the historic reasons and legends about the building of the Wall, its construction reflects a monumental feat of engineering, and required massive use of slave labor.

Shi Huang Ti departed from his predecessors in many ways, not the least of which was the implementation of a new philosophy of virtue and of law, **Legalism**. Shi Huang Ti's prime minister, Han Fei, drafted many of the Legalist positions, according to which very harsh punishments for infractions of the law were necessary in order to compel the population to respect the emperor's authority and to obey the law. The Legalists rejected the Confucian notion of inner virtue and did not believe that people would obey the law without some sort of external force present. One of the punishments for breaking laws was to be sent to work on the Great Wall, as the difficult conditions under which the laborers worked was in essence a death sentence. According to legends, when the husband of a young woman was sent to work on the Wall, she was worried about his welfare in the cold and harsh conditions. She prepared for him warm clothes and a basket of food and went to visit him. When she arrived, she found him already dead and wept so profusely that the Wall itself melted away, revealing his bones in the Wall as well as those of many others. According to legend, there are more dead Chinese in the Wall than there are living Chinese. The young woman took the bones of her husband to the coast, where her spirit and that of her husband can still be seen today as boulders off the coast of China.

This story is an extremely important indicator of just how hated Shi Huang Ti was. Traditionally, women in China were subservient to men and had little rights. The fact that a woman's tears could literally bring down the Great Wall, one of the most potent symbols of Shi Huang Ti's brutal repression, is very telling indeed and foreshadowed his quick demise.

The brutal treatment of workers on the Great Wall was but one of many harsh punishments during the Legalist era. Han Fei was one of the most important Legalists of this era, who instituted such punishments as boiling a victim alive in hot water and cutting off limbs or ears.

Anti-Confucianism of Shi Huang Ti's Reign

The philosophy of Legalism departed radically from Confucianism, which had dominated Chinese thought before the reign of Shi Huang Ti. Confucianism was based on the belief that following traditional rites and rituals, and respecting elders and the emperor, who served as models, could cultivate inner virtue. This inner virtue would dictate following the Way no matter what external circumstances arose; a virtuous person in Confucius's sense could be counted on to act according to the Way regardless of whether there were external reasons compelling him to act in that manner. Confucius had a very highly evolved notion of humankind and its ability to act virtuously, and it was a notion the Legalists did not share. Confucians refused to accept the Legalist ways of thinking. Consequently, Shi Huang Ti ordered the burning of the Confucian classics, and even had Confucian scholars who refused to give up their books and teachings buried alive. In a painting from antiquity, Shi Huang Ti's eyes have been scratched out, reflecting the hatred many Chinese had for him.

Shi Huang Ti's policy of moving forward rather than respecting the rites and rituals of tradition also conflicted with Confucianism. He abolished the law of **primogeniture**, according to which property is passed from the father to the eldest son. This custom had the effect of strengthening the nobility, as they were able to amass great estates and pass them intact to their eldest son. Shi Huang Ti wanted to break the power of the nobility, and so forced them to divide their property among all sons.

Standardization of Weights and Measures

Shi Huang Ti also wanted to unify trade in China, and so found it necessary to standardize the various forms of currency used in China. Before Shi Huang Ti, the currency was called the Ming Tao, or "imitations of useful tools." The 1/2 ounce Pan Liang coin with the square hole in the center became the standard coin. Its circular shape represented the heavens, while the square hole in the center represented the earth. His ministers also saw to it that writing was standardized. Today, there are five styles of calligraphy, which were first standardized in the reign of Shi Huang Ti in the third century B.C.E.

The Tomb of Shi Huang Ti

Shi Huang Ti was, in many ways, a megalomaniac who sought immortality. He brought diviners, astrologists, and apothecaries to court, who concocted special potions for him. It is believed that some of these potions contained mercury and so contributed to his death in 207 B.C.E. At one point, he was told by his advisors that his declining health might be due to the fact that the evil spirits could see him. Shi Huang Ti then built a palace surrounded by walls, so that he could walk through it without being seen. When this failed, his advisors then told him that perhaps the Divine Immortals on the Coast could help him attain immortality; he ordered 3,000 men to go in search of these immortal beings. The 3,000 men never returned, and according to legend, these men then traveled to the islands of Japan and founded Japanese culture. This is surely not historic, as we know that there were indigenous Japanese in Japan, the Ainu, and also other inhabitants who had migrated from Korea, not from China. Japan borrowed a great deal of cultural ideals from China, but almost certainly that borrowing did not begin in this way.

Although Shi Huang Ti believed that he would live forever and reign for 10,000 generations, he still built an enormous tomb to celebrate his power on the outskirts of Xi'an, the ancient capital of China. In 1974, some farmers were digging for a well when they discovered the remains of some terra cotta soldiers. This led to the discovery of the actual tumulus of the emperor, which has never been excavated. This is partly due to the size of the complex uncovered and the difficulty of the excavation project, but it is also due to the accounts of the later Han Dynasty, whose historians were renowned in the ancient world for their record-keeping. The Han accounts state that the tomb was booby-trapped with poison-tipped arrows, which has at least suggested that modern archaeologists should approach this site with care. Excavation work continues at the site. The Han historians also state that the tomb had moving rivers of mercury, a map of the heavens on the ceiling, and a map of China on the floor, clearly putting the first emperor not only in the center of China, but in the center of the universe.

Several massive pits filled with terra cotta soldiers and horses surround the tumulus. The horses are not fully life-size, but reflect the interest in the horse as an art motif in the **Han Dynasty**. During the Han Dynasty, the Chinese pushed westward in order to find better horses to combat the **Huns**, who were expert horsemen.

The excavation project has been difficult, as the site was ransacked by peasants who revolted upon news of the death of Shi Huang Ti's brutal rule and burned the site to the ground. Some of the figures still show burn marks. For centuries, the location of the site was forgotten, and peasants built villages over the pits. Much of the site is still in a state of disarray or even rubble. The Great Wall of China and the tomb of its first emperor, Ch'in Shi Huang Ti, are clear examples of architecture used to symbolize the power of the emperor. Shi Huang Ti was a hated despot, but one whom the Chinese have always respected for uniting China and creating a bureaucratic structure that still exists today.

Despite the fact that China is the most populous nation on earth, there are not nearly as many Chinese dialects as one would expect given the number of people and ethnicities, and there are only about 400 family names.

These are but a few of the ways in which Shi Huang Ti, who took power in 221 B.C.E., helped to mold the China of today.

The Han Empire

Today, the Chinese are known as the "people of the Han." The Han preserved the administrative structure of the Ch'in Empire but reinstated Confucian ethics. For centuries, Chinese government was influenced by the Han fusion of Legalism and Confucianism. The Han buried their rulers in great mounds, which can still be seen in the countryside of China today. The ancient literacy of China flourished in Han record-keeping; the Han were the most accurate and astute historians in the world. The Han reconstructed the *Shu Jing,* or *Classic of History,* and also compiled several other texts that became known as the Confucian Classics. Ssu-ma Chien's history, the *Shih chi,* or "historical record," went back to before the Shang. The brother and sister of one of the Han's most famous generals, Ban Chou, wrote a history of the Han Dynasty, the *Han shu.* Ban Gu, who served in the imperial court as a poet, began the history, and his sister Ban Zhao finished it. She clearly exceeded the traditional boundaries for women.

The most well-known leader of the Han was the emperor **Wu Ti**, who reigned from 141 to 87 B.C.E. Wu Ti conquered Vietnam, Manchuria, and North Korea. He also battled the Hsiung nu, or Huns, who were described as moving "on swift horses, and in their breasts beat the hearts of beasts. They shift from place to place like a flock of birds. Thus it is difficult to corner them and bring them under control." The Han were forced to go in search of better horses with which to battle the Hsiung nu, and this led to the origins of the Silk Road. Wu Ti drove the Hsiung nu out of Mongolia and planted forts along the Silk Road. In his various conquests, Wu Ti's armies traveled farther from home than the Roman armies ever did, but he neglected affairs at home. The high levels of taxation imposed for his many campaigns led to revolt.

The Ch'ang An Period or Western or Former Han

From 202 B.C.E. to 9 C.E., the Han maintained power at Ch'ang An. This era is often referred to as the Ch'ang An period or the western or former Han.

The Later Han

From 25 C.E. to 221 C.E., the Han center of power was the old Zhou site of Loyang, and this era is known as the later Han. The later Han defeated the Huns in 89 C.E. and extended their power to the Caspian Sea and Persian Gulf by 97 C.E.

The Period of Six Dynasties

After the collapse of the Han in 221 C.E., China entered the Period of Six Dynasties that lasted until 589 C.E. In reality, during this Chinese version of the dark ages, there were many more than six dynasties, and culture flourished. Many literary and other cultural artifacts date from this period, which distinguishes the Chinese dark ages from their counterpart in the medieval west following the collapse of Roman rule in Europe.

CHAPTER 8

ANCIENT GREECE

Scholars credit ancient Greece with laying the foundation of all later Western culture, including drama, poetry, literature, architecture, and philosophy. The Greeks were the first civilization to explore a scientific view of the world as opposed to a mythological one. The cultural contributions of the ancient Greeks are all the more remarkable when one realizes that all of Greece can be traversed in less than the time it takes one to travel from New York to Dallas, Texas. The distance from Mt. Olympus in northern Greece to the southern tip of the Peloponnesus, where Sparta was located, is only about 240 miles or roughly half the size of modern New York State. The terrain of most of Greece is very mountainous, and early settlers clustered in valleys and eventually developed independent city-states. Although one often speaks of "Greek culture," there was never a unified Greek empire before Alexander the Great. Rather, there were a collection of independent city-states, each with its own patron deities and other customs. The Greek city-states were fiercely independent. Nevertheless, there were aspects of the culture that all Greeks had in common; a Spartan meeting an Athenian on the road would have recognized something Greek about him or her and vice versa. The fierce devotion of the Greeks to independence, however, eventually erupted in the **Peloponnesian War** and brought about the end of the Golden Age of ancient Greece.

THE MINOANS

The earliest Greek culture was located on **Crete** and dates back to 2800 B.C.E. The Cretans most likely came from Asia Minor, probably as early as 3000 B.C.E., and originally spoke a non-Indo-European language. The Cretans were literate, and they used a style of writing known as Linear A. Linear A has never been deciphered, and its language does not resemble later Greek. The culture produced by the Cretan civilization is called Minoan after the legendary King Minos who ruled here. According to legend, Minos had a palace that housed a labyrinth designed by Daedalus. A Minotaur was in the labyrinth, and each year a virgin from Crete was sacrificed to the beast. One year, the Athenian hero Theseus volunteered to be part of the sacrifice in hopes of freeing Athens from Minoan rule. When Theseus arrived on Crete, he fell in love with Ariadne, the daughter of King Minos, and she gave him a golden thread to find his way out. Legend has it that when Theseus killed the Minotaur, Cretan civilization collapsed.

The first to excavate the site was the English archaeologist Arthur Evans. The remains of the palace at **Knossus**, the chief center of Minoan culture, do indeed resemble a labyrinth. There is evidence that the palace was built and rebuilt over the course of many centuries, and it occupies almost an entire hillside. The palace is a self-contained village, with its own olive gardens, presses, and an arsenal. One of the most interesting sections of the palace is the throne room, the oldest throne room in Europe. Next to the throne room is a room with a large basin that probably held water. This water basin was likely used for ritualistic purposes, and its proximity to the throne room suggests that the king was also the chief priest of the civilization. Storage chambers are also very near the throne room. The king stored large vases full of oil and other goods possibly received from other Minoan centers on Crete as tribute. The goods were then redistributed among the king's subjects.

The Snake Goddess

Other interesting artifacts from the ruins of the palace are the snake goddesses, whose bared and exaggerated upper chest calls forth the idea of fertility. Snakes were another symbol of fertility in the ancient world, particularly in Egypt, with which the Minoans had obvious contact. Although many people from the Judeo-Christian tradition often associate snakes with evil, the ancient cultures associated them with fertility, as snakes lose their skins and then regenerate them. The snake goddesses are akin to the mother earth goddesses of the Paleolithic caves. On the basis of the snake goddess figurines, some scholars have suggested that the Minoans were a matriarchal culture, a hypothesis that lacks general support and seems based on scanty evidence. Their chief deity was, however, clearly a female, who was worshiped in small shrines on hills.

Minoan Frescoes

Minoan culture was very artistic. The palace itself was originally painted in bright red and other colors. Many columns still have traces of their original paint. Many of the frescoes on the palace wall convey the relationship of the Minoans with the sea, such as the beautiful dolphin frescos that Arthur Evans mistakenly placed on the walls rather than on the floors, where they appear in remains on the mainland. The Minoans had a large seafaring empire and contact with many other cultures. They exerted tremendous influence over other cultures through trade. Although scholars debate the extent of their power over other areas through seafaring trade, this sort of control of seafaring routes and areas has been called a thalossocracy. Archaeologists have found artifacts from Egypt and other cultures in the ruins of the palace. Interestingly, later Greeks on the mainland associated the dolphin with Apollo, and Greek myth credits the Minoans with bringing the cult of Apollo to the famous oracle at Delphi.

The House of the Double Ax and the Bull Jumping Ritual

The most famous of all the frescoes in the palace is the Bull Jumping fresco. This fresco is renowned for its lifelike portrayal of the popular sport of bull jumping on Crete. The bull itself seems caught in the act of jumping; its back is arched and its legs are not portrayed in a static fashion. The Minoans are shown in the act of jumping. They first grabbed the horns, then flipped over the bull's back, and then landed behind the animal. This ritual took place in the central court of the palace at Knossus, and there are iconic images of bulls' horns throughout the location. Scholars are unsure of the exact meaning of the bull cult, but clearly the bull sign was the basis for calling the dynasty at Knossus the House of the Double Ax. Two bulls' horns side by side create the double ax image, and the Greek word for ax is *labyrinthos*, a word that is very similar to "labyrinth." The style of the Minoan frescos is very similar to Egyptian art. While the Bull Jumping fresco is very animated, unlike formalized, static Egyptian art, this and other frescos also show people with their torsos facing frontally but with their legs facing the side. This is the same style as Egyptian art.

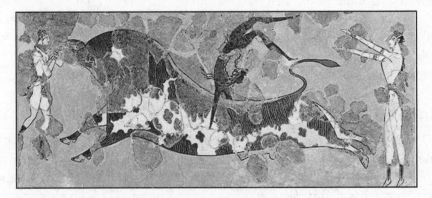

Bull Jumping fresco, Crete. c. 1500 B.C.E.

The Collapse of the Minoans

The traditional date for the collapse of Minoan culture is somewhere around 1450 B.C.E. Scholars are unsure of the reasons for the collapse, and some have suggested that perhaps there was a cataclysmic natural disaster. The palace shows evidence of rebuilding after tidal waves and also earthquakes; further, there was a huge volcanic eruption on Santorini or Thera about the time that the Minoan culture collapsed. Recent studies, however, suggest that eruption may date to as early as 1650 B.C.E., in which case we need another hypothesis to account for the decline of Crete in the fifteenth century B.C.E. Perhaps the eruption on Santorini weakened various elements of Minoan trade, but this is far from certain. As an interesting note, some scholars have suggested that Santorini and the Minoan world may have been the foundation of the legends of Atlantis, mentioned in the works of Plato. This is a very controversial assertion, however, as not only are there many other possibilities for the location of Atlantis, but some doubt the actual historicity of the references to Atlantis.

It has also been suggested that invaders from the mainland might have conquered the Minoans. The **Mycenaeans** on the mainland date back to 2200 B.C.E., but the period in which they flourished, from the seventeenth to the twelfth centuries B.C.E., coincides with the demise of Cretan culture. The Mycenaeans were a warlike people who dominated the Aegean area, and traces of Minoan culture are found in Mycenaean ruins. Whether this was because the Mycenaeans borrowed from an already declining culture or because they conquered the Minoans is unknown.

THE MYCENAEANS

Our knowledge of the Mycenaean world began in 1870 when Heinrich Schliemann excavated Troy, in modern day Turkey, and later Mycenae, in an effort to prove the truth of Homer's *Iliad*.

Before Schliemann, scholars had thought that Greek civilization did not arise until the eighth century B.C.E.; Schliemann's expedition inspired Arthur Evans, an Englishman, to search for the existence of the legendary King Minos, which led to the excavation of Knossus on Crete.

Linear B

The Mycenaeans were a literate society, who borrowed the script of Linear A for their own Indo-European language, the earliest form of Greek known. Their writing is known as Linear B, and numerous Linear B tablets have been excavated in the wreckage of the Knossus. This suggests that the Mycenaeans conquered the Minoans, or at least took over and built upon the ruins of their civilization. The similarity of Linear B to Homer's Greek enabled Michael Ventris to decipher the language. The Mycenaeans migrated to the Greek mainland by about 2000 B.C.E.

Some Hittite writings seem to allude to the Mycenaeans. Mycenaean pottery is found from Naples to Troy to Egypt, which indicates that the Mycenaeans had a vast trading empire.

THE TROJAN WAR

The Mycenaeans are most remembered for the war with Troy, a Greek-speaking colony on Asia Minor. One of the main sources of our information on the **Trojan War** is Homer's *Iliad,* which covers only a ten-day interlude of the war. The *Iliad* dates to the ninth or eighth century B.C.E., whereas the Trojan War allegedly occurred in the thirteenth century B.C.E. The famous story of the Trojan horse actually comes from a much later work, the Roman poet Virgil's *Aeneid.* Virgil wrote the *Aeneid* in the first century B.C.E., and it tells the story of Aeneas, a participant in the war, who fled Troy and later became one of the founders of Rome.

The Legend of the Trojan War

According to legend, the goddess Aphrodite promised the most beautiful woman in the world to Paris, the son of Trojan King Priam. He was awarded Helen, wife of king Menelaus of Sparta. Helen was also the sister of Clytemnestra, who was married to the older brother of Menelaus, Agamemnon. According to legend, Helen was the daughter of Zeus.

During a period in which Menelaus was gone, Paris went to Greece and fell in love with Helen and she with him. They fled together to Troy. Menelaus's brother, King Agamemnon of Mycenae, led an expedition to Troy to "rescue" Helen, and a ten-year-long siege began. Among the Greek heroes of the war was Achilles, whose goddess-mother had dipped him in the river Styx, making him impervious to harm except on his heel. Achilles got angry with King Agamemnon in the beginning of the epic over his failure to give him the honor that was his fair due; Achilles left his fellow Greeks and fought solely for himself. Achilles's fiercely independent actions to achieve glory and his willingness to sacrifice everything for one moment of eternal glory illustrate the Greek ideal of *arete*, or heroism and nobility of character. The Greek ideal of *arete* was very individualistic, as in the early part of the *Iliad*. Since the *Iliad*, however, tells only the story of ten days of the ten-year-long siege of Troy, we must turn to Virgil for an account of the fall of Troy.

According to Virgil, the war ended when the Greeks grew weary of the siege and tricked the Trojans into believing that they had gone by hiding in a nearby harbor. They left a beautiful wooden horse outside the gates of Troy, ostensibly as a tribute to the Trojan patron deities and to buy their safe return home. Some of the Trojans were suspicious, among them the prophetess Cassandra who had been cursed to always tell the truth but never be believed, and the priest Laocoon who made an impassioned plea to them not to bring the horse in.

No one listened, and Athena, the patron goddess of the Mycenaeans, was so angered that she sent two huge serpents to engulf Laocoon and his sons. This famous passage from Virgil was later immortalized in sculpture during the Hellenistic era. During the Italian Renaissance centuries later, this famous Hellenistic sculpture was unearthed and influenced Michelangelo.

According to Virgil, Troy fell in a bloody battle. Achilles's son murdered the son of King Priam before his very eyes and then murdered Priam, dragging him through his own son's blood. Priam lived just long enough to see his son and his city destroyed.

All for the love of a beautiful woman.

Historic Difficulties

Virgil wrote to glorify the reign of **Augustus**, the first emperor of Rome, who claimed descent from Aeneas and the Trojans. Augustus essentially had transformed the Republican form of government of ancient Rome into an imperial one; although he refused to allow the Romans to call him an emperor, he was one in all but name, usurping many of the old Republican offices for himself. Many of the greatest poets of this age tried to make the reign of Augustus appear as the climax of Roman history rather than as the end of Republican Rome. Hence, Virgil's account, written thirteen centuries after the Trojan War, cannot be much trusted as a historic source.

Many elements of Homer, on the other hand, appear factual, such as descriptions of ships. Yet there are also many inaccuracies; Homer always describes the shield of the Greek warrior Ajax as like a tower, and shields of this style had already disappeared by the Trojan War, which likely occurred sometime around 1250 B.C.E. The epic also depicts a transitional type of warfare, from the early period in which the hero such as Achilles fought his opponent in hand-to-hand individual combat to reliance on the phalanx, or group of foot soldiers lined up by rank and file. The phalanx was the preferred model of combat during the period in which the *Iliad* first appeared. Scholars link the so-called hoplite or foot solider revolution to the increased ability of farmers to provide armor and to their increased demands for political participation.

The *Iliad* contains many repetitious phrases known as formularies. In antiquity, epic poems such as the *Iliad* were passed down orally and embellished by the individual bard; the formularies helped the bard remember and organize the epic.

Also, many themes of the *Iliad* resemble those of other ancient epics, such as the *Epic of Gilgamesh*. For example, Achilles has a goddess for a mother, as did Gilgamesh, and his friend Patroclus is much like Enkidu. Patroclus dies in place of Achilles, and a lament follows his death, just as Enkidu dies for what was Gilgamesh's offense, and a lament also follows his death.

Who Was Homer?

Further, there is considerable doubt about whether there ever was a bard named Homer or whether Homer was the name given to a group of bards or the bard who finally wrote down the epic. At any rate, the details of language, construction of shields, and other aspects of the epic suggest that it was told orally for many centuries before it was written. If Homer actually ever lived, he lived in the eighth century B.C.E., making these stories already 500 years old at the time he wrote them down. Further, since many of the details of the war seem to describe an age even before the Trojan War, the story must have been told in some form well before the Trojan War occurred. Homer's epics, then, have to be read very critically and cannot be completely trusted as historical sources.

Heinrich Schliemann and the Excavation of Hisarlik

Although many scholars regard the *Iliad* as a literary masterpiece that is of questionable historical value about the period before the hoplite revolution, Heinrich Schliemann, a wealthy German businessman in the nineteenth century C.E. and an avid fan of Homer, was convinced of the truth behind the legend. From the geographic details in the *Iliad*, he deduced the whereabouts of Troy and was led to a huge tell known as Hisarlik, located in modern Turkey. Schliemann even reenacted the chase of Achilles and Hector around the walls of Troy to see whether the time and distances discussed in Homer matched his own experience.

Schliemann carelessly threw out everything that did not fit the details of Homer's epic poem and dug a deep trench through the middle of the tell. Consequently, many valuable objects were lost, and archaeologists and historians believe that some of these objects might actually have helped to shed light on the Trojan War. During the excavations, a large amount of jewelry and other items were found. Schliemann had married a young Greek woman whom he considered his own Helen of Troy, and pictures of her dressed as Helen in ancient Greek jewelry caused a sensation and strong criticism of Schliemann's methods. Archaeology had not yet been perfected as a science and Schliemann was working under difficult conditions in Turkey. His mistakes helped later archaeologists develop more systematic methods of excavation. They also helped to unearth a part of Greek history that had never been documented.

Hisarlik, the site of ancient Troy, had a very long past. There were nine distinct phases of its history; Phase II of the layers of civilization buried in

Hisarlik represented the level Schliemann thought was legendary Troy. It had a ramp outside the gates, much like the one Homer depicted in the fight between Hector and Achilles. This level was too old, however, to have been the Troy of Homer. Scholars now believe Homer's Troy to have been level VIIa, which was destroyed by a fire somewhere around the thirteenth century B.C.E., about the time of the legendary fall of Troy. Troy VIIa has substantial walls around it fifteen-feet thick, which might have indeed protected its inhabitants from a ten-year-long siege.

The Citadel of Mycenae

Having failed to discover Homer's Troy, Schliemann turned to mainland Greece in search of Mycenae, and here he uncovered many important finds. Mycenae was a fortress with a citadel constructed of limestone walls, twenty-feet thick. The walls are so huge that the ancients believed only the Cyclops could have put them there. The entrance to the citadel is famous for its enormous Lion Gate, which is ten-feet-wide and ten-feet-high. It is topped by a huge lintel weighing twenty tons. Although scholars are unsure of the significance of the lions, they believe they had some sort of heraldic significance and that the lions protected the citadel, like attendants of goddesses of the day.

In the citadel itself, there is only one street that is little more than an alley. The street leads to the palace atop the citadel, and along the street Schliemann found seven grave shafts in a circle protected by a wall. The fact that a wall surrounds the site suggests that the kings there had some sort of religious significance; the circle itself is eighty-five feet in diameter. In one of the grave shafts, Schliemann found a remarkable gold mask. When he came up from the shaft, he made the famous remark that he had "looked upon the face of Agamemnon." Unfortunately, he had not, as these grave shafts were also from an earlier period of Greek history, likely dating back to at least the sixteenth century B.C.E., making them too old to have been the relics of the Mycenaeans who fought the Trojans. Nevertheless, Schliemann had uncovered a previously unknown civilization and had proven that Greek history went back to an era well before the Olympics began in the eighth century B.C.E.

The citadel of Mycenae did prove that the Mycenaeans had a very warlike culture with a thriving kingship. The citadel is located in a very strategic place between mountains, making it difficult to attack, and its huge walls would have defended it well.

The Tholos or Beehive Tombs

Other nearby tombs are also remarkable and are known as the **Tholos** or **beehive tombs**. The culture that produced them is known as the Tholos tomb dynasty. The entrance, or dromos, to one of these famous tombs is twenty-feet-wide and 120-feet-long; the stone lintel over the so-called Treasury of

Lion Gate at Mycenae, c. 1250 B.C.E.

Atreus is estimated to weigh 100 tons. The Tholos Dynasty was also quite definitely an imperial, warlike culture; apparently, they buried their warriors in these tombs. These tombs are a remarkable early western example of the use of the dome.

These tombs date from the fourteenth to the thirteenth century B.C.E., which coincides with the date of the legendary Atreus, after whom the "treasury" is named.

Troy's Later History and the Collapse of Mycenae

Troy was deserted for 400 years after the sack of Troy, and Alexander the Great later visited Troy VIII. Level IX represents Roman Troy, the last of the cities built on the site.

The collapse of Troy VIIa sometime around the thirteenth century B.C.E. also marks the end of the Mycenaean era; despite the fact that Homer claims victory for the Mycenaeans at Troy, after their victory, Mycenaean cities crumbled and their pottery declined in quality. This is oddly consistent with other disasters of the age. The Hittite Empire crumbled, and Egypt endured three serious attacks by People of the Sea. There was a widespread famine throughout the ancient world in the thirteenth century B.C.E., suggesting that whatever happened to the Mycenaeans, their decline was part of an overall decline in all cultures of this era.

THE DORIANS

A group of Indo-European people, the **Dorians**, replaced the Mycenaeans as the dominant power on the Greek mainland. For years, the most common theory was that Dorians, from north of Mt. Olympus, migrated south, gradually replacing the Mycenaean culture. This migration was known as the Dorian Invasion. According to Greek legend, the sons of Heracles and his followers were banished from Mycenae, and they took possession of the Peloponnesus. As we shall see in our study of Sparta, the Spartan kingship traced its genealogy back to the twin sons of Heracles.

The Dorians spoke the same language as the Mycenaeans, and one wonders how they remained isolated for so long. The historian John Fine has suggested that the Dorians were not another group of people at all, but simply another Mycenaean people, long oppressed, who spoke a common dialect and who simply outlived the Mycenaeans.

The Greek Dark Ages

The collapse of Mycenae began the Dark Ages in Greek history; written records disappeared until the eighth century B.C.E.

The Dorians lived in isolated tribal groups. The Greek mountainous regions, leading to the origins of the Greek city-state or polis, hemmed them in. The Dorians were a patriarchical group of people who were ruled by kings and an aristocratic society. Many aspects of Homer's *Iliad* reflect this aristocratic age; for example, Homer has King Agamemnon hold councils with his nobles in the *Iliad* in much the same way as the Dorians held them.

The Age of Colonization and the Formation of the City-State of Athens

The Greeks began to colonize in the eighth to the sixth centuries B.C.E. In this age, there were too many people for the land to sustain and many people left to colonize other regions.

They colonized southern Italy, and the Greeks there battled the Romans during the Pyrrhic Wars.

Corinth was another colony that became important during the Christian era as one of the places to whom the apostle Paul wrote. Greeks also established colonies on the northern tip of Africa. The Greek colonies around Egypt helped further the golden age of ancient Greece by introducing Egyptian papyrus, geometry, and astronomy to the Greeks. Evidence of cultural exchange can also be seen in the Greek statues, whose rigid, formalized poses and wig-like hair is very reminiscent of Egyptian art.

Black Athena

Martin Bernal, in *Black Athena* and other works, has argued that the influence of the Egyptians on the culture of ancient Greece has been underestimated and, consequently, the role of Africa in the development of Western culture has been overlooked. Bernal's thesis is very controversial, but it does highlight for us the fact that the Greeks, as remarkable a culture as they developed in the Golden Age, had other cultural models and influences on which to build.

Ionia (Asia Minor), the Greek colonies in Asia Minor, were conquered by Cyrus the Great in the sixth century B.C.E. These colonies, or Ionia, subsequently went to the mainland Greeks for help against the Persians, beginning the Persian wars.

The Greeks also colonized along the Black Sea. Byzantium was a Greek colony that later became the capital of the Roman Empire in the east. Under Constantine the Great, the first Christian emperor, the city was renamed Constantinople. In 1453 C.E., the Seljuk Turks conquered Constantinople and changed its name to Istanbul.

ARCHAIC CULTURE: THE OLYMPICS

Several characteristic expressions of Greek cultural ideals arose during the Archaic period. The first Olympic festival was held in Olympia in 776 B.C.E. Before Schliemann's excavations, scholars believed that Greek culture originated with the Olympics. Olympia was dedicated to **Zeus**, the chief god of the Greeks. The Greeks valued the life of the mind and were known for producing some of the finest philosophical minds in the history of the world, including **Socrates**, his student **Plato**, and his student **Aristotle**. They also valued the health of the body, and held the Olympics as a tribute to the gods through presenting the most highly developed physical bodies in grueling competitions. Only free Greeks could participate in the Olympics, and a truce was declared during which no warfare could be conducted.

Olympic athletes competed in brutal sports, such as Greek boxing, in which no holds were barred. Many stories tell of athletes whose teeth were knocked out in fights and who kept fighting despite what must have been agonizing pain. In fact, *agon*, or suffering, was a fundamental theme in Greek culture. Through heroic *agon*, true *arete* was displayed. Those who emerged victorious at Olympia were given the laurel leaf wreath of Apollo, the god of wisdom.

The Roman Emperor Theodosius banned the Olympics as pagan practices. In the nineteenth century, the Olympics were revived, and today, every Olympiad begins with the lighting of the Olympic torch at Olympia in the same place where once it was lit in antiquity.

Delphi

Legend has it that **Delphi** was founded when Zeus wished to find the center of the earth and let two eagles fly from the two ends of the earth. They met at Delphi, which was the "navel" of the earth. Delphi celebrated the god Apollo, and his temple contained an *omphalos* or navel stone, and pilgrims offered objects in the shape of the *omphalos*. Delphi was one of the most important cultural centers in the ancient world. According to tradition, Delphi was first recognized as a special place when sheep grew intoxicated while grazing near a crevice. Later, priestesses, called the Pythia, would sit over this crevice on a tripod and breathe in its fumes. Their seat was placed in the middle of the sacred temple of Apollo. The Pythia would spew out garbled prophecies in monosyllables, and a priest would interpret her words for the pilgrims.

Delphi became prominent during the period of Greek colonization; many colonists consulted the oracle there before selecting their destination, including the founders of the colony of Syracuse. Many colonies called themselves Apollonia, after the patron god of Delphi. The spread of the Greek colonies also spread the fame of Delphi, making it a cosmopolitan center of religion for many cultures.

Delphi began to decline in the Roman period, and Theodosius finally shut it down by the fourth century C.E.

Delphi also exhibits the Greek tradition of paying tribute to the gods through developing both the body and the soul. At Delphi, the Greeks held athletic, theatrical, and other festivities in honor of Apollo.

GREEK CULTURE DURING THE GOLDEN AGE OF GREECE

Greek Theater

Theater originally arose as part of the cult of Dionysus, the god of wine and merriment. The philosopher Aristotle believed that seeing horrific tragedies on stage allowed one to experience *catharsis*, or a purging of all unbalanced emotions. Theatrical performances helped to balance the soul and create a better citizen. In such plays as Sophocles's *Oedipus Rex*, created during the Golden Age of Greece, the Greek ideal of *agon*, or suffering, was taken to new levels. While the feats of Achilles and other heroes such as

Odysseus were almost superhuman, Sophocles reminded one of the roles of the gods and human limitations in the face of fate. In *Oedipus Rex*, Oedipus struggles in vain to avoid his fate; upon hearing a prophecy that he would kill his father and marry his mother, he fled the home of his youth and went to Thebes. On the road there, he met a stranger and killed him. Unbeknownst to him, he had killed Laius, King of Thebes, who in fact was his biological father. The rest of the play unfolds like a ticking clock as Oedipus inexorably progresses toward his fate. Oedipus learns the power of the gods and the role of fate in human life. While at Colonus, Oedipus later comes to understand the transcendent value of *agon*. For the Greeks, life was a continuous heroic struggle through which one might display the noblest value, *arete*.

The playwright Euripides explored the aftermath of the Trojan War and the darker side of human nature in his Oresteia trilogy. Seeking revenge for the sacrifice of their daughter Iphigenia, Clytemnestra kills her husband Agamemnon when he returns from war. Their son Orestes then avenges his father by killing his mother, whom the goddess Athena declares not to be a true parent because of her sex. Euripides's play is a frightening commentary on the social roles of women, and many scholars believe the play represents the transition from the matriarchal society of early Greece to the patriarchal society of later Greece. Euripides also wrote the horrifying tragedy *Medea*, in which Medea's husband Jason leaves her for a younger woman, and Medea then kills her own children to cause her husband greater sorrow. Although such playwrights as Aristophanes wrote riotously funny comedies, Greek drama was a profound commentary on social mores as well as the darker parts of the human psyche.

One of the most famous theaters in Greece is located at Epidaurus. The acoustics are so fine that someone sitting in the upper rows can hear a pin dropped on stage or an actor whisper. Epidaurus was not simply a theatrical complex, but also a place where one went for healing spas. Many remnants of Corinthian columns here have carvings of plants known for their healing purposes, illustrating the Greek notion of theater as a healing force.

Greek Philosophy

Greek culture was based on the ideals of reason, order, and balance. The word "philosophy" means "love of wisdom," and ancient Greek philosophers as well as artists, architects, and dramatists sought the same ideals by which life is ordered. The pre-Socratic philosophers probed the structure of the cosmos to determine the underlying principle of its unity. Thales, who was renowned as a general and astronomer, posited the idea that the cosmos was water in various forms; Democritus saw the underlying order of the cosmos in tiny, indivisible particles that collided with one another to create the world as we know it. Pythagoras spoke of the harmony of the spheres, and probed the mathematical structure of the universe and identified that structure with musical harmony.

Socrates began a revolution in Athens when he was tried and convicted of corrupting the young and of heresy against the state religion. Socrates made a career of questioning the beliefs, practices, and principles upon which Athenian society rested, and had the misfortune to live in a tense political period following the Peloponnesian War when questioning the status quo made the Athenians uncomfortable. Rather than accept the Athenian demand to cease his teachings, he insisted on continuing his career as a "gadfly," and argued that the Athenians should be grateful rather than resentful of his attempt to show them what they did not know. Socrates argued that his wisdom, if there was any at all, lay in the fact that he knew only that he did not know anything. The Socratic *elenchus*, or method of questioning, is a reductionist method that frees one from mistaken beliefs so that one may begin to build true knowledge. Although the Athenians offered Socrates a way out of his difficulties by simply ceasing to teach, Socrates established a new form of heroic *arete* when he willingly gave his life for what he believed to be right rather than live by falsehoods. Socrates fought for the right of individual conscience, and he insisted that the welfare of the soul was more important than any other consideration. Socrates also elucidated an interesting argument about why death was preferable to life without questioning. The unexamined life was a known evil, but death was an uncertainty; perhaps death was simply the cessation of consciousness, in which case one would not be in pain. Alternatively, if a reality in and of itself, then perhaps death would represent the chance to dialogue with other great figures of the past.

In the *Dialogues*, Socrates's student Plato recorded the questioning, probing mind of Socrates, but developed some of Socrates's teachings. Plato found the meaning of the universe in the eternal, changeless realm of the ideal forms. Plato was concerned above all else with the form of the Good, which he believed to be the basis for good government. As human souls once lived with the forms before entering bodies, he argued that all knowledge on earth is remembrance of things already known. In *The Republic* Plato attempted to elucidate the nature of the ideal state when governed by the Philosopher King, one who himself was governed by reason.

Plato's student Aristotle was more practically minded, and was the first to categorize animals and plants by species and genus. Aristotle also developed rules for the perfect tragic form in the *Poetics,* rules that if followed might enable the audience to leave the drama more balanced citizens. Aristotle's thought sought the first principles of being, and his unified view of the cosmos was reflected in his activities in philosophy, logic, politics, biology, and drama, among other things.

In ancient Greece, there was no separation between history, mythology, philosophy, theater, and other art forms; all were aspects of the love of wisdom and all expressed the fundamental order of the universe. Werner Jaeger uses the Greek term *paideia* to refer to the Greek ideal of education, culture, and the unity of knowledge. Metaphorically, one might think of Greek *paideia* as that single body of thought from which all later Western culture evolved.

CHAPTER 9

THE GOLDEN AGE OF GREECE

THE GREEK CITY-STATES

Sparta

The word **Sparta** comes from the Greek word *spartos*, which was a prevalent plant in the Peloponnesus. In antiquity, Sparta was called Lacedaemon. Not much remains today of the once-mighty military society that dominated the Greek Peloponnesus in ancient times. The Spartans were a military society, who, unlike the Athenians, did not contribute much to the world's great philosophical, literary, dramatic, or other traditions.

The conditions under which early Sparta evolved account for its military emphasis. Early in their history, the Spartans fought several wars against the Messenians. Once the Spartans conquered them, the Messenians were in the minority. The Spartan government divided their land into equal allotments to support the Spartan military. These allotments were called the *kleros*, and the income from the land gave the Spartan males the wherewithal to survive. Spartan male citizens spent their life in the service of the state. The land could not be sold, and it reverted to the state after the death of its holder and was then handed over to another citizen. Often it was the son of the deceased, but it was not necessarily so. There were approximately 9,000–10,000 such allotments in Sparta, meaning that there were the same number of Spartan male citizens.

State service was a lifelong requirement and, to provide the free time necessary for this, the *kleros* were worked by *helots*, who were bound to the land. The word *helot* comes from the Greek root *hel*, which means "capture," and the *helots* were the remnants of the defeated Messenians. The *helots* were serfs of the state and were assigned by the state to the *kleros*. The Spartans were drastically outnumbered by *helots* and developed a very repressive society as a result. The Spartans developed a secret police force that routinely went on random murdering sprees among the *helots*. The Spartans intended for these terrorist acts to inspire fear among the *helots*, and, indeed, there were no slave revolts in Sparta.

Other Inhabitants of Sparta

There were several independent states surrounding Sparta, whose inhabitants were called *peroicoi*. These were the free inhabitants of those regions, who were obligated to provide military support for Spartans. They worked with the Spartan hoplite force, or armed foot soldiers. The *peroicoi* also conducted trade and business in the Spartan commonwealth. Spartan citizens were forbidden to conduct business, as it was considered demeaning work. The *peroicoi* eventually became part of the Peloponnesian league of Sparta and her allies.

Spartan Society

Sparta was a very closed society that expelled foreigners and was very secretive about their politics and culture. The control that Sparta exercised over its male citizens began at birth. Infants were examined for fitness to serve. Those judged unfit were left exposed on a hillside. Their mothers raised those who survived until the age of seven. At seven, they began the *agoge*, or Spartan system of military training and education. Spartan males were placed in a barrack consisting of fifteen men, called a *pheiditia*. The word *pheiditia* comes from a Greek verb that means sparse or sparing. Meals in the barracks were taken in common, and were very sparse to induce greater strength and fortitude in the Spartans. Attendance at the evening and noon meals was compulsory, and Spartan males were required to contribute a certain amount of food from their *kleros* to support the barracks. One negative vote from any member of the *pheiditia* was sufficient to exclude a prospective member from the barracks. The barracks was the chief social unit in Spartan male society, and the aim was to create harmony and unity.

Life was rough in the barracks. Young Spartan soldiers slept on straw mats without a blanket and had to forage for food at a very early age. In these ways they learned battle tactics and how to survive off the countryside even if their rations ran low.

After six years, at the age of thirteen, the boys took lovers, who also served as teachers from the upper class of soldiers known as *eirens*. The boys formed close relationships with the *eirens*, and Spartans believed such bonds made their soldiers more willing to fight to the death for each other on the battlefield. At thirty, the Spartan males were eligible to enter the Assembly and then marry and live at home. They continued to serve in the military, however, until the age of sixty.

Women also had a place in this system. A physically healthy woman was valued, for she would produce strong children.

Political Structure

Lycurgus was the founder of the Spartan political system, and many ancient commentators regarded Sparta as an ideal state. One of the unique aspects of its government was that two kings ruled Sparta. According to legend, however, the hero Heracles, ousted from Mycenae, had twin sons, Eurysthenes and Proclus, from whom were descended the Agis family and the Euryphons, who held the two posts. The kings judged cases concerning public roads, adoption, and arranged marriages. A board of five ephors limited the power of the kings, who served for one year and who were chosen by acclamation of the Assembly. The ephors presided at the assembly, formulated issues for voting; began military campaigns; and transmitted orders to officers in the field. They also supervised the *helots*. Each month, the ephors exchanged oaths with the two kings. The kings swore to rule according to laws, while the ephors swore to preserve the kingship.

There was also a Council of 30, the *gerousia,* which included the kings. Those who served on the council had to be at least sixty years of age, the age at which military service to the state was completed. The role of councils in Greek society was evident already in Homer; in the *Iliad*, Agamemnon consults his nobles and discusses issues with a council of elders. The Spartan council also limited the power of kings. Not all political thinkers praised the council, however; Aristotle, for example, remarked about the Spartan state that the mind, as well as the body, also declines with age!

Council members were chosen by acclamation in public assembly and served for life. The council advised the kings, prepared business for assembly, and tried cases.

Oligarchy

Many commentators, such as Plutarch, praised the Spartan constitution as democratic for its emphasis on equality. However, the few fragments of text we have about the Spartan constitution, such as the *rhetra*, suggest that the Spartan government was an **oligarchy**, where the kings and elders on the Council introduced proposals that were passed to the people. The *rhetra* also makes clear that should the leaders consider the decisions of the people to be "crooked," they could overrule the vote of the assembly and enact their own measures. In Sparta, all citizens were equal in land allotments and other resources, but it was not the case that the government was structured as a democracy.

Those who favored the Spartan constitution were historically not supporters of democracy. Plato praised Sparta as a model society, but he argued that society should be governed by Philosopher Kings, elite, educated members of society who were the only ones fit to rule. He believed that democracy was the equivalent of mob rule, that it was rule by the unfit and the tyranny of the majority over the minority. Spartan government also influenced the eighteenth-century philosopher Rousseau, who wrote in *The Social Contract* that for the good of society as a whole, individuals should give up rights. Adolf Hitler based the Hitler Youth on the Spartan system of education and the infamous SS on the Spartan secret police, or *kryptaea*.

Athens

Athens is historically credited as being the birthplace of Western democracy and is also renowned for the culture it produced during the fifth-century B.C.E. Golden Age, one of the most profound intellectual and artistic cultures of the ancient world.

Athens was originally governed by nine *archons*, one of whom functioned as king, another as eponymous *archon*, another as the *polemarchos* or military commander, and six as setters of verdicts. The *archons* were from the aristocracy, elected by the assembly, and at least thirty years of age. They served for one year, then "retired" to serve for the remainder of their life on the Areopagus Council, named after the hill west of Acropolis on which they met.

Athenian government, however, was primarily driven by the Assembly, which included all citizens. In ancient Athens, one could be ostracized for failure to participate in government. Athenians wrote the names of such citizens on pottery shards called *ostrakon*. When Athenians wrote the name of any one person on enough pottery fragments, they ostracized or expelled the person. There was widespread participation in ancient Athenian government in contrast to the very small percentage of the American population, for example, that votes today; some estimate voter participation in modern America to be as low as thirteen or fourteen percent, but certainly not greater than thirty percent. In antiquity, there was near 100 percent participation, as Athenians considered those who failed to serve in a public capacity as unfit for society.

Draco issued the first set of laws in early Athens, and they were very harsh laws that mandated the death penalty for many cases.

The Crisis of the Sixth Century B.C.E.

During the sixth century B.C.E., population growth forced Athenians to keep more land under cultivation and for longer periods of time. The Athenians did not understand the fallow system of agriculture, and consequently, the land went bad and so did the crops. Peasants and even the wealthy were forced to borrow against next year's harvest just to survive, and when the next harvest failed, they had to forfeit their holdings or sell themselves into slavery to pay their debts.

The crisis led to several reforms that ushered in the age of democracy in Athens.

Solon

In 594 B.C.E., in the midst of this crisis, the Athenians appointed **Solon** sole *archon*. Solon was a trader, general, and poet. Today, Athenian school-children still memorize his poems as a tribute to Athenian democracy. Prior to his appointment as sole *archon*, Solon was the eponymous *archon*. He initiated several reforms, including:

1) forbidding the export of wheat crops, so that Athenian wheat would be used to feed Athenians.

2) exporting olive oil, which created a very prosperous economy. Olive oil is still an important product in Greece, as seen from the Sea of Olives near the ancient oracle of Delphi overlooking the Aegean Sea.

3) offering citizenship to foreign artisans to stimulate the economy. Prior to this date, Athenian citizens had to be native born.

4) instituting the *Seisachtheia*, or "shaking-off-of-burdens," which canceled all debts on land, forbade the selling of people for debts, and freed all those currently enslaved due to debts. Solon even traveled abroad to find Athenians who had been sold as slaves, and freed them and returned them to Athens. These policies benefited the debtors but hurt those who held the debts.

5) forbidding land from being used for collateral.

Solon established four classes of citizens based on wealth. At the top of the social ladder were the 500 measure men or *pentacosiomedimnoi,* citizens whose estates produced 500 bushels of grain or measures of wine or olive oil annually. Next came the *hippeis,* who produced 300 bushels or measures annually, and then the *zeugitai,* who produced 200. At the bottom of the social ladder were the *thetes*, who produced less than 200 bushels or measures a year. Only members of the top two classes could serve as *archons*. Members of the wealthiest three classes could also hold various magistracies in Athens. The *thetes* could only serve on the popular court or *heliaea*. Athenian citizens could appeal the decisions of the magistrates to this court. Solon also created a Council *(Boule)* of 400 (100 from each tribe), whose responsibility was to propose laws to the assembly *(ecclesia)*. The assembly voted on the proposals and also elected all the magistrates. Solon reduced the power of the Areopagus council, historically controlled by the aristocrats.

Although Solon defined citizenship on the basis of wealth, under later rulers citizenship was defined on the basis of property. Athenian citizenship was offered to all males whose fathers were citizens, and to immigrants and merchants. Citizens had to own property, meaning that only two of four classes could hold office.

Solon's poems insisted that his reforms were moderate and not intended to wipe out the wealthy. He insisted he did not seek to abolish the aristocracy, but rather to elevate the condition of the poor. The poor, however, were dissatisfied with his reforms, while the wealthy resented the steps he had taken. The *hektemoroi*, or six parters, wanted land to free them from poverty and bondage to the wealthy. The *hektemoroi* were called six parters because they had to pay 1/6 of their crops for the use of the land. Solon also did not offer land to freed slaves.

As sole *archon*, Solon implemented these reforms single-handedly without consulting any of the deliberative bodies in Athens. He left Athens and traveled for ten years following the implementation of his reforms, confident that they would survive his departure.

Peisistratus

After Solon left, conflict once again broke out between wealthy aristocrats and the poor. **Peisistratus** declared himself tyrant. He distributed land to the *hektemoroi* and encouraged opposition to the old aristocracy.

Hippias and Hipparchus

After Peisistratus died, his sons **Hippias** and **Hipparchus** followed him as tyrants. Harmodius and Aristogeiton plotted to assassinate both of them, but only killed Hipparchus. Consequently, Hippias was left as sole tyrant and he became more oppressive. The Spartans allied with a family of Athens, the Alcmaeonidae, and overthrew Hippias in 510 B.C.E. Hippias returned later from exile to work against the Greeks at the Battle of Marathon.

Cleisthenes

Athenian democracy really began in earnest when **Cleisthenes** took power in 508 B.C.E. Cleisthenes wanted to further diminish the influence of power cliques. Under Solon, the Athenian Council had 400 members, 100 from each of four tribes. Cleisthenes radically restructured the council to make it a 500-member council known as the *Boule*, with fifty members from each of ten tribes. Essentially, he restructured the ancient tribal life of Athens. Since members of the *Boule* served for only one year, could only sit two terms in a lifetime, and were selected by random lot, any citizen might be expected to serve on the council.

The *Boule* sent proposals to the assembly, where anyone might propose legislation. The assembly met four times a month, and there were often as many as 6,000 people present.

There was also a system of popular courts or *dikasteria,* which were also selected by lot. Athenian democracy has often been called a grass roots democracy, as every citizen represented himself and served in some capacity. Athenian democracy is distinguished from American democracy, or representative democracy, where citizens elect representatives to speak for them.

Over the course of the next several decades, the Athenians would be forced to fight first the Persians and then their fellow Greeks. Athenian democracy changed as a result of these conflicts, in ways we shall see below.

THE PERSIAN WARS

In 546 B.C.E., the Persians, under Cyrus the Great, conquered the Greek colonies of Ionia on the coast of Asia Minor. The Greek colonies had been founded with the full rights and privileges of an independent city-state and were independent from even the Greek city-state from which the colonists came. The Greeks strongly valued independent government, and so it is not surprising that by 499 B.C.E. Ionia rebelled from Persian rule.

Herodotus

Our main account of the Persian wars is that of **Herodotus**, known as the Father of History. His *Histories* not only chronicle the events of the Persian wars, but also offer many insights into Greek customs and beliefs, as well as human nature. For Herodotus, history was almost a Greek tragedy, whose heroes have "fatal flaws" (*hamartia*) even before Aristotle described them in the *Poetics*. For Herodotus, the Persians were fatally flawed by their *hubris*, or pride. The Persian leader Xerxes boasted that one of his Immortals was worth 10,000 Greeks; the Persians would find out how wrong they were in the coming years.

Herodotus paints the Athenians as the great heroes of the war, and the Spartans as self-centered. When Ionia first rebelled, they came to their fellow Greeks on the mainland for help. First they went to the greatest military power on the mainland, Sparta. When they asked the Spartans for help, the Spartans excused themselves, saying it was too much to ask for them to march three months inland to the Persian capitals for the Ionians. Athens did agree to help, and attacked the Lydian city of Sardis, which made the Persians furious. Their anger sparked the first Persian invasion of the Greek mainland under the leader Darius.

While Herodotus chastised the Athenians for their actions in Sardis and for the Persian invasion, he nevertheless painted the Athenians as very astute and aware of the threat to all Greeks that such an invasion posed. In the coming years of the war, Herodotus described the Athenians as continually behaving heroically in the face of great odds, while the Spartans often seemed to care for little other than their own interests, at least in the early stages of the conflict.

The Battle of Marathon

The first Greek victory came in 490 B.C.E. at the Battle of Marathon. The Greeks defeated the numerically superior Persian army with the leadership of Miltiades, who led a charge across the plain where the Persians were stationed. A swamp blocked the Persian escape, and the Greeks allowed the Persians to break their ranks, then flanked them and won the battle. Ironically, at Marathon, 10,000 Athenians defeated the vastly superior Persian army. The Athenians used longer spears and heavier armor than the Persians, which may account for their surprising victory. Darius and his men returned in shame to Persia. The Spartans arrived after the battle was over. Many modern scholars defend the Spartans on this count, as their absence was due to their devotion to their religious rites and rituals.

The Battle of Thermopylae

Darius's son **Xerxes** wanted to avenge his father and launched a second invasion of Greece. The Persian army was the largest ever collected, and according to Herodotus numbered around two million. Although one may doubt the accuracy of this number, nevertheless, the movement of this army was a phenomenal feat of engineering, as the Persians built movable bridges, dug canals through mountain ranges, and drank entire rivers dry on their way to Greece. In 480 B.C.E. the Spartans led a heroic effort to stop them at Thermopylae, a place whose name derives from the hot springs located here. The Spartan King Leonidas, 300 Spartans, and approximately 9,000 other Greeks attempted to hold off the Persians at the narrow pass. The Persians again had a vastly superior force that outnumbered the Greeks by at least 3 to 1. One of the Greeks remarked that the Persian arrows would darken the sky, and another responded that if so, then the Greeks would fight in the dark! Local inhabitants, however, gave away their location and the Persians went in from the back and defeated the Greek force. Spartan mothers and wives taught Spartan men never to return home unless victorious or dead on their battle shields. True to their teaching, the 300 Spartans at Thermopylae fought to the last man, while many of the other Greeks there with them had fled as the fighting intensified. The Persians proceeded through the pass, which is no longer visible today due to shifting terrain. Recent scholarship suggests that the Spartan heroism at Thermopylae was a deliberate strategy designed to hold the Persians long enough to evacuate Athens. The evacuation was accomplished, and the Persians proceeded to Athens, where they razed the Acropolis and burned its temples.

The Battle of Salamis

Meanwhile, the Athenian navy and a Spartan force had located itself behind some outcrops in the harbor of Salamis, near Athens. Confident that victory was near, the Persians allowed the Athenians to trick them into entering the small harbor. Once in the harbor, the Athenian ships swooped down on the Persians, whose large ships proved difficult to maneuver in such tight quarters. The Greeks, led by the Spartans, devastated the Persian navy.

The Battle of Plataea

In 479 B.C.E. a combined force of Athenians and Spartans defeated the Persian army on land, ending the Persian wars. The Spartan Pausanias distinguished himself as the leader of the Greek forces at Plataea. Typically, however, the Greeks fought amongst themselves even as the battle erupted, arguing over whether the Athenians would lead the charge or play a defensive role.

The monumental victory at Marathon and the threat of foreign invasion prompted the fiercely independent Greek city-states to unite under the leadership of the Athenians, who became the moral heroes of the Greeks following the wars.

THE AGE OF PERICLES

After the Persian threat was gone, several Greek city-states formed the **Delian league** to protect the Greeks from future foreign invasions. Athens was the leader of the Delian League, centered on the island of Delos. Sparta, however, worried about Athenian control and refused to join the Delian League. Sparta formed her own confederation known as the Peloponnesian League.

Under the leadership of **Pericles**, Athens entered her golden age. Many have praised Pericles as a model statesmen; he could be seen from the earliest hours of the morning through the latest hours of the day scurrying from one civic responsibility to another. So devoted to Athenian politics was he that he neglected his own family life.

Under Pericles, Athenian citizenship was restricted to native-born landholding males whose parents were also citizens. This was to counter any foreign influence and was a reaction to the Persian wars. Pericles also began the practice of paying citizens for state service, thus encouraging those less wealthy to participate. He also rebuilt the Parthenon after the original temple to Athena had been razed and burned during the Persian wars. It housed a forty-foot-high statue of Athena by the sculptor Phidias, which was covered in solid gold. The gold on Athena in the Parthenon was in effect the treasury for Athens as well as a religious emblem. Many of the most famous structures on the Acropolis were also built during the age of Pericles, including the Parthenon and the Propylaea, the famous entrance to the Acropolis.

Although the Acropolis displayed the artistic genius of Athens, Pericles had used Delian funds to rebuild it. As these funds were intended solely for the defense of the Greek city-states who joined the league, it was felt that Athens had behaved inappropriately and could not be relied upon for protection.

Pericles argued that as long as Athens provided the protection they promised, what they did with the funds was of no importance to the other Greeks. Pericles also used Delian funds to build the fabulous, long walls that connected the Acropolis to the sea.

As Athens more and more dominated the league, Athenians often punished rebellions harshly and required members of the league to take an oath of allegiance to Athens. The Athenians attempted to dictate the form of government member states were to have. The resentment of other city-states, especially of Sparta, over growing Athenian imperial power led to the Peloponnesian War.

THE PELOPONNESIAN WAR, 431–404 B.C.E.

The **Peloponnesian War** was a conflict between Athens and her allies and Sparta and her allies, as represented by the Delian and Peloponnesian Leagues. When the war first broke out, one of the Greeks said that, "this day will be the beginning of great evils for the Greeks." History proved him right.

Thucydides

Our chief account of this war is that of the Athenian general **Thucydides**, who is known as the father of scientific history for his reliance on first-hand accounts, or primary sources. Thucydides was interested above all else in those lessons from history that might help others in the future, and also in human behavior, which he believed to be always and everywhere the same. Thucydides relates how in the early days of the war, Pericles's strategy was to gather the citizens of Athens into the Long Walls and to wait out the Spartan siege. The plan failed, and plague broke out within the close confines of the walls, taking Pericles as one of its first victims. Before his death, Pericles delivered a famous speech known as the *funeral oration* in honor of those who had died fighting to defend Athens. Although Thucydides is known as the father of scientific history, he also often inserted dialogue into his account based on his own memory; at times, he also used dialogue that never occurred to convey the overall message or atmosphere he wanted readers to get. In this case, it is likely that Thucydides heard the speech and later tried to recapture it.

Thucydides clearly believed that had Pericles remained in control, the course of events would have turned out differently. For Thucydides, Pericles was the model leader; he knew how to lead the mob and not be led by it, and how to control the mob instincts of people under a democracy. For Thucydides, Pericles embodied Plato's ideal of the philosopher king, a monarchy of the most able citizen. Pericles fought mainly a defensive rather than an offensive war, a fact later leaders of Athens ignored.

The Revolt of Mitylene

As the conflict grew more tense, the attention of Athens turned to the tiny but strategically located islands in the Aegean. Mitylene revolted from Athenian control, while Melos, a Spartan colony, wanted to remain neutral and refused to submit to Athens. In both cases, Athenians worried that Athens might look weak. The revolt of Mitylene, if allowed to go unchecked, would have made Athens look vulnerable; the refusal of Melos to join would have allowed a strategic location to be up for grabs.

Thucydides chronicles the Athenian debate over how to handle these difficulties, and in the passages of *The Peloponnesian War*, one sees the devastating impact of competing power factions on a democracy. Thucydides paints a disturbing picture of the negative effects of unbalanced leadership that promotes self-interest above the good of the whole. After the revolt of Mitylene, two different factions arose to debate their punishment. The most radical opinion was that of Cleon, who argued that democracy was incompatible with the development of an empire. One could be a democracy at home, but could not act democratically abroad without losing the empire. Any sign of weakness bred further revolt, and in his opinion, the male inhabitants of Mitylene should be executed and their women and children enslaved. Only such brutal punishments could teach the lessons of obedience that were necessary to maintain the Athenian power over its member states.

Against the position of Cleon, Diodotus took a more moderate line, arguing that such brutality would create further resentment of Athenian power. Only those guilty should be punished rather than the entire population.

The moderate position of Diodotus eventually triumphed only moments before the massacre ordered by Cleon was to take place.

The Melian Debate

The same drama was later played out on Melos, with a very different result. The **Melians** attempted to appeal to the Athenian sense of justice, only to find their appeal falling on deaf ears. Although the Melians wanted self-determination, the Athenians insisted that joining them was in the Melians' best interest. Still facing resistance, the Athenians argued that "might makes right" and that justice only applied between two powers of equal stature. They argued, in other words, that power is the basis of the natural law, and that subjugation of Melos was justified.

When the Melians refused to succumb to Athenian might, the Athenians massacred every last male inhabitant of Melos and enslaved the women and children. The Athenians were hated for generations after, proving that Diodotus had spoken wisely.

The behavior of Athens here raises serious questions about the nature of democracy; was Cleon right and must a democracy behave as a ruthless empire abroad in order to preserve its existence at home? Can a democracy treat its allies as it treats its citizens and hope to preserve control over other states? Must a culture create and maintain an empire abroad to protect democracy at home? Do extreme circumstances justify extreme actions to preserve one's way of life?

THE DEFEAT OF ATHENS

In 405 B.C.E., Sparta defeated the Athenian navy at the Hellespont, the narrow passage of water that in later years would defend the eastern capital of the Roman Empire, Constantinople. Of the 179 Athenian ships that fought at the Hellespont, only nine escaped. After the battle, the Spartans ruthlessly executed 4,000 Athenians.

The Spartan victory marked the end of the glorious age of Greek culture. The Spartans had never been devoted to culture, had always been fiercely independent, and had proved uninterested in governing the Greek world. That task was left to the Macedonians, first under Philip and later under his son, Alexander.

CHAPTER 10

ALEXANDER THE GREAT AND THE HELLENISTIC ERA

THE AFTERMATH OF THE PELOPONNESIAN WAR

After the Persian wars, the Greeks failed to sustain the unity that had brought them victory; similarly, they proved unable to keep together the coalition that defeated the Athenian Empire in the Peloponnesian War. The Greek love of independence that was the basis of Athenian democracy proved also to be the seed of the dissolution of Greek culture in the wake of the Peloponnesian War. Ironically, the **Macedonians** took up the task of governing the Greeks and spreading Greek culture throughout the world. The Athenians and other Greeks long had great disdain for the Macedonians; they were primarily farmers who spoke a very rough Greek dialect that the other Greeks regarded as unsophisticated.

Philip of Macedon

The rise of Macedon began in 359 B.C.E., when Philip became king. Philip had studied the works of Xenophon, where he had recounted the famous march of 10,000 Greek mercenaries in Persia. From Xenophon, Philip had concluded that the hoplite **phalanx** supported by cavalry was unbeatable. A phalanx was a block-shaped formation of hoplites, or foot soldiers. Each soldier carried a spear, so when the phalanx formed, there was a line of spears that projected out several feet in front of the men. The phalanx was the tank of antiquity; its only weakness was that when it was necessary to turn, the entire formation had to turn at once.

Philip's war tactics proved the phalanx to be the premier battle machine of antiquity. In 349 B.C.E., Philip attacked the Greek town of Olynthus, as he was worried that his two half-brothers might challenge his throne. In 346 B.C.E., he moved further into Greek territories and attacked the home of the oracle, Delphi. Philip urged the Greeks to unite with him on the pretext of attacking the Persians; in so doing, he attempted to appeal to the civic pride of Greeks who had thrown off the Persian threat.

Only Demosthenes, an orator in Athens, recognized the threat posed by Philip. Demosthenes walked through the streets of Athens carrying a light, and urged the Athenians to resist in the name of independence. His efforts failed, and by 338 B.C.E., Philip defeated the Greeks. During Philip's advances, the Spartans, true to past behavior, did not come to the assistance of their fellow Greeks.

In 336 B.C.E., Philip was assassinated. He had recently taken a second wife, and some scholars suggest that Philip's first wife feared for her son's position and his inheritance. Consequently, they suggest that she had her husband assassinated. Philip's son by his first marriage, **Alexander**, did in fact succeed him. To his credit, he pursued the assassin and punished him accordingly.

Alexander the Great

As a young man, Alexander had tamed the horse Buchephalus, whom no one else had been able to tame. Alexander had led many of his father's campaigns and in 340 B.C.E. had been named regent in Macedonia during his father's absence. Impressed by his son's abilities, Philip had once remarked that he had no kingdom big enough to offer such a talented boy.

Alexander's tutor was the philosopher Aristotle, who perhaps introduced him to Plato's concept of the Philosopher King, the educated statesman who ruled through reason and education. Alexander had a love of Greek culture and spread it throughout the known world, yet at times his oversized temperament seemed to be ungoverned by reason.

Just as the earlier Greeks sought after *arete*, a heroic nobility of character exemplified by bravery on the battlefield, and a god-like sense of honor among men, Alexander's career as a crusading Greek hero raised him to the level of the gods in the eyes of many men. In his lifetime, Alexander was revered as a god in many parts of his empire. In later history, his achievements continued to inspire awe even among the most gifted generals. It was said that the Roman Julius Caesar shuddered when he walked past Alexander's statue.

Alexander was twenty when he came to the throne; by the age of thirty-three, when he died, he had conquered territories from Egypt to the Indus

River Valley, representing almost all the world known to the Greeks. Few have ever achieved conquests as significant as those of Alexander, yet in his own mind Alexander believed his goals incomplete at his death, as there was still more to conquer, more to do. Despite the enormity of his achievement, one must also take into account the fact that his empire fell apart immediately after his death.

Rebellion in Thebes

While Alexander had been away securing the northern frontiers, a rumor had spread that he had been killed. The city of Thebes revolted. In retaliation, Alexander razed Thebes and burned it to the ground in 335 B.C.E. While he virtually destroyed the city, he left the poet Pindar's house untouched, as well as several Greek temples. The destruction of Thebes was the first demonstration of Alexander's tendency towards ruthless conquest, as well as of his veneration of Greek culture.

The Conquest of Persia

Alexander wanted to realize his father's vision of conquering the East, and formulated one of the most ambitious plans of conquest of all time. Alexander planned to attack Persia, the empire that stood between him and his goal, the conquest of the known world. Alexander's teacher Aristotle had taught him that the ocean at the subcontinent of India marked the boundary of the earth. A century after the Persian wars ended, the Persians still outnumbered the Greek forces three to one; they were wealthier and also had a powerful navy bolstered by a series of port fortifications. On paper, never had any plan looked as risky as Alexander's plan to conquer the East.

By the time he died, Alexander conquered not only the Persian Empire, but also the remnants of the Egyptian and the Babylonian cultures. One reason for his success was his style of leadership; Alexander fought in the front lines with his men. By the time of his death, he had been wounded in battle in nearly every part of his body. When his men were without food, he was without food; when they were without water, he was without water. Alexander's boyish good looks, his charisma, and leadership abilities inspired great loyalty not only among his men, but also among his enemies. When he finally defeated the Persian ruler Darius, he told his men to treat Darius's wife and daughter as the royalty they were. When Alexander died, Darius's wife and daughter grieved for him as if he were their own son and brother.

The Battle of the Granicus River

Crossing the Hellespont, the very site where Athens had been defeated in 405 B.C.E., Alexander first met the Persians at the battle of Granicus River in

334 B.C.E. Here, his forces unexpectedly defeated the Persian army. While near Granicus, Alexander visited the site of ancient Troy, and reportedly uttered his famous tribute to Achilles. Alexander wished to be a new Achilles.

The Battle of Issus

Alexander defeated the Persians at the Battle of Issus in 333 B.C.E. Although the Persians caught him off guard by marching on him from behind, Alexander managed to accomplish a stunning victory.

Egypt

Alexander reached Egypt, where he was hailed as a pharaoh at Memphis in 332 B.C.E. After a trip to the oracle in Egypt, his men hailed him as the son of Amon and later also as the son of Zeus. Alexander began to found cities in his name; the famous Hellenistic city of **Alexandria** on the northern tip of Africa became an important center of Hellenistic culture. The lighthouse of Alexandria, the pharos, was one of the seven wonders of the world. The lighthouse once guided international traffic from the Nile, Red Sea, and the Mediterranean into the harbor. An earthquake later toppled it and today it lies beneath the ocean. The library of Alexandria contained a half-million scrolls, but was later destroyed.

The Battle of Arbela

In 331 B.C.E., Alexander continued his pursuit of the Persian ruler Darius III. At the Battle of Arbela, near the Tigris River, Darius met his fate at the hands of his own men. Alexander ordered his wife and daughter to be treated as royalty and with compassion. He later married the daughter of Darius, beginning the fusion of Greek and Persian customs.

Battle of Gaugamela

Alexander decisively defeated the Persians at Gaugamela, and later went on to the two ancient Persian capitals, Susa and Persepolis.

The Wedding Feast of Susa

At the Wedding Feast of Susa, Alexander ordered 10,000 of his men to marry Persian women, insisting that all humanity was united through a common creator. The Wedding Feast of Susa symbolized the new world of the Hellenistic empire. The word "Hellenistic" means "Greek-like," and blending of the fiercely independent Greeks with Persians and other peoples changed the Greek world forever. The Hellenistic world was cosmopolitan, a word made up of "cosmos," meaning the universe, and "polis," harking back to the Greek city-state. In Alexander's cosmopolitan empire, the polis became the known world, thus ending forever the ethnocentricity and localization of the old Greek poleis. Alexander allowed conquered areas to keep their laws and customs, and brought many of those customs back into the old Greek world.

The Persian Treasury in Persepolis

Alexander also traveled to Persepolis, the second Persian capital. Here, Alexander took the Persian treasury; the silver coins from Persepolis created wild inflation as Alexander's forces dumped them on the ancient world. In a drunken fit of rage, Alexander also burned the famous Persian capital. Alexander might have been trained in philosophy, but his oversized personality included the full ranges of unrestrained emotion. Alexander often exhibited ferocious fits of temper that he juxtaposed with the humane treatment of those he conquered.

The Indus River Valley

Alexander reached the Indus River Valley in 326 B.C.E. The impact of the Greeks on India is evident in Indian art of the next several centuries. Alexander's men had been on the march now for almost eight years. Exhausted, for the first time they refused to follow their leader and threatened mutiny. Alexander ordered massive purges in retaliation; it has been estimated that one-third to two-thirds of the men were dismissed or executed. It was at the Indus River that Alexander himself began to deteriorate; having reached the ends of the earth and with a mutiny on his hands, he began to formulate wild plans to conquer Carthage in north Africa and to construct a canal linking Africa with Saudi Arabia. Had his plan worked, the Portuguese would never have explored the coast of Africa in an effort to reach the East during the fifteenth century C.E. or the Age of Exploration; there would have been no need for this as the canal would have made sailing around Africa unnecessary. Alexander also envisioned deporting entire populations to complete the project.

Babylon

Alexander left the Indus and returned to Babylon in 323 B.C.E. In June he died of a mysterious fever. The origin of his illness is unknown, but some speculate it was more the result of his perceived failure to urge his men farther that caused his final decline. Upon his deathbed, his men asked him whom he wished to rule his empire. Rather than cede his conquests to the son he now had with his Persian wife, his response was, "Let the best man win." In death as in life Alexander was a true Achilles, who believed in prowess on the battlefield as the main criterion for leadership. His wife Roxanne and her son were murdered in 310 B.C.E. The chaos in the wake of his death and that of his son fragmented the Hellenistic world. The tomb of Alexander has never been found, although recent excavations near Alexandria may prove to be his final resting place.

THE HELLENISTIC EMPIRE

After Alexander's death, his empire was divided into separate kingdoms. For forty years, various figures battled for power.

The Aetolian League

The Aetolian League was centered on the Gulf of Corinth. In the Aetolian League, citizens of the various city-states retained their own citizenship but also received citizenship in the League. There were two kinds of citizenship offered: sympolity, which provided full civil and political rights, and isopolity, which provided civil but not political rights. Isopolity was given to citizens in the more distant states linked to the League. The League government could raise armies and collect taxes. The transformation of Greek citizenship in this League symbolized the new cosmopolitan world.

The Aechaean League

The Aechaean League was formed from the city-states of the northern Peloponnesus and was very closely related to the old Peloponnesian League dominated by Sparta. The Aechaean League had a common system of coinage and uniform standards of weights and measurements shared by the city-states. There was also a system of federal courts. Unlike the city-states in the Aetolian League, those in the Aechaean League did not exchange citizenship. The League government could raise armies and collect taxes.

The Ptolemaic Monarchy

The Ptolemaic monarchy was founded by **Ptolemy I**, a Macedonian general in Alexander's army, and became one of the wealthiest centers of the Hellenistic world. It extended over the territory of ancient Egypt. Ptolemy believed that the generals could not hold Alexander's empire together, and proposed its division at a council in Babylon following Alexander's death. Ptolemy enacted a policy of protecting Egypt's borders and also exploiting its economy. He used Macedonian commanders to run daily affairs alongside Egyptians, and there is some evidence that he and his men discriminated against the native Egyptians. He founded only one city, Ptolomais, and introduced coinage, which was unknown in Egypt at that time. He also founded the cult of Sarapis, which was a fusion of Greek and Egyptian religions. Ptolemy died in 282 B.C.E. and passed power to his son. The Ptolemies reigned longer than any other monarchy founded on the ruins of Alexander's conquests, and finally succumbed to the Romans in 30 B.C.E. The last Ptolomaic ruler was Cleopatra VII, whose union with Julius Caesar and later Marc Antony threatened to rip the Roman world apart.

The Seleucid Monarchy

Antioch was the capital of the Seleucid monarchy, which extended from Thrace to the subcontinent of India. The Seleucid Empire spanned the outlines of the old Persian Empire. Seleucus I Nicator, one of Alexander's generals, became satrap, or governor, of Babylon in 323 B.C.E., two years after the death of Alexander. When Antigonus I, who inherited Alexander's Macedonian throne, expelled him from Babylon, Seleucus allied with Ptolemy against him. In 312 B.C.E., he defeated the Aontigonids and founded the Seleucid monarchy. In the continuing conflict that surrounded the death of Alexander, Seleucus was later assassinated by the son of Ptolemy I. The Seleucid Empire was one of the most important centers of culture in the Hellenistic world, but their favoritism to Greek culture caused many rebellions. In the second century B.C.E., for example, they erected a statue to Zeus in Jerusalem, causing the rebellion documented in the Hebrew book of Maccabees. The Seleucids began a long process of decline when they were first defeated by the Roman Empire in 190 B.C.E. The Romans finally conquered the last remnants of the Seleucid monarchy in 64 B.C.E.

Pergamene Monarchy

The Pergamene monarchy covered Asia Minor. The capital city of Pergamon was one of the most important cities in the Hellenistic world, with a library second only to that of Alexandria. Pergamon was originally under the control of the Seleucids, but in 263 B.C.E., the Attalid rulers declared independence from the Seleucids. Attalus I fought against the Macedonian dynasty of the Antigonids with the help of the Romans in two Macedonian wars. Attalus I was known as a patron of the arts, and the city of Pergamon was also an important city in Roman times, when its population reached 200,000. After the fall of the western Roman Empire, the Byzantines and then the Ottoman Turks ruled the city of Pergamon.

The Antigonid Monarchy

The Antigonid monarchy was the ruling house of Macedonia from 306 to 168 B.C.E. The Antigonids rose to power when Demetrius I Poiorcetes

Dying Gaul. Roman marble copy of a Hellenistic original.

ousted the governor of Athens and conquered the island of Cyprus. His father, Antigonus I Monophthalmus, then conquered all of the Middle East except Babylonia and was proclaimed king in 306 B.C.E. The Antigonids later clashed with the expanding Roman Empire; in 215 B.C.E., the Romans defeated Philip V of Macedon and his power was confined to Macedonia. His successor, Perseus, fought for Macedonian freedom against Rome, but was defeated by the Romans at the battle of Pydna in 168 B.C.E.

HELLENISTIC ART

Hellenistic art was very realistic and portrayed the psychological pain many Greeks felt in the aftermath of Alexander's conquests. Whereas the artists of the classical era portrayed ideals, the Hellenistic artist attempted to be as realistic as possible and to capture the often strong emotions that reigned in the day. *The Laocoon Group*, a marble statue, was one of the most powerful Hellenistic works. Its artist captured the agony of Laocoon and his sons in the twisting, painful torsion of their bodies as they were engulfed and strangled by the serpent. *The Dying Gaul* is another famous Hellenistic statue. From the realism of this work, historians have learned much about the actual physical appearance of the Gauls, a Celtic people who wore only a torque around their necks and fought ferociously in the nude. The artist has captured the last breath of the Gaul, who places all his weight on his arms. Despite the obvious agony of the *Dying Gaul*, the artist gave him a nobility of bearing and character that haunts us even today.

Laocoon Group. Roman copy of original, c. first century C.E.

The Colossus of Rhodes

The *Colossus of Rhodes* was another of the seven wonders of the ancient world created during the Hellenistic era. It was a huge bronze statue built with the same technique used by Phidias for the giant Zeus of Olympia. The *Colossus* illustrated the extent of creativity during the Hellenistic period. It collapsed after only a few decades, as its legs were not large enough to sustain its massive weight. Scholars debate whether the colossus straddled the harbor of Rhodes, which would have been almost impossible from a technological point of view, or stood on the shore, the more likely alternative.

CHAPTER 11

THE CIVILIZATION OF ROME

Rome began its history as a city on the Palatine Hill, one of seven hills along the Tiber River. According to the historian Livy, the legendary foundation of Rome occurred in 753 B.C.E. when Romulus defeated his twin brother Remus in a cataclysmic battle across the seven hills on the Tiber. Romulus and Remus were the sons of Rhea Silvia and the god Mars. Their uncle had banned their mother from having children due to a family conflict. When they were born, their uncle ordered them placed on the Tiber River; they landed on the Palatine Hill, the exact spot where Rome would later be built. A she-wolf found them and raised them to maturity. Remus, however, crossed a wall built by Romulus and the two fought each other to the death. Romulus became the founder of Rome, which was named after him.

She-Wolf. Etruscan, c. 500 B.C.E.; human figures added later.

Livy further relates that the original inhabitants of Rome were debtors and criminals, and were in desperate need of women. The Romans went to the Sabines and raped several of their women, bringing them home to further their community. The Sabine women became loyal to their Roman husbands and rose to the defense of their husbands when their families tried to rescue them. According to Livy, part of Rome's later greatness was its ability to conquer enemies and then convert them to allies, thereby uniting all of the Italian peninsula and later much of the Mediterranean world. The Romans fought the Sabines in several wars, and several other groups of people, including the Latins. The Latins were named after the volcanic plain on which they lived, the Latium Plain, which was bounded on the north by the Tiber River. The Romans eventually made peace with both the Sabines and the Latins. The Latins gave their name to the official language of the Republic and the Empire.

THE ETRUSCANS

The Etruscans, a group of Indo-Europeans whose roots were in Central Asia, were another important group of people on the peninsula. Traditionally, it has been said that the Etruscans dominated Rome during its first 200 years of history. However, of the first seven kings of the Romans, only two were Etruscan: Tarquinius the Elder and Tarquinius Superbus or Tarquin the Proud, who was likely his grandson. The Tarquins did not take Rome by force, but

Etruscan sarcophagus, c. 500 B.C.E.

rather by election, and recent historians have reevaluated the extent to which the Etruscans influenced Roman civilization. Several recent historians argue that the Greek colonies on the southern tip of Italy had more influence on the Romans than did the Etruscans.

The Etruscans were a self-governing aristocracy with a military ruling class, and they controlled most of the northern Italian peninsula. The Romans borrowed many customs from the Etruscans, including the Triumph, in which victorious generals were led through the center of Rome. The Romans also copied the Etruscan custom of burying their dead in decorated sarcophagi. The Etruscans wore shoes, the idea of which the Roman army would borrow and use to great advantage.

The Foundation of the Roman Republic

The Romans, however, eventually threw off the last Etruscan king, Tarquinius Superbus or Tarquin the Proud, in 510 B.C.E. Ironically, one of the conspirators was Brutus, the name of the later assassin of Julius Caesar. Brutus became one of the two first consuls of the Roman Republic, traditionally said to be founded in 509 B.C.E. Some historians believe the foundation of the Republic was actually later, but this traditional date is still the most widely accepted date.

The Roman Republic was based on the rule of law. The laws of Rome were displayed in the Roman forum on twelve bronze tables. This public display of law illustrated the Roman commitment to **constitutionalism**, which was important in the development of the modern world. The Latin name of the Republic was the *Res publica*, or the Roman "public thing." Indeed, the public proclamation of law was one of Rome's greatest achievements.

Although the twelve bronze tables have disappeared, we know much about the Roman Republic from the historian Polybius. Polybius insisted that the greatest achievement of Rome was the balance of power between the consuls, the senate, and the people. He argued that if one looked at any of these branches of Roman government in isolation, one would have interpreted it as either a despotism, an oligarchy, or a democracy. Rome, however, was a republic, in which all branches were checked and balanced by the others. Yet in many important ways, the Romans never did balance the two competing forces in their society: the patricians or the noble class, and the plebeians, or those considered citizens but without the right to hold office in the early days of the Republic.

At the top of the Roman governmental structure were the two **consuls**, either of which could veto the decrees of the other. Citizens elected the consuls from the patricians for a one-year term and the senate had to approve their election. The consuls were the supreme masters of administration, and all others but the tribunes were subject to them. They were charged to bring matters before the senate for deliberation, carry out decrees of the majority, make preparations for war, and control the military during maneuvers. After the expiration of their terms, they retired to the senate, where they spent the rest of their lives in civic service. According to Polybius, "a survey of these powers would justify calling constitutional Rome a despotic government." Traditionally, one became consul in Rome after having progressively moved through the *cursus honorium*, or list of offices.

In many ways, the most important governing body in Rome was the **senate**, composed of elder statesmen from the patrician class who served for life. The senate oversaw the treasury; in fact, no money was authorized for the state without the decree of the senate. The senate was charged with leading public investigations into treason, conspiracy, and murder. Senators also served as ambassadors to reconcile warring allies. According to Polybius, since they "stayed here while the consuls were away, Rome could be perceived as an oligarchy or government led by the aristocracy." Nowhere were the powers of the senate decisively spelled out, which gave senators the ability to establish supreme power in Rome. During the Age of the Reformers in the second and first century B.C.E., tribunes attempted to change laws to benefit the plebeians, and it was the Senate that masterminded many of their assassinations.

According to Polybius, the third important body in the Roman *Res publica* was the people. The plebeian assembly was the last and final court to decide matters of life and death. The people's assembly met when summoned by the consuls, and later, the office of Tribune was established to look after the affairs of the people.

The difficulty faced by Rome throughout its history, however, was the tension between the patricians, who came from the ancient noble families and whose name was derived from the Latin word for father, *pater*, and the plebeians. Both were defined as citizens, but they did not enjoy the same rights. The patricians were the aristocracy, and they did not intermarry with the plebeians. They held the highest offices, such as senator and consul. The plebeians, on the other hand, were citizens who paid taxes and served in the army, but were barred from holding office in the early Republic. Although there was no obvious law prohibiting plebeians from holding office, in practice, one had to perform certain religious rites and rituals, which were only open to participation from the patricians.

In effect, the history of the Republic was the history of how the patricians and plebeians resolved these tensions so that they could embark on a wave of conquest that would make them masters of the Mediterranean area; the history of Rome as an empire is the story of how they managed to unite such a disparate group of peoples and cultures under the banner of Rome.

ROME BECOMES MASTER OF THE MEDITERRANEAN

Rome began to address the tensions between the patricians and plebeians with the appointment of the tribunes in the fifth century B.C.E. The tribunes were elected by plebian assembly for one year, and could convene the assembly and block measures proposed by the senate by saying "I forbid" or *veto* in Latin. In 367 B.C.E., Rome passed the Sexto-Licinian Laws, according to which plebeians could hold the office of consul and could intermarry with patricians. In 287 B.C.E., Rome passed the Hortensian Laws, which mandated that laws passed in the plebian assembly were binding on the Roman senate. These various measures resolved the class tensions enough to allow Rome to expand beyond the Tiber to conquer the Italian peninsula.

Rome defeated the Greek colonists who still remained at the foot of the Peninsula during the Pyrrhic Wars from 282–272 B.C.E. Pyrrhus, King of Epirus, led the Greeks and in the early days of the conflict defeated the Romans at Heraclea. During the battle, Rome lost 7,000 men while the Greeks lost 4,000. While the Romans lost more soldiers, the Greeks could not afford to lose the 4,000 men who died. Thus, a Pyrrhic victory refers to a victory that is too costly for the victor.

The Punic Wars

Rome's expansion to the southern tip of the Italian peninsula was quickly followed by a leap across the water to Sicily. The Punic Wars began when Rome entered Sicily. The **Phoenicians** had a settlement in Sicily, as well as an important outpost at Carthage in North Africa. The Phoencians were not involved in war and conquest so much as they were interested in trade. They marketed purple dye, which was expensive to make in antiquity. Purple was the symbol of royalty in many cultures. It has been shown that Phoenician ships were capable of crossing the Atlantic. The Latin word for Phoenician was *Punicus*, and when the Romans entered Sicily, the Carthaginians rose to the defense of the Sicilians. During the first Punic War from 264–241 B.C.E., the Romans were forced to fight a sea war. They were ill equipped for such a conflict, yet they eventually devised a bridge known as a corvus to enable them to board the Carthaginian ships and fight what amounted to a land battle on the decks of the ships. Rome eventually won the conflict and exacted a large indemnity against the Carthaginians as well as the surrender of territory.

Hannibal and the Second Punic War

During the First Punic War, Rome had taken Carthage's most important province, Sicily, as well as Sardinia and Corsica. To compensate for these losses, the Carthaginians began to expand their holdings on the Iberian

Peninsula. The leader of the Iberian forces was the general Hamilcar Barca, who brought with him his ten-year-old son, **Hannibal**. The Romans believed that Hamilcar forced Hannibal to promise eternal hatred for the Romans. When Hamilcar died, Hannibal's brother-in-law, Hasdrubal, was appointed commander in Iberia. In 221 B.C.E., however, Hasdrubal was murdered and Hannibal was made commander. While Hasdrubal had pursued more peaceful tactics in Iberia, such as intermarriage with the Carthaginians, Hannibal returned to his father's more aggressive stance and laid siege to Saguntum, a Roman ally. At the time, Rome was occupied with the Second Illyrian War, and Saguntum fell after eight months. Enraged, the Romans demanded that Carthage hand over Hannibal for prosecution. Hannibal continued to expand the holdings of Carthage in Iberia, and Rome declared the Second Punic War (218–201 B.C.E.).

This time, the Carthaginians decided to attempt to outwit the Romans and force them to fight a defensive battle. Hannibal launched a bold attack directly into the heart of Italy. With a force of 50,000 infantry, 9,000 cavalry, and 37 elephants to carry supplies for the troops, he crossed the Pyrenees, and then ferried the elephants across the Rhone River on rafts. Even more remarkably, his forces crossed the Alps in the snow, and by October 218 B.C.E., his remaining forces of approximately 38,000 soldiers and 8,000 knights had reached the plains along the Po River, near the Italian town of Turin. Hannibal's achievement was astonishing. The route Hannibal took across the Alps is the subject of much debate. Our only sources of his route are the Roman historians Livy and Polybius, neither of whose accounts we can completely verify. Hannibal caught the Romans off-guard, and they sent forces to the river Ticinus to meet him. Hannibal defeated them, and the many Gauls who inhabited the region now flocked to his cause. According to legend, Hannibal so mistrusted the Gauls as allies that he continually wore wigs and changed them so as to disguise himself.

Hannibal and his new allies then defeated the Romans again at Trebia. Later, at the lake of Trasimene, two Roman legions were annihilated. The Romans attempted to stop Hannibal and raised a force of 80,000 men to fight him at Cannae. While Hannibal's army only had about 26,000 Carthaginians, 12,000 Gauls, and 7,000 Italians, clever military leadership managed to thwart the Romans again. At the battle of Cannae, Hannibal's troops killed so many senators and patricians that the government was very nearly shut down. Hannibal was thirty years old when he leveled the world's mightiest army. Other Roman provinces revolted, such as Capua, which Hannibal entered triumphantly on his last surviving elephant.

Hannibal's men were exhausted after the campaign, and although Cannae was a tremendous victory, the Romans gradually began to push them further south. Hannibal countered by laying siege to Rome itself, but the Romans launched a counter-offensive in Iberia against Hannibal's brother

Hasdrubal (a different person from his brother-in-law Hasdrubal, who was governor before him), whom he had appointed commander. The young Roman Publius Cornelius Scipio conquered the Carthaginian capital of Iberia, Cartagena, and then proceeded to launch an attack on Carthage itself. Scipio forced Hannibal to leave the peninsula to defend his home ground. Rome sent its expedition to Africa under the leadership of Scipio Africanus, a young Roman who was not yet twenty-five years of age.

In 202 B.C.E., fourteen years after Hannibal's victory at Cannae, Scipio defeated Hannibal in a stunning maneuver at the battle of Zama. Hannibal's forces were tricked into opening the formidable line of elephants. Hannibal had distinguished himself in the earlier part of the campaign with such brilliance one wonders why he allowed himself to be duped in such a manner.

The peace negotiated between Rome and Carthage forced the Carthaginians to give up their fleet, recognize the Roman conquests in Iberia, and pay an indemnity of 10,000 talents in fifty annual installments. A treaty that resolves one conflict only to create further tension through its terms is referred to as a "Carthaginian peace." Tension between Rome and Carthage continued to escalate. The Carthaginians appointed Hannibal consul. Only a year later, when some of his enemies told the Roman senate that Hannibal planned another attack in conjunction with the Seleucid monarchs, Hannibal fled. When Hannibal advised the Seleucid monarch Antiochus to declare war on Greece, the Romans came to their defense. Hannibal fought the Romans once again and their allies at Rhodes, but was defeated. Hannibal fled again, and later led the Bythnians to victory against Pergamum. Once again, though, Rome intervened, and to avoid extradition, in 183 or 182 B.C.E. Hannibal poisoned himself.

Later generations would not forget Hannibal. The emperor Septimus Severus erected a monument at the place where he killed himself, Libyssa, which was still visible in the eleventh century. Throngs of pilgrims came to the site, including many Romans who never forgot the heroic general who led his troops across the Alps. After Hannibal, Roman power was not threatened for 600 years.

The Third Punic War

In this case, the deceptive peace erupted again in a Third Punic War from 149–146 B.C.E. Cato the Elder, a senior statesman of Rome, told the senators that, "Carthago delenda est/Carthage must be destroyed." The Third Punic War was not a war in the sense the other two conflicts were; it was a minor skirmish that ended quickly. This time, the Romans were determined to wipe Carthage out. They destroyed the city of Carthage, sold the citizens into slavery, and salted the ground to prevent Carthage from ever being able to grow crops. The Carthaginians were, as Cato urged, utterly destroyed, leaving Rome the master of the Mediterranean.

Legacy of the Punic Wars

The Romans referred to the Mediterranean as the *mare nostrum*, or "our sea." Following the conquest of Carthage, the Mediterranean literally became a Roman lake, and Julius Caesar eventually rebuilt Carthage as a Roman city. The conquest of Carthage made possible the development of an empire that eventually spread to Byzantium in the east and to the British Isles in the north. Livy, a historian of the Silver Age of Culture, the age of Augustus, first emperor of Rome, wrote that, "God has ordained it that Rome should be ruler of the world."

The Punic Wars not only resulted in the destruction of Carthage, but also left their mark on Rome. During Hannibal's siege of Rome in the Second Punic War, he and his troops and elephants destroyed the Roman countryside, forcing many peasants to enter Rome. Rome was forced to accommodate the refugees, but suffered from overcrowding and unemployment. In the wake of the Second Punic War, many patricians amassed huge estates known as *latifundia* and retreated to lead the shady life, as one Roman historian called it. Preferring life in the countryside to an active life of civic commitment, the patricians forsook public life and therefore, many argue, weakened the fabric of Roman politics. The *latifundia* also became the basis for the later medieval manorial estates.

As the empire expanded, these problems grew more acute. The provincial governments became corrupt; the distance between Rome and the provinces was often far so Rome had no way of adequately overseeing the officials. Tax collectors often collected many times the rate of taxation imposed by Rome and kept the overflow for their own devices. The separation between patricians and plebeians grew more acute than at any time since the early days of the Republic.

THE AGE OF THE REFORMERS

The abuses of patrician power led to the career of several tribunes collectively known as the reformers. In 133 B.C.E., Tiberius Gracchus initiated a land reform package whereby Rome was to reclaim state land taken by the patricians and redistribute it to the landless plebeians. In order to implement his measures, he bypassed the senate and blocked the vote of the Tribune. Further, he tried to have himself illegally reelected to a second term. Tiberius was a good example of what went wrong in Roman politics; he had praiseworthy motives, to help the underprivileged, but the means by which he accomplished his ends were illegal.

Tiberius was clubbed to death by an angry mob led by the senate. The senate, pledged to uphold law and order, now became an angry mob of assassins.

In 123 B.C.E., Tiberius's brother, Gaius Gracchus, came into power. The equestrians in the military, an elite class of soldiers, supported Gaius. He passed measures to ensure their support and for the first time allowed them to become tax collectors. He allowed provincial governors to be tried by equestrians and generally increased the power of the military. Despite having the support of the military, Gaius, too, was assassinated, likely at the hands of the senate. His tenure in office had established, however, a dangerous precedent, that of the loyalty of the military to their leader as opposed to Rome.

In 107 B.C.E., this dangerous precedent reached fruition when Marius, a powerful general, became consul. The patricians no longer wanted to serve in the military, and Marius needed to increase military recruitment. He offered land for service, and further encouraged loyalty to one man as opposed to Rome. Marius reformed the army, making it a professional corps rather than a volunteer citizen army. He also made it more mobile, and Roman soldiers were often called "Marius's mules."

Marius fought a bitter civil war with Sulla, who had been his assistant in the Jugurthine War in Africa. Sulla fought his way up the Italian peninsula and became dictator in 82 B.C.E. After an extended period during which he purged all his enemies, Sulla doubled the size of the senate by packing it with his own supporters.

Julius Caesar

By the time of **Julius Caesar**, the republican values of Rome had been significantly weakened. Caesar formed a triumvirate with Pompey, a powerful general, and Crassus, whose name meant "the thick one." Pompey married Caesar's daughter to solidify their pact, and Caesar was named governor in Spain and Gaul. The historian Livy called the first triumvirate "a conspiracy against the state by its three leading citizens," as Caesar's later actions would permanently bring the Republic to an end.

Caesar's campaigns in Gaul made him wildly popular with the army and the Roman people, to the point where Pompey worried about his motives and growing power. The historian Suetonius wrote in his *Life of Caesar* that Caesar was "every man's woman and every woman's man," meaning that he attempted to win over everyone's support through whatever means possible. Further, Plutarch wrote that he was rather uncultured, having a barbaric type of speech. The Romans valued eloquence, and apparently Caesar did not possess that gift of speech. Nevertheless, Plutarch related that his men adored him, as he became one of them in order to win his victories.

Caesar's most famous campaigns were in Gaul. The Romans had control of Cisalpine Gaul, but in 52 C.E. the Celts joined together in a rebellion to free all of Gaul from Roman rule. The tribes to the north of Roman Gaul were the heart of the rebellion, and Caesar's most formidable enemy was

Vercingetorix. Vercingetorix's father had attempted to make himself king of the Gauls and had been assassinated, apparently at Roman hands. Vercingetorix knew he could not defeat the Romans in battle, and his strategy was rather to cut off their supply lines. The conflict with Vercingetorix came to a climax at the siege of Alesia. Although Vercingetorix had escaped before the siege began, the Gauls fought the Romans from both within and without the city. After thirty days, their supplies ran out, and the situation was hopeless. Vercingetorix surrendered to Caesar and was taken prisoner to Rome. He was imprisoned for six years, and after Caesar's final victory over Pompey in 46 B.C.E., he was strangled.

Caesar was a historian who wrote an account of his conquest of Gaul, and in characteristic direct fashion, he summed up the defeat of the Celts in the simple phrase "veni, vidi, vici/I came, I saw, I conquered." The fierce, warlike nature of the Celts and their heroic struggle against the Roman legions is immortalized in the Hellenistic statue *The Dying Gaul*. The statue captures a Gaul at the very moment of death, still struggling to hold himself up. The Celts fought in the nude and wore collars around their necks. The nobility of bearing portrayed by the statue has often helped to create a romanticized view of the Celts in Gaul.

The Crossing of the Rubicon

Caesar's campaign in Gaul was so successful that the senate and Pompey began to worry about Caesar's power over the masses. Further, Caesar's daughter Julia had died, breaking down the alliance with Pompey. In 49 B.C.E., the senate ordered Caesar to hand over his ten legions to a new governor. Caesar, however, refused to hand over power peacefully, so he gathered his forces and marched towards Rome. Upon deciding to rebel rather than surrender, Caesar uttered his famous remark that "alea iacta est/the die is cast."

On the way to Rome, his forces crossed a small, insignificant river called the Rubicon. Crossing the Rubicon, however, signified that Caesar's troops were committed to revolt. Eventually, in 48 B.C.E., Caesar's army met Pompey's forces near Pharsalus and defeated them.

Cleopatra

Pompey fled to Egypt, his greatest mistake. Ptolemy XIII and his sister, who was also his wife, **Cleopatra**, then ruled Egypt. Cleopatra and Ptolemy were in the midst of a bitter struggle for power and saw the Romans as possible allies. Ptolemy promptly had Pompey killed in an effort to win the support of Caesar against his sister Cleopatra VII. Cleopatra, however, had other ideas, and had herself rolled up naked in a carpet and brought into Caesar's rooms. The historian Plutarch tells us that while she was not terribly attractive from a physical standpoint, she had an inner charisma that drew men to her. Caesar was captivated by her, and took her side against her brother in the Alexandrine War. In 47 B.C.E., Ptolemy XIII was found floating dead in the Nile River. Caesar fathered a son by Cleopatra, Caesarion. Cleopatra followed Caesar to Rome, where Caesar openly declared Caesarion his son. His scandalous affair with a foreigner, along with his progressive usurpation of power in Rome, would eventually bring about his downfall.

Caesar as Dictator

In 46 B.C.E., Caesar was proclaimed *imperator*, or dictator; in 44 B.C.E., he was proclaimed dictator for life. Roman law allowed for the appointment of a dictator in extreme circumstances, but Caesar used the position to transform Rome into that of a monarchy.

During his dictatorship, Caesar implemented some important reforms, such as a unified law code, a new calendar based on the Egyptian calendar, and subsidies for farmers. He ordered Carthage rebuilt and offered the impoverished citizens of the empire a chance to relocate there. Caesar extended some benefits of citizenship to conquered peoples, including some of the Gauls he had defeated. Caesar also began to bring senators from outside of Italy, and packed the senate with his supporters. According to some historians, such as Ronald Syme in *The Roman Revolution*, Caesar overthrew the corrupt patrician centers of power by using those outside Italy to support his cause.

Caesar catered to the *populares* party, and among his most popular acts was the establishment of the gladiator games.

Caesar was elected consul in 48, 46, 45, and 44 B.C.E. Although he shared the consulate in 44 B.C.E. with Marc Antony, in 45 B.C.E. he occupied it alone. Caesar transformed the Republic into a monarchy, and while he could not usurp every office, he accepted the powers of several magistratures without occupying the magistratures themselves. Caesar also named a month after himself, July; previously, months had only been named for gods.

By 44 B.C.E. many powerful patricians were alarmed. Led by Caius Cassius and Marcus Brutus, more than sixty men joined in a conspiracy to assassinate Caesar on the Ides of March, March 15, 44 B.C.E., the date the senate was to meet. Caesar almost foiled the plan when he decided to stay home due to illness. Brutus's brother, however, persuaded him to appear at the senate meeting. While preparing to receive requests, Caesar was caught off guard and was stabbed twenty-three times. Contrary to Shakespeare's colorful story, Caesar never uttered a word or sound during the violent attack. He collapsed at the foot of a statue of Pompey. No one dared to come near him, and for several hours he lay at the statue until three slaves finally carried him back to his home.

Although Caesar wished to be "first among equals," most historians since World War II agree that he established rule by one man. The benefits he brought to the more than sixty million people in the Roman Empire, fully one-third of the world's population, have largely been overshadowed by what many modern historians see as a monarchy reminiscent of the fascist regimes of World War II.

The Civil War and the Rise of Octavian

Although the conspirators hoped Caesar's death would restore the Republic, another civil war ensued. Marc Antony, Caesar's co-consul, immediately confiscated Caesar's papers and treasury. He gave amnesty to the conspirators, but insisted that Caesar's acts remain law. Antony, however, made use of public opinion against the conspirators. When Caesar's corpse was burned on March 20, Antony publicly announced that Caesar had left his gardens to the city of Rome and had granted every inhabitant money from his own funds. The population was so enraged that the conspirators had to flee Rome.

Unfortunately, Antony's path to complete power was blocked by Caesar's great-nephew, Octavius, whom Caesar had also adopted as a son. Caesar had left Octavius two-thirds of his property. Antony had confiscated it with all of Caesar's other possessions, and although Octavius was only eighteen at the time, he confronted Antony and demanded its return. Meanwhile, Antony was forced to leave Rome to fight the brother of Brutus. While he was away, the great orator Cicero urged the senate to rid themselves of Antony. Cicero, like many others, did not regard Octavius as a threat and decided that he must be used as a pawn in the fight against Antony. Cicero remarked that, "We must praise the boy, give him a command and then put him away." In 44 B.C.E., in honor of his adoption by Caesar, Octavius took the name C. Julius Caesar Octavianus, or Octavian, and in 43 B.C.E., he turned the tables on Cicero by defeating Antony in two battles and demanding the consulship in return.

Octavian then made peace with Antony in order to pursue and exterminate the conspirators against Caesar. In 42 B.C.E., he and Antony defeated Brutus and Cassius. Octavian formed the second triumvirate with Antony and Lepidus, and divided the empire between the three. The triumvirate was sealed through the marriage of Octavian's sister, Octavia, to Antony. Antony, however, was still not pacified. Like Caesar before him, he fell in love with Cleopatra and had four children with her. Cleopatra clearly hoped to gain Caesar's inheritance for her son and, through Antony, to rule Rome. Octavian presented Antony's affair with Cleopatra and his campaigns in her interests as a violation of Roman interests and of Antony's marriage to Octavian's sister. Sometime between 32–31 B.C.E., Antony divorced Octavia, and put Cleopatra's name and face on Roman *denarii* that were circulated throughout the Mediterranean area.

These deeds ended the peace between Octavian and Antony, and they met in battle at sea at Actium in Greece, where Octavian defeated Antony in

31 B.C.E. Antony retreated to Egypt, where less than six months later Octavian defeated him again. In 30 B.C.E., Antony committed suicide by falling on his sword. Meanwhile, Cleopatra attempted to negotiate with Octavian, who was not interested in any reconciliation with her or offering any concessions to her. When it became apparent the negotiations were hopeless, Cleopatra allowed herself to be bitten by a poisonous asp. She was thirty-nine years old when she died on August 12, 30 B.C.E. Following her death, Egypt became part of the Roman Empire. Ironically, the last pharaoh of Egypt was a woman, and Egypt had long had very liberal customs regarding women. In defeating Cleopatra, Octavian brought Egyptian women under Roman rule, and never again would they enjoy the autonomy they once enjoyed under the pharaohs.

Following the defeat of Antony and Cleopatra, the way was now clear for Octavian. Octavian would soon become the first emperor of Rome.

Caesar was the last of the so-called reformers before the reign of his adopted heir Octavian. Livy had written about the Roman emphasis on the noble virtues of *pietas*, or piety; *fides*, or faithfulness to duty; *religio*, or the upholding of Roman customs; and *gravitas*, or seriousness and manliness. The word "virtue" comes from the Latin word for "man," "vir." To be virtuous literally meant to be manly; yet as we have seen, few of the most famous Romans seemed to uphold these virtues. Despite the fact that the Reformers had the interest of the most needy in mind, they corrupted Republican values through their willingness to bypass the laws of Rome. The reign of Augustus would forever change the Republic even while he maintained he was strengthening it.

THE FIRST EMPEROR OF ROME: AUGUSTUS

The future emperor had made his first public appearance at his grandmother Julia's funeral, where he gave the eulogy. Julia was the sister of Caesar, likely the connection through which the future emperor came to Caesar's attention. During his career, the young man originally known as Octavius reinvented himself to suit his particular needs, whether it was his assumption of the name Octavian and the formation of the second triumvirate, or his acceptance of the title of *Pater Patriae*, Father of the Country, in 2 B.C.E. In his guise as Octavian, he knew it was important to at least respect tradition, and his achievement was to transform the government of Rome into a monarchy while maintaining the appearance of the Republic. When Octavian ceremoniously walked into the senate and resigned his triumviral powers, the senators implored him to assume command of several important provinces, including Gaul, Spain, and parts of Egypt, while they and the people held command over the rest of the empire. Three days later, the senate gave him the title of "**Augustus**" or "revered one," and now he became officially known as Imperator Caesar Augustus. Augustus was also called *princeps*, or first citizen, and held a continuous consulship for many years and also had the powers of tribune as well as numerous other offices. In 23 B.C.E., he was given the right to convene the senate at will, and in 13 or 12 B.C.E., Augustus became *pontifex maximus*. Most of the powers granted to Augustus were given only for five or ten years, and thus he avoided Caesar's mistake of naming himself dictator for life. At every opportunity the senate renewed the powers they granted to him, thus providing the appearance of election through choice. With the senate's blessing, Augustus was able to assume the powers of many offices without actually occupying them, and he became, for all intents and purposes, the first emperor of Rome.

Augustus and the Arts

Augustus was a master of propaganda, and Rome entered its silver age of culture with such authors as **Virgil**. In the *Aeneid*, Virgil painted the Trojans as the legendary founders of Rome, and Augustus as the direct heir of Aeneas and Romulus. Livy wrote a multi-volume history of Rome in which he glorified the age of Augustus as the high point of Roman history. Livy justified the Augustan transition from Republic to empire by arguing that since the time of Romulus, Rome ruled with a mandate from gods.

Augustus also made use of the visual arts to promote his image, such as in his mausoleum modeled after the fourth-century B.C.E. tomb of Mausolus, located at Halicarnassus in Caria in southwestern Asia Minor. The tomb at Halicarnassus was one of the seven wonders of the ancient world. His autobiography, *The Achievements of the Divine Augustus*, was inscribed on two bronze tablets outside the mausoleum of Augustus in Rome. Although he denied taking power that was not offered to him freely and repeatedly stressed that he refused the title of emperor, Augustus's presence in the visual arts and in the political arena makes clear that he was an emperor in fact. His autobiography is the only first-person narrative of an emperor's career.

The statue of Augustus at his wife Livia's villa at Prima Portia is the most famous portrayal of the emperor. The statue is seven feet tall, much larger than life-sized. Since the statue depicts Augustus as a young man, it is designed to remind the viewer of images of Alexander the Great. His stance in the statue is reminiscent of the famous *Doryphoros*, or spear-bearer, by the Greek sculptor Polyclitus. Augustus's right hand is extended, as it would have been if he were addressing the legions. He also carries a spear. Augustus is depicted barefoot, which was a sign of his divine status. Cupid is depicted on a dolphin by the right foot of Augustus, linking him to Venus, the divine ancestress of his family.

Literary Arts in the Silver Age

The flourishing of culture during the age of Augustus is known as the

Augustus, c. 20 B.C.E.

Silver Age of Roman culture. While Greece had a Golden Age, the achievements of Roman culture are symbolized by silver, as many scholars argue that the Romans were but a pale imitation of the Greeks. Many scholars maintain that Roman poets, philosophers, and other scholars were not as creative and original as those of ancient Greece, and that they merely mimicked the achievements of the Greeks. Nevertheless, the Romans made important contributions to poetry, history, and philosophy, and preserved many Greek bronze statues by copying them in marble.

Ovid (43 B.C.E.– C. 17 C.E.)

Publius Ovidius Naso, who was better known as **Ovid**, was an aristocrat who studied law and rhetoric. He went to Athens, however, and soon developed a greater interest in poetry. His most famous work is *The Art of Love*. Ovid was banished by Augustus, however, because the work appeared around the time Augustus's daughter Julia was charged with immorality and exiled from Rome.

Horace (65 B.C.E.–8 C.E.)

Quintus Horatius Flaccus or **Horace** was the son of a former slave and he studied philosophy in Athens. He served as a tribune under Marcus Brutus, and when Brutus was defeated, he found himself without support. He began to write a series of epistles that addressed social abuses in his poetry. Horace advocated the need for strong moral qualities. He entered the court of Augustus and wrote many other famous works, such as the *Odes* and the *Ars Poetica*. One of the most famous Latin phrases, *carpe diem*, or "seize the day," was taken from a line in the *Odes*. The *Ars Poetica* influenced poetry during the Middle Ages and the early modern period. Dante, for example, listed Horace as the third poet, following Homer and Virgil. While many works of Roman poets were lost after the Roman Empire collapsed in the West, those of Horace were preserved.

Virgil (70–19 C.E.)

Publius Vergilius Maro or **Virgil** was not a Roman by birth but a Gaul. He was born in Gallia Cisalpina, the region that was governed by Julius Caesar. Virgil wrote the eclogues and georgics about life in the country. The work of the Greek poet Hesiod influenced Virgil. Virgil entered the service of Augustus, and after the victory at Actium, Augustus asked Virgil to write a poem glorifying Rome during the Age of Augustus. The result was an epic poem, the *Aeneid*, which was modeled on the epic poems of Homer. The *Aeneid* was the epic story of the Trojan hero Aeneas and the founding of Rome. Although Virgil never finished the *Aeneid*, the Emperor Augustus published it, and it became so famous that the medieval poet Dante chose Virgil as his guide in the *Comedia* through the *Inferno* and *Purgatorio*, but denied him entrance to paradise as Virgil was not a Christian.

Livy (64 or 59 B.C.E.– 17 C.E.)

Titus Livius or **Livy** wrote 142 books of history, only thirty-five of which have been preserved. His history of Rome was unique in that he wrote it in Latin. Earlier historians had written in Greek. Livy, like Horace and Virgil, emphasized the importance of moral qualities in the creation of Rome and thought them necessary for its continued success. Livy was unique in that he was not involved in politics nor was he a member of the senatorial class. Many scholars have found errors in his works and accused him of accepting legend too readily. His lack of involvement in political circles may have deprived him of needed resources, but his *History of Rome* nevertheless stands as one of the greatest works of the age.

Reforms of Augustus

While Augustus was a great patron of the arts and used them to create a grandiose image for himself, he also reformed the military, taking direct command and regulating pay, pensions, and length of service. He mandated that the military's size be permanently fixed at twenty-five legions, and shrunk the borders of the empire to make them more defensible.

Augustus promoted trade, and luxury goods, such as silk and fruits from the East, were brought into the empire. Many famous wall murals, such as the ones at Pompeii, show Roman nobles dressed in silk from *Ceres*, the only word by which they knew China.

During the Principate and the *Pax Romana*, the Roman Empire enjoyed the longest period of unity, peace, and prosperity of its history; moreover, it was to be the longest such period that Western Europe, the Middle East, and the North African seaboard would ever know in their entire recorded history.

Augustus's achievements were remarkable and, although his successors were corrupt, the Rome he recreated would endure for generations to come. Augustus created a new empire that would endure for 500 years in the west and for 1,500 years in the east. Augustus, like Caesar before him, named a month in his honor, August, thus giving him divine status. In later centuries, he would be worshiped as the Divine Augustus. Gone was any semblance of the Republic, and Rome would suffer the consequences of this for many generations to come. Many nobles would fight for the restoration of the Republic, but in the end, it was the Augustan Principate that won.

After Augustus

Despite his many successes, the reign of Augustus created a new problem for Rome. When Augustus died in 14 C.E., there were no established procedures to replace someone with his vast powers. The Romans turned to heredity as a solution and appointed Tiberius, the son of Augustus's wife Livia, as the next emperor. Tiberius, however, grew increasingly corrupt, and the moral depravity at his palace on the Isle of Capri was legendary. During his reign, a Jewish peasant named **Jesus** preached in the Galilee region, and his teachings later gave rise to Christianity.

Caligula was even more depraved and had himself proclaimed a god. The Roman army assassinated Caligula and proclaimed his uncle Claudius emperor. Claudius had physical disabilities and a pronounced stutter, which made him the laughingstock of Rome. Claudius, however, succeeded in conquering Britain and establishing a Roman presence there. He had his wife Messalina murdered for betraying him, and then married his niece, Agrippina, who allegedly poisoned him with a mushroom so that her own son, Nero, could succeed her husband as emperor.

Nero focused on the arts and performed publicly in theatrical events. The Romans were horrified, as theater was a profession dominated by the lower strata of society. Nero often disguised himself and went on binges in public, and even at one point married a young man. Nero had to battle his ambitious mother Agrippina for power, and there were rumors of a sexual liaison between them. He had her murdered. Nero ordered the death of the philosopher Seneca, his tutor, and committed suicide himself when it became clear the Romans had turned on him.

The low point of Roman history came when no fewer than four generals vied for power. The winner was Vespasian, who first commissioned the Flavian ampitheater, known as the Coliseum. Vespasian restored order on the battlefield temporarily, but this was not enough to prevent the further decline of Rome. Vespasian originally served under Nero, who ordered him to conduct a war against the Jews with his son, Titus. Vespasian was one of the least tyrannical emperors and died a natural death when he was near seventy.

Despite the excesses of Tiberius, Nero, and Caligula, there was some good leadership during the period following the death of Augustus.

The emperor Hadrian, for example, engaged in several monumental building projects and attempted to shore up the frontiers. The ruins of several Roman forts in England, however, attest to the fact that the Romans continued to struggle against other peoples along the frontiers. Eventually, in the fourth century C.E., the Germanic peoples would overrun the empire in the West.

Trajan was another effective ruler, whose monumental column in Rome still stands as a testament to his victory over the Dacians.

RELIGION IN THE ROMAN EMPIRE

The Roman Empire incorporated many diverse regions and cultures, including the remnants of Egyptian civilization, Mesopotamian civilization, Hebrew culture along the eastern Mediterranean, and many others. The Pantheon, a temple to all the Roman deities, best exemplifies the plethora of religions in Rome. It is circular in design; the circle often symbolizes completeness in various cultures, and the Pantheon summed up Roman paganism by embracing all the deities of the citizens of Rome.

The Rise of Christianity

The historic Jesus was born during the reign of Augustus, sometime around 3 B.C.E. Although the gospel accounts of the life of Jesus relate his birth and some events of his youth, they are silent regarding the vast majority of his life. The narratives resume during his last three years. The evangelists describe and interpret his ministry in Galilee, his passion in Jerusalem around 30 C.E., and his resurrection three days later. The gospels paint Jesus as having fulfilled the prophecies in Jewish Scriptures, but they also make it clear that Jesus preached a radical new vision of Judaism, one not focused on practice but rather on peace, love, and inner faith as central to spirituality. In the **Sermon on the Mount**, Jesus preached, "Blessed are the poor in spirit, for they shall see the kingdom of heaven." Jesus ministered to the outcasts of society, but clearly his remarks were meant to refer to more than physical poverty. It referred to a kind of inner, spiritual poverty in which the soul was so truly one with the divine that it was emptied of all other, worldly concerns. Many zealots, Jews who opposed Roman rule in Palestine, hoped for a Messiah that would launch a rebellion, but Jesus instead preached a message of peace. Scholars speculate that the disappointment of Judas over Jesus's failure to launch a rebellion led him to betray Jesus to the Romans. In addition, scholars suggest that the fear of Jewish religious leaders that they would be punished for the actions of Jesus and so lead to the downfall of Judaism led them to distance themselves from Jesus and to seek his punishment.

The Jesus of history is quite different from the Christ of faith. About the Jesus of history we know little. There are only a few statements in the Scriptures that were known to be statements of Christ. The Christ of faith, however, is the result of centuries of interpretations about what the life of the historic Jesus means. The gospel of John, the last gospel to be composed, is an excellent example of how the life of Jesus was interpreted. John opens his gospel with the following words: "In the beginning was the Word, and the Word was with God and the Word was God." Here, Jesus is interpreted as the Word or Logos of God, the ordering principle behind the universe. He is interpreted as having existed for all eternity, and moreover, as having been God himself. The gospel of John is a mystical text that laid the foundation for the teachings of the later **Council of Nicaea** in 325 C.E., where Trinitarian theology was formally put forth.

Following the death of Jesus, his disciples disagreed on how to proceed. The disciples were Jews, who continued to worship in the synagogue. In other words, they did not perceive Christianity to be anything other than a sect of Judaism. They also disagreed whether converts to Christianity had to become Jews first. Did they have to be circumcised? Did they have to follow kosher laws of diet? The apostle Peter believed Christianity should be for Jews only; while a later convert to Christianity, Paul, believed it should be for all. Ultimately, it was the apostle Paul who won, and whose missions throughout Greece and Asia Minor began to attract converts to Christianity.

Nevertheless, Christianity was not legal in the Roman Empire until 313 C.E. Christians were persecuted and often executed. The first persecution of Christians occurred during the reign of Nero. Early Christians met in private homes often owned by women. Phoebe, for example, was one of the most important followers of Paul. They also gathered in the catacombs around Rome. Until the time of Constantine the Great, however, they could not openly practice their faith.

The Emperor Diocletian's Persecution of the Christians

Nero's persecution of Christians was one of many, which culminated in the persecution under Emperor **Diocletian** in 303 C.E. As political corruption, problems on the frontiers, and economic instability became progressively more severe for the Romans in the third and fourth centuries C.E., Christians were often blamed for the empire's difficulties. Although Romans practiced many religions, Christianity departed from the common beliefs held by Romans, particularly because Christians placed their God above the Roman Empire and its emperor, and refused to sacrifice in the cult of the emperor. In 303 C.E., the economic instability of Rome and problems on the frontiers led Emperor Diocletian to hold a traditional sacrificial ritual to determine the cause of Rome's difficulties. According to custom, a pure lamb or other animal was sacrificed, and then the markings on its liver were interpreted as signs of things to come. On this particular occasion, a Christian was present. When the lamb was sacrificed and opened, no markings were apparent. Those present were horrified and blamed the presence of the Christian, who did not follow the custom of sacrificing in the cult of the emperor, for the lack of a sign. To calm the disturbance, Diocletian ordered that Christians hand over their sacred scriptures and sacrifice in the cult of the emperor. So began the persecution of 303 C.E. It would culminate in one of the most important debates in the early Church during the reign of Constantine, that of the Donatist heresy.

Diocletian Divides the Empire

Beset by trouble on the frontiers and a collapsing economy, Diocletian had frozen wages and prices and also divided the empire in 284 C.E. into an eastern half, with its capital at Byzantium on the Bosphorus strait, and a western half, with its capital in Rome in order to better administrate it. Each half had an emperor and also a Caesar beneath him. Diocletian was the emperor of the east, while Maximian served as emperor of the west. It was planned that the emperors would resign in 305 C.E. and hand over power to their Caesars in an orderly way, thereby avoiding the decades of civil war Rome had endured.

Civil War Following Diocletian's Abdication

As planned, Diocletian stepped down in 305 C.E. and was succeeded by Galerius; his cohort in the west, Maximian, however, was not similarly inclined, and although he eventually stepped down, he later decided to return to power, waging a civil war before his Caesar, Constantius, was proclaimed Augustus. Constantius, the Caesar in the west, eventually was made Augustus and asked that his son, Flavius Valerius Constantinus, later known as **Constantine**, be appointed Caesar under him. When Galerius refused the request on the basis of Constantine's youth, Constantius asked that Constantine at least be allowed to return from the court of Diocletian. Constantine's mother was Helena, a commoner who was apparently a Christian. Evidence suggests that Constantius and Helena were not legally married, but that Helena was a concubine. In any case, when Constantius became Caesar, he put Helena aside and married Theodora, the daughter of Maximian.

Constantine joined his father in Britain, where he fought in the campaign against the Picts. When Constantius died on July 25, 306 C.E., at Eboracum, now known as York, the troops proclaimed Constantine Augustus. One can still visit the location beneath the York Minster where Constantine was proclaimed Caesar. Constantine appealed to Galerius to recognize him as Augustus, but Galerius refused, accepting him only as Caesar and appointing Severus Augustus of the west. Constantine returned to the continent and married Fausta, the daughter of Maximian.

The Battle of Milvian Bridge

However, in that same year, the senate and Praetorian Guard rebelled from the rule of Severus and proclaimed Maxentius, the ambitious son of Maximian, Caesar in Rome. In 308 Maxentius claimed to be sole Augustus, or emperor, and his supporters eventually executed Severus. The situation was further complicated when Galerius appointed Licinius to succeed Severus as Augustus in the west. When Galerius, the Augustus of the east, died in 311 C.E. followed by Maximian's death in 312 C.E., hostilities between the three main contenders, Maxentius, Licinius, and Constantine, erupted into open conflict. Constantine eventually met his enemy Maxentius at the **Battle of Milvian Bridge** in 312 C.E. Accounts differ of what happened prior to the battle. Lactantius later said that during the night before the Battle of the Milvian Bridge, Constantine had a dream in which he was commanded to place the sign of Christ on the shields of his soldiers. Lactantius was a tutor to Constantine's son and must have been close to Constantine. Twenty-five years later, Eusebius, Bishop of Caesarea in the fourth century C.E., wrote an Ecclesiastical History of the Christian church and the life of Constantine in which he tells us that sometime before the battle, Constantine had a vision in the sky in broad daylight of a cross of light and the words "by this sign you shall conquer/*in hoc signo vinces*." Eusebius also claims that during the next night, Christ appeared to Constantine and told him to place the heavenly sign on the battle standards of his army, which he did. At Milvian Bridge with the sign on their shields, Constantine's army emerged victorious. The new battle standard became known as the labarum, and it is composed of the *chi* and *rho* of the Greek word *Christos*, or the "anointed one."

Many scholars debate the authenticity of both accounts of Constantine's conversion, since even Lactantius's account was not reported until near the end of Constantine's life. Some scientists attempt to explain the experience chronicled in Eusebius's account as a natural phenomena that occurs when light passes through moisture in the air. Such an occurrence will make one see a corona that sometimes may look like a cross.

The Edict of Milan

Further, scholars debate the nature of Constantine's conversion. On the one hand, in 313 C.E., shortly after the victory at Milvian Bridge, he and Licinius issued the Edict of Milan. The edict granted legal toleration for the first time to Christians. Some scholars suggest that this edict might have been promulgated to protect his mother Helena, who was Christian. Moreover, the edict also granted tax-exempt status to the emerging Christian Church and returned to it all property confiscated in previous persecutions. On the other hand, Constantine was a devotee of the sun cult, a common cult in Rome during his youth. The coins he continued to issue still bore the pagan symbol of *sol invinctus*. Why would a Christian emperor mint pagan coins? Practically speaking, it would have been foolish to attempt to change so radically the practices of the Romans. Constantine also continued to serve as *pontifex maximus* and to preside over pagan rituals of the empire. These facts, though having a practical explanation, raise issues about the legitimacy of Constantine's reported conversion. In addition, Constantine was not baptized until he was on his deathbed. Although this was common in the early Christian period, it still raises doubts in modern minds about the authenticity of the conversion.

St. Helena

Some of the most important events in early Christianity occurred during his reign. His mother, Helena, made pilgrimages to the Holy Land and is credited with discovering the location of Golgotha and the fragments of the true cross. She is also credited with founding several churches on holy sites, including a church near the grotto of the nativity in Bethlehem and one on the Mount of the Ascension. Whether Helena became a Christian because of her son's influence or was one before he converted is open to debate. Helena was commemorated in several special coins issued during the reign of Constantine.

THE EMPEROR CONSTANTINE: FIRST CHRISTIAN EMPEROR OF ROME

Constantine continued to battle his enemies for several years following the Milvian Bridge. There is no doubt that Constantine viewed Christianity as the key to solidifying his power in the empire. In many letters and other documents, he asserts that the unity of the church was crucial to maintaining the unity of his empire. For this reason, he was concerned with stamping out heresy and maintaining a united belief system.

The Donatist Heresy

Diocletian's persecution had created issues of great importance for the Christian community. Many Christians had given up their Scriptures as commanded in order to spare their lives; they were known as *traditores*, from the Latin word "to hand over." The English word *tradition* is also derived from the same root word. Others had sacrificed in the cult of the emperor and were known as *lapsi*, from the Latin word "to fall away." The English word *lapse* comes from the same root word. After the legalization of Christianity, the *traditores* and the *lapsi* wanted to reenter the church, but some also wanted to serve as priests and bishops. Herein lay the problem. How could those who had forsaken their religious beliefs now administer the sacraments to others? If they did, would those sacraments be valid? A strong faction argued for purity in the priesthood and was led by Donatus. The Donatists grew so strong that a competing church arose in North Africa, alarming Constantine. The Donatists argued that *lapsi* and *traditores* could not be confirmed as priests or bishops, as the sacraments would not be valid if performed by priests who

Constantine the Great. Early fourth century C.E.

were *traditores* or *lapsi*. When the Donatists refused to accept the consecration of Caecilian as bishop of Carthage, alleging that he was consecrated by one of the *traditores*, the crisis came to a climax. Constantine summoned a council to Arles in the west. In 314 C.E., the council decided that there was no evidence against Caecilian nor was there evidence of the invalidity of his consecration, and Caecilian was allowed to return to his position. The decision supported the view that the validity of the sacraments did not depend upon those administering them. Further, the great theologian **Augustine of Hippo** would later write at great length against the Donatists, and firmly establish the theology of the priesthood when he wrote that it was grace and not human intervention that made the sacraments holy.

The Arian Heresy

Another important heresy of Constantine's reign was the **Arian heresy**. Arius was a priest in Alexandria whose exploration of the Trinity led him to conclude that Christ was not fully divine, which seemed to shake the foundation of Christian views on the redemptive power of the cross. As the followers of Arius grew in numbers, Constantine once again became concerned. He summoned the first ecumenical council to Nicaea, this time in the east. It was the first council to include bishops from both the east and the west. The word "ecumenical" means "a coming together." Constantine presided at the council, while the theologian Athanasius wrote the creed that eventually emerged from the meeting. Today, it is called the Nicene Creed, and it was later modified at Constantinople in the late third century C.E. Christians throughout the world recite it, as it summarizes the essential beliefs of Christians. Christianity, unlike Judaism and other traditions, is defined by what one believes rather than what one practices.

Constantine's role at Nicaea would seem foreign to many today. American culture, for example, is very much based on the separation of church and state. Here, Constantine presided over an important meeting of church officials. In the east, the emperor would be known for centuries as the thirteenth apostle, having every natural right to participate in matters of the church. Constantine's actions represented a form of government called Caesaropapism, according to which the head of state was also the head of the church. Throughout the Middle Ages, the church and state would have to struggle to resolve the tensions created by Constantine's reign.

Impact of Constantine

Although scholars debate the nature of Constantine's conversion, there is no doubt that his legislation to legalize and to protect the Christian Church during his reign forever changed the course of Roman history and Western civilization. His son and immediate successor, Constantine II, was pagan, but his son Constantius was devoted to propagating the Christian religion. Constantius was an Arian Christian, however, and the Arian heresy continued to thrive in the Roman Empire. Most of the Germanic peoples who would infiltrate the empire in the fifth century, such as the Visigoths, were Arian Christians. By the end of the fourth century, however, Orthodox Christianity triumphed within the Roman Empire. The Theodosian Code declared that all Romans must be Christians and that heresy was a crime against the state. Most Romans were still not Christians in the time of Theodosias, and the Code represents a radical transformation of Roman religious beliefs.

Despite the Theodosian Code, it took centuries for Christianity to spread throughout the Roman Empire.

THE DECLINE AND FALL OF THE ROMAN EMPIRE IN THE WEST

Rome had suffered for centuries from civil war, corruption in politics, and economic and other difficulties. By the time the Germanic peoples began to infiltrate the frontiers of Rome in the fourth and fifth centuries, Rome was teetering on the brink of collapse. At first, their arrival was in small groups who came across the frontiers and blended with the Romans. In fact, when the Visigoths entered the empire to escape the westward movement of the Huns and revolted against the Romans at the Battle of Adrianople in 378 C.E., the Roman army was itself largely made up of barbarians, a word the Romans used to refer to the Germanic peoples as other than Roman in custom. The battle of Adrianople sent shock waves throughout the civilized world. The Romans had spread their civilization through the west and maintained order for almost 1,000 years. Suddenly the word's mightiest army had fallen to the barbarian hordes. In 410 C.E., the Visigoths sacked Rome and eventually established a Germanic kingdom in Spain. The onslaught continued as the Vandals made their way into the frontiers and eventually down to North Africa in 429 C.E. North Africa was a hub of trade on the Mediterranean and an important producer of grain in the empire. The Vandal conquest further shook the empire. In 455 C.E., the Vandals crossed the Mediterranean and sacked Rome. Other Germanic tribes, such as the Franks, also established their own kingdoms in what once was Roman Gaul.

The old Roman Empire in the west had disintegrated. In many ways, however, Roman civilization did not disappear. Many Germanic kings, such as **Charlemagne**, would rule with the approval of the eastern emperors in Byzantium and call themselves emperors of Rome in the west. The organization of the Roman Empire was preserved through the structure of the Roman Catholic Church, and Roman law formed the basis for the church's corpus of canon law. Latin, the language of Rome, influenced the development of the vernacular languages of Western Europe, or the languages spoken by the masses, such as Italian and Spanish.

Nevertheless, while the Byzantine emperor **Justinian** would recapture parts of what was lost in the sixth century C.E., and the emperor Charlemagne of the Franks would later also attempt to reform the old boundaries of Rome in the west, the Roman Empire in the west was lost and, after Justinian, never again would the east and the west be under one banner. Eventually, the western Christians would turn against their counterparts in the fourth crusade and capture Constantinople. Never again were eastern and western Romans united; never again was Constantine's dream of a united Christendom fully realized.

Reasons for the Fall of Rome

Historians have long argued over the reasons for the fall of the empire in the west. As the barbarians began to invade, many Romans of the fifth century C.E. believed that the conversion of the Romans to Christianity had so angered the gods that they allowed the barbarians to defeat the once mighty Roman army. In response, St. Augustine, the Roman bishop of Hippo in North Africa, argued in his monumental work *The City of God* that Roman history began in violence and continued to engage in warfare throughout its history. He pointed out that there never was a time when Rome was free of violence and, moreover, he argued that all human civilizations were destined to collapse. Augustine argued that the need for government arose out of human inability to control their more base characteristics; since government arose out of a privation, it was unavoidable that all governments collapse. Therefore, he argued, Romans could not blame the collapse of the empire on Christianity, but rather needed to accept that all human civilizations were destined to fall.

Not all historians agree with St. Augustine. In the *Decline and Fall of the Roman Empire*, Edward Gibbon argued that the long period of peace had weakened the discipline of the army, and that overindulgence in luxurious goods and activities had corrupted the morals of Roman society. In addition, he argued that the Romans used lead pipes to carry water, and that many suffered from the effects of lead poisoning. Gibbon lived during the eighteenth-century Enlightenment, an era in which reason was considered superior to religious faith, and also argued that the Roman conversion to Christianity had led to their downfall. The Christian obsession with life after death drew them away from focusing on the practicalities of this life. When the empire was threatened, Christians retreated to the desert to lead lives of intense prayer and asceticism rather than take to the battlefield. For Gibbon, Christianity was the fatal weakness of the western empire.

In *Muhammad and Charlemagne*, Henri Pirenne argued yet another point of view. Although historians talk about the fall of Rome in the wake of the barbarian invasions, he argued that Roman civilization did not actually collapse in the west until the teachings of Muhammad began to take hold in the seventh century C.E. Prior to Muhammad, Pirenne argued that the barbarian chiefs actually respected Roman culture and made use of it. The spread of Islam, however, cut off the European kingdoms from the Mediterranean coastal regions, thus bringing about the final collapse of Roman culture. Roman unity had been based on the Mediterranean areas. It was Muhammad, then, who made the career of Charlemagne possible, and the spread of Muhammad's teachings that gave rise to feudal society.

Historians differ widely in their interpretation of the reasons why Rome fell in the west. Rome was never truly at peace; not only was it beset with internal class, political, and economic tensions, but in its later days, it teetered on the brink of collapse for centuries as new groups of peoples infiltrated its frontiers. The mystery is not so much about why Roman culture finally collapsed in the west, but rather about how the empire managed to survive for so many centuries despite many fatal weaknesses.

CHAPTER 12

THE RISE OF ISLAM

Approximately twenty to twenty-two percent of the world's population today is Muslim. **Islam** was founded by the prophet **Muhammad**, who believed himself to be the last and greatest in a chain of prophets going back to Abraham. Historians have often been baffled as to the reason for the great success of Islam, for it contains little not already enunciated by the prophets of the Judeo-Christian tradition. Muhammad's religious charisma united the Arab tribes behind the banner of Islam in the seventh century C.E., and the religion of submission, Islam, spread faster than any other world religion. Many historians would place Muhammad among the top ten most influential historical figures. Many consider him the single most influential figure to ever have lived.

THE LIFE AND CAREER OF MUHAMMAD (570–632 C.E.)

Muhammad was born in **Mecca** in 570 C.E. Many legends surround his birth; it is said that a ray of light came out of his mother's breast that was seen for miles away heralding his birth. Muhammad was also said not to have cast a shadow during his lifetime; nevertheless, Islam regards Muhammad as a prophet, and not as a divine figure.

Muhammad was orphaned at the age of six. He was born into a society that was heavily materialistic and polytheistic. He traveled with his uncle, Abu Talib, in the caravan trade. When he was twenty-five he married an older widow, Khadijah, who involved him more deeply in the caravan trade through Mecca. Mecca was the center of the trade, and it was quite lucrative. There was an annual bazaar and pilgrimage to Mecca to pay tribute to the gods, which later became the basis of the hajj, or pilgrimage to Mecca. Muhammad became increasingly dissatisfied with the polytheistic, materialistic life of Mecca.

At the age of forty, he went up into the mountains around Mecca into a cave on Mt. Hira. There he stayed in prayer, solitude, and meditation for six weeks. During that time, he was visited by the archangel Gabriel, who conveyed to him, in the form of a recitation, revelations from Allah (the Arabic word for "lord"). These recitations, which the angel commanded Muhammad to recite to others, became the **Qur'an**, an Arabic word that literally means "recitation."

The Qur'an contains the fundamental beliefs of Islam, expressed in the **Five Pillars**. In contrast to the customs of Mecca in Muhammad's time, the Qur'an emphasizes monotheism, a life of prayer, fasting, and almsgiving. Those who submit to the teachings of the Qur'an are known as "Muslims," while the word "Islam" literally means "to submit." Islam is the religion, then, of submission to the Five Pillars.

According to Islamic tradition, in 621 C.E. Muhammad ascended into heaven. This event is known as the Night Journey, or Israa and Mirag. During that night, Muhammad led all past prophets in prayer on the site of the Hebrew Temple Mount in Jerusalem. The al-Aksa mosque marks the site of the Night Journey.

Muhammad's uncle died, and Muhammad had no protection from those who opposed his teachings. The caravan trade was lucrative, and Muhammad's values and teachings conflicted with both the materialism of Meccans, as well as their polytheistic beliefs. In 622 C.E., Muhammad left Mecca and went north to Yathrib, later renamed "Medina." This event is known as the *Hijra*, and marks the first year in the Islamic calendar. The word "Medina" means "city of the prophet," and this is where Muhammad began to collect his first band of followers. The mosque in Medina is the second holiest site in the Islamic world.

Muhammad and his followers made a continuous series of raids on Mecca, winning the Battle of Badr in 624 C.E. In 630 C.E., they attempted to make the annual pilgrimage to Mecca. As 3,000 of them approached Mecca, the inhabitants assumed that they were making another attack. They surrendered peacefully to Muhammad in 630 C.E.

The Ka'ba in Mecca symbolizes the restoration of the city to the pure practice of monotheism. The faithful circle the Ka'ba during the annual hajj.

Muhammad died in 632 C.E.; according to Islamic tradition, he ascended into heaven in Jerusalem from the Dome of the Rock. Inside the shrine is the actual rock from which Muhammad is believed to have ascended. Muslims believe the rock has the footprints of the archangel Gabriel in it, and that all souls gather under the rock. This shrine is located on the ancient Hebrew Temple Mount, the most sacred site in the world for Jews and one of the most sacred for Christians. The Dome of the Rock dates from 690 C.E., and it is the third holiest site in the Islamic world after Mecca and Medina. Jews believe that the Ark of the Covenant was once on this very site, and since its exact location is unknown, it is forbidden for Jews to walk on the site. Jewish people also believe that it was on this site that Abraham prepared to sacrifice Isaac, whereas Muslims teach that it was Ishmael whom Abraham prepared to sacrifice and that this event occurred at the Ka'ba, not at the Dome of the Rock. For these reasons, Jews regard the Dome of the Rock shrine as a sacrilege, and it is but one reason why there is a continuing conflict between Jews and Muslims today.

After Muhammad's death, there were many **caliphs**, or successors, in the umma, or community of the faithful. Many of these caliphs extended the Abode of Submission (Dar al-Islam), or the regions where Islam was practiced. In fact, Islam is the world's fastest-spreading religion. The religion spread west to North Africa, controlled by the Fatimid caliphate, and Spain, and conquered Damascus, Jerusalem, and other cities sacred to Jews and Christians within 100 years. After Muhammad's death in 632 c.e., Abu Bakr, Muhammad's father-in-law, became caliph. Not all Muslims agreed with this choice, and many supported the claim of Muhammad's cousin and son-in-law Ali to be the legitimate successor. Ali would later become the fourth caliph.

Under Abu Bakr's leadership, Islam expanded rapidly. Abu Bakr united the Saudi Arabian Bedouin tribes, and led a series of *razzia* or raids under the banner of the jihad to expand the religion and domain of the umma. Abu Bakr's Muslims defeated the Byzantines at Yarmuk in 636 c.e., and in 540 c.e. conquered Syria. By 650 c.e., Muslim Arabs had conquered the Sassanid Persian Empire.

Muslim forces also conquered Egypt in North Africa. Today, the official language of North African countries is still Arabic.

The Umayyad Caliphate

The fourth caliph, Muhammad's son-in-law Ali, was assassinated in 661 c.e. Mu'awiyah replaced him and made the succession hereditary. His family was a branch of Muhammad's own clan, the Quraishi, and the caliphate ruled by his clan was known as the Umayyad. The Umayyad caliphate (661–750 c.e.) ruled from Damascus. The Umayyads conquered the Berber tribes in the region of North Africa west of Egypt, and in 725 c.e. conquered the Iberian Peninsula. In 750 c.e., one of the Umayyad princes escaped to Spain and established the Spanish Umayyad caliphate. The Spanish Umayyads channeled the game of chess into Europe, as well as Arabic commentaries on Aristotle, whose works had largely been lost in Western Europe.

The Expansion Halts

Some historians argue that it was Islam rather than the barbarian Germanic tribes that ended Roman civilization in Western Europe. Henri

Pirenne, in *Muhammad and Charlemagne*, argues that it was the expansion of Islam that disrupted trade across the Mediterranean and cut off the coastal areas from the heart of Europe, thus bringing an end to Roman civilization in the Western world. In 732 C.E., Charles Martel and the Franks defeated the Muslims at Tours. This battle is often also called the Battle of Tours or Poitiers, because the actual skirmish happened between these two locations. The battle occurred in southern France.

The Byzantines also defeated the Muslim forces in 717 C.E. at Constantinople. Muslim forces would not succeed in conquering the city until 1453 C.E.

Shi'ites and Sunnis

During the early period after Muhammad's death, a split arose in the Umma between the **Shi'ites**, or partisans of Ali, and the **Sunni**, or followers of tradition. The Shi'ites believed that the succession to Muhammad should be by bloodline, and Ali was the son-in-law and cousin of the prophet. They believed that Muhammad had given Ali some revelations that he did not write down, and so they insisted that only the bloodline succession could preserve the fullness of revelation. Further, they accepted the existence of an oral tradition, which Sunnis did not. They also believed in the coming of the *Mahdi*, or chosen one, who was an imam, or prayer leader, who disappeared in the ninth century. Shi'ites believed that he would return to guide the faithful through judgment day. Shi'ites insisted that only those faithful who accepted these teachings in addition to the Qur'an were Muslims, while Sunnis taught that anyone who submitted to the Five Pillars was a Muslim.

The split between the supporters of Ali and those of the other successors, already evident in the first years after the death of the prophet, became tenser during the Ummayad period when Ali's son, Hussein, launched a revolt against the caliph. Hussein, like his father Ali, was assassinated, but the Shi'ite faction of Muslims continues to flourish today in such modern countries as southern Iraq. In 973 C.E., Shi'ite Muslims established a caliphate in Egypt known as the Fatimids.

The Abbasid Caliphate

Abu Abbas, a descendant of an uncle of Muhammad, led a revolt against the Umayyads and established the Abbasid caliphate. Its capital was Baghdad, which was first built in 762 C.E. Baghdad served as the capital of the Abbasid caliphate until 1258 C.E. and is today located in Iraq. During this period, the caliphs were known as "caliphs of God," and they adopted many Persian ideals of leadership. The most important Abbasid caliph was Harun al-Rashid, or Harun the Upright (786–809 C.E.). The Abbasids were Sunni Muslims.

During the Abbasid caliphate, Baghdad was an important cultural center. The philosopher Ibn Rushd (Averoës) wrote many commentaries on Aristotle, which were eventually transmitted to Western Europe. Averoës believed in the principle of two-fold truth. He argued that philosophy and religion were different kinds of knowledge, each with its own sphere of truth. Religion was for the unlettered masses, and taught through signs and symbols. Philosophy, however, represented truth directly. Teachings in the two areas could conflict with one another, and in that case, philosophy would supersede religion. Ibn Rushd's commentaries on Aristotle created a controversy in the Catholic Church, as many of Aristotle's philosophical arguments conflicted with orthodox Christian teaching. In contrast to Ibn Rushd's theory of double truth, the scholastic theologians of medieval Europe, such as Aquinas, sought to harmonize the teachings of religion and philosophy. Ibn Rushd was born in Córdoba in southern Spain, a region known as Andalusia that was controlled by Muslims. While under Muslim control, culture flourished, and monuments such as the Alhambra in Granada and the mosque in Córdoba were among the greatest architectural masterpieces in Europe. Christians recaptured Córdoba in the thirteenth century and in the fifteenth century, the rulers Ferdinand and Isabella of Aragon and Castille destroyed the remnants of Muslim culture in their zeal to entrench Roman Catholicism within their domains.

Ibn Sinna, or Avicenna, was another important Muslim scholar who was born and worked in Persia. He wrote a medical textbook that was used in medieval universities. Literature also flourished, as seen in the words of Omar Khayyam. Although his *1001 Arabian Nights* and *Rubaiyat* have enjoyed limited popularity in the Middle East, they have become classics in the west. In *1001 Arabian Nights*, Scheherazade tells a story a night in order to avoid death. Her tales of *Ali Baba and the Forty Thieves* and *Aladdin and the Magic Lamp* have become favorite tales and have been translated into many languages.

The Fall of the Abbasids

In 1055 C.E. the **Seljuk Turks**, who converted to Islam, conquered Baghdad. They allowed the Abbasids to continue to control religion, but took control over state affairs.

Seljuk Turks Threaten Byzantium

In 1071 the Seljuks defeated the Byzantines at the Battle of Manzikert. By 1095, Byzantine Emperor Alexius was alarmed at the threat posed by the Muslim Turks, and called upon the Roman Catholic Pope in the west for assistance in delivering his Christian lands from "the infidel." Alexius's call began the first Crusade; he could not have known that the Christian knights would come in their own interests and threaten his control over Byzantium. Western knights established their own kingdoms in the east, and in 1204, during the Fourth Crusade, would actually sack the city of Constantinople itself on the pretense of helping the "legitimate ruler," who was an importer, regain his rightful throne. In 1453 C.E., the Ottoman Turks conquered Constantinople, sending a wave of refugees to Italy, where they helped to fuel the Italian Renaissance.

THE TEACHINGS OF ISLAM

The Muslim world is one of the most diverse groups of cultures today, all united through belief in the Qur'an. The Qur'an contains the fundamental beliefs of Islam, expressed in the Five Pillars. According to tradition, Muhammad did not read or write and dictated the recitation to aides. It is one of the great works of medieval literature, and its style is on a much higher level than comparable poetry found in the west from a similar period. It is written in Arabic, which became the holy language of all Muslims, and in the Foosha, or official dialect of Arabic shared by all Muslims. Dialects can vary so much from one region of the Arabic world to another that they are barely intelligible to those of different regions, and the Foosha enabled all Arabic-speaking peoples to communicate. Arabic does not contain vowels, so when people read Arabic, they have to know which vowel sounds to insert. For example, the letters "bg" could be read as "big" or "bog" or "bag" in English and one must know from the context which word is being used. The Foosha specifies the vowel sounds so as to leave no doubt as to the proper word. Arabic calligraphy became a highly prized art form, as the language was the language of the Holy Qur'an and the Qur'an forbids the use of images.

The influence of Arabic calligraphy on Islamic art can be seen in many Islamic mosques and shrines, such as along the interior of the Dome of the Rock shrine, which is encircled with inscriptions from the Qur'an. Even wrought iron gates make use of designs based on Arabic calligraphy.

The Five Pillars of the Qur'an are as follows:

The first pillar of Islam teaches that there is no God but Allah, and Muhammad is his messenger. This pillar emphasizes the belief in only one God. Muslims are thoroughly monotheistic; to put anything at all on the level of Allah is to worship that thing and to commit the gravest possible sin— shirk. The Qur'an, like the Hebrew Scriptures, forbids the making of idols and images, as they might be potential objects of worship.

The first pillar also emphasizes the humanity of Muhammad, who is not regarded as a divine being, but as a good human who conveyed the word of Allah. According to Islamic tradition, the revelations to Muhammad were the last time that Allah has communicated with humans and the fullest expression of divine revelation. Muslims believe that all the holy prophets in the Hebrew and Christian Scriptures imparted some measure of Truth; it was Muhammad, however, who received the most complete version.

The second pillar commands prayer five times per day facing Mecca, the place of Muhammad's birth. Mecca is a significant place in the Islamic tradition for many reasons. Muslims believe in the truth of the Hebrew Scriptures, and Arabs are, in fact, descendants of the Hebrew patriarch Abraham. Abraham's firstborn son was Ishmael, whom Abraham's wife Sarah expelled along with his mother Hagar, Abraham's concubine. According to Islamic tradition, when Ishmael was expelled, he and his mother journeyed to what is now Mecca. There he struck the ground in anger and a spring arose.

The **Ka'ba**, a shrine that contains a black meteorite revered as sacred since prehistoric times, marks this site. Muslims also believe that the Ka'ba marks the site where Abraham prepared to sacrifice his son Ishmael; Jews believe that Abraham was commanded to sacrifice Isaac, and that this event occurred on the temple mount in Jerusalem. Thousands of Muslims journey to the Ka'ba every year and encircle it while praying.

Muhammad expected Jews to follow his teachings, not only because of the common lineage from Abraham, but also because much of the Qur'an is based on the Hebrew Scriptures. Consequently, Muslims originally prayed towards Jerusalem. When Jews did not embrace his teachings, Muslims separated themselves from the Jewish community and began to pray towards Mecca. Many Islamic prayer rugs have representations of a mihrab in the center, along with the light that usually hangs in the niches. The light symbolizes the presence of Allah. Mosques also contain a mihrab, from which the Qur'an is read.

There are no images in a mosque, as the Qur'an, like the Hebrew Scriptures, forbids the making of idols and the worship of anything but Allah. These beliefs are expressed in the first pillar of Islam.

A mosque usually has a square base and a round dome. The square base symbolizes earth, as it has four corners and there are four cardinal directions. The dome, being round, symbolizes heaven. A circle has no beginning or end, and so, too, the afterlife is without beginning or end. One enters a mosque without shoes on, to symbolize the holiness of the place.

The Islamic prayer ritual symbolizes submission to Allah. The prayer ritual begins with a washing of the hands, feet, and face three times each to symbolize one's cleanliness and ability to come before Allah.

Mosques have fountains in front, where Muslims wash themselves before prayer. At the beginning of the ritual, Muslims put their hands on either side of their head to symbolize that they are in the hands of Allah during prayer and also in life.

The third pillar of Islam commands almsgiving to other Muslims.

The fourth pillar commands fasting for one month a year. This is the month of Ramadan, in which Muslims neither eat nor drink from sunup until sundown. Ramadan commemorates Muhammad's sojourn on Mt. Hira.

The fifth pillar commands every Muslim to make the hajj or pilgrimage to Mecca at least once in a lifetime.

CHAPTER 13

AFRICA ON THE EVE OF THE AGE OF EXPLORATION

Although the ancient Greeks had contact with Africa, and the Romans had extensively colonized the northern part of Africa, Europeans in the medieval period had little knowledge of African geography. Africa is the world's second largest continent. It covers nearly twenty percent of the earth's surface and is three times the size of Europe. Myths were widely circulated in Europe about the boiling waters near the equator and the seaweed that might swallow entire ships. European woodcuts portrayed Africans as strange creatures; sometimes they were depicted with huge feet that they used to cover themselves from the boiling sun, while others portrayed them as Cyclops with one eye.

Africa was known in Europe as "the Dark Continent," not only because of the lack of knowledge about it, but also because of the difficulty of exploring its treacherous terrain and rivers. The geography of Africa isolated the many cultures of the continent from one another, and created one of the most diverse arrays of cultures in the world. The languages of Africa reflect its geographical diversity as well as the impact of the expansion of Islam. Arabic is the language of northern Africa. In addition to Arabic, many other languages are spoken that also reflect the history of the continent. During the Age of Exploration beginning in the fifteenth century, the Portuguese established many outposts along the coastal areas of Africa. Portuguese is still the language of trade in many regions of Africa. In the nineteenth century, the Age of European Imperialism also influenced the development of African cultures. Modern Africans speak English and French in addition to Arabic, Portuguese, and hundreds of African Bantu languages. The **Bantu** are a large family of Negroid tribal peoples who inhabit Africa south of the Sahara.

GEOGRAPHY OF AFRICA

The world's largest desert, the **Sahara**, covers 3.5 million square miles across the center of the African continent. In the thirteenth century, Arab traders established gold routes across the Sahara, and African gold became the foundation of the Mediterranean trade. The word "Sahara" comes from the Arabic word for "tan," the color of the sand. Some traditions suggest it comes from the sound a thirsty man makes when in need of water.

There is evidence that the Sahara was not always a desert. Fossil finds indicate the presence of water in the desert 5,000 years ago; a recent controversial theory suggests that the erosion patterns on the Sphinx at Giza are those of water, making the Sphinx much older than originally thought. The Sahara continues to grow today, and the desertification of this region is one of the world's major ecological issues. The vast expanse of the desert separated North African cultures from those south of the Sahara.

The region south of the Sahara is covered by dense rain forests on the west coast, while flat grasslands, or savannah, cover the central part of the continent and the east coast. Rainfall here is very heavy. African rain forests are very dense and difficult to penetrate; the insect life also presents many health hazards, even in the modern era. The Bantu, a black-skinned people, live in this area and speak over 800 languages. Most of them lived in illiterate societies that preserved their heritage through strong oral traditions. The Greeks described the Bantu as *Ethiopians*, which translates as "people with burnt faces." We still use the word "Ethiopia" today for the East African nation. The Arab description of the area as the *Bilad-al-Sudan*, or "land of the blacks," also survives in the name of the modern West African nation of the Sudan. The Bantu people are enormously important in the history of Africa, as they were the first to introduce the smelting of iron and use of iron tools. While the iron age may have started in Africa as early as the sixth century B.C.E., iron did not spread across Africa until after the first century C.E. The Bantu migrations began from north-central Africa in the first century B.C.E., lasted throughout the first millennium C.E., and resulted in not only the spread of iron-making but also agriculture. Pygmies, short brown-skinned people, inhabit this region.

The Olduvai Gorge is a prominent feature on the eastern coast of sub-Saharan Africa. The earliest known hominid fossils come from the Olduvai Gorge. Although this theory is now being challenged, anthropologists have traditionally argued that human life originated in Africa and later spread elsewhere.

The Kalahari, a much smaller desert, is located on the southern tip of Africa. Cultures here were separated from those in the North by the rain forests and Sahara desert.

The rivers of Africa are very difficult to navigate, and contribute to the isolation of one region of Africa from another. The Nile River was the center of ancient Egyptian civilization. Its cataracts effectively prevented invaders from penetrating Egypt; it is surrounded on the east by high cliffs and on the west by the desert, providing other natural geographic barriers. The Nile is another excellent example of why Africa is known as "The Dark Continent"; it was not until the twentieth century that the British explorer Livingston discovered the source of the Nile River in Lake Victoria.

The Niger River is another important river and the center of the medieval Kingdom of Benin.

ANCIENT AFRICA AFTER THE EGYPTIANS

Kush

The **Kushites** were located to the south of ancient Egypt and were the heirs of Egyptian culture. There are more pyramids standing today in Kush than in Egypt. These pyramids are not as large as those of Egypt, but archaeologists often rely on them to help unravel the mysteries of the great pyramids of Egypt. The capital of Kush was Kerma, and Egyptian influences reached Kush, centered on the third cataract of the Nile, through Nubia, a land centered on the first cataract and conquered by the Egyptians in the New Kingdom. The Egyptians conquered Kush during the New Kingdom, but when Egypt collapsed in 1000 B.C.E., Kush then declared independence and conquered Nubia. At this time the Kushites moved their capital to Napata and assumed Egyptian royal titles. They conquered Egypt itself and became the twenty-eighth pharaonic dynasty of Egypt.

Meröe

The arrival of the Assyrians in Egypt in the seventh century B.C.E. eventually forced the Kushites to move south. When their capital Napata was conquered in 591 B.C.E., the Kushites moved their capital to Meröe. For several centuries, Meröe was the path through which trade went to North Africa, and on to the Middle East and Europe. The king was elected from the royal family through the maternal line, and there were several female monarchs here. Meröe eventually lost its supremacy in trade to Axum in east Africa.

The Nok

One of the earliest examples of sophisticated sculpture in sub-Saharan Africa was the **Nok** culture. The culture takes its name after the town of Nok where archaeologists discovered one of the first objects produced by the culture. Scholars do not know what the people who produced this art called themselves. Nok is in central Nigeria today. Among the most famous products of the culture are unique heads that portray the individuality of the subject. Most artifacts are of fired clay or terracotta sculptures. Some are small-like pendants, while others are life-sized figures. The Nok were an iron age culture that dates from 900 B.C.E. to 200 C.E. Some scholars believe there is a similarlity between Nok sculptures and those of the Yoruba people, suggesting that there may be as yet unknown connections between Nok culture and contemporary Yoruba peoples in West Africa.

Axum and Adulis

The kingdom of **Axum** (**Ethiopia**), which converted to Christianity in 250 C.E., maintained strong ties with Byzantium, and was influential in the conversion of other east African peoples before the expansion of Islam took over the trade in the Mediterranean region. Axum adopted the **Coptic**, or Egyptian, form of Christianity, according to which Christ had only a single, divine nature, as opposed to the Orthodox view that he had both a human and a divine nature. Its main port city of Adulis was a major center of trade in the Mediterranean and a gateway to trade with the east. During the period following Muhammad's career, many Muslims fled to Adulis.

ISLAM IN AFRICA

By the seventh century C.E., followers of Muhammad were spreading their faith and their control west across the northern shores of Africa, and south along the eastern regions of the continent. Egypt, which had previously been a Byzantine province, quickly became an Arab state in 641 C.E. For many of the commoners, life improved, and partially as a result, many Egyptians willingly converted to the new faith of Islam. The Arab conquerors established a new capital at Cairo and used it as a base for further expansion into Africa.

By the early eighth century, much of northern Africa, called the Maghrib, meaning "west," was also under Arab control. From here, they spread into Spain and southwards across the Sahara. The end result was that Axum remained one of the few non-Muslim states in north and eastern Africa. Axum had provided shelter and refuge for many Muslims during the early history of Islam, when Muslims were driven out of Mecca. Out of respect for this help, Muslims never attempted to conquer Axum. Muslims did later control the trade routes, which weakened the kingdom, and despite the cosmopolitan and eclectic nature of Axumite society, the Axumites never converted to Islam. Despite later crises over the succession, and later colonization efforts by Europeans, Axum continues to be largely Christian today and is known as the nation of Ethiopia.

A key result of the Islamic conquest of large portions of Africa was the establishment of a vast trading network. Port cities arose along the east coast that facilitated contact with the Arabian peninsula and even settlements near the Indian Ocean. Ghana and later Mali in western Africa eventually became linked into this trading network, becoming influential partners through their lucrative gold trade. Moreover, many societies along the trade routes had mostly oral rather than written traditions. The introduction of the written Arabic language, as well as Arabic laws, allowed local rulers greater authority and improved administration over their subjects.

Ghana

Ghana, which flourished from 900–1100 C.E., was a military kingdom that conquered a region approximately the size of Texas. Ghana was an important center for the gold trade, and gold from Ghana was the basis of the Mediterranean trade with the east. Its name comes from the Soninke name for "war chief." According to Al-Bakri, an Arab chronicler, Ghana had an army of 200,000 warriors, and 40,000 of them carried bows and arrows. The king maintained a standing royal guard of 1,000 men. Income from conquered areas helped to support the extensive administrative apparatus of Ghana. Taxes were also levied on imported goods such as salt. Social rank in Ghana was based on heredity and on service to the king. The Muslim administrators of Ghana were the highest rank on the social ladder; merchants ranked directly beneath them. Its main city, Kumbi, housed 12 Islamic mosques, an indication of its size and prosperity. After the collapse of Kumbi, the kingdom of Ghana was split into several smaller kingdoms.

Mali

The Mandike people, a successor state, established the kingdom of **Mali**. Under the leadership of Sundiata Mali, a cripple whose exploits are immortalized in the *Epic of Sundiata*, and his descendent Mansa Musa, Mali conquered the warring peoples and established an empire larger in size than that of Ghana. Mansa Musa strengthened his control over his empire by appointing relatives as provincial governors. Mansa Musa made an historic hajj to Mecca; his entourage carried so much gold with them that the economy of Egypt suffered from inflation for generations. Mansa Musa's travels brought many scholars and artists to Africa, and Timbuktu became a renowned center of Islamic learning and trade. The pilgrimage also opened trade with Muslim areas and fostered intermarriage between Muslims and African women.

OTHER CULTURES OF AFRICA

The Great Zimbabwe

The massive walls of the **Great Zimbabwe** are the most important monuments in Africa south of the Nile Valley. The Bantu people were responsible for the great ruins, which were built between the eleventh and fifteenth centuries from local materials and cover more than sixty acres. There are two complexes, a fortress, and the "temple," which is an elliptically shaped enclosure. A massive wall surrounds the entire complex. The buildings were highly decorated with ornaments and carvings, including ceramics from Asia. The massive ruins convey the strength of the economy of the Great Zimbabwe, which was based upon the gold trade. They also convey the power of the Great Zimbabwe as the center of a vast empire. The most well-known walls of the complex date to around the fourteenth and fifteenth centuries C.E., but the site was occupied by Bantu as early as the third century C.E. Great Zimbabwe was the center of a vast trading network, which controlled the export of gold to the coastal cities of East Africa. The gold trade reached its highpoint from 1400–1500 C.E., and scholars have discovered remains of objects imported from Persia, China, and the Near East in the ruins of the Great Zimbabwe. Zimbabwe arose about the time Arab trade was developing on the East African coast, and declined at around the same time that Arab trade on the east coast declined. This suggests a direct relationship between the gold trade and the prosperity of Zimbabwe. The gold trade declined in

Walls of the Great Zimbabwe

the fifteenth century, due to falling world prices and depletion of natural resources, and at the same time, the Great Zimbabwe was abandoned. Other scholars suggest that there were factors in addition to the gold trade that brought about the decline of Zimbabwe. In the fifteenth century, drought and failing agriculture damaged the pastoral economy of the Great Zimbabwe, and some scholars suggest that Zimbabwe may have derived as much of its wealth from cattle as from gold.

Benin

The Kingdom of Benin was a strong, centralized kingdom in West Africa with significant military and economic power. Kings called Obas, who claimed divine ancestry, ruled Benin; they controlled trade so effectively that the Europeans could never manage to dominate Benin. Today, members of this family still rule in Benin. The Obas ruled the land by dividing it into fiefs held by officials, who were appointed by the Oba himself. The Oba in many ways was the absolute ruler of spiritual affairs as well as temporal ones. For example, he could speak with the voices of ancient ancestors of the people. Bronze casting reached a high point in Benin in the fifteenth century, in part fueled by the bronze and copper manilas brought by Portuguese sailors. Nonetheless, the power of the Oba was so strong that the Portuguese were unable to dominate Benin as they would do in a number of other African states.

CHAPTER 14

THE AMERICAS BEFORE COLUMBUS

The native population of the Americas began coming from Asia across a land bridge that once covered the Bering Strait between 50,000 and 20,000 years ago. Over the course of thousands of years, people trickled down to the southern tip of South America.

There were several strong kingdoms and civilizations in the Americas that flourished and collapsed before the arrival of the Europeans in the fifteenth and sixteenth centuries C.E. Although the European explorers who "discovered" the Americas described them as a "New World," clearly there were advanced civilizations here that dated back thousands of years before the arrival of the Spanish.

Native cultures included the Olmec, the Maya, the Aztecs, the Incas, the Mound Builders of the Mississippi region, and the Anasazi of the American Southwest. Some of these cultures, such as the Anasazi and the Maya, had already collapsed prior to the arrival of the Europeans; others, such as the Aztecs and Incas, would collapse as a result of contact with the Europeans. Historians differ over the size of the native population of the Americas in 1500 C.E. The American historian John Tindall, for example, estimates that there were 50 million Native Americans when the Europeans arrived, while other historians claim the figure was closer to 19 million. There can be no certainty about this issue, as official censuses were rare. Further, many Native American cultures were non-literate and relied upon oral traditions.

THE NATIVE AMERICAN CULTURES OF MESOAMERICA

The Olmec

The **Olmec** originated around 1500 B.C.E. at San Lorenzo, south of present-day Veracruz. A small class of hereditary nobles governed them. The Olmec were literate. San Lorenzo fell in 900 B.C.E. La Venta was a prominent Olmec center after the collapse of San Lorenzo in 900 B.C.E. The site is known for its Great Pyramid 110 feet high. La Venta collapsed in 300 B.C.E. Tres Zapotes became prominent after the fall of La Venta and was the last great Olmec site. The Olmec were the foundation of the later cultures in the classic period from 300–900 C.E. in Mesoamerica.

The Maya

The **Maya** of Mesoamerica were the heirs of Olmec culture. The word "Maya" is derived from the word "Zamna," a Maya god. The Mayan civilization flourished on the Yucatan peninsula, and was based on agriculture. The Maya grew maize, chili peppers, beans, squash, and a variety of fruit. The textile arts were an important part of Mayan trade, and their cotton was exported throughout the region. There may once have been 14 million inhabitants in the Mayan cities on the Yucatan peninsula. The largest city was Tikal, which may have had a population of 100,000.

Chichen Itza

Chichen Itza

Chichen Itza was one of the last Mayan centers to be abandoned. Even after Tikal and Palenque had been deserted and overgrown by the jungle, Chichen Itza continued to flourish. One reason Chichen Itza is so well-preserved is that it became a **Toltec** center after the decline of the Maya. Images of the Mayan god Kukulcan, or the "feathered serpent," are omnipresent in Chichen Itza and other Mayan sites; the Toltec identified the "feathered serpent" here with the god Quetzalcoatl, worshiped at Teotihuacán. According to tradition, the Toltec Quetzalcoatl came here after being ousted by the Toltec god Tezcatlipoca. Chichen Itza then appealed to the Toltec as a ceremonial center. The name "Chichen Itza" means "mouth of the Itzas' well," or "at the edge of the well of the water sorcerers." The Itzas were the group of Maya who settled here. In this part of the Yucatan, there is little rainfall and no sources of water on the surface; cenotes, or places where the limestone has collapsed exposing underground water, were very important. Consequently, the cult of Chaac, god of rain and waters, was important here.

The Maya built their cities around a central ceremonial pyramid and other buildings, with a sacred ball court nearby. The Pyramid of Kukulcan, or **El Castillo** is a famous ruin at Chichen Itza. It is a nine-story structure symbolizing the planes of the underworld with a temple on top and another pyramid on the inside of the structure. At 3:00 P.M. on the spring and fall equinoxes (March 20 and September 21), the sun forms a design on the north staircase that looks like an undulating serpent; this design symbolizes the descent of the god Kukulcan to earth, and, hence, the beginning of the agricultural cycle.

There is also a **ball court** here that is one of the largest courts of the Maya. The game played on the ball court near the pyramid had deep religious significance for the Maya. Although the ritual practiced here is not fully understood, the players bounced a large ball back and forth using their hips. The game was dangerous, and the balls were thrown with such force that players had to wear protective padding. The court had metal rings on the walls through which the combatants attempted to drive the ball. The ball court is believed to have represented the cosmos, while the ball represented the sun. The game symbolized the conflict between light and darkness. The losers were sacrificed to the gods after the games.

El Caracol is another famous ruin here, and the Maya and later the Toltec used it for astronomical purposes. It was built between 900–1000 C.E. The movements of the heavens were very important for the Maya and later the Toltec. The Maya developed their sophisticated solar calendar of 365 days through observing the heavens at structures such as this. The solar calendar was divided into eighteen months with twenty days each, with five additional empty days. There was also a ritual calendar that governed the lives of humans and deities. The Maya made very sophisticated observations and calculations of the solar, lunar, and Venusian cycles, eclipses of the sun, and the movements of constellations. The cylindrical observatory tower known as the snail of El Caracol has a small room from which the Maya observed the heavens.

The Nunnery Complex is the largest structure at Chichan Itza dating from the Classic period. It has many small rooms and is thought to have been used by priestesses in the Mayan rituals. For these reasons, Spanish explorers gave it its modern name.

Palenque

Palenque is another important city of the Maya, associated with the ruler Pacal. There are fifteen structures on the palace platform. **The Temple of the Inscriptions** is the highest temple in the complex at 75 feet above ground level. It was built to house the tomb of Pacal, the ruler responsible for many of the buildings at Palenque. His sarcophagus weighs five tons, and several sacrificial victims were placed outside of it.

The Group of the Cross is a group of three temples, including the Temple of the Sun, the Temple of the Foliated Cross, and the Temple of the Cross. Pacal's son Chan-Bahlum built the group to commemorate his coronation.

Uxmal

"Uxmal" means "thrice occupied." Its most famous ruin is the Nunnery Quadrangal, and it also contains the Governor's Palace, the Great Pyramid, and the Pyramid of the Magician. Like other Mayan cities, it had a ball court.

The Decline of the Maya

The Maya reached their peak from 500–800 C.E. but began to abandon their cities between 800–1000 C.E. The reasons for this are unknown, but scholars have suggested that foreign invasions, civil unrest due to disease, overpopulation, crop failures, administrative problems caused by an overly large empire, or natural disaster might have prompted the decline of the Maya. Although the civilization of the Maya who built the ruins above collapsed, over two million Maya continue to survive today in the Yucatan peninsula.

Teotihuacán

Teotihuacán arose as a major center of Mesoamerican civilization around 300 B.C.E. and flourished until 700–800 C.E. It was located around thirty miles northeast of modern Mexico City and had a population of around

150,000 people. Teotihuacán had stratified social classes, with the elite living in a special precinct and the working classes in barrios on the edge of the city. The city contained more than 5,000 ceremonial structures, and was laid out on a north-south and east-west axis. The Pyramids of the Sun and Moon dominated the city. The Pyramid of the Sun had four levels and was over 200 feet high. Each side was 700 feet long. There are many images of Quetzalcoatl on the ruins. In 700 c.e., invaders from the southwest burned Teotihuacán.

Monte Alban

Sometime around 500 b.c.e., the Zapotec people began to build much larger cities and monumental structures at **Monte Alban**. The structures at Monte Alban are built on a stone terrace on a 1,200-foot-high mountain overlooking modern Oaxaca. Approximately 20,000 people lived here on terraces for farming carved into the mountainsides. Monte Alban fell to invaders somewhere around 700 c.e., having flourished for over 1,200 years in Mesoamerica. Teotihuacán was clearly the most powerful influence on the architecture and culture of Monte Alban, whose inhabitants spoke Zapotec. Monte Alban fell shortly after invaders destroyed Teotihuacán.

Toltec Confederation

Under the leadership of Toliptzin (980–1000 c.e.), the Toltecs established themselves as masters of Mesoamerica. Their capital was Tula. The Toltecs intermarried with the remnants of the population of Teotihuacán. Toliptzin even took the name "Quetzalcoatl" to symbolize his position as high priest of the cult of the plumed serpent god worshiped in Teotihuacán. According to later Aztec legend, the Toltec god Tezcatlipoca had a struggle with Teoliptzin-Quetzalcoatl and drove Quetzalcoatl into exile. Coincidentally, the year that Quetzalcoatl promised to return was the same year in which Hernando Cortes arrived in Mesoamerica.

Aztecs (Mexico)

The **Aztecs** wandered for 150 years before settling on the swampy islands of Lake Texcoco, the modern location of Mexico City. They worshiped their god Huitzilopochtili in the city there. In 1428, the Aztecs began a policy of expansion. Although the Toltecs had once looked upon them as barbarians, the Aztecs quickly assimilated the cultural legacy of the Toltecs, and by 1519, the Aztec confederation occupied virtually all of Mesoamerica. In Tenochtitlan, there were 60,000 households, and the total population was somewhere around 500,000. Tenochtitlan was larger than any European city of its time. The population in the Aztec empire was over 5,000,000.

Much of the Aztecs' success can be attributed to the cult of their chief god Huitzilopochtili, the god of the sun. The Aztecs believed that this god had to be kept moving so as not to be overtaken by darkness. They believed that he had to be fed human blood and practiced ritual sacrifice, sometimes on a mass level. There are many theories as to why the Aztecs practiced sacrifice. Some argue that sacrifice was a check on population growth. Others say that it served as an instrument of state terror and controlled nearby populations; and some historians and anthropologists suggest that ordinary people fed on the bodies of the sacrificial victims as a form of protein. Emperor Montezuma II lived in splendor greater than any European monarch of the day; at his coronation, 5,100 people were sacrificed. This religious ritual, for whatever reasons it was practiced, strengthened the Aztec state.

NATIVE AMERICAN CULTURES OF SOUTH AMERICA: THE INCA

In the 1980s archaeologists discovered evidence of great civilizations along the west coast of Peru going back 5,000 years. These civilizations were older than those of the Maya or Aztecs. These civilizations built step pyramids and other large monuments. For reasons unknown to us, these people moved into the Andes highlands, the highest mountain range in the Western Hemisphere. They became known as the **Inca**, a name taken from a ruling family in Cuzco, and then applied to all Native Americans living in the Cuzco basin. The Inca became militaristic during the reign of Pachacuti Inca (1438–1471) and conquered surrounding groups. They controlled their population through strong government; they unified the language and the religion of their subjects.

Macchu Picchu

The Inca settled primarily in the valleys of Huaylas, Cuzco, and Titicaca where they constructed terraces along the slopes of the steep mountains. How or why they made the transition from dependence on the sea for food in the early period to settled agriculture between 600–1000 C.E. is still a mystery. They grew corn and potatoes and learned to preserve the potatoes through freeze-drying. In 1911, Hiram Bingham discovered the most famous Inca site, **Machu Picchu**.

NATIVE AMERICAN CULTURES OF NORTH AMERICA

The Mississippian Culture or the Mound Builders

The **Mississippian** culture arose along the Mississippi River and flourished from 900–1350 C.E. The culture spread along the rivers to many parts of what is now the central and eastern United States. The Mississippians were farmers who grew corn, squash, beans, pumpkins, and tobacco. Among the most important centers of Mississippian culture were Cahokia, Illinois, the largest settlement north of Mexico; Moundville, Alabama; and Ocmulgee, Georgia. The Mississippians are also known as the Mound Builders, due to the enormous flat-topped temple mounds they constructed in the centers of their large, well-organized cities.

Cahokia, eight miles east of St. Louis, reached the high point of its development between 1050–1150 C.E., and the city covered nearly six square miles. There were 120 mounds at Cahokia, the largest of which is Monks Mound, covering 15 acres at its base and soaring 100-feet high. Scholars estimate that the complex had a population of between 10,000-40,000, although 20,000 is the most likely number. Inhabitants built a circle of wooden posts, now called Woodhenge, and used it as a calendar. A ten-foot-high stockade surrounded a large part of the complex. Cahokia began its decline around 1200 C.E. and was completely deserted by 1400 C.E.

Ocmulgee takes its name from the river upon which the Mississippians settled here. The name "Ocmulgee" means "boiling water," and the river water literally seems to boil and bubble as one stands near the shore. At one time, Ocmulgee had a population of as many as 1,000 people. Ocmulgee is primarily known for the remains of several mounds. There are at least seven mounds still remaining on the site, including the largest mound, the Great Temple Mound. The Great Temple Mound is approximately 45 feet high. Its base is 300 feet by 270 feet long. At one time, there were rectangular wooden structures on top of the mound, whose purpose is uncertain. There is also an Earthlodge at Ocmulgee, and the doorway was aligned so that once a year on the winter solstice, sunlight poured through the entrance and flooded the platform. Rituals here may have commemorated the beginning of the spring and harvest season.

Scholars know very little about how the Mississippian mounds were used, except that they were built for public ceremonies.

THE SOUTHWESTERN NATIVE AMERICANS: THE ANASAZI

Spanish explorers first encountered the southwestern Native American tribes in the 1540s. There were three major Native American cultures in the southwest: the Hohokam, who were an agricultural group located in the river valleys of the desert; the Mogollon, who were hunters and gatherers; and the **Anasazi** (called Hisatsinom by their likely descendants, the Hopi), who were cliff dwellers.

The Anasazi were likely the descendants of an archaic desert culture in the southwest from 6,000 B.C.E. known as the Basketmaker I culture, or from the Mogollon. They first appeared in the Four Corners region (the intersection of New Mexico, Arizona, Utah, and Colorado) around the time of the historic Christ. The ruins of the Anasazi culture are the best-preserved ruins in North America. The word "Anasazi" is a later Navajo word that means "ancient people who are not us" or "ancient enemies." The Hopi consider themselves to be descendants of the Anasazi, and prefer that their ancestors be called the Hisatsinom, which means "people of long ago." The Anasazi did not build cliff dwellings for the first 1,000 years of their history, but rather lived in open communities or in caves. They lived near fields where they grew corn, squash, and beans. They also gathered nuts and other wild foods and hunted game. Given the very open nature of their lifestyle, archaeologists argue that the Anasazi had few enemies in their early history.

Sometime between 900–1100 C.E. (called the Pueblo II period), the Anasazi began to build kivas, or communal rooms for ceremonial purposes in their villages. Their population increased, and during this period small Anasazi villages began to spread throughout the southwest.

Starting from 1100–1300 C.E. (called the Pueblo III period), the Anasazi began to build the cliff dwellings for which they are most well-known. Many buildings in these villages under the cliffs were several stories tall. These villages were in places that were easily defensible, suggesting that the Anasazi had perhaps acquired enemies they did not have in earlier periods. For unknown reasons, near the end of this period the western Anasazi sites were completely abandoned, while the eastern sites continued to flourish and expand.

From 1300 until 1598 C.E. (called the Pueblo IV period), the Anasazi moved further south near the homes of the Hopis and Zunis. Many Anasazi cliff dwellings, or **pueblos**, became much larger, often housing thousands of people and standing several stories high.

Chaco Canyon

The ruins of the Anasazi were first discovered in the nineteenth century, and many have since been designated national monuments and World Heritage Centers. The earliest Anasazi site to enter the Pueblo stage of development was **Chaco** in northwest New Mexico. Chaco Canyon was the center of Anasazi civilization by 900 C.E., and may have had a population that numbered in the thousands. There were three major building styles perfected here: great towns with enormous room blocks with up to five levels; great houses with plazas and kivas; and outlying villages probably designed for family groups. The Anasazi here were known for their turquoise jewelry, and traded with other Anasazi groups. They reached the height of their development around 1130 C.E. Some twenty years later, following a long period of drought, the Chacoans abandoned this region. In 1980 Chaco became a national monument. Pueblo Bonito is one of the Great Houses in Chaco Canyon; each pueblo here typically has around 216 rooms.

Mesa Verde in southwestern Colorado was another very important center of Anasazi culture. Anasazi of the Basketmaker III period lived here, perhaps as far back as 575 C.E. The Anasazi began to construct villages on top of the mesas here as early as 800 C.E. By the 1300s the Anasazi were building much more elaborate cliff dwellings protected by caves. Mesa Verde contains more than 4,000 prehistoric sites.

The Anasazi made the shift from the mesa top to the cliff dwellings below sometime in the 1200s. The inhabitants of **Sun Point Pueblo** on the mesa top actually dismantled their stone and wooden structures and carried the materials to the shelter of the caves below. Given the tremendous amount of labor involved, scholars have suggested that there must have been a serious threat to their safety above.

Mesa Verde

Mesa Verde contains some of the best-preserved cliff dwellings in the southwest. Cliff Palace is the largest cliff dwelling in North America. It has 217 rooms and 23 kivas, and probably had a population of 200–250 people. The kivas here were sunk into the ground, and one entered them by climbing down a ladder.

Other large dwellings include **Spruce Tree House**, which has 144 rooms and 8 kivas. There are over 600 cliff dwellings in Mesa Verde and, although there are other large villages such as this in Mesa Verde, seventy-five percent contain only one to five rooms. Balcony House is another famous dwelling in Mesa Verde and is located high on the cliffs 600 feet above the canyon floor. Through tree-ring dating, its first timbers have been dated to 1190 C.E., and its latest timbers to 1290.

Decline of Mesa Verde

The Anasazi abandoned most cliff dwellings in Mesa Verde around 1270 C.E. The reasons for this are uncertain, but drought, climatic change, or depletion of natural resources are the most likely explanations. Most scholars believe that the inhabitants of the villages in Mesa Verde moved south to join the Hopi or many other tribes in the area. The ruins of the villages were not discovered until December 18, 1888, when a Colorado rancher named Richard Wetherhill happened to spot them from the mesa top. In 1906 the site became a national park, was later excavated by the Smithsonian, and was made a World Heritage Center in 1978.

Other Anasazi Ruins

Near Mesa Verde are the misnamed **Aztec ruins**, so-called because the Spanish believed the pueblos to be too sophisticated to have been built by the southwestern Native Americans. The main ruin here has over 500 rooms.

Another important Anasazi site is **Hovenweep National Monument**, straddling the boundary of Utah and Colorado. Hovenweep is a Ute word that means "deserted valley," and contains six separate Anasazi sites. There were no places here to build cliff dwellings, and the Anasazi built their villages at canyon heads near springs. Their pueblos were multi-story dwellings and they lived in the region from 900–1300 C.E. Drought and population increases probably caused the Anasazi to abandon this site.

Betatakin, a Navajo word for "ledge house," is another well-known Anasazi ruin. It has more than 135 rooms. While **Keet Seel**, a Navajo word meaning "broken pottery," has more than 150 rooms and 6 kivas. Inscription House has three stories, eighty rooms, and one kiva. All sites were built into the cliffs by the Kayenta Anasazi on what is today the Navajo National Monument on the Navajo Reservation in northeastern Arizona. The Anasazi only lived here from 1250 to 1300 C.E. Nevertheless, these structures are among the largest ruins, testifying to the organizational strength of the Anasazi communities.

The Anasazi lived much longer at **Canyon de Chelly**, also located on the Navajo Reservation. There are over 700 prehistoric sites here, including Whitehouse Ruins, Antelope House, Mummy Cave Ruin, and others. The Anasazi built these cliff dwellings between 1100–1300 C.E. When the Anasazi (Hisatsinom) left, the Hopi and Navajo later occupied the site. Canyon de Chelly became a national monument in 1931, and is on over 130 square miles of land now owned by the Navajo. The Anasazi also lived in the region now known as the Petrified Forest National Park and, although they did not know what petrified wood was, they used it to build their dwellings. They lived here from 1050 B.C.E. to 1400 C.E.

Decline of Canyon de Chelly

As the Anasazi abandoned their cliff dwellings here, they joined other tribes in the area. For example, one group of Anasazi joined the inhabitants of Pecos somewhere around the twelfth century and began to build their multi-story pueblos. Pecos was an important center of trade between the Pueblo and Plains Indians.

The legacy of the Anasazi can still be seen throughout the southwest. There are many other sites associated with the Anasazi, and other groups of people who believe themselves to be descendants of the Anasazi. The **Sinagua**, whose name means "without water," built smaller cliff dwellings at **Montezuma's Castle** in Arizona. Although it is not certain whether the Sinagua were a branch of the Anasazi or some other southwestern culture, they were very influenced by the Anasazi. Montezuma's Castle, built in the thirteenth century, has two five-story pueblos, the upper of which has twenty rooms while the lower has forty-five rooms. Montezuma's Well, which is nearby, was erroneously named for the Aztec king, as again the Spanish felt it too advanced for the southwestern Native Americans.

Native American culture would change greatly with the arrival of the Europeans in the fifteenth century.

CHAPTER 15

ASIA FROM 500 C.E.
TO 1400 C.E.

Many conquerors established powerful and important empires in Asia during this period. After the fall of the Roman Empire in the west, Europe entered the Middle Ages and Germanic peoples began the establishment of the European monarchies. While Europe struggled to reassert itself following the collapse of Rome, some of the most important and vibrant Asian empires flourished.

CHINA

Yang Jian founded the Sui Dynasty in 581 C.E. Its capital was Chang-an. He patronized both Buddhism and Taoism and founded many monasteries. Yang Jian and his son and successor, Sui Yangdi, built a 1,400-mile-long Grand Canal that linked the Yellow and Yangtze Rivers. Yangdi was a tyrannical ruler and was assassinated by **Li Yuan**, who founded the **T'ang** Dynasty. The T'ang held power in China for over three centuries until it collapsed in 907 C.E. China expanded greatly under the T'ang, who conquered Tibet and forced the Koreans to pay tribute. During the T'ang Dynasty, culture flourished in China. One of the favorite art forms of T'ang China reflected the revived trade along the Silk Road. T'ang artisans produced blue, yellow, and gold ceramic horses and camels that are still highly valued by collectors today. Another milestone of T'ang artistry were the longmen Buddhist caves. Li Po was an important poet during the T'ang period who wrote about the beauty of nature. The Kirhgiz people overthrew the T'ang, and a new dynasty took their place. The Song ruled China from 960–1279 C.E. The Song formed an alliance with the **Mongols**, who ultimately defeated them.

Genghis Khan

The Mongols and Yuan China

Temujin was born in the 1160s. He was destined to become one of the world's greatest conquerors. Although he spent a portion of his childhood as a refugee in the wilderness following his father's assassination, he won a number of victories against rival Mongol chieftains and in 1206 he was elected **Genghis Khan**, or "universal ruler" of the Mongol tribes, at a *kuriltai,* or meeting of all of the Mongol chieftains. Genghis Khan's army was not overwhelmingly large, but he and his forces unleashed terror in the hearts of those who fought them. Mongol warriors wore silk shirts, so that arrows entering their bodies could be easily removed without further tearing of the flesh. They traveled with portable, round felt tents called yurts, which could quickly be disassembled and assembled. They were expert military tacticians, and their skill on the battlefield led to the defeat of the Abbasids in Baghdad in 1258. The Mongol hordes attacked the Song Dynasty in China beginning in the 1260s, and finally defeated them in 1279 C.E. The capital of the Mongol empire under Genghis Khan was Karakorum; today it is located in Outer Mongolia. After the death of Genghis Khan, his principal wife divided his empire amongst his sons in accordance with the Khan's wishes. Ogedai, his third son, was elected universal Khan, but was not as able a leader as his father had been. Various khanates were carved from his territory and ruled by the sons of Genghis Khan, including the Chaghadai Khanate in Central Asia, whose capital was Samarkand; the Khanate of Persia with its capital at Baghdad; and the Khanatwe of Kipchak, or Golden Horde. Genghis Khan's grandson, **Kubilai Khan**, continued the conquest of Song China and established the Yuan Dynasty. His capital was Khanbaliq, the city of the Khan. This city would later be known as Beijing or Peking, the northern capital. Kubilai Khan extended the Grand Canal of the Sui to the capital city Khanbaliq, which was twenty-four miles in diameter. The Italian wanderer Marco Polo lived there during his visit to Asia and wrote of its magnificence. Although his account has been subjected to doubt in many respects, his tales of the grandeur of China under Kubilai Khan earned him the nickname "il millione," as Italians believed his stories were too remarkable to be true and were, therefore, just a million tall tales. Yuan rule collapsed in the 1340s when a poor peasant named **Zhu Yuanxhang** led a rebellion that toppled the fabulous Mongol Dynasty. Zhu's dynasty would be called the **Ming**, or the "brilliant" dynasty, and it ruled China from 1369–1644.

Tamerlane's Empire

Genghis Khan destroyed Baghdad in 1250 C.E. The fourteenth-century Mongol ruler **Tamerlane** founded his empire on the ruins of the Mongol empire begun by Genghis Khan. He took power in 1369 C.E. in Samarkand, which became the capital of his empire. Alexander the Great had once occupied the great city, and it had also been a Mongol outpost. Tamerlane conquered the region east of the Caspian Sea, Mesopotamia, and Baghdad. He entered northern India, where he massacred 100,000 Hindu prisoners before entering Delhi. He then turned to Anatolia and led his armies to the Bosphorus Strait before his death in 1405 C.E.

JAPAN

Prince Shotoku Taishi (572–622 C.E.) sent a mission to Chang-an in China to learn more about T'ang-style administration. Shotoku then launched a series of reforms designed to limit the power of the hereditary nobility. In the seventeen-article constitution, he designed a merit system for promotion in the government and created a centralized government around the person of the ruler. After his death, more reforms were passed, including the famous **Taika**, or "great change" reforms of the seventh century. The Taika reforms established a Grand Council of State and divided Japan into administrative districts.

The **Fujiwara** clan rose to prominence after the death of Prince Shotoku. Their position was primarily due to intermarriage with the royal family; while the Yamato emperor ruled in name, the Fujiwara often ruled in fact. In 710 C.E. the Japanese built Nara, a capital modeled on the Chinese city Chang-an. In 794 C.E., the emperor moved the capital to Heian, where modern Kyoto is located. The Fujiwara continued to control affairs during the Heian period. One of the most famous chronicles of court life during the Heian period was Lady Murasaki's *The Tale of Genji*. *Genji* illustrates the norms for men and women. Courtship was often conducted through exchange of sophisticated poetry; the more beautiful the poetry written, the more attractive the suitor. Women were confined to their households, and their suitors often did not so much as look upon them until they were in their bedchambers. Ironically, women had few rights in Heian Japan, but the most famous record of its culture and customs was written by a woman who served in the imperial court.

Japanese culture was very influenced by its native religion, **Shinto**, and Buddhism, which arrived in Japan from China in the sixth century C.E. The two most important sects of Buddhism in Japan were Pure Land and Zen Buddhism.

In the twelfth century, Minamoto Yoritomo defeated several rivals and established the Kamakura Shogunate. He created the *bakufu*, or "tent" system of government led by a shogun, who was the most powerful military leader. Although the emperor continued to have authority in name, the shogun had actual authority. In 1266 the Yuan emperor Kubilai Khan demanded tribute from Japan. The Japanese refused, and the Khan sent a force of 30,000 to invade the islands. The Yuan invasion was thwarted by bad weather, but one year later in 1281 they returned with a force of 150,000. The Japanese fought them for two months, but eventually a "divine wind," or *kamikaze*, destroyed the invading fleet. No foreign invader would threaten Japan again until World War II, when the Americans dropped the atomic bombs on Hiroshima and Nagasaki in 1945.

In 1333 the Ashikaga overthrew the Kamakura and established a shogun in Kyoto. The unity of Japan was seriously threatened during the **Onin War** from 1467–1477; this period parallels the period of Warring States in ancient China. During this period, the **samurai** played an important role on the battlefield. According to their code of *Bushido*, loyalty was important above all else. During the reign of Hideoshi in the sixteenth century, only the samurai were allowed to carry weapons and have last names. The fighting skill of the samurai was strengthened by the meditative techniques of Zen Buddhism, while their notion of their sword as their soul was influenced by the Shinto veneration of nature.

ANGKOR

Cambodian peasants reported to French colonial powers during the nineteenth century that they had found remnants of "temples built by gods or by giants." No one took them seriously until 1860, when Henri Mahout discovered the ruins of the Angkor kingdom. The temples are spread out over some forty miles, and are located about 192 miles from present-day Phnom Penh, at the magnificent city of Angkor Thom. The Khmer kingdom of Angkor arose in the ninth century and was the most powerful kingdom in southeast Asia before the sixteenth century. The capital city, Angkor Thom, covered an area of more than four square miles. The Thai destroyed the city in 1432 C.E. The temple of **Angkor Wat** was a Hindu site, with as many as 3,000 priests at its apex. It was built between 1113 and 1150 C.E. and has a moat 570 feet wide and four miles long. Its thousands of sculptures portray Hindu mythology from the Mahabarata and Ramayana. Another famous temple is the Buddhist shrine Bayon. The Temple of Bayon was built between 1181 and 1220 C.E. and has 172 giant heads representing the Bodhisattva of Mercy. Buddhists venerate Bodhisattvas as those who have attained Nirvana, but remained behind to teach others the path to salvation. The architectural style of the Temple of Bayon is a mix between Hindu and Buddhist elements and was influenced by the conversion of Jayavarman from Hinduism to Buddhism.

Srivijaya

Srivijaya developed in the eighth century and was a trading society whose primary commodity was spices. Their deepwater port and capital Palembang provided refuge from the monsoons. Srivijaya dominated the trade that passed through the Strait of Malacca. In 1025, the Dravidian kingdom of Cola defeated it, and it gradually lost its hold over trade in the region.

MAJAPAHIT

After the defeat of Srivijaya, Majapahit on Java rose to prominence in the thirteenth century. In the mid-fourteenth century, it had united the archipelago of islands and part of mainland southeast Asia.

EMPIRE OF MAHMUD GHAZNI

In 962 C.E., Turkish-speaking slaves took power from the Sasanid Persians. In 997 C.E. the founder's son, Mahmud Ghazni, took power and began a series of raids in Indian lands. By the time he died in 1030 C.E., he had conquered the upper Indus Valley and areas as far south as the Indian Ocean. By 1200 C.E., successors to the Ghazni controlled northern India and had established the Delhi sultanate.

Kingdom of Cola

Cola was a medieval Indian kingdom that often clashed with the Delhi sultanate to the north. Cola defeated Srivijaya in 1025 C.E.

CHAPTER 16

THE WESTERN MIDDLE AGES

The **Middle Ages** span over one thousand years of European history. Although different scholars cite different dates for the beginning and the end of the Middle Ages, the most commonly accepted date for the beginning of the medieval period is 476 C.E., the date the last Roman emperor of the west, Romulus Augustulus, was deposed. From this point of view, the medieval period is characterized by the disappearance of Roman city life until its revival in the eleventh century, and the development of a localized economy on vast manorial estates. Further, the level of literacy and educational achievements dropped in the wake of the collapse of the Roman Empire in the west. During the medieval period, the church preserved literacy, especially in monastic communities where monks devoted a third of their day to studying and copying the scriptures and other writings of the church fathers.

Another commonly cited date for the beginning of the Middle Ages is 529 C.E., the date of the foundation of St. Benedict's monastery of **Monte Casino**, about 80 miles south of Rome. In the medieval period, Monte Casino was the center of Benedictine monasticism and continues to be so today. The emphasis of the Benedictine monks and nuns on "Ora et labora," or "Prayer and Work," preserved the legacy of Greco-Roman culture and transformed the economy of Europe. In the same year as Benedict founded Monte Casino, the Byzantine emperor Justinian closed the last of the pagan schools. The events in the year 529 C.E. symbolize the beginning of the Christian era in Europe, and for this reason, the Middle Ages are commonly also known as "The Age of Faith." The medieval mind focused on the sacred as opposed to the profane.

The date given as the end of the Middle Ages is also a matter of great debate among historians. The year 1453 C.E. is the most commonly accepted date, as this was the year that the Islamic Seljuk Turks conquered Constantinople, the capital of the eastern Roman Empire. In 1453, the last vestiges of Roman Imperial power collapsed. Under Muslim rule, the beautiful Hagia Sophia basilica, for centuries a symbol of Greek Orthodox Christianity, became an Islamic mosque. Many historians argue, however, that the transition from the medieval period to the early modern era cannot be pinned to a decisive date or event. Interpretations of the differences between the medieval and early modern era vary widely.

THE HISTORIOGRAPHY OF THE MEDIEVAL PERIOD

Not only are the dates of the medieval period a matter of great debate, but interpretations of the period are also varied. In the fourteenth century, the Renaissance Humanist **Francesco Petrarca** (known in English as Petrarch) referred to the Middle Ages as "the Dark Ages." Petrarch, as did many humanists, valued the inner life of the individual; he found awareness of individual growth to be lacking in several respects in the writings of the medievals. The later humanist **Erasmus of Rotterdam**, who poked fun at the convoluted logic of scholastic thought, further developed Petrarch's description of the medieval period as intellectually dark. Erasmus believed that the medieval scholastic theology failed to speak to the individual in terms that would impact his or her growth. The Renaissance Humanists saw their own era as a new beginning, and as a radically different era from the medieval period before. Many scholars, including the nineteenth-century scholar Jacob Burckhardt, argue that the Renaissance was the first modern period, while the medieval period was a time of vast intellectual stupor.

These interpretations of medieval thought tended to be the dominant interpretations for many centuries beyond the Renaissance. There is a resurgence of interest in the Middle Ages today and a reevaluation of these interpretations. In contrast to Burckhardt and other scholars who would disparage the culture of the Middle Ages as lacking in vitality, creativity, and individuality, Charles Homer Haskins argued that there was a Renaissance of the twelfth-century that ran parallel to that of the Italian Renaissance. During the twelfth century, Haskins pointed out that there was an interest in the Greco-Roman culture just as there was in the later Italian Renaissance. Colin Morris, in *The Discovery of the Individual*, argued that such controversial and flamboyant figures as Peter Abelard clearly indicate an awareness of the individual. These two historians are representative of a historiographical school known as "the revolt of the medievalists." Paul Oscar Kristeller argued that the difference between medieval culture and that of the Renaissance was not as black and white as Burckhardt once suggested, and that the two eras were not to be separated on the basis of ideas about the individual or interest in Greco-Roman antiquity but rather on the basis of the disciplines they emphasized and in which they worked. The medieval scholastics emphasized natural theology, while the humanists of the Italian Renaissance emphasized rhetoric, ethics, and history.

These historiographical debates highlight the complexity of the medieval period, a period often referred to as "the crucible of Europe." During the Middle Ages, Europe rose from the ruins of the Roman Empire, and its legacy is still felt today.

THE BYZANTINE EMPIRE DURING THE EARLY MIDDLE AGES

While the western Roman world collapsed in the fifth century, the eastern Roman world remained intact. The eastern Roman world was known as Byzantium, after the name of the capital city there that Constantine later renamed Constantinople. During the sixth century c.e., the emperor **Justinian** attempted to reconquer the western Roman world. His general Belisarius defeated the Vandals in North Africa, and soon thereafter defeated the Ostrogoths, who had taken the Italian peninsula. By 552 c.e., Justinian had reconquered Spain, North Africa, and parts of Italy. General Belisarius took Ravenna in 540 c.e., and a church was built there commemorating Justinian's achievements. At Ravenna he is shown with a halo, suggesting his role as the supreme protector of the church. Justinian married a former actress, Theodora, who played an important role in the creation of laws. At that time, being an actress was considered a despicable profession akin to prostitution, but Theodora managed to wield considerable power. In fact, most of Justinian's accomplishments as a ruler occurred during her lifetime.

Justinian never managed to fully recapture the old outlines of Rome in the west, and his conquests were lost shortly after his death. One of Justinian's major achievements was the revision of Roman law in the *Corpus Iuris Civilis*, or Body of Civil Law. Justinian also codified the Digest, a collection of imperial decrees. His codification of Roman law was the basis for law in the Byzantine Empire until its collapse in 1453 c.e. Justinian also built the **Hagia Sophia**, or the Church of the Holy Wisdom. This church reflects the importance of religion for the Byzantines. Icons played a powerful role in the Greek Orthodox religion, and this image of Christ Pantocrator from the interior of the main dome was one of the most famous images of the Christ. After Justinian's death, the Byzantines had to fight off the Persians and the Slavs; neither of these threats was as serious as that posed by the converts to Islam, who defeated the Byzantines at Yarmuk in 636 c.e. The Muslims took Syria and Palestine from Byzantium. As the Muslims threatened the frontiers of Byzantium, a controversy over the use of images or icons broke

Christ Pantocrator, Hagia Sophia.

out. Muslims forbade the use of images in religious art, and many people began to wonder whether the use of images in art had led to the defeat of the Byzantines. During the Iconoclastic controversy, the Byzantine emperor attempted to abolish all images; the Byzantine people reacted violently, and eventually the emperor was forced to recant and once again allow the production of icons.

THE DEVELOPMENT OF THE MEDIEVAL EUROPEAN KINGDOMS

Anglo-Saxon England

The Romans withdrew from Britain in the fifth century C.E.; in the chaos that surrounded the Roman withdrawal, a hero emerged who in later times was known as **King Arthur**. Many sources do not even refer to this hero as Arthur, but rather as Ambrosius Aurelianus. It is doubtful whether anyone ever lived who did all the things legend credits to Arthur, but he became the symbol of the English monarchy in later centuries.

During the time of "Arthur," Saxons began to arrive in Britain. They settled in Kent, Wessex, and other kingdoms, and merged their culture with that of the native population, the Britons. Another group of people, the Picts, lived in the region now known as Scotland. Roman influences were felt once again in the sixth century, when **Pope Gregory the Great** decided to send a mission to Christianize the "barbarians" in Britain. Roman Catholicism arrived in Britain in 596 C.E., when Augustine of Canterbury landed in Kent and later converted its royal family. Roman Christianity spread to Northumbria, where the missionary Paulinus converted King Edwin. English monks and nuns helped to spread Christianity to the continent. The missionary Boniface traveled to Germany, where he was aided by the nun Leoba and countless other women. Women had considerable power in the Anglo-Saxon Church, and they very often presided as heads of double monasteries for men and women. Among the important monastic foundations of Anglo-Saxon England were Jarrow and Monkwearmoth, where the Venerable Bede spent his life. Bede was the first historian to use the Anno Domini (AD) system of dating, and in the eighth century C.E. wrote a monumental *History of the English Church and Peoples*. His history chronicled the conflict between Roman and Celtic customs, and its eventual resolution at the Synod of Whitby. Before the Synod of Whitby, Celtic Christianity flourished in the northern regions of the island at Lindisfarne and on Iona, off the coast of Scotland.

The greatest Anglo-Saxon ruler was Alfred the Great. In the ninth century, King Alfred defended Wessex and England from the Viking attacks. He had a number of important works translated from Latin into the Anglo-Saxon language.

The Franks and the Church

In 313 C.E., the emperor Constantine legalized Christianity through the Edict of Milan and gave the Christian church tax-exempt status. In 325 C.E., he resolved the Arian heresy, one of the first serious threats to the unity of the new Church, at the Council of Nicea. Constantine officiated at the council and even suggested the key word "homousion," which addressed the Arian claim that Christ was a creature and less than fully divine. Nevertheless, it was not until 381 C.E. that the Roman emperor of the west, Theodosius, proclaimed Christianity to be the state religion of Rome.

Despite its rapid progress in the fourth century from a persecuted religion to the official state religion of Rome, in the following centuries Christianity spread slowly throughout the Western world. Many Romans remained *pagani* for decades and centuries after the Theodosian Code. After the fall of Roman power in the west, the barbarian kings, such as Clovis of the Franks, along with scores of Christian monks and nuns, continued the conversion of Europe. In 500 C.E., **Clovis**, founder of the Merovingian Dynasty of the Franks, became the first barbarian to convert to Catholic Christianity. Other barbarian tribes, such as the Visigoths, had adopted Christianity, but followed the Arian heresy. Clovis's conversion, which was sealed through his marriage to the Christian princess Clotilda, was the beginning of an alliance between the Franks and the other strong power in Europe, the papacy.

Under the leadership of **Charles Martel**, Mayor of the Palace, the Franks defeated the Muslims at the Battle of Tours (Poitiers) in 732 C.E. This monumental victory was a turning point in European history; had Martel not defeated the Muslims, all of Europe might have been conquered. Further, Martel's son, Pepin the Short, was later able to transform his role as Mayor of the Palace into that of King of the Franks on the basis of his father's victory. While the barbarian Lombards besieged Rome, the pope turned to the Franks for military aid. In return for such aid, Pepin was anointed the king of the Franks by a papal legate. Pepin was not of royal blood, but even before Charles Martel, the Frankish kings had been inept, leaving the daily affairs of the kingdom to the Mayor of the Palace. When the papal legate anointed Pepin king through the approval of the pope, the suggestion was clearly made that papal approval could create a king even where there was no legitimate claim through blood. In return for this favor, Pepin carved out a tract of land across central Italy for the pope known as the Donation of Pepin. These estates would later be known as the **Papal States** and would play a central role in Renaissance politics. Pepin forged a new dynasty known as the Carolingian Dynasty after his son, **Charlemagne**.

Charlemagne and the Carolingian Renaissance

Charlemagne's Latin name was *Carolus magnus*, or Charles the Great, and by the time he died, he came close to reestablishing the frontiers of the Roman Empire in the west.

The Frankish emperor Charlemagne continued to support the church through reform of the educational system for priests, Benedict of Aniane's reform of the monastic life, and the forcible conversion of the Saxons in the ninth century. Charlemagne brought the monk Alcuin from Northumbria in England to help him in the reform of the clergy. Alcuin established a school at Aachen that revived the education of the priesthood and so addressed several issues of corruption in the church. Alcuin and his assistants developed a new style of writing, Carolingian miniscule, that helped to preserve the writings of the Greeks and Romans. Many manuscripts were in such a poor state that they were virtually illegible; Alcuin's monks helped to restore many texts that otherwise would have been lost. The revival of learning during Charlemagne's era was known as the Carolingian Renaissance. Einhard wrote a biography of Charlemagne that describes him as a man with a boisterous personality, a great love of meat and wine, and a great love of his "doves," or daughters, but above all else, a devotion to reforming the church. His court at Aachen was a center of education and church reform.

Charlemagne united his realm through the use of the *missi dominici*, who were messengers sent to proclaim his laws and report back to him on events throughout the realm. Through his capitularies, Charlemagne enforced military obligations, the *missi dominici* system, and the reform of the church.

The Campaigns Against the Basques and the Song of Roland

In 778 C.E., Charlemagne led an attack against the Basques, who were Christians, in northern Spain. During the campaign, his rear guard fell behind and was ambushed by the Basques. The leader of the rear guard was Count Roland, and the *Song of Roland*, which was written several hundred years later, commemorates the defeat of these troops. Charlemagne would later successfully conquer the Spanish March, a strip of land that he used as a buffer zone between the Kingdom of the Franks and Muslim Spain.

The Saxons

Charlemagne led several campaigns against the pagan **Saxons**. The Franks found the Saxon custom of leaving their dead out on funeral pyres offensive, as Christianity taught that the body would be resurrected. Since animals often ate the dead Saxon bodies, they believed this practice was an affront to Christian teachings. Over a thirty-year period, Charlemagne tried forcibly to convert the Saxons, and after each assault, the Saxons reverted to paganism as soon as his men withdrew. When the Saxons destroyed one of Charlemagne's forces in 782 C.E., he ordered his men to behead 4,500 Saxons. In 785 C.E. the Saxon leader Widukind surrendered and converted to Christianity, and thereafter Charlemagne made the relapse into paganism a crime against the state. He fortified his conquests by constructing a series of forts, endowing monasteries in Saxony, and deporting Saxons to Frankish areas while replacing them with Frankish nobles.

Conquest of Italy

Pepin had won control over large parts of Italy, but his conquests were already beginning to fall back into Lombard hands. Although Charlemagne had married one of the Lombard King Desiderius's daughters, he repudiated her, causing tension between the two kingdoms. The Lombard king began to support rebellious Frankish nobles against Charlemagne, leading him to attack the Lombards in 773 C.E. Charlemagne shuffled Desiderius off to a monastery, and proclaimed his own son king of Italy. Charlemagne, however, was for all intents of purposes the ruler of Italy. Charlemagne won the allegiance of the Roman Catholic pope in Rome for his victory; when, in 799 C.E., the pope was attacked in the streets, Charlemagne once again sent a contingent of forces to the rescue.

Coronation in 800 *c.e.*

In 800 C.E., while attending Christmas mass in Rome, the pope approached Charlemagne from behind and crowned him emperor of Rome in the west. Although the act did not have Charlemagne's approval, nevertheless it supported the tradition begun with Pepin that the pope anointed the emperor and so created his right to rule. Charlemagne sought to overturn this precedent by ceding his power to his son Louis the Pious before his death, but Louis would later ask the pope to crown him officially and thus further solidified the fusion between the medieval church and state.

The Treaty of Verdun and the Viking Raids

Strong monarchs like Clovis and Charlemagne, who conquered large areas of land had their empires dissolved as their sons quarreled and divided their fathers' holdings. Although Charlemagne had wanted to recreate the Roman Empire in the west, the **Treaty of Verdun** in 843 C.E. divided his empire between his three grandsons.

While his grandsons vied with each other for power, invaders ravaged Europe. Muslims invaded Sicily in 827 C.E. and controlled it for over a century. The Magyars traveled up the Danube River and plundered Bulgaria in 890 C.E. and in 906 C.E. ravaged Saxony. They raided Germany and other regions, and in 937 C.E., traveled as far inland as Rheims in France. The Scandinavians led by far the most threatening of these invasions from Norway, Denmark, and Sweden. One often hears these warriors referred to collectively as "**Vikings**," but in fact, they each had their own characteristics. Europeans called them the Norsemen, or Northmen. The Swedish Vikings ravaged Russia, and established outposts at Novgorod, a medieval Russian capital, and at Kiev, another capital during the Middle Ages. The Swedish Vikings were called the Varangians in Russia, and their center at Kiev was the first true Russian state.

In 787 C.E., the Norwegian and Danish Vikings reached England, and later sacked and burned the monasteries of Lindisfarne and Jarrow. In 841 C.E. Vikings traveled up the Seine in France and ravaged Rouen. In 843 C.E. they went up the River Loire and destroyed Nantes and slaughtered all the inhabitants. By 857 C.E. they had plundered Bordeux, Tours, Orleans, Poitiers, and Paris. In 885 C.E. the Vikings returned to Paris and laid siege to the city for two years.

In England the situation was even worse. The Vikings captured East

Anglia in 870 C.E. and in 876 C.E. occupied a good bit of Northumbria and then moved into Mercia in 877 C.E. Although King Alfred the Great successfully battled the Danes in Wessex, most of East Anglia, eastern Merica, and modern-day Lincolnshire and Yorkshire were controlled by the Vikings and became part of the Danelaw. Viking warriors reached Ireland in the ninth century and eventually attacked the famous monastery of Clonmacnois. The Vikings controlled the Isle of Man and the Scottish Isles until the mid-thirteenth century C.E.

In 874 C.E., the Vikings settled on Iceland, and then went on to Greenland. The king of Denmark ruled Iceland until 1944, and Greenland continues to be ruled by Denmark.

EMERGENCE OF THE MEDIEVAL MONARCHIES: FRANCE AND ENGLAND IN THE CENTRAL MIDDLE AGES

The medieval monarchies emerged during this chaotic period, and many grew out of the settlement of the Treaty of Verdun. The western section of Charlemagne's old territories became the kingdom of France. In 987 C.E., the last Carolingian ruler died, and the Frankish nobles selected Hugh Capet as king. The Capetians, however, never had the power of Charlemagne; although they were overlords of Normandy, Brittany, Burgundy, and Aquitaine, in reality they only controlled the small area of land around Paris known as the Ile-de-France. When William, Duke of Normandy, defeated Harold II of England at the **Battle of Hastings** and became the king of England in 1066, the French king was literally overshadowed by his vassal who was now a king in his own right. William's successors, most notably Henry II of England, gained control of much of the territories surrounding the Ile-de-France; these regions were known as the Angevin kingdom. King Philip II Augustus (1180–1223) won back control of many of these territories from Henry's weak son, King John of England. Philip IV "The Fair" (1285–1314) fought Pope Boniface VIII for control over the French church. In the fourteenth century, the tensions between France and England erupted in the Hundred Years' War. Such tensions within feudal society make it all the more remarkable that vestiges of feudal society survived in France until the French revolution in 1789.

EMERGENCE OF THE MEDIEVAL MONARCHIES: GERMANY IN THE CENTRAL MIDDLE AGES

The eastern section of Charlemagne's territories became the basis for Germany, which would not exist in its modern form until the age of Bismarck in the nineteenth century. The German monarchs, like the Frankish monarchs before them, forged strong alliances with the papacy. Otto I was crowned Emperor of Rome in 962 C.E. by a pope he had selected himself, Sylvester II. German emperors appointed many bishops and archbishops and exerted strong control over the church. In the eleventh century, the church's desire to rid itself of imperial control erupted in the Investiture Conflict. The reforming pope **Gregory VII** issued a decree in 1075 against lay investiture, or the practice of the German emperor, his princes, and nobles of investing clergy with their offices. The church insisted on the right to control selection of its bishops and archbishops. The German emperor Henry IV ignored the decree and continued to invest churchmen. Gregory VII excommunicated Henry; Henry, in turn, eventually appointed his own pope. The struggle waged on until the German nobles began to turn on Henry; in desperation, Henry went to Canossa where Gregory was in hiding and begged forgiveness while standing barefoot in the snow. The crisis was eventually resolved in 1122 by the Concordat of Worms, according to which the empire might still invest the cleric with his temporal benefice, while the church alone might invest them with the symbols of their spiritual office. A similar crisis occurred in England in the twelfth century when Thomas á Becket collided with Henry II over control of church affairs.

Later German emperors would experience some of the same difficulties with the church. The Hohenstaufen ruler Frederick I (1152–1190) attempted to build a holy empire by conquering northern Italy, but the Italian city-states defeated him in 1176. His idea of a "holy empire" was the origin of the description of the German empire as the Holy Roman Empire. As the witty Voltaire in the eighteenth century pointed out, the Holy Roman Empire was "neither holy, nor Roman, nor an empire." In fact, it was in many ways the papacy in Italy that conquered the Germans. Innocent III, the most powerful of all medieval popes, agreed to protect the four-year-old King Frederick II from rebellious Norman barons in Sicily. He guarded him for nine years and then continued to guide him as monarch in later life. Innocent III represents the zenith of papal power. Frederick II also tried to conquer northern Italy but was defeated. The German nobles developed considerable power over their own duchies, leaving the Holy Roman Emperor with little power of his own. The Protestant Reformation would further undermine the political structure of the Holy Roman Empire in the sixteenth century; in 1555 the Peace of Augsburg gave the German princes the power to choose either Catholicism or Lutheranism.

Medieval Russia

Olga, a Russian queen, visited Constantinople around 957 C.E. and was converted to Christianity. Although she requested missionaries from the

German ruler Otto I, most of Russia remained rooted in its pagan traditions. Her brutal grandson **Vladimir**, however, adopted Christianity largely out of political motives. Basil II, ruler of Byzantium from 976–1025, was having difficulty managing various rebellions, and he appealed for help to Russian King Vladimir. Although Vladimir already had several wives and at least 800 concubines, he demanded the hand of the emperor's sister, Anna, and also agreed to convert to Christianity. He later repudiated his pagan wives, and set upon abolishing paganism from Russia. Vladimir ordered the chief deity of the pagans, Perun, thrown in the River Dnieper; upon his command, thousands of Russians were baptized in the same river.

Eastern Europe

The native people, the Slavs, of eastern Europe suffered from the migrations of Asiatic nomads, such as the Huns, Bulgars, Avars, and Magyars. The Slavs were once a single group of people, but they later settled in western, southern, and eastern Europe forming three distinct groups. The western Slavs became the Polish and Bohemian kingdoms. By the tenth century, missionaries from Germany had converted both groups to Christianity. This group of Slavs adopted Roman Catholic Christianity. The southern Slavs, on the other hand, were more influenced by Greek Orthodox Christianity. Cyril and Methodius, two Byzantine missionaries who were brothers, converted the Moravians in the ninth century C.E. The Serbs converted to Greek Orthodox Christianity, as did the Bulgarians, who later conquered the Balkan peninsula. The Croats, on the other hand, converted to Roman Catholicism. The eastern Slavs settled in the region where the modern Ukraine and Russia are located. The Vikings called the eastern Slavs "the Rus," and this is the origin of the modern name of Russia. Hungary was not a Slavic nation, but it adopted Christianity after the tenth century C.E.

Medieval Culture: Feudal Society

During the reign of Charlemagne, a system of landholding and obligations began to develop in Europe that is often referred to as "**feudalism**." Historians prefer the term "feudal society" to describe the complex social, economic, and political relationships that characterized Europe from the ninth century through the French Revolution, which began in 1789. Historians now avoid the term "feudalism," because it implies that there was a single set of features shared by all western European medieval cultures. This is anything but the case, as life in feudal France differed greatly from that of the feudal Germanies or other locations.

Feudal society was based upon private contracts, and the historian Joseph Strayer has described medieval feudal society as having had three main characteristics:

- public power was held in private hands
- power was fragmented
- armed forces were used to obtain and keep power

In order to understand these three characteristics, one must first understand the system of **fief holding** and **investiture** during medieval times. Land was the basis of the feudal economy; with enough land, one could support oneself, a household, and retainers to protect one's holdings. Though there were coins and other forms of currency minted during the Middle Ages, the medieval economy was not based primarily on monetary exchange but rather on barter.

In order to survive in a world based on warfare, a king or lord needed vassals or knights. In order to be a knight, one had to be wealthy. The training of a knight was lengthy and costly; the suit of armor he wore was also very expensive. It has been estimated that the cost of making and owning a suit of armor in the Middle Ages was equivalent to the cost of purchasing a home today. It could take up to two years to make the suit of mail, often called chain mail; it was made by hand and each link was riveted to other links. Further, the battle horse was a costly animal to acquire and to feed and train.

In order to obtain a vassal, then, a lord had to supply the vassal with the means to maintain his profession; in medieval times, that was only possible through the gift of a plot of land known as a fief. A knight or vassal was "invested" with his fief, in return for which he pledged homage (from the French word *l'homme* for "man") to his lord. A vassal was required to fight when his lord demanded it and to ransom his lord if captured on the battlefield. Because vassals became powerful in their own right, a vassal had to seek the permission of the lord before his daughters could marry or before he himself could enter into such a contract. Marriage was often used as a tool to gain political, social, and economic power in the Middle Ages; hence, the right marriage could propel a vassal to greater status than his lord if allowed to occur unchecked. For example, when Henry II of England married Eleanor of Aquitaine, he gained the duchy of Acquitaine and began to amass the territories known as the Angevin kingdom in France.

The agreement between lord and vassal was of a personal nature, and often resulted in conflicts within the feudal system. For example, a knight might have more than one lord and those two lords might wage war on one another, both demanding the services of the knight. Such situations eventually created *liege homage*, where the vassal pledged homage to a particular lord above all others. A vassal of a lord might also divide the fief received and so create his own vassals. This process was called *subinfeudation*.

Those who had the most vassals and were the most successful on the battlefield held power. There was virtually no concept of public power, in the Middle Ages, such as exists in the modern United States. During the reign of the Frankish kings, the territory the kings conquered was the kingdom of the Franks; there was no stable center, as the king's court moved wherever the battles were. The mayor of the palace, a chief officer in the king's personal household, was the one who often ran state affairs on a daily basis. The kingdom of the Franks, then, was considered the property of the one who held the position of king.

Daily Life in the Middle Ages

Medieval agriculture relied on the **rotation system**, where one-third of the land lay fallow every year to allow the land to recover needed nutrients. The diet of the Middle Ages was based primarily on bread and vegetables; peasants consumed very little meat. Land was cultivated on vast manorial estates, which were divided into the lord's *demesne*, or area of land reserved for the lord, and tracts reserved for peasants. The free peasants and serfs, peasants who were bound to the land for life, worked the lord's *demesne* in return for their tract of land. They were required to return to the lord a percentage of the harvest on their lands. The crops could be milled in the village on the estate for a fee to the lord. The system of agriculture and serfdom on the manorial estates created a very localized economy in the Middle Ages. Whereas the Roman Empire thrived on the city, the heart of medieval Europe was the manorial estate.

Peasants lived very difficult lives. Peasants and serfs owed the lord a certain number of days of work per month on the land in return for the use of a tract of land for their own crops. Peasants and serfs had to give the lord a percentage of their harvests, pay fees for the use of the village mill, and seek the permission of the lord to marry off their daughters. Peasants and serfs could not move up the social ladder easily during the Middle Ages. The social hierarchy was generally rigid and based upon status determined by birth.

Medieval Culture: Christian Monasticism

The conversion of Clovis and the subsequent support of the Franks and later the German emperor helped to spread Christianity. As we have seen in the case of Alcuin at the court of Charlemagne, monks and also nuns played an important role in the spread of Christianity. When the Roman Empire in the west collapsed, it was the church that filled the vacuum. The early church in Europe had been organized along the same lines as the Roman Empire. The dioceses and archdioceses of the church had been modeled after the same structures in the empire.

The Desert Hermits and Eremitical Monasticism

Monasticism was an important social, economic, and religious force in Europe. The word "monasticism" is derived from the Greek word "monos," meaning single or alone. The earliest form of the monastic life was in the desert around the Nile River in Egypt, and was inspired by the meditative life of Christ himself in the desert. As Christ had no wife or permanent dwelling, so early desert hermits gave up the world of men in favor of the life of prayer. St. Anthony the Great spent twenty years in a cave along the Nile battling his inner demons, and so influenced his age that it was said the desert literally became a city teeming with monks. The lifestyle lived by Anthony and other monks like him is called "**eremitical**." The desert lifestyle was a very disciplined lifestyle of prayer and fasting, and this discipline of the body and spirit is known as asceticism. John Cassian, a monk who spent several years in the great desert foundation of Scete along the Nile and who traveled widely through the great foundations of the east, transmitted the wisdom of the desert hermits to Europe. His conversations with the desert monks were preserved and spread throughout Europe in his *Conferences*.

Cenobitic Monasticism

Although the eremitical lifestyle was the most influential form of monasticism along the Nile after the legalization of Christianity, in medieval Europe **cenobitic** monasticism was more common. St. Basil of Caesarea was the first to question the isolation of the eremitical life and its consistency with the Christian belief in love of one's neighbor. Basil advocated a form of monasticism called the cenobitic lifestyle. It is based on the "rule" of community and the idea of progressing in holiness through one's relationship with others. Another famous founder of cenobitic communities was Pachomius, whose monastery in Thebes along the Nile had over 1,300 men.

St. Benedict of Nursia

The cenobitic monastic life in Europe was largely modeled on the Rule of St. Benedict of Nursia. Benedict was born in 480 C.E. in Nursia, Italy, in the midst of the collapse of the western Roman Empire. He studied in Rome and found it decadent. As a result, he sought out a spiritual teacher and later became a hermit at Subiaco whose holiness attracted followers. Benedict eventually founded the monastery of Monte Casino in 529 C.E., and it became a symbol of the Christian era.

The success of Monte Casino was largely due to Benedict's genius as expressed in his Rule for monastic life. Although much of it is not original and resembles an earlier document known as the Rule of the Master, Benedict tempered the master's harshness and adapted the regulations found in it to individual circumstances. Benedictines vow obedience, stability, and conversion to the monastic way. The Benedictine day involved work, study, and prayer. The ethos of work, study, and prayer colored all of medieval European culture. Through work Benedictines practiced stewardship of the earth, and they were instrumental in reclaiming vast amounts of wasteland in

Europe as well as in developing new crops. Through study the Benedictines preserved many ancient Greek and Roman manuscripts as they copied texts for one-third of their day. Prayer permeated the Benedictine day, as work and study were simply another expression of the prayerful life.

According to tradition, Benedict's twin sister Scholastica lived at the foot of Monte Casino. Scholastica is the patroness of modern Benedictine nuns. Gregory the Great's biography of Benedict painted him as a new hero for a new age. The many Benedictines who helped to convert Europe, including the monk Boniface and the nun Leoba, who came from England and converted the Germans, carried on the legacy of Benedict and Scholastica.

Celtic Monks

In Europe before the reign of Charlemagne, monasteries often mixed parts of the Rule of St. Benedict with that of Columbanus, an Irish monk whose travels established many of the most famous houses in Europe such as Bobbio. Irish monks, who lived a very ascetic lifestyle not based on the Rule of Benedict, traveled widely and were very instrumental in the spread of monasticism and in christianizing the pagan world. Irish monks from Iona christianized Northumbria in England. **Lindisfarne** is a famous monastery in Northumbria founded by Irish monks, and these monks produced the Lindisfarne Gospels.

Benedict of Aniane and Reform of Monastic Life

Monastic life was revised and reformed on many occasions. In various ages, corruption became a problem. In the reign of Charlemagne, the monk Benedict of Aniane reformed monastic life and mandated the Rule of St. Benedict for all monasteries.

Cluny

In the tenth century, the monastery of Cluny was founded and made subject not to the local overlords, but only to the pope to escape the problems and obligations of feudal society. The Cluniac life was largely devoted to liturgy, and the Cluniacs became fabulously wealthy through donations from nobles.

THE CENTRAL MIDDLE AGES

In the eleventh century, **Pope Gregory VII** began to centralize the church, culminating in the Investiture Crisis, and scholars such as Gratian and Ivo of Chartres worked to reform canon law. Other scholars applied logic to theology, creating the movement known as Scholasticism. St. Anselm of the monastery of Bec believed that reason and faith could be harmonized and formulated one of the most famous proofs for the existence of God, which Kant later called the Ontological argument. **Peter Abelard** first made

Page from the Lindisfarne Gospels, c. 700 C.E.

his reputation as a logician who challenged powerful teachers of his era. He created more controversy when his application of logic to theology resulted in several heretical works, such as his famous *Ethica or Know Thyself*, in which he argued that sin could only come from consent to what is against the will of God. Therefore, there could be no original sin, and those who crucified Christ were not guilty of sin. Abelard believed the Greeks and Hebrews had foreshadowed Trinitarian belief, another aspect of his work that was considered heretical. Abelard also became controversial when his affair with Heloise (Abelard's student and the niece of wealthy canon Fulbert) became public. They had a child together, Astrolabe, and Heloise's uncle had Abelard castrated in revenge. Abelard and Heloise both entered monasteries, and several years later began a famous exchange of letters. Abelard wandered from monastery to monastery, but founded the Paraclesis, a monastery that he later donated to Heloise and her sisters from the monastery of Argenteuil. Heloise was one of the most learned women of her time and became the most famous abbess of the Central Middle Ages. Abelard was condemned at the council of Sens two years before he died. He spent the last two years of his life in a Cluniac daughter house and remains today a symbol of the questioning intellect. Abelard is representative of the new schools of the Central Middle Ages, which were not in monasteries, but in cathedrals. The schoolmen, or scholastics, were those who taught in such schools. **Thomas Aquinas** was the most famous scholastic theologian, and he wrote the *Summa Theologia*, which contains his famous five ways of proving God's existence.

During the Central Middle Ages, the Gothic style of architecture first appeared at the abbey of St. Denis in France. Abelard entered this monastery after his disastrous affair with Heloise. The Abbot Suger first developed the soaring ceilings, stained glass, and flying buttresses of the Gothic style to express his theology of light, the idea that light symbolized the divine presence. Gothic cathedrals such as Chartres and Notre Dame in France are designed to allow as much light in as possible, and their stained glass windows are justifiably famous throughout the world.

The Central Middle Ages was a period of tremendous intellectual vitality. While early scholastics, such as Abelard, developed new theological views, visionaries, such as Hildegard of Bingen, wrote prolifically. Hildegard claimed to experience visions from a young age, but only began to write about them in her forties. She wrote in many areas, including theology, music, and medicinal works. Her chant is some of the most beautiful ever written, and it requires a tremendous vocal range difficult for performers to achieve today. Hildegard was an outspoken critic of the papacy and a promoter of reform.

The Cistercians

The spirit of reform also spread to monastic life. Robert of Molesme, a monk of St. Benedict, wanted to return to the pristine origins of the Rule of Benedict and left his position as abbot of Molesme for a wilderness retreat far from civilization. There he founded a new monastery, the *novum monasterium*, at Citeaux. Eventually, his followers expanded and formed a new order of monks, the **Cistercians**, who lived strictly according to the Rule. The Cistercians interpreted the Rule literally. They revived the manual labor component of monastic life and forbade the use of gold and silver items in their churches. Their monks wore clothes made of harsh white wool to avoid the distraction of color and comfortable clothes, and so they became known as the "white monks," while Benedictines who were not Cistercians were known as the "black monks." So austere was Cistercian life that they avoided color in their stained glass windows, using only monochromatic shades of gray. As the Cistercians expanded, they admitted lay brothers to work their fields. The Rule forbade travel further than one could return in a day, and as their estates grew, they needed workers to manage them so that the monks could continue to pray the liturgy of the word. These lay brethren were known as *conversi*, and they were able to share in the prayer life of the monastery even if they were not able to be choir monks. Vocations in the Cistercian order were becoming so popular that in the minds of some historians, "all Europe become Citeaux." Yet the ideals of the Cistercians, too, evolved over time.

The Impact of Church Reform in the West on the Roman and Greek Churches

By the eleventh century C.E., the western popes were growing stronger in their insistence that the pope in Rome had supremacy over the other patriarchs. This increasing insistence on papal supremacy eventually led the Greek Orthodox Church, led by the Patriarch of Constantinople, to separate from the Roman Catholic Church. In addition to the issue of papal supremacy, various other theological issues were at stake. The Greeks rejected the "filoque" clause from the Nicene creed, which says that the Holy Spirit proceeds "from the father and the son." The Byzantines maintained the Holy Spirit proceeds only from the Father.

The Crusades

The Byzantines had been defeated by the Muslims in the seventh century, and the onslaught of the Islamic Turks continued when in 1071 C.E. they defeated the Byzantines at Manzikert. In 1095 C.E., the emperor Alexius called upon Pope Urban II to send assistance. Urban offered an indulgence to all those who would go on **crusade**. Before the western powers could even gather their official forces, a people's crusade led by Peter the Hermit left for the Holy Land, sacking and pillaging towns in their way, and massacring thousands of Jews. Eventually, thousands of western knights followed suit. Although crusading knights from western Europe came to the east in an effort to support the Byzantine cause, their presence caused greater disruptions as they carved out kingdoms for themselves. Alexius's daughter, Anna Comnena, left an account of the first crusade and the arrival of the western knights. She found their behavior barbaric, as did many of the Muslims with whom they battled. The western knights reached Jerusalem in 1099 and massacred many of its inhabitants, including women and children.

Four crusader states were created from the spoils of victory, but quickly the Muslims fought back.

The Latin Crusader state of Edessa fell in 1144 C.E., prompting the Cistercian monk Bernard of Clairvaux to preach the Second Crusade. Many have criticized Bernard for his active involvement in politics, but his words fueled another crusade. This crusade was an endeavor of kings. Pious King Louis VII of France led this crusade, but it was ultimately unsuccessful.

In 1187 C.E. the Muslims recaptured Jerusalem from the Christian knights, which inspired the Third Crusade. Richard the Lionheart, son of Henry II of England, left on the crusade along with Frederick Barbarosa of Germany and Philip II Augustus of France. Barbarosa, or "red beard," had a dream that he would die at sea and so decided to cross by land; ironically, he drowned while crossing a river and never arrived at his destination. Richard the Lionheart fought bravely during the Third Crusade, especially at Jaffa and Acre, but was not successful in his quest to conquer Jerusalem. He did, however, negotiate a settlement allowing Christian access to Jerusalem with Saladin, who had captured the city in 1187 C.E. following the famous battle at the Horns of Hattin.

Saladin died in 1193 C.E., and the powerful Pope Innocent III called the Fourth Crusade. During the Fourth Crusade in 1205 C.E., the western knights sacked the Christian city of Constantinople. The Byzantines did not recapture their city until 1261 C.E. If Alexius had known what he initiated in 1095 C.E., he might never have asked Urban II for help. In the end, the Muslims pressed on, and the Latin knights left the Holy Land. Several other unsuccessful crusades followed, but in 1453 C.E., the Islamic Turks conquered the once mighty city of Constantinople and converted Justinian's Hagia Sophia into an Islamic mosque. Today the city is known as Istanbul.

The Crusades had the effect of creating ill will between Christians and Muslims, and their lasting negative effect can still be seen today in the Middle East. Crusader castles still dot the landscape of the Middle East, a vivid reminder to modern Muslims of their mistreatment at the hands of the Christian knights. Many new religious orders were founded for knights, such as the Templars and the Knights of St. John, or the Hospitalers. This new kind of warrior knight lived like a monk but fought like a knight, and their orders amassed great fortunes during the Crusades. The Templars owned vast estates in Europe, including some of the most famous vineyards, but were eventually dissolved by the French monarch Philip IV, who desired to acquire their vast holdings. The Hospitalers eventually relocated to Malta, where they continue to have a presence today.

The Central Middle Ages were a period of reform, change, and vast movement of peoples from west to east. The cultural exchanges between the European, Byzantine, and Islamic worlds continue to have an impact on today's cultures.

CHAPTER 17

THE LATE MIDDLE AGES

During the fourteenth century, often called the "century of woe" or the "calamitous fourteenth century," the **Black Death** cycled throughout Europe, the **Hundred Years' War** began, and the papacy grew more corrupt. Ironically, the "century of woe" broke down the medieval worldview and paved the way for the cultural, economic, social, and political shifts of the early modern period symbolized by the growth of Humanism during the Renaissance.

The Calamitous Fourteenth Century: The Black Death

Origins of the Plague

Rumors of a great pestilence that started in China and spread to India, Persia, Syria, Mesopotamia, and Egypt had reached western Europe by 1346. The traditional view was that the plague originated in the Gobi desert in China in the 1320s and that the migrations of the Mongol hordes brought the long-dormant bacterium from the remote desert into contact with various centers of civilization. From here it spread from the east to the west via trade routes. Scholars have suggested that when the Mongols catapulted dead bodies infected with plague into the Genoese stronghold at the port of Caffa, the fleeing Genoese sailors carried the plague with them to Europe as they fled the Mongol attack and landed at Messina on the island of Sicily, where the plague then spread to Europe.

Recently, some scholars have suggested that reports of the great pestilence in China were not necessarily reports of the plague, but rather reports of death and disease from famine, drought, and other causes now thought to have begun in the 1330s. Since the plague appeared in India in 1346, some scholars think the events in China in the 1330s were too early to have been the cause.

Cause of the Plague

The cause of the plague was the bacterium *Yersinia pestis*, which is transmitted by fleas carried by rats. The rat was very plentiful in medieval Europe. Every household was infested with brown rats; rats inhabited the beams of houses and especially the family hearth. Medieval families lived with their animals; a typical house had an area for the animals and another for the family. Sanitation in the towns was also problematic, as families disposed of their waste by throwing it into the narrow streets. All of these customs attracted a sizeable rat population. Black rats were present on every ship and often survived even when the crew did not. When a ship docked, the rats would scurry down the ropes that tied the ship to the dock, go into the town, and then into the homes of the population.

It was not the rats that actually caused the Black Death, but rather the fleas they carried. Fleas ingested the bacilli, bit human hosts, and then vomited the bacilli into the human bloodstream. The sizeable population of rats brought an even more sizeable population of fleas into Europe.

The word "bubonic" comes from the Greek word for groin, *boubon*. One of the first signs that someone had been infected with the plague was a blackish purple pustule at the site of a flea bite, which would swell and become very tender. It could grow as large as an egg. Subcutaneous hemorrhaging caused the skin to appear black. The victim's nervous system began to collapse, causing dreadful pain and neurological disorders.

There were three forms of the plague: bubonic plague, in which an infected flea bites a person or when materials contaminated with *Yersinia pestis* enter through a break in a person's skin; pneumonic plague, in which the bacillus invades the lungs; and septicemic plague, in which the bacillus enters the bloodstream.

Controversy over the Plague Today

Some modern scholars have suggested that the disease that spread throughout Europe in the fourteenth century was not the plague, but rather the ebola or some other hemorrhagic virus. Others have suggested it was anthrax. By far the most convincing thesis remains that the plague was caused by *Yersinia pestis*, as recent excavations of graves in Europe show the bacilli in the pulp of teeth. However, in some parts of Europe, as in Iceland, no rat bones are found in appropriate layers, suggesting that there may have been more than one disease at work.

The Transmission of the Plague in Europe

The plague spread primarily along the major trade routes of Europe. Modern historians estimate that somewhere around twenty-five million people, representing anywhere from one-fifth to as many as fifty percent of the population of Europe, died of the plague in the fourteenth century. Since the medieval world had no accurate census, it is very difficult to state with accuracy the number of victims.

Although the plague itself was deadly, its impact was made worse by the fact that the climate had become progressively colder in the fourteenth century, causing disastrous results for crops. The population had also increased by 2.5 times. When the plague erupted in Europe, the population was at its highest point in many decades, while the food supply was at its lowest point. The population was weakened by famine. Then, when the plague struck, its effects increased dramatically. The population of Europe would not reach its pre-plague levels again until the beginning of the sixteenth century.

One can only imagine the horror of life in medieval Europe from 1347 to 1350. Most historians argue that the plague first erupted in Europe at Messina, a town on the island of Sicily. A ship docked there with the disease, and although it was quarantined, the rats with their fleas nevertheless managed to escape onto the island. Within two months, half of the population of Messina was dead. Another Genoese ship was reported to have carried the disease to Marseilles in 1348. By 1350, the plague had traveled through France, England, Scotland, and Ireland to the northernmost parts of Europe, including Sweden, Denmark, Norway, Prussia, Iceland, and Greenland. When Norwegian sailors finally returned to Greenland again in the early fifteenth century, they found only wild cattle roaming through the deserted villages.

Reactions to the Plague and Popular Remedies

The plague affected people in more ways than the mere physical. So many people died that disposal of the bodies became a problem. In Italy, a group of people known as the *becchini* hired themselves out to carry away the dead; they terrorized the population, and were known to extort them on the threat of carrying them away with the piles of dead bodies.

In Milan, Italy, citizens walled up all the occupants of a house in which there was a victim and left them to die. **Boccaccio** tells us in the *Decameron* that people abandoned their families in order to survive, fleeing to the countryside to escape the plague. Medical knowledge in the fourteenth century was scant. No one understood that it was a bacterium that caused the plague, much less that rats and fleas transmitted it.

The medievals still practiced medicine according to Galen's theories of disease, according to which disease spread by miasmas, or poisonous vapors that corrupted the air. The faculty of the University of Paris, who argued that the plague was the result of the conjunction of the planets Saturn, Mars, and Jupiter in the fortieth degree of Aquarius at 1 P.M. on March 20, 1435, gave the most "scientific" view of the day. This conjunction of planets had corrupted the atmosphere. People attempted not to breathe the air, either by breathing in noxious fumes, or in some cases, by holding their noses and carrying flowers to avoid breathing atmospheric air. According to legend, this latter custom was the origin of the children's folk tune "Ring around the rosie, pocket full of posies, ashes, ashes, they all fall down." Although the tune does not seem to appear before 1881 in literature, nevertheless, popular custom credits its origin to the plague era. The "ring around the rosie" refers to the ring around the initial flea bite; the "pocket full of posies" to the custom of carrying flowers to avoid breathing the fumes; and the "ashes, ashes, they all fall down" to the many deaths that occurred as a result of the plague. Sometimes the line "A tishoo, a tishoo" replaces "ashes, ashes," and may refer to the sneezing that would have characterized early stages of the pneumonic plague.

Flagellants

Many Europeans believed that the plague was due to human sinfulness. In Germany, a penitential movement began in 1348 known as the Brethren of the Cross, or the **Brotherhood of the Flagellants**. The flagellants paraded throughout Germany and other parts of Europe in groups from 200 to 300 to as large as 1,000 in some cases. The penitents beat themselves with leather thongs tipped with metal studs as atonement for sins. They continued the rituals for thirty-three days and eight hours, one day for every year of the life of Christ. Without the use of antibiotics, many must have died before the end of their thirty-three-day pilgrimage. The flagellants might have been partly responsible for the further transmission of the plague.

The most interesting aspect of the movement was its anti-clericalism. The flagellants in Germany denounced the Catholic Church hierarchy, and refused to take the Eucharist. They interrupted masses, drove priests from churches, and even looted church property. The anti-clerical behavior of the Brethren indicated a strong foundation of resentment towards the church well before Luther began his work in the sixteenth century.

The flagellant movement spread from Germany through Hungary, Poland, Flanders, and the Low Countries. Inevitably, the anti-clericalism of the movement turned the church against it. In 1349, Pope Clement VI issued a papal bull condemning the group for their contempt of church practices.

Persecution of Jews

Among other things, the denunciation in 1349 also condemned the flagellants for persecuting Jews. The treatment of Jews and other minorities during the Black Death was one of the many tragedies associated with the era. While Arabs, lepers, and other minorities were accused of bringing the plague, it was by far the Jews who suffered the most. In Germany in particular, the Jews were the money-lending class. They had attained this status primarily because they had been ousted from civil and military functions and prohibited from owning land or working as artisans. Many Jews had large numbers of people indebted to them. This created tension. The church prohibited usury, or the loaning of money to others with interest.

Further, since the Jews were associated with those who persecuted the historic Christ, Jews were often blamed for every ill in society. People argued that Jews poisoned their wells, and that brought about the plague. In point of fact, the Jews had a greater understanding of hygiene, and so avoided the polluted public wells. Their dietary and cooking practices also helped spare them from the transmission of the plague; they appeared to die in far fewer numbers than did the rest of the population. All of these facts created a sense of near hysteria against the Jews.

Whether the Jews survived in greater numbers or not, prejudice against them created a wave of persecutions that would not again be equaled until the twentieth-century Third Reich. At Speyer in Germany, bodies of murdered Jews were put in wine casks and floated down the Rhine River. Some chronicles suggest that as many as 16,000 Jews died in Strasbourg. A total of 350 massacres took place. Over sixty large Jewish communities were exterminated, and 150 smaller communities were also depopulated. The Jewish population shifted in Europe. Today, there are large communities of Jews in Poland and Lithuania, where many persecuted Jews of the fourteenth century fled. It is tragic that in the midst of such torturous physical suffering, the cruelty of humans towards their fellows nearly matched the horrors of the plague itself.

Impact of the Plague on Art, Society, Economy, and Politics

In the wake of the Black Death, the shortage of workers created a demand for higher wages and prices. Peasants' revolts occurred throughout Europe, the most famous being the **Peasants' Revolt** in England in 1381 and the Revolt of the Jacquerie in 1356. In England, Way Tyler and John Ball led the peasants against nobles and the church. Many historians maintain that the plague weakened the feudal system by creating a shortage of labor.

Corruption also increased in the church, as priests, bishops, and other officials died in great numbers. Many who had no particular vocation or calling to the priesthood entered the ranks of the church. The Dominican order, for example, prided itself on learning, but was forced to admit many uneducated brothers into the order. The decline of learning in the church perhaps contributed to the rise of superstition and heresy prior to the Reformation; it helped to create the conditions that led Martin Luther and other reformers of the sixteenth century to attempt to reform and later to separate from the Catholic Church.

Art reflected the omnipresence of death in medieval Europe in the fourteenth and fifteenth centuries. Art became more stilted, less naturalistic, and more focused on death. The art of Sienna, Italy, in particular, is very dark and gloomy.

The *Danse macabre* also became an important cultural phenomenon in Europe following the Black Death. *Macabre* describes the interaction of the dead or death with the living. The dance of death first originated as a set of frescoes at the Cimetière des Innocents in Paris in 1424, and other examples are later found on cemeteries, family vaults, and churches throughout Europe. Death appears as a skeleton chastising sinners for wanton sexual practice, excessive riches, and other sins. Kings and emperors were chastised no less than ordinary people. Even the leaders of the church were not exempt.

Death reigned triumphant in European art and culture in the wake of the Black Death. In 1490 Hieronymous Bosch painted *Death and the Miser,* an allegory about life and death in which the miser must make a choice between the crucifix and a purse full of riches given to him by a devil. In *The Four Knights of the Apocalypse* (1498), Albrecht Dürer portrayed four riders that represent, from left to right, Death, Famine, Discord, and War. An angel watches while the last three figures tread on men and women from all social classes. Death rides a skeletal horse and throws a bishop in the mouth of a dragon emerging from the bowels of the Earth.

Hieronymous Bosch,
Death and the Miser, 1490.

Epilogue: The Plague in Europe and the World After the Fourteenth Century

By 1350, the plague had reached the northern frontiers of Europe. Although it subsided in the 1350s, the plague continued to cycle throughout Europe for the next 300 years. The plague struck several times in the fourteenth century, and other outbreaks occurred in Europe in the fifteenth and sixteenth centuries. In 1665, there was a last outbreak of plague in London. Over 1,000 people died each week during the outbreak of 1665. When the plague finally subsided, there were over 68,576 deaths reported in London alone. Modern historians think the figure is more likely around 100,000.

In 1666, the Great Fire occurred in London, killing off the large black rat population. Many argue that the death of the black rat and its subsequent replacement by the brown rat led to the gradual decline of outbreaks of the plague in Europe.

The plague recurred in Marseilles in 1720, and in the Balkans from 1770 to 1772. Outbreaks have been reported in China, Hong Kong, Manchuria, and, most recently, in 1994, in the Indian city of Surat in the state of Gujarat. There are reports of between 1,000 to 3,000 cases of the plague every year in regions such as Africa, Asia, and South America. There continue to be isolated cases of the plague in the rural areas of the United States, where ten to fifteen people per year are reported infected. It has been estimated that over forty percent of the land in the United States is infested with animals carrying the plague.

Many scholars argue that the Black Death has been with humans for centuries prior to the outbreak in the fourteenth century. The plague struck Pelusium, Egypt, in 540 C.E. and reached Constantinople in 542 C.E. Procopius of Caesarea described the plague that ravaged Byzantium in 542 C.E. During the next ten years, the disease, then called "the plague of Justinian," spread into Europe and Asia. Some historians think the disease that killed the ancient Athenians while they were under siege by Spartans in the Peloponnesian War was the plague. Some even maintain that many instances of "plagues" in the Bible might have been the Black Death. Just as historians and scientists hotly debate the exact cause of the reported deaths and symptoms of the fourteenth century, so, too, they debate the identification of these other historic events with *yersinia pestis*. The medievals regarded the Black Death as a mysterious visitor; in many ways, the modern world continues to regard the historic instances of outbreak as mysteries that science and history have yet to resolve.

THE DECLINE OF THE CHURCH IN THE LATE MIDDLE AGES

King Philip IV and Pope Boniface VIII

The fourteenth century was also a time of crisis for the church. One of the most notorious of all medieval popes was **Boniface VIII**, whose papacy was affected by preparations for the Hundred Years' War. King Philip IV (The Fair) of France and then-King Edward of England were preparing for war and were forced to raise money by taxing the clergy. In 1296,

Boniface VIII issued a papal bull in protest of the taxation of the clergy, *Clericis Laicos*, which forbade clergy in any state to pay taxes to a prince or monarch without the consent of the pope. Boniface was attempting to assert the church's independence from the state and its right to govern itself.

Unfortunately, he chose the wrong monarch with whom to wrestle. In response to the bull, Philip IV banned exports of gold and silver from France, cutting off the flow of money to Rome. Boniface recanted the bull, but Philip continued to interfere in church politics, charging a French bishop with heresy. Heresy was an issue that the church should determine.

Boniface believed that the independence of clergy was again at stake and promptly reissued the basic doctrine behind the bull *Clericis Laicos*. King Philip IV summoned the estates general, who declared Boniface a heretic. In response, Boniface excommunicated Philip and then issued another bull in 1302, *Unam Sanctam. Unam Sanctam* rejected the famous "theory of two swords," which maintained that there were two separate spheres of power, the church and the state. Boniface, in contrast, argued that while there may be two swords, they were both to be put in the same sheath. That sheath was the church.

In one of history's most memorable remarks, Philip told Boniface that "your weapons are theory, mine are fact." He then hired one of the most well-known henchmen to kidnap Boniface at Anagni, and he was tortured and then released. Although he was apparently not seriously hurt, he died soon afterwards. Some would maintain that he died more of the shame of defeat rather than the torture itself.

The Babylonian Captivity

With Boniface out of the way, the French elected their own pope, Clement V, who moved with his curia to Avignon. The papacy at Avignon was clearly a pawn of the French monarch. During the Hundred Years' War, the English refused to pay the Peter's Pence, an annual tithe directly to the papacy. To have done so would have been to further fuel the power of the French to resist their campaigns. Over ninety percent of the cardinals elected during the time the pope resided in Avignon were French. The popes lived in lavish luxury here, constructing an enormous palace. The papacy remained at Avignon until 1378, a period of seventy-three years. The phrase "Babylonian Captivity" builds upon imagery associated with the period during which the ancient Hebrews were in captivity in Babylon. Just as the Hebrews were literally held captive, so Martin Luther and other later Protestant reformers would argue the Roman Catholic Church was held captive during the Avignonese papacy.

The Great Schism

In 1377, Pope Gregory XI moved the curia back to Rome and died shortly thereafter in 1378. To counter French control of the papacy, the cardinals elected an Italian to replace him, Pope Urban VI. However, the French cardinals later challenged the election and voted Clement VII the new pope. Clement VII resided in Avignon, while Urban continued to reside in Rome. So began the **Great Schism**. As the Hundred Years' War raged on, the states of Europe were divided in their papal loyalties largely based upon which side they supported, the English or the French.

Popular resentment of the church grew during the Avignonese papacy and the later Great Schism. In 1324, Marsilius of Padua wrote the *Defensor Pacis* and published it anonymously. According to Marsilius of Padua, all power resides in the people. The people delegate authority to a legislator, or king. The state has complete authority and delegates power over spiritual matters to the church. Within the church, Marsilius argued that the councils had supreme authority, and that the pope's claim to coercive power over the state disrupted Christendom. The pope consequently had spiritual authority only, and that only on the authority of the state. According to Marsilius, ultimate authority rests with the state.

John Wycliffe, an Englishman, argued that all Christians were equal. He also stated that monarchs should be able to tax the church, as these were temporal affairs. He insisted that practices be based solely on the Bible as a standard and insisted that the church should return to its simple teachings. His insistence on biblical authority was certainly an outgrowth of the uncertainty surrounding papal status and the obvious corruption of the Avignonese papacy and the Schism; it was also very similar to the later Protestant insistence on *sola scriptura*, or the Bible alone as authoritative versus the traditions of the church. Wycliffe criticized the doctrine of the real presence in the Eucharist and challenged the efficacy of confession. He attacked the Church itself as corrupt, arguing that "dominion is founded in grace," and that those who sin lose the dominion given to them by God. This included the church as well as the temporal overlords. Wycliffe issued these doctrines immediately before the Peasant's Revolt in 1381; in the wild outbreak of passion following the revolt, the church was even more alarmed about his teaching. The church regarded many of his teachings as heretical and condemned his doctrines in 1382. His career in many ways foreshadowed the Protestant Reformation of the sixteenth century.

The Conciliar Movement

The conflict culminated in a debate over the nature of power within the church. The Conciliar movement was based on the idea that power resided in the hands of the people rather than the pope, and that this power was best represented by the general council of the church. A church council met at Constance from 1414–1418. The council deposed the competing popes and elected Martin V. The declarations of the council were contained in *Haec Sancta.*

The Papal Response

While the Conciliar movement held much promise for the governance of the church, in 1459, the pope issued the bull *Execrabilis,* in which he firmly declared that ultimate authority in church affairs rested with the pope. This decree negated one of the most important platforms of the Conciliarists, that appeals could be made to the church councils.

THE HUNDRED YEARS' WAR

The Hundred Years' War was a very significant series of battles from the mid-fourteenth through the mid-fifteenth centuries that resulted in the alteration of many political institutions in France and England. The war contributed to the collapse of feudal society and ushered in the beginnings of the nation state and more modern ways of waging war.

Origins of the Conflict

The origin of the Hundred Years' War can be found in the conflicts within feudal society. The feudal conflicts between France and England began in the eleventh century. The French were still a very loose confederation of duchies or provinces united under the leadership of a single monarch. One of these provinces, Normandy, was under the control of a group of people who became known as adventurers and crusaders. In 1066, William of Normandy, on the pretext that he was the true heir to throne of England, crossed the English Channel and, at the Battle of Hastings, defeated Harold II, the English monarch. In addition to being Duke of Normandy, vassal of the French king, William now became the King of England. In effect, the French monarch now had another king as a vassal. This proved to be a difficult situation. As vassal to the French monarch, William was obligated to support him. As king of the English, he was obligated, and of course had a natural desire, to protect his own interests. Thus, the Norman conquest of 1066 initiated the friction that would later erupt into one hundred years of war.

During the reign of **Henry II**, one of the descendants of William, this friction and tension became even stronger. Henry II acquired much territory in France, in particular, the wealthy duchy of Aquitaine through marriage to Eleanor of Aquitaine. The English king now controlled an enormous expanse of land now called the Angevin kingdom, and was actually more powerful than his overlord, the French king.

The English and French attempted to resolve these tensions by the marriage in 1303 of the English King Edward II and Isabella, the daughter of the French King Philip IV, or Philip the Fair. This was to prove a crucial event that would ultimately provide the pretext for formal hostilities. Edward II and Isabella had an uneasy marriage, but did produce a son, Edward III. Philip IV died, and so did his three sons soon afterwards, leaving only Isabella and her son, then King **Edward III** of England. Philip of Valois, a nephew of Philip IV, claimed the throne. Edward III, the only other male descendant, could make a claim only through his mother's line, a succession forbidden by the Salic Law. Although the French rarely followed this law, they used it now to bypass the claim of Edward III to the throne. Philip of Valois was eighteen years older than Edward, was French, and had lived in France all his life. Edward, on the other hand, although a more direct descendant of Philip IV, had not been raised in France and was accustomed to English styles of government. The Normans had learned to manage the English nobles very well, and the French feared the tight restrictions Edward might make on their powers.

Although Edward gave Philip liege homage in the early part of his reign, hostilities started in 1337, when Philip of Valois, now king of France, confiscated Aquitaine, accusing Edward of acts of rebellion. Among the points of dispute were the English support of a candidate for leadership of the duchy of Brittany against a French candidate, and French concern over the connection between Flanders, near France, and the English wool trade.

The First Battles of the Hundred Years' War

In 1346 Edward III finally launched his attack, basically to aid his candidate in Brittany. He landed in Normandy, swung to Paris, and was headed out again when the French caught up with him. Edward's men were tired from the long march, and chose a strong defensive location near Crécy on a hill. The Englishmen were armed with longbows that were very powerful and were shooting downhill. They totally disrupted the unorganized charges of the French, who attacked seventeen times. Although the French army outnumbered the English army by at least three to one, the English had superior leadership and military skill. The **longbow** had a greater range than the crossbow, the French weapon of choice, and the longbow could penetrate a suit of plate armor at 200 yards. The English experience fighting the Welsh had perfected their use of the longbow. Philip violated the rules of chivalry when he fled the battle.

The following year after Crécy, the English laid siege to Calais, thus capturing a stronghold on the French coast. That year as well, the English captured the King of the Scots, as well as the French candidate for the kingdom of Brittany.

Poitiers

Recovering from the eruption of the plague in the 1340s, in 1356 England began a three-pronged attack on France, meeting the French at Poitiers. The son of Edward III, known as the Black Prince, defeated the French and captured the French king, sending him to the Tower of London. Again, the English were numerically inferior to the French but won by superior tactics and arms. The French never ransomed their king. The French in Aquitaine protested the rule of the Black Prince, eventually causing the French monarch to confiscate the duchy once again, renewing hostilities. The war continued into the fifteenth century.

Agincourt

During the fifteenth century, the French monarchy again faced a huge problem. The king at this time was Charles VI. He was mentally incompetent and degenerating more each day. He had become king while still a child, and his uncles ruled as regent for him. Of these, the most important were Philip, the Duke of Burgundy, and his brother, Louis of Orléans. The rivalry between these two became intense when Philip died, and his son John the Fearless became Duke of Burgundy. John had his uncle Louis of Orléans assassinated in 1407, and Louis's relatives, known as the Armagnacs, became bitter enemies of the Burgundians.

The English took advantage of the civil war raging in France. The king of England at this time was Henry V, who decided to end the conflict in a decisive series of attacks. Henry V made an alliance with the Burgundians and proceeded to invade France in 1415. He landed with 2,000 men at arms and 6,000 archers. The English besieged Harfleur, which fell after about six weeks in September. The English were considerably weakened by an epidemic of dysentery. Despite the physical weakness of Henry's men and the shortage of supplies after the siege, he decided to march to Calais. The French army, led by the Armagnacs, or the supporters of the Duke of Orléans, caught up with the English at Agincourt. Henry's men were too tired to flee, and they prepared for battle. It had been raining for three days prior to the battle. The French once again tried to march against the English archers; the archers broke up the first assault, and the arrows quickly killed the French horses. The dismounted French knights then advanced, but fifteenth-century armor had become so heavy that the knights sunk down quickly in the mud.

When the battle was over, the French had lost 1,500 nobles and 3,000 men at arms, and the Duke of Orléans was captured. The English lost less than 100 men. Agincourt is perhaps the best example of the poor military leadership of the French; they never mastered the art of fighting against the English longbowmen.

Following Agincourt, the Duke of Burgundy made another alliance with Henry V, and this led to the Treaty of Troyes in 1420. This was a most important treaty, for the English and the Burgundians agreed to disinherit the dauphin, the son and heir of Charles VI. His mother agreed to claim that he was not the legitimate son of Charles VI, and upon the death of the mad king Charles, Henry V was to become king of France as well as king of England. To seal the deal, Henry married the French king's daughter Catherine. The Duke of Burgundy acquired full sovereignty in his own lands.

In 1422, both Charles VI and Henry V died, and the throne of both countries passed to the young Henry VI of England. Since Henry was a child, the English nobles seemed more concerned with obtaining more power at home and were not very concerned with their monarch's French holdings. The disinherited French dauphin, meanwhile, had a stronghold of support in the south of France with the Armagnacs. He was unable to effectively muster this support, however, since unscrupulous nobles who consistently stole his revenue also dominated him.

Orléans

In 1429 the English decided to wipe out resistance in the south of France and besieged Orléans. The situation looked grim for the French, until a young woman from the small village of Domremy, Jeanne d'Arc, or **Joan of Arc**, appeared in the camp of the dauphin claiming to have had visions that directed her to free Orléans and escort the dauphin to Rheims. The English King Henry VI had been crowned king of France in Paris; French monarchs were traditionally crowned in Rheims. Joan's voices told her that the English were evil usurpers and that the dauphin Charles was the legitimate monarch. Although the medievals venerated visionaries, Charles's men were suspicious of this young village girl. After having her questioned and examined for witchcraft, they escorted her to the dauphin. When Joan entered his chambers, he was in the company of several other men and disguised to test her visions; although she had never seen Charles, she immediately recognized him in the crowd. Charles told her she was mistaken, but again, she insisted he was the true monarch. Charles was intrigued, and told her that if she could tell him a secret he had never confided to anyone, he would recognize her. Joan told him such a secret; unfortunately, the sources do not reveal the secret. After having her once again questioned about witchcraft, Charles, too, began to listen to her story.

Some scholars have suggested that all of this was prearranged since it seems to be such an unlikely story, and that Joan was, in fact, an illegitimate daughter of the dead King Charles. She knew how to fight and to ride like a knight, unlikely knowledge for a girl to have, especially one from a small peasant village. This theory has never been strongly supported. Quite simply, the French were desperate, and there was something about this young girl, all of eighteen at the time, that convinced men of her sincerity and ability to lead them to victory. The men who rode with her all testified to her innate charisma; her closest male companions said that although she was quite beautiful, they never had carnal desires for her. According to them, she radiated purity and sanctity. Whatever Joan possessed, the French followed her to Orléans and successfully defeated the English.

The victory at Orléans made Joan a legend. According to the earlier medieval prophecies of Merlin, a maid of Lorraine was to save the French in just such a situation. Joan was identified with this legend. Although she likely did not actually lead the French army but only served as a moral incentive, she was hailed throughout France as a hero.

Rheims

After the battle of Orléans, Joan of Arc led the dauphin to Rheims, the traditional site of French coronations, and he was crowned king of France as Charles VII. Although the English Henry VI had also been crowned king of France, he had been crowned in Paris. This point was not lost on the French. Joan had appealed to their patriotism, and now the French were determined to defeat the English. Charles VII, however, was not far-sighted enough to continue the fight. Having been crowned, he thought his struggle was over and quickly dismissed the Maid of Orléans.

Compiègne

Joan of Arc continued to fight to oust the English after her success at Orléans in 1429. She was eventually captured by the Burgundians and English outside of Compiègne, and held prisoner and tried on charges of witchcraft. Charles did nothing for her, even though the Burgundians appeared to be willing to sell her to her friends; Charles also had the military might at that time to rescue her. He seemed to forget the Maid of Orléans as soon as he had achieved his goal. Joan was convicted and burned at the stake for heresy. Charles later seemed to have second thoughts about owing his coronation to a convicted heretic and, in 1429, her case was reopened with the help of her family and she was cleared of all charges. In the twentieth century, Joan of Arc was canonized.

Joan of Arc is one of the most remarkable women in world civilization, if for no other reason than that we know so much about her. It is rare for the historian to have access to so many primary sources on the life of any woman from this period, much less that of a simple peasant woman from Domremy. We have the records of her trial and the later trial of rehabilitation, at which many people who knew her as a child and as a leader testified. While her cross-dressing behavior has been the subject of much debate, Joan of Arc continues to be a symbol of the French fight for liberty today.

Impact of the Hundred Years' War

Although Charles seemed to forget Joan, the French did not. By 1453, the English had lost all their possessions on the continent except Calais. For all practical purposes, English power on the continent was ended. Although English kings up through George III, king during the American Revolution, would continue to proclaim themselves kings of France, it was an empty title. Despite their poor military record during the Hundred Years' War, the French had succeeded in resolving disputes amongst the various dukes and creating a new and more centralized government, which was well on its way to becoming a unified nation state.

The Hundred Years' War was important in many ways. It helped resolve the complex feudal relationship between France and England and within France herself. It also had many other momentous results. Both France and England had to develop new ways of assembling an army. The old feudal ways did not work well. First of all, many nobles were not really very skilled on the battlefield and could not always provide enough men. Both the French and the English resorted to the use of private soldiers who were paid for their services. They came to recognize that leadership did not depend on birth but on ability. The power of the medieval nobility was thus compromised, another hallmark of modernity. This was the beginning of a professional military. Many English and French saw the need to keep a standing army ready at all times; and the English, in particular, argued that there was a real need to develop a navy that could respond to attacks on the English coastline. The English did, in fact, develop a navy, which was, for a very long while the most powerful naval force in the world.

During the conflict, the English monarch was forced to consult Parliament. He had to transport men and supplies while fighting an aggressive war overseas. Parliament's power rose, and it acquired the structure it has today. It is divided into the **House of Lords** and the **House of Commons**, and during the war, the English monarch agreed that he could not levy taxes without the permission of Parliament.

In France, on the other hand, the French monarch was able to muster the support of the **Estates General** and the nobles. The English ransacked and pillaged the French countryside and defeated the French army. To raise finances, the French monarch acquired a monopoly over the salt tax, and became more and more master of the Estates General. This chain of events laid the groundwork for the French Revolution in 1789, when nobles would protest taxation.

The Hundred Years' War destroyed the French countryside. The English found it difficult to besiege towns, as they were well protected. Medieval towns depended on the countryside for food, and the English discovered that destroying the countryside also eventually weakened the resistance of the towns. The new professional soldiers roamed the countryside in search of plunder during interludes of peace. The peasants suffered most in all this. The suffering of the peasants awakened social consciousness and debates on the nature of war and its limits. Many tracts argued that war should be fought only between armed combatants, and the population should be spared. Also, many argued that wars ought to be fought only for the good of the state rather than for personal gain.

During the Hundred Years' War, **nationalism** began to emerge. The strengthening of the French monarchy and the English parliamentary system helped to pave the way for the later nation state. During the Reformation, Martin Luther's *Address to the Christian Nobility of the German Nation* was symptomatic of a new era, as he played upon budding national sentiment in his argument that the church in Germany should separate from the Roman Church.

The medieval worldview was definitely on the decline, and the humanists of the Renaissance would only further separate themselves from the medieval outlook.

CHAPTER 18

THE RENAISSANCE

Many scholars have hailed the **Renaissance**, or "rebirth," as the beginning of the modern era. The Renaissance began in Italy, in part due to its unique economic position throughout the Middle Ages. After the collapse of the Roman Empire in the west, urban life virtually ceased to exist in western Europe. The Italian city-states, however, survived and had developed apart from many of the restrictions of feudal society. Many merchant and banking families not of the hereditary nobility amassed great wealth, and this wealth helped to fuel the artistic Renaissance. Of these, the **de Medici** family in Florence and the Fugers in the North were prime examples of a new class of people known as the **popolo grossi**, or fat people, primarily because their newfound wealth made them physically more comfortable. They were literally better fed, but also "fat" from the point of view of disposable wealth. The Medici came to power after the Revolt of the Ciompi in 1378, one of many peasant revolts in the wake of the Black Death. They were the bankers for the papacy, and they received deposits from England, France, and Flanders. They also had banking branches in Lyon, London, and Antwerp. The Medici lent money at exorbitant interest rates for wars or other endeavors to various European heads of state. With the revenues, they bought English wool, had it shipped to Florence, and exported the fabrics created with a large profit. The Florentine gold florin became the monetary standard for much of Europe. While the medieval church taught that usury, or the making of a profit from interest, was a sin, the Renaissance redefined the role of money and profitable business. The patron saint of **Florence** was John the Baptist, and in many paintings he appears in his loin cloths surrounded by gold florins. Surely, money was not a part of John the Baptist's historic mission, but in the hands of the Renaissance families such as the Medici, even an ascetic figure such as John the Baptist was associated with the wealth of Florence.

Cosimo de Medici, known as the *pater patriae*, or "Father of the country," of Florence, was a great patron of the arts. He founded the

Neoplatonic academy and commissioned many works. His son Lorenzo the Magnificent was also a patron of the arts and himself a poet. Patronage is one of the most important factors leading to the rise of artists such as **Michelangelo**, who was the first wealthy artist in history. During the Renaissance, the artist came to be valued as a "genius" rather than a mere craftsman in the service of church or state. The explosion of artistic genius during the Renaissance was partly due to the fact that for the first time, artists were supported by wealthy patrons and now had the time and financial resources to devote themselves to their art. Many artists had their own workshops and developed their own unique styles. While medieval artists rarely signed works of art, the Renaissance artist did not have to, as his style was immediately recognizable. Artists also often signed works in ways that conveyed their own individuality, such as **Raphael**, who signed his name on one of his Madonnas right across her chest!

Another factor in Italy's economic development was the fact that many of the Italian city-states had maintained a thriving trade with Constantinople and other areas during the Middle Ages. This was particularly true of Venice, and when Constantinople fell to the Seljuk Turks in 1453, many Greek scholars fled along with their texts to Venice. The Italian Renaissance was in large part characterized by its fascination with the culture of Greco-Roman antiquity. Many Greek churchmen and scholars had attended the Council of Ferrara from 1438–1445; although the Council failed in its goal to reunite the Greek Orthodox and Roman Catholic Churches, many of the attendees, such as Manuel Chrysoloros, stayed in Italy and helped to spread their knowledge of Greek philosophy and culture. Many Italian humanists, such as Pogio and Boccaccio, were avid hunters of long forgotten Greco-Roman manuscripts and art works, and this mania for antiquity infused Italian art and literature with a new character that nevertheless continued to build on the achievements of the medieval world.

Medieval art was formalized and rigidly stylized, and it was often difficult to distinguish the work of one icon artist from another. In fact, with only a few exceptions, we often do not even know the names of medieval artists and architects. Art was for the glory of God and not for the glory of humanity. We cannot even name the authors of such literary masterpieces as *Beowulf*. Medieval artists had never developed much skill with perspective and art was not very realistic.

The rediscovery of many works of Greco-Roman art, whose sheer technical mastery and startling realism departed from that of the medieval artisan, prompted an explosion of new artistic creativity. The rediscovery of many ancient Greco-Roman scholarly manuscripts opened a new world to the humanists, as many ideas contained in them departed from those of the medieval church. While the medieval church taught that pagan works were not particularly relevant to the Christian world and, in many cases, should be avoided, the humanists found inspiration in the Greco-Roman interest in the human condition and in their belief in the power of human reason. The Renaissance zeal for Greco-Roman antiquity was one source of the humanist interest in individual achievement.

The changes that marked the advent of Renaissance art can be seen in the proto-Renaissance art of Giotto, who for the first time painted religious scenes where individual faces and expressions displayed the powerful emotions that must have been felt by those who witnessed the events surrounding the life of Christ. One achievement of the Renaissance artists was to portray the Holy Family as fully human, and to have explored the human experience and feelings of the historic Christ. The Renaissance artists portrayed the same events as the medieval iconographers, yet they had more awareness of these events as happening in human time and being experienced by human followers. While the humanists of the Renaissance found the hand of God in the beauty of the world and the human form, the medieval church had taught that worldly interests were evil and the body sinful. The artist Michelangelo, who was influenced by the philosophy of Neoplatonism, depicted the nude human body in the famous S curve, a symbol for the tension between the soul and the body. For Michelangelo, however, the body was an image of the soul, and the more beautiful the soul, the more beautiful the body. **Leonardo da Vinci** studied human anatomy through dissecting cadavers, thought to be a moral sin, but his emphasis on realism resulted in several fine self-portraits. During the Middle Ages, the self-portraits would have been considered profane and vain, but da Vinci, like other humanists, valued the uniqueness of each individual.

Michelangelo also incorporated Greco-Roman figures in the Sistine Chapel ceiling and painted the ceiling with a Neoplatonic agenda. Jacob Burckhardt, one of the most important interpreters of the Renaissance who wrote *The Civilization of the Renaissance in Italy*, argued that the humanist interest in Greco-Roman antiquity distracted them from Christianity. Although the humanists thought they were Christians, Burckhardt argued that their thought often deviated from orthodox Christianity and gravitated far into the pagan realm. This was perhaps true of the Sistine Chapel ceiling, as well as of the art of Sandro Botticelli and other Neoplatonists. Botticelli's *Birth of Venus*, for example, depicts a pagan myth, but its iconography is Christian. Botticelli intended Venus, the pagan goddess of love, to be a symbol of Christian love; her birth from the sea to be an allegory of baptism; and the pagan gods of wind in the corner to be an allegory of the Holy Spirit. In Burckhardt's view, the humanists created a new, pagan-infused Christianity through their efforts to incorporate Greco-Roman influences. Orthodox Christianity differed on several fundamental points from pagan philosophies; nevertheless, the humanist Pico della Mirandola's *Oration on the Dignity of Man* suggested that pagan and Christian works might be fully harmonized.

Botticelli. Birth of Venus, *1480.*

The advent of the **Gutenberg movable type printing press** in 1446 also made books more widely available. During the Middle Ages, the Bible and other texts had to be hand copied. Manuscripts were rare and, for the most part, housed within monasteries. The more widespread availability of books, coupled with the wealth of families such as the de Medici, promoted an intense flourishing of the arts. During the Renaissance, the literary, visual, and architectural arts would flourish and politics would take a decisive turn away from the attitudes and values of the medieval church and more towards the secular orientation of modern politics. There were more geniuses that emerged during the Italian Renaissance than perhaps at any other time in world history.

Humanism

The term often used to describe Renaissance culture, "humanism," was not in use in the Renaissance. However, the word "humanist" was used in the Renaissance. The term "umanista," or "humanist," technically referred to a professional teacher whose subject matter was the *studia humanitatis*. The *studia humanitatis* consisted of all those educational disciplines outside of theology and natural science, two important areas of medieval learning. While the most important aspect of the trivium in the Middle Ages was dialectic or logic, the Renaissance humanists focused on another area of the trivium, rhetoric, and highly valued eloquence of speech. In their view, if one could not interest an audience sufficiently for them to learn, all the logic in the world was wasted. If one could not move an audience toward ethical action, natural theology was useless. The humanists found Scholastic theology dry and so abstract that it had little bearing on the ways to live a good, Christian life. The humanists were not so interested in the medieval Scholastic's abstract, logical explorations of theology as they were in teaching one how to become a better person. While the medieval Scholastic focused on dialectic, theology, and natural science, the humanists focused on grammar, rhetoric, history, literary studies, and moral philosophy.

Baldesar Castiglione's *Book of the Courtier* (1516) reflected the interest of the humanists in developing personal skills and *virtu* to a high point. Castiglione was a count and a diplomat who described the ideal man as a *uomo universale*, more commonly known as a "Renaissance man" or "universal man." Castiglione's *uomo universale* was master of a wide variety of knowledge and skills. His model of the well-rounded individual has become the emblem of the Renaissance.

Education in the Renaissance

The humanists insisted that education was an important foundation of the virtuous man. Peter Paul Vergerio promoted the study of the liberal arts, but especially history, ethics, and rhetoric. History, he said, was valuable for its illustrations of past models of virtue, ethics for its exploration of the virtuous person in society, and rhetoric for its emphasis on how to teach, please, and move people.

In his *Oration on the Dignity of Man*, Pico della Mirandola described humans as able to reach any heights they desired. Humans alone, he argued, were created without natures that limited what they might achieve. Humans alone, then, might transform themselves into whatever they desired to be.

The humanists insisted on the value of education, and Erasmus, a northern humanist, wrote that education should be made available to even the ploughboy in the field, who might then transform himself. Despite such lofty sentiments, humanist education was an elitist endeavor. Humanists promoted the study of languages, in particular, Latin and Greek, so that one might gain a better understanding of Greco-Roman texts. **Erasmus**, for example, thought the Scriptures would be better understood through knowledge of their original languages. He published a new translation of the New Testament with the Greek text alongside his new Latin translation. He also included notes on the Hebrew. Luther's reading of the *Novum Instrumentum*, or *Testamentum*, helped to fuel the Reformation.

Another example of the importance of linguistic studies in the Renaissance was **Lorenzo Valla**. Valla was a Renaissance philologist who studied the origins and use of language. His study of the **Donation of Constantine** created a shockwave throughout Europe. The Donation of Constantine was allegedly written during the reign of the first Christian emperor, Constantine. Upon the death of Constantine, it purported to give the pope in Rome both temporal and spiritual power over the domain of Constantine. Valla proved, however, that the document used language not in existence before the ninth century. For example, it used terminology related to feudal society, and that terminology was not in use prior to the reign of Charlemagne. If so, Valla had proven that the document was a medieval forgery and not written during the age of Constantine. His discovery encouraged further criticisms of the church.

The Vernacular Languages

Other humanists, such as **Dante**, began writing in the vernacular languages, or languages actually spoken. Dante was the first to write in vernacular Italian, and although his *Comedia* contained many medieval ideas, the use of the Italian opened new frontiers. During the Reformation, Luther translated the Bible into his native German, thereby allowing Germans to actually read the Scriptures in a language they spoke.

Humanist Awareness of Their Own Uniqueness

The humanist interest in language reflected awareness that words could change meaning from age to age and from culture to culture. It reflected as well their awareness of their own age as distinct from that of other ages. The fourteenth-century humanist Petrarch is credited with being the Father of Humanism. In many texts, Petrarch argued that his own age was vastly different from the culture of the Middle Ages. In fact, he argued that the medieval period was dark culturally, that it was lacking in literary and artistic masterpieces, and that it reflected no awareness of the potential of the human spirit. Petrarch coined the term "Dark Ages" to refer to the medieval period, and that appellation and its negative overtones has plagued the historiography of the Middle Ages ever since.

The humanists saw their own era as vastly different from earlier eras. The humanists may have exaggerated their own uniqueness, as some scholars have seen more continuity between the Middle Ages and the Renaissance than Petrarch admitted. Dante, for example, structured the *Comedia* around the mystical Christian number three; there are three large parts to the *Comedia*, the *Inferno*, the *Purgatorio*, and the *Paradisio*. The *Comedia* also makes numerous use of the number 10 in its structure, the perfect Christian number. The numerology of the *Comedia* is entirely medieval. Dante's view of sin in the *Inferno* was also very medieval; Dante based the punishments given to sinners on the medieval notion of retributive justice, or to each according to what he or she deserves. Beatrice is symbolic of Divine Love and the desire of all Christians to unite with the Godhead. Nevertheless, his use of the vernacular Latin as well as the pagan poet Virgil as his guide marked new attitudes.

Indeed, the cultural flourishing of the Italian Renaissance was accompanied by tremendous changes in culture and political structures throughout Europe.

Politics in Renaissance Italy

Italy was not united as a nation state until the nineteenth century, and Renaissance Italy was a collection of Republics and duchies that were often at war with one another.

Milan

Milan was one of the richest city-states in Italy. Many mercenaries used in the Hundred Years' War came from Italy. Francesco Sforza came from a *condottiere*, or mercenary family, and in 1447 he took control of Milan. The Sforza were well-known patrons of the arts. Leonardo da Vinci worked for the Sforza for a portion of his career and designed a number of military devices and fortifications for them.

Republic of Venice

Venice maintained a thriving trade with Constantinople through the Middle Ages. In the Fourth Crusade, the Venetians helped to support a false claimant to the Byzantine throne, and eventually led the western knights in their conquest of Constantinople. Venice was governed by a small oligarchy of elite merchants and led by the Doge. The Doge's palace in Venice is a masterpiece of Gothic architecture. It contains a number of Renaissance masterworks, including a painting of the Battle of Lepanto in 1571, when an alliance of Europeans, including the Venetians, defeated the Ottoman Turks at the Gulf of Patros. The important military victory in 1571 stopped the advance of the Ottomans, whose various conquests threatened to turn the Mediterranean into a Muslim sea. Another famous location in Venice is St. Mark's Cathedral, which was designed on the plan of a Greek cross. The Venetians maintained a thriving trade with Constantinople and the influence of Greek culture is seen in the cathedral.

Republic of Florence

Florence was located in Tuscany and it was an important center of the arts during the Renaissance. Michelangelo was born near Florence and worked here; Leonardo da Vinci also worked in Florence. The Revolt of the Ciompi brought Cosimo de Medici to power in 1434. Although Florence was a republic, the Medici ruled it as despots. The Medici ousted **Machiavelli**, and he wrote *The Prince*, which may have been intended to satirize their political practices. In *The Prince*, Machiavelli advocated the separation of politics from ethics and/or theology, and many consider him to be the founder of modern politics. Machiavelli was also an advocate for a unified Italy, which he argued could only be achieved by such a man as he described in *The Prince*. The Medici were important patrons of the arts, and their palace is famous for its use of several different styles of architecture. Lorenzo de Medici was a poet who patronized the artist Michelangelo. Hans Baron, a modern scholar, argues that the political conflicts of the Medici and others helped to prompt the shift from medieval to Renaissance thought. He believes that civic humanism, an interest in leading an active, public life, originated in large part from the political crisis in early modern Florence. Civic humanism and interest in public life led to the creation of open, public spaces, and to such architectural masterpieces as the Duomo in Florence. The Duomo was a masterpiece of engineering that could be seen from miles away. It came to be the symbol of the Renaissance itself.

Urbino

The Montefeltro dynasty ruled Urbino. Federigo da Montefeltro was a *condottiere*, or mercenary, but was also a benevolent and classically educated ruler.

Ferrara

The most famous person to emerge from Ferrara was Isabella d'Este, daughter of the Duke of Ferrara. She was known as the "first lady of the world" for her learning and patronage of the arts. She married Francesco, Duke of Mantua, and after his death ruled Mantua alone. An important scholarly question about the Renaissance is to what extent there was a Renaissance for women. Isabella is an excellent example of an educated woman who managed to function in a man's world and in a man's role.

Mantua

Francesco Gonzaga, Marquis of Mantua, ruled Mantua and was the husband of Isabella d'Este, daughter of the Duke of Ferrara.

Siena

The art of Siena was much darker than other Renaissance art, particularly in the wake of the Black Death.

Papal States

The Donation of the Frankish ruler Pepin created the tract of land known as the Papal States. Revenue from the Papal States helped the medieval and Renaissance popes centralize the church and develop vast political power.

During the Renaissance, the Borgia family largely controlled the Papal States. Rodrigo Borgia, the family patriarch, was born in Spain in 1431. His favorite son was Cesare, who was accused of murdering his brother Juan. In

1502, he pillaged the Dukedom of Urbino and took four large cartloads of art treasures that contained tapestries, silver, and paintings; these treasures were worth an estimated 150,000 ducats. Cesare tried to establish a hereditary monarchy in central Italy, and Machiavelli praised him as the ideal prince. He also used his sister, Lucrezia, as a pawn in the marriage game to increase his power. When she was only thirteen, Cesare married her to Giovanni Sforza, but later had the marriage annulled when a more suitable partner appeared, Alfonso of Aragon. Cesare later murdered Alfonso, and Lucrezia married the Duke of Ferra. Cesare died in battle in 1507.

The Borgia family produced two popes, Pope Callistus III and Pope Alexander VI, father of Lucrezia and Cesare. Pope Alexander was openly devoted to his many children, and procured for his sons powerful positions in the church. He appointed Cesare a cardinal in the church. Alexander VI was the epitome of the corruption of the Renaissance papacy. Alexander was also a patron of the arts and learning, and as Pope issued a bull dividing the new world between Spain and Portugal. He also imposed a tithe for crusades against the Turks.

Political Outlines of Renaissance Europe

Spain

The marriage of **Ferdinand and Isabella**, in 1469, united Aragon and Castille and created a new Spain. Spain would profit greatly when Isabella convinced Ferdinand to finance the first voyage of **Christopher Columbus** in 1492. The wealth generated from the Spanish colonization of the Americas not only strengthened the Spanish monarchy, but caused a price revolution in Europe. The power of Spain also propelled it to leadership of the Catholic world during the Reformation. Ferdinand and Isabella had permission from the church to select the most important churchmen in Spain. To deal with issues surrounding the conversion of significant Jewish minorities in Spain, they also requested that the pope start the **Inquisition** in 1478. In 1492, Ferdinand and Isabella conquered Muslim Granada and expelled all professed Jews from Spain; in 1502, all professed Muslims were also expelled. The intense orthodox Catholicism of the Spanish monarchs also attracted the attention of the Catholic Queen Mary of England. Mary was a staunch opponent of her father Henry VIII's reformation. She married Philip to restore Catholicism to England. When she died, Philip launched the Armada, the largest naval fleet ever assembled, against her Protestant half-sister Elizabeth. In 1588, the legendary "Protestant Wind" grounded the Armada before it could attack, thus assuring the success of the Protestant Reformation in England.

England

The victory of Henry VII, a member of the Tudor family, over the infamous Richard III in 1485 brought an end to the Wars of the Roses and ushered in a new era in England. Henry VII enacted various policies to curtail the power of the English nobles, thus ending their constant squabbles in the Wars of the Roses. Henry planned for his eldest son, Arthur, to succeed him. Unfortunately, Arthur died, and Henry's second son became **King Henry VIII.** Henry VIII separated the English Church from the Roman Catholic Church and began the Reformation in England.

The English humanist **Thomas More** objected to Henry's actions and refused to sign the Act of Supremacy. For that crime against the state, he was beheaded. More's *Utopia* was one of the most famous works of English Humanism. The fictional Utopians were a pre-Christian society whose monastic-style practices made those of his own Christian England seem immoral by contrast. More exemplifies a style of writing common to many humanists. While the Scholastics wrote argumentative treatises, the humanists wrote humorous works designed to suggest ideas rather than to prove them.

Henry VIII's daughter Elizabeth later succeeded her half-sister Mary as queen. She was known as the "Virgin Queen." Although she never married, she used the possibility of the marriage bed as an effective diplomatic tool. During her reign, English culture enjoyed a Renaissance. Shakespeare worked during the reign of Elizabeth.

France

France developed a strong monarch as a result of the Hundred Years' War. King Louis IX won control of the *taille*, an annual tax on land and property. He used the funds from this tax to strengthen his control over troublesome provinces such as Maine, Anjou, and Provence.

Holy Roman Empire

Voltaire once said that the Holy Roman Empire was neither holy, nor Roman, nor an empire. During the Renaissance, the Holy Roman Empire was increasingly fragmented. Each German state often acted independently of the emperor. The first **Hapsburg** to become Holy Roman Emperor was Rudolph I in 1273. Although the Hapsburg rulers were themselves successful at forging alliances through marriage and thus strengthening their own position in Europe, the Protestant Reformation dealt a fatal blow to the empire. Luther's claim that "all Christians were of the same estate" was taken by the German princes to mean that they had the power to revolt against the emperor, while peasants took it to mean they could revolt against their overlords. By the end of the Reformation era, thirty percent of Germans lay dead on the battlefield. The Peace of Augsburg in 1555 and the Treaty of Westphalia in 1648 vastly curtailed the authority of the Holy Roman Emperor.

The Ottoman Turks threatened parts of the Holy Roman Empire during the Renaissance era. In 1529, the Turks besieged Vienna, but failed to capture it. In 1683, the Turks attempted once again to capture the city through siege, but were defeated a final time.

Hungary

Hungary became the most important state in eastern Europe during the Renaissance era. **King Matthias Corvinus** (1458–1490) managed to control the wealthy nobles and create a centralized government. In 1526, the Ottoman Turks defeated the Hungarians at the battle of Mohács. The Turks also conquered the cities of Buda and Pest. Pest fell to the Turks in 1526, and Buda fell fifteen years later. During the seventeenth century, the Hapsburg rulers conquered Hungary.

Poland

Powerful nobles who controlled the Sejm, or national diet, thwarted the attempts of the Polish kings to centralize the government. By 1511, the nobles reduced the peasantry to serfdom and established their right to elect their kings.

Russia

Russia was converted to Christianity during the Middle Ages, but it had been conquered by the Mongol hordes in the thirteenth century. Moscow gradually rose to prominence under Ivan III. Ivan III annexed other Russian principalities and defeated the Mongols in 1480.

Byzantium

The Byzantine Empire declined during the Renaissance period. In the thirteenth century, the Byzantines had to deal with a new threat, the Ottoman Turks. In 1453, the Turks conquered Constantinople, the mighty bastion of Roman culture in the east. The Hagia Sophia, one of the greatest Christian churches from the reign of Justinian, was converted to an Islamic mosque. Many Christian scholars fled Byzantium and went to Venice, with whom the east had a thriving trade. Their presence helped to fuel the Italian Renaissance.

The Northern Renaissance

The Renaissance of the north had a considerably different character than that of the Italian Renaissance. Whereas Burckhardt argued that the Italian Renaissance was secular in its orientation, the northern humanists were concerned with reforming Christianity so as to promote a deeper awareness of spirituality, and the art of the northern Renaissance in Germany had a decidedly fierce overtone. The art of Dürer, for example, focused on God as a judge who wrought vengeance on sinners.

Erasmus, Prince of the Humanists, lived and worked in Rotterdam. Erasmus corresponded with many important humanists and leaders of Renaissance Europe, including Thomas More. Erasmus emphasized the value of education, which he wanted made available to even the ploughboy in the field. Erasmus published a new translation of the Bible known as the *Novum Testamentum*. In this new translation, Luther read in the Pauline Epistles the words "be penitent" where the Latin Vulgate had read "do penance." The emphasis on inner spirituality rather than outward piety distinguished the thought of Erasmus; Luther, however, acted on these notions and eventually separated from the Roman Church. Erasmus, on the other hand, debated Luther and insisted on the need to reform the church. When Luther split the church, Erasmus later remarked that Luther had blown out his candle—he had destroyed the possibility of reform from within.

Flanders

Flanders supported the English during the Hundred Years' War. Artists here during the Renaissance developed the use of perspective. Jan van Eyck, for example, literally played with his technical virtuosity in such paintings as *Giovanni Arnolfini and His Bride*.

The Renaissance was a time of tremendous change, and these changes created a willingness to question that helped to usher in the Reformation.

Giovanni Arnolfini and His Bride, *Jan Van Eyck, 1434.*

CHAPTER 19

THE AGE OF EXPLORATION

Around 20,000 B.C.E., during the Ice Age, a hunting-gathering people crossed a land bridge between northeastern Asia and Alaska and thus "discovered" the American continent. This group of people, who ultimately became known as "Native"Americans, probably had no sense of having entered a new continent, and it was not until a much later era that one finds a more deliberate effort to explore and discover "New Worlds." The Europeans of the fifteenth and sixteenth centuries are often credited with the "discovery" of the "New World," not because they "discovered" something previously unknown but because they exploited what they found. The so-called "New World" was already known to the Native American inhabitants, and had already been visited by Europeans as early as the ninth century. The exploration of the Americas by Europeans, however, created a new global economy and forever transformed Europe, Africa, and the Americas. In this sense, the European experience of the Americas in the fifteenth and sixteenth centuries was far different from earlier "discoveries" or explorations of the continent.

The first European to land on the North American continent was **Leif Erikson**, who sailed from Scandinavia in the late ninth century. His voyage, however, occurred at a time when Europe was still in the throes of illiteracy, superstition, and localism, and thus went almost unnoticed; there were no attempts to follow up on his experience for hundreds of years.

Between the tenth and the fifteenth centuries, however, several concurrent movements began that would lead Europeans into the Age of Exploration and Discovery. During the Crusader era, beginning in the eleventh century, Europeans were introduced to desirable products from East Asia: spices such as pepper, cinnamon, ginger, nutmeg, and cloves; tropical foods such as figs, rice, and oranges; luxury goods including perfumes, silk, cotton, dyes, and precious stones. The complicated trade routes involved tariffs at many ports of entry as products went overland to Constantinople, through the Mediterranean on Venetian sailing vessels, and ultimately to west European ports. This trade was costly not only because of the number of handlers, but also because every petty tyrant whose land Arab caravans crossed exacted a tax on the goods. Scholars have estimated that the price of pepper in Europe was fifteen times more expensive than in the East Indies. The balance of trade was unfavorable from the standpoint of the European countries; the necessity to cut out the middlemen was crucial.

The fifteenth century was also a time of economic, political, and intellectual recovery as the Renaissance introduced new ideas and encouraged new ways of thinking. During the fourteenth century, Europeans suffered from famine and died in great numbers from the Black Death. As the plague subsided, Europeans developed new ideas that emphasized individualism, secularism, and humanism. A desire to challenge old ways and old ideas swept Europe and, at the same time, strong rulers emerged. Called the "new" monarchs, these kings unified their countries, sought ways to expand their economies, and competed with each other at every turn.

A number of technological tools of both European and Asian origin were important in the fifteenth-century explorations. By 1350, the Europeans had perfected the cannon, capable of firing iron or stone balls that, when mounted on a seagoing vessel, created a formidable force. A new sailing vessel, the caravel, replaced the old galleys that had relied on rowers for motion. Although slower than the galleys, the caravel relied on wind power and was designed to carry larger cargoes. The lateen sail, which had replaced the ancient square sail in the early Middle Ages and was widely used in the Mediterranean region, made it possible for ships to sail into the wind through a movement known as tacking. When combined with square-rigged sails in the Renaissance, the caravel now had increased maneuverability on the seas. Earlier inventions used in navigation included the compass, perfected by the Chinese many centuries before, and the astrolabe, a tool developed by the Arabs. The astrolabe allowed sailors to determine the altitude of the sun and thereby to plot latitude. Improvements in cartography gave navigators more exact information on distances, sea depth, and geography.

THE VOYAGES OF EXPLORATION

The Portuguese were the first Europeans to become involved in the voyages of exploration. Following the lead of their king, **Prince Henry the "Navigator,"** they set sail down the west coast of Africa in search of a sea route to the "Spice Islands" of the East Indies. In 1487, Bartholomew Diaz reached the tip of South Africa, and in a second Portuguese effort from 1497 to 1499, Vasco da Gama reached India. The Portuguese had limited success in their conquest of Africa, however, due to the difficulty of penetrating the continent's harsh terrain and the strength of the African monarchies.

King Manuel I of Portugal was impressed by the samples brought from India by Vasco da Gama and sent an expedition the following year, 1500, under the leadership of Pedro Cabral, to set up trading posts in India. Following what he thought was the route defined by da Gama, he headed for India. The fleet was, however, blown off course, and on April 22, 1500, it sighted **Brazil** and claimed it for the Portuguese crown. After spending a few days on the east coast of South America, Cabral and his crew continued on to India, arriving in 1501. From that point on, ships were sent from Lisbon each March headed for India and the Spice Islands. Lisbon harbor became the entry point for goods from the east.

While the Portuguese were attempting to reach the east by sailing around the tip of Africa, the Spanish turned to another route suggested by **Christopher Columbus**. Columbus was an Italian from Genoa who had studied the ancient maps of Ptolemy, a second-century geographer whose works were still highly regarded in the Renaissance. Ptolemy's map of the ancient Mediterranean area was very accurate, and scholars had always assumed, without proof, that his other geographical works were equally accurate. Ptolemy, however, overestimated the landmass from Europe to Asia and extended Asia much farther to the east than it actually is; on the other hand, he underestimated the amount of water on the planet. According to his map, the measurements of the known world were about 4,580 miles from north to south and 8,250 miles from east to west. All of these factors led Columbus to conclude he could more easily reach the east by sailing west across the seemingly limited expanse of ocean that separated Asia from the western coast of Europe than the Portuguese could reach it by sailing around the enormous continent of Africa. Of course, Columbus had no idea that the Americas separated Europe from Asia.

Columbus first approached John II of Portugal with his plan of sailing west to reach the east. In 1485, Christopher Columbus approached Ferdinand and Isabella of Spain; at the same time his brother Bartholomew tried to sell the idea to Henry VII of England. Although the Spanish were at first disinterested in Columbus's ideas, Spain was newly unified and eager to counter the rising power of the Portuguese resulting from their initial voyages around Africa. It was Queen Isabella who was converted first to the plan of Columbus, and in 1492, shortly after the fall of Granada to the crown, she promised Columbus everything he had asked for. That year, Christopher Columbus set off on his first voyage. In October, he reached the Caribbean, convinced that he had in fact attained his goal of sailing west to reach the east.

Columbus made four journeys in all to the islands of the Caribbean, embarking in 1492, 1493, 1498, and 1502. Although Columbus was convinced that he had reached the East Indies, and called the natives he encountered

"Indians," he failed as governor of Hispaniola, and, in 1500, spent time imprisoned in Hispaniola and Spain. His last voyage in 1502, during which he was marooned for a year in Jamaica, was his most adventuresome. He returned to Spain in 1504, however, arthritic and poor. He died in 1506.

OTHER VOYAGES TO THE AMERICAS

In 1499 and 1500, **Amerigo Vespucci** took part in an expedition led by the Spanish explorer Alonso de Ojeda. In the course of this trip, Vespucci wrote at length about the "New World" reached by the Europeans. Because of his descriptions and his realization that indeed the Europeans had not reached the Indies, but continents previously unknown, the German mapmaker, Martin Waldseemuller, suggested that the new land be named for Vespucci. Columbus never received even this recognition for having charted new lands.

Other crowns also financed voyages. **John Cabot**, a native of Italy, and born Giovanni Caboto, sailed under the English crown in 1497, the first Englishman to reach North America. He, like Columbus, da Gama, and Cabral, was interested in a shorter route to India and chose a more northern one. Embarking in May 1497, he reached land, probably either Newfoundland or Cape Breton, in June. Cabot made a second voyage in 1498. His voyages gave England claim to the North American mainland; it would lead to future English colonization. The next English expedition did not take place until the late sixteenth century.

Magellan, a student of astronomy and navigation, further developed some of Columbus's pioneering ideas. He believed that a shorter route to India was possible if, instead of sailing around the tip of Africa, ships sailed west and rounded the tip of South America. The Portuguese king would not support his request for ships, men, and money, so Magellan turned to the Spanish King, Charles I. Magellan set sail in 1519 and became the first European to circumnavigate the globe. Magellan's route took him from Europe around the tip of South America; through the Pacific Ocean, the Philippines, and the Indian Ocean; around the Cape of Good Hope; and back to Spain. He set out with a fleet of five ships and returned home three years later with one ship and only seventeen of the original crew.

One of the surviving crew members was an Italian, Antonio Pigafetta, who painstakingly recorded the events of the trip. Although Magellan failed to find a shorter route to India, his voyage contributed to the geographical knowledge of the world.

In 1535, Jacques Cartier sailed under the French flag towards the "New World," and was the first European to explore the St. Lawrence River. The following year the French attempted their first colony in Canada.

Dividing Up the Conquests

The early success of both the Portuguese and the Spanish in exploration led to many disputes. On May 4, 1493, Pope Alexander VI attempted to adjudicate the controversy. Essentially, he established an imaginary line running north and south through the mid-Atlantic, 100 leagues (480 km) from the Cape Verde Islands. Spain would have possession of any unclaimed territories to the west of the line and Portugal would have possession of any unclaimed territory to the east of the line. In 1494, The **Treaty of Tordesillas** redrew the line at 370 leagues (1,770 km) west of the Cape Verde Islands. Portugal came up the big loser in the Americas, as it received only Brazil. The Spanish became the beneficiaries of the vast wealth of the Americas.

The Spanish in the "New World"

Just as technological advances spurred exploration, so also did they aid the Spanish in their conquest of the natives of Meso- and South America. Many Spaniards sought fame as conquistadores, but their abuse of the Native Americans have made their names live on in infamy.

Juan Ponce de León might have begun his career as a *conquistador* on the second voyage of Columbus. By 1502, he was serving as a captain under the governor of Hispaniola. After he suppressed an Indian uprising, he was made governor of eastern Hispaniola. In 1508–1509 he explored Puerto Rico, as he had heard reports of gold there. He founded the oldest settlement there, the city of Caparra. Although he was named governor of Puerto Rico, he lost the position due to political rivalries. Hearing reports of a fountain on an island called Bimini whose waters could rejuvenate humans, he set out from Puerto Rico in 1513, the same year Balboa first sighted the Pacific Ocean. He landed on the coast of Florida near modern St. Augustine. Like Columbus, he did not realize he had reached the mainland, and thought he was on an island that he named "Florida," as he had reached it at Easter, or *Pascua Florida* in Spanish. He explored the Florida Keys and then returned to Puerto Rico. Somewhat later he returned to Spain, where he was made governor of Bimini and Florida. In 1521 he again sailed to Florida, but upon his landing, he was attacked by **Seminoles** and wounded by one of their arrows. He was taken back to Cuba, where he died. One of the largest cities in Puerto Rico is named "Ponce" in his honor.

Balboa

Vasco Núñez de Balboa was the first European to see the Pacific Ocean and the leader of the first stable colony in South America. In 1500, Balboa sailed along the coast of modern Colombia with Rodrigo de Bastidas, and later lived in Hispaniola. He was a poor farmer, however, and when his creditors threatened to take him, he became a stowaway on an expedition to a colony in Colombia. When the expedition arrived, they found the colonists, but on Balboa's suggestion they moved to the isthmus of Panama where they founded the town of Santa Maria de la Antigua, which was the first stable European settlement in South America. In 1511 King Ferdinand made Balboa governor of the colony. In September 1513, Balboa went in search of the fabled riches to the south, which may have been a reference to the Inca empire. On September 25 or 27, 1513, he sighted the Pacific Ocean. A few days later, he reached the Gulf of San Miguel and took the South Sea in the name of the king. He and his men carried ships in pieces over the mountains to the Pacific, and from 1517 to 1518 he explored the Gulf of San Miguel. During the period from 1511 on, Balboa had endured a number of assaults from Pedrarias, his father-in-law, and others who accused him of various misdeeds. Pedrarias charged him with treason, rebellion, mistreatment of the natives, and other crimes, and in January 1519, Balboa was beheaded.

Cortes

The Aztecs of Central America and the Incas of Peru had well-established nations by the end of the fifteenth century. Nevertheless, in less than two years, **Hernando Cortes** destroyed the monarchy, took possession of Tenochtitlan, and defeated most of the Aztecs.

Cortes was a notary and farmer on Hispaniola in the early years after the Spanish discovered the Americas. Here he contracted syphilis, but had recovered sufficiently by 1511 to accompany Diego Velazquez in his conquest of Cuba. Cortes later became clerk under Velazquez. For his service, Cortes received a *repartimiento*, or gift of land, and native slaves. He also received the first house in Santiago. Cortes was imprisoned and was involved in other scandalous incidents here when he came into conflict with Velazquez, but was twice the mayor of Santiago. In 1518, Cortes was put in charge of an expedition to establish a colony on the mainland. He sailed for the Yucatan coast on February 18, 1519, with eleven ships, 508 soldiers, and sixteen horses. Cortes captured an Indian slave, Malinche, who spoke both Mayan and the Aztec language, Nahuatl. She was known as the "tongue" of Cortes, and was eventually baptized as Doña Marina. Doña Marina was likely one of the reasons Cortes was initially able to charm **Montezuma**. Through his interpreter Doña Marina, Cortes learned of unrest among the subjects of the Aztecs. He swayed over 20,000 of the Aztec subjects to his side and marched to Tenochtitlan. At first, Montezuma welcomed Cortes, as he identified him with **Quetzalcoatl**, the legendary god of the Aztecs who had, by coincidence, promised to return in this very year. Although Cortes enjoyed momentary success in Tenochtitlan, his troubles with the Spanish had not subsided. After Cortes founded Vera Cruz, the explorer Narvaez attacked him in 1520.

While Narvaez distracted Cortes, the Aztecs, who had become increasingly resentful of the Spaniard's lust for gold and found Cortes's deputy particularly noxious, finally revolted and attacked the Spaniards. On the *noche triste*, or "sad night," of June 30, 1520, the Aztecs drove Cortes and his men down the causeway of Tenochtitlan. Cortes laid siege to the city, which finally surrendered on August 15, 1521. Meanwhile, Cortes was still under attack from the Spanish. His old enemy, Velazquez, began to attack him in Spain, which prompted Cortes to write five letters to King Charles V.

In 1524, Cortes led an expedition to Honduras. His health deteriorated during the two-year trek, and those he had left in charge of the empire he had conquered had confiscated his property and abused the natives. These events prompted his famous fifth letter to Charles V, and, in 1528, he returned to Spain to defend himself. In 1530, he returned to the Spanish empire in the New World, now known as New Spain, and found it in a state of anarchy. His subjects accused him of murdering his first wife and, in 1540, Cortes returned to Spain. He died, in his own words, "old, poor, and in debt." Towards the end of his life, he had intended to return to New Spain, but died before he could even reach Seville in Spain.

His troops numbered 600; the Aztec population was close to 5,000,000.

Pizarro

The Incas met a similar fate in 1532 at the hands of 175 Spanish troops led by **Francisco Pizarro**. Francisco Pizarro first traveled to the New World in 1510 on an expedition led by Alonso de Ojeda to what is modern Colombia. In 1513 he accompanied Balboa on the expedition that first sighted the Pacific. From 1519 to 1523, he served as mayor of Panama. In 1523, at the age of forty-eight, Pizarro left on the expedition that would discover the empire of the Incas. From 1524 to 1527, he journeyed to the south, and his men endured many hardships. Upon finding traces of civilization, Pizarro sent for reinforcements from Panama. The governor told him to return, whereupon Pizarro drew a line across the ground asking those who desired wealth and glory to cross it. Thirteen men crossed the line, and Pizarro continued south. He named the land "Peru," which was derived from the name of the river Viru. In 1528, Pizarro traveled to Spain to ask for further help, at the same time as Hernando Cortes had returned from the New World. In 1529, Charles V gave Pizarro a coat of arms, and made him governor of the region now called New Castille, which extended 600 miles south from Panama along the coast. In January 1530, he and four of his brothers set sail with 180 men for Peru, and in April they made their first contact with **Atahualpa**. Pizarro attempted to convert the Inca king, who threw the Bible to the ground. Pizarro attacked and quickly defeated the Incas. He ordered Atahualpa to be put to death by strangulation on August 29, 1533. In November, Pizarro then took Cuzco, the Inca capital, without a struggle. Pizarro founded Lima, Peru, in 1535. During the last years of his life, his rival Almagro attacked him. On June 26, 1541, Almagro attacked Pizarro's palace in Lima. Pizarro was killed in the attack, and, as he lay dying, drew a cross on the ground with his own blood.

Cabeza de Vaca

Álvar Núñes Cabeza de Vaca was treasurer for the expedition of Narvaez to Tampa Bay, Florida, in 1528. By the time the expedition reached Galveston, Texas, only about sixty men were left. By the next spring, only fifteen men were still alive, and, eventually, only Núñes and three others were left to explore the remaining way into northern Mexico. His accounts of the Seven Golden Cities, or El Dorado, inspired the expeditions of de Soto and Coronado. Núñes was appointed governor of Rio de la Plata. From 1541 to 1542, he explored the region from Brazil to Paraguay, and later wrote a valuable work on the geography of the region. He was eventually deported to Spain for misconduct in office and sentenced to work in Africa.

Coronado

Francisco Vásquez de Coronado and his men explored the North American southwest, discovered the Grand Canyon, and were the first Europeans to see the enormous herds of bison in the southwest. Coronado earned a reputation for pacifying the Native Americans and was made governor of Nueva Galicia in 1538. Other explorers had returned with tales of the Seven Golden Cities of Cibola, which we now know were the Zuni Pueblos. In 1540, Coronado was put in charge of the main force sent to look for what the Spanish believed were cities of gold. He moved up the west coast of Mexico to Culiacan, and sent a smaller force that captured the Pueblos of Zuni. He and his men spent that winter along the Rio Grande River, where they were attacked several times by natives. In 1541, Coronado discovered the Palo Duro Canyon in Texas, and then proceeded with a smaller contingent to Kansas. Coronado was indicted in the *residencia*, or investigation, of his expedition for misconduct, but later was exonerated. He was also indicted and condemned after his governorship.

De Soto

Hernando de Soto accompanied Pedrarias Davila to the New World on his explorations along the coast from 1516 to 1520. Balboa had recently reached the Pacific, and competition and greed had begun to divide the *conquistadors*. Pedrarias was Balboa's father-in-law, and he had him beheaded over a squabble. De Soto participated in the conquest of what is now Nicaragua and became the military commander there. When Pedrarias died in 1531, he joined the expedition of Pizarro, and he was Pizarro's ambassador to the Inca king Atahualpa. De Soto became friends with Atahaulpa, and when Pizarro executed the king, de Soto returned to Spain. De Soto sailed again for the New World in 1538 as leader of an expedition with 10 ships, 600 to 1,000 men, and 300 horses. He landed in Florida, just south of Tampa Bay, in 1539. He encountered the small village of the Apalachee Native Americans. The next year, he forged on to Alabama near modern Mobile; there he fought with the local chief. He traveled on through Tennessee to the **Mississippi River**, first sighted on May 21, 1540. The name "Mississippi" means "Father of the Water." His forces made their way into Arkansas and Oklahoma, where they encountered hostile natives on many occasions. Later that same month, he turned back to the Mississippi River, where he died a few days later. De Soto brutally mistreated the Native Americans by chaining them together with iron collars and using vicious dogs to keep them in line. He was so hated by the natives that his companions interred him in the Mississippi River for fear the natives would desecrate the corpse.

REASONS FOR THE SUCCESS OF THE SPANISH CONQUEST

The superstitious conviction of many natives that the Spanish were somehow either divine or extraterrestrial and European technology contributed to the defeat of the Native American populations. Aztec and Inca warfare was no match for the well-trained Spanish troops, the strange men in "floating houses," and their cannon.

Frightened and then defeated by European technology, the Meso- and South American Indians fell prey to the Spanish *conquistadores*. The scenario that followed has been described as a New World "holocaust," which resulted from the policies of the Spanish overlords and the devastation caused by European disease. Falling victim to the **encomienda** system of forced labor in mines and sugar cane fields and exposed to such European diseases as smallpox, the Indians died in droves. Although there is dispute among historians as to the exact number of Indians who died, some believe that in Peru the population of Native Americans fell from 1.3 million in 1570 to 600,000 in fifty years. In Central America, of the 25.3 million Indians living there at the time of the arrival of Cortes in 1519, only 1.3 million remained by 1620.

The Spanish treatment of the Native Americans gave rise to the "black legend," first discussed by **Bartolome de las Casas** in 1552. De las Casas was the Dominican Bishop of Chiapas, who participated in a debate in 1550 concerning the treatment of the Native Americans. He argued that the Spanish abused and exploited the Native Americans, whom he portrayed as innocent, noble beings. The Spanish, he said, did not realize the achievements nor their commonalities with the inhabitants of the Americas. Sepulveda, a Spanish bishop, challenged his arguments, and presented what was the more common

European view of the Native Americans. De las Casas wrote nine essays, eight of which were published in 1552 and the ninth in 1553.

Historical Issues

Since the onset of the quincentennial celebration of Columbus's first voyage, historians have debated many aspects of the voyages of exploration, the contributions of Columbus, the actual site of his first "landfall," and the impact of the European presence on the Native Americans. Before 1992, most historians appear to have agreed with Samuel Eliot Morison who insisted in *Admiral of the Ocean Sea* that "the whole history of America stems from the four voyages of Columbus."

Since 1992, however, there has been an endeavor to subject Columbus to a re-examination, leading some writers to emphasize that his treatment of the Native Americans was cruel and inhuman, that he was ineffective as a colonial governor, and that he had not indeed "discovered" America. The actual discovery had taken place tens of thousands of years earlier, by the Asians crossing the land bridge between Siberia and Alaska.

Most historians in the twenty-first century, however, insist that the merits of Columbus and his experiences must be measured in terms of fifteenth-century standards and values and not in terms of those of the twentieth century. He was a product of the crusading zeal of the Renaissance period, a religious man, who did indeed accomplish what he set out to do. He sailed west and encountered continents previously unknown to fifteenth-century Europeans, and the subsequent crop and animal exchange revolutionized the lifestyle of Europeans. Historians refer to this process as the "**Columbian Exchange**," and it introduced into the New World such previously unknown commodities as cattle, horses, goats, sugar, barley, oats, wine grapes, melons, olives, bananas, tea, and coffee, as well as snap, kidney, and lima beans. Tobacco, potatoes, chocolate, corn, and tomatoes made their way from the New World into the Old World. Europeans also discovered iguanas, flying squirrels, catfish, rattlesnakes, bison, cougars, armadillos, opossums, sloths, anacondas, electric eels, vampire bats, toucans, condors, and hummingbirds in the Americas.

Not all exchanges were beneficial, of course, and European diseases such as smallpox, for which the Native Americans had no resistance, were responsible for the significant depopulation of the New World.

Because of such crops as the potato, the sweet potato, and maize, however, Europeans and later the Chinese were able to vary their diets and participate in the technological revolution that would begin within 200 years of Columbus's voyage.

In addition, silver from the mines in the Americas flooded the European markets. From 1503 to 1650, the Spanish brought six million kilograms of silver and 185,000 kilograms of gold into Seville. Although the influx of New World silver has often been blamed for the rampant inflation that hit Spain and later Europe in the sixteenth century, prices had already risen sharply before 1565, while silver imports did not reach their peak until 1580 to 1620. However, Phillip II of Spain paid his armies and foreign debts with New World silver, and transmitted the rising prices and inflation to the rest of Europe. This surge in prices is known as the "**Price Revolution**."

In Wittenberg in 1517, the year Martin Luther posted his 95 theses, prices had risen by 100 percent over what they were in 1492, the year of Columbus's first voyage. Those who owed debts actually benefited from the inflation, as their debt decreased in value, while the nobles, to whom the debts were owed, suffered, as did the poor, who had to combat rising prices for food and other necessities.

The European Voyages of Exploration also created a global economy through sea trade. The Portuguese reached India and then went on to Japan and China. They brought back spices to Lisbon and often paid for these goods with textiles from India and gold and ivory from eastern Africa. From the Portuguese outpost at Macao, they took Chinese silk to Japan and the Philippines. There, they traded silk for Spanish silver. Spanish silver from the New World had a dramatic effect on the Chinese economy; the Single Whip Reform united the taxation system of China through a single tax payable in silver. The Portuguese also brought horses to India from Mesopotamia and copper from Arabia, and carried hawks and peacocks from India to China and Japan. The Portuguese also traded in African slaves; African slave labor produced the sugar on their plantations in Brazil, which produced the bulk of Europe's sugar supply in the sixteenth and seventeenth centuries. Portuguese became the language of trade in eastern Africa and in the Asian trade. The legacy of the Portuguese trading empire continued until the late twentieth century; Macao was ceded back to the Chinese in 1999, and the Portuguese are also planning to relinquish control of other areas conquered during the Age of Exploration.

The Spanish also established a large maritime empire in the Age of Exploration. Miguel Lopez de Pegazpi established Spanish control over the Philippine Islands. Manilla linked Spanish trade in the Americas with the Eastern trade. The Portuguese brought silk to the Philippines, and the Spanish carried it to the New World where it was exported to Spain. The silk trade transmitted huge amounts of bouillon from the New World to Manila; in 1597, 12 million pesos made the journey across the Atlantic to fuel the silk trade. This was almost the total value of the entire transatlantic trade.

The Dutch also established a large trading empire based on spices. In 1599, a Dutch fleet brought over 600,000 pounds of pepper and large quantities of other spices, such as cloves and nutmeg, to Amsterdam, and made over a 100 percent profit. The Age of Exploration brought Europe into contact with not only the Americas, but with the Asian trade market. It forever changed the world view of the Europeans and created the first global economy.

Some historians call the voyages of the fifteenth century the "last crusade," explaining that the explorers searched for "God, Gold and Glory." Columbus, himself, in commenting in his journal about his first voyage, explained, "God made me the messenger of the new heaven and the new earth of which he spoke in the Apocalypse of St. John . . . and he showed me the post where to find it." Whatever the motives of the explorers, the Spanish presence in the Americas forever changed the course of world history. The Voyages of Exploration created the first true global age in world history.

CHAPTER 20

THE REFORMATION

The **Reformation** was, in many ways, an outgrowth of the Renaissance. It was also an outgrowth of centuries of general problems in the church, dating back to the Babylonian Captivity of the fourteenth century and the Great Schism that followed. The corruption evident in the church during these periods had sparked a great deal of dissent and literature of protest. Other problems included absent bishops, or those who held appointments by virtue of family standing or wealth but who were rarely present in their bishoprics and, therefore, did not meet the needs of the people.

Modern scholars, such as Haiko Obermann, insist that the late medieval period was not as corrupt as once thought, but rather its obvious concern for corruption was a mark of a deep and intense piety on the part of the laity. In other words, appearances are deceptive in that there was no more corruption than in earlier periods, but people were more concerned due to a resurgence in popular piety. Whatever one's scholarly view on the subject, the Renaissance helped to create more criticism of the papacy and of the church in general.

The Renaissance humanists had opened up a new era in which existing authorities were subject to thorough critique. Lorenzo Valla, for example, had shown through a sophisticated study of language that the so-called Donation of Constantine was a forgery and dated well after the time of Constantine. This document had purported to cede the temporal or earthly power of the emperor Constantine to the pope in Rome, thus giving him power over secular and sacred affairs. This document was a fundamental plank of arguments in support of papal power over secular affairs in the Middle Ages, yet Valla had shown that it could not date to a period before that of Charlemagne in the ninth century, during which some of its language, relating to feudal society, first came into being.

Erasmus of Rotterdam was another good example of the links between humanist critique and the desire for reform in the church. He published the *Novum Instrumentum*, or *Testamentum*, a new critical edition of the New Testament based on the study of its original languages. It was this edition of the New Testament that helped Luther frame his revolutionary idea of justification by faith, but the approaches of Erasmus and Luther to reform were radically different.

Erasmus was very dissatisfied with the attitudes and methodology of the medieval Scholastic theologian. He argued that Scholastics tried to systematize everything, even the most remote mysteries of the faith. In so doing, their ideas often became unintelligible to the ordinary man and so could not contribute to one's spiritual growth. In the *Praise of Folly*, he pointed out that even the Apostles could not have understood the Scholastics, and in his *Paraclesis*, the preface to the *Novum Instrumentum*, he argued that the Scriptures ought to be made accessible to the ploughboy in the field. Erasmus urged Christians to go back to the basics as contained in the Scriptures. In the *Praise of Folly* and other works, Erasmus criticized the corruption of the clergy and of monks and nuns, whom he felt focused on outer manifestations of piety without any true inner piety. For this reason, he was very critical of the practice of selling indulgences, whereby one might earn forgiveness for sins or less time in purgatory by being in the presence of the bones or other relics of saints or by donating money to the church. Erasmus argued that one's inner state was more important for forgiveness than the mere act of donating money, which one could do while still not repenting inwardly.

MARTIN LUTHER

Many, including the young German monk **Martin Luther**, shared Erasmus's desire for reform. Luther's parents were very harsh and authoritarian, which may have contributed to his obsession with his own faults and sins. As a young man, Luther was caught in a storm while out walking one day; he was terrified and prayed to St. Anne that if she rescued him, he would dedicate his life to religion and become a monk. So he did and joined the Augustinian order. As a monk, Luther was obsessed with his sinfulness and spent hours beating his back in penance. He went so often to his confessor Staupitz that he was finally told not to come back unless he had something really important to confess. In other words, Staupitz tried to free Luther of his overwhelming sense of guilt, but did not succeed.

Luther was terrified by his vision of God as a God of vengeance, rather than one of mercy. In the art of his time in Germany, Judgment Day was a frequent theme. Artists, such as *Durer*, portrayed Christ as a fearsome Judge, rather than as the merciful Son of Man.

Luther was troubled by the sinfulness of man, but he carried his worries to an extreme. While the Italian humanists glorified man and his achievements, Luther focused on man's sinfulness, as well as his own.

When Luther celebrated his first mass, he trembled at the altar out of fear of the Almighty and of God as a Transcendent Judge.

Luther was respected in the Augustinian order for his austerities and penances, and they selected him to make a trip to Rome, the heart of the Roman Catholic Church. While there, he viewed many shrines of saints, including a famous set of stairs that one climbed on one's knees as an act of penance. His trip to Rome began to enlighten him on areas of corruption and the need for reform, and on the impossibility, in his view, of achieving true forgiveness and purity through acts of penance. In Luther's Wittenberg, there were so many relics that one could erase one million years in purgatory by touching or viewing all of them!

In 1517, the papacy hired the infamous Tetzel to sell indulgences in order to finance the construction of St. Peter's in Rome. The church wanted the dome to rival that of the cathedral in Florence, the famous Duomo, a symbol of the Renaissance. The pope also changed the doctrine of indulgences in a way that truly alarmed Luther. Before, one could obtain absolution here on earth from punishment by performing satisfaction or penance; now, the church suggested that the pope could remit time in purgatory. The pope was arguing that indulgences drew from a storehouse of good works.

Luther was incensed by the sale of indulgences, but whereas Erasmus used humor to make a point, as in *The Praise of Folly*, Luther's language was a crude one of hellfire and brimstone, and downright crude at times.

Luther was not comfortable with indulgences because he was troubled by the relationship of good deeds to salvation. If God really is a just God, then man could never be saved. Man could never do enough good to merit salvation in the eyes of God, and this is what had driven Luther virtually mad as a monk. No amount of penance was satisfactory in his view; every bad deed must immediately be confessed. If one lived in such a manner, one could never attain peace, much less salvation.

In 1517, Luther posted his **95 theses** on the door of the church at Wittenberg. This was a common area for posting matters for debate, and Luther chose October 31, or the Eve of All Saints' Day, on which to make his statement. He asked the church to consider 95 points of dispute, among them the claim that the pope had any power at all to forgive sins. Luther believed only God had this power.

The outcry over Luther's 95 theses led to the Leipzig Disputation, in which the church attempted to refute Luther's ideas, and eventually, when they failed to silence him, to his being summoned to appear in Rome during the Diet of Augsburg. He refused to go to Rome, but met the papal legate Cajetan at Augsburg in October 1518. Luther refused to recant and returned to Wittenberg on the anniversary of his posting of the 95 theses.

By 1520, Luther's appeal to Rome for reform had become an appeal to Germans for open revolution against the church. Luther published three famous treatises in this year that attacked the cornerstones of Catholic theology.

"The Freedom of a Christian"

Luther had never resolved his intense inner struggle with sin and repentance. It was a passage from Erasmus's new translation of the Bible that prompted a flash of insight that would forever change not only Luther's life, but the life of many Christians then and now. In Romans, Erasmus translated the words of Paul to read "be penitent," whereas the Latin Vulgate translation used by the Roman Catholic Church for centuries had read "do penance." This passage reinforced Luther's disgust with indulgences and helped to explain his theological struggle with penance. All the outer penance in the world cannot affect inner repentance, and this can only come as a gift of grace, not as an act of the human will, because humans can never do enough good to earn salvation.

Luther argued that man has two natures, an inner and an outer. The inner nature cannot be touched by the outer nature; therefore, only one thing is necessary for the Christian: the Word of God. This word cannot be practiced through works. Luther argued that the Ten Commandments, for example, teach us what we ought to do, and they are only given to us so that we may despair of our own ability to do good. We will fail to live up to the commandments no matter how hard we try. For Luther, humans are totally depraved and have no ability whatsoever to do good. When one has totally despaired, as Luther did, of ever achieving salvation through good works and penance, then one turns to the one thing that may save him—faith, which alone can justify one in the eyes of God. This he took from Romans 10: 10, an epistle from the apostle Paul.

For Luther, faith was a gift of God and not something one freely chooses. As his career progressed, Luther would also argue that humans have no free will whatsoever. We are totally dependent for our salvation on faith, a gift preordained for us. Luther did argue that a good tree will bear good fruit, or that those with faith would do good works, but he insisted that good works do not effect our salvation.

In this treatise, Luther decisively broke with the theology of the Roman church, in which good works were an integral part of spirituality. Erasmus challenged Luther on this issue, asking why the commandments were given if we could not follow them, and at this point, the methods of Erasmus and Luther were easily differentiated. Erasmus wanted to reform the church that was, whereas by 1520, Luther wished to create a new church, one that totally broke from Rome.

"On the Babylonian Captivity of the Church"

This was another of the 1520 treatises, in which Luther denied the seven sacraments of the Roman church and insisted that there was biblical proof for only three: baptism, the Eucharist, and penance. He would later reject penance as a sacrament, keeping only baptism and the Eucharist. Luther also rejected the **apocrypha**, a group of books in the Old Testament that he argued were rejected by Jews but included in the Septuagint translation. If Jews rejected them, then so should Christians.

"The Address to the Christian Nobility of the German Nation"

In this 1520 work, Luther argued that the "three walls of the papacy" were invalid. These were the claims that the papacy had power over the temporal sphere, such as asserted by Boniface VIII over Philip IV; that only the pope can summon a church council, such as the claim made in the bull *Exacrabilis*; and that only the pope can interpret the Bible for all Christians. Luther argued that "all Christians are of the same estate," not that all Christians are social equals, but that insofar as they are Christians, they are spiritually equal and able to interpret scripture for themselves. Luther also suggested that the king, as a Christian, need not be under the power of the pope. Similarly, many German princes immediately used Luther's statement of spiritual equality to create open rebellion against the Holy Roman Emperor. Peasants rebelled from their masters, too, and looted and pillaged the estates of nobles. These claims inspired an intense movement of German nationalism, as kings and princes separated from Rome in the name of German interests. Some scholars argue that nationalism was a strong force in this region in later times because of Luther's explicit appeal in this treatise to the German nation, which did not come into being until the nineteenth century. Later German thinkers emphasized the distinctiveness of cultures, especially that of Germany. Some would tie these later ideas to Luther's work.

Luther's writings also initiated a massive social rebellion that he had not anticipated. Although Luther condemned these revolts and upheld the power of the state, nevertheless, he had started a mass movement that would ultimately fragment the Holy Roman Empire. Many historians debate whether the Reformation would have happened or unfolded with the viciousness it did without the complicated set of social, political, and economic conditions that existed in Luther's age. For what it is worth, Luther's protest was motivated by theological concerns, but spoke to the social, political, and economic interests of the Germans.

In his treatise, Luther also denied the value of Holy Orders or the validity of the priesthood. He argued that all Christians are able to be their own priests and to interpret the Scriptures for themselves. Similarly, he insisted that the monastic life was not a special state of life, and that every person's work is God's work. Luther urged the dissolution of monasteries and himself married an ex-nun, Catherine von Bora, with whom he had six daughters. He rejected the idea that clergy should be celibate, and insisted on the family as the center of Christian life. In Lutheran households, women gained new respect as those primarily responsible for teaching the word of God.

Luther also denied that the chalice or cup of wine in the Eucharist should be administered only to the clergy, as in the Roman Church, but rather insisted that it be given to all Christians. He insisted that the mass be said in German, the language of his people, rather than the Latin of the Roman mass, a language many did not understand. In 1534, Luther published a new translation of the entire Bible in German, making the scriptures available to many. Many scholars argue that this translation marks one of the high points in the history of the German language. Luther also used hymns, as opposed to the Gregorian chant used in the Roman Church.

In 1520, the pope issued the bull *Exsurge domine*. Amidst the wild uproar of students, Luther burned the papal bull. In 1521, the Diet of Worms later condemned Luther as well, through the **Edict of Worms**. According to a pious but inauthentic tradition, he responded with the simple words that "here I stand. I can do no other." Luther was a very courageous man of conviction when it came to theological beliefs, and whatever one may say about some of his more controversial beliefs and actions, one may still remain respectful of the courage of Luther's fight against Catholicism. Luther could be very vehement in his condemnation of ideas and practices and could use very forceful, even crude, language. He remarked on one occasion that since the Anabaptists, a group in Munster, advocated adult baptism when one reached the age of understanding, they should be thrown into a river with rocks around their necks and allowed to drown! Luther was also very anti-Semitic in his opinions, and some have linked the growth of anti-Semitism in Germany to Luther. This movement, some would argue, culminated in Hitler's attempt to eradicate the world of Jewry in World War II. Certainly, these aspects of Luther's character were controversial and can be condemned on many grounds. When compared, however, to such men as Erasmus, who was often unable to abide by the restrictions of Lent or to fulfill his commitment to the monastic life, one in the end may perhaps still remain respectful of Luther's single-minded commitment to fighting abuse in the church.

In 1530, Emperor Charles V summoned the Diet of Augsburg to address the conflict between the Lutherans and Catholics. Luther's supporter Melancthon drafted the Augsburg Confession, designed to reconcile the two opposing viewpoints, but the Diet rejected the Protestant assertions. The Protestants formed their own league, the Schmalkald League, a group of Lutherans. They did not include other dissenting groups, such as the followers of Zwingli. Despite Luther's insistence that every Christian was capable of interpreting the Word, he was convinced that only the Lutheran interpretation was correct!

THE AFTERMATH OF LUTHER'S CAREER

Luther died in 1546, and with his last breath wished for the end of the Roman church. In 1537, he had allegedly wished for his epitaph to read: *"Pestis eram vivus, moriens ero mors tua, Papa* / Living I was a pest to thee, O Pope, dying I will be thy death." Luther did succeed in unleashing a movement that the Roman Church could not contain: the Protestant Reformation. In 1555, the Peace of Augsburg finally addressed the differences between the Lutherans and Catholics. The fundamental principle of the Peace of Augsburg was *cuius regio eius religio*, or "his the region, his the religion." In other words, the prince had the right to determine the religion of his territory. This freedom did not apply to the followers of Zwingli nor to those of Calvin, but only to Lutherans and Catholics. Denmark, Sweden, Scandinavia, and North Germany became and still remain predominantly Lutheran, but the movement was too distinctively German in its origin to spread further during this period. The Peace of Augsburg effectively destroyed the Holy Roman Empire, though it would linger on for years, neither holy, Roman, nor an empire in the true sense of the word.

John Calvin in Geneva

In 1536, **John Calvin** published the Institutes of Christian Religion, considered by many to be the definitive work of Protestantism. At the Marburg Colloquy, differences between Luther and Calvin were already apparent. Both denied the Catholic doctrine of **transubstantiation**, whereby the host and wine become the body and blood of Christ in the Mass. Both argued that the host and wine were a symbol rather than the reality of Christ himself, but Luther believed in consubstantiation, the idea that the presence of Christ was there should one's faith be great enough. Calvin continued to view the sacrament as primarily symbolic rather than the reality of the presence of Christ.

Calvin believed that the religious community, or the church, should control the state. He believed, like Luther, that the laity should control church affairs. Calvinist churches were led by elders and were called presbyteries.

Calvin advocated the idea of the calling, the notion of doing God's work as a holy endeavor. The historian Weber argued that Calvin encouraged capitalism, as making a profit from doing God's work well is a holy thing. According to the controversial Weber thesis, the Protestant work ethic led to an economic revolution and also to greater democracy, as the laity controlled the affairs of state through their church structure. In New England in the Americas, Calvinism is linked to the town hall meeting; today in America, many presidential campaigns symbolically begin in New England town halls, which many regard as the seat of democracy.

The Huguenots in France

The **Huguenots** were French Protestants who followed the teachings of Calvin. These Protestants refer to themselves as *"réformees"* (reformers) rather than "Huguenots." The origin of the name "Huguenot" is uncertain, but appears to date from approximately 1550 when it was used in court cases against heretics. The absolute monarchy of France refused to tolerate any dissent, especially that of such Protestant groups as the Huguenots. Luther's teachings had ripped apart the Holy Roman Empire, and the French were deeply suspicious of Protestantism. The Wars of Religion erupted in France when 1,200 Huguenots were massacred at Vassy on March 1, 1562. The St. Bartholomew's Day Massacre, during the nights of August 23–24, 1572, was the most infamous event of these wars. More than 8,000 Huguenots were murdered in Paris. The massacre occurred during the wedding of Henry of Navarre, a Huguenot, to Marguerite de Valois, the daughter of **Catherine de Medici**. Many Huguenots were in Paris for the wedding. Catherine de Medici had persuaded her son Charles IX to order the massacre, which lasted three days and eventually spread to the countryside. On the morning of August 24, 1572, a Sunday, she personally walked through the streets of Paris to inspect the carnage. Even the pope rejoiced at the massacre and the victory of Catholicism over the heretics. Catherine and Charles spared Henry's life

Massacre of the Huguenots *by Francois Dubois depicted the St. Bartholomew's Day Massacre of 1572.*

when he pretended to support Roman Catholicism. In 1593, he renounced Protestantism, and within five years he became King Henry IV, known as *le bon Henri*, the good Henry, of France. On April 13, 1598, Henry eventually signed the Edict of Nantes, which allowed the Huguenots to practice their faith openly in twenty selected French cities, now known as "free cities." Unfortunately, later figures such as Cardinal Richelieu and Louis XIV were not as tolerant of the Huguenots and continued to persecute them. Many fled to the Americas and other parts of the world to practice their faith.

Ulrich Zwingli

Ulrich Zwingli was another important leader of the Reformation and, like Luther, was first ordained a Catholic priest, serving at the Great Minster Church in Zurich. Zwingli preached powerful sermons straight from the New Testament rather than from the lectionary, and so launched the Reformation in Switzerland. While Luther believed that "the Word worked" and relied only on the Scriptures rather than the traditions of the Roman Church, he also believed that what the Bible did not prohibit was acceptable. Zwingli, on the other hand, believed that everything not specifically mentioned in the Bible should be prohibited. Like Luther, he emphasized the ability of the masses to interpret the Bible for themselves. Following Zwingli's teachings, the Swiss in Zurich rejected the prohibition of meat during Lent and ate sausages right before Easter in protest of Roman policies. Zwingli met with Luther and Calvin at the Marburg Colloquy, and rejected transubstantiation in favor of the view of the Lord's Supper as a memorial. He also rejected Luther's view of consubstantiation as a form of cannibalism, while Luther rejected his view of the Lord's Supper as empty. Like many reformers, Zwingli urged the return to the Apostolic church as described in the New Testament. Just as Luther married an ex-nun, Zwingli secretly married Anna Reinhart, a widow with three children, while still a priest. They had four more children together. Zwingli fought for the Swiss against the Holy Roman Emperor Charles V, organizing a defensive force and being wounded at the Battle of Capel. He later died of the plague in 1531, a hero of the Swiss Reformation.

THE ENGLISH REFORMATION

King Henry VIII (1509–1547) was originally a defender of the Roman Catholic faith, having written a *Defense of the Seven Sacraments* against the teachings of Luther. However, his marriage to his brother Arthur's widow and Hapsburg heiress, Catherine of Aragon, had produced only a daughter, Mary. Out of desire for a son, Henry sought permission from the pope to obtain a divorce. The pope would not give permission, as the papacy had already given permission for Henry to marry his brother's widow in an earlier decision. Consequently, Henry separated from Rome to marry **Anne Boleyn**, who bore him a daughter, Elizabeth, later to be known as Elizabeth the Great. Anne's failure to produce a son resulted in the loss of her head and in a traumatic childhood for her daughter Elizabeth, who became a Protestant, while her half-sister Mary remained a staunch Catholic.

In 1534, Henry passed the Act of Supremacy, whereby he became the head of the Church of England. His Lord Chancellor Thomas More refused to support the act and consequently was beheaded. More was a friend of Erasmus and wrote the famous work *Utopia*.

Henry confiscated church property, dissolved the Roman Catholic monasteries and took their land and other possessions, but everything else about religion remained the same.

King Henry VIII.

In 1539, the Six Articles articulated the structure of the Church of England, and they retained bishops, archbishops, and essentially the rest of the structure of the Roman church without the pope.

The Six Articles affirmed the Catholic doctrines of transubstantiation and of the celibacy of clergy, but did insist on the mass in English, a Protestant plank.

Henry finally did produce his long awaited son, Edward, by his third wife, Jane Seymour. He would marry three more times, beheading all but the last wife, who outlived him.

As for Edward, he, like his mother, was sickly and frail and died at an early age, leaving only his half-sisters to rule. Under Edward, the *Book of Common Prayer* more clearly defined the Protestantism of the Church of England, or the Anglican Church.

Henry's daughter Mary, by Catherine of Aragon, was staunchly Catholic, and through her vicious persecution of Protestants became known as **Bloody Mary**. To further the Catholic cause, she married Philip of Spain, the strongest Catholic monarch on the continent and a relative of her mother.

Philip despised Mary, but allied with her to defend Catholicism from the rising ride of Protestantism. Spain would be the leader of the Counter-Reformation and the Spanish Inquisition, one of the most brutal and intolerant episodes in history.

When Mary died childless in 1558, her half-sister Elizabeth came to the throne. During the reign of **Elizabeth the Great**, the Church of England rejected saints and allowed the clergy to marry, all Protestant ideals. Elizabeth never married, thus earning her the nickname of the Virgin Queen, but she used the possibility of marriage to make many alliances. As a woman monarch in a man's world, she managed to rule for sixty years. Many scholars argue that her rule was not an especially great one, but it was against the backdrop of the Renaissance in England and the careers of such notables as William Shakespeare.

In 1588, Elizabeth achieved perhaps the most important victory of her reign. Philip of Spain summoned the largest armada ever collected to invade England and rid it of the Protestant Elizabeth, but before the fleet could reach England, a massive wind, called the **Protestant wind**, blew the fleet around the island and wrecked it. England did not become Catholic, and Protestantism would rule the church there. The victory over the armada also made it possible for England to later rule the seas.

THE COUNTER REFORMATION

The Roman Church fought the growing threat of Protestantism in a movement known as the Counter Reformation. **Ignatius of Loyola** founded the Jesuits or Society of Jesus as an imitation of Christ, and he insisted on complete submission in matters of faith. According to Loyola, if the church says that white is black, then white is black. The immense learning of the Jesuits was for the purpose of refuting Protestant doctrines and teaching the Catholic faith. The Jesuits would carry the faith to the Far East, and also make numerous contributions to science.

The Council of Trent met sporadically from 1545 to 1563. There would not be another church council until 1870. The council, like the Jesuits, reaffirmed the basic tenets of Catholicism. It rejected the Protestant justification by faith and argued that good works were necessary for salvation. The council affirmed the doctrine of transubstantiation and that priesthood was a special vocation, and insisted on the Latin Vulgate as the only authoritative translation of the Bible. This was perhaps unfortunate, as we now know the Vulgate was not a particularly good translation.

The council also issued a list of banned books, the Index of Prohibited Books. They regulated art, affecting Michelangelo's painting in the Sistine Chapel. The council rejected the conciliar movement and kept the papacy as the authoritative center of the church. They insisted on the unity of the church, and rejected those doctrines of the Protestants that resulted in the plethora of sects seen today. Luther's notion that any Christian could interpret the Bible as well as any other was rejected in favor of the consensus of the faithful and the need for the church as a mediating authority.

The council also affirmed the seven sacraments in the face of Luther's criticisms. Many scholars have suggested that their rigidity on theological points of debate with the Protestants kept the Roman Church from reconciliation with them. On the other hand, the council also implemented many reforms in the priesthood and other areas. They reformed the controversial sale of indulgences, forced bishops to reside in the region they presided over, and forbade the practice of simony, or the buying and selling of church offices. Despite these achievements, it was not until **Vatican II** in the 1960s that many of Luther's ideas were implemented by the Roman Catholic Church, such as giving the chalice to the laity and the mass in the languages spoken by those in attendance. The Council of Trent completely separated the Protestants from the Catholic world; it would not be until the twentieth century that some Protestant groups, such as the Anglicans, would begin dialogues with the Roman Church about reunification. Although the Anglicans and Catholics remain separated over the issue of female ordination, the Catholic and Lutheran Churches recently issued a declaration on the idea of justification by faith that makes a beginning towards reaching agreement as to language.

Erasmus argued that Luther had blown out his candle; what he meant was that perhaps if Luther had approached the problem in another, less vehement and inflammatory way, some of his reforms might have been accepted.

Many others, such as Erasmus, had agitated for reform, but Lutheranism firmly stopped the movement within the Catholic Church for the next several hundred years.

Many wars would be fought over these religious issues. The Wars of Religion from 1618 to 1648 would leave over 30 percent of Germans dead on the battlefield. The Peace of Westphalia in 1648 following the Thirty Years' War finally included Calvinists and gave them the freedom of religion offered to Lutherans in the Peace of Augsburg.

CHAPTER 21

THE SCIENTIFIC REVOLUTION AND THE ENLIGHTENMENT

The **Scientific Revolution**, like the Renaissance, helped to end the old medieval ways of thinking and to usher the world into the modern era. During the Renaissance, there was increased interest in the secular world, but it was during the Scientific Revolution that a new, scientific attitude towards the study of the world emerged, one whose conclusions often clashed with the teachings of established religions. During the subsequent movement known as the **Enlightenment**, the **philosophes** would ultimately reject the religion of past eras as superstition in favor of the use of reason. While the medieval work relied upon authorities, such as the Bible and the church, the figures of the Scientific Revolution helped to establish the attitude that one should not believe anything unless one could empirically verify it or prove it mathematically.

The seventeenth century was an age of genius, in which such figures as Galileo, Kepler, Bacon, and Descartes flourished. All of these men believed that the universe is a rationally ordered harmonious whole, and that humans have the ability to penetrate and to understand its structure.

This attitude was in direct contrast to the medieval worldview, according to which nature is a manifestation of God's will and Truth is given to us in revelation. Everything else in the world is interpreted through revelation, and the church taught that many truths of revelation cannot be understood or rationally explained. Although the Scholastic theologians believed that much could be explained, many articles of faith remained "mysteries."

For the figures of the seventeenth-century Scientific Revolution, nature was no longer a manifestation of some transcendent entity, but an "it" to be understood and manipulated for human benefit.

Humans could understand nature because it operated according to mathematical principles. The new thinkers of the seventeenth century, in large part, insisted on the use of experience rather than on revelation, and sought to correlate experience with the truths and principles of mathematics.

NICHOLAS COPERNICUS (1473–1543)

Copernicus was from Poland and in 1543 published *On the Revolutions of the Heavenly Orbs*, in which he articulated the theory that the universe was heliocentric, or sun-centered. He argued that the earth and planets revolved around the sun in circular orbits. The most common theory of the time was that of the ancient Greco-Roman geographer Ptolemy, who taught that the universe was made up of a series of concentric circles that revolved around each other. According to this theory, the earth was in one glass sphere, while the other planets were in others. Further, the universe was geocentric according to this model.

Tycho Brahe (1546–1601) developed many instruments for astronomical observations and made detailed observations over a long period. These observations highlighted anomalies on the orbits of the planets, and he hired Johann Kepler to help calculate the orbits. Brahe's observations proved that Copernicus's remarks on the circular orbits of planets were not correct and, therefore, not many adopted Copernicus's theory. Most preferred to maintain the Ptolemaic conception, as it also supported various passages in the Scriptures that suggest that the earth stands still while the heavens move around it.

JOHANN KEPLER (1571–1630)

Kepler was the first to make detailed observations and to plot the elliptical orbits of the planets. Kepler also noted that the closer a planet is to the sun, the faster it moves. Its length of orbit also varies according to its distance from the sun.

GALILEO (1564–1642)

Galileo's observations rocked the world when he proved that Copernicus was right about the sun-centered structure of the solar system. Galileo observed four of Jupiter's moons, and thereby decisively proved that the Ptolemaic concept of the universe was inaccurate. He also proved that the planets were not just luminous objects, as taught by the ancients, but that they had mass and that the laws of mathematics applied to them as to everything else. Further, he observed spots on the sun and proved that the sun rotated, thereby again contradicting Ptolemy. The church condemned Galileo, who

Galileo.

argued that Scripture was infallible when it taught about salvation, but that in other places, as for example where it said that the earth stood still but the sun moved, Scripture was meant to be read figuratively. The church ordered Galileo's works to be burned and forbade him to teach; according to tradition, when the sentence was given, Galileo uttered under his breath, "It still moves."

Ironically, the church admitted the error made about Galileo only in the twentieth century, and further, the method of exegesis, or interpretation of Scripture Galileo referred to in his defense, was an accepted method of interpretation!

ISAAC NEWTON (1642–1727)

Newton's achievement was to synthesize all previous systems by asking the simple question, why? Other figures, such as Galileo and Kepler, had observed and described, but Newton wanted to know why the universe behaved as it did. Why, for example, did not the planets fly off in a straight line as they rounded the sun?

In 1687, he produced perhaps the most important work ever published, the *Principia Mathematica*. It had been written while students were in exile from Cambridge due to the outbreak of the plague in the seventeenth century, and had sat in his desk for many years as a collection of notes he thought unimportant. In these notes was perhaps the most important discovery ever put forth, that of **universal gravitation**. Newton had discovered three laws of motion that applied to all bodies, no matter what they are:

- Every object in a state of uniform motion tends to remain in that state of motion unless an external force is applied to it.

- The relationship between an object's mass m, its acceleration a, and the applied force F is $F = ma$. Acceleration and force are vectors (as indicated by their symbols being displayed in italicized bold font); in this law the direction of the force vector is the same as the direction of the acceleration vector.

- For every action there is an equal and opposite reaction.

These three laws explained the tides by the gravitational pull of the moon and many other events not previously understood.

The poet Alexander Pope expressed the importance of Newton when he wrote that, "nature and nature's laws lay hidden in night and God said 'let Newton be' and all was light!"

Newton believed that his mathematics allowed him to look directly into the mind of God. Although the philosophes of the Enlightenment that followed in the eighteenth century would become agnostics or even atheists, Newton remained profoundly religious. He believed, if anything, that the mathematical nature of the universe proved the existence of God, and like the medieval Scholastics, he believed that God had made it possible for the human mind to penetrate many of the mysteries of the universe and so come that much closer to an awareness of its maker.

BLAISE PASCAL (1623–1662)

Similarly, the brilliant mathematician **Blaise Pascal** believed that a wagering person must believe in God. Pascal became a profound mystic and, in his famous *Pensées*, he pointed out that it is more reasonable to have faith than to not. If one supposes the teachings of orthodox Christianity to be false and they are false, then one has not lost much except the false promise of an afterlife. If one believes the teachings of orthodox Christianity to be true and they are true, then one's faith is aptly rewarded. If one believes these teachings to be true and they are not true, then one has lost nothing. However, if one believes the teachings of orthodox Christianity to be false and they turn out to be true, then one has lost more than one can imagine. Therefore, the odds suggest faith is more productive than lack thereof. Pascal used reason to prove the reasonableness of having faith, whereas many of his colleagues rejected religion altogether.

FRANCIS BACON (1561–1626)

Francis Bacon's *New Organon* criticized old forms of knowledge and ways of attaining it. Plato, for example, spoke of an ethereal, transcendental world of ideal forms and believed that humans do not see perfection in their world, but only weak copies of the forms.

Knowledge comes from the world of forms, which humans in this life do not directly experience but which they recognize and remember from their lives as souls before entering bodies.

Bacon also criticized medieval Scholastic learning, as he thought it was based on idle speculations rather than on direct experience.

More importantly, Bacon criticized the method of Aristotle, widely used by medieval Scholastics, as relying on faulty principles. Aristotle pioneered the syllogism, according to which one moved deductively from general principles to more specific ones.

For example, from the claim that "All men are animals" and the statement that "Socrates is a man," one can deduce that "Socrates is an animal." Bacon argued that this syllogism, however, does not tell us anything that we do not already know, that all men are animals. For him, the deductive syllogism was like a pyramid, where one might pick out blocks that were already there.

Bacon argued that old knowledge served to perpetuate errors rather than to uncover truth. For example, the principle "all men are animals" is asserted in an Aristotelian syllogism, rather than proven. Aristotle argued that such principles could not be proven, but rather must be accepted. Bacon rejected such logic, and argued that the world needed a new form of knowledge that tells us what is actually there; he argued that we needed to obtain knowledge from experience, rather than from predetermined principles. Bacon suggested that one needs to move from the ground up, to build the pyramid of knowledge from the blocks, rather than to take the blocks from a preconstructed pyramid.

Bacon's method is known as the inductive method and is the method according to which most scientific hypotheses are formulated today.

David Hume (1711–1776), a Scottish philospher, raised some questions, however, about the integrity of the inductive method. Like Bacon, Hume believed in the primacy of human experience in the knowledge process. In other words, both Hume and Bacon were empiricists. Hume argued that to validate induction, however, we have to make an induction, and that this departs from our actual experience. For example, how do we know that since we have seen 999,999 white swans that the 1,000,000th swan will be white? We can only say that, in the past, such inductions appear to be reliable, but if the question is whether the process is valid, then to use induction itself to prove its validity is to make a circular argument. Hume's questions here are now known as "the problem of induction."

RENE DESCARTES (1596–1650)

Descartes, unlike Bacon, was a rationalist. Like the scientific figures of his age and even Bacon, he was interested in obtaining true knowledge as opposed to the reliance on authority of past eras. Descartes argued that this was only possible if one proceeded by foundations that were known for certain to be true. Many things we think are true are just opinions, so one must discover the foundations that are certainties. Just as a building cannot be built on a weak foundation, so knowledge cannot be built on mere opinions.

In the *Discourse on Method*, Descartes argued that one should not accept anything as true unless it is certain, and to proceed from the simple to the more complex.

In the *Meditations,* Descartes introduced the method of radical skepticism when he supposed that there might be an evil demon deceiving us all along the way in everything we think we know or experience. In such a case, Descartes argued that almost everything we think we know must be rejected, as it was susceptible to even this wild supposition. The only thing we cannot doubt, however, is the contents of our own minds, particularly, the notion that if "I think, therefore I am" or the famous *cogito ergo sum.* Actually, in this work, Descartes never said this phrase exactly, but argued that the absolutely clear knowledge we have of the contents of our own minds was the certain foundation for all knowledge for which he was looking. Descartes said that the contents of the mind were "clear and distinct," and this became his new criteria for knowledge. Descartes's method was entirely based on the use of reason; one could come to his conclusions without ever leaving one's armchair, and therefore, Descartes differed from the empiricist methods of Bacon, Hume, and also John Locke, who believed that all knowledge came from experience.

The Cartesian view fundamentally separated mind from body, and the Cartesian idea that the mind was transparent would not be challenged until Sigmund Freud argued that there were areas of our psyches that were opaque to us.

BARUCH SPINOZA (1632–1677)

Spinoza was a Jewish philosopher who argued that science had demonstrated that the only thing we need to understand nature was nature itself.

Therefore, Spinoza equated God with nature; that is, he believed in pantheism, the idea that God does not exist apart from the world.

CRITIQUE OF THE BIBLE

The emphasis of the seventeenth century on observation led to a new interest in the historical scholarship and critique of the Bible. In a *Critical History of the Old Testament*, Richard Simon attempted to unravel some of the mysteries of the Bible. He raised doubts about the integrity of the Hebrew texts, explored the question of the authorship of the Books of Moses, and dealt with other issues. Since the Protestant world, for example, recognized the Bible as its infallible source, Simon's book shook the religious world, although it presented little that was new in the world of biblical scholarship.

JOHN LOCKE (1632–1704)

Locke was an English philosopher who pushed the Newtonian worldview to its logical conclusions. In *Two Treatises of Government,* Locke developed a natural rights theory of government, according to which the laws of government and of society were embedded in nature itself. Newton had proven the universe to be mechanical, and now Locke insisted that according to nature itself, humans had the rights of life, liberty, and property, and that these rights were to be respected and protected by their governments. He pushed to its logical conclusion Newton's third law of motion relating to cause and effect by arguing that there should be checks and balances in an efficient and acceptable system of government. Locke wrote that when the government did not respect the natural rights of man, people had a right and even a duty to rebel. Locke's theories justified the Glorious Revolution in England against the Stuart monarchy.

THE ENLIGHTENMENT

The Enlightenment was an eighteenth-century outgrowth of the Scientific Revolution. The most basic feature of Enlightened thought was reliance on reason above all else. The German philosopher **Immanuel Kant** wrote a work on "What is Enlightenment?" in which he stated it was the move from immaturity to maturity, a progression in critical thought in which one is not reliant on the "guardians of truth" or authorities to inform one about the nature of reality. Kant and others of the Enlightenment insisted on the public use of reason, meaning that past authorities made assertions without proof and merely expected others to follow.

All thought now was to be subjected to public scrutiny, and there would be no repositories of mysterious wisdom, such as the church.

An important consequence of this rationalizing attitude was Deism, a movement in which God was seen as a watchmaker who set the world in motion and then left it to run alone. David Hume, for example, suggested that the existence of a creator God might be inferred from the presence of an orderly universe. An orderly machine must have a builder, he argued. The Deist God did not interfere in the world, but rather, the laws of nature continue to govern the unfolding of the universe. The God of the Deists was not the compassionate and involved God of the past, but a secular God identified with nature.

Many French philosophes carried this idea further. While Deists were willing to believe in the existence of a watchmaker God, some philosophes saw no need for one.

FRANCOIS MARIE AROUET (1694–1778)

Arouet, more commonly known as **Voltaire**, was born in Paris. He produced many satiric plays, for which he was imprisoned in the Bastille for eleven months. He then spent three years in England, and learned to like the freedom there following the Glorious Revolution, when the absolute Stuart monarchs had been overthrown. Voltaire even wrote a work on Newtonian physics before he retired to Switzerland. Here, he communicated often with Frederick the Great, and was a prolific writer with many friends and visitors. Voltaire's ideas were typical of the period. In the *Philosophical Dictionary* (1764), he attacked religion as fanaticism and superstition.

In *Candide* (1759), he attacked the rationalist argument put forth by the philosopher Leibnitz that this is "the best of all possible worlds." Every misfortune possible befalls Candide; he is beaten, sees death and destruction on the battlefield and in the earthquake at Lisbon, and eventually comes to believe that the best possible thing to do is to cultivate one's own garden. In *Candide*, Voltaire advocated reform close to home as an appropriate beginning place, and suggested that that is the only thing one might be able to control. In this statement, he differed from some of his colleagues, whose idealism about human nature and the possibilities of reform he came to doubt by the end of his life. Although Voltaire criticized the church, he received last rites on his deathbed, and so while the Enlightened philosophe found much to doubt about religion, still the possibility of its truth lingered with him.

THOMAS PAINE (1731–1814)

Similarly, **Thomas Paine** rejected institutionalized religion. In the *Age of Reason*, Paine wrote that since even Jews who witnessed the life of Christ did not believe in his teachings and his own apostle Thomas rejected him, then why should anyone believe? Paine was also well known as a revolutionary and migrated from England to America, where his pamphlet *Common Sense* made the case for independence. Later, he went to France and wrote in support of the French Revolution.

DENIS DIDEROT (1713–1784)

Diderot's compilation of the writings of various authors, the *Encyclopédie*, was an important work that critiqued many aspects of life. This work contained an article by Diderot in which he wrote about the fictitious Voyage of Bouganville. His main character comes to a place where Christian morality is foreign, and even evil and strange. There, very different morals were tolerated. Diderot wrote in favor of greater sexual liberties and toleration of moral systems outside of Christianity, as did many other authors, such as Thomas Paine.

EDWARD GIBBON (1737–1794)

Gibbon's masterpiece was the massive work on the *Decline and Fall of the Roman Empire*. In this work, he argued that Rome fell because of the pernicious influence of Christianity. Gibbon's thesis has since been strongly challenged, but his condemnation of Christianity reflects the opinions of his age. Gibbon also suggested that the Romans suffered from lead poisoning, due to their system of plumbing.

MARIE JEAN ANTOINE NICOLAS DE CARITAT CONDORCET (1745–1794)

The Marquis de Condorcet is best known for his belief in the *infinite* perfectibility of humankind. Like Pico in the Renaissance, Condorcet believed humans were capable of any achievement they so desired.

OTHER ENLIGHTENED THINKERS

Condorcet's belief was reflective of the Enlightenment emphasis on progress. For example, Cardinal Beccaria led a movement for penal reform, and advocated abolishing cruel and unusual punishments. Enlightened thinkers criticized the slave trade, leading to emancipation and abolition movements on the continent and in the Americas. Many principles of the Enlightened thinkers also resulted in the women's rights movement. Mary Wollstonecraft wrote the *Vindication of the Rights of Woman*, arguing for rights for women that had been denied to them, especially the right to equal education. Enlightened thinkers also argued for freedom of the press, believing that humans could teach themselves and also formulate their own opinions. Jean Jacques Rousseau argued in his famous *Emile* that education should be left to nature, that when one returned to nature, one could truly learn.

These ideas resulted in the strong critique of the absolute monarchy in France and other places, and would profoundly influence the course of both the French and the American Revolutions.

CHAPTER 22

CLASSICISM

The Scientific Revolution and Enlightenment profoundly influenced music and other art forms. Musicians translated Newton's third law of motion, that for every action there was an equal and opposite reaction, into love of perfectly ordered form, balanced phrases of the same length, and rhythmic emphasis on the beat as opposed to off the beat, creating a sense of stability. Various rhythmic formulas became standard, such as the Alberti bass, as did various melodic motifs, such as the Mannheim rocket, a short motif based on rapidly ascending triadic harmony. The sonata-allegro form became the standard form for many works, and it represented a balanced exploration of

Hampton Court, England.

two or more themes within a standardized harmonic framework. At the end of a piece in sonata-allegro form, one came back to the starting point, both tonally and thematically. No matter how much the composer varied the themes in the middle, development section, the themes reappeared in their original key in the recapitulation, or final section of the piece. A gifted composer such as **Beethoven** or **Mozart** might considerably develop these themes in the development section, but Beethoven's use of motivic development almost treated the themes as if they were made of atoms, breaking them into their natural component segments and exploring the ways in which they could be combined. Another important composer of the classical era was Haydn.

Musical sonata-allegro form paralleled the Enlightened view in the laws of nature as stable and as guiding the unfolding of the universe.

There was also a revival of interest in classical architecture. In many ways, the Greek love of balance, order, and harmony complemented the enlightened emphasis on the laws of nature. Greek-like temples dotted the landscapes of many estates, and landscape architecture also forced nature to comply with the "laws" of nature. Unruly vegetation was sculpted into ordered designs. Gardens, such as the famous gardens of Versailles in France or Hampton Court in England, defied the unruliness often inherent in nature to present a fabricated sense of order in nature itself.

CHAPTER 23

LOUIS XIV

Louis XIV developed an absolute monarchy in France, whose complete power was summed up by his famous motto, "*l'etat c'est moi*," or "the state is me." Events during Louis XIV's childhood had convinced him of the need to forge a strong monarchy, one able to curb the power of nobles and the church. **Cardinal Richelieu** dominated his father's reign, while Cardinal Mazarin dominated his mother's reign after the death of his father. During the Revolt of the Fronde in 1648, the nobility and the French *parlements* asserted territorial privileges. The nobles had even called on Spanish forces to help them. At one point, a group of rebels had burst into the young Louis's room, an event he never forgot.

Louis was known as the **Sun King** and his reign as the age of *gloire*. His palace at **Versailles** was an apt symbol of his power; just as rays of sun spread across the earth, so, too, the symbolic rays of the Sun King spread throughout France and, later, Louis attempted to spread them throughout Europe.

The location of the palace of Versailles, on the outskirts of Paris and away from the population, was perhaps due to events during the revolt of the Fronde. The grandeur of Versailles accompanied the grandeur of culture during the Age of Louis.

All life here centered around Louis and, in the process, Louis reduced the nobility of France to his own personal valets. Each day he began his routine at 7:45 A.M., when he would be found in bed with his sheets turned down to his waist. His valet, who slept in the room with him, would then awake, dismantle Louis's bed, and light a fire. Another valet wound his watch, while others helped him to dress. A long line of nobles passed down his shirt; the one closest to him was the most important noble. When Louis's dinner passed in the palace, all were supposed to bow, sweeping the floor with their plumes.

Elaborate etiquette existed for all areas of life and behavior. For example, one knocked by scratching a door with one's little finger, whereas for a lady of

Palace of Versailles

standing one knocked once on the door. Louis controlled the nobility by giving them duties in the court rituals, and one's status depended on one's proximity to the king. Nobles left their estates in order to maintain a costly life at the palace. In effect, Louis reduced the nobles to servants, and some scholars have suggested that while the nobility was absorbed in the rules of etiquette, they neglected the most important aspect of status, which was power.

THOMAS HOBBES

Bishop Bossuet first articulated the philosophy behind Louis's reign that the king is God. The English philosopher **Thomas Hobbes** also articulated the philosophy of **absolutism** in his 1651 work, *The Leviathan*. The Leviathan was a mythical creature of enormous proportions mentioned in the Biblical books of Enoch, Job, Psalms, and Isaiah as living in the deep realms of the ocean. According to Hobbes, humans are wicked creatures who cannot be trusted. The only way to protect oneself was to give all power to a central monarch, who then implemented laws to protect the people from each other and other nations and to create a state of peace. Even a people's assembly, such as the French *parlements*, could not be trusted, as they would act in their own self-interest. Although the sovereign's power derived from the people, the people were bound by complete submission to its power. The sovereign was the new Leviathan of the early modern era, a power that dominated every aspect of life.

The government of France under Louis XIV implemented the philosophy of *The Leviathan*.

COLBERT AND ECONOMIC REFORM

Louis developed a vast, centralized bureaucracy, supported by the economic reforms of **Jean Baptiste Colbert**, the comptroller of finance. Colbert's economic policies were likely motivated by the need to finance Louis XIV's grandiose lifestyle and foreign policy. By 1661, the treasury was broke. The nobles and clergy were exempt from the taxes in existence at this time, which included the *aides, douanes, gabelle*, and *taille*. The *aides* and *douanes* were customs taxes, the *gabelle* was a salt tax, and the *taille* was a land tax. Colbert first attempted to reform the system of taxation. The old way was corrupt, as the nobility purchased offices and then could make a profit from them, developing an independent source of wealth. Only one-third of the funds generated were channeled into the treasury. Colbert allowed no tax exemptions for the nobility and taxed them for the first time.

Colbert's greatest achievement was the encouragement of mercantilism. He wanted the flow of bullion to come into France, rather than out of it. He encouraged production at home, and focused on commerce rather than on agriculture, following the examples of the Dutch East India Company and the Spanish in the New World. He developed new industries and allowed for the formation of new monopolies to increase revenue. These monopolies drove the price of necessities up, and the peasantry bore most of the burden through the payment of the *taille* and *gabelle*. He charged heavy tariffs on imported products, but no tariffs on internally produced goods. In France, there was a free market known as the Five Great Farms, the largest tariff-free area in Europe. To further increase trade, he developed a navy, leading to the creation of the French East India Company.

THE CENTRALIZED BUREAUCRACY

Louis also centralized the management of the government, as opposed to the independent regions that existed before his reign.

The Council of State oversaw foreign policy, while the Council of Dispatches was responsible for internal affairs. The Council of Finances addressed the economic needs of the realm, and the Privy Council served as the court of the king's justice and the final court of appeal in the land. This apparatus was overseen by intendants, who carried out the king's orders in the Generalities. They supervised and observed activities of local *parlements* and nobility, but did not issue orders. The intendants reported everything back to the controller general, who in turn reported to the king.

All papers went through the king; to demonstrate his power, Louis always vetoed at least one proposal, though no one could predict which one.

Each region had a *parlement*, the one in Paris being the most important. The Paris *parlement* had the privilege of registering the king's decrees (*lettres de cachet*), which they took to mean that they could also reject them. Louis's army often ran disruptive *parlements* out of town, and he later took away the privilege of resisting his commands, having the power to issue a *lit de justice* ("bed of justice"), or the command to accept his orders.

Louis also had the right of evocation, by which he could move a case in court to whatever location he so chose.

To maintain order, Louis developed a strong and centralized army. Before Louis XIV, colonels had been responsible for their own units and were very independent and not accountable to the crown. Louis established a chain of command, recruiting rather than buying and selling positions. He commissioned officers, and the government was responsible for equipping troops and providing uniforms. The army of Louis was four times larger than it had been previously.

CONTROL OF THE THREE ESTATES

The **three estates** of France were the nobility, the clergy, and the commoners. The commoners made up the vast majority of the population. In order to curb the power of the nobility, Louis ennobled those who were not hereditary nobility, making them grateful to Louis and also enlarging the court treasury. The best example of the newly created noble was Louis's comptroller of finance, Jean Baptiste Colbert. The use of intendants and the virtual enslavement of the nobles at Versailles were other ways in which Louis controlled the nobility.

Louis controlled the church through emphasizing unity in religion, which he believed was supportive of and necessary to achieve unity in the political sphere. The French church had always had a strong identity, as illustrated by the battles of Philip IV to control the church over the will of Pope Boniface VIII and the French control of the papacy at Avignon during the Babylonian Captivity.

Louis wished to control the church in France, and although he professed Catholicism, he wished to be in control of its resources. In 1682, Louis passed a decree that the councils were to be considered superior to the pope. The French church was once again in service to the state.

Louis viewed Protestant movements, like the Huguenots, and conservative Catholic movements, like the Jansenists, as threats to the royal authority. In war, he feared that the French Protestants might side with other Protestant nations. He suppressed movements like the Jansenists, an austere ascetic sect who believed in predestination and removal from the secular world, because he feared their dedication to religion over the state and thought them too fanatical. He razed the Jansenist convent at Port Royal in 1661, while he "encouraged" the Huguenots to convert by quartering the army in their homes, holding guns up to their heads, and offering them money. In 1685, believing that most Huguenots were gone, Louis revoked the Edict of Nantes. Many Protestants fled; since the Huguenots were often successful in business, Louis may have unwittingly thwarted the efforts of Colbert.

NEC PLURIBUS IMPAR: NONE HIS EQUAL

Louis wished to have more power than any other leader, and expanding French rule on the continent was one of his most important goals. In 1667, he started the **War of Devolution**. "Devolution" is a term invented by his aides, and referred to the idea that property in certain areas of the Netherlands to which France had some shaky claims arising out of a 1659 settlement with Spain could only be passed to children of a king's first marriage. The Spanish King Charles II was weak and mentally incompetent. Moreover, Charles had no children, and was himself the child of his father's second marriage. Louis had married one of his sisters, who was the child of her father's first marriage. On this basis, Louis claimed that this property should "devolve" to France.

The war brought France into conflict with the Dutch, as the Spanish Netherlands had previously been a buffer for them against France. The Dutch were at the height of their imperial and cultural prosperity, as this was the age of the artists **Rembrandt** and **Vermeer**, and of the inventor of the microscope, Huyghens. The Dutch had established a vast trading empire in the New World with the Dutch East India Company. They had also captured the Cape of Good Hope on the southern tip of Africa from Portugal in 1652. The Bank of Amsterdam, founded in 1609, was then the financial center of Europe. It had established a universal system of coinage, whereby the population of Europe often exchanged their native coins, which fluctuated in value, for those of the Dutch.

The Dutch were a distinct threat to France, which was trying to establish an overseas trade of its own. The French, on the other hand, were a threat to the Dutch, as they had an absolutist form of government, while the Dutch had a republican form of government. Further, the Dutch were Calvinists, an immediate conflict with the policies of Louis. The Dutch intensely disliked the pomp and circumstance of Versailles, as well as the lack of freedom for Protestants in France.

The Dutch immediately allied with the Swedish and English. In 1668, the Treaty of Aix-la-Chapelle forced the French to surrender their initial gain in the War of the Franche-Comte, but the French managed to keep eleven towns in Flanders.

In 1672, Louis made another attempt at conquest, leading to the Franco-Dutch War. This time Louis bribed Sweden and obtained the support of the English King Charles II through a treaty. The French were so successful on the battlefield this time that they were referred to as Huns. The Dutch, for their part, opened their dikes and flooded their land in an effort to halt the progress of Louis. Eventually, the Dutch elected **William III of Orange** as their leader, who would become Louis's most important enemy and the leader of the Protestant opposition to the Catholic Louis. William went to the Austrian and Spanish Habsburgs, who stood to lose the most to the consolidation of Louis's absolutism in France and its expansion in Europe, for help.

In 1678, the Treaty of Nijmegen ended the war, allowing Louis to take the Franche-Comte. In 1679, Louis invaded the Holy Roman Empire. Vienna was under siege from the Ottoman Turks, distracting the Holy Roman Emperor. Moreover, Louis had considerable support from important principalities in the Holy Roman Empire, such as Brandenburg, and the church states of Cologne and Trier. In 1681, he succeeded in taking Strassburg and set up the infamous *chambres de reunion*, courts that had no authority in the Holy Roman Empire, but to which Louis delegated the responsibility of deciding territorial questions in his favor.

War of the League of Augsburg

Louis's flagrant violation of the Holy Roman Empire and his frightening wave of expansion galvanized the Protestant world behind the Dutch leader, William of Orange. The Catholic world united against Louis under the Holy Roman Emperor Leopold. The combined Protestant forces created the League of Augsburg. Among their leaders were the Holy Roman Emperor, the kings of Spain and Sweden, the Holy Roman prince electors of Bavaria, Saxony, and the Palatinate, and the leaders of the Dutch republics and England in 1689.

From 1688 to 1697, Louis fought this impressive force in the **War of the League of Augsburg**. The combined fleet of Dutch and English was simply too large for him to defeat, and in 1697, the war ended with the Peace of Ryswick, which established a system of trade with the Dutch. Moreover, the treaty forced Louis to recognize William of Orange as leader of the Dutch and as King of England, a position he obtained in the Glorious Revolution of 1689.

The War of the Spanish Succession

The War of the Spanish Succession (1701–1714) was the second war that engulfed Europe, but which was also a global conflict. In North America, the War was called Queen Anne's War. The War of the League of Augsburg had barely ended when the conflict over the Spanish succession broke out.

Exhaustion on the part of all parties contributed to their decision-making process.

The war arose as a result of the ill health and mental incompetence of the Spanish King Charles II. Charles never produced heirs, but his half-sister, the child of her father's first marriage, was married to Louis XIV and had produced an heir. Louis, of course, earnestly wished for his son to obtain the Spanish crown, as then France would control Spain's vast wealth in the New World. Since France was already threatening to take over much of Europe, this choice was problematic for other rulers.

The other choices were Emperor Charles VI and Prince Joseph Ferdinand of Bavaria, an elector of the Holy Roman Empire. The former frightened many with the possibility of resurrecting the Spanish-Austrian Habsburg Empire of the sixteenth century. Consequently, England and the Netherlands favored Prince Joseph Ferdinand.

Due to exhaustion from the War of the League of Augsburg, England and France quickly negotiated the First Partition Treaty, giving the crown to Joseph Ferdinand, while Louis's son and the Archduke Charles received territory in Italy.

The next year, Joseph Ferdinand suddenly died, and the parties negotiated the Second Partition Treaty. According to this treaty, Charles was now heir to the crown, but the Italian territories awarded in the First Partition Treaty were now to go in their entirety to France. While France, the Netherlands, and England happily accepted these new terms, Austria did not and now attempted to gain the entire Spanish inheritance. At this point, Charles II unexpectedly named Louis's grandson, the Duke of Anjou, as his heir, thus preventing Louis from having direct control over France. Louis refused to honor the treaty, but the Spanish crowned his grandson King Philip V.

The situation grew more tense when Louis recognized James Stuart, the son of the exiled Catholic King of England James II, as the legitimate king of England, Scotland, and Ireland. The English were furious and determined to defeat Louis. During the war, the British captured Gibraltar in Spain, which they continue to hold today. The Austrian and English forces defeated the French at the Battle of Malplaquet, but at a tremendous cost.

The war ended with the Peace of Utrecht in 1714. Louis's grandson Philip became the Spanish king, but was forbidden to be in line for the French throne. Austria received the Spanish Netherlands, Naples, and Milan, and Savoy received Spanish Sardinia. More importantly, the treaty gave Britain the exclusive right to trade slaves in Spanish America and to maintain control of Gibraltar as well as Minorca, both former territories of Spain. The British also gained several French colonial possessions, making them by far the greatest beneficiaries of the treaty.

Historical Evaluations of Louis's Reign

Louis's foreign wars were costly, and detracted from Colbert's success in the economic sphere. On the other hand, the author Voltaire credited Louis with the excellence of French culture during this period, as Louis was a great patron of the arts. Louis made Paris the beautiful city that it is today, with paved streets and streetlights. He had a system of hospitals that performed charitable work, highways, and a thriving commerce. There are, however, more negative evaluations of Louis; perhaps the most well known is that of the Duke of Saint-Simon. Saint-Simon called Louis the "King bee" and argued that Louis chose his advisors for their ignorance rather than for their knowledge. According to him, Louis had an "intellect beneath mediocrity," being not very well educated and having little knowledge of history. Contemporary historians argue that while Louis deified himself and flaunted morality, he divided the labor of government to maintain power, and thus began the age of bureaucracy. While Louis's centralization of the French government might be praised from this point of view, Louis also brought the French one step closer to the massive uprising of the population in 1789 against the abuses of absolute monarchy. By the end of the eighteenth century, the French Revolution would dismantle much of the apparatus of Louis's absolutist monarchy and establish a Republic in France whose revolutionary motto continues to inspire the French Republic today.

CHAPTER 24

THE RISE OF PRUSSIA AND THE HOUSE OF HOHENZOLLERN

The origins of Prussia go back to **Brandenburg**, one of the German states of the Holy Roman Empire. In 1415, Emperor Sigismund granted the margravate of Brandenburg to the house of **Hohenzollern**, who would rule Brandenburg until the end of World War I. The margrave of Brandenburg was an elector of the Holy Roman Empire until the empire collapsed in 1806. Brandenburg converted to Protestantism during the Reformation. In 1614, the Hohenzollern annexed Cleves, which had a mixed population that was one-half German and one-half Polish. Its population was also divided by religion, as it was one-half Lutheran and one-half Catholic. The Hohenzollern dynasty was limited as a European power by its lack of sea ports, poor mineral resources, and lack of natural frontiers to protect it from invasion. Its domains were disconnected and widely scattered.

In 1618, the Hohenzollern acquired the **Duchy of Prussia**, which gave them access to the sea. In 1701, Frederick III assumed the title of "king of Prussia." Prussia was outside of the legal boundaries of the Holy Roman Empire, but the Holy Roman Emperors did not agree to his use of the title until 1713, when the Treaty of Utrecht officially named the Elector of Brandenburg the King of Prussia. Brandenburg remained the heart of the kingdom, but increasingly became identified with Prussia.

FREDERICK WILLIAM, THE GREAT ELECTOR (1640–1688)

Frederick William was a dedicated Calvinist. He created a standing army, which he funded through the resources of the crown domain and taxes. The officers of the army collected the very taxes that supported their existence. Frederick created a hereditary class of officers through the landed aristocracy, called Junkers. They were forbidden to sell their land to non-nobles, and their service was based on duty, obedience, and service to the king.

FREDERICK WILLIAM I (1713–1740)

Frederick William I devoted his reign to the improvement of the army. He spent little money on his own coronation and cut three-fourths of the royal household from state expenses. He channeled the money saved into the military. He rearranged the order of the court by elevating the officers of the army and relegating civilians to lower ranks. His army appeared in uniform. Its might was symbolized by the height of many soldiers, who were often six to seven feet tall. Frederick doubled the size of the army through a system of recruitment from the cantons. His militaristic attitude was manifested in his discipline of the citizens with a walking stick on his regular strolls. His militaristic bearing prompted one biographer to call him the "Potsdam Führer." Frederick worked constantly and developed the bureaucracy necessary for further development.

FREDERICK II (THE GREAT) (1740–1786)

The reforms of Frederick William I made it possible for **Frederick the Great** to maintain an army of 200,000. Prussia was very small and ranked thirteenth in Europe in terms of the size of its population. Nevertheless, it maintained the third largest army.

Frederick wanted to expand Prussia and violated the Pragmatic Sanction by annexing Silesia, an Austrian territory. He strengthened Prussia as well in the Seven Years' War.

Despite his military actions, he was an **enlightened despot** who encouraged education and provided for his subjects. He supported freedom of the press and religious toleration. Frederick abolished the use of torture, and the death penalty could only be given on his authorization. He instituted the first law code and improved the plight of the people through education and the construction of roads. While it is tempting to romanticize Frederick as an enlightened ruler, one must also remember that he firmly believed in nobles as the basis for a strong state and insisted that they all serve as soldiers. Serfs and peasants were simply for work. Frederick did little to overturn the old class structure.

Like many *philosophes* of the Enlightenment, he rejected religion; like Thomas Hobbes, he believed that it was necessary to relegate power to a judicious monarch. Nevertheless, he claimed to be the "first servant of the state."

Frederick made Prussia one of the strongest nations in Europe, and in the nineteenth century, Bismarck would further transform it through the unification of Germany into one of the most powerful empires in the world.

CHAPTER 25

THE AUSTRIAN HAPSBURGS AND THE HOLY ROMAN EMPIRE

In 1278, the **Hapsburgs** became the rulers of Austria and, despite the turmoil of the Reformation and succeeding eras, they managed to rule Austria until World War I. Austria was the center of the Holy Roman Empire in the early modern period. Frederick Barbarossa first described his empire as the "Holy Roman Empire," but the term itself dates from 1254. In the Middle Ages, the German duchies were never firmly united, and neither was the Holy Roman Empire during the early modern period under Austrian rule. The Austrian Hapsburgs ruled over a tremendously diverse group of people, making it very difficult to achieve any kind of unity. At its height, the empire contained most of the territory of modern Germany, Austria, Slovenia, Switzerland, Belgium, the Netherlands, Luxembourg, and the Czech Republic. It also contained parts of eastern France, northern Italy, and western Poland. Therefore, many of the movements of the early modern world, in particular the rise of nationalism, rocked the empire as various groups fought for their own self-interests.

CHARLES V (d. 1588)

The abdication of Emperor Charles V in 1556, also known as King Charles I of Spain, resulted in the division of the Hapsburg holdings between an Austrian and a Spanish line. To his brother Ferdinand in Austria, he ceded the Holy Roman Empire, while to his son Philip, he ceded his personal kingdom of Spain. Philip is better known as Philip II of Spain. Charles had numerous problems during his reign, including the invasion of the Ottoman Turks into Hungary and the siege of Vienna. He bitterly fought the Reformation and summoned Luther to the Diet of Worms. He also invaded Italy in order to prevent the pope from annulling the marriage of the Hapsburg heiress, Catherine of Aragon, and Henry VIII of England. His son Philip II would marry the Catholic Mary, daughter of Henry VIII and Catherine, and further pursue the fight against Protestants.

The Wars of Religion devastated Hapsburg holdings; as much as half the population was killed and the countryside destroyed. The Hapsburgs had no great trading markets, in contrast to the Netherlands and France. Further, there were some 300 states in the Holy Roman Empire capable of independent action. In 1648, the Peace of Westphalia ended the Thirty Years' War, and gave the various regions and territories almost complete power to determine their own fate. There were nine electors who chose the Holy Roman Emperor, and among them was the Duke of Brandenburg, who became King of Prussia according to the Treaty of Utrecht in 1713. This treaty also marked the defeat of the Spanish Hapsburgs, and the Austrian Hapsburgs thereafter controlled the Holy Roman Empire.

THE THREE CROWNS OF THE HOLY ROMAN EMPIRE

The Austrian Hapsburgs controlled three separate regions, and their power in these areas was known as the "**Three Crowns of the Holy Roman Empire.**"

The Crown of St. Stephen represented Hungary, Transylvania, and Croatia. The Ottoman Turks under Sulieman laid siege to Hungary and defeated the Hungarians at the Battle of Mohacs in 1526. The Turks also laid siege to Vienna, but failed to take it, and tried again in 1683. The Hapsburgs defeated the Ottomans in 1699 and reconquered Hungary.

The Crown of St. Wencelas represented Bohemia, Moravia, and Silesia. The attempt to impose Catholicism on Bohemia led to the Thirty Years' War, as citizens of Prague threw the emperor's governors out the window in the second "defenestration of Prague." After the war ended, the Hapsburgs imposed Catholicism on Bohemia and were seen as very repressive.

The Hereditary Holdings of the Hapsburgs Austria represented the hereditary holdings of the Hapsburgs and was the third crown held by the Holy Roman Emperors. After 1806, the imperial title was recognized only within Austria. There was little unity in terms of culture or religion within the Holy Roman Empire.

The Pragmatic Sanction

Charles VI (1711–1740) had no male heirs, and so forged a treaty known as the Pragmatic Sanction (1713). The Pragmatic Sanction made Hapsburg territory indivisible, and mandated one line of heirs through his daughter, Maria Theresa.

Maria Theresa (1740–1780)

In that time it was unusual to have a woman heir, and Maria Theresa consolidated holdings by bringing government to Vienna. She centralized the government, reformed the army and the economy, and introduced a public system of education. Maria Theresa was an "enlightened despot," who ruled with a firm hand but nevertheless implemented reforms based on enlightenment thought. Along with Frederick the Great, Maria Theresa was one of the most well-known enlightened rulers of her time. During her reign and those of her successors, Vienna became a renowned center of culture, a city where Haydn, Mozart, and Beethoven created some of their finest compositions.

Napoleon

Napoleon defeated the Austrians at Austerlitz in 1805. In 1806, the Holy Roman Emperor was essentially emperor in Austria only.

Franz Joseph

Prussia defeated Austria in the 1866 Austro-Prussian War. A dual monarchy of Austria-Hungary was created in 1867 under Emperor Franz. Prussia became the basis for a new German empire unified by Bismarck.

World War I

During World War I, the Allies defeated the Austro-Hungarian Empire, and Hapsburg rule ended in both Austria and Hungary in 1918.

CHAPTER 26

PETER THE GREAT (1682–1725) AND THE WESTERNIZATION OF RUSSIA

THE GEOGRAPHICAL LOCATION OF RUSSIA

There has been considerable debate among scholars about whether to include Russia as a part of Europe or not. Russia had some western influences from the Vikings, but their only inlet from the west was the port of Archangel, which was ice-locked for most of the year. Russia was geographically isolated, with no warm water seaports and little communication with the west. The Poles, Swedes, and Prussians surrounded the Russians. Even ancient Roman civilization had never reached Russia.

Russia was very influenced, too, by Asiatic cultures. Russia's vast plains from the Baltic Sea to the Ural Mountains made it easy to invade, as it had no natural frontiers. The Mongol Hordes, who conquered Russia, brought Asiatic influences, and the assimilation of the Tartars by the Great Muscovites around Moscow led to the colonization of Asiatic Siberia, which stretches 5,000 miles across Asia. The greatest Russian River, the Volga, flowed into the Caspian Sea in the east. Persians, Afghans, Indians, and Chinese frequented Russia's bazaars. Dress followed Asiatic customs, as Russian women wore veils and men wore beards. Russian architecture was also influenced by Asiatic traditions, and even Russian Christianity was imported from the Greek world, or eastern half of the old Roman Empire.

The union between the Russian world and old eastern half of the Roman empire, the Byzantine empire, was evident in the marriage of Ivan the Great and Sophia Paleologus, niece of the last Byzantine emperor, Constantine Paleologus. Ivan called himself a tsar after the Latin word "Caesar," and referred to Moscow as the third Rome, heir to the Byzantine world and protector of the Orthodox Church.

In these respects, Russia was more Asian than European, and it was also considerably underdeveloped compared with the European world at this time.

Some of the obstacles to Russia's modernization included their devout **Russian Orthodox** faith. The **Old Believers**, an ultra-Orthodox group, were so-called because they steadfastly held to old beliefs in the face of new scientific developments and new scholarship. For example, they refused to give up their spelling of the name of Jesus as *Isus* in the face of new textual scholarship suggesting that *Jisus* was more correct. They believed the Russian church was under the influence of Greek scholars and resisted even the suggestion to make the sign of the cross with three fingers rather than their customary two.

Many other Russians were equally resistant to change and followed a religious calendar that began with the biblical account of creation. In Russia, as in many Christian cultures, it was an offense to miss church during Lent, but unlike other Christian cultures, it was also an offense to look at the new moon and to play chess. Many Russians regarded eclipses as magic and used no Arabic numerals but relied upon the abacus. Even the Russian archbishop said that, "anyone who loves geometry is abhorred of God." In Russia, there were no courtly manners of Versailles and no social charity, as under Louis XIV. Cruel punishments and the use of torture were common.

There were harsh laws against fugitive **serfs**, and lords could recover their serfs up to fifteen years after their flight. In 1625, the only punishment for killing a peasant was to have to replace him. In 1646, Russians passed a law mandating that peasants had to be registered and bound to the land. Such harsh treatment led to the serf uprising in 1667 led by Stephen Razin, who marched his forces up the Volga, killing lords as he went. In 1671, he was executed and in 1675, Russia passed a law allowing peasants to be sold without their land, resulting in their loss of tenancy and a near state of slavery. This law created a mobile workforce of poor peasants.

Both peasants and Old Believers saw the church and government as repressive.

THE RUSSIAN MONARCHY

Russia had a history of autocracy even before Peter the Great. **Ivan the Terrible** had created a domain under his complete control called the *oprichnina;* the tsar used the *oprichnina's* secret police, the *oprichniki*, to terrorize his subjects.

Although Ivan the Terrible conquered the Tartars and established a kingdom that went all the way east to the Urals and west to Poland and Sweden, following his death there was chaos during the "time of troubles," which lasted from 1604 to 1613. The nobles became more powerful and elected Michael Romanov as tsar, since he was not a member of any faction. His descendants ruled Russia until 1917.

He was fanatically pious, attending church four or five times a day. Michael's death created a controversy, as he had two wives. By his first wife, there were several daughters and two sons; by his second wife, there was one son, who became **Peter the Great**. Michael's eldest son died and the other by his first wife was a weak candidate. The Russian nobles or boyars wanted Peter to rule with his mother as regent. One of his stepsisters, Sophia, stirred up the *streltsy*, or Russian army, against Peter. They invaded the Kremlin and killed Peter's grandfather and his mother's brothers before his very eyes, and forced the *boyars* to accept his half-brother Ivan as tsar with his half-sister Sophia as regent.

Peter never forgot these atrocities, and he was determined to create a strong position where nobles, church, or family could not threaten him. In 1869, one of Peter's many supporters among the boyars sent a false message to him that Sophia planned to have him arrested; he and the boyars then deposed Sophia as regent and exiled her to a convent. His half-brother Ivan yielded his power to Peter, and Peter became the new tsar.

Peter was a striking figure at seven feet tall. He was larger than life in both stature and power, yet had very crude manners. He and his companions were known for trashing hotel rooms in Europe, and for his brutality. Peter wanted to make Russia a powerful nation with a powerful monarch who could control serfs, nobles, and the church. He wanted to make Russia a major power that could fight off Turks, Poles, and Swedes, who surrounded Russia.

Peter's Search for a Warm Water Seaport

The Swedes held the key to warm water seaports, so Peter, in 1696, captured the port of Azov, giving Russia access to the sea. But without a navy, this gain was meaningless. Peter also tried to capture more of the Black Sea coast, but he could not hold it and he quickly learned the inferiority of the Russian army against European forces.

In his youth, he was exposed to western scholars. His half-sister Sophia pioneered western ideas, such as freedom for women. In 1697, Peter visited Europe, traveling incognito. Russia was so backwards that his subjects might have revolted had they known of his journey and goals. While traveling in

Europe, Peter became enchanted with the arts of shipbuilding and navigation. He brought 1,000 Western experts to Russia to bring it into line with
western technological advances.

The Revolt of the Streltsy

While he was away, however, events at home further convinced him of
the inadequacy of the army and the need to modernize Russia. In 1698, the
streltsy revolted. Peter viciously put down the revolt, ordering the execution
of over 1,200 rebels, whom he had put on public display. Peter personally
executed many of them.

The Great Northern War

Peter's continued quest for an adequate seaport led to the Great Northern War (1700–1721). When the Swedes crowned Charles XII king at the
young age of fifteen, Peter thought this was the perfect opportunity to attack.
At the Battle of Narva in 1700, however, Charles defeated Peter's force of
40,000 with a force of only 8,000. This failure once again highlighted to
Peter the weaknesses of the Russian army and convinced him to rebuild the
army after western models. Peter implemented the use of European officers
and western uniforms, and drew soldiers from each territory. He armed the
regiments with western weapons, so that by 1703, Peter, disguised as Pyotr
Mikhailov, led his forces to victory at the mouth of the River Neva. Following the victory, Peter founded the city of **St. Petersburg**. In 1704, Peter's
forces retook Narva.

In 1709 Peter successfully drew the Swedes into the Russian winter
and defeated them at the Battle of Poltava. The Treaty of Nystadt awarded
Russia the much sought after warm water seaport.

THE MODERNIZATION OF RUSSIA

St. Petersburg was known as the "window to the West," and it symbolized a revolution. It was a new city facing Europe, and Peter gave very favor-
able terms to foreign merchants. St. Petersburg was built on piles in swampy
ground. Thousands of people died while constructing it. Many Swedish prisoners of war died here, but so did many Russians. The toll taken by the project
is symbolic of the hardships Russians suffered as Peter the Great stopped at
nothing to drag Russia into the modern era. Peter himself said that "Russia
must be coerced" to enter the modern era. Peter westernized Russia over the
protests of Slavophiles and others who resisted westernized customs.

The new European-style city symbolized a complete revolution in
society and the westernization of Russian belief systems. Peter ordered the
long Asiatic style beards of boyars trimmed. This was controversial because

Cathedral of Saint Basil, Moscow.

Russians believed that the beards were necessary for salvation, as the apostles and prophets wore them. Some Russians saved their beards after they had been shaved and had them placed in their graves.

Dress changed to a more western style, and women appeared in public. Peter imported printing presses from Europe and printed Russian newspapers and a book of western etiquette. Peter reformed the alphabet and the Russian calendar to bring it more in line with the Julian calendar. Under Peter, the year now began in January, and many Russians wondered why God would have chosen the middle of winter in which to create the world. Peter also encouraged his subjects to study abroad.

Peter secularized the Russian Orthodox Church by abolishing the office of patriarch; after 1721, there was not another put in place. He created the Holy Synod, headed by the procurator, who was a government official and directly controlled by Peter. He taxed the Old Believers heavily for continuing to wear beards and holding on to the old ways. Many were burned to death, tortured, or imprisoned for life. Many went to their deaths holding their fingers in the characteristic two-finger gesture with which they crossed themselves.

Peter tolerated many faiths, and while he had traveled in the west, he had attended many Protestant services. Peter allowed Calvinist and Lutheran churches to be built on the Nevsky Prospect, which became known as the Prospect of Toleration.

Repression of the Boyars

The Russian boyars still sought too much power, so Peter created a Table of Ranks, according to which rank was independent of one's noble status. One's rank in society was now equated with one's rank in Peter's bureaucracy and Peter required service to the state. This reform was perhaps one reason his overall package of reforms endured.

Peter supported his new westernized state with taxes on just about everything, from the right to marry, to wear a beard, or to be an Old Believer. Peter instituted a tax on each head, which Russians pejoratively referred to as the soul tax. Previously, taxation had been by household, and it was possible for many to cheat the government out of money. Peter had no toleration for those who cheated the government, and even executed boyars who stole tax money.

The new government was organized into ten territorial governments. There were no heads of departments, but rather committees to run affairs of state.

Peter brought new industries to Russia, which had been primarily a backward agricultural land, and used peasants as conscripted labor.

His reforms succeeded in further distancing the aristocracy from the rest of the population. The boyars now spoke western languages, while the peasants spoke Russian. The condition of the serfs was worse than ever before, and Peter regarded them as brutes for their lack of the new western culture. He simply exploited them as a supply of cheap labor.

Peter the Great was one of the most hated rulers during his time in world history. Even his own son wanted him dead. In retaliation, Peter ordered his son put to death. The Russian Orthodox Church hated his reforms and saw him as the anti-Christ. Those dedicated to Russian culture, known as Slavophiles, were in open revolt. Peter's reforms may have westernized the boyars, but this only further separated them from the masses. Nevertheless, Peter is justifiably credited for dragging Russia "kicking and screaming" into the modern age.

CHAPTER 27

THE STUART MONARCHY AND THE GLORIOUS REVOLUTION IN ENGLAND

The **Glorious Revolution** in England occurred during the Age of Absolutism, in which the power of European monarchs was reaching an all-time high. England, by contrast, had a long tradition of representative government going back to 1215, when English barons made King John sign the **Magna Carta**. The Magna Carta established the idea that the king, just like everyone else in society, was subject to the law. During the Hundred Years' War, the power of the parliament increased, while that of the monarch decreased.

In 1603, Elizabeth the Great died childless, leaving her cousin Mary Stuart's son James VI of Scotland as her heir. He became James I of England and established the Stuart line in England.

The Stuart monarchs did not subscribe to the English parliamentary tradition and behaved as autocrats. James wrote the *True Law of Free Monarchy*, in which he asserted that there should be no parliamentary power. He argued that the king got his authority from God, and so should be responsible to God alone.

During the English Civil War, the conflict between the Stuarts and Parliament were resolved in favor of the Parliament.

THE PURITANS

The Parliament at that time was made up of **Puritans** who were landed gentry (wealthy), and were composed of at least three different factions who, to varying degrees, supported Presbyterianism. The Puritans fought for religious freedom and wanted to abolish the rites and rituals of the Anglican Church, as well as the structure of the clergy, and to establish a Presbyterian structure for the church. Some of the more radical Puritans were known as Separatists, for their desire to separate from the Church of England. The Pilgrims who went to the Americas were Separatists.

THE CATHOLICISM OF THE STUARTS

King James was Catholic, and relaxed many of the prohibitions against Catholics instituted during the reign of Elizabeth the Great. He also reaffirmed the use of Anglican rites in the face of the Puritan desire for simplicity.

ABSOLUTIST POLICIES OF THE STUARTS

Both James I and his son Charles attempted to raise funds without the consent of Parliament. Charles attempted to use these funds to keep the navy armed in a time of peace. In 1628, Parliament passed the Right of Petition, according to which Charles could not billet soldiers in private homes, arbitrarily tax without the consent of Parliament, or arbitrarily imprison anyone.

In response, Charles dissolved the Parliament in 1629 and did not recall it until 1640.

Under Charles, the Archbishop of Canterbury, William Laud, bitterly repressed the Puritans, many of whom went to the New World. He believed in the total uniformity of the Anglican Church and expelled clergy who failed to conform, censored the press, and allowed no religious meetings outside of the Anglican Church. He also persecuted the Presbyterians, followers of Calvin in Scotland. Charles further outraged the Puritan and Protestant world when he married the Catholic sister of Louis XIII.

THE LONG PARLIAMENT

Problems with the Presbyterian rebellions in Scotland starting in 1637 forced Charles to summon the Parliament in 1640. This session was known as the Long Parliament, and it sent Archbishop Laud to the Tower of London and attempted to limit the king's power through regular meetings of Parliament. The Long Parliament also abolished the Court of the Star Chamber, and passed legislation so that the king could not levy taxes without the consent of Parliament. Many of the members of the Parliament wanted to go further and completely transfer all authority from the king. Charles ultimately sent troops into Parliament to contain the situation, but the legislators passed the militia ordinance giving Parliament control over the army.

THE ENGLISH CIVIL WAR

By 1642, England was in a state of civil war between the Roundheads, who were Puritans and got their names because of their round haircuts, and the Royalists, known as the Cavaliers.

OLIVER CROMWELL

Oliver Cromwell, a staunch opponent of the Anglican Church, rose to prominence as the leader of the Roundheads and created a New Model Army that defeated the forces of the king in 1645.

The Rump Parliament

In 1648, Cromwell's extreme Puritan supporters purged Parliament of moderates and other foes, in an event known as Pride's Purge after the colonel who led the soldiers. The resulting Parliament was known as the Rump Parliament, and Cromwell and his supporters abolished the House of Lords.

The End of Monarchy and the Establishment of the Protectorate

The Rump Parliament was responsible for the trial and execution of King Charles I as a public criminal. Following this event, it established a Puritan commonwealth that ruled England from 1649 to 1653. In 1653, Cromwell dismissed the Rump Parliament and established the Protectorate, with himself as Lord Protector.

Cromwell viciously crushed Ireland, where the Catholics there favored the Stuarts. He was intolerant of Anglicans and vigorously enforced Puritan morality in England.

The money needed to maintain his army caused grave financial difficulties, and these were compounded by the wars with Spain and the Dutch.

Rising opposition forced Cromwell to resort to military rule. When he died in 1658, many Englishmen were ready to go back to the old monarchy. Cromwell was initially buried in Westminster Abbey, the traditional burial place of England's monarch, but a few years after his death, angry crowds removed him from his coffin and dragged his body through the streets to Tyburn, where criminals and traitors were often executed. Cromwell's body was hanged there and displayed for twenty-four hours, and his head placed on a spike. Later, his remains were thrown on a dunghill. Cromwell's dictatorial methods seem to contradict his desire for religious freedom, especially from intrusion by the monarch and a state church. He set up exactly the sort of system he worked to defeat.

THE RESTORATION

The Stuarts were restored to power when **Charles II**, the son of the executed King Charles I, was crowned in 1660. He ruled until 1685. Upon the restoration of the monarchy, Charles agreed to limit his power, not to pass taxes without the consent of Parliament, and to make no religious changes. However, Charles II very much admired Louis XIV, a fellow Catholic and one who shared the Stuart belief in absolute monarchy. They negotiated in secret the Treaty of Dover in 1670. According to the treaty, England would join in Louis's war with the Dutch, and in return, money would flow from France to England.

The Declaration of Indulgence

Charles II's Catholic sympathies also led him to enact the Declaration of Indulgence in 1672, whereby there was toleration for those who dissented from the Church of England.

The Titus Oates Plot

Meanwhile, James, Charles II's brother, publicly announced his conversion to Catholicism, creating further ill will for the Stuarts. The Titus Oates plot, a conspiracy to place James on the throne, made fears of a Catholic monarchy more intense. Although Charles II ordered the conspirators put to death, the damage was done.

The Cavalier Parliament

The Cavalier Parliament, a royalist Parliament that met through 1679, enacted several laws in reaction to Cromwell's Puritanism. It attempted to diffuse Puritan influence by reinstating the Anglican Church. The Conventicle Act of 1664 forbade dissenting religious assemblies of more than five people; the Act of Uniformity required the use of all rites and rituals in the Book of Common Prayer in church services; and the Five Mile Act forbade dissenters from living in incorporated and chartered towns. Since the king was the head of the church in England, the church and king worked to support one another.

Two parties dominated the Cavalier Parliament: the Whigs and the Tories. The Whigs supported the Act of Exclusion proposed in 1678 and again in 1681 to bar James, a Catholic and the brother of Charles, from the throne; they wanted a Protestant monarch. The Tories supported the traditional succession and monarchy.

In 1679, the Cavalier Parliament was dissolved. Charles did not summon the new Parliament in 1681, renewing old fears about the monarchy.

The Rye House Plot

In 1683, Charles's Catholic leanings led Whig leaders to conspire to assassinate Charles in what was called the Rye House Plot. Charles ordered the execution of the Whig leaders.

James II

In 1685, James II became king and would rule until 1688, when he would be deposed in favor of Protestant monarchs.

James's reign began on a negative note, when in the Bloody Assizes he put to death a thousand Protestant rebels. He then suspended the Test Act, which barred Catholics and other dissenters from holding office, and issued two Declarations of Indulgence that provided tolerance for Catholics and other dissenters.

William and Mary

When James's second wife, Mary of Modena, bore him a male heir, the Parliament worried that their desire to see his Protestant daughter Mary (from his first wife) on the throne would be thwarted. The Parliament invited Mary and her husband William of Orange, the most important leader of the Protestant forces in Europe, to take the throne.

The Glorious Revolution

On November 5, 1688, William and Mary landed in England and became the new rulers of England in a bloodless revolution known as the Glorious Revolution.

The Penal Codes

James fled to Catholic Ireland and later to France, where he spent the rest of his life. The English never forgave the Irish for harboring James and bitterly punished them. Penal codes were enacted according to which, among other things, Catholics did not have the freedom to worship, receive education, enter a profession, hold public office, engage in trade or commerce, live in a corporate town or within five miles thereof, own a horse of greater value than five pounds, purchase or lease land, bear arms, or vote.

Legislation after the Glorious Revolution

In 1698 Parliament passed the Bill of Rights, giving Parliament the right to levy taxes, make new laws, and raise a standing army. The Bill guaranteed free elections, the right of citizens to petition and keep arms, trial by jury, and freedom of speech. In that same year, the Act of Toleration granted freedom of worship to Puritans, but did not revoke the Test Act. Puritans still did not have full civil and political equality. The Act of Settlement, passed in 1701, restricted the succession to Protestants. After William died, James's daughter Anne, whose mother was a Protestant, became queen, and during her reign the Parliament passed the Act of Union in 1707. This Act created Great Britain by finally fully uniting England and Scotland. Ireland, repressed by the penal codes, did not join the Union until 1801.

John Locke and the Right of Rebellion

John Locke explained the political rationale behind the Glorious Revolution in the *Second Treatise on Government*. Despite the fact that the revolution was bloodless, the English had overthrown a legitimate monarch. Locke argued that people were born with natural rights, including life, liberty, and possessions, and when the government deprived them of these rights, they had a natural right of rebellion. Much to Britain's chagrin, Locke's ideas became the basis for the American Revolution in 1776.

CHAPTER 28

JAPAN FROM THE WARRING STATES THROUGH THE MEIJI RESTORATION

THE WARRING STATES

By 1467, during the Ashikaga Shogunate (1338–1567), there were almost 260 feudal houses or *daimyo*. Each *daimyo* was independent and maintained its own separate army, making Japan, in reality, 260 separate countries. Since the Ashikaga had no powerful central administration, there was constant armed conflict between the *daimyo*. During the Onin War (1467–1477), Japan was literally in the "sengoku jidai," meaning "the age of the country at war." This age is commonly called **Warring States Japan**. Powerful warlords arose, such as **Nobunaga**, who tried to remedy this situation by taking strong control of the *daimyo*.

Oda Nobunaga (1534–1582)

Nobunaga made the first attempt to unify Japan at the end of the Warring States period; he attempted to bring all of Japan "under a single sword" (*tenka-fubu*). He destroyed the Buddhist monastery on Mt. Hiei, as the monks there had often been involved in Japan's political and military struggles. To further thwart the influence of Buddhism, Nobunaga encouraged Christianity and was especially interested in the teachings of the Jesuits. The Jesuits would not enjoy such freedom in the Tokugawa Shogunate. He also embraced the use of western firearms and retrained his army to accommodate new weapons, including the pike, built stone forts, and became the first Japanese leader to clad his ships in iron. Nobunaga, however, never managed to eradicate the warring lords, and he was assassinated by two of his generals.

Toyotomi Hideyoshi (1536–1598)

Hideyoshi, the son of a peasant, became the complete master of Japan by 1590.

Hideyoshi had no last name when he began to serve Oda Nobunaga; by the end of his life, he had assumed the family name Toyotomi, or "Abundant Provider."

Hideyoshi, like the Hong Wu emperor of Ming China, was concerned about the ability of people such as himself from lower classes to rise to power. Consequently, he froze the social classes, making class status permanent for people and their children. In 1586, he ordered farmers to stay on their land. Hideyoshi gave the samurai, who had helped to create the chaos of the warring states and who were the professional soldiers of Japan, special status. In 1587, Hideyoshi decreed that only the samurai could carry their famous long sword, or katana, or wear armor, and only the samurai had "last names"; others in Japan were simply known by their functions.

Hideyoshi invaded Korea in 1592 and 1597 in order to prepare for an eventual invasion of China. He died without accomplishing his goal. His ambitions abroad perhaps account for his failure to completely unite Japan. While Nobunaga had used force in his attempts to pacify the *daimyo* and rebellious Buddhist monks, Hideyoshi relied on personal loyalties. When he died, those loyalties died as well.

Although the emperor had refused to give Hideyoshi the title of Shogun due to his poor lineage, the Japanese named him a Shinto deity shortly after his death and gave him the title "Hokoku," or "Wealth of the Nation."

TOKUGAWA JAPAN 1600–1867

Ieyasu Tokugawa (1542–1616)

In 1600, Ieyasu **Tokugawa** won the Battle of Sekigahara and began a process that would eventually create a centralized government and unite Japan. The Tokugawa ruled Japan until 1867, and created the longest period of peace in Japanese history. The Tokugawa period is also known as the Edo period, after the place of residence of the Shogun.

The emperor gave Ieyasu the title of Shogun, or chief military leader. The Tokugawa Shogunate relied upon the *bakufu* domain system, and the Shogun became the most important leader in Japan. Under the Tokugawa

Shoguns, the emperor lived in Kyoto, while the Shoguns resided in Edo, a city later known as Tokyo. The emperor became a mere figurehead, and the *daimyo* became mere vassals of the Shogun.

Various methods of controlling the *daimyo* were developed, such as the requirement to march to the Shogun's court in Edo every year. At the court, it was forbidden to draw weapons, and along the way, *daimyo* stopped at Inns of the Shoguns, thus generating revenue for the Shogunate and keeping the *daimyo* under control as they marched. Their absence from their territories further contributed to their inability to wage wars with one another or revolts against the Shogun, and the Shoguns held their families hostage during the period when the *daimyo* were not in Edo.

Lord Asano and the 47 Ronin

The samurai lived by the **Code of Bushido**. There were about two million samurai during the Tokugawa period, out of thirty million in the total population. One of the most famous stories of the period, which continues to be told and retold in Japanese cinema and in books, stories, and other forms, is the story of Lord Asano and his 47 samurai. Lord Asano was angered by Lord Kira while at the Shogun's court and drew his sword against him. He was ordered to commit seppuku (also known by the slang term *hara kiri*, or "belly slashing"). According to the samurai code of honor, this was the only way to restore one's honor when one disagrees with and then morally protests an order of the Shogun. Seppuku was a ritual in which one disemboweled oneself while still alive, as the Japanese believed the seat of all life or the life force was to be found in the abdomen.

Asano's 47 Ronin believed he had been treated unjustly by Kira and by the Shogun, and so plotted their revenge. For two years, they gave the appearance of accepting the verdict and watched Asano's estate dismembered. They lived as Ronin, or unemployed samurai. In the middle of winter two years later, they stormed Kira's palace, killed him, put his head on a pike, and took it back to Asano's gravesite, where they displayed it in triumph. Because they had violated the Shogun's codes here, they, too, committed seppuku. They are the greatest heroes of Japanese literature, but they also illustrate the many contradictions of Japanese life during this period. One was forced to display loyalty to the Shogun in one's outer life, no matter what the contradictions might be in one's inner life.

JAPAN AND THE WEST

During the Tokugawa period, Dutch traders appeared in Japan. They were restricted to the port of Dejima in Nagasaki. Jesuits also were in Japan, but while Hideyoshi allowed them to teach to thwart the influence of Buddhism, Ieyasu ordered them expelled in 1616. Those who failed to leave were killed, and converts to the faith were executed or forced to recant. The Shogunate adopted an increasingly isolationist strategy, and expelled all westerners after 1638. The Tokugawa forbade Japanese to travel abroad.

Japanese isolationism resulted in the development of an interest in Japanese culture. A branch of scholarship called *kokugaku*, which means "Native Studies" or "Nativism," became prominent in this period. Since the Japanese had imported much from China, it was always difficult for them to separate out their native traditions, such as Shinto.

Motoori Norinaga (1730–1801) concentrated on the recovery of the Japanese language, and he argued that the use of the Chinese writing system interfered with the understanding of Japanese itself. He studied the *Kojiki*, or the oldest history of Japan. Although the work was written in Chinese, he discovered that it was meant to be read in Japanese. Norinaga also explored the first collection of Japanese poems, the *Manyoshu*. These studies led him to develop his theory of the sensitivity to things or the *mono no aware*, according to which one experienced the world and was touched by it, and used Japanese to directly express it.

Haiku

Norinaga's studies led to the popularity of haiku, a three-line form of seventeen syllables, in which one captured, through attention to a single moment in nature, the deepest aspects of life. The most famous haiku poet of the time was Basho.

Contact with the west would not occur again until Commodore Matthew Perry's expedition in 1853.

The Bunraku Puppet Theater

The playwright Chikamatsu Monzaemon wrote for the Bunraku Theater, the famous puppet theater of Japan. The Japanese preferred puppets to live actors, as the puppet had no personality of its own and so could not interfere with the meaning of the play. Chikamatsu emphasized the conflict between duty and human feelings, such as that felt by the 47 Ronin as they sacrificed their own well-being and family life in order to avenge Lord Asano. His father was a Ronin who moved the family to Kyoto. His most famous plays were the *Kikusenya Kassen* or *Battles of the Kikusenya*, the story of a Tartar king's invasion of China; and *Sonezaki shinj* or *The Love Suicides at Sonezaki*, the story of an apprentice clerk and his prostitute lover, who committed suicide in order to be together.

The Kabuki Theater

The word "kabuki" comes from Japanese words meaning "slanted" or "inclined," which was a reference to a way prostitutes tried to entice men in the Floating World, or *ukiyo*, a district four miles outside of Edo. The word "ukiyo" is a pun on the Japanese word for waves. Prostitutes made their living here, but many were of a very high class and refused most customers. The world here, like everywhere else, was dominated by ritual.

Because of its origins in prostitution, the Tokugawa forbade female actresses in the Kabuki Theater. Male actors, known as *onnagata*, portrayed females. The *onnagata* believed they could portray women better than women themselves could, as they were outside observers who noticed mannerisms and other details that women took for granted about their own behavior.

Ukiyo-e Woodblock Prints

The *ukiyo-e* woodblock prints became an important art form during this period. The most famous woodblock print artist was Hokusai, whose *Thirty-Six Views of Mount Fuji* (1823–1831) influenced the late-nineteenth-century impressionist movement in Europe.

Hokusai, Great Wave, from Thirty-Six Views of Mount Fuji.

Ihara Saikaku (1642–1693)

Ihara Saikaku was the most famous novelist of the Tokugawa period, and like Chikamatsu, he wrote about the conflict between outer duty and inner emotion. He believed the Tokugawa period emphasized empty external rites of behavior to the neglect of the inner world. His most famous novels were *The Life of an Amorous Man* (1682) and *Five Women Who Loved Love* (1686). He often poked fun at the Floating world. Saikaku first became famous for his ability to compose linked verse, or *haikai*, and once composed over 23,000 in a single day.

The Meiji Restoration

In 1866, Saigo Takamori, the leader of the Satsuma domain, and Kido Takayoshi, the leader of the Choshu domain, formed the Satcho Alliance, whose purpose was the overthrow of the Tokugawa in order to restore the emperor to power.

On November 9, 1867, the fifteenth Tokugawa Shogun, Tokugawa Yoshinobu, resigned, and imperial rule was restored. This event is known as the *Taisei Houkan*, or "restoration."

In January 1868, the Boshin War, or the War of the Year of the Dragon, started with the Battle of Toba Fushimi. The armies of Choshu and Satsuma defeated the Tokugawa army at the siege of Hakodate on the second largest island of Japan, Hokkaido, in 1869.

The fourteen-year-old heir to the imperial throne, Mutsuhito, became emperor and took the title **Meiji**, meaning "enlightened rule." Shortly thereafter, he signed the Five Charter Oath, according to which the feudal order was abolished, the Tokugawa freezing of classes was abandoned, the isolationism of Japan ended, and the formation of a deliberate assembly was promised. The latter never happened, as in fact, the only real change of the Meiji period was that the Tokugawa were removed in favor of the powerful *daimyos* that overthrew them.

CHAPTER 29

CHINA FROM THE MING TO THE CHING DYNASTY

THE MING DYNASTY 1368–1644

The Yuan dynasty of the Mongols may have been successful in many areas, but there were still many patriotic rebellions on the part of the Chinese against Mongols, whom they saw as invading conquerors. Among other issues was the fact that the Mongols tended to hand all-important positions to Mongols, employing Chinese bureaucrats in non-Chinese areas of their empire.

According to Chinese historians, in 1351 a group of laborers digging along the Yellow River found a statue with only one eye and an inscription indicating a coming rebellion. There had been a number of natural disasters, such as floods and landslides, and the Chinese took these signs as an omen that the Mongols had lost the Mandate of Heaven. In the 109 years of Mongol rule, only Emperor Khubilai Khan had any kind of success as an emperor, while the short reigns of the other monarchs had allowed the eunuchs to rise in power. The Mongol rulers supported their lavish lifestyle through heavy taxes, and the peasants bore most of the burden. Towards the end of the Mongol rule, very high inflation was common throughout China.

Chu Yuan Chang (Hong Wu Emperor)

The rebels were mostly peasants who were affected by the flooding of the Yellow River, which brought about serious famine. One of the most important of these rebels was a Han Chinese peasant, Chu Yuan Chang, whose father was an itinerant agricultural worker. At the time of the famines, Chu Yuan Chang had become a Buddhist monk. He served as general for one of many rebellious warlords, Kuo Tzu-hsing. Chu Yuan Chang successfully defeated the Mongols, and became one of only two peasants to have founded a dynasty. By 1368, he had conquered southern China, and by 1369, he had driven out the Mongols. Chu Yuan Chang took the reign name of **Hong Wu**, which means "great military power." He reigned from 1368 to 1398, and most scholars see him as one of the greatest emperors in Chinese history. So began the **Ming Dynasty**, whose name means the "brilliant dynasty." The Ming leaders did create a period of brilliance in culture and in their care for their people. They were also the last native dynasty to rule China. Under the Ming, China experienced its greatest social and economic revolution prior to the twentieth century. The Ming were also the first dynasty to interact with Europeans on a large scale.

The Reconstruction of the Economy

The Mongol conquest had, in fact, left the border areas of China virtual deserts. Even today, much of this region remains desolate. In order to reclaim useless land, the Ming transferred a segment of their population to deserted regions. The government planted over one billion trees in an effort to reforest China. Fifty million trees were planted in Nanjing alone in 1391, and these became the material that built the ships used in the maritime expeditions of the Yung-lo emperor, the third Ming ruler. These trees also created the basis of the Chinese merchant marine; during the sixteenth century, this merchant marine was one of the most successful in the world, as China entered the new global trade created in the wake of the European Age of Discovery.

Governmental Reforms

The Hong Wu emperor instituted an absolute monarchy, comparable to that established by Louis XIV. He was very conscious of his peasant origins, and so distrusted the nobles, eunuchs, and scholars. His capital was Nanjing, and he forced nobles to live at his court there and to participate in many elaborate rituals designed to establish the court as divine.

The Hong Wu emperor publicly beat any officials who criticized him or dissented in any way. This involved having 100 men beat the offender on the buttocks, and most offenders did not survive. The emperor demanded complete submission, as opposed to the Confucian ideal that the superior man should not be beaten or subjected to punishment. The emperor, at one point, tried one of his comrades on suspicion of cooperating with Mongols and the Japanese; over 15,000 people were involved in the trial.

To take complete control of the government, the Hong Wu emperor abolished the Imperial Secretariat, the main central administrative body under previous dynasties. Six ministries of the government were under the Hong Wu emperor's direct supervision. The emperor now ran the government, in great contrast to earlier dynasties. The Hong Wu emperor had to hold court three times a day to manage the government, a task Ming emperors were able to maintain for the first three reigns, but not thereafter. The emperor forbade eunuchs to read to lessen their power, and reduced their numbers. Later, dissatisfaction with the repressive government would result in their resurgence.

The emperor also took control of the army and developed the Guards with Brocade Uniforms, a secret police that spied on political officials.

Civil Service Exams

The Hong Wu emperor revived the **civil service system of exams**, and created a three-part exam that was held at the district, provincial, and imperial levels. He created an extensive system of examinations that was very difficult to pass. One had to write answers in eight parts and to explain portions of sentences according to various interpretations. Under the Ming, one had to use the interpretation fostered by the state. These essays were known as the "eight legged essay," and one had to make use of no more than 700 characters. Only about ninety scholars a year passed these exams. The exams represented an old Chinese idea going back to Confucius and even before, that one's advancement should be on the basis of competence as opposed to high social standing. Nevertheless, only those who abided by Ming philosophies passed.

Functional Division of the Population

The emperor had risen from the peasantry to the imperial house and, as a result, he greatly feared social mobility. He ordered a functional division of population, whereby anyone born a peasant, soldier, or craftsman remained in this station throughout life. The Chinese system of taxation led to the need for a census, and they divided the population into *li-chia,* or groups of ten families responsible for levying taxes equitably among their members and maintaining order. The poor of China often became dependent on the gentry.

The Hong Wu emperor's greatest achievement was the creation of the Ta-Ming lü, a code of laws. These laws were considered the *lü,* or "unchanging laws." The emperor also developed a set of laws to address changing situations, and these laws were known as the *li.* Later Ming emperors abused the *li,* and the constant changes in the set of laws resulted in their losing the trust of the people.

EXPANSION UNDER LATER EMPERORS: THE MARITIME EXPEDITIONS OF THE YUNG-LO EMPEROR

The **Yung-lo** emperor (1403–1424), the third emperor of the dynasty, began a series of naval expeditions in 1405. The Hung-hsi emperor (1425) and the Hsüan-te emperor (1426–1435) continued the expeditions. The Yung-lo emperor liked exotic goods and also wanted to expand trade, and he sent seven expeditions led by the eunuch Cheng Ho, a Muslim from Yunnan, to such places as Ceylon, Calcutta, South Vietnam, and Africa. Cheng Ho commanded sixty vessels with 500 troops. His ships were 400 feet long and weighed 500 tons, far bigger and faster than those of the Portuguese seamen, for example. The expeditions brought back zebras, ostriches, and tribute from other kings. Cheng Ho left stelles proclaiming that these areas were vassals of the Ming, and inhabitants of some of these areas still revere him as a god. In Southeast Asia, for example, he is revered as the god San-Pao. In 1391, over fifty million trees had been planted in Nanjing to prepare for maritime exploration, and during this period, the Ming were the most powerful sea empire in the world. The Yung-lo emperor's empire was bigger than all of Europe in size, and his expeditions were far larger.

The expeditions started by the Yung-lo emperor ended in 1435, after astrologers convinced the Ming rulers that the exotic goods imported would bring about the downfall of the dynasty. Ironically, it was in part the European presence in China during the nineteenth century that contributed to the downfall of the following dynasty, the Ch'ing.

At any rate, the maritime expeditions led to great commercial success, particularly in the sixteenth century. As the silver mined in the New World made its way across the globe, about one-half of it ended up in China. The influx of silver from the Americas made it possible for the Ming to take thirty or forty taxes and reduce them to one payable in silver. This was known as the **Single Whip Reform**.

Similarly, plants from the New World led to agricultural reform in China, as maize and the sweet potato became staples of the Chinese diet. These products could flourish in poorly irrigated areas.

ARTISTIC AND CULTURAL ACCOMPLISHMENTS OF THE MING

During the Ming period, there was a cultural renaissance, in part fostered by successful trade. The Ming was famous for their style of porcelain, featuring blue on white. Much of this porcelain was sent out on the merchant fleets to Europe, whose merchants coveted the secret of making the delicate white china.

The Dutch imported tea from China, which became a very popular drink in Europe. Success at trade made China one of the leading manufacturing centers in the world.

Other cultural accomplishments occurred in the Ming period, such as in music. Chu-tsai yu became the first person to define the equally tempered musical scale. In the west, Bach's *Well-Tempered Clavier* would not appear until the seventeenth century.

The Ming produced a treatise on botany, listing nearly 2,000 plants with medicinal uses. Hsu Hsia Ko first traced the origin of the Yangtze and other rivers, and Chinese printing presses produced literature in spoken dialects. The most famous example of Ming learning is the Great Canon of the Yung-lo emperor, which represented 11,000 volumes of encyclopedic knowledge. The Yung-lo emperor's expeditions also left their mark on literature, as travel literature began to appear in China. The most famous piece of travel literature is the *Voyage to the West* (1570), about the adventures of a monk and a monkey on a pilgrimage to the Indies.

China encountered Europeans through trade, but also through the work of Catholic missionaries, who followed Portuguese to the east. In the sixteenth century, the Jesuit **Matteo Ricci** came to China to convert them to Christianity. The Jesuits helped to bring about a resurgence of long-forgotten Chinese mathematical and astronomical skills. Christianity, however, was too foreign an influence to take hold in China. The Chinese were not acquainted with the idea of a transcendent being. Confucianism was a practical system of ethics not involving the worship of deities; the Chinese were more prone to worship ancestors than deities. Although the Jesuits respected the ethical values of Confucianism and used stories and parables to teach in hopes of reaching the Chinese, they forbade their cult of ancestor worship. The Chinese experience with the Jesuits eventually led to great mistrust of foreigners.

THE DECLINE OF THE MING

Ming emperors spent too much money supporting the aristocracy with maintenance payments. Some had as many as 94 heirs and relatives. Many expeditions against the Mongols, including five under the Yung-lo emperor, had forced the Ming to levy higher and higher taxes. They built lavish tombs while the peasantry suffered. After the Yung-lo emperor, later Ming rulers did not handle the demands of the Hung Wu emperor's bureaucracy well. By the time of the Chia-ching emperor (1522–1566), the emperor had become a figurehead who retreated into his private world while the eunuchs ran China. During the Chia-ching emperor's rule, the grand secretary, Yen Sung (1480–1568), brought China to its knees with an abusive style of leadership. By the seventeenth century, the corruption of the eunuchs was so intense that the Ch'ung-chen emperor (1628–1644) attempted to oust them from power by running the government alone. This proved an impossible task and contributed to the downfall of the Ming.

Though the Ming emperors had all they could handle with the eunuchs at home, they had to contend with pirate raids along the coast from the Japanese, whom they referred to as the Woukou, from the word "wo," meaning "dwarf."

Further Mongol attacks from 1438 to 1449 caused them to build a second line of defense, a set of inner walls that were double or triple in some places and 5,000 kilometers long. In fact, the Ming built most of the remaining sections of the Great Wall.

THE CHING (QING) DYNASTY (1644–1911)

By far the greatest threat to the Ming were the **Manchus**, members of the Jurched tribe who lived in Manchuria. Their dynasty, founded in the twelfth century, was the Chin, or "Gold," dynasty. Their leader, Aixinjueluo Nurgachi (1559–1626), forged them into a tightly unified single political unit by 1616, and the Mongols so respected him that they gave him the title Kundulen Han, or "Respected Emperor."

Abahai

Nurgachi's second son, Abahai, succeeded him, and he launched an attack on Korea and then marched on China. Abahai looted Beijing and then set up a civil administration like that of China. A Manchurian prince administered each ministry or board. Each prince had five assistants, including at least one Mongol and one Chinese. Abahai called his people the "Manchu" and renamed the dynasty the "**Ching**," or the "Pure," to avoid the negative associations with the third century B.C.E. Ch'in Empire. Given its use of Manchurians and Mongols, it was anything but "pure" from the Chinese point of view.

When the rebel peasant Li Tzu-ch'eng entered Beijing on April 25, 1644, the Ming emperor, the Ch'ung-chen emperor, committed suicide by hanging himself. So ended the "brilliant" dynasty.

Fu-lin and Dorgan

At the time Li was in Beijing, Abahai's son, Fu-lin, who was only six years old, led the Manchurians. Two regents, Jirgalang and Dorgan, controlled the government. Dorgan moved on Li in Beijing and buried the Ming emperor. He eventually succeeded in finding the rebel Li and killed him in 1645. Dorgan then placed the child Fu-lin on the throne, inaugurating the Ching rule in China. The Ching were the last imperial dynasty to rule China.

Rebellion in support of the Ming continued in southern China for twenty years into the Ching period. Three generals ruled for the Ching in southern China and, although two of these generals and the son of the third revolted, the Ching eventually won control of the south. This was known as the Revolt of the Three Feudatories.

The Manchu, or Ching, were in the minority of the population and made up only two percent of the people. Chinese held ninety percent of the posts. During this period, the Manchu leaders enforced their custom of males wearing their hair braided into a pigtail. They forced all Han Chinese to wear their hair this way, and any male caught without their pigtail in public was beheaded.

The Ching rid China of the corruption of the Ming after the Yung-lo emperor, and relieved the burdens on the peasantry. They also encouraged the arts.

The Kangxi and Qianlong Emperors

The learning of the Jesuits influenced the Ching, and they became great patrons of the arts. The most famous Ching ruler was the **Kangxi** (1622–1723) emperor, the third son of Fu-lin. The Yong Zheng (1723–1736) and Qianlong (1736–1796) emperors were two other important rulers. The Qianlong emperor's reign was one of the longest in history, and during his reign China controlled the largest expanse of territory in its history, including Mongolia, Tibet, Nepal, Taiwan, and portions of central Asia. Qianlong also sponsored a compilation of the Confucian Classics called the Five Classics, a standard of Chinese learning. His mother was a Manchurian and he was a grandson of Kangi. He retired after 60 years so as not to exceed the reign of his grandfather.

During their reigns, the *History of the Ming* was published, as well as catalogues of paintings and calligraphy, a dictionary, and a 5,000-volume encyclopedia. Ku Yen-wu published an important work in the area of philology, the study of languages, relating to textual and historical criticism. Tai Chen pioneered the use of scientific reasoning seeking proofs as opposed to mere hypotheses. Chang Hsueh Cheng wrote a philosophy of history, arguing that history had the same value as the classics.

Literature flourished during the Ching period, including China's greatest novel, *The Dream of the Red Chamber*, which is also sometimes known as *A Dream of Red Mansions*, or *The Story of the Stone*.

The Ching interest in learning earned the loyalty of the literati, who had opposed the Ming as repressive.

Prosperity

During the Ching, the population exploded, increasing by two or three times what it had been under the Ming. China became the most populous region in the world, reaching a population of 450 million by 1850. The need to feed such a large population led to innovations in agriculture and the development of two rice crops per year. Due to lack of land, the Chinese learned to terrace, or create fields from mountainsides.

The English economic theorist **Adam Smith** praised the Ching economy, saying that its provinces were the equivalent of all of Europe operating in a self-sufficient manner. Robert Fortune remarked that, "in no country in the world is there less misery and want than in China."

The Ching had numerous problems during their reign, including the White Lotus Rebellions, a rebellion in Nien in 1853 led by an offshoot of the White Lotus Sect, Muslim rebellions in the southwest from 1855–1873, and the Taiping Rebellion.

The White Lotus Rebellion

The **White Lotus Sect** had beliefs that combined aspects of Buddhism, Taoism, and other schools, but their most central belief was in the impending reincarnation of the Buddha as Maitreya. The return of the Buddha would bring a new government and a new era of peace and prosperity. The Qianlong emperor banned it in 1775, but it reappeared under the leadership of Liu Chi-she in 1796. He claimed to have found the Buddha-Maitreya in the son of his own master Liu-Sung. Further, he attempted to drum up support for a surviving member of the Ming dynasty as the legitimate emperor. The Ching reacted strongly, intending to exterminate the White Lotus Sect. The government used very harsh methods to attack White Lotus strongholds, with the result that more splinter groups joined the movement. These groups protested Ching taxation. Unfortunately, the Ching entrusted leadership to Ho-shen, who stole money for himself and misreported his activities in the countryside. In 1799, the new Emperor Chia Ch'ing removed Ho-shen, who committed suicide, and thereafter their fights against the White Lotus were more successful. The Ching resettled large portions of the population in areas of rebellion and gave amnesty to White Lotus deserters. The Ching finally crushed the rebellion in 1804, but it resurfaced in the Nien and Boxer Rebellions.

The Taiping Rebellion

Hung Hsiu-ch'üan, the son of a poor farmer near Canton, led the **Taiping Rebellion**. He had failed the civil service examinations twice and had a nervous breakdown, after which he began having visions that he believed were God the Father and Jesus, his Elder brother, speaking to him. He believed himself to be the Younger Brother, sent to earth to wipe out demon worship. Seven years later he studied with a Baptist minister, Issachar J. Roberts, and then formed a new Christian sect, the **God Worshipers**. He believed that the overthrow of the Manchu (Ching) dynasty would bring about the Kingdom of Heaven. Many western scholars argue that the famines of the 1840s contributed to revolts such as this one, as peasants looked for new ways and groups to provide for them. In the 1840s, the organization began to amass weapons and develop a military structure, and in the 1850s, the government saw them as a big enough threat to attack them. Hung Hsiu-chuan's followers successfully repulsed the attack, and in 1851, Hung declared that the Kingdom of Heavenly Peace had been founded, and humans were now in the era of Taiping, or peace, with Hung as the Heavenly King. Taiping was to be a classless society with all wealth distributed equally. Women were equal to men. The Taiping then began to advance toward Nanjing, moving primarily through rural areas and encountering little resistance. In 1853, they conquered Nanjing and renamed it T'ien-ching, or "Heavenly Capital." The generals of the movement claimed to receive visions from God and the Heavenly King himself tolerated no dissent. The movement failed to maintain authority in the areas it conquered; Hung withdrew from public life and immersed himself in a wanton life in the large harem he had accumulated. In 1864, faced by the desertion of his most important general, Hung committed suicide by poisoning himself. The Chinese found his body in a sewer, wrapped in imperial yellow. The twenty-year-long rebellion was over.

The Opium Wars

The Ching also had to manage issues related to an increased European presence in Asia. The Ching initially allowed the Europeans to be only in Canton. In 1793, the Europeans asked for more privileges, but the Chinese were not interested and had forbidden the importation of **opium** in 1800, a drug more and more commonly used for recreational purposes. By the 1830s, the Chinese were no longer masters of the trade market; rather, Europeans had the advantage and they wanted fewer taxes on their goods and the right to trade opium. By the 1830s, more than 30,000 chests of opium, each of which held about 150 pounds of the extract, were coming into China a year. Some scholars have suggested that the loss of Chinese supremacy in trade was the result of the opium trade. By 1839, the Chinese were desperate to stop the trade, as it was damaging the health of their citizens and bringing in unwanted foreign intrusions. They burned several tons of opium in Canton. The British reacted by surrounding Canton, and in 1842, the British defeated the Chinese. In the Treaty of Nanjing, the Chinese lost Hong Kong to the British, who held it until the late twentieth century, when it reverted back to China. The treaty forced the Chinese to open other ports to the British, and by 1844, the French and Americans had a trading presence in China as well. The French allied with the British to fight a second opium war, which led once again to the defeat of China in 1856. The Treaty of Tientsin (1858) opened new ports to trading and allowed foreigners with passports to travel in the interior of China. The Chinese granted Christians the right to spread their faith and to own property, and in separate treaties, the United States and Russia received similar privileges.

The Boxer Rebellion

The defeat of China in the Opium Wars led to mass outpouring of anti-foreign sentiment. This culminated in the **Boxer Rebellion**, led by the Society of Harmonious Fists, which first arose in Shandong province. The name of the rebellion came from the fact that members of the society practiced shadow boxing, which they believed made them impervious to bullets. In 1900, the Boxers invaded Beijing, with the complete support of the Dowager Empress Cixi. The Dowager controlled the country through her son Guang Xu, whom she in effect kept under house arrest. She was a strong opponent of reform, and so supported the Boxers. In Beijing, the Boxers attacked foreign embassies, including those of Britain, Germany, Japan, Russia, and the United States, while Chinese troops watched the events. The foreign ambassadors survived the assaults for two months before an international relief force came, known as the Eight Power Allied Forces. They occupied Beijing and put down the rebellion, and the American Foreign Secretary John Hay formulated the Open Door Policy, allowing all nations access to the China market.

The Fall of the Ching

In 1908, the captive Emperor Guang Xu died, followed quickly by his mother, the Empress Dowager Cixi. As successor, she had chosen her two-year-old nephew, Pu Yi. The conservative Prince Chun ruled as regent. In 1911, the harvest failed and revolts began.

The Double Ten Incident

By October 10, 1911, the "Double Ten" incident occurred, when soldiers from the Wuchang armory, led by Yuan Shi Kai, joined in the rebellion. On February 12, 1912, Pu Yi abdicated, ending 270 years of Qing rule.

Sun Yat-sen

The leaders of the rebellion formed a republic, with **Sun Yat-sen** as provisional president.

The new government allowed Pu Yi to continue living in the Forbidden City until 1924, but forced him to live in the inner court of the complex. In November 1924, the National Army gained control of China and, on November 5, they abolished all of Pu Yi's titles and ousted him from the Forbidden City. He ended his life as a humble gardener in the streets of Beijing; his ashes were moved to the western Ching tombs in 1995. Bernardo Bertolucci depicted Pu Yi's tragic last years in the film *The Last Emperor*, but despite Pu Yi's personal tragedy, the Chinese were ready to end 5,000 years of imperial rule. Unfortunately, the twentieth century would bring many more upheavals.

CHAPTER 30

THE ISLAMIC WORLD FROM THE OTTOMANS THROUGH THE EARLY TWENTIETH CENTURY

THE OTTOMAN EMPIRE

Mehmed the Conqueror (1451–1481)

The Ottomans were a Turkish dynasty that rose to prominence when **Mehmed**, Turkish for Muhammad, conquered Constantinople in 1453. After 1930, the city was officially known as Istanbul, from the Greek words *stan poli*, meaning "at the city," or "city of the cities." The city had been the capital of the eastern Roman Empire and of Byzantium, and would also be the capital of the Ottoman Turks. The Hagia Sophia, the great Basilica of Justinian, became a mosque.

Mehmed's success was largely due to huge cannons, developed for his forces by a Hungarian engineer. One cannon was twenty-six feet long and eight inches in diameter and could fire a 1,200-pound ball as far as one mile. Mehmed attacked the walls of the great city from the west, the only part of the city not protected by water. His army arrived on Easter Monday, April 2, 1453, and fired cannon volleys at the Byzantines for seven weeks. The Byzantines had protected the waterways across the Golden Horn with a large chain, and so he built a road of logs across the north side of the Golden Horn. He then rolled his ships across and attacked on May 29, 1453. The Ottomans entered the city through the Kerkoporta gate in the Blachernae section, which had been left unlocked, and looted it for three days.

Many Greek scholars fled and sought refuge in Italy, particularly in Venice, where they helped to fuel the Italian Renaissance. Some remained behind and served as advisors to the sultans. These Greeks were called Phanariots.

The fall of Constantinople marked the end of Roman rule in the east, and many scholars date the end of the Middle Ages from 1453. Even today, the Greeks still speak of reconquering Constantinople, but it remains one of the most important cities in the Islamic world.

The Ottomans

The Ottomans practiced brutal customs, and as each leader rose to power as sultan, he killed all of his male relatives except one brother to prevent rebellions. He also killed his brother's children and wives.

Selim

Under the next two sultans, the Ottomans became an Asian as well as a European power. Selim conquered the Egyptian Mamluks, North Africa, and Syria-Palestine, and brought Mecca and Medina under Ottoman Rule. After conquering Mecca and Medina, he took the title of Caliph, or successor of Muhammad. This title had not been used since the Mongols captured the capital of the Abbasid Caliphate, Baghdad, in the thirteenth century.

Sulieman the Magnificent (1520–1566)

Sulieman extended the Ottoman Empire to Mesopotamia (modern Iraq), Kurdistan, and Georgia. He captured Belgrade in 1521, and in 1526 the Ottoman Turks defeated the Hungarians at the battle of Mohács. The Turks also conquered the cities of Buda and Pest. Pest fell to the Turks in 1526 and Buda fell fifteen years later. Sulieman besieged Vienna from 1526 to 1529, and lost only because of torrential rains that caused his heavy carts to bog down. Sulieman's presence as a European monarch contributed to the ferocity of the Wars of Religion, as he aided Protestant nations in an effort to destabilize Europe. Many scholars believe the Reformation succeeded in part because of Sulieman's financial support. During his reign, he also took the island of Rhodes from the Knights of St. John, or Hospitalers, and laid siege to their new stronghold at Malta.

Sulieman's conquests earned him the title of the "protector of the sacred places," which were Mecca and Medina, and also the title of padishah, or emperor. The Ottomans became the new heirs to the Abbasid Caliphs.

Sulieman built magnificent walls around Jerusalem, which still surround the Old City today. Under Sulieman, the Ottoman Empire reached its high points and ruled an empire from Hungary to Yemen on the Saudi

Arabian Peninsula to Persia to Oran. Sulieman's empire encompassed six of the ancient Seven Wonders of the World.

Sulieman restructured the Ottoman legal system, and Muslims referred to him as the Kanuni or the lawmaker. He codified the **kanun**, a system of laws dealing with cases not covered by the Shari'ah. Mehmed had begun to compile the kanun, and in the early sixteenth century it was added on to, but after Sulieman it was never changed again.

Sulieman created a military state, where the *ulema*, or school of study of Islamic law, was a part of the government. He controlled the aristocracy by creating the *devshirme*, a system of conscripting Christian boys from the provinces, raising them as Muslims, and using them as soldiers. Although many increased their lot in life through the *devshirme* and families often competed for the honor, these boys were in essence conscripted slave soldiers. As the system evolved, it became highly selective.

The Janissaries

The conscripted troops made up the elite force of infantry soldiers known as the **Janissaries**. Members of the Janissaries could not wear beards, as free Muslims did, and could not marry until 1566 in the reign of Selim II. Their chief loyalty was to the empire and they were taught to consider the sultan their father. Since the empire controlled their property, there were no claims based on heredity from members of their families. One of the most famous boys who began their career through the *devshirme* was the architect Sinan, who built over 400 structures, including the Suleymaniye Mosque.

In 1683, the Janissaries had become so successful that the sultan Mehmed IV abolished the *devshirme*, allowing Turkish boys to enter the elite ranks. Starting in 1449, the Janissaries led revolts and demanded higher wages and other rewards. Through palace coups, they even succeeded in controlling the sultanate.

Sulieman's relationship with a captured Russian slave girl, Roxelana, hastened the decline of the empire. Roxelana convinced Sulieman to marry her, something unheard of for sultans, and she increased the power of the harem. She was suspicious of Sulieman's boyhood friend and chief assistant in his rise to power, Ibrahim, and had Sulieman arrange for his death. Roxelana feared the sultana and her son, Mustafa, and fought for the succession of her own son, Selim. Although Sulieman loved Mustafa, he ordered him killed and Selim became his successor.

Sulieman also advanced his personal favorites and progressively retreated into isolation in the Topkapi palace.

The Fall of the Ottoman Empire

The Ottoman Empire was never again as great as it had been under Sulieman, and they were defeated at Vienna in 1683. Napoleon invaded Egypt in 1798, thus severing this portion of the empire. The Ottomans fought for the Crimea against Russia starting in 1854 and lost it. World War I brought the final collapse of the empire, which officially ended in 1922 when Turkey became a Republic.

Ataturk

A group of liberal nationalists who favored western-style governments, called the "young Turks," led the revolution. Their leader was Mustafa Kemal, who wished to modernize and westernize Turkey. He is known today as **Ataturk**, or "Father of the Turks." Ataturk was president of Turkey from 1922 to 1928, and during this period he introduced a series of legislative reforms adopting European legal systems and civil codes. In so doing, he overthrew the Islamic law of the *Shari'ah* and also the Ottoman laws, the *kanun*. He implemented European-style Roman writing, and secularized the state by eliminating the Arabic call to prayer, the caliphate or the Muslim civil and religious leadership of an Islamic state, and the mystical Sufi orders of Islam. His radical reforms survived, and the Turkish republic remains an independent and secular Islamic state.

The Safavid Shi'ites in Iran

The Safavid rulers of Persia were descendants of Sufi mystics. According to their own histories, which they rewrote to suit their purposes, their founder was **Sheikh Safi al-Din** (d.1334) from Ardebil, leader of an order of Sufi mystics in Persia. His tomb became the headquarters of the Safavids, who took their name from their founder. In 1501 the fourteen-year-old **Shah Ismail I** (1501–1524) defeated the Turkoman ruler of Iran at Sharur and occupied Tabriz. The population had originally been Sunni, but the new Shah rigidly enforced Shi'ite traditions and laws. Shi'ites believed that there had been twelve infallible *imams* since Muhammad. *Imams* are prayer leaders and rulers that claim descent from Muhammad. The twelfth *imam* had gone into hiding, but would one day return. In some accounts, Ismail was presented as the hidden *imam*. His followers wore red hats with twelve points in memory of this tradition. The Shah lost considerable territory to the Ottomans, who defeated him in 1514 at Chaldiran.

The leaders of the Safavids were known as Shaykhs or Shahs. The Shi'ites rejected the first three caliphs and the Sunni kingdoms. The Shah Abbas I (1588–1629) defeated the Ottomans in Iraq and Azerbaijan, largely with the help of British mercenaries.

Under Abbas I, the capital of the empire was Isfahan, still a renowned center of Islamic architecture. Many of its buildings were built during the reign of his great-grandson, Abbas II. Many of these rulers feared members of their own family, and were known for killing their brothers and even their own mothers to prevent revolt. The severity of the Hussein's rule led to revolt among Sunni Afghans, who forced the abdication of the Shah in 1722. After a brief period of Afghani rule, Tahmasp II recovered the empire for the Safavids. Under Tahmasp's son, Abbas III, the general Nadir Khouli (1736–1747) recovered much territory that had earlier been lost to the Ottomans. Nadir eventually became Shah and abandoned Shi'ism as the official religion of the empire.

Persian became the common language in Safavid lands. The art of the Safavid kingdom reflected Chinese and other Asian influences.

The Mughals in India

The word "mughal" is the Persianate form of "Mongol." The **Mughals** were descendents of the Mongols from Turkestan, and they brought Persian influences to India, especially that of Sufi mysticism. The Mughals were not the first Muslim power in India, as Arabas had invaded in the seventh century C.E. and Rajput, in southeastern India, was ruled by the Delhi sultanate, whose ruler was an Islamic Turk.

Babur the Tiger

Babur the Tiger was a descendant of Genghis Khan on his mother's side and on his father's side from Timur. Starting in 1483, he conquered Afghanistan and captured Kabul in 1504, the Delhi sultanate, and Hindustan and came to power in 1483. His success may be attributed in part to the arrival of the Portuguese in 1510, who weakened the Delhi sultanate enough for Babur to later conquer it. Although his army was small, their firearms more than balanced their numbers. Babur was the first Islamic leader to use firearms and created what many scholars call the first gunpowder empire.

Humayun (1556)

Babur's son, Humayun, lost much of his father's territory between 1530 and 1540, but by 1555 he had managed to regroup his army while in exile in Persia. They succeeded in reconquering significant amounts of lost territory, but Humayun fell down a flight of stairs and broke his neck. Humayun, however, encouraged the appreciation of Persian culture, especially in his son Akbar, who became the most famous Mughal ruler.

Akbar (1556–1605)

Akbar was only thirteen when he came to power, but he continued the wave of conquests started by Babur, and by the time he died, had conquered most of northern India and Afghanistan. His empire was larger than Babur's and he believed that any empire not expanding must be in decline.

Akbar's bureaucracy was very efficient in the world, and he put military governors, or *mansabars,* in charge of each region. Each governor was responsible for the military of the province. Akbar severely punished abuses of power and mistreatment of the poor or weak, sometimes with death.

Akbar's rule was benevolent, as he canceled the poll tax on non-Muslims and offered tolerance to all faiths. He stopped the pilgrimage tax on Hindus, and so earned their support. Many Hindus served in his bureaucracy, and he even married a Hindu, who was his favorite wife and mother of his son, Jahangir. He had over 5,000 wives, many of them daughters of the various kings of regions. He allowed Hindus to be governed by their own law, the *Dharmashastra,* as opposed to the *Shari'ah,* or Muslim code of law.

Akbar's political theorist was Abu'l Faz'l, who, like Akbar, was influenced by Shi'ite thought, especially the doctrine that the Divine Light was passed to the world through the *Imam.* Abu'l Faz'l believed that the *Imam* in the world was the just ruler, and this ruler was to guide humanity. Akbar adopted this idea and developed a new religion that he called the Din-i Ilahi, or "The Religion of God," based on the belief that all religions contained a grain of truth about the single unifying principle of reality, God.

In 1578, Akbar completed the construction of a new city designed to symbolize his new religion, Fatehpur Sikri.

Akbar was opposed by the Islamic *ulema*, or elite body of learned Muslim spiritual leaders, who were threatened by the suggestion that the *Imam* in the world, or the just ruler, was above the *Shari'ah*. Akbar also supported the notion of the divine kingship, equally disturbing to them.

Jahangir (1605–1628)

Although Jahangir added Bengal to his father's domains, Jahangir focused on patronage of the arts. His reign is known as the age of Mughal splendor.

In 1627, Jahangir gave the British East India Company permission to build a fortified factory at Surat, the most important Mughal port. Within ten years, they were headquartered at Bombay. The British would eventually control India.

Shah Jahan (1628–1658)

Shah Jahan continued Akbar's wave of conquests. Shah Jahan conquered parts of the Meccan and turned back the Portuguese intrusion at Bengal. He moved the capital from Agra to Delhi and built a magnificent palace for himself within the famous Red Fort. His famous Peacock throne symbolized the success of the Mughals, and some estimate that it cost as much as five million dollars in today's money. In 1739, the Afghans who conquered the Safavids entered India and took the Peacock throne back to Iran, where it remains today.

The Taj Mahal.

Shah Jahan's most famous project was the Taj Mahal, built to commemorate the memory of his favorite wife, Mumtaz Mahal, who died following the birth of her fourteenth child. The monument took more than 20,000 people to build and is intended to be representative of paradise. The tomb was so expensive to build, however, that taxes were raised from the one-third of the crop value they were under Akbar to over one-half of the crop value. The heavy tax was a burden for poor Hindus.

Aurangzeb (1658–1707)

Late in his reign, Shah Jahan's two sons fought over the succession. His son Aurangzeb viciously took power, had his father imprisoned, and gouged out his eyes so that he could no longer see the Taj Mahal. Aurangzeb also had his brother executed. He continued the wave of conquests, but was also a very pious Muslim who insisted that the *Shari'ah* be followed. No laws that were not found in the *Shari'ah* could be enacted, and Aurangzeb overturned years of tolerance for Hindus and other non-Muslims when he reenacted the *jizya*, or poll tax for non-Muslims. He also abolished the practice of *sati* among the Hindu warrior caste in some areas of India, such as Rajasthan, where widows threw themselves on their husband's funeral pyres.

Hindu resistance to Aurangzeb increased. Aurangzeb had conquered the Marathas of the Deccan, and by 1740, the Marathas controlled more territory than the Mughals.

The Sikhs

The **Sikhs** were also a threat to Aurangzeb. The word "Sikh" means disciple, and in this case, they were disciples of the Gurus. The religion dates back to the reign of Babur, and teaches that God is one and present in all creation. They believe that God can be directly apprehended by the human mind, and there is no need for churches, rites, or other practices. Since all humans have God within them, there are no castes. The Guru, leader of the movement, reveals to his followers the Name of God, through which one can experience unity, and the Word of God, which provides the acceptable methods of achieving union. Under Aurangzeb, the most influential Guru was Gobind Singh, who transformed the Sikhs into a radical brotherhood, or *khalsa*. Aurangzeb regarded them as heretics but, by the eighteenth century, the Sikhs had a separate kingdom within Mughal territory and were allies of the British as they incorporated India into their empire in the 1850s. The Sikhs continue to be a revolutionary force, as it was the Sikh bodyguards who assassinated Indira Ghandi in the twentieth century.

The British in India

The progressive intrusions of the **British East India Tea Company**, which sought to control the economy of India, further complicated the situation.

After the British established factories at Bombay, Madras, and Calcutta, the East India Tea Company expanded to the interior of India and bit by bit won rights to govern areas there. Robert Clive defeated the army of Siraj-ud-daulah, the Nawab of Bengal, at the Battle of Plassey in 1757. He bribed the Nawab's soldiers and his chief rival, and so began the British *Raj* domination of India and the transformation of the East India Tea Company from traders to the rulers of Bengal and eventually to all of India.

In 1760, the British defeated their French rivals for India at Wandiwash and in 1761, at Pondicherry, thus paving the way for complete domination. In 1765, the East India Tea Company acquired the right of the *diwani* of Bengal, or the right to collect revenue in the name of the Mughal emperors in the Bengal region. British rule in India would last nearly 200 years.

In 1803, the British General Wellesley, who was governor general of British India, continued to expand British control when he defeated the Maratha chieftains. He began to build an empire in India through conquest of several native rulers or making treaties with them.

The Sepoy Mutiny

The British controlled their conquests with British forces, supplemented by larger numbers of Indian troops called sepoys. Rebellions against the

British culminated in the 1857 **Sepoy Mutiny**. The chief cause of this revolt was the refusal of the Hindu troops to use animal grease on the cartridges of their Enfield rifles. Soldiers had to bite off the end of the cartridges to load the rifles, which violated both Islamic and Hindu beliefs. Muslims worried that the fat might be from pigs, prohibited animals under their dietary laws, while Hindus feared it was from cows, prohibited by their beliefs.

In 1857, the British disbanded three regiments for refusal to use rifles with animal grease. Then the British imprisoned eighty-five sepoys, stationed at Meerut, for refusing to load their rifles, after which the remaining regiments mutinied on May 10, 1857. These regiments marched to Delhi in support of the last Mughal emperor, Bahadur Shah Zafar, as the ruler of all India.

By June, nearly 90,000, about seventy percent of the Bengal army's sepoy force, were involved in the mutiny. The sepoy defeated the British at the Kanpur garrison and Lucknow, but the British army, helped by their Sikh and Gurkha forces, eventually stopped the rebellion. This marked the final defeat of the Mughal Empire.

The British Parliament then replaced the East India Tea Company with a secretary of state for India, who was directly responsible to the British Cabinet. In November 1858, Queen Victoria gave the governor-general of India the title of Viceroy.

British Contributions to Indian Society

The British built railroads and telegraph lines, and developed a postal system, all of which improved communication. They cleared large areas of forest and planted coffee, tea, and opium crops for trade in their growing imperial world.

English goods produced by machine, however, weakened the market for the traditional Indian village artisan. Poverty increased, and when the American Civil War (1861–1865) forced the British to find an alternate supply of cotton in India, Indian agriculture collapsed. A serious drought in the 1870s created widespread famine throughout India.

The British united all of India, including present-day Pakistan and Bangladesh, as well as Sri Lanka, or Ceylon, under a single government. The British hoped to consolidate their presence by transforming India through western education. Many of those so educated became officials in the British government, and served as lawyers, businessmen, and teachers.

The newly educated Indians, however, became the backbone of strong opposition groups to the British. Although the British had hoped to eradicate many native traditions through education, believing western ways to be superior to those of the native Indians, if anything, education provided a force for strengthening opposition by exposing the Hindus to such ideals as freedom, justice, and equality.

The Indian National Congress

The **Indian National Congress** was first established in 1885 and eventually became the force behind the rise of Indian nationalism.

Extremists opposed to the British eventually assumed control. The extremists were also anti-Muslim and built on memories of past Hindu glory. The anti-British movement paved the way for the nationalistic efforts of Mohandas Gandhi, Rabindranath Tagore, and Jawaharal Nehru, who eventually led India to independence on June 11, 1947.

CHAPTER 31

THE BRITISH COLONIES IN THE AMERICAS AND THE AMERICAN REVOLUTION

THE EUROPEAN COLONIES IN THE AMERICAS

While the Spanish dominated the colonization of the New World in the sixteenth century, the French and English dominated the colonization efforts in the seventeenth century. The Spanish had primarily been concerned to take wealth and riches from the New World and to convert the heathen natives. The French and English, on the other hand, saw the benefits of developing a self-sustaining economy in the New World, and focused on trade with the natives and the cultivation of crops. The various European powers established three types of colonies in the seventeenth century: plantation colonies, settlement colonies, and trading colonies. Plantation colonies were based on the cultivation of crops for profit. Sugar was one of the first crops cultivated on the plantation colonies of the Spanish, French, and English in the Caribbean; the cultivation of sugar led to the use of African slaves in the eighteenth century and the development of the Triangle Trade. Tobacco and rice, however, became important crops in North America. Settlement colonies, such as the New England colonies, were based on farming for subsistence. Both plantation and settlement colonies resulted in significant conflicts with the Native American population, as both required large tracts of land to cultivate. The European colonists believed in the ownership of land, while the Native Americans believed land belonged to all in common.

When the native populations refused to vacate land Europeans desired for cultivation, conflicts often erupted.

FRENCH EXPLORATIONS AND COLONIZATION OF THE AMERICAS

In contrast to the plantation and settlement colonies that competed and often conflicted with the Native American population, the trading colonies were dependent on the goodwill of the native population. The French had begun to explore the Americas when, in 1524, Giovanni da Verrazano had sailed along the North American coastline from the Carolinas to perhaps as far north as Maine. Colonization began ten years later, but the French were preoccupied with the wars of religion that raged across Europe and resulted in a civil war in France itself. French colonization of the Americas began again in the seventeenth century. Jacques Cartier explored the Gulf of St. Lawrence and traveled up the St. Lawrence River to what is modern Montreal. In 1542, he founded Quebec. It did not survive for long, and Samuel de Champlain reestablished Quebec in the seventeenth century. The French concentrated on trade in beaver furs in Canada and in the west of North America, and cultivated their relationships with the Native Americans, as did many of the Dutch traders at New Amsterdam. In the French and Indian War, known as the Seven Years' War in Europe (1756–1763), the British defeated the French, who were pushed off the continent, except for two small islands off the coast of Newfoundland. Britain acquired all French possessions, including Canada, in the Treaty of Paris in 1763. The British presence in Canada forced many French down to Louisiana, forming the Cajun population that is still a strong presence there.

DUTCH COLONIZATION

New Netherland (New York)

New York was once known as New Netherland and was founded by Henry Hudson. In 1602, Hudson sailed for the Dutch East India Company in search of a northern passage to China. Hudson discovered Delaware Bay in 1609 and sailed up the Hudson River to Albany, where he made a friendly pact with the Iroquois. In 1614, the Dutch founded fur-trading posts on Manhattan Island and at Fort Orange. In 1626, Governor Peter Minuit purchased Manhattan from the Indians and founded New Amsterdam as the capital of New Netherland. Although the Dutch were primarily interested in the fur trade, the Dutch West India Company made provisions for stockholders to obtain estates if they stocked them with at least fifty people. In 1664, the

English—led by James, Duke of York, and later King James II—took New Netherland from the Dutch governor Peter Stuyvesant in a bloodless coup d'etat. The English changed the name of **New Amsterdam** to **New York**, and Fort Orange to Albany.

ENGLISH COLONIZATION OF THE NEW WORLD

Roanoke Island

In 1584, Sir Walter Raleigh first discovered Roanoke Island off the outer banks of North Carolina, and in 1597, the first settlers arrived. The first English child born in the New World was Virginia Dare, the granddaughter of the colony's governor, John White. White left one month after their arrival and did not return until 1590. By the time he returned, the colonists had disappeared, leaving behind only the word "Croatoan" inscribed on two trees. The fate of the lost colony of Roanoke is still a mystery today. The historian Karen Ordahl Kupperman has called Roanoke the "twice-lost colony," as not only were its original inhabitants lost, but also history has long emphasized the importance of Jamestown while failing to credit Roanoke's significance as the first English colony.

Jamestown, Virginia

The first successful English colony in the Americas was founded by the Virginia Company, chartered by James I, the heir and successor of Elizabeth the Great of England. The Virginia Company was a joint stock company, in which stockholders hoped to make a profit from their investment. The London branch of the Virginia Company planted the first permanent colony in Virginia, which was named after Elizabeth, the Virgin Queen. On May 6, 1607, three ships landed on the Chesapeake Bay. They settled on the River James, as they thought it might provide a northwest passage to Asia. The colonists were not adept at farming, and so forged trading alliances with a confederation of thirty Algonquin tribes under Powhatan (Wahunsonacock).

Captain John Smith

Captain John Smith was the leader of the colonists, and managed to keep them alive by forcing them to work. He was captured by Powhatan, and according to unsubstantiated legends, was freed through the intervention of Pocahontas. After Smith returned to England in 1609, the colonists endured a time of famine known as the "starving time" and disintegrated into anarchy. By 1610, there were only about sixty settlers left in the colony.

John Rolfe and Pocahontas

A turning point occurred in 1612 when John Rolfe took charge, married Powhatan's daughter Pocahontas, and began the cultivation of tobacco in Virginia. After Sir Francis Drake brought tobacco to England in 1586 from the Caribbean Islands, tobacco had grown in popularity. After Virginia began to cultivate it and export it, the English smoked more tobacco per capita than any other European nation. The cultivation of tobacco is labor intensive, which eventually resulted in the need to import labor. In the seventeenth century, labor came in the form of **indentured servants**, whose price of passage was paid in return for a specified number of years of service. Although indentured servants had rights, two of five died from the difficult working conditions in the hot, moist climate of the Chesapeake. In the eighteenth century, the colonists would turn to slaves from Africa in order to meet their labor needs.

The cultivation of tobacco also had consequences for the colonists' relations with Native Americans. Tobacco depletes the soil, forcing planters to continually search for new lands. Three crops of tobacco can be grown before a field must lie fallow for several years. This need for new land brought about new conflicts with the Algonquin, who were no longer led by Powhatan but by his brother Opechancanough. In 1622, the Algonquin killed John Rolfe along with 350 colonists in an attempt to keep the colonists from further expansion. After this event, the English deliberately embarked on a policy of extermination, and, in 1623, Captain William Tucker killed 200 Indians with poison-laced wine under the pretense of negotiating a treaty. In 1644, the Algonquins attacked again, but were firmly routed by the English. Thereafter, the English promoted a view of the Indians as savages whose destruction was warranted in order for civilization to advance.

Plymouth

Plymouth was founded by Separatists who had fled to Holland after having been persecuted under James I in England. Although the Dutch were sympathetic to the Puritans, they had discriminated against them. In 1620, William Bradford secured a land patent from the Virginia Company, and 101 Puritans left Leyden aboard the Mayflower for the journey to the New World. Less than one-third of the passengers were among the "elect," or those believed to be predestined for salvation. After a stormy voyage, the Puritans arrived in Cape Cod and eventually settled at Plymouth. They signed the **Mayflower Compact** on November 21, 1620. Although revisionist historians now challenge the intended scope of the document, many traditional historians see the Mayflower Compact as the predecessor to the Constitution, as it established the ideal of consensual government.

The Pilgrims at Plymouth endured much hardship and famine, but were aided by Wampanoag Indians, especially Squanto, who taught the settlers to grow maize. In 1621, they produced a bountiful crop and celebrated with a feast now known as Thanksgiving. The colony was absorbed by the larger Puritan colony of Massachusetts Bay in 1691.

Massachusetts Bay

Puritans who, unlike the Separatists at Plymouth, hoped to reform the Church of England, founded Massachusetts Bay. They were known as non-separating Congregationalists. In 1629, Charles I granted the Massachusetts Bay Colony a charter for the area north of Plymouth. Their leader, John Winthrop, was a lawyer who wanted to establish a Christian utopia in the New World. In 1630, the Puritans left on the *Arbella* and six other ships. Winthrop delivered his famous speech, "A Model of Christian Charity," during the voyage. Boston became the capital of the colony, and soon a Great Migration of some 80,000 more people followed. Only official churchmen could be stockholders, later known as freemen, in the Massachusetts Bay Company. The Massachusetts Bay Company eventually became the governing body of the colony, and status as a "visible saint" as indicated by membership in the Puritan church became the criteria for voting. The colony had a general court, a representative body with two houses. Massachusetts Bay was intolerant of dissent, and banished Roger Williams and others whose views conflicted with those of the freemen. The tensions caused by rigid adherence to norms erupted in the Salem Witch Trials in 1692.

Maryland

Sir George Calvert, Lord Baltimore, converted to Catholicism in 1625 and sought a charter to found Maryland as a refuge for Catholics. His son, Cecilius Calvert, founded Maryland in 1634 at a place known as St. Mary's on a stream of the Potomac. Maryland was the first proprietary colony granted to an individual as opposed to a joint stock company. Its primary crop was tobacco. Maryland's Toleration Act granted equality and freedom of religion to all Christians.

Rhode Island

Roger Williams founded Providence in 1636, after being banished from the Massachusetts Bay Colony for his advocacy of the separation of church and state. In 1640, the dissenters who had come to the area formed a confederation, and in 1643 received their first charter. Rhode Island was the smallest colony in America and was also the first colony to legislate freedom of religion.

Connecticut

In 1636, three congregations of Puritans from Massachusetts traveled south on the "Great Road" to Withersfield, Windsor, and Hartford. Under the leadership of Thomas Hooker, they founded Connecticut in 1637. In 1639, the Connecticut General Assembly passed the "Fundamental Orders of Connecticut." Unlike Massachusetts, those who were not members of the Puritan church were allowed to vote. John Davenport and a group of Puritans founded New Haven on Long Island Sound in 1638. This location was propitious for trade. New Haven became a very rigid Puritan colony and never developed its own self-governing charter. It was absorbed into Connecticut in 1662.

New Hampshire

The territory now known as New Hampshire and Maine was the result of a grant in 1622 from the Council for New England to Sir Fernando Gorges and Captain John Mason. Gorges and Mason divided their territory at the Piscataqua River, Gorges calling his northern part Maine, and Mason calling his southern part New Hampshire.

The Carolinas (North)

The Carolinas were a proprietary colony run by eight lord proprietors. The northernmost part of the Carolinas was known as Albemarle Sound, and it was separated from Virginia by the Dismal Swamp. There was no governor until 1664 and no assembly until 1665. Bath, founded in 1704 by a group of French Huguenots (Calvinists), was the first town. North Carolina remained a proprietary colony for ten years after South Carolina became a royal colony in 1719.

South Carolina

The lord proprietors of the Carolinas focused their attention on South Carolina as opposed to the desolate northern reaches of the Carolinas, Albemarle. In 1669, they brought three ships from London, stopped in Barbados for more settlers, and finally arrived at a place on the Ashley River. There they founded Charles Town (Charleston), which remained there from 1670 until 1680, when it was moved across and downstream to Oyster Point. The colony exported furs and cattle, and, in the 1690s, developed rice into a major export crop. Planters from Barbados, who developed trade in Indian slaves, dominated South Carolina. Lord Ashley-Cooper, one of the eight proprietors of the colony, drew up the "Fundamental Constitutions of Carolina." His secretary was the philosopher John Locke, whose works justified the English Glorious Revolution. The document was unique in the degree of religious toleration it granted to Jews and non-Christians. South Carolina became a royal colony in 1719.

New Jersey

New Jersey was a gift from James, Duke of York, to Sir George Carteret and Lord John Berkeley. The land between the Hudson and Delaware rivers was called New Jersey in honor of Carteret's native island of Jersey. Dissenting Puritans from New Haven founded Newark in East Jersey. West Jersey and East Jersey were united as a royal colony in 1702.

Pennsylvania

Pennsylvania was a proprietary colony founded by Quakers. The Quakers were almost in direct contrast to the Puritans, as they believed in individual inspiration, or the "inner light." They rejected formal sacraments and ministries, called everyone by the familiar "thee" and "thou," refused to accept hierarchical authority, and were pacifists. George Fox founded the Quakers in 1647, and he returned from the New World in 1673 with a vision of a Quaker commonwealth in the Americas. William Penn received a charter for the colony in 1681 from Charles II. He named the colony "Pennsylvania," which literally meant "Penn's Woods," after his father. Penn's *Frame of Government* was based on the idea of a Quaker state that supported freedom of individual conscience. There was no established church in Pennsylvania, and Philadelphia was an unfortified city. William Penn was on very friendly terms with the Indians. William Penn signed a "Great Treaty" in 1682 at the village of Shackamaxon with the Delaware Indians, according to which he paid 1,200 pounds for their land, which was a fair price. The treaty has not survived, and historians have questioned its terms.

Delaware

James, Duke of York, granted the portion of Dutch territory that became Delaware to William Penn in 1682. In 1710, Delaware obtained the right to elect its own assembly, but had the same governor as Pennsylvania until the American Revolution.

Georgia

Georgia was founded as a buffer zone between the English colonies and the Spanish in Florida. It was also a place where debtors and other persecuted people could make a fresh start. In 1732, King George II gave the land between the Savannah and Altamaha Rivers to twenty-one trustees. General George Oglethorpe founded Savannah in 1733. Georgia became a cosmopolitan center that was home to many ethnicities and faiths, including Protestants from central Europe, Scottish Highlanders, Portuguese Jews, and Welsh. In 1753, the province became a royal colony, which exported rice, lumber, and other goods, and traded with the West Indies. Slavery was not permitted in Georgia.

MERCANTILISM

British colonial rule in the Americas was based on the economic philosophy of **mercantilism**, a theory articulated in detail by the Scottish economist Adam Smith in his *Wealth of Nations* (1776). According to mercantilism, colonies supply raw materials for the mother country. This philosophy led to many of the taxes levied on the colonies and to other policies protested by the colonists.

BRITISH COLONIAL RULE

The British colonists who went to the Americas, however, often went with very different assumptions. First, they went on the assumption of having full rights of a British subject. These rights included all the assumptions of the Glorious Revolution, which occurred in 1688.

For many years, the colonists were allowed to live virtually unaffected by taxation.

Debt from the Seven Years' War

However, the Seven Years' War (1756–1763), known as the **French and Indian War** in the Americas, drastically affected England's financial situation. The British were in debt and needed to raise revenue.

The American colonies were a special problem, as they represented one-quarter of the population of the empire, yet they paid only 1/100 of the cost to maintain the colonies. The American colonists only paid some 2,000 pounds a year in taxes, yet it cost 8,000 pounds a year to collect them.

The New Colonial Policy

In 1763, the crown enacted the New Colonial Policy, which was an attempt by the British to collect what was rightfully their due.

Their first attempts to collect taxes were actually very mild. There was already a tax on molasses in 1733, for example, yet no one paid it.

The Sugar Act (1764)

The new colonial policy resulted in the Sugar Act in 1764, which increased duties on imported sugar and other items such as textiles, coffee, wines, and indigo. It doubled the duties on foreign goods reshipped from England to the colonies and also forbade the import of foreign rum and French wines.

The Currency Act (1764)

Also in 1764, the British prohibited the colonists from issuing paper money in the Currency Act. Colonists feared it would destabilize the colonial economy.

James Otis responded to the new taxation with "The Rights of the British Colonists Asserted and Proved," in which he argued that governments should not take the property of citizens without their consent. He also advocated the natural law theory of government, although his version of natural law was God's law.

Boston merchants responded by boycotting British luxury goods.

The Stamp Act (1765)

The British were undisturbed by colonial protests and implemented the Stamp Act in 1765, the first direct tax on the colonists. The act levied a tax on newspapers, cards, legal documents, and other items, such as dice and playing cards, enraging colonists. Those who united against the tax were those most affected, such as lawyers, merchants, and landowners.

In response to Otis's points and those of other colonists, the British asserted that colonists were "virtually" represented by the Parliament at home. The colonists, for their part, insisted that the interests of the Parliament and of the English at home were far different that those of the colonists in the Americas.

The colonists argued that external taxation might be permissible, but internal taxes should only be passed with the consent of those taxed.

VIRGINIA RESOLUTIONS

In May 1765, Patrick Henry presented seven Virginia Resolutions to the Virginia House of Burgesses. The Virginia House of Burgesses was the first democratic assembly in the colonies, and Virginia was the most populous colony. Henry argued that only the House of Burgesses could legally tax Virginia residents.

The Sons of Liberty

Rebellion increased, and, in July 1765, the Sons of Liberty were formed. The Sons of Liberty was an underground organization whose members opposed the Stamp Act and used violence and intimidation against British stamp agents and American colonial merchants who ordered British goods.

The Stamp Act Congress (1765)

In October 1765, representatives from nine colonies met in New York and drafted a petition to **King George III**, asserting that only the colonial legislatures could tax the colonists.

On the date when the tax was implemented, November 1, 1765, people appeared in public wearing black armbands and carrying coffins down the street. Almost all daily business ground to a halt as colonists refused to use the stamps.

In 1766, the British repealed the Stamp Act, but also passed the Declaratory Act, which asserted their right to tax the colonists and their power to pass laws to govern them. Continued rebellions occurred over the Quartering Act, as British General Thomas Gage, commander of all English military forces in America, attempted to force the New York Assembly to house and supply his troops.

In 1767, England's continuing economic difficulties forced it to take a stronger stance towards the colonists, and the British appointed four admiralty courts to judge cases. This was the equivalent of martial law in the opinion of the colonists. In that same year, the Townshend Revenue Acts imposed a new series of taxes on the colonists. Imports such as paper, tea, glass, lead, and paints were now taxed.

Even moderates, such as John Dickenson, began to protest. Dickenson wrote "Letters from a Farmer in Pennsylvania," rejecting the distinction between internal and external taxes and insisting that all taxes must be self-legislated.

The Virginia Resolves expressed opposition to taxation without representation.

The Boston Massacre (1770)

In 1770, a mob was angrily harassing British soldiers in Boston. The soldiers fired on the crowd, killing three colonists. The Boston Massacre was a breaking point, after which the colonists could no longer see the British as friends or protectors, but as an armed enemy.

Repeal of the Townshend Duties

In 1770, the British repealed the Townshend duties. American colonists had learned the power of collective action.

The British had given up on taxation, but there was a general feeling that the colonists had been unreasonable, and perhaps they were, as they did not pay a comparable share of the taxes for their maintenance yet wanted the full protection and benefits of the British government.

Tea Act (1773)

The British passed the Tea Act, enforcing a tax on tea already in existence, but allowing the British East India Tea Company to sell directly to colonial agents, thus creating a virtual monopoly on the tea trade and undercutting colonial merchants. The first tea ships affected by the act arrived on November 28, 1773. The Boston Tea Party occurred on December 16 when colonists disguised as Mohawk Indians dumped several tons of tea into the harbor rather than pay taxes.

Coercive Acts (Intolerable 1774)

In 1774, the British shut down the port of Boston and forced Bostonians to reimburse the British East India Tea Company for lost goods. The Bostonians were also forced to pay taxes on the tea. There were several other provisions of these acts, which represented an attempt by the British to gain further control over the colonies.

In March 1775, Patrick Henry summed up the attitudes of many colonists when he said, "Give me liberty or give me death!" to the delegates of the Virginia House of Burgesses.

In April 1775, the first shots were fired in what would become known as the American War for Independence. In 1775, it was not yet clear, however, that all the colonists or even most of them wanted independence.

Also in April, the British General Gage attempted to suppress rebellion and marched with the intent of destroying the colonists' arms there. Paul Revere rode to Lexington to warn the colonists, and the first skirmish of the war occurred on the Lexington common. The first shot fired is known as the "shot heard around the world." The British killed eight colonists and wounded ten others, and then marched on to Concord, where the British again skirmished with a colonial militia.

On June 17, 1775, the first major battle between British and American troops occurred in Boston at Breed's Hill. The battle is known as the Battle of Bunker Hill.

The Olive Branch Petition

During the first year, colonists continued to hope the British would address their grievances. In July 1775, the **Continental Congress** drafted the *Olive Branch Petition*, which attempted to reconcile the colonists to the monarchy. It was addressed directly to King George III and asked for his help. The king refused to look at the petition and instead declared the colonists to be in a state of rebellion.

The Declaration on the Causes and Necessity of Taking Up Arms

By this time, George Washington had assumed command of the Continental Army, and the Congress drafted the *Declaration on the Causes and Necessity of Taking Up Arms*, explaining their reasons for continuing to fight and "die as free men" rather than to live "as slaves." King George III then closed the colonies to trade.

THE DECLARATION OF INDEPENDENCE

The Second Continental Congress, representing the colonial governments, adopted the **Declaration of Independence** in July 1776. Thomas Jefferson drafted the document, but the declaration was influenced greatly by John Locke's *Two Treatises on Government*. The Declaration opened with a statement of principles and concluded with a list of the "injuries and usurpations" of the British monarch. Since many of the ideas articulated by Jefferson had, in fact, been the basis of the Glorious Revolution, the document presented a reasonable argument for independence. Jefferson had a flair for writing, and while Locke had said that the rights of life, liberty, and property were inalienable, Jefferson changed "property" to the "pursuit of happiness."

The war for independence had begun. The colonies, now states, had no central system of government, inadequate military forces, and no European ally. What they did have, however, was a common experience as colonials and a common determination to escape from the system of "tyranny" imposed on them by the British.

Perhaps as many as one-half of the colonists in the Americas remained loyal to Britain. Many of these loyalists left during the Revolutionary War. Some scholars have referred to the ensuing struggle for independence in the colonies as "England's Vietnam," as the British fought a desperate battle to maintain control.

The first year of the war, from the spring of 1775 to summer 1776, saw inconclusive action as the British tried to figure out whether, indeed, they were engaged in warfare, or simply caught up in the irritating plots of a group of spoiled colonists. At first, the war was a struggle localized in and around Boston. Following the Declaration of Independence, the conflict spread. In the fall of 1776, the largest British fleet ever sent abroad arrived in New York harbor. On Christmas night, 1776, the Americans won their first victories at Trenton and then at Princeton, New Jersey.

The campaigns of 1777 brought mixed success to the British. Under such capable leaders as the Howes and John Burgoyne, they devised a plan to divide the United States into two sections. This plan failed and the American victory at Saragota brought an end to their New York campaign.

Saratoga resulted in more than just a defeat for the British in New York; it convinced the French, and their new king, Louis XVI, that the new American states might actually win the conflict, and, in February 1778, the French government extended official recognition to the United States. A military alliance and military aid were forthcoming.

The final phase of the war took place in the South. With the surrender of Cornwallis at Yorktown, the war for independence ended. The American Revolution, however, had just begun.

The Second Continental Congress

At the time independence was declared, and until the fighting had ended, the central "government" consisted only of the Second Continental Congress, a body of men charged originally with considering the redress of grievances submitted to the mother country in 1774. The Congress had no authority from the old colonies, or the new states, to conduct a war or to make laws.

The Articles of Confederation

In November 1777, the Continental Congress proposed the **Articles of Confederation**, which created a national system so weak that it barely had more power than the Congress itself. The conflict between those who wanted to emphasize the rights of the states as opposed to the rights of the whole dominated American history until the Civil War. The thirteen states ratified the Articles of Confederation in 1781. They were in effect until 1789. Under the Articles of Confederation, the first "national" laws were passed, and these laws addressed the issue of lands west of the Appalachian Mountains.

The Constitution of 1789

Delegates to a constitutional convention met in 1789 to address the weaknesses of the Articles of Confederation. They expected to revise the Articles of Confederation, but instead created a radically new kind of government for the new nation based on the ideas of the French philosopher Montesquieu. Montesquieu had discussed the need for a strong central government comprised of branches empowered to check each other. James

Madison proposed that the government's powers be divided among three branches, the legislative, judicial, and executive. The legislative branch was to be bicameral, following the model of the British Parliament. There were checks and balances established to prevent any one branch from controlling the government.

The Great Compromise, credited to Roger Sherman of Connecticut, resolved disputes between large and small states about representation by having representation in the lower house in proportion to population and equal for every state in the upper house. In 1791, a Bill of Rights was added to the Constitution guaranteeing individual rights. The Bill of Rights represents the first ten amendments to the constitution.

How Revolutionary Was the American Revolution?

Just how "revolutionary" was the American Revolution? Certainly, the English colonials won their independence, and the system of government they would eventually adopt would not be a monarchy, but neither was it a democracy, a reality later reflected in the Constitution of 1789. George Washington took office as president in that same year.

Without question, land ownership was more widespread than it was in England. There were no titles of nobility, or any of the other trappings of monarchy, and religious freedom was guaranteed in most state constitutions and in the Constitution of 1789. On the other hand, slavery continued, and women did not win the right to participate.

Many issues, including slavery, the presence of the Native Americans, and the international position of the new United States, remained to be addressed by later generations.

CHAPTER 32

THE FRENCH REVOLUTION

THE REVOLT NOBLESSE

Discontent with the absolutist government created by Louis XIV boiled over in the eighteenth century. The financial crisis following the Seven Years' War contributed to the rise of revolutionary sentiment. Fully half of the royal budget went towards interest payments on the royal debt, and although the nobility had great wealth, they found numerous ways to escape the payment of mandated taxes. Louis's ministers Turgot and Necker both attempted to stabilize French finances, but to no avail. When the government attempted to reform the tax system so that the nobility paid those taxes they were intended to pay, the Parlement of Paris resisted and revolted, followed by other Parlements throughout France. The Parlements then demanded that the estates general be summoned, something that had not been done since 1614. This initial stage of the revolution is known as the "**Revolt Noblesse**," or the "Revolt of the Parlements."

Summoning of the Estates General

Although there was great hope among the masses surrounding the first meeting of the estates general in 1789, that hope was quickly dashed. The estates general voted by body, that is one vote per estate. The three estates were the clergy, the nobility, and the commoners. The first two could and did always outvote the third estate, which represented the majority of the French population. The famous pamphlet by the Abbe Sieyes, "What Is the Third Estate?," pointed out the folly of this process when he argued that the answer to the title question was "everything." The third estate performed most of the work in France and paid most of the taxes, and, therefore, was entitled to more rights. When the estates met for the first time after the Revolt Noblesse, the first two estates, dressed in their finery, marched in and sat in their traditional locations. The third estate soon realized that nothing would change for them through this process.

The National Assembly

On June 1, 1789, the third estate left the assembly and then invited the clergy and the nobles to join them. By June 17, they had declared themselves the National Assembly. On June 20, they took the famous **Tennis Court Oath**, promising not to disband until the assembly had created a new constitution. The majority of the clergy and a large number of nobles joined with them.

The French Revolution is considered the first movement in which the masses participated. The role of the people became intense about the time the National Assembly began its work. In 1788, there was a great famine, leading to bread riots in 1789. The royal family had little or no understanding of the needs of the masses. Although Marie Antoinette, the German queen of Louis XVI, never made the infamous remark, "let them eat cake," the remark symbolized the distance between the royal family, who led a life of great pomp at Versailles, and the masses, who led lives of misery. While Marie Antoinette frolicked in a country village constructed on the grounds of Versailles for her amusement, the masses did not even have bread to eat. Rarely had royals been so distant from those they governed.

The Storming of the Bastille

The bread riots alarmed the monarchy, and it already had many troops in Paris due to the revolutionary activities of the third estate. The masses became further agitated when Louis dismissed his minister, Necker, whom the people saw as their champion against the aristocracy. This volatile situation erupted on July 14, 1789, and culminated in the **storming of the Bastille**, a fortress prison where the monarchy traditionally kept dissenters. The rioters killed troops, released seven prisoners, and formed a new municipal government, the commune.

General Lafayette and the National Guard

In response, the government created a militia in Paris, which became the national guard. Its emblem was a cockade made up of the two colors of the city of Paris, blue and red. Louis XVI gave command of the guard to General Lafayette, despite his involvement in the American Revolution, of which the monarchy had disapproved. Lafayette added the royal color, white, to the cockade, thus creating an emblem of the revolution. Ironically, the revolutionaries forced Louis XVI to wear the very symbol of his future execution.

The Great Fear

The situation became progressively more volatile, as the "great fear" swept through France in 1789. Fear of an aristocratic conspiracy to overthrow the third estate in the National Assembly, desperate needs in time of famine, and long-standing anger over feudal dues brought about violent protest against ancient manorial privileges. Peasants still paid fees for use of village mills and other privileges known as banalities, and they paid rent for land.

Abolition of Feudal Obligations

On the night of August 4, 1789, while the nobility was absent, the National Assembly abolished feudal society in France. The assembly outlawed banalities and tithes to the church, and mandated that jobs be made open to all. Peasants, however, still had to buy their land to legally own it, which for most of them amounted to the same thing as the old rent payments.

The Declaration of the Rights of Man

On August 27, 1789, the assembly issued the **Declaration of the Rights of Man**, by which everyone in France was considered born free and equal in rights, especially those of life, liberty, property, security, and resistance to oppression.

Although the document contained many lofty sentiments, including freedom of the press, the delegates' use of the word "man" clearly left "women" out of the equation. Mary Wollstonecraft would later write a rebuttal of the assumptions that women were not equal to men in her "Vindication of the Rights of Women."

The Civil Constitution of the Clergy

In July 1790, the assembly passed the Civil Constitution of the Clergy, whereby they secularized the French Catholic Church. They confiscated church lands, especially those owned by monasteries, and dissolved the monasteries. The assembly used these lands as the basis for selling bonds called *assignats*. The clergy was now to be paid a salary by the state and elected by the appropriate parishes. Such clergy would feel no real allegiance to the Roman pope, but rather would be loyal to the new republic. The assembly forced the clergy to take an oath to uphold the Civil Constitution; some did not, and were called refractory clergy. King Louis XVI, who was required to publicly support the document but who privately did not, made the fatal mistake of using a refractory cleric as his chief priest. The Roman Catholic pope repudiated the Civil Constitution in 1791, but it reflected centuries of seething resentment towards the church.

Active and Passive Citizens

The term of the National Assembly expired in September 1791, and their achievement was a new constitution. The constitution distinguished between active and passive citizens, on the basis of the amount of taxes paid. Active citizens could fully participate in the government, while passive citizens were more limited. Only males were considered citizens. Passive citizens had to have had French parents or to have been born in France. In order to become active citizens, one had to take a civic oath, be twenty-five years of age, and pay a tax equivalent to three days' wages.

The revolutionary leader Marat, one of the most radical revolutionaries who advocated universal male suffrage, was horrified by this distinction and cried out in a famous pamphlet, "The Worst Has Happened."

The Legislative Assembly

After the National Assembly was dissolved, the Legislative Assembly took its place. Girondists, Feuillants, and Jacobins dominated the assembly. The Girondists were primarily deputies of the department of the Gironde, and supported the idea of a foreign war in the belief that war would unite France and help to spread the revolution to other countries. They were also interested in a constitutional government. Jacques Brissot de Warville was the leader of the Girondists, and so they were also known as Brissotins. The Feuillants were a group that supported a constitutional monarchy, but since they opposed a foreign war, many associated them with the royalist factions. The Jacobins opposed all counter-revolution, but wished to limit the power of the king and to institute a republic. They customarily met at a Dominican monastery, giving rise to their name, as Parisians called Dominicans "Jacobins."

The Storming of Versailles

Meanwhile, the revolution was beginning to fragment as the revolutionaries disagreed, and European monarchs began mustering forces to oppose them. Peasant revolts had erupted all over Europe in response to the French revolutionary motto of **"liberty, equality, and fraternity."** European monarchs rightly believed that the revolution threatened their own monarchies, and this was further confirmed when an angry Parisian crowd stormed Versailles on October 5, 1789, and brought the king and queen, whom they mockingly called "the baker and the baker's wife," to the Tuileries palace in Paris.

Louis XVI and the Flight to Varennes

Louis XVI's wife, Marie, was the sister of the Holy Roman Emperor. Louis believed they could expect help from the emperor, as well as other monarchs, and so attempted to leave France. Revolutionaries got wind of his desperate flight on June 20 and 21, 1791, and halted him at Varennes. The king and queen were escorted back in humiliation and Louis was eventually forced to accept the new constitution.

Declaration of War Against Austria in 1792

As the revolution gained in momentum, the Feuillants fell. In August 1791, the Holy Roman Emperor and King of Prussia met at Pillnitz, and issued an ultimatum to the French in the Declaration of Pillnitz. That ultimatum demanded the protection of Louis XVI on the threat of war. The Brissotins (Girondists) hoped that the declaration would be interpreted as a declaration of war, and, on April 20, 1792, the second revolution began when the Legislative Assembly declared war on Austria.

In addition to Marie Antoinette's brother, the Holy Roman Emperor, among the foreign leaders that now aligned themselves against France were

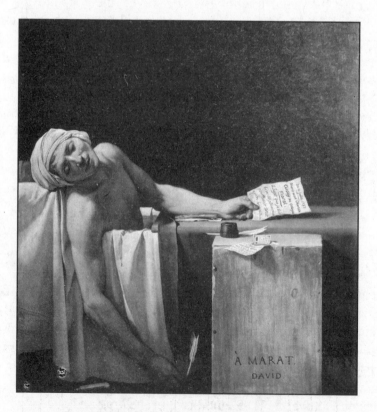

Death of Marat. *Jacques-Louis David*, 1793.

the King of Sweden, the Russian Tsarina Catherine the Great, the King of Prussia, and even Alexander Hamilton of the United States.

The National Convention and September Massacres

The war went very unfavorably, and the masses began to turn against the king and queen as they feared a royal conspiracy. In August, they stormed the Tuileries, where the king had been kept since his flight, and imprisoned him. The rebels set up an insurrectionary commune that replaced the legally elected one of the early revolution. They rejected the constitution of the National Assembly and demanded new elections by universal manhood suffrage for a national convention, whose task would be to draw up a new constitution. There were mass arrests of royalists, and, in September, a wave of massacres in which approximately 2,000 prisoners died.

The *Sans-culottes*

Radical revolutionaries dominated the national convention, especially members of the *sans-culottes*, or "those without fancy breeches." Although often portrayed as frenzied commoners, the *sans-culottes* were lawyers, clerks, tradesmen, and the working people of France. Among their leaders were the most radical revolutionaries, such as Georges Jacques Danton, Jean Paul Marat, and Camille Desmoulins.

The Mountain

A faction of Jacobins went to their side, and since they sat high in the convention hall, they were called the Mountain.

Abolition of the Monarchy

The National Convention met for the first time on September 21, 1792, and immediately abolished the monarchy. It proclaimed Year One of the French Republic. Not only were the years to be dated from this event, but also new names were to be used for the months, and weeks were to have ten days. The convention then accused the king of treason and on January 21, 1793, executed citizen Capet, as Louis was then known. Mass citizen uprisings in areas of strong support for the royalist cause occurred in the Vendée. The opposition of foreign monarchs became more intense and civil strife in France increased.

The Jacobins of the Mountain finally succeeded in ousting the Girondists in June 1793. The convention created a democratic constitution that was approved by 1.8 million voters in a plebiscite, but it was never implemented.

The Reign of Terror

From 1792 to 1795, the Emergency Republic ruled France, dominated by the Committee of Public Safety, created in April 1793. The committee was essentially a dictatorship, whose tasks were to manage the war abroad and the growing chaos at home. Wages and prices were frozen, and the French were ordered to use the worthless assignats as money. The most important leaders were Danton and **Maximillian Robespierre**, who vigorously argued in defense of any measures to ensure the survival of the "Republic of Virtue." Robespierre instituted a Reign of Terror starting in 1793. Robespierre supported such lofty ideas as universal suffrage, but the society he created was anything but utopian. He turned against any and all whom he believed did not support the revolution and who might see its reforms turned back. The Girondists, for example, were now enemies of the spread of the revolution. In 1793, Charlotte Corday, whose brother had been denounced and condemned by the Committee of Public Safety, assassinated Marat while he was soaking in his bathtub. Robespierre condemned many of his own friends, such as Danton, to the guillotine. In 1794, Danton tried to restrain some of Robespierre's excesses, but in the end, lost his life. He asked the executioner to display his severed head to the people in the hope that it would ignite further action against Robespierre.

The Cult of the Supreme Being

In the Constitution of 1793, the government dechristianized the state and founded the Cult of the Supreme Being. The Supreme Being was designed to counter the influence of Jacques Héber's goddess of reason, and Robespierre had Héber executed. No longer were religious holidays to be celebrated in honor of Christ.

Fall of Robespierre

By July 27, 1794, however, many feared that Robespierre would turn against them, and they shouted him down in the assembly. Robespierre fell victim to his own extremes and was executed on July 28, known as the ninth of Thermidor in the revolutionary calendar.

Thermidorian Reaction

The conservative reaction that followed is known as the Thermidorian reaction. A new constitution created a directory and a two-chamber legislature. There were five directors, but, unfortunately, they and their colleagues were corrupt.

Napoleon Bonaparte

Many feared the return of the royalists, but at the same time many royalists were able to reassert their ideas. The Abbe Sieyes, once a leader of the third estate, now called for direction from above and supported the efforts of a French war hero, **Napoleon Bonaparte**, to restore order. Napoleon had recently crushed the Austrian armies and the First Coalition (Spain, Holland, Austria, Prussia, England, and Sardinia). The Treaty of Campo Formio in October 1797 ended the first phase of the Napoleonic wars.

The Battle of the Nile

The Directors feared Bonaparte, and so, in May 1798, they sent him out of France to capture Egypt. The possibility of his success greatly worried the British, for if the French dominated the Middle East, they would control the land route to India. In August 1798, at the Battle of the Nile (or Aboukir Bay), Lord Nelson wiped out the French fleet while it was anchored in shallow water, leaving 38,000 French soldiers stranded.

The Second Coalition

Now a Second Coalition formed against the French to take advantage of their defeat on the Nile. From 1799 to 1801 the Second Coalition, made up of Turkey, England, Austria, and Russia, fought France. In 1799, Austria drove the French back across the Rhine, a Russo-Austrian army defeated the French and drove them out of Italy, and Britain pushed the French out of Holland. A three-pronged attack was planned on France, by Britain, Austria, and Russia.

The Consulate

Meanwhile, Napoleon returned to France, and on the nineteenth of Brumaire, or November 10, 1799, Napoleon established the consulate and named himself as first consul. In 1801, Napoleon shocked many revolutionaries by making peace with the Roman Catholic pope. He argued that since Roman Catholicism was the religion of the people, peace was good, but at the same time he kept all the church lands previously confiscated.

Napoleon continued to insist that the clergy swear an oath of loyalty to the state and submitted a new constitution to the public for ratification according to universal male suffrage.

The Napoleonic Code

Napoleon also instituted the **Napoleonic Code**, which tended to favor employers over their employees, and males over females within the family. Prior to the code, France did not have a single set of laws. The code was also the first established in a country where there was a civil law system, and it followed Roman law, particularly the sixth-century C.E. Byzantine emperor

Justinian's *Corpus Juris Civilis* in dividing civil law into personal status, property, and acquisition of property.

Napoleon Becomes Emperor in 1804

In 1802, Napoleon made peace with Britain, thus ending the threat of the Second Coalition. However, Napoleon alienated many of his supporters in 1804 when he declared himself emperor. The ceremony occurred in the Cathedral of Notre Dame, and at the point when the pope had blessed the regalia, Napoleon took the crown and placed it on himself.

The Third Coalition

The Third Coalition of Britain, Russia, and Austria formed against France, and on October 21, 1805, Admiral Horatio Nelson defeated the French at the Battle of Trafalgar. The British now had control of the sea. On land, the story was different. Napoleon occupied Vienna, and in December 1805, he defeated Austria and Russia at Austerlitz. Austria retreated from Italy, leaving Napoleon in control of everything north of Italy. Napoleon proclaimed himself King of Italy and annexed Genoa. He appointed his relatives in control of his new territories. In 1808, Napoleon made his brother Joseph king of Spain after obtaining the abdication of Charles IV and his son Ferdinand VII.

Napoleon also defeated the Prussians at Jena in 1806. As a result of the Treaty of Tilsit in 1807, Prussia lost half of its territory, and Russia recognized the French gains and eventually lent support to Napoleon in his defeat of the Swedes.

The Berlin Decrees and the Confederation of the Rhine

Europe was now virtually unrecognizable from the pre-revolutionary period. The Holy Roman Empire was essentially dissolved in 1806, and Napoleon now controlled most of the West German princes through the Confederation of the Rhine. Napoleon made the Prince Electors of Bavaria, Württemberg, and Saxony kings; created the kingdoms of Holland and Westphalia; and made his brothers Louis and Jérôme Bonaparte their kings. In 1806, the Berlin decrees forbade his allies to import British goods. Napoleon instituted the continental system and imposed his codes all over Europe.

Napoleon Marries Marie Louise

The Austria Hapsburgs were so weakened by this time that the Holy Roman Emperor was now calling himself the "emperor of Austria." In 1810, after Napoleon had his marriage to Josephine annulled, he married Marie Louise, the daughter of the Austrian emperor Francis I, formerly the Holy Roman Emperor Francis II. Together they had a son, the "king of Rome," later known as the duke of Reichstadt, or Napoleon II.

Revolts

Many Europeans as well as Napoleon's allies were beginning to turn against his heavy-handed policies. The continental system ruined the economies of many of Napoleon's allies. There were revolts in Spain, and, in 1810 Russia withdrew from the continental system.

Napoleon Invades Russia in 1812

In 1812, Napoleon collected the largest army ever seen and **invaded Russia**. The Russians tried to slow them down by following a scorched earth policy, but both sides suffered huge numbers of casualties at the Battle of Borodino on September 7. The French lost 30,000 men and the Russians twice as many. Napoleon reached Moscow on September 14, only to find that the Russians had burned the city.

The French army now was caught in the Russian winter and began a disastrous retreat on October 19, 1812. Those who did not die of exposure died of sheer hunger. Napoleon left with 600,000 men and returned with only 100,000.

Capture of Paris in 1814

Nevertheless, upon his return to France, Napoleon was once again planning war. Many former allies now turned against him. Prussia allied with Russia in 1813, soon followed by Britain and Sweden, and, finally, by Austria. At the Battle of the Nations at Leipzig in October, they defeated Napoleon. The allies now offered peace if Napoleon would stay within French borders, but he refused, and the allies then took Paris on March 31, 1814.

Napoleon Abdicates and Then Returns for the 100 Days

Napoleon abdicated in 1814 and went into exile on the island of Elba. The Bourbon monarchy was restored, and King Louis XVIII took power. While the allies debated the future of Europe at the Congress of Vienna (1814–1815), Napoleon made a return, landing at Cannes on March 1, 1815. Many French were still suspicious of the Bourbons and remained loyal to their former emperor. Napoleon entered Paris on March 20, 1815, and for 100 days ruled again.

Defeat of Napoleon at Waterloo

The Continental Congress declared Napoleon an outlaw and sent the Duke of Wellington to defeat him. At **Waterloo**, in what is now Belgium, Napoleon was finally defeated on June 18, 1815. Napoleon abdicated and was sent into exile on the remote and tiny island of Saint Helena in the Atlantic, off the coast of Africa, where he died of stomach cancer in 1821. In 1840, Louis Philippe ordered the return of Napoleon's remains, and they remain enshrined today in the Invalides in Paris.

German Nationalism

Napoleon's return made the attitudes of the allies towards France more harsh and generated an intensely conservative reaction. Napoleon's attempt to dominate the German principalities spurred a wave of German nationalism. Later figures, such as Herder, would write about the *Volksgeist*, or special spirit, of the German people. Napoleon succeeded in inspiring a wave of nationalistic sympathies that would culminate in the unification of Germany and Italy in the nineteenth century.

The Congress of Vienna

The Congress of Vienna created a balance of power in Europe that would dominate Europe for the next century. The allies agreed that no single nation should dominate Europe, and that the Bourbon monarchy should be restored to prevent France from becoming a threat again. They erected a series of powerful border states to contain French expansion, such as the Netherlands and Prussia, but they failed to revive the once mighty Holy Roman Empire, leaving in its place the German Confederation.

The Holy Alliance

The Holy Alliance of Russia, Austria, and Prussia was founded to uphold the Congress and to preserve Christian ideals.

The Quadruple Alliance and the Concert of Europe

The Quadruple Alliance of Great Britain, Austria, Prussia, and Russia, which had successfully defeated Napoleon, later evolved into the Concert of Europe and included France, making a Quintuple Alliance, in 1818. The Concert of Europe was founded in order to preserve peace through diplomacy. In the wake of Napoleon's attempt to conquer Europe, peace and the balance of power were desired at all costs. The Ottoman rulers, as Muslims, were left out of both alliances, one of the weakest decisions of the aftermath of Napoleon.

In hindsight, the Anglo-Irish philosopher **Edmund Burke**, in his *Reflections on Revolution in France*, had warned against the attempt to level the traditions of centuries overnight. He believed the French Revolution to be too radical, and that it was sheer folly to obliterate centuries of wisdom. Perhaps the revolutionaries should have listened to Burke, for what followed in France was a long period of conservative backlash.

CHAPTER 33

THE AMERICAN AND FRENCH REVOLUTIONS SPARK OTHER MOVEMENTS FOR INDEPENDENCE

THE HAITIAN REVOLUTION

On the island of Hispaniola in the Caribbean, the ideas of the French and American revolutions did not fall on deaf ears. There were both French and Spanish colonies on the island, and the French colony of Saint-Domingue was one of the most productive colonies of all European colonies in the Caribbean. During the American Revolution, French support had meant that many *gens de Couleur*, or free people of color, had been sent to aid the American colonists. The white colonists in Saint Domingue took advantage of the opportunity created by the French Revolution to establish their own government, but had not conceded rights to the *gens de Couleur* nor to any of the large slave population.

In 1791, Boukman, a Voodoo priest, led a slave revolt that ignited the struggle into a full-scale civil war. Many former or escaped slaves, known as maroons, joined in the revolt. Boukman died, but his revolt did not. Francois **Dominique Toussaint** rose to leadership of the slave revolt, calling himself "**L'ouverture**," meaning "the opening." By 1797, he controlled most of the island, and by 1801, he had created a constitution that granted equality and citizenship to all residents of the colony. Although Toussaint did not declare independence from France, in 1803, his successors did. On January 1, 1804, the new nation of Haiti became the second independent republic in the Western Hemisphere. As for Toussaint, invading French forces took him in 1802, and he died in a French jail in 1803. Nevertheless, his name is synonymous with slave revolts and with the fight for human rights among repressed peoples everywhere.

Latin America

A struggle for independence in Latin American countries also followed in the wake of the French revolution. When Napoleon invaded Spain and Portugal in 1807, he weakened their power and inspired revolution in their colonies. In Mexico, **Miguel de Hidalgo** led a rebellion against the Spanish. The white inhabitants of European ancestry there were called Creoles, and they executed Hidalgo. Later, a Creole general, Augustin de Iturbide, conquered the capital and named himself emperor. Although he declared Mexico's independence, other Creoles deposed him later and declared a republic. Shortly thereafter, the southern regions of the Spanish empire in Mexico declared independence and formed the Central American Federation. In 1838, the federation split into Guatemala, El Salvador, Honduras, Nicaragua, and Costa Rica.

Simón Bolivar

In South America, the Creole **Simón Bolivar** worked to create an independent and unified Latin America. Venezuela, Colombia, and Ecuador formed a republic called Gran Colombia. By 1830, however, differences between these three had broken Gran Colombia apart.

Meanwhile, Napoleon's invasion of Portugal, in 1807, had driven the royal family into exile in Rio de Janiero. Although the king returned to Portugal, in 1821, following the defeat of Napoleon, his son Pedro stayed behind as regent. Revolution erupted only one year later. Pedro disobeyed his father's command to return home and eventually revolutionaries established him as Emperor Pedro I.

Benito Juárez

Revolutionary activity would not succeed in changing the face of Latin America until after World War II. The revolutions of the early nineteenth century succeeded in strengthening the white, Creole elite, as well as their European traditions of Roman Catholicism and slavery. In Mexico, **Benito Juárez** attempted to curtail the influence of the church and of the military. In the Constitution of 1857, Juárez limited the privileges of priests and other elite members of society. Church properties were confiscated, and Mexicans received such civil liberties as freedom of speech and universal manhood suffrage. Juárez was a native Mexican and not a Creole, and he intended his *La Reforma* to benefit the native peoples. Not surprisingly, Creoles bought much of the confiscated church lands.

Villa and Zapata

Over ninety-five percent of Mexican peasants remained landless until the Mexican revolution on 1911–1920. **Emiliano Zapata** and **Francisco Villa** (Pancho Villa) fought for *terra y libertad*, or "land and liberty." The U.S. had supported the Mexican government, and Villa attacked U.S. citizens. Zapata seized land and redistributed it to peasants. The Mexican Constitution of 1917 allowed for land redistribution and restrictions on foreign owner-ship of Mexican land and resources. Other provisions mandated minimum wage levels, limits on hours that could be worked, and a state system of education. Zapata and Villa continued their fight, however, and were both assassinated.

Juan Manuel de Rosas

Creole leaders continued to abuse native populations, however, in places such as Argentina, where the caudillo (regional military leader) Juan Manuel de Rosas (1835–1852) put down rebellions through brutal means. Rosas ruled as a despot, but did succeed in establishing a centralized government.

CHAPTER 34

THE INDUSTRIAL REVOLUTION

The **Industrial Revolution** began in the late eighteenth century in Britain. There were reasons why this revolution occurred in Britain, as it had good natural resources, such as a good water supply for mills and steam power, waterways for transportation of goods, and a budding colonial empire with which to trade these goods. The geographic location of Britain, for the most part, protected it from invasion, so they enjoyed peace and liberty in this era. The Glorious Revolution, engineered by the Puritan landed gentry, created freedom from the constraints of an absolute monarchy and encouraged development of capitalistic enterprises. The enclosure movement, whereby the wealthy enclosed the common pastures, displaced many peasants from the countryside, and they flocked to the developing cities providing a good, cheap supply of labor. The stage was thus set for the Industrial Revolution.

The revolution began in the area of textile manufacturing, Britain's chief industry. The British were always in search of cheaper and newer ways to make cotton. In 1733, John Kay invented the **fly shuttle**, a machine that was able to weave thread together better than a one-person loom. It performed the work of two weavers and increased the speed of weavings, as the shuttle was passed mechanically across the warp threads. Prior to this invention, one could not weave a piece of cloth wider than the human body, as the shuttle had to be passed from hand to hand. The device cut the cost of labor in half, and in 1753, weavers sacked Kay's house in protest.

In 1760, James Heargreaves invented the **spinning jenny**, a device named for his wife. The jenny could spin eight spindles of thread at once and later was expanded to a sixteen-spindle device. This was the first machine to improve on the spinning wheel. In 1769, Richard Arkwright became the father of the industrial revolution when he produced the first power-driven spinning mill, the **water frame**. It took six spinners to keep a weaver busy, and although the spinning jenny helped that situation, it had to be operated by highly skilled laborers. Arkwright's invention eliminated that difficulty and also produced stronger warp thread. Arkwright's invention enabled the rise of the factory system. The first factories were very small in comparison to modern factories.

In 1793, Eli Whitney's **cotton gin** was developed to mechanically remove the seeds from cotton, a very laborious process by hand; therefore, the demand for and supply of cotton increased dramatically, thus contributing to the use of slavery in the Americas, for example. The manufacture of cotton in England increased fivefold after 1793. By 1820, it made up one-half of all exports.

THE STEAM ENGINE

During the 1700s, there was a severe wood shortage in England that led to the search for other sources of fuel, such as coal. Coal, however, was deep in the ground and demanded new techniques to get it out of deep shafts and to pump out the water that inevitably filled the shafts. Thomas Newcomen invented the first steam engine in 1702 and **James Watt** further perfected the steam engine in 1763. **Robert Fulton** used the steam engine in his riverboats in 1807, and in 1829, George Stephenson first pioneered the Rocket, which used the steam engine in a locomotive. The Rocket traveled at 16 mph from Liverpool to Manchester. The steam engine on boats and locomotives made communication between various parts of England, and later the world, possible, increased trade, and contributed to the expansion of the economy.

In the nineteenth century, railroads expanded virtually across the world. Although they brought many benefits, they also contributed to the decline of the Native American lifestyle in the American West and of tribal cultures of Africa, and also impacted the indigenous industries of India. The Industrial Revolution of the nineteenth century was centered on the production of steel to produce railroad tracks, and was a direct outgrowth of the impact of the steam engine developed in the first Industrial Revolution. The Industrial Revolution of the nineteenth century was centered in factories in America, Britain, and in continental Europe.

City life increased dramatically as a result of the Industrial Revolution. Cities such as Manchester, England, increased their population from 25,000 in 1772 to 455,000 in 1851. By the mid-nineteenth century, half of the English population lived in cities, whereas before the revolution most lived in the country. A similar trend occurred in the late nineteenth century in North America; following the second Industrial Revolution, the population began to move from the rural areas to the urban areas, to the point where today the majority of Americans reside in urban areas. Such a rapid rate of expansion naturally led to problems in urban areas with sanitation and overcrowding.

Slums developed in the factory cities, and whole families lived in single rooms or on the streets. Working conditions were equally squalid, as child labor and long hours were common. Workers had little or no rights in the early factories and received no workers' compensation for injuries (which were frequent), no minimum wage, and no breaks or other rights enjoyed by modern workers in America, for example. America addressed these issues during the Progressive era of the early twentieth century, implementing minimum wage guidelines and prohibiting the noxious practice of **child labor**, but not before many children worked themselves to death in coal mines. In many parts of the world today, people continue to work in abusive conditions, some even worse than the conditions following the Industrial Revolution.

CHAPTER 35

THE REVOLUTIONS OF 1848

The fires of revolution spread across Europe in 1848, fanned by economic hardships. Social movements, such as nationalism, liberalism, and socialism, brought diverse groups together, all striving to better their society. Revolutionaries were primarily bourgeoisie, a Marxist term for wealthy members of society who controlled the means of production. The bourgeoisie protested the conservative, reactionary governments created in the wake of the Napoleonic Wars. Revolts occurred throughout Europe that affected France, Italian and German states, and the Austrian Empire. Only England and Russia were spared. By the end of 1849, the revolutions had failed, but the idea of revolutionary social change would live on.

TERMS

Liberalism was based on the ideals of liberty and equality. Liberalism advocated representative government; equality before the law; freedom of speech, assembly, and the press; and freedom from arbitrary arrest. Liberalism also promoted free enterprise and lack of government control of the economy, also known as *laissez faire*, or classical liberalism.

Nationalism was founded on the belief in cultural unity based on a common language, history, territory, and ethnicity. The nationalists sought to create nations based on cultural unity.

Socialism advocated help for the poor, government control of the economy to ensure economic equality between the rich and poor, and regulation or abolition of private property.

REVOLT IN PARIS AND THE ABDICATION OF LOUIS PHILIPPE

The people of Paris revolted in February, forcing Louis Philippe to abdicate. He had abdicated in favor of his grandson, but the people would not accept another king. A provisional republic was declared and the Second Republic was born. This French revolution was interested in social reform, reform of the government, and working conditions. It freed colonial slaves, abolished the death penalty, and recognized rights for the working classes.

Louis Napoleon

While liberal socialism dominated Paris, political moderates dominated the rest of France. Free elections brought a majority of moderates to the Constituent Assembly. By June, this clash of ideologies resulted in more violent uprisings in the streets of Paris. The army put the uprisings down at a cost of thousands of lives. The elections in December brought Louis Napoleon to power.

Revolt of Hungary from Austria

The revolution in France inspired liberal uprisings throughout Europe. Hungarian revolutionaries demanded freedom from Austria. When the Austrian government did not respond positively, protestors filled the streets of Vienna and were active in the countryside as well. Emperor Ferdinand I freed the serfs and gave in to the protestors' demands. Metternich fled, but the various revolutionary groups that had united to bring about change in the Austrian government had differing goals and so could not remain united for long.

The revolutionaries that wanted an independent Hungary for Hungarians could not cope effectively with the other ethnic groups that would be half of an independent Hungary's population. Croats, Serbs, and Rumanians, as well as Hungarians, lived in the territory that would be Hungary. Each of these groups wanted its own independent country. They did not want to exchange being a minority in the Austrian Empire for being a minority in Hungary.

The monarchy and its supporters, which regrouped around a new emperor, **Francis Joseph**, after the abdication of Ferdinand I, exploited these ethnic divisions. The Austrian army was brought in to end the revolts. With the aide of the Russian military, the Hungarian revolution was crushed and Hungary was occupied to deter further uprisings.

Revolt in Prussia

In March 1848, revolution reached Prussia. Working class and middle-class protestors joined together in Berlin to rally against the monarchy. **Frederick William IV** of Prussia responded with a promise of a liberal constitution and a willingness to allow Prussia to be a part of a new united Germany.

A threat to German unification arose in the matter of Schleswig and Holstein. Schleswig and Holstein were two Germanic provinces. Holstein was also a member of the German Confederation, and Germans were the primary inhabitants of both. The King of Denmark, however, controlled both. When Frederick VII of Denmark attempted to solidify his control over these two provinces, he sparked a revolt among their German residents.

The German National Assembly called on Prussia, as the largest of the German states, to deal with Denmark. Frederick William IV sent his Prussian army forth to settle the matter. Meanwhile, the National Assembly finished the constitution and elected Frederick William IV of Prussia as the new emperor of Germany. Frederick William IV refused, not wishing to be bound to the liberal constitution.

In Prussia, he terminated the Prussian constitutional assembly and instead issued a conservative constitution. He then attempted to have himself elected emperor of Germany on his own terms. Austria blocked him and, since Austria was backed by Russia, it was strong enough to force Frederick William to back down. The liberals had failed, and those wishing for German unification had failed also.

THE ITALIAN STATES

Italians wanted liberal government and the expulsion of Austria from the Piedmont region. In the 1830s, **Joseph Mazzini** organized a secret society called *Young Italy*. In 1847, the hated Austrians took the town of Ferrara in the Papal States, but were forced out. When the Milanese threatened, in January 1848, to quit using goods that contributed to the Austrian financial machine, such as tobacco, Austrian soldiers shot and killed sixty-one Italians. The Austrians laid siege to Milan, but were repulsed by armed citizens. Mazzini, who had been in hiding in South America, returned in June 1848. Most inhabitants of Milan still supported the Austrians, and many potential allies, such as the Kingdom of Naples, abandoned the revolutionary cause. Only Lombardy and the Piedmont provided aid.

Field Marshal Radetzky, who defeated the Italians at Custozza in the end of July, commanded the Austrians. The Italians retreated to Milan and, when the Austrians gave permission to leave for those who wished to do so,

Milan promptly lost half its population and fell on August 7. The Kingdom of Piedmont alone continued to fight, and the rebellion ended at Novarra on March 23, 1849.

On November 15, 1848, the prime minister of the Papal States was assassinated in Rome, and the pope fled to Geata in the south. Mazzini then took charge and improved the plight of the poor. He distributed some of the church's land to the poor, reformed prisons and insane asylums, granted freedom of the press, and provided secular education.

The French invaded on April 20, 1849, and eventually the pope returned. Garibaldi, who had helped to delay the French arrival, escaped to the United States. In the 1850s, he would return to fight for Italian unification. Mazzini fled to England.

Venice continued to fight on, and the Austrians blockaded the city during the winter of 1848–1849. Venice surrendered at the end of August.

The revolution in Italy of 1848 had failed to achieve a united Italy.

THE AFTERMATH OF THE REVOLUTIONS

The Hungarians won more self-determination from the Hapsburgs by 1867. Prussia eliminated feudalism by 1850.

A group of the German liberals who failed in the revolution of 1848 migrated to the United States. There they were called the "Forty-Eighters," and almost 177,000 of them fought for the union against slavery and other issues of interest to their radical mindset. Whereas they failed to unify Germany in 1848, by 1871, Bismarck had succeeded in so doing.

The Italian Risorgimento eventually succeeded in uniting Italy in 1860, with Rome and the Papal States coming into the union in 1870.

CHAPTER 36

THE UNIFICATION OF ITALY AND GERMANY

ITALY

Italy entered the nineteenth century not as one single country, but rather as a collection of small kingdoms that had evolved from the city-states of the Middle Ages. The relations of these kingdoms with each other varied from cooperation to competition, sometimes hostile, sometimes friendly, but always independent of each other.

The **Congress of Vienna**, in 1815, confirmed the disunity of Italy. Lombardy and Venetia were handed over to Austria. One king ruled Sardinia and the Piedmont, another king ruled in Sicily and Naples (formerly the kingdom of the Two Sicilies), and the pope controlled the Papal States in central Italy. Other small kingdoms filled in the rest of northern Italy.

The move towards unification began following the Congress of Vienna. There were three distinctive early movements. The first, led by **Giuseppe Mazzini**, called for the formation of an Italian democratic state, with universal suffrage. A priest, Vincenzo Gioberti, who wanted to form a federation of Italian states with a pope as president, an idea that was too impractical, led the second. The third group wanted to form a united Italy with Sardinia-Piedmont as the central power.

Italy had been touched by the revolutions of 1848, just as most of the rest of Europe had been. In Italy, as elsewhere, the revolutions of 1848 failed. Revolts in support of Mazzini's efforts had occurred in the provinces controlled by Austria. The revolts were crushed by the Austrians and Mazzini's support faded.

Victor Emmanuel of Sardinia had responded to the uprisings in 1848 by granting a liberal constitution. This constitution had the unexpected effect of making Sardinia appealing to the Italian middle class, and so Sardinia became the natural center of unification goals.

Cavour

Count Camillo Benso di Cavour was the leading figure in Sardinian politics from 1850 to 1861. Cavour was the chief minister of Victor Emmanuel. Cavour's original aim was to unite northern and some of central Italy into a Sardinian-dominated state. Cavour worked on strengthening the infrastructure of Sardinia, supporting civil liberties, and opposing the privileged status of the church.

To unify northern Italy, Cavour had to free Lombardy and Venetia from Austria. To this end, he negotiated secretly with Napoleon III of France for military support against Austria. In July 1858, Austria attacked Sardinia and found itself defeated at the hands of the combined forces of Sardinia and France.

Sardinia expected to be able to claim Lombardy and Venetia at last. Instead, Napoleon III suddenly changed his position. He had no stomach for war and, as the pope had declared Sardinia to be an enemy of the church, French Catholics were not happy to be aiding Sardinia. As a result, Sardinia did not obtain the territorial gains it sought. Instead, it received only Lombardy. Deeply angered by this turn of events, Cavour resigned.

In other parts of Italy, particularly in central Italy, nationalists rose in successful revolt and called for a united Italy, demanding that their particular regions be joined to Sardinia. Cavour returned in 1860 to control most of Italy in the name of Sardinia.

Garibaldi

Giuseppe Garibaldi had been active in the fight for Italian unity and in the fight to liberate parts of Italy from foreign control since the 1830s. His followers, guerrilla fighters, were known as the "Red Shirts." In 1860, Garibaldi turned his attention to the Kingdom of the Two Sicilies. Cavour supported Garibaldi, but only in secret. While Garibaldi's goals seemed to match Cavour's, Cavour recognized that Garibaldi's appeal to the common people could make him a most dangerous enemy. Cavour wanted to use Garibaldi to further Sardinia's cause, but at the same time, he wanted to remove Garibaldi as a potential threat.

Garibaldi liberated Sicily and Naples in 1860, claiming them in the name of Victor Emmanuel. Following this victory, he intended to march on to Rome. Cavour blocked Garibaldi, realizing that an attack on Rome, which meant an attack on the pope, would almost certainly mean war with France.

Giuseppe Garibaldi.

A Unified Italy

Cavour organized elections in Sicily and Naples. The people voted as Cavour had expected. They voted to join Sardinia. Garibaldi and Victor Emmanuel met and rode through the streets in triumph. Italy was united, with the exception of the Papal States and Venetia. Venetia was brought into the newly united Italy in 1866. Rome was the only part of Italy not a part of the unified country. As a result of the Franco-Prussian War of 1870–1871, the French lost control of the Papal States, and Italy took Rome. In 1870, Rome became the capital of a united Italy.

In reality, the unified Italy was not the liberal state that so many of Sardinia's supporters had believed it would be. It was a state governed by a monarch and a parliament that allowed limited voting rights for Italian males. There was a gap between the landed upper class and the rest of the population. While Cavour's efforts had made it possible for northern Italy to rapidly industrialize, southern Italy remained a rural, mainly agricultural society.

GERMANY

Prussia and Austria were the two strongest Germanic states. Each wished to dominate a unified Germany, and each feared the results if the other succeeded. In 1848, Frederick William of Prussia almost succeeded in becoming the ruler of a united Germany. He was thwarted at the eleventh hour by Austria, backed by its occasional ally, Russia. In this case, the need to stop the growing power of Prussia drew Austria and Russia into an alliance.

By 1853, the economy had become a factor in German unity. A customs union, the **Zollverein**, had been established in 1834. The Zollverein was intended to increase trade and thereby generate revenue for its membership. The Zollverein, led by Prussia, worked out quite well, and soon every German state, with the exception of Austria, was a member.

The revolts in Italy in 1859 had caused Austria numerous problems, and Prussia had learned important lessons. Prussia was now under the rule of William I. William was well aware of the potential of a war involving Prussia and was greatly concerned that Prussia was not prepared as well as it should be. The energetic and militaristic William I set about military reform. His goal was to restructure the Prussian army and double its size. To do this, William I needed a larger defense budget, which meant higher taxes.

However, William I was not an absolute monarch. He could not simply raise taxes, no matter how just the reason. The Prussian Assembly had been formed in 1848 and had some power. The liberal members of the Assembly wanted to increase their power and to make the Assembly more powerful than the king. The people the members represented were not enthusiastic about increasing the military. They did not want to live in a military state, and there was no obvious, undeniable military threat to Prussia's borders to sway the people to William I's position. The Assembly rejected his proposed military budget in 1862.

Otto von Bismarck

William I reacted decisively. He created a new ministry and appointed **Otto von Bismarck** as its head. Bismarck, an aristocrat, was devoted to Prussia, the King of Prussia, and Prussian supremacy in Germany. His career began in the Prussian Assembly in 1848, where other members considered him to be a conservative. He served as the Prussian ambassador to the German Confederation from 1851 to 1859, working for Prussia and against Austria. He then served as Prussian ambassador to Russia and France, gaining valuable experience in dealing with the other powers in Europe.

In 1862, Bismarck took control. He ignored the Prussian Assembly, which declared it alone had the right to authorize taxes. Bismarck ordered taxes collected even though the Assembly refused to approve the budget. He then set about reorganizing the army according to the wishes of William I.

Otto von Bismarck.

Meanwhile, the people of Prussia continued to elect liberal representatives who were absolutely opposed to Bismarck's policies and methods. Bismarck refused to give in to the lack of popular approval and continued to do his duty as he saw it.

Schleswig-Holstein

In 1864, Bismarck found an opportunity to raise Prussia's standing and possibly convince some of the people that his methods and aims were justified. The Danish king again tried to add Schleswig-Holstein to Denmark. The people of Schleswig-Holstein, a Germanic province and member of the German Confederation that was ruled by the king of Denmark, did not want to be part of a larger Denmark. The people of Schleswig-Holstein were Germans, no matter who their king happened to be. Austria joined Prussia in this nationalistic cause, fighting for the rights of oppressed Germans. Prussia and Austria succeeded in defending Schleswig-Holstein.

Bismarck felt that Prussia was the natural leader of the German states, or, at the very least, of the northern, Protestant German states. Prussia was the largest and strongest of the northern states and was bound to them by culture and religion. Austria, on the other hand, was one of the southern states that were predominately Catholic. Bismarck was determined to end Austria's dominant role in the German Confederation.

The situation was delicate, but Bismarck had laid his plans carefully. First, he neutralized Austria's casual alliance with Russia by supporting Alexander II of Russia, in 1863, when he had put down an uprising among the Poles. If war came between Prussia and Austria, Russia would remain neutral. France was the other major question mark. Bismarck used diplomacy to bring Napoleon III of France to a neutral stance. With Russia and France committed to neutrality, Bismarck had only to be concerned about angering other German states when declaring war on Austria.

Austro-Prussian War

The **Austro-Prussian War** (1866) was a short, contained war. The careful reorganization of the Prussian army paid off, and Prussia defeated Austria at the Battle of Sadowa. The war lasted seven weeks. Bismarck wanted Austria out of German affairs, but Bismarck also did not want to create a permanent enmity between Prussian-led Germany and Austria. The terms of the truce were generous, not punitive, but Austria would no longer interfere in German affairs. The German Confederation, in which Austria had played a leading role, was ended.

North German Confederation

The new North German Confederation was formed from the Protestant German states north of the Main River. Prussia, as the largest state, dominated the group. The Catholic southern German states became independent allies of Prussia. Bismarck constructed the new constitution for the confederation. The constitution gave each state a certain independence and each state continued to have its own government, but the King of Prussia became the central authority governing the confederation as its president. The constitution created an office of chancellor of the confederation. The chancellor would answer only to the president. Bismarck became the chancellor. The chancellor and the president directly controlled the military and the foreign relations of the confederation.

The constitution established a legislature with two houses, each of which could make laws. One house consisted of representatives appointed by the different states; the other consisted of representatives elected by the all-male voting population. This move by Bismarck created a way for the common man to actively participate in the government of the confederation. It gave the people a sense of empowerment they had not previously had while not really giving them any power. Bismarck and his king retained the real power.

Although occupied with the formation of the new government of the confederation, Bismarck did not neglect Prussia. He knew that he had offended many with his rough tactics of ignoring the Assembly. He also knew that everyone loves a winner, and he had come out of the war with Austria feeling that Bismarck had made Austrians winners, too. Bismarck asked the Assembly to approve the taxes he had already collected to fight the war he had already won. The Assembly did so, and the middle-class liberals fell in line.

Still, the dream of German unity was not truly realized. The southern states remained independent allies, not actually part of Bismarck's confederation. Bismarck realized that if he could but find a way to appeal to their nationalistic passions, he could bring about the unity he so devotedly sought. A well-planned war would serve his purposes. France conveniently appeared as the enemy.

Franco-Prussian War

The official reason for the conflict was a potential heir to the Spanish throne. In reality, France was alarmed by the power of the militaristic Prussian-led confederation so near its own border. War broke out in 1870. The southern German states supported the North German Confederation, just as Bismarck had planned. Austria, having been well treated by Bismarck after its own war with Prussia, now repaid its debt by not involving itself in this war. Russia, too, stayed out. On September 1, 1870, the French were defeated at the Battle of Sedan. The blow was too much for the government of Napoleon III, and it fell three days later. The French formed the Third Republic of France and attempted to carry on the war, but abandoned the effort five months later.

Bismarck was not as kind to France as he had been to Austria. He had no need to be. There was great sympathy and loyalty to Austria among the other German states. No such feelings existed among the Germans for France.

The New German Empire

The southern German states now joined with the North German Confederation to form the new German Empire with King William I of Prussia as Emperor William of Germany. The emperor, his chancellor, his army, and his people were united as the power straddling central Europe.

Nationalism

Nationalism was a major force in the 1848 revolutions, and now had resulted in the unification of Italy and Germany. Although the thirteen colonies of Britain had become the "United" States after the revolutionary war, there was still a great deal of disunity in American politics. The northern states, for example, bitterly disagreed with the southern states over slavery. The issue of state's rights as opposed to the power of the central government was still hotly debated. From 1861 to 1865, the Americans fought the Civil War to decide these and other issues. One can view the Civil War as the culmination of the attempt to forge a union that began with the Articles of Confederation.

Emancipation of Slaves

Scholars often debate whether the issue of slavery alone might have provoked a civil war, but almost all scholars believe that slavery was the one issue without which Americans might not have gone to war. During the Civil War, President Abraham Lincoln issued the Emancipation Proclamation of 1863, which applied to areas under rebellion. America become one of many nations to free its slaves in the wake of the French Revolution 100 years earlier and the cry for "liberty, equality, and fraternity." Britain abolished slavery throughout its empire by 1833; France abolished slavery in its colonies in 1848, Russia in 1860, and Portugal in 1869. Brazil became the last state in the Americas to abolish slavery in 1888. Although Britain abolished slavery by 1833, when it moved into Africa, British practices there led to renewed use of slavery. Britain abolished slavery in the parts of Nigeria it still controlled in 1900.

Saudi Arabia was the last nation to abolish slavery in 1962. Slavery continues to be an issue in parts of the world in the twentieth and twenty-first centuries. For example, there are reports of slavery today among the peoples of Africa. In various parts of the world, the plight of women also continues to be a problem that nearly resembles slavery. Thai women taken to Japan for use in the sex industry, for example, are often treated in ways resembling slavery.

CHAPTER 37

ROMANTICISM

In addition to nationalism, liberalism, communism, and socialism, **romanticism** was another force that dominated European culture in the late nineteenth century.

The reactionary forces that led to the revolutions of 1848 were paralleled by tidal waves in the arts. Musicians reacted to the formalized music of the eighteenth century. According to the canons of classicism, phrases were uniform in length, rhythm was also in tight, tidy little balanced units, and the form of the entire composition was also balanced and codified. Romanticists broke those boundaries, creating phrases of vast, sweeping length that often covered a tremendous range from low to high notes; rhythm was more syncopated, and romantic composers preferred the minor mode, for its pathos, to the major mode. **Beethoven** was one of the first composers to break the classical mold, when he exploded sonata-allegro form by lengthening it and creating long codas. Beethoven's late piano sonatas, such as the *Opus 111*, also broke tonal boundaries to the point where contemporary audiences attributed the dissonance they heard to the composer's tragic deafness.

Composers, such as Franz Liszt, dazzled the world with sheer virtuosity and pyrotechnic etudes, such as the *Transcendental Etudes*; the Polish composer Chopin wrote melodious nocturnes that made use of rubato, a technique for bending the rhythm in the melodic line over a stable base to create a more emotional affect; and Franz Schubert wrote melodious and beautiful pieces that often threatened to flow on without end.

Music also took on a nationalistic tone, as seen in Tchaikovsky's *1812 Overture*—a tribute to the Russian victory over Napoleon, in 1812—which contained Russian melodies. Smetana wrote *Má vlast* about his native Czechoslovakia; Dvorak wrote *The New World Symphony*—a tribute to his newfound home in America—which combined the musical styles and influences of African-American spirituals and other American and even European influences; Chopin wrote many polonaises for piano, a form used in his native Poland; Liszt wrote a number of Hungarian rhapsodies; and Bartok, in the twentieth century, continued to explore Hungarian music in his Hungarian dances.

Visual artists developed a love for the exotic, non-European, and mythological subjects. Delacroix, for example, painted *The Death of Sardanapalus* and *Arabs Skirmishing in the Mountains*. The English **J.M.W. Turner**'s swirling, misty paintings created amorphous, mysterious impressions of his subjects that defied the classical belief in the ordered universe.

Poets also broke form. **Samuel Taylor Coleridge**'s *Kublai Khan* captured the exotic world of the East; he claimed the poem came to him in a dream while he was intoxicated with opium. Many romanticists tried to portray the supernatural as real. The American poet Walt Whitman, on the other hand, tried to portray reality itself as remarkable and out of the ordinary. His *Song of Myself* made use of long, unbroken lines that poured forth inner emotion and rejected formalized use of stanzas, lines, meters, and other poetic techniques. Whitman's boundless lines paralleled the American belief in its Manifest Destiny, by which it was sweeping across the continent to occupy both east and west. Just as America itself was breaking out of its geographical boundaries, so, too, Whitman broke the boundaries of formal poetry.

The Battle of Trafalgar, *J.M.W. Turner*, 1806.

CHAPTER 38

AMERICA IN THE NINETEENTH CENTURY

The United States expanded rapidly in the years following its Revolutionary War. Britain ceded to the United States the area west of the Appalachian Mountains to the Mississippi River, almost doubling the size of the territory occupied by the thirteen original colonies. In 1803, Napoleon knew he could not defend French territories from the Mississippi to the Rocky Mountains, and so chose instead to gain the revenue from their sale. The Louisiana Purchase again doubled the size of the U.S. Meriwether Lewis and William Clark then mapped the new territory from 1804 to 1806. In 1845, Texas entered the union, forcing a war between Mexico and America from 1845 to 1848. The U.S. paid Mexico fifteen million dollars for Texas, California, and New Mexico, according to the Treaty of Hidalgo.

As America expanded west, it encountered many native peoples. In 1830, the Indian Removal Act forced Native Americans east of the Mississippi onto reservations in what would later become Oklahoma. Among those who suffered the most were the Seminoles in Florida and the Cherokee, whose Trail of Tears (1838–1839) serves as a symbol of the suffering of Native Americans throughout this period. Conflict between the American settlers and natives culminated in the Battle of Little Big Horn, in 1876, where thousands of Lakota Sioux wiped out an army under George Armstrong Custer. In 1890, American soldiers slaughtered more than 200 Sioux at Wounded Knee, where Sioux were engaged in the Ghost Dance. As the Ghost Dance involved beliefs in a world free of whites, the government felt threatened by it.

Native Americans were not the only population to suffer as the United States expanded. Slavery continued to grow in the southern states, where the plantation economies were in stark contrast to the industrialization of the north. During the American Civil War from 1861 to 1865, the north and south fought one another over many issues, some economic and some political.

President Abraham Lincoln had issued the Emancipation Proclamation in 1863, in which he freed slaves in areas of rebellion. Leaders of the reconstructed union would have to decide upon civil rights for the freed slaves of the south. Although former slaves became citizens and earned the right to vote during reconstruction, discrimination continued in the form of the Jim Crow laws, and finally erupted in the civil rights movements of the 1960s.

The nineteenth century became the era of Manifest Destiny for Americans. Landscape paintings reflected endless boundaries and no visible horizons. Americans believed it was their Manifest Destiny to control all of North America from sea to shining sea, and some even talked of an American presence in Canada, Cuba, Latin America, and South America.

In the late nineteenth century, the United States would expand on the notion of Manifest Destiny as it emulated many European powers in a wave of imperialist expansion.

CHAPTER 39

EUROPEAN AND U.S. IMPERIALISM IN THE NINETEENTH CENTURY

Europeans had established colonies in other parts of the world since the Age of Exploration. In the late nineteenth century there was really nothing new about Europe extending its control and power over other parts of the earth. Europeans first used the word "imperialism," however, in the mid-nineteenth century to describe the web of colonial empires built between 1870 and 1914. The word refers to the European domination of other nations and cultures, such as those in Africa and eastern Asia, the only parts of the world not already dominated by Europeans.

In this era the word "**colonization**" took on a new meaning, and referred to the political, economic, and social structures created by Europeans in foreign lands that supported their efforts to dominate native cultures. Many political leaders viewed imperialism as the only way to preserve national security, and also saw new colonies as a possible outlet for the population explosion.

J. A. HOBSON

The British economist, J. A. Hobson, however, attributed the wave of European imperialist expansion in the late nineteenth century to special new economic forces arising out of the industrialized nations of western and central Europe. Although the British author Rudyard Kipling wrote about the "**white man's burden**," the duty of the Europeans to civilize the barbarous native peoples of other lands, and the French spoke about the *mission civilisatrice*, or civilizing mission, of the Europeans, Hobson argued that their true motives were based on capitalistic greed for cheap raw materials, advantageous markets, good investments, and fresh fields of exploitation. Cecil Rhodes is one of the best examples of Hobson's point of view, as he had made a fortune in the Kimberly diamond fields of South Africa. Ninety percent of the world's diamonds came from these fields, and Rhodes vigorously supported British imperialism in order to preserve his business enterprises. In 1889, Rhodes founded the South Africa Chartered Company to develop the Zambezi valley.

Hobson argued that the "economic taproot of imperialism" was "excessive capital in search of investment," and that this excessive capital was, in essence, the result of unequal distribution of wealth.

Lenin on Imperialism

In his 1916 pamphlet, *Imperialism the Highest Stage of Capitalism,* V. I. Lenin also suggested that capitalism gave rise to imperialism, and that World War I was the ultimate result of European attempts to dominate world markets. Lenin argued that while the standard of living increased for workers in imperialist countries, Europeans were now exploiting a new kind of proletariat in the colonies.

Interpretive Problems

The main problems with the theses of both Hobson and Lenin were that France led the way in the race towards an empire, doubling her colonial holdings between 1815 and 1870 and establishing outposts in Senegal, Indochina, and Algeria. France was, in fact, the least industrialized of all western nations. Lenin's argument, too, about the quality of life in imperialist countries could not be easily demonstrated, as the standard of living in France, for example, was relatively low for workers as compared to Denmark or Sweden, who had no colonies in the late nineteenth century.

Negative Perception of Imperialism

Nevertheless, the presumption that economic motives and capitalistic greed motivated imperialism has left a bad taste, and with good reason. Attitudes, such as those of Kipling and the French, contributed to the disrespect and neglect of native cultures, and ultimately, in various parts of the world, even to their demise. While building railroads across India, for example, workers discovered bricks with script and eventually were led to the city of Harappa. The British plundered the bricks of this once-mighty place, thinking it unimportant and not even wondering about the possible contributions of the magnificent ruins. In Africa, Europeans assumed that Africans could not have built the Great Zimbabwe, as natives surely had not the gifts or techniques to do so!

JOSEPH ARTHUR DE GOBINEAU AND HERBERT SPENCER

Europeans also justified their behavior and attitudes through new, allegedly "scientific" views, such as those developed by **Count Joseph Arthur de Gobineau**, a French noble who divided humanity into four basic races. Each race had unique characteristics. In his four-volume *Essay on the Inequality of the Human Races*, Gobineau argued that Europeans were superior to the other races. Modern sociologists argue that race is a social construct, and biologists, that there is no such thing as a "pure" race. Gobineau's views, however, combined with Charles Darwin's thesis concerning the survival of the fittest, became "social Darwinism." **Herbert Spencer** argued that stronger and more able individuals competed better and so became more successful. Therefore, European domination of less well-developed cultures was a natural and just situation.

While many scholars now reject these viewpoints and are making an effort to recover the indigenous history and cultural contributions of those areas of the world colonized by European and U.S. powers, the Age of Imperialism created much tension in the world. European attitudes of supremacy created a legacy of ill-will and a negative appraisal of European motivations, especially in those areas whose cultures were so denigrated.

NEW DEVELOPMENTS IN TECHNOLOGY

The European powers were aided in their efforts to create new empires by the development of military vessels powered by the steam engine. The Opium War was brought to a conclusion in part by an expedition up the Yangtze, in 1842, by the British gunboat *Nemesis*. Steam-powered military boats made the most inaccessible regions more accessible.

New canals enabled these new ships to travel to remote parts of the world more quickly. The **Suez Canal** (1859–1869) and the **Panama Canal** (1904–1914) linked oceans and seas and made trade between the imperialist powers and their colonies more profitable. Steamships could now travel between Britain and India via the Suez Canal in less than two weeks. Steam power also made it easier to import goods into Britain from her colonies. Communication was also revolutionized by the development of undersea telegraph cables, which were capable of transmitting messages from Britain to India in about five hours.

Railroads also contributed to the ease of travel and trade, and to the demise of native cultures.

Perhaps the most frightening tools of the imperialist age were the more accurate rifles and machine guns. The power of these weapons is illustrated by events in 1898 near **Khartoum**, when a British force with only twenty machine guns killed a force of 11,000 Sudanese at Omdurman. The British were fighting for their lives against the Mahdi, or "divinely guided one," who led a massive insurrection against Turkish rule in Egypt, but the Sudanese were no match for the machine gun. The British were one of many European powers involved in a mad "scramble for Africa." They eventually established a regime in the Sudan, but not before the Mahdi defeated the British Gordon Pasha in a shocking victory at Khartoum in January 1885. The Mahdi died shortly thereafter, with shock waves still emanating through the British Empire. Four years later, the British Kitchner led a combined force of British and Egyptians to Khartoum and recaptured it. In 1889, they did eventually succeed in controlling the Sudan. The British remained there until the Sudanese won their independence in 1956.

EUROPEAN EXPLORATIONS OF AFRICA

European explorers helped to chart remote places of Africa. **David Livingstone**, a Scottish minister, explored central and southern Africa in search of suitable locations for missions. The American journalist Henry Morton Stanley traveled throughout Africa in search of Livingstone to report on his activities. Richard Burton and John Speke, both English, explored east Africa in search of the origin of the Nile River. Serpa Pinto explored the headwaters of the Cuanza River in Angola and followed the course of the Zambezi River to Victoria Falls in present-day Zimbabwe. Similar events would be recorded in India and other places where the British ruled.

The Scramble for Africa

The "scramble for Africa" officially began when Henry Stanley claimed the Congo River Valley for Belgium. **King Leopold II** of Belgium, in essence, created a personal colony there, using forced labor on rubber plantations. He essentially thrust out the Portuguese, who had established a colony in the Congo in the fifteenth century. He declared the Congo a free trade area, but his legacy of repressive rule there eventually forced the government of Belgium to take control of the colony in 1908. It then became the Belgian Congo.

The British in Egypt

In 1882, the British occupied Egypt to ensure their access to the Suez Canal, which they virtually stole from the French by becoming the major stockholders.

The French in West Africa

As early as 1659, the French established a trade port on the West African coast at St. Louis in present-day Senegal. Unlike other European powers following the Age of Discovery, France never played a major role in the slave trade and was primarily interested in Africa for trade. During the wave of imperialist expansion in the nineteenth century, the French, at first, began to move eastward into the savanna regions. Military men, such as General Louis Faidherbe, primarily led their expansion. By the twentieth century, France controlled much of present-day Senegal, Mali, Burkina Faso, Benin, Guinea, Ivory Coast, and Niger. France also controlled Algeria and Morocco in Africa and Dahomey. Out of various territories in West Africa, the French created French West Africa. Their base remained St. Louis in Senegal, and only there did they allow the native populations any voice in the government created. The French attempted to rule nine million West Africans with a force of only 3,600 men.

France also conquered the region on the north bank of the Congo and created French Equatorial Africa. On the east coast, France claimed part of Somaliland. By 1896, France had also conquered the island of Madagascar.

THE BERLIN WEST AFRICA CONFERENCE 1884–1885

Fourteen European nations and the United States determined that any European nation could found a colony in unclaimed territory if it notified the other nations of its intentions. Effective occupation of an area was to take the place of history, and Portugal was officially thrust out of the Congo. The conference awarded Mozambique, Angola, and Guinea to Portugal. Not one African attended the conference.

South Africa

The British also established a presence in South Africa well before their occupation of Egypt in 1882. In 1652, the Dutch East India Company had founded Cape Town as a supply station on the route to Asia. Company employees settled there, as well as other Europeans, and were known as **Boers**. Later, they were called Afrikaners, from the Dutch word for "African."

In 1806, the British took over the Cape of Good Hope and drove the Afrikaners further inland. The British abolished one of the key features of Afrikaner life, slavery, prompting the Great Trek, or movement eastward, of Afrikaners. This eastward movement led to conflict between the Afrikaners and the native populations. The *voortrekkers,* the Afrikaans word for "pioneers," eventually defeated the **Zulu** and other groups and created the Republic of Natal, the Orange Free State, and the South African Republic.

The Boer War (1899–2002)

The discovery of diamonds and gold, in 1866 and 1867, in Afrikaner territory and subsequent competition for resources eventually led to the South African or **Boer War** between the British and Afrikaners. The British defeated the Afrikaners in the war, and, by 1920, had carved up Afrikaner territory and created the Union of South Africa. As the British sought to reconcile Afrikaner interests with British interests, they often discriminated against black Africans. In fact, black Africans fought on both sides of the Boer War, but the British treatment of them was foreshadowed by their imprisonment of over 100,000 black Africans.

The British method of colonization involved what Frederick Lugard, the British colonial administrator, called indirect rule, or relying on indigenous, tribal authorities and local populations to manage the colonies.

Other British Colonies in Africa

By the end of the nineteenth century, the British also took Bechuanaland (1885), Rhodesia (1889), and Nyasaland (1893).

Other Powers in Africa

Germany established German Southwest Africa and German East Africa. The German East Africa Company developed this region. By 1914, Germany had acquired new territories of one million square miles and as many as thirteen million people.

Italy formed the Italian East African Empire in Eritrea by 1885, and appropriated Asmara and the southern coastal strip of Somaliland in 1889. The Italian Benadir Company developed the Somaliland. Italy attempted to form a protectorate in the African kingdom of Abyssinia, but the Abyssinians defeated them at Adowa in 1896.

Governments granted monopoly rights to the various companies formed to develop the regions. The Royal Niger Company, for example, colonized Nigeria.

Impact of European Colonization on Africa

In 1875, Europe had colonized less than one-tenth of Africa. By 1895, Europe failed to dominate only one-tenth of the world's second largest continent. Between 1870 and 1900, Britain added 4.25 million square miles and 66 million people to her empire; France added 3.5 million square miles and 26 million people. At the turn of the century, the only independent states south of the Sahara were Liberia and Abyssinia.

Belgium added new territory to its empire of 900,000 square miles and 8.5 million inhabitants. The colonial empires of Portugal and the Netherlands, established during the Age of Discovery, became increasingly powerful in this era. Portugal, for example, controlled much of the western coast of Africa and Mozambique.

The languages of modern Africa reflect the colonial period. Portuguese is still the language of trade in Mozambique and areas along the west coast. French and English, for example, continue to be spoken in areas colonized by the Europeans during the nineteenth century.

The British in Asia

In the 1850s, the British established rule in India. For review of these events, consult Chapter 30, "The Islamic World from the Ottomans through the Early Twentieth Century." The British also expanded economic interests in China and won a victory over the Ching in the Opium Wars. For review of these events, consult Chapter 29, "China from the Ming to the Ching Dynasty."

British imperial rule in India and other parts of Asia transformed the economic production of those areas. The American Civil War prompted the British to search for a new source of cotton in India, and Indian cotton began to be produced for export rather than internal use. Export of cotton increased from 10 million rupees in 1849 to 410 million rupees in 1913. Simultaneously, the British imported textiles, and these imports undermined the native Indian market for finished cloth. India was once the principal producer of cotton cloth, but was now transformed into a consumer of British imports and their chief supplier of raw cotton.

In Malaysia and Sumatra, the British planted rubber trees in the 1870s and began to export these commodities to the rest of the world.

From China, the British brought tea to Ceylon and India, where they cleared forests to plant tea plantations. Native women were used in the labor force, and tea was then exported to Europe. The approximate monetary value of tea exported from south Asia rose from 309,000 pounds sterling in 1866 to 6.1 million pounds sterling in 1900.

EUROPEAN IMPERIALISM IN THE PACIFIC

The Aboriginals of Australia

In 1770, Captain **James Cook** landed in Botany Bay, Australia. The voyages of Captain Cook opened up Australia to European colonization. In 1788, a group of migrants, who were mostly convicted criminals, founded the colony of New South Wales. The British argued that Australia was *terra* *nullius*, or land belonging to no one, that could be seized and used at will. By 1900, they had pushed the aboriginal population into reservations in regions that were largely desert.

The Maori of New Zealand

As in the New World during the Age of Discovery, the Europeans brought smallpox and other diseases that devastated the native populations. This was also true in New Zealand, where the native **Maori** population dropped from 200,000 to 45,000 within a century. The British also forced the Maori to reservations after a series of wars from 1860 to 1864.

Other Islands

The European powers that colonized Africa wasted no time in competing for the Pacific Islands. France had created colonial governments, by 1880, in Tahiti and New Caledonia, Britain took Fiji, and Germany took most of the Marshall Islands. The Berlin Conference of 1884–1885 also divided up the Pacific Islands, with the United States and Germany dividing Samoa.

THE UNITED STATES EMERGES AS AN IMPERIAL POWER

Although the United States historically had pursued a policy of isolationism going back to its founding fathers, in the nineteenth century it became a world power that intruded often into international affairs. The Monroe Doctrine, in 1823, effectively put the Western Hemisphere under U.S. domination, as Monroe warned European nations against imperialist activity in the Western Hemisphere.

In 1867, the purchase of Alaska increased U.S. territory in North America, while in 1875, Hawaii became a U.S. protectorate. In 1893, a group of white planters overthrew the last queen, **Lili'uokalani**, with the help of John Stevens, the U.S. Minister to Hawaii, and a contingent of marines from the warship *U.S.S. Boston*. Acting without the permission of the U.S. State Department, Stevens declared that Hawaii was now a U.S. protectorate. Most native Hawaiians opposed this action. Although the next President, Grover Cleveland, strongly criticized Stevens and the overthrow of Queen Lili'uokalani, Hawaii became a republic in 1894. When rebellion erupted, many natives were arrested along with Queen Lili'uokalani. The U.S. eventually annexed the islands in 1898.

Those who subscribed to the U.S. doctrine of Manifest Destiny had always hinted at the desire to annex Cuba, one of the last remaining bastions of Spanish power. When the U.S. battleship *Maine* exploded in Havana harbor in 1898, the U.S. accused Spain of treachery and the Spanish-American War began. In 1899, the United States defeated Spain, taking Cuba and Puerto Rico; soon thereafter, the U.S. took the Philippines and Guam from Spain. President William McKinley paid Spain twenty million dollars for the Philippines, but soon became involved in a bloody revolt led by Emilio Aguinaldo. The main thrust of the revolt ended in 1902, but it took a massive toll on human life, and insurrections continued until 1906.

The new empire of the United States required the construction of the Panama Canal. President Theodore Roosevelt incited rebellion in Colombia to accomplish his goal, and helped the rebels establish a new state, Panama. Roosevelt's policy of the Big Stick also contributed to the further development of imperialistic aspirations and behavior.

THE RISE OF JAPAN AS AN IMPERIAL POWER

Japan began to expand in the Pacific in the 1870s, when it encouraged Japanese settlers to live on Hokkaido and the Kurile Islands in an effort to block Russian expansion. By 1879, they had hegemony over Okinawa and the Ryukyu Islands, and now controlled the islands to the south and north of the four islands of Japan.

In 1876, they expanded control over Korean trade through an unequal treaty such as that imposed on Asia by the western powers after the Opium Wars. In 1894, the Koreans began a series of protests over foreign intrusion, leading the Chinese to send a force to restore order there and to reassert their authority. In August 1894, the Meiji government in Japan declared war on China. In a five-hour battle, the Japanese defeated the Ching navy on the Yellow Sea and within only a few months took control of Korea. China recognized it as independent, and ceded Taiwan, the Pescadores Islands, and the Laiodong peninsula to Japan. Japan also gained unequal rights in China that paralleled those of the United States and Europe.

These gains created tension with Russia, who had desires for much of the territory controlled by Japan, in particular Korea and the Liaodong peninsula. Manchuria was also a common interest. The Japanese escalated their military buildup, and, in 1904, the **Russo-Japanese War** broke out. The Russian Baltic fleet sailed halfway around the world to meet the Japanese, but the Japanese quickly routed them and won control of Sakhalin Island and a railroad in Manchuria. The Russo-Japanese War firmly established acceptance of Korea as a colonial territory of Japan.

Like the Europeans, the Japanese often justified their brutal imperialist regimes on the basis of their alleged racial superiority. Just as European imperialism has been condemned on this basis, so, too, many scholars condemned the Japanese racist views that emerged as they became one of the major world imperial powers. The long-term effects of their quick rise to prominence culminated in World War II.

IMPERIALISM AND THE LABOR FORCE

In the nineteenth century, approximately fifty million Europeans left Europe and migrated to other areas in search of work. The poor of central and eastern Europe migrated to the United States in the late nineteenth century, whereas earlier in the century, many from Britain, Ireland, Germany, and Scandinavia had gone to the United States. Their labor helped to support the U.S. move toward industrialization in the late nineteenth century, such as in the steel and railroad industries.

Other migrants went to newly formed parts of the British Empire, such as Australia and New Zealand, where they often became herders or cultivators.

There was also a mass migration of Asians, Africans, and Pacific Islanders in the nineteenth century. Most of these migrants sold their services as indentured laborers. Many European powers had abolished slavery in the nineteenth century, and plantation owners needed another labor force. Workers got free passage and food and shelter in exchange for their services. They pledged to work from five to seven years in most cases. Most indentured labor originated in India, but there were also laborers who came from China, Japan, Africa, the Pacific Islands, and Java. While the European migrants went to temperate climates, the indentured laborers went to tropical and subtropical areas in the Americas, Africa, the Caribbean, and Oceania. After the Opium Wars, Chinese migrants went to sugar plantations in Cuba and Hawaii, mines in various parts of the world, and railroad construction sites in the United States and other parts of the Americas.

The new migrations changed the makeup of the population in many parts of the world. As the ethnic makeup of various areas became more diverse and complex, tension often erupted. In the United States, for example, an effort was made to stop the flow of foreign migrations from certain areas, especially those from central and eastern Europe and Asia. The Johnson-Reed Act of 1924 (the Permanent National Origins Quota Act), for example, implemented a quota system according to which countries could send legal immigrants to the United States in proportion to the percentage of the population (in 1924) who were of that particular nationality.

CHAPTER 40

RUSSIA IN THE EARLY TWENTIETH CENTURY

THE REVOLUTION OF 1905

The **Crimean War** served as a motivating force for change in Russia and forced its leaders to realize that Russia was a barely industrialized, agricultural backwater compared to the rest of Europe. If Russia was to keep up with the world, great changes would have to be undertaken. So, in the latter half of the nineteenth century, Tsar Alexander II's government embarked on a program of social reforms and modernization schemes.

In 1861, Alexander II freed the serfs. No longer tied to the land, they were now allowed to own it but with certain caveats. This was a major step forward for Russia, but it was not as revolutionary as it might have been. While the serfs were now free to own the land, they could not own it outright as individuals. They had to own it as part of their local community or village. The serfs were free, but yet still bound.

Alexander's government implemented other reforms, changed the legal system, altered the local government, and reformed industry, but political life in Russia remained largely unchanged. Alexander II had seen the need for reform, but the measures his government put forth did not go far enough to suit everyone. In 1881, an assassin tossed a bomb into his carriage and ended his attempts at reform.

Tsar Alexander III was naturally affected by his father's violent death and remained steadfastly opposed to political reforms. He was not blind to economic realities, however, and so it was in his reign, in the 1890s, that Russia truly joined in the industrial revolution.

Sergei Witte was the driving force behind the economic reforms. Witte's accomplishments include constructing the trans-Siberian railroad and modernizing the Russian railway system, employing tariffs to protect the fledgling industries of Russia, and placing Russia on the gold standard, the same standard used by most of the world. Witte encouraged western investment in Russian industry with amazing results. In just forty years, Russia went from a static, agricultural nation to a world leader in the production of steel and oil.

The surging Russian economy spurred an interest in imperialistic expansion, with the Far East as the target. Japan, however, thwarted Russia's desires. In August 1905, the well-oiled military machine of imperial Japan defeated Russia.

This defeat brought forth a backlash from the public. In January 1905, a peaceful protest occurred in St. Petersburg. A priest led the protestors as they sang songs and approached the Winter Palace, home of **Tsar Nicholas II**. The tsar, however, had already left St. Petersburg. Troops opened fire on the protestors. The resulting massacre turned the people against the tsar. Revolutionary political groups became openly active as the summer of 1905 dragged on, and they organized revolts.

By October 1905, opposition to the government had grown so great that a general strike was carried out, effectively shutting down the country. Tsar Nicholas responded with the October Manifesto that promised civil rights for the people, free elections for the **duma**, and more power to that body as well. It appeared that the revolutionaries had won. In reality, the elections for the duma did not constitute direct representative government. The tsar still chose and controlled his ministers and the ministers ran the government, not the duma. The duma did have the power to make laws, but the tsar had the power to veto any legislation the duma passed. The tsar also held ultimate control over the duma, being able to dismiss it as he pleased.

With the duma failing to toe the line, the tsar dismissed it in 1906. New elections, in 1907, brought in even more members opposed to the tsar's government. Again, the tsar dissolved the duma. The tsar's ministers then took steps to see to it that the tsar's supporters would gain the majority in the duma by altering the election laws. They were successful, and the next election, also held in 1907, yielded the results the tsar had sought.

All was not lost for the revolutionaries. The new leader of the duma, Peter Stolypin, a supporter of the tsar, recognized the need for real reform. He took on the agricultural policies and rewrote them to make it easier for the peasants to truly own the land they farmed. Although these and other reforms did much to modernize Russia, they failed to end the hardships that sparked revolution. Within a decade, Russia would be in flames.

THE REVOLUTIONS OF 1917

Long-standing social unrest in Russia was brought to a boil by World War I. In 1914 Russia entered the war with Germany with the same patriotic fervor that swept the rest of Europe. War seemed to be an opportunity for the various factions of Russian politics to make gains and so it had widespread support. But unlike Germany, Russia was ill-prepared for an all-out extended military campaign. Its army was ill-equipped and soon ran short of weapons and munitions. The Russian army suffered two million casualties in 1915 alone.

Tsar Nicholas II failed to provide effective leadership and failed to work with the duma, the legislative body of Russian government. By 1915, factions in the duma were openly critical of the tsar and each other. The tsar, distrusting the duma and dissatisfied with the progress of the war, dismissed the duma and headed to the front, leaving his wife, Tsarina Alexandra, in charge in his absence.

The situation in Russia rapidly deteriorated and social unrest exploded into open revolt. Continued bad news from the front and shortages of food in the cities created an ugly mood among the people. Bread riots broke out in Petrograd (St. Petersburg) in March 1917. The tsar ordered his troops to restore order but they joined the revolt instead. The duma declared a provisional government and the tsar abdicated, ending centuries of Romanov rule. Alexander Kerensky, a hero in the duma, became the new leader of the Provisional Government. In 1918, the new government executed Tsar Nicolas II, his wife Tsarina Alexandra, their children, and their servants.

The Russian Revolution was a revolt against the Russian monarchy and the Russian government as it then existed. The revolutionaries were diverse groups with differing goals, values, and ideals. Once their common goal of removing the tsar was achieved, they then turned against each other, each determined to see their vision for a new Russia realized.

The government formed after the abdication of the tsar was still pro-war, including Kerensky. They granted freedoms to the people, but did not engage in the social reforms the more radical revolutionary groups sought. Petrograd itself was in the control of the Petrograd Soviet, a collective of workers and soldiers that was determined to give power to the people. By the summer of 1917, Russia was in turmoil and the government faced a total breakdown.

Vladimir Ilyich Lenin (1870–1924) rose to prominence in the chaos of revolutionary Russia. Lenin had always been a revolutionary, but it was not until he became a law student that he found his revolutionary philosophy. In the works of Marx, Lenin found the theories that spoke to him. From Marx's *Communist Manifesto,* Lenin drew his first principle of revolution: that violent revolution was necessary to destroy capitalism. Lenin believed that revolution was necessary and possible even when a society did not have fully developed capitalism.

Lenin also believed that only dedicated revolutionaries, with the intellect to fully understand the importance of revolution, could successfully lead a revolution. These revolutionary leaders would need an organized army of workers, but it would be up to the leaders to keep the revolution on course to take control of a nation.

Lenin had been living and plotting revolution in exile, but in 1917, Germany helped transport him back to Russia and even gave him financial aid, hoping that Lenin would destabilize the fragile provisional government. Lenin immediately took the lead of the **Bolsheviks** and refused to cooperate with other groups. He demanded an end to the war, land reforms, and power to the soviets. In July 1917, Kerensky ordered the arrest of the Bolsheviks, but he was unsuccessful in stopping their rise to power. When Kerensky's general, Kornilov, revolted and marched on Petrograd, Kerensky turned to the Bolsheviks for help, as they controlled the Red Guards and the Soviets. Lenin agreed to help defend Petrograd, but at the same time made a clear statement that he was not fighting for Kerensky. General Kornilov ultimately committed suicide, but now Kerensky was in deep trouble, as the Bolsheviks could clearly muster significant military forces against him. In October, he ordered the arrest of the Military Revolutionary Committee and shut down the Bolshevik papers.

Leon Trotsky supported Lenin and urged him to overthrow the provisional government. He helped the Bolsheviks gain control of the Petrograd soviet and from there, control of Russia. On October 24, 1917, Lenin gave the order to take the railroad stations, and then for the Red Guards to march on the Winter Palace, the center of the provisional government. By October 26, 1917, Lenin's Bolsheviks had succeeded in their attempt to topple the government. The all-Russian Congress of Soviets officially handed over power to the Soviet Council of People's Commissars. They elected Lenin chairman and put Trotsky in charge of foreign affairs.

The Bolsheviks succeeded because, by late 1917, the democratic dream of the provisional government was dead. Lenin and Trotsky were strong, charismatic leaders, and the Bolsheviks tried to appeal to the common people.

Lenin moved quickly to solidify his position. He declared the peasants' right to seize land. He signed a treaty with Germany ending World War I for Russia. The terms were harsh: Russia gave up its western territories, areas that would eventually become Poland, Finland, Lithuania, and more, with a loss of one-third of its population. Not everyone supported Lenin's surrender to Germany; even members of the Bolsheviks balked at the terms. But when the threat of invasion by Germany returned in 1918, the Treaty of Brest-Litovsk was approved.

Elections were held for the Constituent Assembly that was to be the new Russian government. The Bolsheviks, however, did not manage to take a controlling majority in the elections, so Lenin used his Bolshevik troops to dismiss the assembly and take control. The Bolsheviks who became the Communists were referred to as the "Reds." The "Whites" represented the other revolutionary groups, groups that wanted a more democratic government for Russia. Once it became clear that Lenin intended to increase the power of the state and to control Russia as a dictator, the Whites revolted. The Whites were primarily conservative members of the Russian military. From 1918 to 1920 the armies of the Reds and Whites fought for control, and eventually the Reds defeated the Whites. Trotsky had managed to mold a formidable army for the Reds, while the Whites were never able to truly unite. Soviet Russia was born.

THE SOVIET UNION FROM 1920 TO 1927

By the 1920s, the Bolshevik revolution in Russia was complete and Lenin could now devote his attention to controlling what remained of the country. Russia lay in ruins. Over half the people were starving due to famine brought on by drought combined with the devastation of war. The economy had been destroyed. The population, stretched to its limits, rioted once more.

Lenin reacted quickly. In 1921, he issued the **New Economic Policy**, or NEP, which allowed for some economic freedom by encouraging cottage industries and small farms to produce and trade. Major industries remained in the hands of the government. By 1926, the economy had rebounded to its pre-1913 levels.

Lenin died in 1924, leaving the government scrambling to determine his successor. Trotsky was an obvious choice, having been so instrumental in the success of the revolution, but he was not alone. **Joseph Stalin**'s star was rising as well. Stalin, born Joseph Dzhugashvili, was talented, daring, and determined, but lacked the style of Trotsky. Still, Stalin was able to garner the support needed to become general secretary of the Central Committee, the most important committee in the government, and he used that position to gain even more power, influence, and supporters.

Trotsky believed that in order for the revolution in the Soviet Union to last, the revolution had to be taken to the rest of Europe. This position did not sit well with a nation of war-weary people just beginning to dig out of an economic grave. Stalin held the opposite position, believing that the Soviet Union could stand on its own as a socialist nation, a position far more appealing to party members than Trotsky's. Stalin achieved total power by 1927 and would lead Russia through World War II. He succeeded in having Trotsky exiled in 1929, and on August 20, 1940, had Trotsky murdered. Stalin would ultimately be known as the grave-digger of the October Revolution, and his reign of terror in Russia would result in the death of millions of Russians.

CHAPTER 41

WORLD WAR I (1914–1918) AND ITS AFTERMATH

World War I was the first war to encompass more than half the globe. It was also known as *The Great War*, or "the war to end all wars," at least before World War II usurped that distinction. The term "world war" was first coined in the 1920s by Lieutenant Colonel à Court Repington in *The First World War 1914-18*. Some scholars have suggested that the First World War is more properly thought of as the first phase of a thirty-year-long war that began with World War I and ended with the termination of hostilities in World War II in 1945.

In World War I, twenty-eight nations, the **Allies** and Associated Powers, fought four others nations or empires known as the **Central Powers**: Germany, Austria-Hungary, Bulgaria, and the Ottoman Empire. World War I was the first "total war" in history, as those involved used every resource available for the war effort. For the first time, people referred to the "home front," which referred to the mobilization at home of resources for the military front. Mobilization at home drained countries of their males who were old enough to fight, creating a vacuum in the workforce. Many women, particularly in Britain and the United States, went to work in factories making war products. The work was often very dangerous and women demanded more equal wages. In the wake of the war, women earned the right to vote in America, Great Britain, Germany, and Austria.

The Great War brought about the end of the German, Ottoman, Russian, and Austro-Hungarian empires. It created nine new nations. The First World War also brought about the end of the global supremacy Europe had enjoyed beginning in the Age of Discovery and reaching a high point during its imperialist phase in the nineteenth century.

NATIONALISM

The rise of nationalist movements in the nineteenth century culminated in World War I. Although Germany and Italy were unified, many other movements had never achieved their goals. This was particularly true of various areas within the Austro-Hungarian Empire, where the Slavic peoples, such as Poles, Czechs, Slovaks, Serbs, and Croats, bitterly struggled for independence. Of these, the Serb struggle was the most threatening to the Austro-Hungarian Empire and to peace in Europe. Tsarist Russia's support of Pan-Slavism furthered these rebellions in the hopes of eventually annexing them as part of the Russian Empire.

IMPERIALISM

The late-nineteenth-century colonial empires of Britain, France, Russia, and Germany had created conflict across the globe. Although Germany was rather late in joining the imperialist colonization of Africa, for example, Germany often conflicted with Britain and France over its aspirations in Africa. Britain had several disputes with other powers, such as France, as a result of its expanding presence as a colonial empire, leading to the creation of some of the treaties described below. While these treaties resolved some of the tensions in the nineteenth century, they created a system of alliances that quickly came into place during the early phases of World War I. European involvement in various parts of the globe during the late nineteenth century had created tensions that colored the more immediate events that gave rise to World War I.

EARLY TWENTIETH-CENTURY CONFLICTS

Starting in 1905, a series of conflicts created tensions that contributed to the outbreak of hostilities in World War I. In Morocco in Africa, the Germans supported the movement for independence against France. In 1912 to 1913, the Balkan states of Bulgaria, Greece, Montenegro, Serbia, and Romania fought two wars over territories held in Europe by the Ottomans.

ALLIANCE BUILDING

In the latter half of the nineteenth century, the nations of Europe participated in alliance building on a grand scale. The purpose was to form alliances for mutual defense, to isolate potential enemies, and to negate the potential of other nations to engage in wars that would threaten the security of one's own nation.

The great German statesman Bismarck led the way, making his Prussian-dominated Germany a great power in central Europe through treaties that, he hoped, would keep Germany's enemies weak and Germany's neighbors at peace.

MAJOR TREATIES THAT CREATED THE SYSTEM OF ALLIANCES

1873—Three Emperor's League: An alliance of Germany, Austria-Hungary, and Russia

1879–1918—Austrian-German Alliance (Dual Alliance)

1881–1887—Alliance of the Three Emperors: An alliance of Germany, Austria-Hungary, and Russia

1882–1914—The Triple Alliance: An alliance of Germany, Austria-Hungary, and Italy

1887–1890—Russian-German Reinsurance Treaty, whereby Germany and Russia pledged neutrality in the event of an attack by a third party, provided Russia did not attack Austria or Germany attack France

1894—Franco-Russian Alliance

1902–1915—Anglo-Japanese Alliance

1904—Anglo-French Entente

1907—Anglo-Russian Entente

1907–1914—Triple Entente: An agreement between Russia, France, and Great Britain

The alliances, treaties, and agreements were intended to prevent war between the various nations of Europe. Instead, they formed an inescapable web so that what affected one, affected all.

By 1914, Europe's major powers were divided into two opposing camps: the Triple Alliance and the Triple Entente. The Triple Alliance became the Central Powers of World War I, and had grown out of the Dual Alliance of the treaty of 1879, formed for mutual protection against Russia. In 1882, Italy joined this alliance, creating the Triple Alliance. This alliance was tenuous at best, as Italy threatened German relations with the Ottomans and Austria-Hungary's possessions in the Balkans.

During the Franco-Prussian War of the nineteenth century, France had suffered a humiliating defeat. They were determined to contain the Germans. Russia feared the German-Austrian-Hungarian alliance, and Great Britain still feared events such as had happened in the Napoleonic Wars and tried to preserve the balance of power. Great Britain, France, and Russia, then, together formed the Triple Entente, or the Allies of World War I. Between

1904 and 1914, Britain and France had signed a treaty (Anglo-French Entente) and so had Britain and Russia (Anglo-Russian Entente) over their colonial possessions.

The Event that Sparked a World War: The Assassination of Archduke Ferdinand and Sophie

On June 28, 1914, a Serbian revolutionary and member of the radical Black Hand group, Gavrilo Princip, assassinated **Archduke Franz- Ferdinand** of Austria-Hungary and his wife Sophie. The Black Hand wanted the unification of all Yugoslavs, or south slavs, to form Serbia. Austria-Hungary determined to punish the Serbs for this event. As a result of a treaty of alliance, Germany supported its neighbor Austria-Hungary while Russia supported its ethnic kinsmen the Serbs and their bid for independence, setting the stage for war in Eastern Europe. On July 23, the Austrians issued an ultimatum to Serbia, demanding the right to participate in the investigation of the assassination. The Serbs declined, and on July 28, the Austrians declared war on Serbia. In July, Austria-Hungary declared war on Russia, as Russia was mobilizing to defend the Serbs. In August, Germany responded by declaring war on Russia, followed by a declaration of war on France. Russia had been allied with France since the Dual Alliance between Russia and France in 1894, and in the Triple Entente, which included Great Britain. Therefore, Germany would have expected the French to join in the hostilities. Further, the war plan Germany developed, the **Schlieffen plan**, involved a quick first strike against France.

War Strategies

The alliances and plans for military mobilization based on projected points of conflict ensured that war could not be confined to one region. Austria moved against Belgrade, while Russia mobilized and prepared to attack both Austria and Germany.

The French based their maneuvers on Plan XVII, which relied on offensive attacks without concern for the opponent's strategy. French actions helped account for many of the massive casualties in the war.

The Germans wanted to avoid a war on two fronts, as this might mean that Germany would be surrounded. They relied on the Schlieffen plan developed by Count Alfred von Schlieffen, in 1905, that directed their first assaults on France and then focused on defending Germans from Russian attacks. Germans believed it would take a few weeks to mobilize the Russian forces, giving them the necessary time to knock the French out of the conflict.

German Advance

Germany, confident in its military, then marched west rather than east in their effort to knock France out of the war. Standing between Germany and its target of France was neutral Belgium. Belgium's neutrality in such conflicts had been recognized and supported by its more aggressive neighbors since 1839. Victory for Germany in France depended on its ability to invade swiftly. The German armies would have to enter France through Belgium. Belgium refused to grant Germany permission to pass its borders. Germany refused to be denied and attacked the neutral country in August 1914.

Germany failed to achieve the expected swift victory, its offensive stalling short of Paris. The two combatants flanked each other in a series of moves known as the "race to the sea." Paris was the objective of the German push. With the capture of Paris, France would fall and the Western Front of the war would be under German control. The German army drove hard into France, pushing the allied forces before it. The year ended with the two sides digging into a line of trenches marking the Western Front. The opposing armies then engaged in the meat-grinder horrors of **trench warfare**. For the next four years, though great battles were waged, the armies of Germany and France would advance and retreat repeatedly over the same ground with neither side able to make real headway.

The German plan failed in part because Germany had expected Belgium to either allow the German army to pass or to offer minimal resistance. Instead, the Belgian army fought well against the overwhelming superior German forces and withdrew in orderly fashion to the allies in France rather than breaking and running. Their efforts delayed the progress of the German army, allowing the British forces time to join with the French. German fear of a potential French invasion across the border between Germany and France had prompted them to leave behind some of their forces to protect the homeland, and so they sent a smaller number of troopers into France than mandated by the Schlieffen plan. Consequently, the Germans were unable to counter the unexpected resistance of the Belgians, especially after being reinforced by the French.

Germans Halted at the Battle of the Marne

In September 1914, a gap in the German lines gave the French the opportunity to counterattack. The Battle of the Marne halted the German advance and forced the Germans back, but the allies were not able to mount an offensive strong enough to drive the Germans out of France.

Trench Warfare

Technology determined the style of warfare played on the fields of France. Advances in weapons, particularly the invention of the machine gun, made traditional battle tactics obsolete. With a machine gun, one man could defend a large area against an attacking force and scores of soldiers could be shot down within a matter of seconds. No longer could armies stand and face each other across a field and fire their weapons and have any hope of surviving. Other traditional tactics, such as the charge, were now suicidal efforts but still used.

Soldiers dug into the earth to protect themselves from enemy fire until the order came to go "over the top," leaving the comparative safety of the trenches for the no-man's land of the torn battlefield between the trench lines. There, if they could negotiate barbed wire and avoid land mines, artillery shells, and the automatic weapons fire of the enemy, they had a chance to actually see their enemy and engage him in close combat with rifles and bayonets. **Poisonous gas**, first used by the Germans in the Second Battle of Ypres in 1915, was one of the greatest horrors of the war, inflicting a terrible death from which soldiers had no protection. Chances of survival were slim for front-line soldiers on the Western Front, no matter which army they served. The trench areas became known as "no man's land."

Time and again soldiers were sent forward, only to die or be repulsed by the enemy. The majority of the action on the Western Front took place along a narrow line running from the coast of France to Alsace-Lorraine. Within this thin area, the combatant forces pushed back and forth, gaining a few miles here and there only to lose it again, neither able to achieve the breakthrough victory it sought.

The loss of life was on a scale difficult to imagine. In 1916, over 1,800,000 men were killed or wounded in just two battles; there were 1,100,000 combined casualties in the Battle of the Somme, while there were 700,000 casualties in the longest battle of the war at Verdun. Those who did survive the war on the Western Front were forever transformed by the carnage.

Battles of Verdun and the Somme

In 1916, the Germans attempted to break out of the trenches with an assault on Verdun, a fortress. The French were determined that "they shall not pass," and although they succeeded in stopping the Germans, the loss of life was frightening. At the Battle of the Somme, British forces attacked the Germans to help relieve pressure on Verdun. By November, the British had advanced only a few yards at tremendous cost of life. By 1916, neither side had managed to gain a strategic advantage.

The Eastern Front

The Eastern Front with Germany and Austria-Hungary opposing Russia was a different type of war. The Russian army mobilized and moved into eastern Germany where it faced stiff opposition from the German forces. The Germans were well commanded by Generals Paul von Hindenburg and

Erich Ludendorff. The Battle of Tannenberg in August and the Battle of the Masurian Lakes in September 1914 drove the Russians back. They would not be able to mount another major offensive against Germany for the rest of the war.

In the Austro-Hungarian campaign, the Russians fared little better. Unable to make any progress against the Austro-Hungarian forces, they were soundly repulsed when the Germans were able to join the campaign. By 1915, the Russians had been driven back to their own territory, having suffered 2.5 million lost, captured, injured, or killed.

Other nations weighed in. In 1914, Italy had declared itself neutral only to reverse its position and join the Triple Entente of Great Britain, France, and Russia in 1915. Italy had not been able to resist the possibility of territorial gains at the expense of Austria. Bulgaria was neutral in 1914, but followed the Ottoman Empire in joining the Central Powers of Germany and Austria in 1915, lured by the possibility of defeating Serbia.

The Ottoman Empire

The entry of the Ottoman Empire into the war is significant because it broke the war from the confines of Europe and spread it to the Middle East. In 1915 Winston Churchill, who was then first lord of the admiralty, suggested a strike against Ottoman territories in an effort to distract the Germans. The British launched an attack in the Dardanelles, a strait through which supplies might be shipped to Russia. At **Gallipoli**, a heavy force of Ottomans defended the straits. The Allies dug their trenches and the result was a disaster. There were over 250,000 casualties at Gallipoli. Although the British led the campaign, many of its colonials actually fought. Following the war, the resentment of the Canadian, Australian, and New Zealander soldiers weakened the British Empire. The leader of the Turkish defense, Mustafa Kemal, formed the Turkish Republic and became known as Atatürk. Lawrence of Arabia, a British colonel, aided the Arab revolt of Ibn Ali Hussain, sheriff of Mecca and king of the Hejaz, against the Ottoman Turks in 1917. The Ottoman Empire came to an end in 1918 as a result of defeat at the hands of the British, who employed troops drawn from the far reaches of the British Empire.

The colonial territories of the warring European nations played significant parts in the war. British and French colonies remained loyal, feeding men and supplies to the war effort and helping to take control of German colonies, thus removing Germany's ability to draw on its colonial resources. The Japanese, allies of the British, were able to move against German possessions in the Pacific and in China. This Japanese aggression added to the tension existing between China and Japan.

The United States Enters the War

In February 1917, the United States ambassador to the United Kingdom, Walter H. Page, obtained a copy of the Zimmermann Telegram, which helped to thrust the U.S. into the World War. In the telegram, which was sent by Germany to Mexico, the Germans offered to return the southwestern portion of the United States to Mexico if Mexico would declare war on the United States. The resumption of unrestricted submarine warfare also contributed to the United States' decision to enter the war. The sinking of the passenger liner *Lusitania*, in 1915, with 139 Americans on board had outraged the United States. Germany had quickly changed its policy for submarine warfare from one of total blockade in which any ship was a legitimate target to a more relaxed stance and so avoided war with the United States. By 1917, Germany felt the possibility of starving Britain was worth risking the enmity of the United States and had gone back to a policy of unrestricted warfare. U.S. President Woodrow Wilson declared Germany's new stance to be "warfare against mankind." The United States entered the war on the side of the Triple Alliance in April 1917.

Russia Makes Peace with Germany

The Russian Revolution crippled the already failing effort of the Russian army to combat Germany. In February 1918, Russia accepted Germany's peace terms, leaving Germany free to turn its attention back to the Western Front.

The Second Battle of the Marne

In the spring of 1918, Germany launched a new offensive in France, attempting once again to reach Paris. The Germans were stopped at the Second Battle of the Marne in July 1918. One hundred and forty thousand American troops joined the exhausted allies in stopping the German advance. By August, the Americans had committed two million men to the war effort.

This influx of fresh Americans into the lines of the war-weary allies proved to be the deciding factor in the war. By October 1918, the Allies had pushed the Germans back and the Germans were prepared to ask for peace terms.

Kaiser Wilhelm II Abdicates

The peace negotiations dragged on beyond the endurance of the German people. By November, mutiny and revolution were realities in Germany. Austria-Hungary surrendered, leaving Germany fighting on its own, but not for long. Before the end of November, Kaiser Wilhelm II abdicated, a German republic was declared, and Germany surrendered. By the end of the war, the Ottoman, Austria-Hungarian, German, and Russian empires no longer existed.

The Treaty of Versailles

In 1919, the victorious powers met in Paris at the Paris Peace Conference to negotiate the fate of the nations. Woodrow Wilson went to Versailles with high hopes of crafting a lasting peace. He presented his **Fourteen Points**, advocating open treaties, free navigation of the seas, and equality of trading conditions. Chief among the Fourteen Points was his call for the creation of "a general association of nations," which became the **League of Nations**. Other allies had other priorities, specifically the punishment of Germany. Clemenceau of France was particularly determined to see Germany punished and permanently crippled so that it could never again threaten France. Lloyd George of Britain was not as strident, but had to consider the opinion of the British people who, having had their lives forever changed by the war, were still angry and wanted retribution.

Wilson was able to deny France's most punishing demands with the support of the moderate Lloyd George. Clemenceau did not achieve the secure buffer zone he sought for France, but gained the promise from Britain and the United States that each would come to the aide of France should France be attacked again. Germany lost little territory within Europe, but all of its colonial holdings were divided among the victorious allies.

Germany was allowed to maintain an army, but its size was limited to no more than 100,000. Germany was allowed to keep the Rhineland, but was not allowed to place military installations there. Germany returned Alsace-Lorraine to France. A part of northeastern Germany that was inhabited largely by Poles was given to the newly created Poland, an action in line with the national self-determination beliefs espoused by Wilson and others.

Wilson could not block the demand for reparations. The Allies insisted the fault for the war be laid squarely on Germany and Austria. Further, Germany would have to pay an undetermined amount of reparations for the destruction resulting from the war. Germany protested the terms of the treaty, but as it, too, suffered from the devastation wrought by the war, it had no choice but to sign the treaty on June 28, 1919.

The League of Nations

The League of Nations was the first permanent international security organization. Its purpose was to maintain world peace, but it had two basic flaws in its structure. First, it had no means to enforce its decisions, and second, it relied on the notion of collective security to preserve global peace. "Collective security" essentially meant that a threat to any one country was a threat to all, but since participation by the various powers was essential, the League could never attain its aims. Many important powers were, at one time or other, absent from the League. Wilson had been the driving force for the formation of the League of Nations and for getting a treaty that would promise peace for Europe, but Wilson was unable to deliver American ratification of the treaty. The Senate had not been able to agree with the terms of the League of Nations, but the rejection of the treaty also meant that the United States was not bound by its promise to come to the defense of France. Britain then refused to ratify its defense agreement with France as well. France was left with no defensive buffer zone and no promise of aid in the case of German aggression. Germany left the League in 1933, as it believed it to be dominated by the Allies. The Soviet Union joined in 1934 and was expelled in 1940. The League utterly failed to stop World War II and so collapsed in 1940.

The Aftermath of War

One of the most important consequences of the World War was the beginning of the breakdown of the colonial empires of Europe.

Malaise in the Arts

The carnage of the First World War was the worst the world had ever experienced, and it left an indelible imprint on literature and other art forms. Gertrude Stein said that the postwar generation was a **lost generation**. Ernest Hemingway's *A Farewell to Arms* and Erich Maria Remarque's *All Quiet on the Western Front* expressed the malaise and disillusionment of the postwar era and captured the seemingly meaningless suffering of the Great War. Sigmund Freud, whose psychological theories first began to appear in 1896, created a new view of the self whereby much of one's inner life is not conscious. While Descartes had earlier told one that the contents of one's mind were clear and distinct, now Freud wrote about the id: the seething, churning desires that are not conscious but that often dictate our behavior. For Freud, God was a mechanism of the superego, a projection of the moral authority of parents and other figures. Salvador Dali and other artists and writers incorporated Freudian psychology into their works, often creating disturbing images of the world that matched the horrors of World War I.

Similarly, theologians reminded one that God's kingdom is not of this world, and Karl Barth's *Epistle to the Romans* questioned the belief that progress is the realization of God's purpose. The Russian orthodox writer Nikolai Berdiaev claimed that "man's existence had been one of steady failure," and claimed there was no evidence to suggest this would ever change.

Old Values Fall

Many scholars and political activists of the far right or far left questioned the value of democracy, while others questioned the power of the ordinary citizen to control a world of such chaos. Jose Ortega y Gasset, a Spanish philosopher, wrote the most famous argument to this effect in the "Revolt of the Masses," where he warned that the masses may be unduly swayed by demagogues. He argued, too, that the masses have the power to destroy the greatest achievements of Western society, due to the attempt to impose a mass will on everyone and everything.

Relativism

Einstein developed the **theory of relativity**, according to which space and time are relevant to the person measuring them. Gone were all the absolutes of past ages, and reality or truth were merely mental constructs. Werner Heisenberg developed the "**uncertainty principle**," according to which it is impossible to specify simultaneously the position and velocity of a subatomic particle. The more accurate the position, the less accurate the velocity. Heisenberg's theory suggested that one cannot accurately observe electrons, because the very act of observation interferes with them. One could not be objective, then, thus undermining some of the assumptions of the Age of Reason and its emphasis on observation.

In art, the belief that there were objective measures of good and evil was rejected. Pablo Picasso was a leading exponent of cubism, according to which multiple perspectives on objects were displayed at the same time. Picasso and other artists, such as Gauguin, also incorporated non-European influences into their work, such as from Africa and, in the case of Gauguin, Tahiti. Gauguin argued that in primitive cultures there was a sense of wonder present that Europeans had lost.

GLOBAL DEPRESSION IN THE WAKE OF WORLD WAR I

Under President Warren Harding, the United States reacted against the idealism of Woodrow Wilson, and entered a period in which it sought to "return to normalcy" in the 1920s. His successor, President Calvin Coolidge, known as Silent Cal, seemed to be a living expression of "normalcy," as he had a quiet and understated demeanor. One of the main planks of the return to normalcy was rejection of Wilson's belief in America's international role and a renewal of the former stance of isolationism. In fact, by the mid-1930s, a Senate committee chaired by North Dakota Republican Gerald Nye concluded that American involvement in World War I had been a mistake, contributing to American reluctance to enter World War II.

In the 1930s, however, the United States and the rest of the world were caught in the **Great Depression**. The complex system of reparation demanded by the Treaty of Versailles was the basis for much of the economy in the 1920s, and Austria and Germany, for example, relied on U.S. loans to pay these debts. The French and British relied on reparations payments to pay their own loans from the United States during the war. By 1928, U.S. lenders had started to withdraw capital from Europe, straining the financial system.

Other factors contributed, as the use of oil began to undermine the coal industry, and techniques for using reclaimed rubber, perfected during the war, hurt the rubber export industry of the Dutch East Indies, Ceylon, and Malaysia. In fact, overproduction contributed to the global depression. During the war, European agricultural production had fallen for obvious reasons. The United States and other parts of the world had expanded their production, and after the war, European production resumed. The result was a worldwide surplus. Demand declined and prices dropped. By 1929, the price of a bushel of wheat was at its lowest level in 400 years. This contributed to the inability of farmers to purchase manufactured goods, leading businesses to cut jobs.

The Stock Market Crash of 1929

On **Black Thursday**, October 24, 1929, investors across the world pulled out of the market. Stocks plummeted. Many lost their life's savings, and banks began to call in loans. President Herbert Hoover's response to the collapse of the American economy, calling for increased volunteerism, proved ineffective.

By 1932, industrial production was at one-half the level of 1929, and the national income was also only one-half of what it had been. Almost half of the banks in the United States went out of business and took with them the deposits of millions of people. Since so much of the world was dependent on the U.S. economy, the world economy collapsed as well. Germany and Japan, as well as Latin America, Africa, and Asian countries, were hard hit. These were nations that relied on exports. In Germany, the unemployment rate reached thirty-five percent by 1932 and their production fell by fifty percent. Although there had been no military engagements on German soil and so Germany itself was largely spared, leaving its industries and economy intact, the post-war economic collapse destroyed the German home front.

Economic difficulties forced Latin American nations to develop their internal economies. In Brazil, the dictator Getulia Dornelles Vargas created the *Estado Novo*, or New State. Vargas ruled with the support of the military and created new industries, such as iron and steel, while also protecting workers with safety and health regulations, minimum wage laws, unemployment compensation, retirement plans, and limits on working hours.

Only China remained unaffected by the global depression. China's market did not rely upon foreign trade, while many parts of colonial Africa also escaped the ravages of the global slump.

World production declined by thirty-eight percent in the three years following the crash of 1929. Trade dropped by over sixty percent, as nations imposed tariffs on imports in an attempt to become self-sufficient. The U.S., for example, enacted the Smoot-Hawley Tariff in 1930, raising duties on manufactured imported goods.

Unemployment backfired on women, who lost some of the gains of World War I. Many still believed women should not work but rather manage the home, and some argued that a solution to the world's employment problem would be to return women to the home.

The author John Steinbeck described the suffering of the depression in such works as *The Grapes of Wrath*. In the 1930s, President Franklin Delano Roosevelt responded to the plight of many Americans with his New Deal, a massive program of social reform legislation based on federal intervention in the economy. The government created new jobs through the Works Progress (Projects) Administration, the Civilian Conservation Corps, and other agencies. The government created Social Security and other measures for the relief of its beleaguered population.

New Economic Theories

The economist John Maynard Keynes put forth a new economic idea in 1936, rather like the New Deal, in *General Theory of Employment, Interest and Money*. Keynes argued that the problem was lack of demand, and that governments should create more jobs and put more money into circulation, which he thought would lower interest rates and increase investment.

Russian Response to the Post-War Period

Lenin's revolution had occurred in the midst of World War I, and the Bolsheviks were still rebuilding Russian society when the global depression hit. Lenin enacted the NEP, or New Economic Policy, whereby he returned industries with less than twenty employees to the private sector. The NEP also allowed peasants to sell surpluses for free market prices. Lenin died in 1924 and Stalin took power. The "man of steel" enacted several **Five Year Plans**, intended to promote rapid economic development. The first plan focused on heavy industry, which was to become centralized through the efforts of Gosplan, the central state-planning agency. Stalin created collective farms, and all private land was subsumed into these units. Members shared the profits. Peasants revolted, and many starved to death on their own lands when they were unable to meet production quotas set by the government. By 1931, when the plan ended, half the land in Russia was contained within collective farms.

As Russia focused on industry, consumer goods were virtually nonexistent. Rebellions emerged not only among those whose land was taken, but within the Communist party as well. Stalin embarked on a series of purges starting with the Congress of Victors in 1934, an event that was to celebrate achievements. It was later known as the Congress of Victims, due to the numbers of people purged. Over two-thirds of the members of the 1934 Central Committee and one-half of the army's highest-ranking officers were removed, while three million citizens died and eight million were imprisoned.

As Stalin gained power in Russia, fascism and National Socialism took root in Italy and Germany, movements that would bring the world to war again in World War II. These movements will be further addressed in Chapter 43.

ASIA AFTER WORLD WAR I

India

Beginning in the 1850s, the British ruled India. World War I weakened the empire, leading to, among other things, a movement for Indian independence. The Indian National Congress was founded in 1885, and after World War I the congress increasingly turned against the British. The Muslim League, founded in 1906, feared that Hindu domination would replace the British, and considerable conflict arose between Hindus and Muslims that continues today. Wilson's Fourteen Points encouraged self-determination, and the Indian population eagerly embraced the ideal. The British responded with more repressive measures, creating a wave of rebellions and violence across the subcontinent of India.

Mohandas Gandhi emerged as an important leader. He was a Hindu who had been educated in law in London and had spent twenty-five years in South Africa, another British colony. While in South Africa, he had organized resistance within the Indian community to racial segregation. There he also developed his philosophy of **ahimsa**, or nonviolence and tolerance, and satyagrha, meaning "truth and firmness," but referring to his method of passive resistance. He renounced worldly pleasures, including sex, and, although he was a member of the merchant caste, he lived a life of simplicity. Ghandi returned to India in 1915 and became active in the Indian National Congress. He helped to launch the Non-Cooperation Movement of 1920–1922 and the Civil Disobedience Movement of 1930. These were mass movements that boycotted British goods and institutions. Gandhi urged the people to wear Indian spun cloth as opposed to British manufactured clothing. In general, he opposed industrialization in India. Although Gandhi advocated nonviolence, the movements inevitably did result in violence, and the British arrested the offenders. In 1919, in Amritsar in the Punjab, colonial troops dispersed an unarmed crowd with rifles and killed 379 demonstrators.

In 1937, the British government gave in and enacted the Government of India Act, which gave India the institutions for a self-governing state.

The Muslim League, led by Muhammad Ali Jinnah, however, rejected this compromise, as it feared Hindu domination. Jinnah advocated the formation of separate states, one for Hindus in India and another for Muslims in Pakistan, which would be the "land of the pure." In 1947, following World War II, Jinnah's dream became reality. Pakistan separated from India, but into an eastern and a western section. In 1971, East Pakistan seceded and became the separate nation of Bangladesh.

CHINA AFTER WORLD WAR I

The revolution that ended Ching rule and established Sun Yat-sen as president of the Chinese republic did not end China's problems. Many generals of the old imperial army became warlords in the provinces, and they preserved and supported the old opium trade. Although Sun Yat-sen's government controlled affairs in Beijing, China was not united as long as the warlords ran the provinces. Sun Yat-sen eventually relinquished the presidency to Yuan Shikai, a warlord who controlled the Beijing armies. Yuan Shikai, unfortunately, did nothing but reinvigorate aspects of imperial rule. Some historians now argue that Sun Yat-sen did not play an important role in the 1911 revolution that overthrew the Ching Dynasty, as he was out of the country at the time. They further suggest he was chosen as president as a compromise candidate, because he had not been directly involved in these events. Nevertheless, Sun Yat-sen is known today as the "Father of the nation," or the "father of China."

Mao Zedong and the Chinese Communist Party

The unequal treaties of the Opium Wars had resulted, too, in the influx of foreign trade in China. China had hoped that Wilson's Fourteen Points and the Treaty of Versailles might end foreign domination of China's trade and obliterate the unequal treaties, but they were bitterly disappointed when the United States actually helped Japan to increase its activities in China. Resentment boiled over in China in the May Fourth Movement, led by intellectuals and students. They protested foreign imperialism and wanted the restoration of national unity. As the United States had apparently abandoned its own principles, especially in the context of China, and while the Russians advocated anti-imperialism, many turned to Communism. **Mao Zedong** was one of the most important members of the Chinese Communist Party, founded in 1921. He supported the equality of women and fought against such practices as foot binding and arranged marriages, which had kept women from advancing. Although Sun Yat-sen also advocated the end of special privileges for foreigners and national reunification, he wanted a democratic republican government based on universal suffrage. Sun Yat-sen organized the Nationalist People's Party, or Guomindang, in 1912, and by 1926, communists accounted for one-third of its membership. Soviet advisors lent aid to the process.

Jiang Jieshi (Chiang Kai-Shek)

Sun Yat-sen fled to Japan during the tenure of Yuan Shikai, but returned in 1917, and, in 1921, was elected president of what the Guomindang called the Republic of China in Guangzhou in southern China. He died in 1925, and Jiang Jieshi (**Chiang Kai-Shek**) replaced him as leader of the Guomindang. Jiang Jieshi began the Northern Expedition campaign to unite China and establish Guomindang rule through the land. In 1926 and 1927, he defeated thirty-nine warlords. He then moved on to Shanghai, where the communists opposed his entry. He ordered a massacre of the communists and took control of the city. This convinced him that Sun Yat-sen's attempt to work with the Communists was dangerous, and he abandoned them by 1927. The Communists retreated to south China, while Jiang Jieshi marched on Beijing in 1928 and then established his headquarters in Nanjing. At this point, he declared the Guomindang the official government of a united China.

The Long March

Despite rhetoric to the contrary, China was not united. Jiang Jieshi began a vicious battle to rid China of the communist threat, and the Communists were forced to flee to their retreat in southeastern Asia. In 1934, they began their historic **Long March** from their hideout in Jianxi, traveling 6,215 miles north to Shaanxi province in northwestern China by October 1935. Thousands died along the treacherous march. They established headquarters in Yan'an and had attracted many new members as a result of what many Chinese perceived as heroism. Mao Zedong emerged as the leader of the Communists in China, and modified the teachings of Marx and Lenin about the revolutionary power of the urban, industrial proletariat to suit conditions in China. Among other things, he argued that the peasant was the foundation of revolution in China. The struggle between the nationalists and Communists continued through World War II.

JAPAN IN THE POST-WAR ERA

Japan joined the League of Nations and became one of the big five powers. In 1928, Japan signed the Kellogg-Briand Pact, renouncing war as an instrument of national policy. Earlier, it had pledged in pacts with the United States to respect China's territorial integrity.

Nevertheless, Japan invaded Manchuria in 1931. Instability in China made the invasion feasible, while the Japanese military presence there to maintain the Manchurian railroad created a jumping off point. On September 18, 1931, Japanese troops blew up a portion of the South Manchuria Railroad that the Japanese had built. They blamed the Chinese, creating the pretext for war. This act of treachery became known as the Mukden Incident. By 1932, the Japanese had set up a puppet state called Machukuo. The Chinese protested to the League of Nations, who eventually called for the withdrawal of Japan, but since the League lacked the power to take action, Japan went unpunished. The conquest of Manchuria set the stage for future aggression, which ultimately culminated in World War II.

CHAPTER 42

THE RISE OF FASCISM

THE RISE OF HITLER

At the end of World War I, the Allies, particularly France, demanded severe reparations from Germany. The purpose was two-fold: first to re-pay France for the damage caused by the war, and second to punish Germany so harshly that it would never again be a threat to the peace in Europe and the security of France.

The harsh terms of the treaty that ended World War I had the unintended but not altogether unpredictable effect of galvanizing a nationalistic feeling in the hearts of the German people. The very measures designed to keep Germany down had in fact primed it to rise to the call of a strong leader.

Adolf Hitler was an Austrian, born in Austria to Austrian parents. His father died while Hitler was young. Hitler had difficulty in finding a direction for his life. He went to Vienna, intent on entering the Academy of Fine Arts and becoming an artist, but his application was rejected. With no particular place to go and no plans, Hitler stayed in Vienna. His time there was critical to his development.

It was in Vienna that Hitler was first exposed to the ideas that would later be the foundations of his Nazi doctrine: German nationalism, the natural superiority of the Germanic peoples, the natural inferiority of the Semitic and Slavic peoples, and the evil conspiracies of Semites to undermine German nationhood and destroy German culture. Capitalism and Liberalism were threats to German unity. Hitler watched, listened, and absorbed the radical, somewhat irrational, ideas swirling among the Austro-German nationalists. He believed what he learned there and found the road to his ultimate destiny.

In 1913, Hitler moved to Munich, Germany, to avoid service in the Austrian army. Soon World War I broke out and Hitler found himself in the German army. He found a home in the army and a purpose in life. In the army, although a lowly enlisted man, Hitler was proud to be serving the cause of German nationalism. He was really doing something for the first time in his life that he felt had any real meaning. When the war ended with the defeat of Germany in 1918, Hitler was devastated. He was not prepared to give up the fight and move on. The defeat of Germany by the combined forces of the Allies convinced Hitler that all he had learned in Vienna was true. Hitler began preaching what he believed. In the grim aftermath of World War I, he found Germans willing to listen.

In 1919, Hitler found himself once again in Munich. He became a member of the **German Worker's Party**. The German Worker's Party was small in size, radical in outlook. It was anti-Semitic, anti-Marxist, anti-democratic, and anti-capitalistic. It was for "national socialism," building Germany into one large community of Germanic, and only Germanic, people.

The party grew, and Hitler's power within the party grew as well. In 1921, he took control. Honing the skills and ideas he first learned in Vienna, Hitler kept the party moving forward and growing with radical propaganda and mass meetings at which he delivered mesmerizing speeches railing against his usual targets and the government of Germany, the Weimar Republic itself. Hitler had transformed from a youth without direction into a charismatic leader with a dangerous message.

By 1923, the Weimar Republic was clearly becoming unstable. Hitler seized the opportunity to launch a revolt in Munich. Hitler's revolt failed and he was arrested. Hitler turned this defeat into something of a victory. He used his trial as a platform to expound on his ideals, gaining increased notoriety and exposure. He served less than a year in prison—just long enough to become a near-martyr to his supporters and to write *Mein Kampf*. This book served as the guide for all things Nazi. This defeat and imprisonment also gave Hitler time to rethink his tactics. He decided that rather than attempt to overthrow the Weimar Republic by open rebellion, he would do better to use his ever-growing base of support to take over the government by political means.

His party, now the **National Socialist** German Workers' Party or **Nazi** Party, continued its growth, reaching a membership of one hundred thousand by 1928. These members were dedicated, disciplined, and devoted to the Nazi cause. Hitler continued to build the party and broadened its appeal by targeting Bolshevism as a menace to be fought while lessening his protests against capitalism. This made the party more appealing to middle-class Germans.

The Nazis were still just a small part of the total German political system, but in the elections of 1928 they did manage to win twelve seats in the Reichstag. This represented only 2.6 percent of the total vote, but it was enough of a start for the Nazis to begin their attack on the Weimar Republic from the inside.

In 1929, the Great Depression gripped Germany as it did the rest of the industrialized world. As the economy of German entered a severe downswing, it gave the Nazis the opening they needed to find an issue to appeal to the masses. By 1932, forty-three percent of German workers were unemployed. The crisis was worsening. As Nazi power was on the rise, the Weimar Republic continued to slide towards extinction. The government could not contain the economic crisis. In desperation the government took emergency measures. The president, General Hindenburg, agreed to Chancellor Bruning's suggestion of rule by decree. This was a legitimate move under the constitution, but an unpopular one with the lower and middle classes. Bruning was attempting to arrest the economic slide by cutting government spending and driving down prices and wages. His well-intentioned attempt failed to do anything other than increase popular support for Hitler's ideas. In 1932 Hindenburg forced Bruning to resign, but the situation did not improve.

Hitler seized his opportunity. He altered his speeches to appeal directly to those most affected by the failing economy. The middle and lower classes had traditionally supported the conservatives and moderates. In the face of economic disaster, the Communist Party was rising in power. Reacting to the threat of communism, the danger of personal financial ruin, and the promise of Hitler that the Nazi Party, if given the chance, would turn the economy around and stamp out communism as well, the middle- and lower-class voters turned their support to the Nazis.

Meanwhile, Hitler sought the support of big business by promising to help them bring back their profits, even sacrificing workers' wages if need be. To the army leadership, he promised that, given the opportunity, he would overturn the Treaty of Versailles with its punitive conditions and rearm the German military. To the youth of Germany, he promised a purpose for living, a chance to make a difference, to build a better Germany and to be a leader in the new Germany. German nationalism appealed to the young. They flocked to the Nazi Party in droves. Almost forty percent of the party was under the age of thirty in 1931. No other political party in Germany could compete with the Nazis for their appeal to German youth.

In 1932, the work of Hitler and his party paid off. They won 14.5 million votes and took control of the Reichstag as the largest single party represented there. If the other two major parties, the Social Democrats and the Communists, had been able to cooperate, they would have had enough votes to block the Nazis. But the two parties had been enemies too long to become allies. Still, the Social Democrats tried, even going so far as to appeal to the Soviet Embassy, but to no avail. Hitler now had his chance to put his ideas into practice.

Hitler demanded to join the government as the chancellor. The conservatives believed that as they held the majority of government posts, they could control Hitler, even if he were the chancellor. They agreed to his demand and on January 30, 1933, President Hindenburg appointed Hitler as chancellor of

Germany. Hitler immediately called for new elections. The campaigning was violent; part of the Reichstag was burned. Hitler blamed the communists and convinced President Hindenburg to grant him emergency powers. The new election gave the Nazis an even greater number of seats in the Reichstag. With his support in the Reichstag and the streets growing, Hitler was able to outlaw the Communist Party and arrest its Reichstag representatives. In March, he pushed the Enabling Act through the Reichstag that made Hitler absolute dictator for a year.

Hitler moved quickly with his new power to end opposition to the Nazi Party. He kept his opponents divided until he could remove them as threats to his party. The Nazi Party became the only party in Germany. Elections continued, but served no real purpose as the only candidates were Nazi Party members. Hitler was now the **Führer**. He did not dismantle the government; he simply replaced non-Nazi officeholders with Nazi Party members.

Hitler banned strikes and established the Nazi Labor Front to replace the labor unions. Professional organizations were also replaced with Nazi organizations. No independent organizations were allowed in Germany. Only those related to the Nazis could exist. Anything that did not fit the Nazi mold was banned. The Nazis controlled virtually every aspect of German public life by 1934.

Hitler took control of the army by winning the loyalty of its officers. The SA, the "brown shirts," who had supported Hitler in the beginning and who were known for their thuggish ways, had become a powerful group of three million. They expected to be rewarded for their loyalty, but as a group, they were powerful enough to threaten Hitler and they were powerful enough to create problems in other areas as well. They wanted to take control of the army. Hitler decided the best course of action was to remove the SA leadership. He had a thousand of them executed. To do this, he used the SS, the Nazi elite and Hitler's most trusted guards. The army responded by swearing allegiance to Hitler. The SS grew in power and, with the Gestapo, became a dreaded organization with few limits on its power.

The Nazis' attitude towards the Jews had never been a secret as anti-Semitism was a founding principle of the party. Once Hitler took control of Germany, life for the Jews became increasingly difficult. Jews found themselves unemployed, and barred from working. In 1935, the Nuremburg Laws were passed. These laws declared that anyone with at least one Jewish grandparent was Jewish and as such could not be German citizens. By 1938, a quarter of all the Jews in Germany had left the country. They were the lucky ones.

In the latter half of 1938, the situation for the Jews grew suddenly worse. Organized attacks against the Jews began. Their homes, property, and synagogues were damaged and destroyed, and the Jews themselves were forced to pay for the damage. At the same time, they were no longer as free to leave Germany as they had once been. A government that viewed them as the enemy within now trapped them.

While Hitler's persecution of the Jews, along with the other groups Nazis viewed as inferior or deviant, increased, he also enacted policies that did improve the situation for the average German. The work programs, the improving economic picture, the rearmament begun in 1936, and the better opportunities and greater equality for the masses that Hitler introduced helped maintain the popularity of his government. It helped keep quiet those who might criticize his persecution of the Jews and others. Those who would not be quiet in their opposition were imprisoned or executed.

As Hitler had made clear in 1924 in *Mein Kampf*, he believed in the superiority of the German race, and due to its superiority, its right to take whatever space it needed to fulfill its destiny. Nazi Germany had the right, even the duty, to expand. Those nations opposed to such expansion did not know how to handle Hitler. They tried appeasement and failed, not understanding that Hitler's ambitions for expansion would not be limited to what other nations were willing to give up.

Still, Hitler felt that if he moved carefully, he would be able to gain much before the other nations offered any real resistance. In 1933, Germany withdrew from the League of Nations. Austrian Nazis assassinated the Austrian chancellor in 1934 with the goal of joining with Germany as one united Germanic nation. Mussolini, sensing the danger of a union between Germany and Austria, blocked the move with his troops at the Brenner Pass. Hitler was stopped, but not for long.

In 1935, Hitler issued a general draft and fulfilled his promise to the army by declaring that the Treaty of Versailles would no longer bind Germany. Italy, France, and Great Britain protested, but the protest was weak and an alliance of the three nations failed to form.

Germany Takes the Rhineland

Instead, Britain tried appeasement, first with the Anglo-German naval agreement, then in other ways. In 1936, the German army occupied the Rhineland in direct violation of the Treaty of Versailles. France had specifically demanded the Rhineland be a de-militarized buffer zone as a defensive area to protect France from German aggression. Now, Hitler was ignoring the treaty and putting troops in the Rhineland and no one but France seemed alarmed. German troops occupying German territory did not seem to be such a terrible thing to the British. The French were afraid to do anything alone and so did nothing.

There were several reasons why the British tried appeasement. For one, the overwhelming loss of life in World War I still scarred the minds of the British public. They did not want to enter another devastating war. Also, the British felt that Germany had been harshly punished for World War I, perhaps too harshly, and so could understand some of Hitler's demands, such as rebuilding the army and moving into the Rhineland. Russia, Stalin, and communism had been the foremost threats in the minds of the British. They did not believe that Hitler was as dangerous as Stalin. Hitler was something of a champion against the spread of communism, as he had stamped it out in Germany. This made Hitler at least somewhat sympathetic in the eyes of the British. As long as Hitler did not do anything that could not be excused or ignored, the British were not going to move against him. Without the British, the French would do nothing as well unless forced to act in the defense of France.

THE RISE OF MUSSOLINI

Before World War I, Italy had been a largely rural society. Most people were poor, the country was controlled by a small middle and upper class, and the Church had power but was often at odds with the government. Further, the head of the government was a constitutional monarch who was ineffective. As far as European governments of the time went, Italy was fairly liberal. The people had civil rights and universal male suffrage. Still, the difference between the classes was a gulf not a gap, and the poverty most people experienced spawned social movements. The Socialist Party in Italy was opposed to any involvement in World War I, but was unable to keep Italy out of the war.

Italy had joined the war on the side of the Allies believing that if the Allies won, Italy would be able to gain territory for itself. They were wrong. The Italians left Versailles practically empty-handed. Worse, the government had made promises of reforms to the working classes during the war and now that the war was over, failed to deliver. The situation was ripe for revolt.

In 1920, revolutionary socialist elements in Italy were on the move. They seized factories and land. These seizures made no real gains for the socialists, but caused the property owners to become more active themselves. At the same time, a Catholic party was gaining strength and conservatives were flexing their muscles as well. These groups were all very different from each other, but all united in their opposition to the current Italian government. The government's days were numbered.

Benito Mussolini began life in an Italian village. His mother was a schoolteacher, his father a blacksmith. As a young man, Mussolini became a Socialist, and worked on a newspaper. In 1914, Mussolini urged Italy to join the Allies in World War I, which was the opposite of his party's stand on the subject. But Mussolini did not restrict himself to following his party's policies. In this instance, he was listening to anti-democratic groups. The Socialists threw him out of the party. Mussolini joined the army and was wounded at the front in 1917. Upon his return to Italy, Mussolini began organizing war veterans into a new group, the **Fascists**.

His early ideology was a blend of nationalism and socialism. He wanted territorial expansion and land reform, both of which had been promised by the Italian government but never delivered. He also wanted benefits for the working class. As many of his ideas were also the ideas of the Socialists, Mussolini had difficulty in bringing people to his party, as they were already happy with the Socialists. By 1920, Mussolini had discovered that by attacking the Socialists he could draw Conservatives to his cause. He had found a winning formula and his party grew.

His Black Shirt supporters were sometimes violent. They would attack Socialists, usually at night. They pushed them out of the northern Italian city governments. Although they usually stopped short of killing, their tactics were enough to intimidate their Socialist opponents.

In 1922, the government of Italy broke down, due in part to the activities of Mussolini's supporters. Mussolini stepped to the fore. He demanded the resignation of the current government and that he be appointed by the king to form a new government. His supporters marched on Rome to make their demands clear. The king, Victor Emmanuel III, agreed and made Mussolini dictator for a year.

Mussolini changed the election laws so that in 1924 his party was able to gain a clear majority in the government. Then, supporters of Mussolini kidnapped and murdered the Socialist leader, Giacomo Matteotti, causing Mussolini's first political crisis as opposing parties demanded Mussolini disband his Black Shirts. Mussolini responded with force. He declared that Italy would be a Fascist nation. He enacted restrictive laws, abolished independent unions and freedom of the press, put the schools under the control of fascists, and created fascist unions, organizations, and a youth movement. Mussolini summed it up in 1926, "Everything in the state, nothing outside the state, nothing against the state." Still, in many ways, Mussolini's take-over of the government was a nonrevolution. Unlike Hitler and Stalin, Mussolini was not personally dedicated to an extreme ideology that he felt he must force on the people. Rather, Mussolini wanted power for himself and found a way to get it. Thus, he did not do away with old institutions, he did not fight the church, he did not enact great land reforms, he did not liberate women, he did not persecute the Jews, and he did not hunt down and execute his political opponents. He simply did what he had to do to gain power and to keep power. For example, in 1929, in the Lateran Agreement, he recognized the Vatican as an independent state and agreed to give it financial support. The Pope, in turn, encouraged Italians to support Mussolini. Mussolini was a dictator, but a very different style of dictator than Hitler.

Mussolini Attacks Ethiopia

Germany was not alone in looking to flex its muscles in 1935. Mussolini decided to attack **Ethiopia**. Ethiopia was an independent African nation on the east coast of Africa. Italy had colonies in East Africa and used these to launch the attack. The reason for the attack really had nothing to do with Ethiopia, beyond its convenience as a target. Mussolini, like Hitler, felt that expansion was an important part of his doctrine. While he could not expand in Europe without engaging in a war he could not win, Africa provided opportunities for colonial expansion with little risk of all-out war. Publicly, Hitler supported Mussolini; privately, he supplied arms to Ethiopia.

Haile Selassie

The Ethiopian Emperor, **Haile Selassie**, personally led his troops into battle, but was eventually forced to flee. The League of Nations condemned Mussolini's actions, but otherwise did nothing to help Selassie. Only in 1941, with the help of the British, did Selassie regain his throne. Many of his followers are Jamaicans and are known as **Rastafarians**, from the original name of their emperor, Ras Tafari. The Rastafarians believe that Negroids are descendants of the Hebrew King Solomon through the Queen of Sheba, whom they believe was Ethiopian, and their son, Menelik I. Rastafarians continue to venerate Haile Selassie as the Messiah. Selassie was, however, a Christian.

The Rome-Berlin Axis Agreement

Thankful for Hitler's public support, and apparently unaware of his private dealings with Ethiopia, Mussolini signed the Rome-Berlin Axis agreement with Hitler. In Asia, Japan was engaged in imperial expansion and joined the Axis.

The Spanish Civil War

Meanwhile, the **Spanish Civil War** raged. Both Hitler and Mussolini gave support to the fascist forces of General **Francisco Franco**, who eventually was the victor in the war.

Hitler Invades Austria

In 1938, Hitler, by threatening invasion, convinced the Austrian chancellor to give control of the government to the Nazis. Hitler then invaded anyway and divided Austria into two provinces, absorbing both into Germany.

Hitler Invades the Sudentenland and Czechoslovakia

Hitler demanded that the Sudetenland, an area of Czechoslovakia with some German-speaking citizens, be given to Germany. This was a more difficult problem than the Austrian situation. Czechoslovakia did not want to cooperate. Their position was strengthened by their alliance with France and by France's agreement with the Soviet Union. If Germany attacked Czechoslovakia, France was obligated to declare war on Germany and the Soviet Union was pledged to come to the defense of France.

Neville Chamberlain, prime minister of Great Britain, negotiated feverishly with Hitler to avert the almost certain war. Chamberlain and France agreed to Germany's immediate annexation of the Sudetenland. Czechoslovakians had no choice, being unable to stand alone in the face of the German army. The Sudetenland went to Hitler. Chamberlain proclaimed that he had achieved "peace with honor" and "peace for our time." Seeing this betrayal of Czechoslovakia as a sign of weakness, Hitler then used his army to occupy the remainder of Czechoslovakia in 1939. The British and French finally realized that appeasement would not work.

CHAPTER 43

WORLD WAR II

HITLER INVADES POLAND

In 1939, Hitler turned his attention to Poland. There were Germans in Danzig. Chamberlain promised that this time there would be no appeasement. If Germany moved into Poland, Britain and France would rise to defend her. Hitler did not believe that Britain and France would take action; they had never made a stand before and he felt certain that he could continue to push and they would continue to give.

Germany's Nonaggression Pact with Stalin

Hitler did not move until he secured a nonaggression pact with Stalin in August 1939. This agreement was to last for ten years. Germany and the Soviet Union each pledged to remain neutral if the other country became involved in a war. The agreement included a secret plan for the division of Eastern Europe between Germany and the Soviet Union. Britain and France had hoped to make Stalin their ally and trap Germany into a potential two-front war. Stalin never trusted the west, and while he did not trust Hitler either, an alliance with Hitler offered territorial gains, while one with the Allies did not.

Britain and France Declare War on Germany

On September 1, 1939, Hitler invaded Poland. Britain and France did not back down and declared war on Germany, officially beginning World War II. Poland was able to fight against the German invasion for just four weeks. The German military used its *blitzkrieg* ("lightning war") tactic of hitting hard and fast in an attempt to so overwhelm the enemy that they could not form a significant defense. After Poland was occupied, Hitler honored his agreement with Stalin. The Soviets took eastern Poland, Lithuania, Estonia, and Latvia.

Dunkirk

The French and British forces dug in to defend France. Germany turned its attention west, launching another *blitzkrieg* through Denmark, Norway, and Holland, then moving through Belgium and finally into France. This divided the British from the French and trapped the British on the coast at Dunkirk. In a famous rescue effort, the British employed practically anything that would float, be it military or civilian, to save its army. The soldiers were brought home, but the loss of equipment and supplies was enormous.

The Vichy Government in France

German forces then took France, something they had not been able to do during the four years of World War I. Marshal Henri-Philippe Petain of France formed the **Vichy** government and accepted defeat. With the defeat of France, Germany occupied most of continental Europe and the rest was in the hands of nations friendly to Germany. In 1940, Hitler controlled northern Europe from the Atlantic to eastern Poland. Italy was firmly in the hands of Mussolini, Spain was in the hands of Franco's fascists, and the Soviets were pleasantly neutral. The only European power opposed to Hitler lay across the English Channel. Chamberlain was out of office. The prime minister of Britain was Winston Churchill, a man who would prove an implacable enemy to Hitler's Germany.

The Battle of Britain

Britain would not cooperate. Britain would not surrender. Germany launched its air attack in what became known as the **Battle of Britain**. German forces hoped to cripple Britain's ability to defend itself or to launch a counter-attack through massive air assaults on British military targets. Britain would then be unable to interfere with Germans forces on the continent and would be crippled in the face of an invasion. Both sides sustained heavy losses, but the British held on. Hitler then made the mistake of ordering the attack to strike civilian targets as well as military ones. He hoped to break the morale of the British people. Instead, this change of tactics steeled the British against the German aggressors. The people pitched in and pulled together. Factories increased production. British pilots flew as if their world depended on them, which it did. By October 1940, German losses in the air outnumbered British losses three to one. The East End of London became a symbol of British defiance, and that defiance became a source of national pride. The air war against Britain was not working for Germany.

THE GERMANS BEGIN THE TWO-FRONT WAR

Instead of trying another means to soften up Britain for invasion, Hitler turned his armies east, to the Soviet Union. This dangerous move ultimately put Germany into a two-front war. Britain had survived the German air onslaught and was steadily building up its forces. Its supply lines had not been cut. The Soviet Union was not as susceptible to the strategy of *blitzkrieg* as was the rest of Europe. The logistics of launching such an attack successfully over the vast distances required to be effective against the Soviet forces made it a long shot at best.

The attack against the Soviet Union began in June 1941, along a broad front. At first, the momentum was with the Germans, and within five months they were threatening Leningrad and Moscow and had taken much of the Ukraine. The Soviets held on, and the winter caught the Germans unprepared. The unforgiving Russian winter punished the Germans and stopped them in their tracks.

THE WAR IN THE PACIFIC AND THE U.S. DECLARATION OF WAR

In the Pacific, the third Axis power, Japan, continued its aggression against China and launched a successful campaign against French Indochina in July 1941. The United States protested this act by cutting off its sales of rubber, iron, oil, and aviation fuel to Japan. On December 7, 1941, Japan replied with the devastating attack on the U.S. fleet at anchor in **Pearl Harbor**. The Japanese attack practically destroyed the naval base. The ships that had been in the harbor were all damaged or destroyed, including the *Arizona*, which was left where it sank in Pearl Harbor as a memorial to the servicemen who lost their lives in that fateful attack. Roosevelt called December 7, 1941, a "date which will live in infamy."

The Japanese navy had planned on destroying the U.S. Pacific fleet, especially its aircraft carriers, but the carriers were not in the harbor at the time. Although the blow Japan struck that day was a heavy one, it was not the crippling stroke they had hoped it would be. The Japanese had hoped to knock the United States out of the war before the United States really had a chance to enter. Instead, the attack, seen as an unprovoked, unannounced, sneak attack on the American people, galvanized support for President Franklin D. Roosevelt and instantly gave him the ability to bring the United States openly into World War II on the side of Britain. The U.S. had been feeding supplies to Britain all along, but public opinion did not support joining the war. The attack on Pearl Harbor changed the face of the war in an instant. Hitler declared war on the United States in support of Japan. Japanese forces moved quickly to conquer more territory in Southeast Asia, from deep in Manchuria in the north, to New Guinea in the south, to Burma in the west, to an area beyond Wake Island in the east. In February 1942, the British surrendered Singapore, a symbol of European power in Asia, to the Japanese. The area was too large, with too much ocean and too many islands to be easily defended.

The United States reacted by rounding up over 120,000 Japanese-Americans in the United States and sending them to camps without charges or trials. Many argue this event represents the most serious civil rights violation in the history of the United States.

Hitler's Racism

As Hitler's army was stalled on the Eastern front, Britain was pulling itself together in the west and the U.S. war machine was now being pushed into war-time production mode, Hitler went ahead with his plans for a German dominated-Europe as if victory was assured. This "New Order" meant that the superior peoples, Germans and their closest kin, the Scandinavians, were treated as privileged people. Slavic peoples were among those considered most inferior, as little better than pack animals, and the Germans treated them accordingly. Those who fell into Nazi hands were treated as disposable slave labor and were worked to death. The French were considered to be better than Slavs, but still definitely inferior to the Germans. They were not treated particularly harshly, but did have to suffer the indignity of paying taxes to fund the German war effort.

The Jews were considered to be so low as to warrant extermination as rapidly as possible, along with Gypsies, Jehovah's Witnesses, and communists. Their rights had been taken away before the war began. The Jews who did not make it out of Germany or the areas conquered by Germany found themselves herded into ghettos, treated as sub-humans, and forced to wear the Star of David to identify themselves as Jews. Then, in 1941, Germany enacted its "**Final Solution**." German forces executed some Jews in the villages where they lived. Nazis shipped others off to the concentration camps where the weak were sent straight to the gas chambers. The Nazis worked the stronger ones until they became weak and died. Some became test subjects in medical experiments. Once dead, the Germans pulled the gold fillings from the victims' teeth and used them to fund the war effort. Germans cremated the bodies in ovens that belched black smoke into the skies day and night over the camps. Germans treated their Jewish victims in much the same way as an animal carcass might be handled and used, because to Hitler and his supporters, Jews were animals who pretended to be people. An estimated six million Jews died at the hands of the Nazis. Although there is a very controversial movement led by David Irving of Britain that denies the reality of the **Holocaust** today, there is so much evidence that the case is very difficult to make. Survivors of Auschwitz, Dachau, Buchenwald, and other infamous camps make it hard to deny the reality of the suffering endured there and of Hilter's "Final Solution." The American professor Deborah Lipstadt has heavily criticized Irving and eventually won a legal suit against him when he accused her of libel in Britain.

Allied Strategy

Britain, the United States, and the Soviet Union now found themselves bound together as allies by their common enemy, the Axis Powers. The United States agreed to join with Britain and the Soviet Union in fighting Germany first, with Japan remaining as the secondary target. The United States became the "arsenal of democracy," giving roughly $50 billion in military aid to its allies. Britain continued to stand firm, and soon U.S. troops and equipment were pouring into the country as Britain and the United States prepared to push against Hitler's Western Front.

On the Eastern Front, the Soviet had regrouped from Germany's initial push into Soviet territory. The Nazi invasion helped spark a nationalistic fire in the hearts of the Russian peoples. They responded to the call of their country with great determination and personal sacrifice. The supply lines to the Red Army kept up a steady flow and, unlike the Germans suffering in the cold, the Soviets were in better shape with each passing day.

There was resistance to Hitler both within the German-occupied territories and within Germany itself. An underground resistance network was formed. Governments in exile from those countries now under German control operated in London, bringing together information to aid the Allied forces.

The Battle of Stalingrad

The standstill on the Eastern Front ended in July 1942 as the Germans mounted a major offensive against **Stalingrad**. The Germans managed to take part of the city, the first time during the war they had managed to actually enter a major Soviet city, and occupied it for a month of intense combat.

The Surrender of the German Sixth Army

The Soviets launched their first major offensive of the war, a counter-attack in November 1942. Facing Romanian and Italian troops, the Soviets dealt with them and quickly positioned themselves to trap the German Sixth Army. When the Sixth finally surrendered in January 1943, only 123,000 of its original 300,000 were left standing. The Soviets had been able to successfully encircle the German Sixth Army because Hitler had refused to allow the army to retreat. The defeat was a hard blow for the Germans. The Soviets now had the momentum and were on the offensive.

War in North Africa

War raged in North Africa as well. At the Battle of El Alamein, the British defeated the German and Italian desert forces. The British also launched attacks in Egypt, and British and American troops landed in Morocco and Algeria. These were French possessions in Africa, and they went willingly over to the Allied side. By spring 1943, the Axis powers were out of Africa.

Fall of Mussolini

With the Axis out of Africa, the Allies could now concentrate on Europe. They launched an invasion through Sicily in 1943 and deposed Mussolini. The new Italian government surrendered unconditionally in September 1943. The Allied victory was short-lived. The Germans launched a counteroffensive, rescued Mussolini, and captured Rome and Northern Italy, and the fighting continued. In the end, Italians killed Mussolini.

D-Day

On June 6, 1944, the Allies launched a massive invasion of Normandy, France, known as **D-Day**. This offensive, launched from Britain, was the beginning of the liberation of France and Western Europe. American and British forces hit the beaches and marched inland. The Allies pushed the Germans slowly back. American General Dwight D. Eisenhower served as supreme commander of the Americans and British. His plan was not to run straight for Berlin, but rather to roll the Germans back all along the front, liberating Europe with the Allied progress. His forces crossed the Rhine in March 1945.

British troops at the Normandy beachhead for
D-Day invasion in France, June 6, 1944.

The Surrender of Germany

The British firebombing raid on Dresden, in February 1945, was the culmination of two years of bombing of German industrial targets. Meanwhile, the Soviets had continued their offensive on the Eastern Front. They made Warsaw in August 1944, and then turned south, clearing the Germans from Romania, Hungary, and Yugoslavia. Then, in January 1945, they turned for Germany once more. The Soviets and Americans met at the Elbe River and the Soviets broke into Berlin. Hitler was not captured, but chose to commit suicide. His aides burned his body to ash. The Germans surrendered on May 7, 1945. May 8, 1945, is celebrated as VE day, or "victory over Europe" day.

The Battle for the Pacific

In the Pacific, the Americans had their fleet able to sail again and stopped the Japanese advance at the fiercely fought Battle of the Coral Sea, in May 1942. In the Battle of Midway, on June 4, 1942, the Japanese navy suffered a devastating blow. The United States had managed to break the Japanese code in an operation known as *Magic*, and knew of Japanese plans to attack Midway. All four of the Japanese aircraft carriers involved in the battle were sunk. The United States, rather than Japan, now had the superior navy in the Pacific. Midway marked the turning point in the war in the Pacific.

In August 1942, land troops finally entered the war in the Pacific. American marines landed on Guadalcanal in one of the most famous and hard fought battles of the war. The Americans and their Australian allies pushed on and forced Japan into fighting a defensive war, using the strategy of "island-hopping," or taking one island at a time. Midway had been the last U.S.-controlled island in the Pacific, but the United States fought bitter battles closer to Japan on Iwo Jima and Okinawa. Joe Rosenthal's Pulitzer-prize-winning photograph

Raising the Flag on Iwo Jima.

of what was actually the second flag raising on Iwo Jima still stands as a symbol of the heroism of the Allied army in the Pacific.

Fighting continued on Okinawa for two months, and the Japanese introduced for the first time *kamikaze* pilots, who flew their planes loaded with just enough fuel to reach Allied ships and then made suicide dives right into them. The Japanese flew over 1,900 *kamikaze* suicide missions and many Okinawans also died in the battle, convincing the United States that victory over Japan would not come quickly or easily. Saipan fell in July 1944, thus bringing the islands of Japan closer to the reach of U.S. bombers. U.S. bombers unleashed a wave of napalm firebombs over Tokyo in March 1945, destroying twenty-five percent of the city's buildings and killing over 100,000 people.

THE ATOMIC BOMB

The war in the Pacific did not look promising. The Allies were making progress, one island at a time, but there was so much territory to retake from the Japanese, and the Japanese put up a determined fight. U.S. President Harry Truman felt the circumstances justified drastic measures. An important consideration was to prevent greater loss of life through months or even years of continued fighting, and thus Truman authorized the use of the **atomic bomb**, developed through the efforts of the Manhattan Project. In August 1945, the first bomb fell on Hiroshima, Japan. It was the first time such a bomb had been used in war in the history of the world. Japan did not surrender. Three days after the Hiroshima bombing, the United Stated dropped a second atomic bomb on Nagasaki, Japan. The world had never seen bombs with the destructive force of these. The cities of Hiroshima and Nagasaki were blown from the face of the earth in an instant. One hundred thousand people were killed in the blink of an eye, and others suffered horrible injuries. Over fifty percent of the population of Hiroshima and Nagasaki in 1945 either died in the attack itself or were dead from thermal and nuclear radiation exposure by 1950. The magnitude of the devastation was shocking, even in comparison to the two days of fire-bombing of Tokyo in March 1945. One hundred thousand people died in the fire bombing of Tokyo, but it took two days and hundreds of tons of bombs to accomplish what two bombs did in a split second. Japan finally surrendered on August, 14, 1945, ending World War II. The war formally ended on September 2, 1945, when Japan signed the terms of surrender aboard the battleship *Missouri*. This date is now celebrated as VJ day, or "victory over Japan" day.

AFTERMATH

Approximately sixty million people died in World War II. The U.S.S.R. lost over twenty million people, only one-third of which were soldiers. China lost fifteen million people, who were primarily civilians. Germany lost four million, while Japan lost two million. Great Britain lost 400,000 and the United States lost 300,000. The Poles suffered the loss of six million inhabitants. Six million European Jews died. Scholars estimate that Nazi persecutions also resulted in the deaths of one million other people from minority groups, including gypsies, homosexuals, Serbs, anti-Nazi political dissidents, and those with mental illnesses. Over 3.3 million Soviet prisoners of war died in Nazi camps, and six million Soviet citizens died. World War II devastated Europe and left it in need of reconstruction. The agreements made by the Allies during and after the war eventually led to the Cold War and the creation of a bipolar world split between the world's democratic superpowers and the world's communist superpowers.

As in World War I, women entered the workforce in great numbers. In the United States, the WAVES, or Women Appointed for Volunteer Emergency Service, made great contributions to naval efforts. WAVES did not, however, engage in direct combat. Many of these women worked on factory assembly lines. In Britain, over 350,000 women contributed to the war effort. In the U.S.S.R. and China, however, women did engage in combat, while in Japan, the government forcibly recruited women to serve in military brothels. Over 300,000 women from ages fourteen to twenty might have served as gifts of the emperor to Japanese troops. Many of these women came from Japanese occupied territories or from colonies. These women were called "**comfort women**," and Japanese soldiers massacred many of them following the war. The Japanese earned a reputation for brutal treatment of women during their occupation of Nanjing, where they engaged in mass rape.

World War II left virtually no one untouched. Attempts such as David Irving's denial of the reality of the Holocaust seem misguided efforts to forget the terrible suffering caused by World War II.

CHAPTER 44

THE COLD WAR

The **Cold War** refers to the conflict between the communist nations of Eastern Europe, led by the Soviet Union, and the western democracies, led by the United States. Although the United States and the Soviet Union were allies during World War II, united to fight Nazi Germany, the two nations were ideological opposites with a deep-seated mistrust of each other.

In 1943, an agreement was reached between Stalin, Roosevelt, and Churchill concerning the conduct of the war. The United States and Britain would launch their offensive against Germany from France, leaving the Soviets to open an offensive on their own in the east.

YALTA

In 1945, the Big Three met again at **Yalta**. Soviet forces controlled Poland, Bulgaria, Hungary, and Romania, as well as parts of Czechoslovakia, Yugoslavia, and Germany, while the forces of Britain and the United States were still struggling to get out of France. At Yalta, they agreed that when victory came, they would divide Germany into zones under the control of the Big Three, and Germany would pay reparations to Russia. Free elections for all the Eastern European countries under Soviet control were guaranteed, but those countries had to remain friendly to the Soviet Union.

Potsdam

The agreement did not hold up for long. Roosevelt, who had been the key figure in trying to work with Stalin and hold the Big Three together, died. When the Big Three met at Potsdam, in July 1945, the new president, Harry Truman, represented the United States. Truman insisted Stalin allow the promised free elections. Stalin refused, as he believed that such elections would result in anti-Soviet governments in the Eastern countries. One reason why Stalin wanted pro-Soviet countries along his western border was that they would serve as a buffer against future German aggression.

Truman and Churchill were in no position to force Stalin to comply. At the same time, they could not simply ignore the situation. Truman cut off U.S. aid to Russia and declared that the United States would not recognize any government that was not freely elected, and so the "Cold War" was on.

THE COLD WAR

Why the "Cold War"? Although armed conflict would erupt around the world between Soviet and U.S.-backed factions, and the leaders of these two nations would engage in tough talk, these two "superpowers" managed to avoid engaging in direct military conflict with each other. Thus, the war was "cold."

The Iron Curtain

Elections in Britain ousted Churchill from office, but he remained adamant in his opposition to Stalin. In one of his most famous speeches, he coined the phrase "the **Iron Curtain**" to describe the division of Europe into free democracies and states under communist control.

Stalin encouraged communist organizations in other countries in Europe and other areas of the world. France, Italy, Greece, Iran, Turkey, and China all felt his influence. The "communist threat" was considered serious enough for Truman to issue his Truman Doctrine.

THE TRUMAN DOCTRINE

The Truman Doctrine was a plan to stop the spread of communism. The plan involved offering military and economic aid where needed. Under the Marshall Plan, military aid went to Greece and Turkey and economic aid to Europe. Stalin refused aid for the Eastern bloc nations. He then solidified his control over them by removing all noncommunists from governmental positions. Such was the case in Soviet-occupied Czechoslovakia, which had attempted to restore a democratic-style government following the war. Stalin opposed any form of democratic government and insisted that the Czechs refuse aid under the Marshall Plan. In 1948, members of the Cabinet who were not communists resigned, hoping to force a new round of elections. Jan Masaryk, the foreign minister, was the only remaining opposition leader. Two weeks after the coup, he fell from a window, in what was the third "defenestration of Prague." Although his own secretary believed that he committed suicide, many have accused Soviet sympathizers of orchestrating the event. The new Czech government then deposed the president, Edvard Benes, and replaced him with the leader of the Czech communist party, Klement Gottwald. The government also imprisoned many advocates of democracy.

Stalin then blocked access to Berlin. The Big Three had divided Germany into zones, each zone controlled by a different nation. Berlin was situated in the zone controlled by the Soviet Union, but was also divided into zones. The United States and its allies launched the **Berlin Airlift** to bring supplies to West Berlin despite the Soviet blockade. The airlift succeeded.

NATO AND THE WARSAW PACTS

In 1949, the United States and its allies formed NATO, the North Atlantic Treaty Organization. Its main purpose was to thwart the advance of communism in Europe. Stalin answered by strengthening his control over Eastern Europe in what would ultimately become known as the **Warsaw Pact** of eastern European nations and the Soviet Union.

THE KOREAN WAR (1950–1953)

The Marshall Plan had failed to stop the spread of communism, and during the period from 1946–1949, the United States had formulated a new policy of "containment." Meanwhile, communism still continued to spread. The revolution in China resulted in a communist government for that country. North Korea, too, was a communist nation. With the support of Russia, North Korea invaded South Korea in 1950. Truman responded with military aid, including troops of fifteen members of the United Nations' countries. General Douglas MacArthur led the United Nations' forces. When he drove the Koreans back past the **38th parallel**, communist China entered on the side of North Korea. Russia provided aid, but did not directly enter the conflict, and the United States chose not to confront them openly in order to avoid a direct conflict. On October 19, 1950, the Chinese assault began under the command of General Peng Dehuai. Some 380,000 People's Liberation Army troops pushed the United Nations' troops back to the 38th parallel. The communist Chinese and North Korean forces captured Seoul on January 4, 1951. United Nations troops were defeated at the battle of Chosin Reservoir. After MacArthur suggested the possible use of atomic weapons, Truman removed him from command in 1951. That same year, peace negotiations started in Kaesong, and parties agreed to a cease-fire. A **demilitarized zone** (**DMZ**) was created around the 38th parallel, which is still in existence today and defended by North Korea on one side and South Korean and American troops on the other. No peace treaty was ever signed; the conflict was officially a police action rather than a war. Japan provided much of the supplies for the conflict; its manufacturing economy grew by over fifty percent in the early stages of the war. The peace treaty of 1951, signed in San Francisco, ended the six years of Allied military occupation since the end of World War II, and restored full sovereignty over Japan and its territorial waters to the Japanese people. According to the treaty, Japan renounced its previous claims to Korea, Taiwan, Formosa, and several other areas; Japan also did not regain her sovereignty over Okinawa and the Ryukyu Islands. The treaty is considered the formal end to the Pacific portion of World War II. Provisions of another treaty signed in the same year between the United States and Japan permitted United States' troops to remain in Japan in order to launch maneuvers in the Korean War.

CASTRO IN CUBA

In 1958, Fidel Castro led his supporters to a successful revolution in Cuba, establishing a communist country within striking distance of the U.S. coastline. Tensions remained high for decades, culminating in the **Bay of Pigs** invasion in April 1961. President John F. Kennedy authorized the invasion of armed Cuban exiles to overthrow the Castro government. The fighting lasted only two days, as the exiles did not receive the support of their fellow Cubans nor of the Americans on the air or on the ground. Castro imprisoned several, but twenty months later he released them in exchange for $53 million worth of food and medical supplies.

The Cuban Missile Crisis

Tension continued to mount, culminating in the **Cuban Missile Crisis**. Under the Soviet leader **Nikita Khrushchev**, sixty ships were sent to Cuba in May 1962, many carrying military material. The Soviets wanted to shift the advantage in the nuclear arena from the United States and place missiles in Cuba. A U-2 flight of October 14 photographed an SS-4 site under construction near San Cristobal. By October 19, surveillance photographs showed four sites operational. While the Soviets had made no special attempt to keep secret their placement of missiles in Turkey, for example, they had not informed Washington of missiles in Cuba. This alarmed the administration, as not only was Cuba well within easy striking distance of the United States, but the United States could not be sure of Khrushchev's motives.

Kennedy addressed the nation on October 22 and announced a naval quarantine or blockade within 500 miles around the Cuban coast. On October 25, Adlai Stevenson brought the case to an emergency session of the United Nations. The Soviets at first denied the charges, but later made two offers of settlement, offering to withdraw their missiles for an American promise not to invade Cuba. In addition, the U.S. was to withdraw missiles from Turkey. On October 27, a U-2 was shot down over Cuba, while Russians almost intercepted another U-2 flying over Russia. After several tense days, Kennedy accepted both offers of the Soviets, and the crisis was over. Khrushchev never recovered politically, since he had not only backed down in the face of U.S. threats but also initiated the crisis in the first place. In 1964, the Politburo removed him from power, and he died under house arrest in Moscow seven years later. Given the proximity of nuclear warheads and the fact that the Soviets had given authorization to the Cubans to use them when deemed necessary, many of Kennedy's advisors believed his response to the crisis was too weak to guarantee national safety. The crisis was clearly the closest that the United States and the Soviets came to nuclear war in the Cold War era, and Kennedy's choice of diplomacy over a military response kept an invasion and conflict from happening. The Cuban Missile Crisis also prompted the two superpowers to seek a better means of communication, and they established a "**hot line**" between Washington and Moscow. The crisis also likely contributed to the development of détente.

THE VIETNAM WAR (1964–1975)

The conflict in Vietnam was also an outgrowth of the Cold War, and, in the U.S., of the belief that once communism was allowed to flourish in South Vietnam, all of the other governments in southeastern Asia, such as those of Thailand, Laos, Cambodia, Malaysia, and Indonesia, would fall to communism. This idea was known as the "domino theory." The United States, the Republic of Vietnam or South Vietnam, Australia, and South Korea fought against the Democratic Republic of Vietnam or North Vietnam and the National Liberation Front, a South Vietnamese guerrilla movement led by communists. The Russians provided aid to the North Vietnamese, but, as in the Korean conflict, did not directly participate in hostilities.

The First Indochina War

The origins of the war go back to the French struggle in the First Indochina War against communist party leader **Ho Chi Minh**, who led a movement for independence of the colony from France. The Vietnamese communist forces, or Viet Minh, defeated the French army at the Battle of Dien Bien Phu, in 1954. Following this event, the French granted the colony independence. At a settlement reached in Geneva, Vietnam was divided into a communist North and a noncommunist South, with hopes that the South would be a democracy. Elections in 1956 were intended to unify the two Vietnams, but the southern President Diem and President Eisenhower of the United States worried about a possible victory for Ho Chi Minh and the elections were never held.

The Viet Cong

The communists in the North launched a guerilla movement against the South known as the National Liberation Front. This movement was also known in the United States and in South Vietnam as the **Viet Cong**, from *Viet Nam Cong San*, meaning "Vietnamese Communist." The United States began sending support to the South, while the U.S.S.R. and the North Vietnamese communists provided arms, advisors, and military to the Viet Cong along the Ho Chi Minh trail.

The Gulf of Tonkin Resolution

The United States never declared war in Vietnam. In 1964, the Senate approved the *Gulf of Tonkin Resolution*, which authorized the use of armed forces in support of freedom in Southeast Asia. On March 8, 1965, President Lyndon Baines Johnson sent 3,500 marines to South Vietnam, which escalated to over 500,000 troops by 1968. The commander of the U.S. forces was General William Westmoreland.

The Tet Offensive

The guerilla war in Vietnam was very difficult to win, and although victory often seemed near, it never came. On January 30, 1968, the Tet Offensive in South Vietnam suggested renewed vigor at a time when the American public desperately wanted an end to the conflict. Opposition further increased with the My Lai massacre, in which forces led by Lt. William Calley entered a village and massacred Vietnamese civilians, including children.

The Nixon Doctrine

By 1968, President Johnson was in political trouble, and eventually announced he would not seek reelection. Robert Kennedy, who might have drawn on the mystique of his brother, the former president, ran for the nomination, but his bid was cut short when he was assassinated by Sirhan Sirhan. Richard Nixon, a Republican, won the presidency, and initiated the Nixon Doctrine, according to which South Vietnam would be enabled to fight on its own. Although he gradually withdrew troops from Vietnam, Nixon continued air raids and more U.S. servicemen eventually died during his presidency than during Johnson's tenure in office. Nixon also pardoned Lt. Calley, who led the My Lai massacre.

In 1970, Nixon ordered a strike in Cambodia against the Viet Cong. Protests against U.S. involvement in Vietnam had been escalating since 1966, but the events at Kent State, in 1970, horrified many Americans, who were having increasing difficulties understanding the goals of the conflict and Washington's justification of its decisions. When several students on the campus of Kent State University protested the war, the National Guard was called in and several students were literally shot down.

The conflict further escalated in 1971, when South Vietnam invaded Laos with the help of the United States. Although George McGovern ran as an anti-war candidate against Nixon in 1972, Nixon triumphed and ended heavy bombing in North Vietnam that same year. In 1973, the Paris Peace Accords officially ended U.S. involvement in Vietnam, and, in 1975, Congress made the end more official when it refused further aid to South Vietnam.

The North Vietnamese invaded South Vietnam in 1975, captured Saigon, and formed the Socialist Republic of Vietnam in 1976. Saigon became Ho Chi Minh City, a painful reminder of the failure of the United States in Vietnam to stop the spread of communism.

Meanwhile, the communist Khmer Rouge seized power in Cambodia in 1975, beginning the infamous reign of terror of Pol Pot, who tried to return Cambodia to its ancient agricultural ways and to wipe out its religion. By the end of his regime, he had exterminated a sizeable proportion of Cambodia's population in the infamous killing fields.

CHALLENGES TO THE SUPERPOWERS

The Cold War, which polarized the world in a standoff between communism and democracy, renewed desires of Europe to assert itself. Under President Charles de Gaulle, France resisted attempts of Americans to dominate Europe. They feared that American protection would be insufficient against the threat of nuclear attack by Russia, and also wished to regain the status they had enjoyed before the world wars. The French wanted independence from NATO, and, in 1963, refused to sign a treaty banning the testing of nuclear weapons. In 1964, they detonated their first atomic bomb in the Sahara Desert. Over the next four years, the French created a *force de frappe*, or nuclear strike force, which they hoped would encourage other European nations to disengage from NATO and American domination.

Yugoslavia

Meanwhile, the Soviet Union's influence was also challenged. In Yugoslavia, **Marshal Tito** (Joseph Broz) ruled from 1945 until 1980, and fought for Yugoslavian independence from Soviet control. In 1948, Stalin ousted Yugoslavia from the Soviet Bloc.

Rise of Khrushchev and de-Stalinization

In the Soviet Union itself, Nikita Khrushchev took control after Stalin's death in 1953 and attempted to "de-Stalinize" Russia. He ended Stalin's reign of terror and freed many prisoners from Siberian camps, such as Alexander

Solzhenitsyn. Solzhenitsyn won the Nobel Prize for literature in 1970 for many of his works depicting the horrors of Stalin's prison camps.

Solidarity in Poland

Eventually, though, communism began to crumble in the Eastern Bloc. The realities of communist society had never matched the ideals. By the 1980s, economic problems sparked public unrest. Poland was the first to break ranks with the Soviet Union and hold free elections. These elections were the result of revolutionary activity by Solidarity, the workers' union turned political party led by **Lech Walesa**, and **Mikhail Gorbachev**, the new leader of the Soviet Union. Gorbachev was less reactionary and more tolerant than were his predecessors. He could have attempted to use the Soviet military to violently put down any uprisings in Eastern Europe. Instead, he pledged to honor the wishes of the people of the Eastern Bloc nations by ending the Brezhnev Doctrine of 1968 of combating antisocialist forces.

Czechoslovakia and the Velvet Revolution

The revolution in Poland was followed by revolutionary actions in Czechoslovakia, where Alexander Dubcek led reforms in 1968 known as the Prague Spring. These ended when the Soviet Union invaded Prague and took Dubcek to Moscow to force him to accept Soviet demands. Responding to Gorbachev's new policy of openness, in 1989, the Velvet Revolution, a peaceful movement, took power and ousted the communists and held democratic elections. In 1993, Czechoslovakia split into the Czech Republic and Slovakia.

Hungary

The communist regime in Hungary had embraced the de-Stalinization movement, but its citizens wanted a democracy. Massive rebellions ensued, and the Hungarian army joined the people in their effort to overthrow Soviet influence. Imre Nagy and János Kádár formed a new government that declared neutrality and withdrew from the Warsaw Pact. In 1956, the Soviets invaded, executed Nagy in secret, and installed Kádár as a puppet leader loyal to the Soviets. Gorbachev's new policy of openness in the late 1980s resulted in reform in Hungary. In 1989, the Communist government initiated reforms that led to a multiparty system and competitive elections.

The Fall of the Berlin Wall

The fall of communism in Hungary opened once again the border between Hungary and Austria. Hungary allowed East Germans to pour over the border to Austria and to freedom in the west. Back in East Berlin, resistance to the communist government grew, and, by 1990, the Berlin Wall fell. A few months later Germany was once again a united country for the first time since the end of World War II.

Romania

Romania was not so fortunate. The Romanian military violently resisted the attempt to overthrow the communist government of **Nicolae Ceausescu**. Eventually, anticommunist forces won the day and arrested and executed Ceausescu.

Détente

The many difficulties faced by the superpowers in the Cold War eventually led them to agree to **détente**, or a reduction in hostilities, in the 1960s. In 1973 and 1974, Soviet and U.S. leaders began to agree to a number of treaties, the most important being the SALT treaties growing out of the Strategic Arms Limitation Talks. By the end of the 1970s, however, détente was weakening, as the U.S. established full diplomatic relations with the People's Republic of China in 1979, and announced the sale of weapons to the Chinese military in 1980. Both events created hostility among the Soviets.

The Soviets in Afghanistan

In December 1979, the Soviets invaded Afghanistan, further creating renewed tension with the United States. In 1978, a pro-Soviet faction of Muslims took power as the People's Democratic Party of Afghanistan. The PDPA implemented radical reforms, leading to massive protests from Islamic leaders. By 1979, the rebellions had become so intense that the Soviets intervened and installed Babrak Karmal as president. He was a confirmed Marxist. The United States supplied ground-to-air missiles to the **mujahideen**, the Islamic resistance in the countryside. In 1986, the Soviets replaced Karmal, who had not succeeded in pacifying the revolt, with Muhammad Najibullah, who had been head of the Afghan Secret Police and who had a close working relationship with the Soviets. This move was not successful either, and so, in 1988, the Soviets agreed to a cease-fire in the United Nations, and, in 1989, withdrew their forces. The mujahideen, however, disintegrated into tribal and ethnic factions who warred against one another. In 1996, the **Taliban**, an army of religious students, took Kabul and executed Najibullah. So was born the Islamic State of Afghanistan. In 2003, the United States toppled the regime, accusing it of harboring the terrorists of the radical al-Qaeda organization responsible for the terrorist actions in the United States on September 11, 2001. The al-Qaeda evolved out of the mujahideen, and, ironically, the U.S. helped to train and provided weapons for many of their terrorists.

President Ronald Reagan

President Ronald Reagan also contributed heavily to the deterioration of Soviet-U.S. relations through his description of the U.S.S.R. as the "evil empire." He supported a massive military budget and the creation of the Strategic Defense Initiative, or Star Wars, a system that allegedly would have provided protection from nuclear attack.

The Philippines

Surprisingly, Reagan, who had funneled arms to the Contra in Nicaragua in an effort to halt what he perceived as Sandinista support of communism, also supported the regime of **Ferdinand Marcos**, one of the world's most hated and notorious dictators. Marcos was elected president of the Philippines in 1965 and became the first president to be reelected in 1969. He implemented educational and agricultural reforms and earned the support of the United States as a result of his anticommunist rhetoric. In 1972, he declared martial law and dissolved the democratic political institutions of the Philippines. The regime also did not respect human rights. While the people of the Philippines suffered, Imelda Marcos flaunted her thousands of pairs of shoes. The Communist New People's Army and the Muslim Moro National Liberation Front led fierce resistance to Marcos, and, in 1981, he declared an end to martial law and began to restore "democratic" reforms. His problems increased when Benigno Aquino was assassinated at the Manila airport in August 1983. In 1986, Aquino's wife, Corazon, won election as the new president of the Philippines. President Reagan asked Mrs. Aquino to attempt to reconcile with Marcos, as he respected Marcos for his fight against communism, but the people of the Philippines had the final say.

The Fall of the Soviet Union

In the Soviet Union itself, Gorbachev was caught between opposing groups—those who wanted to end communism and those who wanted to take a hard line and crack down on those who would end communist control. In 1986, Gorbachev initiated a radical period of reform by **glasnost**, or "openness," and **perestroika**, or "restructuring." In 1988, Gorbachev abandoned the policies of Brezhnev and allowed the Eastern Bloc countries to move away from communism and even to adopt democracy. This move encouraged many of the revolutions described above, and Gorbachev received the Nobel Peace prize in 1990.

In 1990, Gorbachev was elected as the first executive president of the Soviet Union, but Gorbachev seemed to be leaning towards ending communism, and, in 1991, a force of communist hardliners kidnapped him and detained him in the Crimea. Boris Yeltsin, elected president of Russia in 1991, rushed to the White House in Moscow and convinced some of the armed forces to switch sides. He sent forces to rescue Gorbachev, who returned and arrested the Gang of Eight that had led the attempt to oust him. Yeltsin, who had urged Gorbachev to more reform, outlawed communism in Russia. In 1991, the Ukraine voted for independence, and soon thereafter the presidents of Russia, Ukraine, and Belarus created the Commonwealth of Independent States. As Russia was, in fact, the very heart of the Soviet Union, this was the death blow for the U.S.S.R. By 1991, the Soviet Union no longer existed and Gorbachev resigned. Boris Yeltsin served as president of Russia until December 31, 1999, and Russia took the place of the U.S.S.R. in the United Nations.

Today, most of the former Soviet republics are now part of the Commonwealth of Independent States. With the fall of the stronghold of communism, the Cold War ended. It is ironic that although Yeltsin fought for the independence of Russia, he bitterly repressed the revolts in Chechnya, whose population is largely made up of Sunni Muslims who declared independence from Russia in 1991. The situation there has reached genocidal proportions. Vladimir Putin succeeded Yeltsin as Prime Minister.

CHAPTER 45

DEVELOPMENTS IN THE POST-WORLD WAR II ERA IN CHINA, INDIA, THE MIDDLE EAST, LATIN AMERICA, AND AFRICA

CHINA AFTER WORLD WAR II

Taiwan

In the wake of World War II, the nationalist and communist Chinese attempted to reach an agreement about the future of China. In 1947 and 1948, however, the communists defeated the nationalists in several engagements. By 1949, the **People's Liberation Army**, or the communist forces, controlled most of the Chinese mainland. The nationalists, still led by Jiang Jieshe (Chiang Kai Shek), fled to Taiwan, and proclaimed his government there the legitimate government of China. Most of the country's gold resources went with him.

The People's Republic of China

On October 1, 1949, **Mao Zedong** established the People's Republic of China, led by the Chinese communist party. Chairman Mao reformed Chinese society, using Soviet Russia as his model. The close relationship between the Soviets and the communist Chinese resulted in Soviet support for the removal of Taiwan on the Security Council of the United Nations. Approximately one-half of Chinese exports went to the U.S.S.R., and the Soviets further supported the development of communism in China with loans. Later, the Chinese argued that the Soviets had not helped enough, especially in their quest to reassert authority in **Tibet**. The Soviets remained neutral in this conflict and even made loans to India. The Chinese believed India helped to encourage the rebellion of Tibetans. Although the relationship between China and the Soviet Union broke down in the 1960s, the Soviet model profoundly influenced Mao's programs in China.

A new constitution took effect in 1954. One of the most significant reforms of this period was the attempt to create greater equality for women and to make them productive members of the workforce. Forced marriages were outlawed, as was foot binding and other repressive measures. The advancement of women was one of Mao's greatest achievements. Women of the Mao era remain committed to reform and professional advancement today, whereas many younger women have returned to a desire to be homemakers.

In other areas, Mao was not as successful. As in the U.S.S.R., the Communist Party controlled the nation through its Central Committee and Politburo, but the constitution did create, at least on paper, a national assembly to be chosen through popular election. Just as Stalin had purged all those who opposed him, Mao and his followers purged China of nationalist supporters and others who opposed their policies. In 1951, for example, he executed thousands of Chinese and thrust many more into labor camps.

Mao introduced his own version of the Five-Year Plans in 1955. Like Stalin, Mao wanted to transform China into an industrial nation that was self-sufficient. The policies of the first plan mimicked those of Stalin by focusing on heavy industry to the detriment of the production of consumer goods and equalizing land holdings in the countryside. Even today, as one travels through rural China, one sees peasants with their small strips of land in the villages. Each peasant received an equal amount of land.

The Great Leap Forward

Mao's **Great Leap Forward** (1958–1961) moved the country further on the road to industrialization. Private farms were abolished, and collective farms eventually marketed the goods produced on these lands. Just as Stalin's attempt to collectivize the farms of Russia resulted in disaster, so did Mao's Great Leap Forward really result in a "great leap backward." Production fell as the peasants could not meet quotas, and a series of bad harvests doomed the program. Mao refused to accept responsibility and blamed the failures on the eating habits of sparrows, to which he referred as "counterrevolutionaries." When he ordered sparrows killed, he left the way open for insects to devour the remaining crops. By 1962, The Great Leap Forward had created a situation in which twenty million Chinese had died of starvation.

The Great Proletarian Cultural Revolution

Mao's Great Proletarian **Cultural Revolution** (1966–1976) was another attempt to weed out opposition to his reforms. He had accused the Soviets, by this time, of being revisionists, a term that was very offensive within the communist world. Now, he found revisionists throughout China, and targeted the intellectuals, professionals, and others associated with foreign influences or bourgeois values. The so-called "revolution" set China back many years as it stripped China of its educated population and sent thousands to jails, rural labor camps, or their deaths.

Deng Xiaoping

Chairman Mao died in 1976, having brought China to its knees. Deng Xiaoping took power in 1981 and began a series of reforms known as "Deng's revolution." Deng reversed the isolationism of Mao Zedong, and allowed foreign capitalist investments in China. He also permitted many Chinese students to study at foreign universities. Here, they were exposed to new views, such as democracy, and, in 1997, students staged a sit-down protest at **Tiananmen Square** in Beijing in front of the Forbidden Palace, once home to the emperors of China. Deng Xiaoping had himself been persecuted and condemned to labor during the Mao era, and he feared revolutionary movements of any kind. He responded with vicious force to the students in Tiananmen, mowing them down with tanks and guns. Many students died, while reporters filmed the events and showed them to a worldwide audience.

Return of Hong Kong and Macao

When Deng died in 1997, China was changing rapidly. The British abided by earlier treaties and returned Hong Kong to Chinese rule. Deng promised a "one country, two systems" style of rule, according to which the Chinese socialist system would not be implemented in Hong Kong. Macao would soon follow, in 1999, from the Portuguese. Deng had allowed China to enter the worldwide economy, and the return of its possessions from the European colonizers forced him to address issues for which Mao's isolationism had left no precedents. China continued to progress toward global superpower economic status, and, in 2001, China joined the World Trade Organization.

INDIA AFTER WORLD WAR II

Indians continued to resist British Imperialism in India following World War II. World Wars I and II unleashed a tidal wave of colonial revolts, which resulted in the end of British rule in India after World War II. The Indian National Congress had failed to coalesce the Indians into a unified front, as Muslims disagreed with Hindus over the fate of India. The British made few attempts to reconcile the two groups, and in the end, made decisions that ensured a permanent split.

The Great Calcutta Killing

The leader of the Muslim League, Muhammad Ali Jinnah, advocated a Day of Direct Action in 1946, and as rioting erupted, approximately 6,000 people died in the **Great Calcutta Killing**. Jinnah took a hard line stance on the issue of Indian independence, rejecting any possibility that Hindus and Muslims might live and work together to build a new and united India. According to him, the only solution was a separate state for Muslims, Pakistan.

Partition of India

Other Indian leaders, such as Mohandas Gandhi and Jawaharlal Nehru, did not want to see India partitioned. On August 15, 1947, however, Britain partitioned India into two separate regions, and Pakistan was born. Gandhi called the event a vivisection, the cutting up of a living body. By 1948, ten million Muslims or Hindus had migrated to either India or Pakistan, amidst tremendous violence. Gandhi went on hunger strikes to persuade Indians to follow *ahimsa*, or nonviolence, but in the end he fell to the violent outbursts and was assassinated by a gunman.

Nehru

Nehru, devastated by the death of Gandhi, then pursued a policy of non-alignment with the superpowers of the Cold War, which he articulated most clearly at the Bandung Conference in April 1955. At the Bandung Conference, twenty-three Asian and six African leaders met to formulate a "third path," or an alternative to alliance with either of the superpowers of the Cold War.

Unfortunately, Nehru could not stop the violence between Hindus and Muslims, and war erupted between India and Pakistan over the province of Kashmir in 1947. Pakistan lost its bid to annex the province, and then turned to the United States for help. Nehru accepted help from the Soviets, but continued to pursue his policy of neutrality.

Indira Gandhi

Nehru's daughter Indira Gandhi became prime minister in 1966, and twice served in that capacity. She attempted to revive Indian agriculture through the "Green Revolution," but her policies created further misery among the poor. Overpopulation contributed to the problem, and, in 1975, she declared a state of national emergency. Her methods during the next two years were repressive, as she forced millions to undergo involuntary sterilization. In 1977, elections ousted her from office. She returned in 1980, but now faced growing rebellion from the Sikhs. She ordered an attack on the Sikh temple in Amristar, and as a result, two of her Sikh bodyguards assassinated her in 1984.

Her son Rajiv Gandhi attempted to resolve the Sikh situation, but he was assassinated in 1991.

THE MIDDLE EAST AFTER WORLD WAR II

Jordan

Jordan gained independence from Britain in 1946, and King Hussein ruled there until he died in 1999. King Hussein was a member of the Hashemite monarchy, whose origins date back to Muhammad's great grandfather, Hashim.

Syria

After World War I, the League of Nations created a French mandate in Syria, but when France fell in 1940 during World War II, they eventually had to evacuate Syria. In 1946, Syria's republican government, formed during the mandate period, took control of the new country.

Iraq

After World War I, the League of Nations created a British mandate in Iraq and carved Iraq from Ottoman territories. Britain installed the brother of the king of Jordan, Emir Faisal ibn Husayn, as leader there. In 1921, the Iraqis later elected and proclaimed him king. The discovery of huge oil fields near Kirkuk helped Iraq considerably, though the British-dominated firm, the Iraqi Petroleum Company, had the rights to develop the fields. The British mandate in Iraq ended in 1932. In 1945, Iraq joined the United Nations and helped to found the Arab League. In 1958, a coup d'etat overthrew the monarch in Iraq and established the Republic of Iraq led by Abdul-Karim Qassem, who was known as "il-Za`im."

Kuwait and Iraq

In 1961, Kuwait gained independence from Britain, but the Iraqis attempted to annex it. The British sent forces, and, in 1963, Iraq was forced to recognize the sovereignty of Kuwait. In 1963, the Ba'ath party overthrew Qassem's government following his assassination. Nine months later, the Ba'ath were overthrown as well, but, in 1968, they retook the government. Ahmed Hasan al Bakh led the government, and, in 1979, the United States supported Saddam Hussein, who succeeded al Bakh as president and chairman of the Revolutionary Command Council. Hussein fought a bitter war with Iran (1980–1988), and became the strongest military power in the Persian Gulf.

Invasion of Kuwait

In 1990, Iraq invaded Kuwait, accusing it of not respecting Iraq's borders. The United Nations condemned the invasion, delivered an ultimatum, and authorized a complete embargo on trade with Iraq. Hussein failed to be moved, and, in 1991, the United States launched **Operation Desert Storm**, which pushed Iraq out of Kuwait in just over a month. On the way out of Kuwait, Iraqi troops set fire to several hundred oil wells and fields, creating one of the worst ecological disasters of the century.

The United Nations continued to impose strict embargoes on Iraq through resolution 661. Hussein's brutal use of chemical weapons on the Kurds in the north led the United States to declare "air exclusion zones." The development of chemical and biological weapons continued to worry the United States, finally culminating in the 2003 invasion.

In 1993, an assassination attempt failed against former President George H. W. Bush, and President Clinton bombed the Iraqi Intelligence Headquarters in Baghdad. Hussein's rule became more brutal when his two sons, Uday and Qusay, were given vice-presidential authority in 1995. They ruthlessly purged all dissidents and others who had offended the family in any way. In 2003, the administration of President George W. Bush argued that Hussein had continued to develop weapons of mass destruction in violation of a United Nations Resolution. The U.S. decision to invade Iraq in 2003 without the sanction of the United Nations Security Council remains one of the most controversial military actions of the recent past. The Security Council was deeply divided on the issue of the invasion of Iraq, and while the Bush administration maintained that Iraq posed a serious threat, various intelligence sources contradicted the Bush administration, arguing that the regime had not continued to develop weapons of mass destruction and that Hussein posed no imminent threat. Further, several high-ranking officials in the U.S. government, as well as numerous reporters, accused President Bush of erroneously claiming in his State of the Union address in 2003 that the Hussein regime had sought supplies for nuclear weapons in Africa.

Operation Iraqi Freedom

Hussein's brutal regime controlled Iraq until the United States and Great Britain, along with help from Australia and a few other minor forces, defeated Hussein in Operation Iraqi Freedom in 2003. As of October 2003, no credible evidence of the existence of weapons of mass destruction has been found, and the United States is still attempting to establish order in Iraq. There have been as many as 9,000 civilian casualties in Iraq since the United States began the invasion. On July 22, 2003, a United States occupation force in Iraq killed Uday and Qusay Hussein after an informant turned them in for a reward. The former dictator himself was captured on December 13, 2004.

Iran

Iran was called Persia until 1935. In 1953, the United States Central Intelligence Agency, with help from the British, put Mohammad Reza Pahlavi in power as the Shah of Iran and supported his controversial regime. The Shah was an abusive dictator at home who did not respect civil liberties. Under his regime, Iranians were tortured, and there were numerous other human rights violations. Eventually, Iranians rebelled and overthrew the regime in 1979. The **Ayatollah Khomeini** took power and established a strict Shi'ite state, the Islamic Republic of Iran. In 1979, resentment of U.S. support of the Shah led to the capture of the U.S. embassy in Tehran. For two years, Shi'ite militants held U.S. hostages. President Jimmy Carter's covert attempt to rescue the hostages was a disaster, and combined with economic and other difficulties at home, the Iranian hostage crisis helped to usher him out of office. The hostages finally returned home during the early presidency of Ronald Reagan. After Khomeini's death in 1989, Iran relaxed some of its conservative tendencies. Since the fall of Saddam Hussein, however, the Shi'ite population of Iran has attempted to influence the largely Shi'ite population of southern Iraq.

THE CREATION OF ISRAEL AND THE PROBLEM OF PALESTINE

Zionism

Since the 1890s, **Zionism** had been an important movement in Europe. Zionists fought against anti-Semitism and sought to create a homeland for Jews, an idea first suggested by Theodor Herzl, a Hungarian Jew, in *Der Judenstaat* (1896). Hertzl organized the first Zionist World Congress (1897), which created the World Zionist Organization.

At first, their interests were not in Palestine, as they planned the creation of a Jewish state in Africa, but various factions within the movement returned to biblical teachings developed after the return of the Jews from the Babylonian Captivity. At this time in antiquity, biblical Scriptures reflected a growing emphasis on Jerusalem, first established by King David and the capital of the southern Hebrew Kingdom of Judah. Gradually, the focus of Zionism became Palestine. Some Jews continued to believe that the Jewish nation would return to their homeland only with the coming of the messiah, and these Jews opposed the radical Zionist movement.

Other Jews, however, saw occupation of this land as necessary to their salvation. These Jews called Palestine *Eretz Yisrael*, a term that referred to the ancient Hebrew kingdoms. The land ruled by the two ancient kingdoms encompassed the modern state of Israel, but also the West Bank and Gaza Strip, as well as parts of modern Jordan, Syria, and Lebanon. Some Jews believe that the end of the world will come when the Jews once again occupy their ancient homeland, and this belief has, in part, led to many conflicts between Jews and Arabs and to what many scholars of the Middle East interpret as expansionistic behavior.

Balfour Declaration

The **Balfour Declaration** (1917) promised to establish a secure homeland for Jews in Palestine, and this declaration was supported at the Paris Peace talks following World War I. After World War I, the League of Nations established, in 1922, a British mandate in Palestine. A mandate was a territory surrendered by Turkey or Germany to the victorious allies in World War I and governed by a European power.

Increased Jewish Immigration and Arab Resistance

Arabs resented both the British and the Jewish settlers and rioting erupted in the 1920s and 1930s. As World War II progressed and Hitler's Final Solution threatened the very existence of European Jewry, Jews flocked in increasing numbers to Palestine. Simultaneously, rising Arab nationalism in the wake of the formation of Arab states after World War II contributed to the hostility. The British tried to allay Arab fears by limiting Jewish immigration. Leon Uris's *Exodus*, a fictionalized account of the many Jews forced to enter Palestine illegally due to British blockades, portrays the Catch-22 that entrapped all parties. In 1945, Jewish resistance to British rule began in earnest, led by the Haganah, an underground military organization founded to protect Jewish settlers and refugees. By 1947, the British announced their intention to withdraw and allow the United Nations to decide the matter.

Creation of Israel

The U.N. proposed to divide the area into a Jewish and Palestine state and, before the Arab outcry could even be heard and the matter further debated, Jews took matters into their own hands and announced, in May 1948, the creation of the state of Israel.

Arab-Israeli Wars

Arab states mobilized in support of the Palestinians, and Egypt, Syria, Jordan, and Iraq declared war on Israel. The Arab-Israeli wars had begun. Nevertheless, in 1949, the U.N. forged a truce and partitioned Palestine. Significantly, Jerusalem was partitioned between Israel and Jordan, with Jordan in control of East Jerusalem. The West Bank went to Jordan, while the Gaza Strip went to Egypt. Israel controlled the coastal areas of Palestine and the Negev Desert to the Red Sea. Many Palestinians fled their homelands and sought refuge in other Arab lands.

EGYPT

Nasser

Led by Gamul Abdel Nasser, the Egyptians deposed King Farouk in 1952. Nasser wanted to unite and lead the Arab world against the Israelis. Nasser also refused to become allied with any of the superpowers of the Cold War, and terminated British rights to the **Suez Canal** in 1954. In 1956, he nationalized the canal, resulting in the combined attack of British, French, and Israeli forces. The United States condemned the military invasion of Egypt, and so did the Soviets. The forces withdrew, and Nasser became the acknowledged moral leader of the Arab world. Nevertheless, Israel had not been toppled, and both the United States and the U.S.S.R. supported its right to exist.

The Six-Day and Yom Kippur Wars

In 1967, Israel defeated Egypt and Syria in the **Six-Day War**, and created further tension when it occupied the Gaza Strip, Golan Heights, the West Bank (formerly a territory of Jordan), and the Sinai Peninsula. The loss of the Sinai meant loss of access to the Suez Canal. Egypt lost again to the Israelis in the 1973 **Yom Kippur War**, and its attack on Israel on Yom Kippur, a major holy day for Jews, brought tremendous condemnation. It had, however, managed to regain a portion of the Sinai Peninsula. As a result of a 1979 peace treaty, Israel withdrew from the Sinai entirely by 1981.

Anwar Sadat

During the succeeding presidency of Anwar Sadat, the U.S. President Jimmy Carter initiated the Camp David talks, which resulted in the **Camp David Peace Accords** with Israel, led by Prime Minister Menahem Begin.

Sadat was assassinated, however, in 1981, and many planks of the peace accords were never enacted. In retaliation, the Arab states and the PLO attempted to isolate Egypt.

The Intifada

Palestinians have launched several uprisings, **or intifada** ("shaking off"), against Israeli occupation of the West Bank and the Gaza Strip. In 1987, a massive rebellion began on the Gaza Strip as a result of the stabbing of an Israeli while shopping in Gaza. One day later, four residents of the Jabalya refugee camp in Gaza died in a traffic accident. Rumors spread that Israelis had killed them. While the violence was at first spontaneous, it later became more organized, as protestors bombarded the Israeli troops with Molotov cocktails and other devices. The intifada dissipated by 1990, but it created a new center of resistance independent of the PLO.

PLO and Israeli Peace Treaties

In 1993 and 1994, however, the leader of the **Palestine Liberation Organzation**, Yasser Arafat, was willing to negotiate. Yitzhak Rabin, the prime minister of Israel, and Arafat secretly negotiated a peace agreement, the Oslo Accords, whereby there would be limited Palestinian self-rule in territories occupied by Israel. This led to the creation, in 1994, of the Palestine National Authority (PNA) to administer the West Bank and Gaza Strip, and plans were that eventually the PNA would become an independent Palestinian state. Transfer of power and territory was to occur in stages, but an interim period of self-government was proclaimed. Many Jews were outraged by Rabin's attempts to make peace, as they believed it threatened Israel's security and also meant the loss of numerous Israeli settlements in those areas. In 1995, a Jewish extremist assassinated Rabin. The peace process seemed hopelessly stalled when the Israelis sent occupation forces in 2002 into the PNA.

The peace plan had failed, and although efforts to achieve peace between Israel and the Palestinians continue, no agreements have been reached. Prime Minister Benjamin Netanyahu attempted to galvanize the United States and other powers against terrorism, further aggravating Palestinian and Israeli peace talks. When the Palestinians elected a new prime minister, Mahmud Abbas, hopes were that the peace process would accelerate. However, the current prime minster of Israel, Ariel Sharon, has often expressed the belief that peace is impossible between Arabs and Jews. Sharon has authorized the construction of a barrier to separate the Israelis from the PNA and also the Gaza Strip. Palestinians and human rights activists throughout the world have criticized this action as a serious threat to the peace process.

Lebanon

Lebanon became a French mandate following World War I. It declared independence in 1943, and the French withdrew in 1946, after World War II.

Tension between various groups has always been present in Lebanon. In 1958, U.S. marines were sent to help the Lebanese put down an insurrection, and the arrival of Palestinian refugees from the 1967 Arab-Israeli war further complicated the situation.

The Palestine Liberation Organization

Yasser Arafat was one of those who fled to Lebanon, and eventually his Palestine Liberation Organization (PLO) established headquarters in Beirut and Damascus (Syria). The PLO was founded in 1964 and joined the Arab League in 1976. It launched a wave of terrorist activity. Its agitation for Palestinian autonomy ultimately led to the creation of the Palestinian National Authority in 1994.

Civil War

Tension between Christians and Muslims increased and erupted in 1975 in civil war. Various Muslim factions fought against the predominantly Christian Lebanese army. An Arab Deterrent Force headed by Syria arrived to help calm the situation, but when the PLO blew up a bus in Israel, the Israelis launched Operation Litani and invaded in 1978. During the operation, Israelis massacred civilian inhabitants of three villages at Abbasieh, Khiam, and Kawnin. The United Nations issued a resolution calling for Israel to withdraw, which it did. However, it left an ally, the South Lebanon Army, to protect a buffer zone between Lebanon and Israel.

PLO Occupies South Lebanon

In 1981, the PLO occupied south Lebanon and escalated terrorist attacks against Israel. The PLO and other factions virtually tore Lebanon to shreds and it had no effective government. Although the U.S. negotiated a cease-fire in 1981, the PLO continued to shell Israel.

Operation Peace for Galilee

In 1982, Israel launched Operation Peace for Galilee against the PLO. Within six months, the Israelis withdrew, again leaving the South Lebanon Army in charge of a smaller buffer zone. In 1982, the United States again attempted to intervene and established a multinational force, including U.S. marines, in Lebanon. Syrian and PLO forces were to withdraw from Beruit.

Two Governments in Lebanon

Lebanon elected a candidate supported by the Israeli president, but he was soon assassinated, and the Israelis entered West Beirut. The Israeli army took no action as the Lebanese Christian militias massacred almost 800 Palestinian civilians in the Sabra and Shatila refugee camps. Ariel Sharon, the Israeli Minister of Defense, was indirectly blamed for the incident and forced to resign.

TERRORISM ON THE RISE IN 1983 AND 1984

During this period, significant terrorist attacks occurred against the United States, including a suicide bombing at the U.S. Embassy in West Beirut.

Hizballah

The terrorist organization **Hizballah** also emerged during this period from militant Shi'ite groups who were opposed to intervention from the United States and Israel, and they bitterly resented perceived advantages of this foreign aid for the Christian population of Lebanon. Syria and Iran supported the Hizballah.

The Amal Militia

To further complicate affairs, an Iranian Shi'ite founded the Amal militia to protect Shi'ite interests in Lebanon. "Amal" is the word for "hope" in Arabic. It is also the acronym for *Afwaj al Muquwamah al Lubnaiyyah,* which means "Lebanese Resistance Detachment." The Amal, a moderate faction, clashed with Arafat and the PLO.

The Amal militia captured West Beirut in 1984, and U.S. marines withdrew in 1984.

The Hizballah and Amal militia fought one another bitterly in the War of the Camps (1985–1986) and conflict erupted again in Beirut in 1988. In 1988, Lebanon was further divided as a Christian government was formed in East Beirut to compete with a Muslim government in West Beirut.

The Tai'if Agreement

A committee appointed by the Arab League negotiated the Ta'if Agreement of 1989, which finally brought the civil war to an end. The Lebanese ratified the accord in November and elected Rene Mouawad president. The new president was assassinated in a car bombing only a few days later, and Elias Hrawi succeeded him, serving until 1998.

End of Lebanese Civil War

Muslims have been given a greater voice in Lebanon since the civil war, but the government has since fought Sunni rebels in the north and Hizballah still retains its weapons. Branches of the **al-Qaeda** terrorist organization have also been linked to Lebanon. Syria still maintains troops in Lebanon. In 1996, Israel launched "Operation Grapes of Wrath" in response to Hizballah bombings of northern Israeli villages. During the operation, Israel was accused of killing through bombing attacks 106 civilians who had taken refuge in a United Nations shelter in Cana. Another 110 civilians were injured. In April, Israel and the Hizballah agreed to the "April Understanding" according to which the combatants were to avoid civilian targets. On May 23, 2000, the Israelis withdrew their armies from the south and the Bekaa Valley. Hizballah forces have continued to launch periodic attacks on Israel.

LATIN AMERICA IN THE POST-WORLD WAR II ERA

Latin America had been dominated by European powers since the Age of Exploration, and it had to deal with constant U.S. intervention as the United States became more and more imperialistic. The Argentine economist Raul Prebisch argued that Latin American economies, in fact, were damaged by their dependence on industrial nations, especially those of North America and Europe. Prebisch divided these nations into two groups, the "center" and the "periphery." Latin American nations on the periphery of international trade needed to diversify their domestic trade and to promote their own industrial growth. In the wake of World War II, many Latin American countries fought vigorously against U.S. and other foreign influences, and especially against U.S. intervention in their politics and economies. Despite the warnings of Prebisch and others, Latin American countries had enormous foreign debts. During the recession of the 1970s and 1980s, the debt problem became worse. Despite the movements to separate Latin America from U.S. interference, economics continues to force many Latin American areas to accept aid and so to also accept U.S. terms.

Mexico

In the nineteenth century, Mexico lost territory to the United States. In 1910, there was a revolution in Mexico against foreign interests, and a new constitution was created in 1917. The revolution reached a high point during the presidency of **Lázaro Cárdenas** (1934–1940), who stripped foreign investors of control in Mexican oil wells and returned over forty-five million acres of land to peasants. Cuauhtemoc Cárdenas, the son of the president, fought conservative backlash groups for years after Cárdenas left office in 1940. Peasant revolts against the succeeding conservative governments and the Institutional Revolutionary Party in Chiapas disrupted stability in Mexico.

Argentina

Like Mexico, Argentina also fought against U.S. intervention and foreign control in Latin America. Argentina has avoided U.S. intervention, and **Juan Perón** eventually won the presidency in 1946 on the basis of his opposition to foreign, and especially U.S., intervention. Perón was the culmination of the increasing power of the military in Argentina's politics. His wife Eva was herself from the lower classes and personally implemented aspects of his program of assistance to the poor by seeing long lines of people at their house, the casa Rosada (the Pink house). Perón also advocated industrialization and protection of workers. The couple was very popular with the lower classes of Argentina, though others saw them as opportunistic and as having sympathy for fascism. Perón left office in 1955 and returned in 1970. After Perón, Argentina was controlled by a series of brutal military dictators. During the 1970s and 1980s, these dictators persecuted opponents in a "dirty war" that ultimately took the lives of over 23,000 people.

Guatemala

Similarly, Guatemala also fought U.S. intrusion into its internal affairs. Foreign investors virtually controlled Guatemala's economy after World War II. In 1953, President Jacobo Arbenz Guzmán took the property of the United Fruit Company, which was controlled by U.S. investors, and redistributed it to peasants. Although he offered compensation for the land, the U.S. President Dwight Eisenhower reacted by ordering the CIA to overthrow the government. Eisenhower believed that communist influences were at work behind the nationalization of the United Fruit Company land, and the U.S. trained noncommunist forces under Colonel Carlos Castillo Armas to combat the government. Armas toppled the government in 1954 and returned the land taken from the United Fruit Company. He also ruled as a military dictator, killing and torturing opponents. Under Armas, the deaths and disappearance of over 200,000 people have been reported. These events are being investigated by various agencies as acts of genocide against the Mayan Indians. His brutality resulted in intense rebel activity and his assassination in 1957. Guatemala fought a civil war until the 1990s.

Nicaragua

While the United States engineered the coup d'etat in Guatemala, it also provided arms to Nicaragua and Honduras, both of which bordered Guatemala. Nicaraguans, such as Augusto Caesar Sandino, had also fought U.S. influence, but members of the Nicaraguan National Guard, led by **Anastacio Somoza Garcia Sandino**, assassinated Caesar Sandino. Somoza strongly supported U.S. policies, and later outlawed the communist party in Nicaragua. He and his sons controlled Nicaragua for over forty years. Protests erupted in Nicaragua over U.S. influence as well as over the corruption of the Somozas. The **Sandinista Liberation Front** was founded in honor of Sandino, and the Marxist organization took power in 1979. President Jimmy Carter refused to aid the Samozas in their fight for survival.

The Panama Canal Treaty

President Carter also signed the Panama Canal Treaty in 1979, giving Panama control over the canal and all its territory. Carter generally did not support Cold War anticommunist policies or rhetoric, nor U.S. imperialist activity. Unfortunately, he was relatively alone in the political arena and was strongly criticized for focusing on human rights abroad rather than on issues many Americans felt required more immediate attention at home, such as economic issues. His failure to resolve the Iran Hostage Crisis also contributed to the election of Ronald Reagan in 1981.

The Iran-Contra Scandal

The new president reacted strongly to the Sandinistas and to their Marxist ideology. Reagan believed the Sandinistas were supporting communist insurrections in Latin American countries, and his fierce anticommunist rhetoric renewed with vigor the Cold War. He cut off aid to Nicaragua, instituted an economic boycott, and began to support a rival movement, the **Contras**. The Contras led terrorist attacks on Sandinista strongholds, and the CIA helped to train them. In 1984, Congress banned aid to the Contras, but Reagan was undeterred. He secretly sold arms to Iran and funneled the money to the Contras. The most shocking aspect of Reagan's flaunting of a Congressional act was the fact that he had made a deal with Iran, who had held American hostages in Tehran during 1979 and 1980 and was then under an embargo. The sale of arms to Iran had also been made in exchange for hostages in Lebanon. The scandal exploded in 1986. Reagan later admitted that the arms sale was, in part, to resolve the hostage crisis in the Middle East, but the idea of selling arms to a power that was then hostile to America never sat well with the American public nor with the Congress.

In 1989, the United Nations stepped in to help resolve the civil war in Nicaragua. Elections held in the 1990s brought about more democratic policies.

Chile

Chile was another example of U.S. interference. Prior to 1973, Chile had a relatively stable, democratic style government. In 1973, the military junta of **Augusto José Ramón Pinochet Ugarte** took power in a U.S.-supported coup d'etat. Pinochet would lead Chile through massive economic reforms called the Miracle of Chile before open elections removed him as president in 1990. He remained commander-in-chief of the army until 1998. Pinochet's regime was one of the most brutal in history. Thousands fled to avoid torture and other abuses, while thousands more simply disappeared. Although he was arrested for human rights abuses in London in 1998, the British refused to extradite him to Spain, where his trial was to be held. The Chileans eventually dropped the charges against him. Some see him as saving Chile from communism, and his brutality as necessary in the face of increasingly violent resistance. However, Pinochet was one of the most brutal rulers in Chile's history, and the U.S. support of his reign of terror is a black spot in U.S. history, along with U.S. support of the Shah of Iran, Saddam Hussein, and other rulers known to have abused human rights. U.S. support of such figures is indicative of policy in this period, which sought to obtain political and other benefits for the United States while often overlooking the miseries of the various populations governed by U.S.-supported governments abroad.

AFRICA AFTER WORLD WAR II

The breakdown of European imperialism in Africa created a volatile situation. Africa accounts for only one percent of the world's industrial output, but has ten percent of the world's population. The continent has the highest number of low-income states in the world. Mali, for example, is one of the poorest states in the world and most of its territory is desert. The population continues to explode, rising between 2.5 and 3 percent a year. Many Africans suffer from poverty, health issues, such as AIDS, and serious famines, such as in Ethiopia. The Organization of African Unity was founded in 1963 by thirty-two states to prevent foreign influence and conflicts among themselves. Pan-African movement arose, as well, to promote African unity.

Nevertheless, violent conflicts arose in the former colonial territories of Africa, and continue today. Many African states have become dictatorships, arguing that such brutal measures are necessary to ensure stability against so many competing forces. This is true even in Ghana, which was led by the founder of the Pan-African movement, **Kwame Nikhrumah**. He was overthrown in 1966 and Ghana became a dictatorship. Haile Selassie, who was instrumental in the foundation of the Organization of African Unity, met a similar fate. The Marxist dictator Mengistu Haile Mariam overthrew Selassie's Ethiopian regime in 1974. The emperor, who had abolished slavery in Ethiopia and had valiantly fought against Mussolini's invasion, was widely regarded as one of the most important symbols for African progress and the development of unity. Unlike Nikhrumah, he favored slow and small steps in the process of forging unity from chaos. Haile Selassie's remains were buried under a toilet and not recovered until 1992.

Zaire (Democratic Republic of the Congo)

The Belgian Congo became Zaire in 1971. Mobutu Sese Soko took power in a coup d'etat with U.S. assistance, and established a "vampire elite" who brutally abused the inhabitants of Zaire. In 1997, Laurent Kabila overthrew Mobuto, and established the Democratic Republic of the Congo. His promise of reform, however, soon became just another dictatorship, and he was assassinated in 2001.

South Africa

The situation in South Africa was one of the most tense on the continent. South Africa remained in the control of European settlers, but had a predominantly black population. The black inhabitants had been dispossessed of rights. Black resistance movements led to the formation, in 1948, of the Afrikaner National Party, an attempt to fight against rising demands for black freedoms. The party essentially created **apartheid**, or separateness, a system of segregation that forced blacks to use, for example, separate water fountains, restroom facilities, and telephone booths. Apartheid attempted to divide the non-white population further by differentiating between Indians, Bantus, Zulu, and other colored populations. Over eighty-seven percent of the land in South Africa was reserved for whites.

Nelson Mandela and the African National Congress

Under leaders such as **Nelson Mandela**, the African National Congress fought apartheid. In the Year of Africa, 1960, the government killed several black demonstrators in Sharpeville, near Johannesburg. The government then banned the African National Congress and, in 1963, arrested Nelson Mandela. In 1961, South Africa separated from the British Commonwealth and declared itself a republic.

The End of Apartheid

International condemnation followed. Many conscientious investors refused to buy the krugerrand, the gold coin of South Africa, and the United Nations imposed sanctions. In 1989, F.W. de Klerk became president and began to address these concerns. He freed Nelson Mandela in 1990. He collaborated with Mandela and other groups, and, in 1994, elections put Mandela in office as the new president of South Africa. Apartheid was over. Mandela has become one of the most respected human rights activists in the modern world.

Africa Today

Civil war continues to plague many states in Africa. Serious and violent revolts and revolutions have occurred in Sierra Leone and Liberia. Human rights abuses are reported throughout the continent in countries such as Mali, formed out of the Sudanese Republic after it became independent of France in 1960. Dictators ruled in Mali until 1992, when Mali's first democratic presidential election put Konare in power.

The rule of **General Idi Amin Dada** in Uganda from 1971 until 1979 is one of the most notorious examples of abuse. His unpredictable, egomaniacal, and brutal personality resulted in the death and torture of over a million Ugandans. Dada brought a highjacked airliner with Israeli citizens to Entebbe airport, prompting the Israelis to launch the famous Raid on Entebbe.

These are just a few of the political troubles that have affected the volatile continent of Africa since the end of World War II.

A NEW WORLD ORDER

A new world order began to emerge in the post-World War II period, as colonial empires were broken apart and nationalistic movements dotted the landscape. Although the Cold War broke the world into two opposing camps for many years after World War II, the bipolar world of the Cold War eventually broke down, too. The world entered a global age of unprecedented change.

CHAPTER 46

EMERGING GLOBAL TRENDS

The foundation of the **International Monetary Fund**, in 1944, at the Bretton Woods Conference helped to initiate a new era of global cooperation, as the fund encourages free trade and high growth rates. Free trade across borders was one of the most important issues that affected the post-World War II era. The 1947 General Agreement on Tariffs and Trade, supported by the U.S., helped to establish the World Trade Organization, which took the agreement's place in 1995. Asia experienced an "economic miracle" after World War II, especially in Japan. Deng Xiaoping opened China to outside markets, and in 1992 created a socialist market economy. The transformation of Japan made it one of the technological giants of the world. Meanwhile, the "Little Tigers" of Hong Kong, South Korea, Singapore, and Taiwan also experienced phenomenal growth. By the 1980s, the Little Tigers were a force to be reckoned with on the international scene. Asia was rocked by a severe financial crisis in 1997, however, whose impact was felt in the West. The crisis began when foreign investors began to pull out of Thailand. The Thai stock market dropped by seventy-five percent, and the crisis spread to Malaysia, Indonesia, South Korea, and the Philippines. In an earlier era, the crisis would not have spread so quickly, but the new global economy has created a system whereby the world is linked through a vast economic network. Television, radio, telephones, and other communication devices have made it easier than ever to communicate. The rise of the Internet as a global means of instant communication has furthered the interconnections among world societies. English has become an important language of communication, arising out of the long-lasting legacy of British colonial rule.

Global **corporations** now dominate the business world. In the last twenty years, perhaps as many as 50,000 such corporations have been created.

Whereas earlier forms of international business took the form of a multinational corporation, operating under the restrictions of a particular country but doing business abroad, global corporations are operated from offices across the world. One of the motivating factors of the global corporation is the search for cheap labor and places that offer few restrictions, thus lowering operating costs. Many global corporations manage to escape local tax laws, leading to a depletion of resources from tax revenues in various parts of the world. In fact, United States corporations are among the leaders of this trend.

Old alliances, however, are not easily undone, and various nations have formed trading blocs to protect their interests in the global market. The European Economic Community was first formed in 1957, and, in 1993, the Maastricht Treaty established the **European Union** of fifteen nations. In 1999, eleven members implemented a system of common currency, and members of the union today are attempting to write a constitution.

OPEC, or the **Organization of Petroleum Exporting Countries**, was established in 1990. The association of Southeast Asian Nations, ASEAN, was established in 1967. Meanwhile, the United States, Canada, and Mexico established **NAFTA**, or the **North American Free Trade Agreement**, in 1993. These associations have tremendous power, as demonstrated by OPEC's embargo on oil shipments to the United States in 1973 in retaliation for its support of Israel. The cost of a barrel of oil increased by four-fold, triggering a global recession.

THE POPULATION EXPLOSION

In 1798, Thomas Malthus published a paper on "The Principles of Population," in which he asserted that population increases geometrically, far outstripping the supply of food, which only increases arithmetically. He argued that disease and famine were nature's ways of controlling the population. Although Malthus has often been criticized, not least for his mathematics, his predictions about the potential rapid growth of population in future generations have been confirmed.

The population of the world has rapidly increased due to better health care. Malthus was mistaken in one respect, however, as increased supplies of food in various parts of the world have also contributed to growth. The United Nations has estimated that the population of planet Earth will reach 11.6 billion by 2200 and become more stable, but in the last 300 years it has increased by five times what it was in the seventeenth century. In 1972, a group of scholars known as the Club of Rome warned that the planet's resources are finite and in danger of being exhausted by continued growth in population. Their predictions that natural resources would be exhausted have not yet materialized, but their message about the dangers of overpopulation continues to resonate.

Malthus would be interested to learn of mass epidemics in the twentieth century, such as **AIDS**, that particularly threaten underdeveloped regions, such as Africa. The Center for Disease Control in Atlanta, Georgia, reports that in 2003 there are forty-two million people living with HIV infections or full-blown AIDS. A large percentage of these cases are in sub-Saharan Africa. Experts predict that deaths among women, who make up the largest percentage of victims, will lead to a drop in population of seventy million by 2010. Two of three children are orphans due to the ravages of AIDS in some parts of Africa, and experts have suggested that the deaths of so many young adults will lead to a rise in child labor.

Many experts believe that AIDS began in Africa, as the virus that causes the disease, HIV, has the most mutations there. Similarly, Africa has also seen the outbreak of the Ebola virus and other frightening hemorrhagic diseases. In 2003, SARS (Sudden Acute Respiratory Syndrome) circled the globe, beginning in Asia and makings its way to the Americas. Although preventative vaccines helped to eradicate smallpox and diphtheria in the twentieth century, epidemic diseases still threaten the globe. Our increased interconnectivity helps to make us more vulnerable than ever to killer diseases that now can circle the globe within days or weeks.

POVERTY

Despite advances in agriculture and technology, poverty remains a significant issue in the world today. According to the World Bank, poverty is defined as between $1 and $2 per day in 1993 Purchasing Power Parity (PPP), which measures the relative purchasing power of currencies across countries. In 1999, an estimated 1.2 billion people worldwide had consumption levels below $1 a day, which represents twenty-three percent of the population of the developing world. An estimated 2.8 billion people survived on less than $2 a day. Although every nation of the world has a significant population of those who live in poverty, the vast majority of the world's impoverished are in Europe, Central Asia, and sub-Saharan Africa. Asia has by far the largest population of those in poverty. An estimated 490 million people live in poverty in South Asia. Although the number of impoverished people has declined in the last two decades in Asia, the AIDS crisis in Africa threatens to dramatically raise the level of poverty there.

Poverty is related to infant mortality rates. In Africa, an average of 151 of every 1,000 children die before reaching the age of 5. Worldwide, infant mortality rates have dropped to around fifty-nine per 1,000 in 1999 and life expectancy has dramatically increased by an average of four months per year since 1970. Unfortunately, these gains do not eliminate the pressing need to address the world's impoverished.

Poverty brings with it other social problems, such as illiteracy. Although the level worldwide of adult literacy has risen from fifty-three percent in 1970 to seventy-four percent in 1998, illiteracy still remains a major problem in Africa and the Middle East, the two geographic areas that have not reported gains in the number of children enrolled in primary schools. Across the world, over 110 million primary-school-age children in developing countries are not in school, and sixty percent, or sixty-six million, of these children are female. In 1998, 879 million adults in developing countries, representing one in four adults, were illiterate. Most of these were women, representing sixty-four percent of the total figure. In South Asia, only forty percent of women are literate, while sixty-five percent of men are literate. In Afghanistan, only about twenty percent of women are literate. While the overall rate of illiteracy in the world has fallen since 1970, the population explosion has resulted in an additional forty-one million illiterate adults. This decrease was most dramatic in East Asia. Since 1990, however, illiteracy increased in South Asia, the Middle East, North Africa, and sub-Saharan Africa.

These statistics on poverty reflect continuing inequities throughout the world between industrialized nations and underdeveloped nations, and between men and women. Most of the world's women continue to live in poverty and to be uneducated, and, despite gains in employment in certain parts of the world, much still needs to be done to address these serious global issues.

TERRORISM

Terrorism can be seen in parts of the world as an outgrowth of movements related to nationalism or to ethnic and religious identity; it can also be seen as a response to increasing globalization. Members of the **al-Qaeda** ("the base") organization, for example, have strong feelings of resentment for increasing American military presence in the Middle East. Many terrorist organizations in the Middle East fight for Palestinian autonomy against the Israeli occupation of Palestinian territories. The Hamas, formed in 1987 during the Palestinian uprising against Israel, is just one of literally hundreds of terrorist groups in existence today.

While the current population explosion and modern diseases can often lead to deep fears about the future, the rise of terrorist organizations have created an even deeper feeling of insecurity. This is especially true for Americans, who felt relatively immune from terrorism. Americans watched the PLO launch innumerable terrorist attacks against Israel, and Presidents Clinton and George W. Bush even lifted a ban on funding the PLO, found in the 1987 Anti-terrorism Act. Americans also watched the Irish Republican Army lead attacks against Britain, and Protestant terrorists lead attacks against Irish Catholics, but it was not until September 11, 2001, that Americans recognized that their own daily security might be an issue. American embassies were bombed in the 1990s in Africa, for example, but nothing on such a large scale had ever occurred within U.S. borders. Osama bin Laden's al-Qaeda organization reflects the new global culture of the twentieth century, as it has spawned operations across the globe from Indonesia, to America, to the Middle East, to Africa. Bin Laden rose to prominence as an American-funded mujahideen in Afghanistan, and fled there after the attacks of 9-11. The U.S. pursued him there and toppled the Taliban regime. President George W. Bush's subsequent "war on terrorism" has not yet achieved the goal of finding Bin Laden or of stopping continued al-Qaeda attacks.

ETHNIC CONFLICTS

Despite the increasing globalization of the world, it is still not quite a "world without borders," as various ethnic clashes continue to rip at the fabric of unity.

Bosnia and Herzegovina declared sovereignty in 1991, and independence from Yugoslavia in 1992, and have since fought a series of ethnic wars between Catholic and Orthodox Christians and Muslims. Slobodan Milosevic of Serbia further complicated the situation. Serbian nationalism led Serb minorities in Bosnia and Croatia to attempt to secede, prompting furious fighting. In 1995, a U.N. force went to Bosnia to help implement the Dayton Cease-Fire Agreement. The force still remains, and so does hostility between Christians and Muslims. Similarly, the situation in Kosovo erupted into war in 1999 when Albanians protested Serbian rule. Kosovo was declared an autonomous region of Serbia following World War II, and its boundaries were redrawn to form an Albanian majority. During the Kosovo War of 1999, many Serbs left, and Milosevic was later prosecuted by the United Nations for war crimes, including genocide in Bosnia and war crimes in Kosovo and Croatia. Serbian nationalists continue to resent Milosevic for the Dayton Agreement.

Such simmering ethnic clashes, along with poverty and continued inequities for women, underdeveloped peoples, and classes in the world's societies, suggest that the world has far to go before truly becoming a "world without borders."

IMPACT OF GLOBALISM

Globalism has reduced the role of governments in shaping the economy. Critics argue that global corporations have contributed to environmental problems. Some argue that indigenous cultures and diversity are threatened as a more homogenous global culture emerges. The spread of American culture throughout the world has disturbed many, as McDonald's and other corporations can even be found now on the streets of China. One of the most potent symbols of the McDonaldization of the world is, oddly enough, the Barbie doll. Barbie has been exported to many parts of the world, and to women in the countries of the Middle East and other non-western countries, Barbie represents a stereotype of the modern American woman, a woman whose values often clash with those of the Islamic and Asian worlds. Barbie's svelte body revealed under skimpy clothing, her flashy makeup, and her various hairstyles clash with the insistence in many parts of the Muslim world that the woman's body be covered, sometimes from head to toe, and that she rarely be seen alone or outside of the home. Conservative Muslims and Asians see the Barbie doll as a dangerous symbol of western permissiveness. Nevertheless, the new globalism may be a valuable tool in the face of such worldwide problems as global warming and the destruction of natural habitats.

The race into space, a product of the Cold War conflicts between the U.S.S.R. and the United States, began with the Soviet launch of *Sputnik* on October 4, 1957. Americans were the first to put a man on the moon in 1969, and Neil Armstrong put it well when he remarked, "that's one small step for [a] man, one giant leap for mankind." Armstrong and the Apollo XI team landed on the Sea of Tranquility. The space race has opened up even newer boundaries for the world's nations. A picture of the earth taken by the *Voyager* spacecraft has shown us what a tiny speck of the universe the earth represents. As globalism ties together the world's communities through trade, communication, and other avenues, we may need to find new ways to cooperate as we explore the vast, uncharted regions of space. Although we have not yet managed to defeat the problems of sectarianism, poverty, disease, global warming, and other issues, our collective memory of Armstrong's walk in the Sea of Tranquility and the possibilities of what humankind can achieve may yet inspire the creation of a "world without borders."

SAT Subject Test
World History

Practice Test 1

This test is also on CD-ROM in our special interactive SAT World History TEST*ware*®. It is highly recommended that you first take this exam on computer. You will then have the additional study features and benefits of enforced timed conditions and instantaneous, accurate scoring. See page xix for guidance on how to get the most out of our SAT World History software.

SAT WORLD HISTORY
PRACTICE TEST 1

ANSWER SHEET

1. Ⓐ Ⓑ Ⓒ Ⓓ Ⓔ
2. Ⓐ Ⓑ Ⓒ Ⓓ Ⓔ
3. Ⓐ Ⓑ Ⓒ Ⓓ Ⓔ
4. Ⓐ Ⓑ Ⓒ Ⓓ Ⓔ
5. Ⓐ Ⓑ Ⓒ Ⓓ Ⓔ
6. Ⓐ Ⓑ Ⓒ Ⓓ Ⓔ
7. Ⓐ Ⓑ Ⓒ Ⓓ Ⓔ
8. Ⓐ Ⓑ Ⓒ Ⓓ Ⓔ
9. Ⓐ Ⓑ Ⓒ Ⓓ Ⓔ
10. Ⓐ Ⓑ Ⓒ Ⓓ Ⓔ
11. Ⓐ Ⓑ Ⓒ Ⓓ Ⓔ
12. Ⓐ Ⓑ Ⓒ Ⓓ Ⓔ
13. Ⓐ Ⓑ Ⓒ Ⓓ Ⓔ
14. Ⓐ Ⓑ Ⓒ Ⓓ Ⓔ
15. Ⓐ Ⓑ Ⓒ Ⓓ Ⓔ
16. Ⓐ Ⓑ Ⓒ Ⓓ Ⓔ
17. Ⓐ Ⓑ Ⓒ Ⓓ Ⓔ
18. Ⓐ Ⓑ Ⓒ Ⓓ Ⓔ
19. Ⓐ Ⓑ Ⓒ Ⓓ Ⓔ
20. Ⓐ Ⓑ Ⓒ Ⓓ Ⓔ
21. Ⓐ Ⓑ Ⓒ Ⓓ Ⓔ
22. Ⓐ Ⓑ Ⓒ Ⓓ Ⓔ
23. Ⓐ Ⓑ Ⓒ Ⓓ Ⓔ
24. Ⓐ Ⓑ Ⓒ Ⓓ Ⓔ
25. Ⓐ Ⓑ Ⓒ Ⓓ Ⓔ
26. Ⓐ Ⓑ Ⓒ Ⓓ Ⓔ
27. Ⓐ Ⓑ Ⓒ Ⓓ Ⓔ
28. Ⓐ Ⓑ Ⓒ Ⓓ Ⓔ
29. Ⓐ Ⓑ Ⓒ Ⓓ Ⓔ
30. Ⓐ Ⓑ Ⓒ Ⓓ Ⓔ
31. Ⓐ Ⓑ Ⓒ Ⓓ Ⓔ
32. Ⓐ Ⓑ Ⓒ Ⓓ Ⓔ

33. Ⓐ Ⓑ Ⓒ Ⓓ Ⓔ
34. Ⓐ Ⓑ Ⓒ Ⓓ Ⓔ
35. Ⓐ Ⓑ Ⓒ Ⓓ Ⓔ
36. Ⓐ Ⓑ Ⓒ Ⓓ Ⓔ
37. Ⓐ Ⓑ Ⓒ Ⓓ Ⓔ
38. Ⓐ Ⓑ Ⓒ Ⓓ Ⓔ
39. Ⓐ Ⓑ Ⓒ Ⓓ Ⓔ
40. Ⓐ Ⓑ Ⓒ Ⓓ Ⓔ
41. Ⓐ Ⓑ Ⓒ Ⓓ Ⓔ
42. Ⓐ Ⓑ Ⓒ Ⓓ Ⓔ
43. Ⓐ Ⓑ Ⓒ Ⓓ Ⓔ
44. Ⓐ Ⓑ Ⓒ Ⓓ Ⓔ
45. Ⓐ Ⓑ Ⓒ Ⓓ Ⓔ
46. Ⓐ Ⓑ Ⓒ Ⓓ Ⓔ
47. Ⓐ Ⓑ Ⓒ Ⓓ Ⓔ
48. Ⓐ Ⓑ Ⓒ Ⓓ Ⓔ
49. Ⓐ Ⓑ Ⓒ Ⓓ Ⓔ
50. Ⓐ Ⓑ Ⓒ Ⓓ Ⓔ
51. Ⓐ Ⓑ Ⓒ Ⓓ Ⓔ
52. Ⓐ Ⓑ Ⓒ Ⓓ Ⓔ
53. Ⓐ Ⓑ Ⓒ Ⓓ Ⓔ
54. Ⓐ Ⓑ Ⓒ Ⓓ Ⓔ
55. Ⓐ Ⓑ Ⓒ Ⓓ Ⓔ
56. Ⓐ Ⓑ Ⓒ Ⓓ Ⓔ
57. Ⓐ Ⓑ Ⓒ Ⓓ Ⓔ
58. Ⓐ Ⓑ Ⓒ Ⓓ Ⓔ
59. Ⓐ Ⓑ Ⓒ Ⓓ Ⓔ
60. Ⓐ Ⓑ Ⓒ Ⓓ Ⓔ
61. Ⓐ Ⓑ Ⓒ Ⓓ Ⓔ
62. Ⓐ Ⓑ Ⓒ Ⓓ Ⓔ
63. Ⓐ Ⓑ Ⓒ Ⓓ Ⓔ
64. Ⓐ Ⓑ Ⓒ Ⓓ Ⓔ

65. Ⓐ Ⓑ Ⓒ Ⓓ Ⓔ
66. Ⓐ Ⓑ Ⓒ Ⓓ Ⓔ
67. Ⓐ Ⓑ Ⓒ Ⓓ Ⓔ
68. Ⓐ Ⓑ Ⓒ Ⓓ Ⓔ
69. Ⓐ Ⓑ Ⓒ Ⓓ Ⓔ
70. Ⓐ Ⓑ Ⓒ Ⓓ Ⓔ
71. Ⓐ Ⓑ Ⓒ Ⓓ Ⓔ
72. Ⓐ Ⓑ Ⓒ Ⓓ Ⓔ
73. Ⓐ Ⓑ Ⓒ Ⓓ Ⓔ
74. Ⓐ Ⓑ Ⓒ Ⓓ Ⓔ
75. Ⓐ Ⓑ Ⓒ Ⓓ Ⓔ
76. Ⓐ Ⓑ Ⓒ Ⓓ Ⓔ
77. Ⓐ Ⓑ Ⓒ Ⓓ Ⓔ
78. Ⓐ Ⓑ Ⓒ Ⓓ Ⓔ
79. Ⓐ Ⓑ Ⓒ Ⓓ Ⓔ
80. Ⓐ Ⓑ Ⓒ Ⓓ Ⓔ
81. Ⓐ Ⓑ Ⓒ Ⓓ Ⓔ
82. Ⓐ Ⓑ Ⓒ Ⓓ Ⓔ
83. Ⓐ Ⓑ Ⓒ Ⓓ Ⓔ
84. Ⓐ Ⓑ Ⓒ Ⓓ Ⓔ
85. Ⓐ Ⓑ Ⓒ Ⓓ Ⓔ
86. Ⓐ Ⓑ Ⓒ Ⓓ Ⓔ
87. Ⓐ Ⓑ Ⓒ Ⓓ Ⓔ
88. Ⓐ Ⓑ Ⓒ Ⓓ Ⓔ
89. Ⓐ Ⓑ Ⓒ Ⓓ Ⓔ
90. Ⓐ Ⓑ Ⓒ Ⓓ Ⓔ
91. Ⓐ Ⓑ Ⓒ Ⓓ Ⓔ
92. Ⓐ Ⓑ Ⓒ Ⓓ Ⓔ
93. Ⓐ Ⓑ Ⓒ Ⓓ Ⓔ
94. Ⓐ Ⓑ Ⓒ Ⓓ Ⓔ
95. Ⓐ Ⓑ Ⓒ Ⓓ Ⓔ

SAT WORLD HISTORY PRACTICE TEST 1

Time: 1 Hour
        95 Questions

DIRECTIONS: This part consists of a number of incomplete statements or questions, each followed by five suggested completions or answers. Select the most appropriate choice and blacken the corresponding space on the answer sheet.

1.   The Velvet Revolution marked the fall of communism in

   (A) Hungary   (D) Yugoslavia

   (B) Czechoslovakia   (E) Bosnia-Herzegovina

   (C) Poland

2.   The Soviet leader whose policies of glasnost and perestroika encouraged the fall of communism in the Eastern Bloc was

   (A) Brezhnev   (D) Gorbachev

   (B) Khrushchev   (E) Putin

   (C) Stalin

3.   The civilization known for its massive Pyramids of the Sun and Moon was

   (A) Aztec   (D) Teotihuacan

   (B) Maya   (E) Monte Alban

   (C) Cahokia

4. The African country most affected by famine in the late twentieth century is

(A) Mozambique

(B) Egypt

(C) Ethiopia

(D) Mali

(E) Sudan

5. The doctrine according to which South Vietnam would be enabled to fight on its own while American forces withdrew was called the

(A) Nixon Doctrine

(B) Marshall Plan

(C) Truman Doctrine

(D) Monroe Doctrine

(E) Johnson Plan

6. Which country did Stalin oust from the Soviet bloc in 1948?

(A) Romania

(B) Yugoslavia

(C) Czechoslovakia

(D) Lithuania

(E) Hungary

7. Which of the following was most responsible for the defeat of the Soviets in Afghanistan?

(A) The United States

(B) Iraq

(C) Pakistan

(D) Taliban

(E) India

8. The nation that resulted from the desire of Muslims to form an independent state from India's Hindus in the post-World War II era was

(A) Afghanistan

(B) Pakistan

(C) Sri Lanka

(D) Myanmar

(E) Bangladesh

9. Which of the following was considered the least successful Mughal ruler?

(A) Babur the Tiger

(B) Humayan

(C) Akbar

(D) Shah Jahan

(E) Jahangir

10. Which of the following was NOT a Central Power of World War I?

    (A) France

    (B) The Ottomans

    (C) Austria-Hungary

    (D) Germany

    (E) Both (B) and (C)

11. Which of the following was NOT a member of the Axis in World War II?

    (A) Germany

    (B) Russia

    (C) Italy

    (D) Japan

    (E) Both (C) and (D)

12. Which of the following areas was NOT assigned to Spain as a result of the Treaty of Tordesillas?

    (A) Mexico

    (B) North America

    (C) Peru

    (D) Brazil

    (E) Both (B) and (C)

13. Which of the following dictators most favored U.S. policy in Latin America?

    (A) Peron

    (B) Somoza

    (C) Sandino

    (D) Guzmán

    (E) Cárdenas

14. Which of the following colonial kingdoms became Zaire?

    (A) Rhodesia

    (B) The Belgian Congo

    (C) Mali

    (D) South Africa

    (E) Ghana

15. Who implemented the Great Leap Forward in China and a series of reforms based on the Soviet model?

    (A) Sun Yat-sen

    (B) Chiang Kai-Shek

    (C) Mao Zedong

    (D) Deng Xiaoping

    (E) Pu Yi

16. Who was president of the Republic of China in 1911?

    (A) Sun Yat-sen   (D) Deng Xiaoping

    (B) Chiang Kai-Shek   (E) Pu Yi

    (C) Mao Zedong

17. Who founded the government of Taiwan?

    (A) The Chinese communists under Mao Zedong

    (B) The Nationalist Chinese under Chiang Kai-Shek

    (C) The Qianlong emperor

    (D) The Kangzi emperor

    (E) Deng Xiaoping

18. The Long March refers to

    (A) the flight of the Nationalist Chinese communists to Taiwan

    (B) the flight of the Chinese communists from southern China to Shaanxi province in the north

    (C) the Japanese invasion of Manchuria

    (D) the German march into Russia during World War II

    (E) the return of Buddhists from Tibet to India

19. The man who was the head of the provisional government in Russia following the first revolution in 1917 was

    (A) Lenin   (D) Stalin

    (B) Trotsky   (E) Molotov

    (C) Kerensky

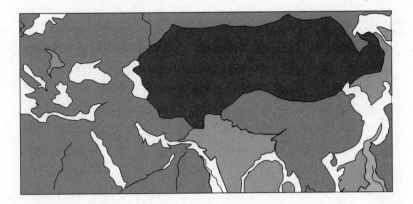

20. The darkly-shaded area in the map above reflects the boundaries of which empire in the early thirteenth century?

    (A) Abbasid Caliphate   (D) Mongol

    (B) Safavid Persians   (E) Mughals

    (C) Ottoman Turks

21. Which of the following artists was NOT influenced by Neoplatonism in the Italian Renaissance?

    (A) Botticelli   (D) Giotto

    (B) Titian   (E) Both (B) and (D)

    (C) Michelangelo

22. The Middle Eastern nation torn by civil war for sixteen years and occupied in the south by the Palestine Liberation Organization and by Israeli forces was

    (A) Jordan   (D) Israel

    (B) Lebanon   (E) Iraq

    (C) Syria

23. Which reformer created a system of radical equality among citizens by equalizing land holdings?

    (A) Solon   (D) Leonidas

    (B) Cleisthenes   (E) Pericles

    (C) Lycurgus

24. The twentieth-century Egyptian leader who nationalized the Suez Canal and who vowed to unite the Arab world in opposition to Israel was

    (A) Sadat

    (B) Nasser

    (C) Saladin

    (D) Hosni Mubarak

    (E) King Farouk

25. The brutal Cambodian regime that exterminated thousands of citizens was

    (A) the Khmer Rouge

    (B) the Viet Cong

    (C) the Laotian Liberation Front

    (D) the Kampuchean Democratic Republic

    (E) the Mujahideen

26. The Israeli prime minister who attempted to make peace with the Palestinians through the creation of the Palestinian National Authority was

    (A) Yitzhak Rabin

    (B) Menachem Begin

    (C) Benjamin Netanyahu

    (D) Ariel Sharon

    (E) Shimon Peres

27. The Safavid Persians were

    (A) Sunni Muslims

    (B) Hindus

    (C) Shi'ite Muslims

    (D) Sikhs

    (E) Buddhists

28. The battle in which Greeks defeated the Persian navy for the final time in the Persian wars was

    (A) Marathon

    (B) Thermopylae

    (C) Plataea

    (D) Salamis

    (E) Sardis

29. Who led the forces that conquered Constantinople in 1453?

    (A) Sulieman the Magnificent

    (B) Selim II

    (C) Ibrahim

    (D) Mehmed the Conqueror

    (E) Selim I

30. The elite corps of the Ottoman troops were the

    (A) Junkers

    (B) Junta

    (C) Janissaries

    (D) Mujahideen

    (E) Sepoy

31. Which of the following areas was NOT colonized by European powers in the nineteenth century?

    (A) India

    (B) Indochina

    (C) New Zealand

    (D) (Siam) Thailand

    (E) Both (B) and (C)

32. During the Opium Wars, the British defeated and earned trading rights from the

    (A) Ming Chinese

    (B) Ching Chinese

    (C) People's Republic of China

    (D) Koreans

    (E) Japanese

33. Which of the following areas is NOT included in the Palestine National Authority?

    (A) The West Bank

    (B) The Gaza Strip

    (C) Jerusalem

    (D) The Sinai Peninsula

    (E) Both (C) and (D)

34. Which of the following is NOT consistent with statements made by Machiavelli in *The Prince*?

    (A) It is better for leaders to be feared than loved

    (B) Politics is based on eternal laws of morality

    (C) It is better to cultivate the appearance of virtue or whatever the public demands than to exemplify such virtues in reality

    (D) Expediency should determine the course of conduct

    (E) The ends justify the means

35. Which document pledged to create a secure homeland for Jews?

    (A) Treaty of Tilsit   (D) Unequal Treaties

    (B) Dayton Agreement   (E) Tai'if Agreement

    (C) Balfour Declaration

36. The desire of Serbs to unite as a nation led to conflict in

    (A) Bosnia and Herzegovina

    (B) Romania

    (C) Poland

    (D) Czechoslovakia

    (E) Hungary

37. The greatest Buddhist ruler of antiquity in India was

    (A) Chandragupta Maurya

    (B) Ashoka

    (C) Aurangzeb

    (D) Humayan

    (E) Akhbar

38. The Gulf of Tonkin Resolution

    (A) mandated an end to hostilities in Vietnam

    (B) was an official declaration of war against North Vietnam

(C) condemned the My Lai massacre

(D) authorized the use of military force by the United States in Vietnam

(E) separated North from South Vietnam

39. "Nonviolence is the greatest force at the disposal of mankind. It is mightier than the mightiest weapon of destruction devised by the ingenuity of man. . . . Noncooperation is directed not against men but against measures. It is not directed against the governors, but against the system they administer. The roots of noncooperation lie not in hatred but in justice, if not in love." Which figure most likely said this?

(A) Aurangzeb   (D) Abbas I

(B) Jinnah   (E) Akhbar

(C) Mohandas Gandhi

40. The nation that most rapidly increased its economic productivity following the two World Wars and became a leader in the production of high-tech goods was

(A) India   (D) the United States

(B) Japan   (E) China

(C) Russia

41. Which nation was the first to declare war in World War I?

(A) Germany   (D) France

(B) Russia   (E) The Ottoman Empire

(C) Austria-Hungary

42. The center of the *Risorgimento* was

(A) Naples

(B) the Kingdom of the Two Sicilies

(C) Rome

(D) Sardinia

(E) Venice

43. "The Mass is the greatest blasphemy of God, and the highest idolatry upon earth, an abomination the like of which has never been in Christendom since the time of the Apostles." Who said this?

    (A) Calvin

    (B) Luther

    (C) Zwingli

    (D) Melancthon

    (E) Henry VIII

44. Which figure first observed the moons of Jupiter and spots on the sun?

    (A) Galileo

    (B) Kepler

    (C) Brahe

    (D) Copernicus

    (E) Newton

45. The Church Council most identified with the Counter-Reformation was

    (A) Constance

    (B) Constantinople

    (C) Vatican II

    (D) Trent

    (E) Augsburg

46. Who wrote the most famous account of court life during the Heian period?

    (A) Lady Murasaki

    (B) Prince Shotoku

    (C) Hideyoshi

    (D) Nobunaga

    (E) Sei Shonagun

47. The Glorious Revolution

    (A) installed William and Mary on the throne

    (B) confirmed the reign of the Stuart James II

    (C) freed Ireland from English domination

    (D) established Catholicism as the religion of England

    (E) freed Scotland from English domination

48. The geocentric theory of the solar system was first established by

    (A) Galileo

    (B) Kepler

    (C) Brahe

    (D) Copernicus

    (E) Newton

49. The leader of the Protestant Reformation in Zurich was

    (A) Calvin

    (B) Luther

    (C) Zwingli

    (D) Melancthon

    (E) Charles VII

50. Which Egyptian ruler created the Amarna revolution?

    (A) Ramses II

    (B) Pepi II

    (C) Akhenaton

    (D) Thutmosis III

    (E) Hatshepsut

51. The figure during the Age of Reason who emphasized induction as a valid method of reasoning was

    (A) Descartes

    (B) Hume

    (C) Voltaire

    (D) Bacon

    (E) Locke

52. The Byzantine ruler who attempted to reconquer lost western territories was

    (A) Sophia Paleologus

    (B) Justinian

    (C) Alexius Comnenus

    (D) Basil

    (E) Diocletian

53. Which of the following most correctly describes the enlightened *philosophes*?

    (A) They adhered to old values, especially the teachings of the Roman Catholic Church

    (B) They rejected institutionalized religion as superstition

(C) They advocated for reform of government based on "natural laws"

(D) They supported the established monarchies and their methods of government

(E) Both (B) and (C)

54. The French military hero who overthrew the directorate during the French Revolution was

(A) Napoleon

(D) Marat

(B) Robespierre

(E) Sieyes

(C) Danton

55. The bronze head pictured above originated in

(A) Ghana

(D) Benin

(B) Mali

(E) Axum

(C) Nok

56. "The program of the world's peace, therefore, is our program; and that program, the only possible program, as we see it, is this: Open covenants of peace, openly arrived at, after which there shall be no private international understandings of any kind but diplomacy shall proceed always frankly and in the public view. Absolute freedom of navigation upon the seas, outside territorial waters, alike in peace and in war, except as the seas may be closed in whole or in part by international action for the enforcement of international covenants."

The quotation above represents

(A) the process of peace envisioned at Yalta and Potsdam in World War II

(B) the process of peace envisioned by the United States following the War of 1812

(C) the process of peace at the end of World War I envisioned by Woodrow Wilson in the Fourteen Points

(D) the process of peace envisioned by the Congress of Vienna following the Napoleonic Wars

(E) the process of peace envisioned by the Monroe Doctrine

57. Whose leadership inspired the formation of the Gran Colombia?

(A) Hidalgo

(B) Zapata

(C) Rosas

(D) Bolivar

(E) Cárdenas

58. The first successful permanent British colony in the Americas was

(A) Maryland

(B) Jamestown

(C) Roanoke

(D) Delaware

(E) Plymouth

59. The final battle of the American Revolution was

(A) Saratoga

(B) Trenton

(C) Yorktown

(D) Bunker Hill

(E) White Plains

60. The careers of Ibn Rushd (Averoees) and Ibn Sinna (Avicenna) flourished during which caliphate?

    (A) Abbasid

    (B) Fatimid

    (C) Umayyad

    (D) Spanish Umayyad

    (E) Ottoman

61. The religion that most influenced the development of sub-Saharan Africa before the Age of Exploration was

    (A) Christianity

    (B) Hinduism

    (C) Judaism

    (D) Islam

    (E) Buddhism

62. Which leader attempted to distribute church property to the poor and established basic human rights in Mexico?

    (A) Hidalgo

    (B) Rosas

    (C) Juárez

    (D) Bolivar

    (E) Cárdenas

63. Toussaint Louverture led a slave revolt that eventually established an independent

    (A) Gran Colombia

    (B) Mexico

    (C) Argentina

    (D) Haiti

    (E) Dominican Republic

64. The Spanish conquistador who discovered the Grand Canyon was

    (A) Ponce de Leon

    (B) Coronado

    (C) Cortez

    (D) Pizarro

    (E) Balboa

65. During the Cold War, the U.S. President Ronald Reagan supported

    (A) Marcos in the Philippines

    (B) the Contra in Nicaragua

    (C) the Sandinistas in Nicaragua

    (D) Aquino in the Philippines

    (E) Both (A) and (B)

66. The first European explorer to reach the southern tip of Africa was

    (A) Vasco da Gama   (D) Diaz

    (B) Pedro Cabral   (E) Balboa

    (C) Magellan

67. Which U.S. president returned the Panama Canal to Panama?

    (A) Ronald Reagan   (D) James Earl Carter

    (B) Harry Truman   (E) George H. W. Bush

    (C) Dwight Eisenhower

68. The image above is of a tablet written in

    (A) Egyptian hieroglyphics   (D) Sanskrit

    (B) Arabic   (E) Hebrew

    (C) Cuneiform

69. Which of the following countries or regions in Africa escaped European domination during the nineteenth century?

    (A) South Africa   (D) Liberia

    (B) The Congo   (E) Both (A) and (C)

    (C) Rhodesia

70. According to Noel Barber, his sixteenth-century "empire stretched from the gates of Vienna to Yemen and Aden, from Persia to Oran, and he ruled over the Six Wonders of the World." Whose reign was the author describing?

    (A) Charles V of the Holy Roman Empire

    (B) Ismail of the Safavids

    (C) Mehmed I of the Ottomans

    (D) Sulieman the Magnificent of the Ottomans

    (E) Selim II

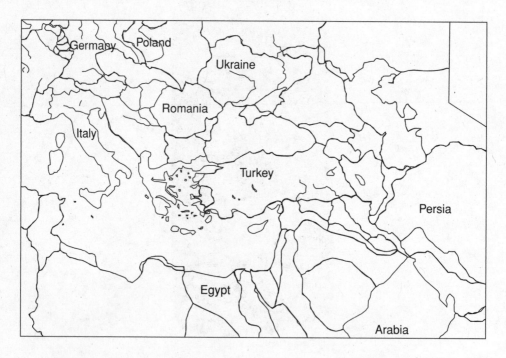

71. The map above reflects the Middle Eastern world after

    (A) World War II ended in 1945

    (B) World War I

    (C) 1935

    (D) 1950

    (E) 1890

72. "If the people be led by laws, and uniformity sought to be given them by punishments, they will try to avoid the punishment, but have no sense of shame. If they be led by virtue, and uniformity sought to be given them by the Rules of Propriety, they will have the sense of shame, and moreover will become good." Which figure most likely said this?

    (A) Lao Tzu

    (B) Han Fei

    (C) Wu Ti

    (D) Confucius

    (E) Shi Huang Ti

73. The image depicts the brutal policies of which Chinese emperor?

    (A) Qianlong

    (B) Kangxi

    (C) Shi Huang Ti

    (D) Hong Wu

    (E) Wu Ti

74. "Thus this person when embraced by the intelligent self, knows nothing that is without, nothing that is within . . . then a father is not a father, a mother is not a mother, the worlds not worlds, the gods not gods."

    The statement above reflects

    (A) the Muslim doctrine of jihad or struggle against evil

(B) the Hindu doctrine of *moksha*

(C) the Chinese view of ancestor worship

(D) Sufi mysticism

(E) the Hindu doctrine of samsara

75. Which statement is true about the Ka'ba?

(A) It is the place where Abraham was commanded to sacrifice Isaac.

(B) It marks the place where Ishmael and his mother Hagar settled after being ousted from the house of Abraham and Sarah.

(C) It marks the place where Muhammad ascended into heaven.

(D) It marks the place where Muhammad received his first revelations.

(E) It marks the place where Muhammad won the Battle of Badr.

76. Which of the following is NOT a location primarily associated with Buddhism?

(A) Magao   (D) Drepung Loseling

(B) Poltala palace   (E) Both (B) and (C)

(C) Angkor Wat

77. Communists were NOT in control of which of the following governments in the post-World War II era?

(A) North Vietnam   (D) India

(B) North Korea   (E) Both (C) and (D)

(C) Cuba

78. Which of the following structures is the earliest?

(A) The pyramids in Mesoamerica

(B) The Acropolis in Athens

(C) The pyramids in Egypt

(D) The Gate of Ishtar in Babylon

(E) The lion gate in Mycenae

79. According to the Code of Hammurabi, if a noble were to break the arm of a slave, what would his punishment be?

    (A) His arm would be broken

    (B) He would pay to the slave the value of his arm

    (C) He would pay to the slave's master a fine representing the loss of labor

    (D) He would be reduced to slavery

    (E) He would have to give the slave's master two slaves to replace the lost labor

80. Which of the following Chinese dynasties ruled the longest?

    (A) The Ch'in (Q'in)   (D) The Chou (Zhou)

    (B) The Ching (Q'ing)   (E) The Han

    (C) The Shang

81. "L'État c'est moi." This statement is representative of what style of government?

    (A) Constitutional monarchy   (D) Socialism

    (B) Absolutism   (E) Communism

    (C) Republicanism

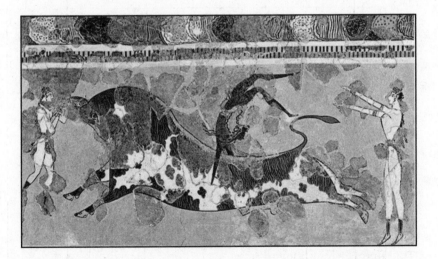

82. The image on the preceding page was likely produced by the

    (A) Egyptians   (D) Minoans

    (B) Mycenaeans   (E) Athenians

    (C) Hittites

83. Germany's invasion of which country prompted the British and French to declare war, starting World War II?

    (A) The Rhineland   (D) Austria

    (B) Poland   (E) France

    (C) Sudetenland

84. "If the spring of popular government in time of peace is virtue, the springs of popular government in revolution are at once *virtue and terror*. . . . Subdue by terror the enemies of liberty, and you will be right, as founders of the Republic. The government of the revolution is liberty's despotism against tyranny." Who said this?

    (A) Danton   (D) Robespierre

    (B) Marat   (E) Louis XVI

    (C) Napoleon

85. What does the following chart illustrate?

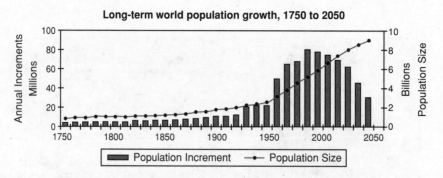

Long-term world population growth, 1750 to 2050

    (A) The population of the world remains relatively stable.

    (B) The rate of growth in world population has remained stable over the past fifty years.

    (C) The rate of population growth is declining since 2000 while overall numbers continue to rise.

(D) The rate of population growth continues to increase as overall numbers remain stable.

(E) The rate of population growth decreased from 1750–1850 and overall numbers remained stable.

86. Which of the following is NOT known as a Little Tiger of the Pacific?

(A) Hong Kong   (D) Singapore

(B) Thailand   (E) Both (A) and (C)

(C) Taiwan

87. The leader who single-handedly reformed ancient Athens and freed those sold into debt for slavery was

(A) Cleisthenes   (D) Solon

(B) Pericles   (E) Hipparchus

(C) Pisistratus

88. Alexander the Great did NOT conquer which of the following areas?

(A) Egypt   (D) Persia

(B) Mesopotamia   (E) Asia Minor

(C) Italy

89. The Roman who transformed the military into an army of professionals was

(A) Sulla   (D) Augustus Caesar

(B) Marius   (E) Romulus

(C) Julius Caesar

90. The heresy that led to the first ecumenical Christian council at Nicaea was the

(A) Donatist heresy   (D) Arian heresy

(B) Nestorian heresy   (E) Monophysite heresy

(C) Montanist heresy

91. Julius Caesar defeated which leader at the siege of Alesia?

    (A) Pompey

    (B) Vercingetorix

    (C) Tarquin the Proud

    (D) Ptolemy of Egypt

    (E) Sulla

92. Which emperor divided the Roman Empire into an eastern and western half?

    (A) Constantine the Great

    (B) Maximian

    (C) Septimus Severus

    (D) Diocletian

    (E) Nero

93. Which medieval ruler forcibly converted the Saxons?

    (A) Otto I

    (B) Charlemagne

    (C) Charles the Bald

    (D) Clovis

    (E) Dagobert

94. The Investiture Controversy was initiated when which pope protested lay investiture?

    (A) Gregory the Great

    (B) Innocent III

    (C) Boniface VIII

    (D) Gregory VII

    (E) Sylvester I

95. European crusaders conquered Jerusalem in

    (A) 1095 C.E.

    (B) 1099 C.E.

    (C) 1205 C.E.

    (D) 1187 C.E.

    (E) 910 C.E.

SAT WORLD HISTORY
PRACTICE TEST 1

ANSWER KEY

1.	(B)	25.	(A)	49.	(C)	73.	(C)
2.	(D)	26.	(A)	50.	(C)	74.	(B)
3.	(D)	27.	(C)	51.	(D)	75.	(B)
4.	(C)	28.	(D)	52.	(B)	76.	(C)
5.	(A)	29.	(D)	53.	(E)	77.	(D)
6.	(B)	30.	(C)	54.	(A)	78.	(C)
7.	(D)	31.	(D)	55.	(D)	79.	(C)
8.	(B)	32.	(B)	56.	(C)	80.	(D)
9	(B)	33.	(E)	57.	(D)	81.	(B)
10.	(A)	34.	(B)	58.	(B)	82.	(D)
11.	(B)	35.	(C)	59.	(C)	83.	(B)
12.	(D)	36.	(A)	60.	(A)	84.	(D)
13.	(B)	37.	(B)	61.	(D)	85.	(C)
14.	(B)	38.	(D)	62.	(C)	86.	(B)
15.	(C)	39.	(C)	63.	(D)	87.	(D)
16.	(A)	40.	(B)	64.	(B)	88.	(C)
17.	(B)	41.	(C)	65.	(E)	89.	(B)
18.	(B)	42.	(D)	66.	(D)	90.	(D)
19.	(C)	43.	(B)	67.	(D)	91.	(B)
20.	(D)	44.	(A)	68.	(C)	92.	(D)
21.	(D)	45.	(D)	69.	(D)	93.	(B)
22.	(B)	46.	(A)	70.	(D)	94.	(D)
23.	(C)	47.	(A)	71.	(B)	95.	(B)
24.	(B)	48.	(D)	72.	(D)		

DETAILED EXPLANATIONS
OF ANSWERS

PRACTICE TEST 1

1. **(B)**
The Velvet Revolution occurred in Czechoslovakia in 1989.

2. **(D)**
Gorbachev retreated from the Brezshnev Doctrine and allowed Eastern Bloc nations the freedom of self-determination.

3. **(D)**
Teotihuacan flourished from 300–800 C.E. and influenced Monte Alban and other Mesoamerican cultures.

4. **(C)**
Ethiopia suffered a severe famine in the 1980s and another one beginning in the late 1990s and continuing into the twenty-first century.

5. **(A)**
Nixon campaigned on the promise of ending the Vietnam War.

6. **(B)**
Marshal Tito of Yugoslavia openly disagreed with Soviet policies, resulting in a split with Stalin and the Soviets.

7. **(D)**
Although the United States provided aid, it was really the guerilla tactics of the mujahideen, from which the Taliban would emerge, that toppled the Soviets.

8. **(B)**
The activities of the Muslim League, led by Jinnah, helped to inspire the creation of Pakistan.

9. **(B)**

Humayan lost much of Babur's territory in the early part of his reign and, although he later recovered much of it, he is considered the weakest of the Mughal rulers.

10. **(A)**

France was a member of the Allied powers.

11. **(B)**

Although Germany and Russia signed a nonaggression pact in 1939, Germany attacked Russia in 1941. The Axis powers were Germany, Italy, and, later, Japan.

12. **(D)**

Brazil became a Portuguese territory, and Portuguese is still the language spoken in Brazil today.

13. **(B)**

Somoza's support of U.S. policies in Nicaragua incited rebellions, including those of the Sandinistas.

14. **(B)**

Mobutu Sese Soko overthrew the leaders of the Belgian Congo in 1971 and it then became Zaire.

15. **(C)**

Mao Zedong attempted to rapidly industrialize China, but his Great Leap Forward is often called a Great Leap Backward.

16. **(A)**

Sun Yat-sen became the first president of the new Republic in 1911.

17. **(B)**

The communist Chinese defeated the nationalists and forced them to flee to Taiwan in 1949.

18. **(B)**

Jiang Jieshi's campaign to rid China of the communists resulted in their flight from southeastern China to Shaanxi in 1934.

19. **(C)**

Alexander Kerensky was a hero of the duma, first created in 1905, and he was selected to lead the provisional government established in the first revolutionary phase of 1917.

20. **(D)**

These are the boundaries following the death of Genghis Khan in 1226. The empire would expand further by the end of the thirteenth century.

21. **(D)**

Giotto was an early, proto-Renaissance artist whose naturalistic paintings broke from the rigid formalism of medieval art. The other three artists were, however, profoundly influenced by Neoplatonism, an idealistic school of philosophy.

22. **(B)**

Lebanon fought a civil war between Muslims and Christians. Syria lent support to the predominantly Christian Lebanese army while the PLO continued to launch terrorist attacks against Israel.

23. **(C)**

Lycurgus reformed the social, political, and economic system of Sparta, creating a system in which citizens were equal in terms of land ownership. This system of land ownership was also the basis of their service in the Spartan military.

24. **(B)**

Nasser vigorously fought Israeli expansionism and vowed to rid the Arab world of both Israel and undue foreign intrusion.

25. **(A)**

Pol Pot exterminated literally thousands and thousands of Cambodians in his attempt to return them to their primitive agricultural past.

26. **(A)**

Yitzhak Rabin was assassinated in 1995 following the 1993 peace accords with the Palestinians.

27. **(C)**

Beginning with Ismail, the Safavid rulers rewrote their history tracing it back to Sufi origins and implemented Shi'ite customs and laws.

28. **(D)**

At Salamis, the Greeks tricked the Persians into entering the harbor while they hid behind the island. The Greeks later defeated the Persian land forces at Plataea.

29. **(D)**

Mehmed used, among other tactics, heavy cannons to level Byzantine defenses.

30. **(C)**

The Janissaries were initially made up of conscripts from the Christian slave population. Later, Turks were also admitted.

31. **(D)**

Thailand is the only Southeast Asian country never to have been colonized by Europeans.

32. **(B)**

The opium trade brought the Ching Empire to its knees, as Europeans demanded and won trading rights throughout China in the unequal treaties that followed the Opium Wars.

33. **(E)**

Neither Jerusalem nor the Sinai Peninsula are currently included in the PNA.

34. **(B)**

According to Machiavelli, politics should be divorced from morality and should be based on expediency and the need for the prince to get power and to maintain it. Machiavelli is credited with founding modern political science.

35. **(C)**

The Balfour Declaration of 1917 pledged to create a secure homeland for Jews.

36. **(A)**

Following the declaration of independence of Bosnia and Herzegovina in 1991, ethnic Serbs attempted to secede from Bosnia and Herzegovina and were aided in their struggle by Serbia.

37. **(B)**

Ashoka spread Buddhism throughout India through the Rock Pillar Edicts, and eventually his influence led to the spread of Buddhism elsewhere.

38. **(D)**

The resolution authorized President Lyndon Johnson to use force in Vietnam. The U.S. Senate never officially declared war in Vietnam.

39. **(C)**

Gandhi was disturbed by talk of the partition of India and attempted to unite Muslims and Hindus as well as other factions in their bid for independence from the British through a program of nonviolent resistance.

40. **(B)**

Despite its defeat in World War II, Japan benefited from the Korean War, enabling it to rapidly industrialize following World War II.

41. **(C)**

Austria-Hungary declared war on Serbia, thus beginning World War I.

42. **(D)**

Victor Emmanuel of Sardinia created a new constitution following the Revolutions of 1848, and Sardinia led the drive toward unity.

43. **(B)**

Luther's language was often vehement and inflammatory. By 1520, he regarded Catholic theology as the instrument of the anti-Christ.

44. **(A)**

The Roman Catholic Church later condemned Galileo for asserting a heliocentric view of the solar system.

45. **(D)**

The Council of Trent achieved many positive reforms, but also permanently separated Protestants from Catholics by its rigid stand on the issues of justification of faith, papal supremacy, and other matters.

46. **(A)**

Lady Murasaki wrote the *Tale of Genji*, considered by many to be the world's first novel. She lived in the Heian court and her fictional novel is our best account of Heian courtly rituals.

47. **(A)**

The Glorious Revolution rejected the Catholic Stuarts, and so also resulted in the persecution of Catholics.

48. **(D)**

Although Copernicus was the first to suggest the solar system had the sun at its center, his ideas were not generally accepted until Galileo's observations confirmed them and Kepler explained the discrepancies in the planets' orbits as attributable to their elliptical orbits. Copernicus had described the orbits as circular.

49. **(C)**

Zwingli fought with the Swiss against Charles V and led them to reject Catholic customs such as the prohibition of meat during Lent.

50. **(C)**

Akhenaton instituted the worship of Aton, the creator god, as the sole God of Egypt and founded a new capital at a place known today as Tel el-Amarna. Akhenaton ruled during the New Kingdom period.

51. **(D)**

Bacon's *New Organon* rejected the syllogism as providing knowledge already had, and advocated the use of induction based upon experience.

52. **(B)**

Justinian's general Belisarius succeeded in reconquering much lost territory of the old Roman Empire in the sixth century, but following Justinian's death, much of this territory was later lost again.

53. **(E)**

Enlightened thinkers viewed religion as superstition and emphasized reason and natural law.

54. **(A)**

Napoleon was asked by those who believed order could only be restored from the top down to overthrow the directorate.

55. **(D)**

The artisans of Benin produced many thousands of heads of their obas during a renaissance of bronze casting in the fifteenth century.

56. **(C)**

The quotation represents two of Wilson's famous Fourteen Points.

57. **(D)**

Bolivar led the Gran Colombia Republic, composed of Colombia, Ecuador, and Venezuela. Hidalgo led an early rebellion that was crushed before achieving much success in Mexico; Rosas led Argentina; Zapata led a revolt in Mexico that sought to give land to the peasants.

58. **(B)**

While Roanoke was the first British colony in the New World, it quickly disappeared. Jamestown was the first permanent British settlement in the New World.

59. **(C)**

Cornwallis's surrender at Yorktown ended the Revolutionary War.

60. **(A)**

Islamic culture reached a high point during the Abbasid caliphate, and Baghdad was a renowned center of learning.

61. **(D)**

Islam spread in Africa starting in the seventh century, and influenced the cultures of Ghana, Mali, and other African states. Although Axum was Christian and North Africa was influenced by Christian culture during the late Roman period, sub-Saharan Africa was primarily influenced by Islam.

62. **(C)**

Hidalgo's rebellion was crushed before achieving much success; Rosas led Argentina; and Bolivar led the Gran Colombia Republic.

63. **(D)**

Toussaint Louverture led the only successful slave revolt in history at the French colony of Saint Domingue on Hispaniola, which later became Haiti.

64. **(B)**

Coronado explored the American southwest and was the first European to see the Grand Canyon.

65. **(E)**

Reagan sold arms to Iran to fund the Contras against the enactments of the U.S. Senate, and supported the abuses of the Marcos regime because Marcos fought against communism.

66. **(D)**
Bartholomew Diaz first reached the Cape of Good Hope in 1487. Vasco da Gama followed ten years later.

67. **(D)**
Carter cut off all aid to the Somozas in Nicaragua and returned the Panama Canal to Panama. The other presidents escalated the Cold War. Reagan supported the Contra in Iran and used inflammatory rhetoric against the Soviet Union; Eisenhower authorized a coup in Guatemala; President Truman's positions after World War II helped to create the Cold War.

68. **(C)**
The first written records in world history are cuneiform tablets.

69. **(D)**
Only Liberia and Abyssinia escaped colonization by Europeans.

70. **(D)**
Sulieman never successfully captured Vienna, but he did establish a presence in Europe.

71. **(B)**
The map reflects the new Turkish Republic and the partition of the Ottoman Empire. Since it refers to Persia, it is a map of this area before 1935, when Persian became Iran. Israel does not yet exist on the map, again pointing to the period before 1948, when Israel proclaimed its existence.

72. **(D)**
Confucius believed in the development of virtue through example and the leadership of virtuous rulers. Virtue would create an ordered society, rather than law and punishments.

73. **(C)**
The illumination depicts the burial of live Confucian scholars, who opposed the progressive policies of Shi Huang Ti and his emphasis on law and punishment as opposed to the rule of virtue.

74. **(B)**

The Hindu tradition teaches that ultimate enlightenment is loss of self and unity with the Absolute, called *moksha*.

75. **(B)**

The Ka'ba is a symbol of Islam and of monotheism, and the place where tradition holds Ishmael struck the ground and a spring flowed forth. It contains a black meteorite that dates back to prehistoric times, but which is associated with Abraham.

76. **(C)**

Angkor Wat is predominantly a Hindu complex built by the Khmer of Cambodia.

77. **(D)**

India's prime minister Nehru declared a policy of nonalignment with neither the United States nor the Soviet Bloc. India today is the world's largest democracy.

78. **(C)**

The pyramids were mostly built in the fourth dynasty of Egyptian antiquity, in approximately 3200 B.C.E. The pyramids of Mesoamerica were the last of the structures to be built.

79. **(C)**

The code applied the principle of "an eye for an eye" to those of the same social class, but mandated lesser punishments, such as fines, for injuries to those of lower classes. The law provided for compensation to masters for injuries to slaves.

80. **(D)**

The Chou ruled the longest of any Chinese dynasty, and established a feudal system in China as well as the notion of the Mandate of Heaven.

81. **(B)**

Louis XIV made this statement about the far-reaching powers he enjoyed during the Age of Absolutism.

82. **(D)**

Minoan art shows the influence of Egypt but is very distinctive in its approach to color and nature.

83. **(B)**

While Europe watched as Germany invaded the Rhineland, Austria, and the Sudetenland, they would not tolerate Hitler's invasion of Poland.

84. **(D)**

Maximilian Robespierre led France during the Reign of Terror, and ruthlessly attempted to exterminate counter-revolutionary movements.

85. **(C)**

While the birth and infant mortality rates have dropped worldwide, the average life expectancy has increased. The population of the world continues to grow.

86. **(B)**

Actually, Thailand was the center of a massive economic crisis in Asia beginning in 1997.

87. **(D)**

Solon became sole archon in 594 and while he instituted sweeping reforms without consulting the Assembly, his reforms put Athens on the road to democracy.

88. **(C)**

Alexander's armies concentrated on the Persian Empire, but also conquered the remnants of ancient Egypt.

89. **(B)**

Marius reformed weapons and taught the soldiers to carry large amounts of supplies. They were called "Marius's mules."

90. **(D)**

Arius taught that Christ was not fully divine and the first creature. The Nicene Creed combats Arian assumptions in many of its clauses.

91. **(B)**

Vercingetorix led the Gauls, a group of Celts, against Caesar, and Caesar trapped him at Alesia.

92. **(D)**

Diocletian attempted to combat civil war by establishing the tetrarchy and dividing the empire between two emperors and two Caesars.

93. **(B)**

Charlemagne led several campaigns against the Saxons before succeeding in forcibly converting them.

94. **(D)**

Gregory VII was one of the most important reforming popes in history. The Concordat of Worms resolved some of these issues in 1122.

95. **(B)**

Crusaders reached Jerusalem and killed every Muslim and Jew that could be found in 1099.

SAT Subject Test
World History

Practice Test 2

This test is also on CD-ROM in our special interactive SAT World History TEST*ware*®. It is highly recommended that you first take this exam on computer. You will then have the additional study features and benefits of enforced timed conditions and instantaneous, accurate scoring. See page xix for guidance on how to get the most out of our SAT World History software.

SAT WORLD HISTORY
PRACTICE TEST 2

ANSWER SHEET

1. Ⓐ Ⓑ Ⓒ Ⓓ Ⓔ
2. Ⓐ Ⓑ Ⓒ Ⓓ Ⓔ
3. Ⓐ Ⓑ Ⓒ Ⓓ Ⓔ
4. Ⓐ Ⓑ Ⓒ Ⓓ Ⓔ
5. Ⓐ Ⓑ Ⓒ Ⓓ Ⓔ
6. Ⓐ Ⓑ Ⓒ Ⓓ Ⓔ
7. Ⓐ Ⓑ Ⓒ Ⓓ Ⓔ
8. Ⓐ Ⓑ Ⓒ Ⓓ Ⓔ
9. Ⓐ Ⓑ Ⓒ Ⓓ Ⓔ
10. Ⓐ Ⓑ Ⓒ Ⓓ Ⓔ
11. Ⓐ Ⓑ Ⓒ Ⓓ Ⓔ
12. Ⓐ Ⓑ Ⓒ Ⓓ Ⓔ
13. Ⓐ Ⓑ Ⓒ Ⓓ Ⓔ
14. Ⓐ Ⓑ Ⓒ Ⓓ Ⓔ
15. Ⓐ Ⓑ Ⓒ Ⓓ Ⓔ
16. Ⓐ Ⓑ Ⓒ Ⓓ Ⓔ
17. Ⓐ Ⓑ Ⓒ Ⓓ Ⓔ
18. Ⓐ Ⓑ Ⓒ Ⓓ Ⓔ
19. Ⓐ Ⓑ Ⓒ Ⓓ Ⓔ
20. Ⓐ Ⓑ Ⓒ Ⓓ Ⓔ
21. Ⓐ Ⓑ Ⓒ Ⓓ Ⓔ
22. Ⓐ Ⓑ Ⓒ Ⓓ Ⓔ
23. Ⓐ Ⓑ Ⓒ Ⓓ Ⓔ
24. Ⓐ Ⓑ Ⓒ Ⓓ Ⓔ
25. Ⓐ Ⓑ Ⓒ Ⓓ Ⓔ
26. Ⓐ Ⓑ Ⓒ Ⓓ Ⓔ
27. Ⓐ Ⓑ Ⓒ Ⓓ Ⓔ
28. Ⓐ Ⓑ Ⓒ Ⓓ Ⓔ
29. Ⓐ Ⓑ Ⓒ Ⓓ Ⓔ
30. Ⓐ Ⓑ Ⓒ Ⓓ Ⓔ
31. Ⓐ Ⓑ Ⓒ Ⓓ Ⓔ
32. Ⓐ Ⓑ Ⓒ Ⓓ Ⓔ

33. Ⓐ Ⓑ Ⓒ Ⓓ Ⓔ
34. Ⓐ Ⓑ Ⓒ Ⓓ Ⓔ
35. Ⓐ Ⓑ Ⓒ Ⓓ Ⓔ
36. Ⓐ Ⓑ Ⓒ Ⓓ Ⓔ
37. Ⓐ Ⓑ Ⓒ Ⓓ Ⓔ
38. Ⓐ Ⓑ Ⓒ Ⓓ Ⓔ
39. Ⓐ Ⓑ Ⓒ Ⓓ Ⓔ
40. Ⓐ Ⓑ Ⓒ Ⓓ Ⓔ
41. Ⓐ Ⓑ Ⓒ Ⓓ Ⓔ
42. Ⓐ Ⓑ Ⓒ Ⓓ Ⓔ
43. Ⓐ Ⓑ Ⓒ Ⓓ Ⓔ
44. Ⓐ Ⓑ Ⓒ Ⓓ Ⓔ
45. Ⓐ Ⓑ Ⓒ Ⓓ Ⓔ
46. Ⓐ Ⓑ Ⓒ Ⓓ Ⓔ
47. Ⓐ Ⓑ Ⓒ Ⓓ Ⓔ
48. Ⓐ Ⓑ Ⓒ Ⓓ Ⓔ
49. Ⓐ Ⓑ Ⓒ Ⓓ Ⓔ
50. Ⓐ Ⓑ Ⓒ Ⓓ Ⓔ
51. Ⓐ Ⓑ Ⓒ Ⓓ Ⓔ
52. Ⓐ Ⓑ Ⓒ Ⓓ Ⓔ
53. Ⓐ Ⓑ Ⓒ Ⓓ Ⓔ
54. Ⓐ Ⓑ Ⓒ Ⓓ Ⓔ
55. Ⓐ Ⓑ Ⓒ Ⓓ Ⓔ
56. Ⓐ Ⓑ Ⓒ Ⓓ Ⓔ
57. Ⓐ Ⓑ Ⓒ Ⓓ Ⓔ
58. Ⓐ Ⓑ Ⓒ Ⓓ Ⓔ
59. Ⓐ Ⓑ Ⓒ Ⓓ Ⓔ
60. Ⓐ Ⓑ Ⓒ Ⓓ Ⓔ
61. Ⓐ Ⓑ Ⓒ Ⓓ Ⓔ
62. Ⓐ Ⓑ Ⓒ Ⓓ Ⓔ
63. Ⓐ Ⓑ Ⓒ Ⓓ Ⓔ
64. Ⓐ Ⓑ Ⓒ Ⓓ Ⓔ

65. Ⓐ Ⓑ Ⓒ Ⓓ Ⓔ
66. Ⓐ Ⓑ Ⓒ Ⓓ Ⓔ
67. Ⓐ Ⓑ Ⓒ Ⓓ Ⓔ
68. Ⓐ Ⓑ Ⓒ Ⓓ Ⓔ
69. Ⓐ Ⓑ Ⓒ Ⓓ Ⓔ
70. Ⓐ Ⓑ Ⓒ Ⓓ Ⓔ
71. Ⓐ Ⓑ Ⓒ Ⓓ Ⓔ
72. Ⓐ Ⓑ Ⓒ Ⓓ Ⓔ
73. Ⓐ Ⓑ Ⓒ Ⓓ Ⓔ
74. Ⓐ Ⓑ Ⓒ Ⓓ Ⓔ
75. Ⓐ Ⓑ Ⓒ Ⓓ Ⓔ
76. Ⓐ Ⓑ Ⓒ Ⓓ Ⓔ
77. Ⓐ Ⓑ Ⓒ Ⓓ Ⓔ
78. Ⓐ Ⓑ Ⓒ Ⓓ Ⓔ
79. Ⓐ Ⓑ Ⓒ Ⓓ Ⓔ
80. Ⓐ Ⓑ Ⓒ Ⓓ Ⓔ
81. Ⓐ Ⓑ Ⓒ Ⓓ Ⓔ
82. Ⓐ Ⓑ Ⓒ Ⓓ Ⓔ
83. Ⓐ Ⓑ Ⓒ Ⓓ Ⓔ
84. Ⓐ Ⓑ Ⓒ Ⓓ Ⓔ
85. Ⓐ Ⓑ Ⓒ Ⓓ Ⓔ
86. Ⓐ Ⓑ Ⓒ Ⓓ Ⓔ
87. Ⓐ Ⓑ Ⓒ Ⓓ Ⓔ
88. Ⓐ Ⓑ Ⓒ Ⓓ Ⓔ
89. Ⓐ Ⓑ Ⓒ Ⓓ Ⓔ
90. Ⓐ Ⓑ Ⓒ Ⓓ Ⓔ
91. Ⓐ Ⓑ Ⓒ Ⓓ Ⓔ
92. Ⓐ Ⓑ Ⓒ Ⓓ Ⓔ
93. Ⓐ Ⓑ Ⓒ Ⓓ Ⓔ
94. Ⓐ Ⓑ Ⓒ Ⓓ Ⓔ
95. Ⓐ Ⓑ Ⓒ Ⓓ Ⓔ

SAT WORLD HISTORY
PRACTICE TEST 2

Time: 1 Hour
        95 Questions

DIRECTIONS: This part consists of a number of incomplete statements or questions, each followed by five suggested completions or answers. Select the most appropriate choice and blacken the corresponding space on the answer sheet.

1. The earliest form of writing is called

   (A) pictography

   (B) cuneiform

   (C) phonetic

   (D) alphabetic

   (E) numeric

2. What great ancient empire was weakening by about 1000 B.C.E. and eventually was lost to invasions by the Hittites, Nubians, Assyrians, and then Persians?

   (A) Babylonia

   (B) Sumeria

   (C) Olmec

   (D) Egypt

   (E) Greece

3. What is Leonardo da Vinci's most famous work of art?

   (A) *Garden of Earthly Delights*

   (B) *Mary and Joseph*

   (C) The painting on the ceiling of the Sistine Chapel

   (D) *Lamentation*

   (E) *The Last Supper*

4. What is the name of the famous law code of the ancient world that included such laws as "If a son strikes a father then his hand shall be cut off"?

    (A) The Ziggurat Codes   (D) The Code of Ramses

    (B) The Philistine Laws   (E) The Code of Hammurabi

    (C) Pharaoh's Code

5. Who was the first king of the Persian Empire?

    (A) Darius   (D) Amenhotep

    (B) Xerxes   (E) Tutankamen

    (C) Cyrus

6. Priests in India were called

    (A) kohanim   (D) Indo-Europeans

    (B) brahmans   (E) pharaohs

    (C) vedas

7. What is the official language of Kenya and the language spoken by a majority of its people?

    (A) Luo   (D) Kush

    (B) Bantu   (E) Swahili

    (C) Arabic

8. The first Chinese dynasty, which until recently was considered only folklore, was called

    (A) Shang   (D) Zhou

    (B) Han   (E) Tang

    (C) Ch'in (Qin)

9. Which of the following describes the most famous characteristic of Olmec art?

    (A) Paintings of nude women

    (B) Pottery made especially for housewives

    (C) Tiny balls made of stone and decorated with etchings

    (D) Statues of giant dogs

    (E) Colossal heads made of stone, some of which are nine feet high

10. The ruins of what ancient city are located near Mexico City?

    (A) Cuzco

    (B) Cahokia

    (C) Teotihuacan

    (D) Sumer

    (E) Machu Picchu

11. Which of the following defines the ancient Greek *polis*?

    (A) School for boys

    (B) City-state

    (C) Monarchy

    (D) Penal system

    (E) Musical theater

12. Which of the following is considered one of the great poets of the Age of Augustus in the Roman Empire?

    (A) Homer

    (B) Ovid

    (C) Amos

    (D) Hoplite

    (E) Sophocles

13. Who was the American president during the dropping of atomic bombs on Japan in 1945?

    (A) Woodrow Wilson

    (B) Theodore Roosevelt

    (C) Franklin Roosevelt

    (D) Harry Truman

    (E) Dwight Eisenhower

14. Which emperor became a Christian and issued the Edict of Milan?

    (A) Constantine

    (B) Nero

    (C) Claudius

    (D) Agamemnon

    (E) Mark Antony

15. Which of the following can be described as the most famous feudal document and the forerunner of trial by jury?

    (A) Runnymeade

    (B) The Tournament

    (C) The Magna Carta

    (D) First Estates-General

    (E) The Saint Louis

16. Which of the following describes Constantinople in the Byzantine Empire until the 1200s?

    (A) It was a city ruled by nomads

    (B) This great commercial center exhibited beautiful architecture and had a huge population

    (C) The city did not exist yet; it was built by the Turks

    (D) It was empty, bleak, and without commerce

    (E) It was in flux; it had been taken over by Muslims 200 years earlier

17. In the year 570, Muhammed was born. His teachings would later form the religion of Islam, which means

    (A) submission to the will of Allah

    (B) people from Mecca

    (C) Muhammed is God

    (D) the people of the book

    (E) followers of Allah, Muhammed, and Ali

18. Which people built the temple shown here in the twelfth century?

(A) The Thai people

(B) The people of southern India

(C) The Tibetans

(D) The Khmer people

(E) The Romans

19. Which of the following was a popular religion of the ancient Persian Empire and featured a god named Ahura Mazda?

(A) Islam

(B) Zoroastrianism

(C) Judaism

(D) Buddhism

(E) Taoism

20. What ancient Greek structure was dedicated to the goddess Athena?

(A) Marathon

(B) The Theatre at Epidaurus

(C) Kouros

(D) The Parthenon

(E) The Oracle at Delphi

21. After the assassination of Julius Caesar, who ruled Rome in the restored Republic?

(A) Augustus

(B) Trajan

(C) Cleopatra

(D) Jesus of Nazareth

(E) Plutarch

22. Pol Pot is most infamous for

(A) being the first modern president of Cambodia

(B) turning the economy of Cambodia from an agricultural one into an industrial one

(C) the slaughter of hundreds of thousands of Cambodians

(D) starting the Vietnam War

(E) being the first president of a Southeast Asian country to become a communist

23. In his work *The City of God,* what bishop wrote that the world of secular government and the world of religion should exist side by side?

    (A) Constantine   (D) Justinian

    (B) Augustine   (E) Saint Benedict

    (C) Jesus of Nazareth

24. Who were the Huns?

    (A) Roman lawmakers

    (B) Chinese traders

    (C) Greek women who owned businesses

    (D) Barbaric invaders

    (E) Germans

25. What is the Hagia Sophia?

    (A) A Byzantine code of law

    (B) A church built in Constantinople, now a mosque

    (C) A famous museum in Athens

    (D) The state religion of the people of the Byzantine Empire

    (E) The most famous ruler of the ancient empire of Iraq

26. Who do Muslims consider to be the "People of the Book"?

    (A) Buddhists   (D) Scholars and teachers

    (B) Confucianists   (E) Jews and Christians

    (C) Jews

27. Which of the following was a student of the Greek philosopher Plato?

    (A) Alexander the Great   (D) Thucidides

    (B) Sappho   (E) Aristotle

    (C) Athena

28. Which is the holy month during which Muslims fast from sunrise to sunset?

    (A) Ka'ba

    (B) Tishrei

    (C) Mecca

    (D) Ramadan

    (E) Jihad

29. What famous book by Machiavelli proposed that leadership could not be restricted by morality?

    (A) *The Prince*

    (B) *Utopia*

    (C) *The Handbook of the Christian Knight*

    (D) *The Folly*

    (E) *Spiritual Exercises*

30. In what year was a printing press with moveable type first used to print the Gutenberg Bible?

    (A) 600 B.C.E.

    (B) 600 C.E.

    (C) 900 C.E.

    (D) 1450 C.E.

    (E) 1650 C.E.

31. Who conquered the Aztecs in 1519 and established their capital on the ruins of Tenochtitlan, the great Aztec capital?

    (A) The Olmecs

    (B) The Maya

    (C) The Portuguese

    (D) The Spanish

    (E) The English

32. Which of the following was a Chinese empress?

    (A) Empress Wi

    (B) Empress Song

    (C) Empress Wu

    (D) Empress Chi

    (E) Empress Li

33. What was the basic belief of the Crusaders (1088–c.1300)?

    (A) Christianity must be spread among all Buddhists and Hindus.

(B) The philosophy of the modern world, namely freedom, must be spread.

(C) All carriers of smallpox must be destroyed.

(D) All Christians must convert to Islam.

(E) A holy war must be waged against the Muslims, and later the Jews, as well.

34. For what purpose was the structure shown above originally built?

(A) To keep political prisoners from escaping

(B) To offer a tribute to former Chinese emperors

(C) To deter the invasion of the Koreans and Japanese

(D) To keep evil spirits away

(E) To deter the invasion of the Huns and Mongols

35. Which two Hindu gods represent the Mighty Lord and the Supreme Being/Creator of Life?

(A) Aryan and Ahimsa

(B) Brahman and Karma

(C) Asoka and Buddha

(D) Shiva and Vishnu

(E) Nirvana and Shanay

36. Which of the following is one of the Four Noble Truths of Buddhism?

    (A) Life is joyous

    (B) Life is suffering

    (C) Never kill another human being

    (D) God is good

    (E) Buddha loves you

37. The empire of Axum existed from about 50 B.C.E. until 650 C.E. In what modern-day country was this empire located?

    (A) Egypt

    (B) Ethiopia

    (C) Nigeria

    (D) Israel

    (E) Iran

38. Who was the famous Mongol leader known for his bloody war tactics?

    (A) Ashoka

    (B) Yang Guang

    (C) Justinian

    (D) Genghis Khan

    (E) Koryo

39. Which culture invented gunpowder?

    (A) The Greeks

    (B) The Hellenistic Empire

    (C) The Chinese

    (D) The Persians

    (E) The Romans

40. In approximately what time period did the illness known as "the plague" spread across Europe?

    (A) 500

    (B) 750

    (C) 900

    (D) 1350

    (E) 1600

41. A hunting lodge and village was turned into the extravagant palace shown above by which French monarch?

    (A) Napoleon   (D) Eleanor of Aquitaine

    (B) Louis XIV   (E) Louis XV

    (C) Louis XIII

42. Which culture reintroduced Western ancient philosophy to late medieval European thinkers?

    (A) Medieval Chinese culture

    (B) The Aztecs of the 1500s

    (C) Early medieval Islamic culture

    (D) The Japanese

    (E) Jewish culture

43. Which of the following is a famous tragedy written by William Shakespeare?

    (A) *Much Ado About Nothing*

    (B) *Twelfth Night*

    (C) *The Merchant of Venice*

    (D) *Love's Labour's Lost*

    (E) *Hamlet*

44. What seventeenth-century thinker believed that at birth the human mind is a *tabula rasa*, or blank slate?

    (A) John Locke   (D) Thomas Hobbes

    (B) Rene Descartes   (E) Isaac Newton

    (C) Baruch Spinoza

45. What city was the capital of the Inca Empire?

    (A) Cuzco   (D) Lima

    (B) Oaxaca   (E) Chinampa

    (C) Buenos Aires

46. What eighteenth-century Russian leader made laws forcing almost all Russians to wear Western dress?

    (A) Alexander II   (D) Alexis Romanov

    (B) Alexander I   (E) Peter the Great

    (C) Catherine the Great

47. In what year was the steam engine first used commercially?

    (A) 1176   (D) 1776

    (B) 1300   (E) 1900

    (C) 1576

48. The most solemn day in the Jewish religion, known as the day of atonement, is

    (A) Yom Kippur   (D) Shabbat

    (B) Chanukah   (E) Passover

    (C) Purim

49. What was one result of the Seven Years' War (1756–1763)?

    (A) The British took over France for ten years

    (B) The French won India from the British

    (C) The French won several islands from the British

    (D) The British won control of Canada from the French

    (E) The British and French agreed to a joint currency

50. The creation of the first encyclopedia was an example of what historical period?

    (A) The Enlightenment

    (B) The Protestant Revolution

    (C) The Catholic Counter-Revolution

    (D) The Renaissance

    (E) The Dark Ages

51. When America's Founding Fathers created three branches of government in order to separate political power, which Enlightenment thinker most influenced them?

    (A) Gibbon   (D) Voltaire

    (B) Hume   (E) Rousseau

    (C) Montesquieu

52. In what year did the French Revolution begin?

    (A) 1760   (D) 1815

    (B) 1789   (E) 1830

    (C) 1799

53. *A Vindication of the Rights of Woman* was written in 1792 by

    (A) Mary Wollstonecraft   (D) Immanuel Kant

    (B) Marie Curie   (E) Ida B. Wells

    (C) Hannah Arendt

54. Which writer is famous for his work entitled *Faust*?

    (A) Byron   (D) Blake

    (B) Coleridge   (E) Goethe

    (C) Wordsworth

55. Which of the following describes a nineteenth-century movement that advocated the end to the state and to capitalism?

    (A) Socialism   (D) Quakerism

    (B) Communism   (E) Anarchism

    (C) Libertarianism

56. Whose work, entitled *The Interpretation of Dreams*, became the foundation for psychoanalysis?

    (A) Karl Marx   (D) Leo Tolstoy

    (B) Emile Zola   (E) Karl Jung

    (C) Sigmund Freud

57. The entire island of Singapore came under whose control in the early 1800s?

    (A) China   (D) The Netherlands

    (B) Thailand   (E) France

    (C) Great Britain

58. What country attacked Ethiopia in 1935?

    (A) Germany   (D) Portugal

    (B) Italy   (E) Spain

    (C) Uganda

59. What ideas were espoused in the Truman Doctrine?

    (A) Communism would be supported everywhere in the world.

    (B) All people of Latin America would be protected by the U.S.

    (C) All nations would be supported in their fight against communism.

    (D) All women of the world would be allowed the right to vote.

    (E) Racism would end globally.

60. Who was the British monarch when the Americans declared their independence from Great Britain?

    (A) King George II   (D) Queen Elizabeth II

    (B) King George III   (E) Queen Victoria

    (C) Queen Elizabeth I

61. Its citizens speak Portuguese; it is one of the largest and fastest-growing cities in the world; and it was founded as a Native Indian mission in 1554. Which city is it?

    (A) Buenos Aires   (D) Sao Paulo

    (B) Lisbon   (E) Sao Tome

    (C) Oaxaca

62. What movement did Ho Chi Minh create in 1930?

    (A) A revolutionary movement against communism in Indochina

    (B) A communist movement against French rule

    (C) A fascist state

    (D) A communist movement against American rule

    (E) An anti-globalism, anti-ecological political party

63. Who fought against one another in the Six-Day War?

    (A) Italy and Ethiopia

    (B) France and Great Britain

    (C) Several Latin American nations and the United States

(D) Iran and Iraq

(E) Egypt (and Syria and Jordan) and Israel

64. Who fought in the so-called "Opium War"?

(A) France and Vietnam

(B) Great Britain and Thailand

(C) The United States and China

(D) Great Britain and China

(E) India and Thailand

65. What led to the Boxer Rebellion in China?

(A) Sports had been outlawed in China

(B) Many Chinese wanted to end Western influence in China

(C) A Chinese politican was murdered by a Westerner

(D) A Chinese woman was raped by a British soldier

(E) The Japanese exerted too much influence over Chinese poetry and music

66. While Mao Tse-Tung was the Chinese communist leader during the Chinese Civil War, who was the nationalist leader?

(A) Lin Piao

(B) Wu Chuan Chi

(C) Yuan Shih-Gai

(D) Chiang Kai-Shek

(E) Nanking

67. The Minoan civilization was developed

(A) on the island of Crete

(B) on mainland Greece

(C) in Turkey

(D) in the Hawaiian Islands

(E) in China

68. When did Communists officially take over the Chinese government?

    (A) 1920   (D) 1949

    (B) 1929   (E) 1960

    (C) 1940

69. Of what movement was Vladimir Lenin the leader?

    (A) The Russo-Nationalists

    (B) The Capitalists

    (C) The Mensheviks

    (D) The Dumas

    (E) The Bolsheviks

70. What African kingdom invaded Egypt in 750 B.C.E.?

    (A) Mauritania   (D) Kush

    (B) Persia   (E) Bantu

    (C) Somalia

71. Which of the following happened during the Russian Revolution of 1916/1917?

    (A) Anarchists set all palaces and important monuments ablaze

    (B) Stalin was murdered by a mob

    (C) The tsar and his family were murdered

    (D) Lenin was assassinated by Tsar Nicholas II

    (E) Stalin was named dictator

72. What was Julius Caesar's title and length of office?

    (A) Senator for four years

    (B) Senator for life

    (C) Dictator for life

    (D) *Nobil* for one decade

    (E) *Tribune* for twenty years

73. Which of the following statements is NOT true of World War II?

    (A) It was fought on two fronts in Europe as well as in Africa and the Pacific.

    (B) German aggression in Europe occurred before Japanese aggression in Asia.

    (C) Hitler's invasion of Poland prompted the allies to declare war.

    (D) Mussolini invaded Ethiopia in the prelude to World War II.

    (E) The Germans launched a blitzkreig against the British that ultimately failed.

74. What was the name of the first spacecraft to circle the earth?

    (A) *Sputnik I*   (D) *Molotov II*

    (B) *Orbiter*   (E) *Explorer*

    (C) *Malenkov*

75. Which Russian author wrote *War and Peace*?

    (A) Alexander Pushkin   (D) Leo Tolstoy

    (B) Nikolai Gogol   (E) Anton Chekhov

    (C) Fyodor Dostoevsky

76. Who led a revolution to overthrow Cuban leader Batista in 1959?

    (A) Peron   (D) Castro

    (B) Jose Marti   (E) Machado

    (C) Martinez

77. Why was the United States interested in building a canal through Colombia (later Panama) in 1903?

    (A) The canal would allow U.S. shipping to cut through South America.

    (B) The canal would help end communism in Panama.

    (C) The canal would provide many jobs for Americans in South America.

    (D) Christian Americans would be able to proselytize in Panama and Colombia.

(E) The canal would provide water for America's southwestern states.

78. What are the two major religions of modern-day India?

(A) Buddhism and Christianity

(B) Hinduism and Islam

(C) Islam and Jainism

(D) Judaism and Hindu

(E) Zoroastrianism and Buddhism

79. Which country shares a border with China?

(A) Cambodia   (D) Mongolia

(B) Malaysia   (E) Philippines

(C) South Korea

80. Mali is known as the first great _____ in West Africa.

(A) Christian empire

(B) Muslim empire

(C) empire led by a woman

(D) modern cosmopolitan empire

(E) architect

81. Of which of the following political organizations was Nelson Mandela the leader?

(A) African Revolutionaries (AR)

(B) South African Freedom Fighters (SAFF)

(C) African National Congress (ANC)

(D) Dutch Nationals for Democracy (DND)

(E) White South Africans Unite (WSAU)

82. What is the former name of the country of Zimbabwe?

(A) Botswana   (D) Tanzania

(B) Mozambique   (E) Ivory Coast

(C) Rhodesia

83. Afonso I made Catholicism the state religion of which African nation around 1491?

(A) Sudan   (D) Kongo (Congo)

(B) Uganda   (E) Algeria

(C) New Guinea

84. From 1890 until about 1920, most immigrants to America were from

(A) China and Japan

(B) Denmark and Norway

(C) India

(D) China and Japan

(E) Italy and Jewish Eastern Europe

85. Which event pulled America into World War I?

(A) The decline in trade with European nations as a result of the war

(B) The predominant philosophical belief in the righteousness of the war

(C) The death of the president's wife, Ellen Wilson

(D) The Zimmermann telegram

(E) The need for Wilson to win the election of 1916

86. What was the intent of Martin Luther when he posted his 95 theses on a church door in Wittenberg?

(A) To begin the Protestant Reformation

(B) To voice his concerns about indulgences and other church practices

(C) To change the leadership of the Catholic Church, especially the Roman leadership

(D) To start rioting in Germany

(E) To merge the Roman Catholic and Eastern Orthodox Churches

87. Ferdinand Marcos was a dictatorial leader of which of these countries?

    (A) Philippines   (D) Singapore

    (B) Brunei   (E) Laos

    (C) Thailand

88. The current conflict between India and Pakistan involves

    (A) trade disagreements between the two countries

    (B) a rumored genocide by India over 300 years ago

    (C) India's southern border region

    (D) the territory known as Kashmir

    (E) fishing rights in the Arabian Sea

89. Nearly every aspect of Mexican life has been under the control of what political party since 1929?

    (A) Madero Party (PM)

    (B) Mexican Revolutionary Party (PRM)

    (C) Liberal Party (PL)

    (D) Republican Party (PR)

    (E) Institutional Revolutionary Party (PRI)

90. Gothic architecture introduced

    (A) the flying buttress

    (B) columns

    (C) stone sculpture

    (D) the steeple

    (E) the facade

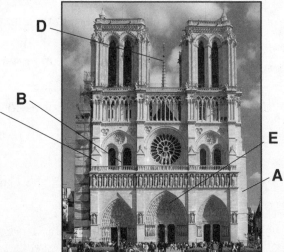

91. One of the largest apartment buildings built in North America before the Industrial Revolution was made by which native peoples?

    (A) The Navajo   (D) The Anasazi

    (B) The Iroquois   (E) The Creek

    (C) The Inuit

92. Which ethical or religious system does the following describe: a set of ethical rules wherein social order is seen as a series of status groups, such as father-son, subject-ruler, etc.

    (A) Buddhism   (D) Christianity

    (B) Jainism   (E) Confucianism

    (C) Islam

93. Modern Islam's division into these two main branches stems from a seventh-century struggle over Islamic leadership. The correct names of these branches are

    (A) Muslims and Muhammeds

    (B) Shi'ites and Sunnis

    (C) Sunni and Sufi

    (D) Shi'ites and Sufi

    (E) Muslims and Jews

94. What are Sufis?

    (A) Native American healers

    (B) Muslim mystics

    (C) Very religious Christians

    (D) Muslims who do not follow the word of Muhammed

    (E) Chinese politicians

95. In medieval European universities, what language was used to study classical texts?

    (A) Latin

    (B) Greek

    (C) Aramaic

    (D) Hebrew

    (E) Italian

SAT WORLD HISTORY
PRACTICE TEST 2

ANSWER KEY

1.	(B)	25.	(B)	49.	(D)	73.	(B)
2.	(D)	26.	(E)	50.	(A)	74.	(A)
3.	(E)	27.	(E)	51.	(C)	75.	(D)
4.	(E)	28.	(D)	52.	(B)	76.	(D)
5.	(C)	29.	(A)	53.	(A)	77.	(A)
6.	(B)	30.	(D)	54.	(E)	78.	(B)
7.	(E)	31.	(D)	55.	(E)	79.	(D)
8.	(A)	32.	(C)	56.	(C)	80.	(B)
9	(E)	33.	(E)	57.	(C)	81.	(C)
10.	(C)	34.	(E)	58.	(B)	82.	(C)
11.	(B)	35.	(D)	59.	(C)	83.	(D)
12.	(B)	36.	(B)	60.	(B)	84.	(E)
13.	(D)	37.	(B)	61.	(D)	85.	(D)
14.	(A)	38.	(D)	62.	(B)	86.	(B)
15.	(C)	39.	(C)	63.	(E)	87.	(A)
16.	(B)	40.	(D)	64.	(D)	88.	(D)
17.	(A)	41.	(B)	65.	(B)	89.	(E)
18.	(D)	42.	(C)	66.	(D)	90.	(A)
19.	(B)	43.	(E)	67.	(A)	91.	(D)
20.	(D)	44.	(A)	68.	(D)	92.	(E)
21.	(A)	45.	(A)	69.	(E)	93.	(B)
22.	(C)	46.	(E)	70.	(D)	94.	(B)
23.	(B)	47.	(D)	71.	(C)	95.	(A)
24.	(D)	48.	(A)	72.	(C)		

DETAILED EXPLANATIONS OF ANSWERS

PRACTICE TEST 2

1. **(B)**
The earliest form of writing is called cuneiform. It was used by the Sumerians, in the Near East, in about 4500 B.C.E. It was comprised of wedge-shaped marks, a type of early pictograph. Pictographs were later used by the Chinese around 1500 B.C.E.

2. **(D)**
The ancient Egyptians suffered internal difficulties and economic problems, but wars with foreign invaders finally tore apart their vast empire. The empire was very large at its height, encompassing parts of Mesopotamia and Anatolia. Beginning in approximately 1000 B.C.E. and ending at about 500 B.C.E., Egypt lost much of its territory to its neighbors. The heart of the empire was even occupied by the Assyrians for a short time.

3. **(E)**
Leonardo da Vinci (1452–1519) painted *The Last Supper*, depicting the final supper of Jesus Christ and his disciples. The gestures of each figure in the painting show inner workings of their minds and souls. The painting is considered one of the greatest Renaissance works.

4. **(E)**
The Code of Hammurabi is attributed to King Hammurabi of Babylonia in 1800 B.C.E. This complex system of laws tells us much about the Babylonian people, ethical beliefs, and power structure.

5. **(C)**
Cyrus the Great (559–530 B.C.E.) was the first king or emperor of the Persian Empire. He is known for his remarkable leadership in maintaining an empire of enormous geographic space and with many varied ethnic and religious groups by allowing the peoples of his empire to keep their religions, local administrators, and even financial means.

6. **(B)**

Brahmans, or priests, performed rituals in Aryan society from 1400 B.C.E. until about 700 B.C.E. The Aryans migrated from central Asia into what is now called India. The Brahman priests used the *Vedas*, the *Mahabarata*, and the *Ramayana* as their religious texts.

7. **(E)**

Most Kenyans speak Swahili, although over thirty different major languages are spoken in the nation. Many Kenyans speak English. Swahili is a mixture of Arabic and local African languages.

8. **(A)**

The Shang Dynasty is believed to have existed between 1500 and 1050 B.C.E. For years it was believed to be fictional; however, scholarly research and archaeological findings prove that the Shang Dynasty did exist. One finding was of tombs containing artifacts that date back to 1300 B.C.E. Among the remarkable findings were the remains of an early Chinese writing system that contains over 3,000 characters.

9. **(E)**

The Olmec civilization (1200–400 B.C.E.) existed in the region of the coast of Mexico. The Olmecs pre-dated the Mayans and probably influenced later Mayan writing and architecture. Olmec art is best known for its very large stone heads, believed to be representative of Olmec rulers.

10. **(C)**

The ancient city of Teotihuacan, which thrived c. 700 C.E., is in the modern-day country of Mexico, outside Mexico City. Some of the remaining structures include the enormous pyramids of the sun and moon.

11. **(B)**

The *polis*, or city-state, was the form of government for the ancient Greeks. Each *polis* was governed differently, with no uniform code of laws for all Greek people. For example, the city-states of Athens and Sparta were drastically different. The former was democratic, and the latter was mostly oligarchical (rule by the few).

12. **(B)**

Ovid (43 B.C.E.–18 C.E.) wrote poems intended to shock the upper class members interested in improving morals. The emperor Augustus had enacted new laws to stop what he considered immoral behavior, such as adultery, hedonistic parties, and a low birth rate. Ovid objected to this new political and moral environment, and in his poems, such as "The Art of Love," he wrote about how to seduce women.

13. **(D)**
President Truman made the difficult decision to drop atomic bombs on the cities of Hiroshima and Nagasaki to end the Pacific front of World War II. Truman became president in April 1945, after Franklin Roosevelt's death, and the bombs were dropped on Japan in August 1945.

14. **(A)**
The Roman Emperor Constantine (306–337 c.e.) became the first Christian emperor and was baptized near the end of his life. The Edict of Milan (313 c.e.) legalized the existence of Christianity in the Roman Empire after many years of Christian persecution.The Emperor Theodosius (378–395 c.e.) made Christianity the official religion of the empire.

15. **(C)**
The Magna Carta was written by British barons in 1215 and approved by King John. It set the stage for trial by jury, due process of law, freedom of cities and regions to maintain their own local customs, and protection of people from their government.

16. **(B)**
Constantinople was the largest city in Europe during this time period and was part of a Greek state—the Byzantine Empire. It was overtaken by crusaders in the 1200s and then overtaken by Muslim Turks in the 1400s. Beginning in the 400s, the city was a bustling urban, metropolitan center with unique architecture and a thriving commercial trade industry.

17. **(A)**
Islam means "submission to the will of Allah," and Allah refers to God. Although Muslims consider Mecca to be a sacred place, Muslims do not come from only Mecca. Muhammed is the Islamic prophet, but not the Islamic God. The phrase "people of the book" is used by Muslims in reference to Christians and Jews.

18. **(D)**
The Khmer people built the monument in what is now Cambodia. This empire was Hindu, and Angkor Wat was dedicated to a Hindu god.

19. **(B)**

Zoroastrianism features a god named Ahura Mazda, who is the creator and embodies goodness, truth, and life. Ahriman is Ahura Mazda's opposing counterpart and embodies the evil spirit. Persian leaders, Darius included, practiced Zoroastrianism as a monotheistic religion, with Ahura Mazda as the only god.

20. **(D)**

The Parthenon, part of the Acropolis, was built between 447 and 432 B.C.E. as a temple for the goddess Athena. The structure still exists, but without the giant Athena statue believed to have originally been in the center of the building.

21. **(A)**

Octavian, later called Augustus, ruled Rome from 31 B.C.E. until 14 C.E. Among his accomplishments was the addition of Egypt to the Roman Empire. He also enacted social legislation aimed at aiding the moral actions of Romans, as he believed that Rome had been punished for being immoral when the first empire fell into chaos.

22. **(C)**

Pol Pot and his regime, the Khmer Rouge, murdered or starved approximately one-third of the total population of Cambodia from 1976 until 1979.

23. **(B)**

Augustine's two famous works are *The City of God* and *Confessions*. He helped spread Christianity in the pagan Roman world and had a great influence on medieval Christian thought.

24. **(D)**

The Huns were people from central Asia who migrated into Germanic lands. They were depicted as being very "savage," or violent, and without advanced culture or laws.

25. **(B)**

The Hagia Sophia (Church of Holy Wisdom) was built by the Emperor Justinian in 537 C.E. It had an enormous dome and dozens of windows around the base of the dome. One of the greatest buildings in Constantinople, it was converted into a mosque in the 1600s.

26. **(E)**

Through Hebrew and Christian traditions, the religion of Islam was born. The Koran, Islam's sacred text, refers to Jewish and Christian traditions and to Abraham and Jesus Christ.

27. **(E)**

Aristotle (384–322 B.C.E.), Plato's most famous student, is best known for his writings on logic. He founded a school, and his most famous student was Alexander the Great.

28. **(D)**

The observance of Ramadan is considered one of the five pillars of Islam. They also include believing in Allah (God) and Muhammad, praying five times a day, making a pilgrimage to Mecca, and giving alms to the poor.

29. **(A)**

Machiavelli's *The Prince*, written in 1513, is a famous example of Renaissance literature. In the book, Machiavelli crafts a form of political power intent on maintaining order, even if this order can be maintained only by ignoring Christian principles of morality. He has been considered the founder of modern political ethics.

30. **(D)**

The "moveable type" metal printing press was first used in the 1450s to print the famous Gutenberg Bibles. The use of printing presses spread quickly throughout Europe and became one of the largest industries in Europe. Printing presses revolutionized education, scholarly research, and literacy.

31. **(D)**

The Spanish arrived in what is now Mexico in 1519 and found a large militaristic Aztec empire. The Spanish overthrew the empire and destroyed the capital, building what is now Mexico City on top of its ruins.

32. **(C)**

One of the few female political rulers in Chinese history, Empress Wu (627–705) ruled during the Tang Empire. The names of the other answer choices are not real historical empresses.

33. **(E)**

Muslim Turks took over much of the Eastern Orthodox Byzantine Empire in about 1088. The Crusades began as a war against these non-Christians who had taken over Christian lands, especially the Holy Land (Jersusalem and Nazareth).

34. **(E)**

The Great Wall of China was built in the fifteenth century during the Ming Empire. It is a 2,000-mile-long wall along China's northern borders, originally built to keep out invading nomads such as the Huns and Mongols.

35. **(D)**

Only answer choice (D) lists two Hindu gods. Shiva is the Mighty Lord; Vishnu is the supreme being and preserver of life. One of Vishnu's incarnations is Krishna.

36. **(B)**

The Four Noble Truths can be summarized as: life is suffering; suffering has a cause; the cause is desire; suffering can be ended by the Eightfold Path.

37. **(B)**

The Ethiopian empire of Axum was mostly agricultural but also had many cities, the city of Axum being its capital. The population of Axum was probably about 20,000 people. One of the most famous aspects of this culture were the stelas built in honor of royalty. The only one that still stands is seventy feet high.

38. **(D)**

Genghis Khan (also spelled Chinggis Khan) was the Mongolian leader from approximately 1162 until 1227. Conquering much of central Asia and some of Europe, he was known for being relentless and aggressive.

39. **(C)**

The Chinese invented gunpowder in the ninth century. Gunpowder was being used in the Arab world and in Europe by the thirteenth century.

40. **(D)**

The Black Death, or plague, spread from China, to India, Persia, and Eastern Europe, and finally to Western Europe via trade routes. It infected the populations of England, France, Italy, and other Western European countries in 1347 and 1348.

41. **(B)**

In 1624, Louis XIII began building a hunting lodge in the small village of Versailles. Louis XIV commissioned the Palace of Versailles to be one of the greatest palaces ever built. The Palace of Versailles is now a historical museum and art gallery.

42. **(C)**

Early medieval Islamic thinkers introduced European thinkers to Aristotle and other ancient Western philosophers. One Islamic thinker who was influential in this movement was Ibn Rushd, also known as Averroes (1126–1198).

43. **(E)**

In 1603, Shakespeare wrote *Hamlet*, one of the greatest tragedies of the Elizabethan era and of all time. The plot centers on a Danish prince who seeks to avenge the murder of his father.

44. **(A)**

John Locke (1632–1704) was an English thinker whose ideas became the most influential political ideas of the century. Many of his ideas are incorporated into American values and laws. He believed that at birth the human mind is a blank slate, without even basic moral values; society teaches us morals.

45. **(A)**

Around 1435, Cuzco, a state in southern Peru, became the capital of the Inca Empire. Answer choice (D) is the modern-day capital of Peru.

46. **(E)**

Peter the Great (1682–1705) was fascinated by the West. He decreed that all Russians except peasants and clergy should wear Western dress. He moved the capital of Russia from Moscow to St. Petersburg, closer to Western Europe. In many ways, he moved Russia towards being a modern state.

47. **(D)**

James Watt invented the steam engine. It was first used to pump water from mines, and then to power cotton mills. By the 1800s, it was used for steam engine ships and then for steam-powered trains. This invention revolutionized transportation and helped give birth to the Industrial Revolution.

48. **(A)**

Yom Kippur, also known as the day of atonement, is the most solemn and important day of the year for Jews. It is a day of fasting that follows Rosh Hashanah, the Jewish New Year.

49. **(D)**

In 1759, the British were victorious over the French at the Battle of the Plains of Abraham (in Quebec).

50. **(A)**

The first volume of the *Encyclopedia* was printed in 1751 in France. It was the work of two French Enlightenment thinkers, Diderot and d'Alembert. Many of the articles were secular in nature and aimed to educate readers with scientific and historical knowledge.

51. **(C)**

One of Montesquieu's (1689–1755) most important contributions to the Enlightenment was the idea of separation of powers. He wanted to limit the power of the monarch and the elite by having them balance one another.

52. **(B)**

The French Revolution began in 1789 with an outcry from the Third Estate (everyone in France except the king, clergy, and aristocracy) for more political power. It ended with the Constitution of 1791, which established a constitutional monarchy recognizing the rights of the common man.

53. **(A)**

Mary Wollstonecraft wrote *A Vindication of the Rights of Woman* to argue for women's rights. Wollstonecraft, an English writer, believed that women did have different social roles than men but that they still should be allowed to participate in government and be educated.

54. **(E)**

The German Romantic writer Goethe (1749–1832) wrote *Faust*, published in 1808 and 1832, which tells the story of a man who makes a pact with the devil. The book depicts the spiritual struggle of the time, that of maintaining Christian values on the one hand and abandoning them and modernizing them on the other.

55. **(E)**

Anarchism is a political movement that began in the 1840s and is sometimes aligned with socialism. It advocates an end to governments, the state, systems like the banking system, and capitalism. Anarchists' means were sometimes peaceful and sometimes violent in this time period.

56. **(C)**

Sigmund Freud is considered the father of psychoanalysis. He investigated what within the dreamer's mind leads to his or her dreams and studied the unconscious desires that create those dreams. *The Interpretation of Dreams* was published in 1900.

57. **(C)**

Singapore, a small country in Southeast Asia, came under British control in 1824, although Great Britain had controlled Singapore's harbor since 1819. It became an independent country in 1965.

58. **(B)**

Fascist Italy, under the dictatorship of Mussolini, attacked Ethiopia in 1935. This attack was perceived to avenge Ethiopia's defeat of the Italians in the late nineteenth century. Ethiopia was quickly defeated, and Italy began its quest to regain the glory of ancient Rome.

59. **(C)**

During the Cold War, capitalist nations and communist nations, led by the United States and the Soviet Union, respectively, had an ideological and political war over the future of many nations in the world. The Truman Doctrine was first introduced in reference to Greece and Turkey, as both were fighting communist revolutions.

60. **(B)**

King George III (1760–1820) was king of Great Britain during the American Revolution. Although mentally ill, the king was the first modern monarch to exercise his individual power aggressively.

61. **(D)**

Sao Paulo, the capital of Brazil, is the correct answer. The people of Buenos Aires, Argentina, speak Spanish, not Portuguese. Lisbon is the capital of Portugal, but the city is significantly smaller than Sao Paulo, and it was not founded as a Native Indian mission. Oaxacans, who live in Mexico, speak Spanish. Sao Tome is a small African island discovered by the Portuguese.

62. **(B)**

Ho Chi Minh, a Vietnamese revolutionary, created the Communist Party in Vietnam and pushed for freedom from French rule. In 1945, at the end of the Second World War, he declared independence from France.

63. **(E)**

The Six-Day War began in 1967 with Egypt's attack on the newly created Israel. The Israelis defeated Egypt, along with Syria and Jordan, in six days and gained the Sinai Peninsula and the West Bank.

64. **(D)**

Opium smuggling became a profitable business for Western (European) traders in China in the 1800s. Due to the destructive nature of opium, the Chinese tried to stop the trade. In 1839, China seized a British opium shipment and the British declared war on the Chinese. The British won the war and gained the use of several Chinese trading ports.

65. **(B)**

As a result of many treaties that the Chinese considered unfair to their economic interests, and the overall Chinese feeling that too many Westerners had influence in Chinese trade and other affairs, a secret society called the Boxers began a rebellion. A terror campaign against Europeans and Americans ensued, until in 1900 an international army was called in to protect the Westerners and the rebellion was crushed.

66. **(D)**

Chiang Kai-Shek was the Nationalist leader who broke away from the communists during the Civil War. He was later captured by the communists and forced to agree to a truce; however, he and his followers continued the Nationalist struggle by retreating to Taiwan instead of giving up their goals.

67. **(A)**

The Minoan civilization is considered the first civilization of ancient Greece. It was developed on the island of Crete starting in 2200 B.C.E. The Minoans developed a writing known as Linear A. Their most famous structure, the Knossos, is a large palace.

68. **(D)**

In September 1949, the communist dictatorship known as the People's Republic of China was created. The government quickly took over all of the country's factories, newspapers, large businesses, and transportation systems.

69. **(E)**

In the 1890s, there was much social and political unrest in Russia. The Bolsheviks offered one solution to the problems of Russia, as they wanted to start a communist revolution to overthrow the tsar. They succeeded with a small group of communist idealists leading the masses.

70. **(D)**

The Kingdom of Kush (also referred to as Nubia) invaded Egypt in 750 B.C.E. and ruled for nearly one hundred years. After leaving Egypt, the kingdom was centered in Meroe and disappeared by about 350 C.E.

71. **(C)**

Tsar Nicholas II proved to be incapable of quelling the Communist Revolution and instead made several moves that angered the educated class of Russians all the more. He ordered the Russian Parliament (the Duma) to dissolve itself. The tsar and his family were imprisoned at their winter palace in 1917 and murdered in 1918.

72. **(C)**

Julius Caesar became dictator in 47 B.C.E. and became dictator for life in 44 B.C.E. He instituted many changes that were good for some Romans, such as establishing new colonies, starting new building projects, and changing the calendar (the basis of the modern calendar). However, he made enemies within the empire. Many saw his rule as the end of the republic and conceived a plot to assassinate him. The plot was carried out in 44 B.C.E.

73. **(B)**

Japanese imperialism was already evident in the Russo-Japanese war of 1905 and in the invasion of Manchuria in 1931. Japan then later invaded China and French Indochina. The Japanese war with Russia occurred much earlier than Hitler's invasion of the Rhineland, as did its invasion of Manchuria. One could actually go back earlier to the Sino-Japanese War between Japan and China in the late nineteenth century.

74. **(A)**

In 1957, the Soviets launched *Sputnik I*, the first spacecraft to orbit the earth. This accomplishment surprised Americans and started the "space race," which included a race to put a man on the moon. Americans were the first to land on the moon, in 1969.

75. **(D)**

Tolstoy wrote *War and Peace* in 1865. This novel is about the French invasion of Russia in 1812. Tolstoy is also famous for his work entitled *Anna Karenina*. The book focuses on the uselessness of romantic love and hails the ideals of duty and family.

76. **(D)**

Fidel Castro, a Cuban physician and revolutionary, helped overthrow Fulgencio Batista in Cuba's revolution. Castro's regime quickly nationalized the sugar industry, thus alienating American interests, and soon became a communist government. An attempt by the U.S. to overthrow Castro's government failed in 1961 and the U.S. has had no diplomatic relations with Cubans in several decades.

77. **(A)**

After the British completed the Suez Canal, which allowed for British shipping to pass freely through Egypt, the Americans wanted all the more to realize their dream of cutting through Latin America. The canal was opposed by the Colombians, and a revolution by Panamanians (formerly Colombians) was encouraged by the United States. Once Panama declared independence, the United States made a treaty granting the United States rights to the canal.

78. **(B)**

The two major religions of India are Hinduism and Islam. About fifteen percent of the population of India is Muslim (Islamic), and the majority of Indians are Hindu.

79. **(D)**

Mongolia shares a northern border with China. The Philippines is an island chain south of China but does not share any borders. Cambodia and Malasyia both lie to the south of China but do not share a border. South Korea does not share a border, but North Korea does.

80. **(B)**

Mali was the first great Muslim empire in West Africa. Its greatest ruler, Mansa Musa, converted to Islam and ruled the empire for twenty-five years. His reign began in 1312.

81. **(C)**

Mandela, the first black president of South Africa and a winner of a Nobel Prize for Peace, was the leader of the ANC. After he left the presidency in 1999, the ANC chose Thabo Mbeki as its leader.

82. **(C)**

Zimbabwe won independence from England in 1980 and changed its name at that time. Since then, it has been a relatively successful African state, with a one-party regime and a moderately prosperous farming and mining economy.

83. **(D)**

Afonso I of the Congo tried to Christianize his people and renamed the capital Sao Salvador. Today, the ethnic Kongolese are the major influential political group in the Democratic Republic of the Congo.

84. **(E)**

Nearly forty percent of the "new immigrants" came from Italy or were Eastern European Jews. They tended to settle in big cities like New York, Chicago, and Philadelphia, working in factories and doing other low paying jobs. The other groups were small minority immigrant populations for this time period.

85. **(D)**

In January 1917, the British intercepted a coded telegram that proved to be a communication from German Foreign Minister Zimmermann to the German Ambassador to Mexico. Zimmermann offered to return Texas, New Mexico, and Arizona to Mexico in return for Mexico's cooperation in World War I against the United States.

86. **(B)**

Martin Luther, a university professor, posted ninety-five theses on a church door in Wittenberg, Germany, in 1517 and began the Protestant Reformation. His concerns included the sale of indulgences for the absolution of sins. Luther did not then intend to change the course of Christianity, only to begin a debate among Christians.

87. **(A)**

In 1965, Marcos became president of the Philippines and quickly became a dictatorial leader. He used his power to help the wealthy, especially his inner circle of friends, and hurt the massive population of poor people in his country. He was voted out of office in 1986, and Corazon Aquino became president.

88. **(D)**

Kashmir lies between modern-day India, primarily a Hindu country, and Pakistan, a Muslim country. This territory not only has abundant natural resources but is also considered an important historical site for both countries.

89. **(E)**

The PRI has been the party in control since the 1920s, and every Mexican president since 1929 has been a member of this party except for the current president, President Vicente Fox of the National Action Party (PAN). The PRI controlled not just politics but the educational system, cultural activities, and the economy as well.

90. **(A)**

The flying buttress is the quintessential element of Gothic architecture, a European movement of the Middle Ages. Massive piers were placed outside the church instead of inside to allow more space inside for stained glass and in order to send one's gaze upward, toward the heavens.

91. **(D)**

The Anasazi built towns, beginning in the eleventh century, in the region of the Southwest. The largest apartment building found had about 500 homes. By about 1300 the Anasazi were disappearing due to fighting between towns and fighting with the Navajo and Apache.

92. **(E)**

Confucianism is an Eastern Asian religion or ethical system that began in the fifth century B.C.E. in China. Confucius and his most famous protégé, Mencius, devised an ethical system that millions of Asians still follow today. It is based on practicality with a focus on encouraging people to behave well in society.

93. **(B)**

Shi'ite Muslims believe that Ali was the true successor to Muhammed, the prophet. They attach special religious meaning to the teachings of Ali. Sunnis, on the other hand, believe in succession through learning or knowledge, not through blood lines.

94. **(B)**

Sufis practice a mystical form of Islam, with the intention of purifying the soul through monasticism, meditation, and chanting.

95. **(A)**

Most of the classical texts were in Latin, the written language of educated people; therefore, it was used in the university. A typical student listened to up to seven hours of lecture a day in reference to these classical texts.

PHOTO CREDITS

Page 97, Dying Gaul, Photo by Erich Lessing/ Art Resource, NY

Page 146, Macchu Picchu, photo by Matthias Ripp

Page 161, Byzantine mosaic of the Deesis: Christ.
Hagia Sophia, Istanbul, Turkey, Scala/Art Resource, NY

Page 389, British troops at the Normandy beachhead, AP Photo/Official British photo.

Page 449, Qin Shi Huangdi, founder of the Qin dynasty, burning all Chinese books and throwing the academics into a deep ravine. From the Lives of the Emperors. Qing manuscript. 17th c. Art Resource/NY

Page 474, Angkor Wat, photo by Manfred Werner.

Page 490, Notre Dame, photo by Tristan Nitot

INSTALLING REA's TEST*ware*®

SYSTEM REQUIREMENTS

Pentium 75 MHz (300 MHz recommended) or higher or compatible processor; Microsoft Windows 98 or later; 64 MB Available RAM; Internet Explorer 5.5 or higher

INSTALLATION

1. Insert the SAT World History Subject Test TEST*ware*® CD-ROM into the CD-ROM drive.
2. If the installation doesn't begin automatically, from the Start Menu choose the RUN command. When the RUN dialog box appears, type d:\setup (where D is the letter of your CD-ROM drive) at the prompt and click OK.
3. The installation process will begin. A dialog box proposing the directory "Program Files\REA\SATWorldHistory" will appear. If the name and location are suitable, click OK. If you wish to specify a different name or location, type it in and click OK.
4. Start the SAT World History Subject Test TEST*ware*® application by double-clicking on the icon.

REA's SAT World History Subject Test TEST*ware*® is **EASY** to **LEARN AND USE**. To achieve maximum benefits, we recommend that you take a few minutes to go through the on-screen tutorial on your computer. The "screen buttons" are also explained there to familiarize you with the program.

SSD ACCOMMODATIONS FOR STUDENTS WITH DISABILITIES

Many students qualify for extra time to take the SAT World History Subject Test, and our TEST*ware*® can be adapted to accommodate your time extension. This allows you to practice under the same extended time accommodations that you will receive on the actual test day. To customize your TEST*ware*® to suit the most common extensions, visit our Website at http://www.rea.com/ssd.

TECHNICAL SUPPORT

REA's TEST*ware*® is backed by customer and technical support. For questions about **installation or operation of your software**, contact us at:

> **Research & Education Association**
> **Phone: (732) 819-8880 (9 a.m. to 5 p.m. ET, Monday–Friday)**
> **Fax: (732) 819-8808**
> **Website: http://www.rea.com**
> **E-mail: info@rea.com**

Note to Windows XP Users: In order for the TEST*ware*® to function properly, please install and run the application under the same computer-administrator level user account. Installing the TEST*ware*® as one user and running it as another could cause file-access path conflicts.

Index

B

F

N

O